D0161163

ABNORMAL PSYCHOLOGY

Second Edition

Robert G. Meyer
University of Louisville

Paul Salmon
University of Louisville

ALLYN AND BACON, INC.

Boston • London • Sydney • Toronto

Dedication

To Ken and Sue—Brother and Sister, and fine friends.

R.G.M.

To Sue, Kaki, Charles, and my parents.

P.G.S.

Series Editor: John-Paul Lenney
Developmental Editors: Tom Mancuso and Wendy Ritger
Senior Editorial Assistant: Leslie Galton
Cover Administrator: Linda Dickinson
Manufacturing Buyer: Bill Alberti
Editorial-Production Service: York Production Services
Cover Designer: Design Ad Cetera
Production Administrator: Rowena Dores

Library of Congress Cataloging-in-Publication Data

Meyer, Robert G.
    Abnormal psychology.

    Bibliography: p.
    Includes indexes.
    1. Psychiatry.   I. Salmon, Paul, 1948–
II. Title.
RC454.M478   1988   616.89   87-30736
ISBN 0-205-11177-7

Copyright © 1988, 1984 by Allyn and Bacon, Inc.
A Division of Simon & Schuster
160 Gould Street, Needham Heights, Massachusetts 02194.

All rights reserved. No part of the material protected by this copyright notice may be reproduced or utilized in any form or by any means, electronic or mechanical, including photocopying, recording, or by any information storage and retrieval system, without written permission from the copyright owner.

Printed in the United States of America.

10 9 8 7 6 5 4 3 2 1 93 92 91 90 89 88

Contents

III

P A R T _____

DISORDERS INVOLVING PSYCHOSIS   226

7

C H A P T E R

THE SCHIZOPHRENIC DISORDERS   228

8

C H A P T E R

THE PARANOID DISORDERS   274

9

C H A P T E R

THE AFFECTIVE DISORDERS AND SUICIDE   302

V

VI

P A R T _____

LEGAL AND ETHICAL ISSUES

640

17

C H A P T E R

Preface

The field of abnormal psychology is undergoing a series of dramatic changes. The system designed to diagnose and classify abnormal behavior has again been revised; both research and practice are branching widely to include the study of disorders in children and the aged, as well as the adult population; we are becoming more global in our view of psychopathology by observing how cultures other than our own diagnose and treat psychological disorders; many of our clinical colleagues are becoming receptive to a wide range of treatment; advances in biology are broadening our perspective on the etiology of disorders as neuropsychologists approach new frontiers of study in the physiological bases of mental disorders.

This changing scene is an exciting one, for it is a period of dynamic evolution. For many of us, this excitement makes the Abnormal Psychology survey a teaching joy; and when instructors are excited about the subject matter they teach, student response is usually enthusiastic as well. When trying to capture this excitement in a textbook though, we were faced with the challenge of integrating the recent innovations in abnormal psychology with the traditional content that we long sought to convey to our student population.

Many texts spend what we feel is an inordinate amount of time on introductory material before arriving at the actual focus of the course, the study of the abnormal behavior patterns themselves. In this book, we have increased the coverage of the actual disorders, with correspondingly less time devoted to the introductory topics. We have confined background material to the first four chapters—Chapter 1 provides introductory concepts and a historical perspective, Chapter 2 gives an overview of the relevant theories of abnormal behavior, Chapter 3 discusses the assessment and diagnosis of mental disorders, and Chapter 4 looks at the wide variety of treatment approaches available to the clinician.

The next two chapters discuss some common disorders such as adjustment, anxiety, phobic, dissociative, and somatoform disorders. These disorders cause significant disruption to a person's world. However, the intensity, duration, and difficulty in changing these behavior patterns are not usually as great as those for changing the schizophrenic, paranoid, and affective disorders studied in Chapters 7, 8, and 9. Suicide is discussed in Chapter 9 along with the affective disorders, Chapters 10, 11, and 12 focus on disorders that involve some violation of legal or social standards, like sexual variations, alcohol and drug abuse patterns, and impulse disorders and violence.

Chapter 13, on neuropsychology, goes far beyond the simple cataloging of organic brain disorders found in many textbooks, emphasizing the dynamic relationship between patterns of behavior and the various syndromes of central nervous system impairments. Chapter 14 deals with mental retardation, and childhood psychological disorders are the subject of Chapter 15. Chapter 16 presents an extended developmental perspective by considering disorders of adolescence, adulthood, and aging. Chapter 17 ends the book with a discussion of how legal and social issues are related to the patterns of abnormal behavior discussed throughout the book.

Special Coverage

Major innovations in the study of abnormal behavior are again being generated by the new edition (DSM-III-R) of the *Diagnostic and Statistical Manual of Mental Disorders,* usually referred to now as the DSM. While many texts on abnormal psychology acknowledge and discuss the DSM, we have fully incorporated it in this textbook. Though there are certainly some valid criticisms of the DSM, it is the only accepted comprehensive classification system in the field of mental disorders, and thus it provides a logical organizational framework for this book.

Two important developments in modern abnormal psychology are the increasing emphasis on cross-cultural aspects of abnormal behavior, as well as on the legal and ethical issues directly related to abnormal behavior in general. Our coverage includes the various rates of occurrence, the symptoms and manifestations, and the types of treatment of societal responses to disorders as they are found in diverse cultures. While the results of cross-cultural research are consistently interspersed in the narrative text, we also highlight cross-cultural topics of special interest in boxed inserts. Legal and ethical topics are discussed within the chapters, and also by a thorough exposition of these issues in the final chapter.

Another central strength of this book is its emphasis on the diversity of techniques used in the treatment of mental disorders. Most texts put a treatment chapter at the end of the book. Beginning with an overall perspective on treatment in Chapter 4, we then follow up by discussing in detail the most important treatment approaches relevant to the specific disorders in each chapter. In that sense, the orientation of this book is eclectic, though we often employ terminology from social learning theory, which incorporates the major concepts and insights of most other thematic approaches.

While a spirit of eclecticism is found throughout this book it especially emerges in the emphasis on a multimodal approach to treatment. The multimodal approach holds that it is rare when a single treatment technique will be a sufficient response to an individual suffering from a mental disorder. Complexity is a common component of such disorders; complexity in treatment response is usually similarly required, an emphasis carried throughout this text.

Modern psychological theory has emphasized the developmental aspect of disorders; they can be a response to the common challenges and stresses of all the various life periods. Most textbooks discuss the disorders of childhood, and a few discuss the disorders related to adolescence. However, very rarely are the disorders related to the challenges of adulthood and aging, as they are in this book. A section on the college student is also included.

Special Features

Several format features of this text have been designed to enhance the interest and accessibility of the material for the student. There is a short summary of topics at the beginning of each chapter, and each chapter ends with a list of summary points, a list of key terms, and a list of suggested readings. A glossary at the back of the text provides an easy reference to increase familiarity with new terms. We have found in our own teaching that case studies especially spark interest in the topic at hand, so each chapter is introduced by a short case history that is subsequently referred to throughout the chapter, and another case is highlighted in a box in the body of each chapter. Also, a judicious use of humor, quotes, and anecdotes should help increase interest in the material.

In addition to numerous exhibits that clarify or demonstrate specific points, three types of boxes are used in this text. Research Profiles help the student gain an understanding of research approaches in abnormal psychology that reach beyond the text itself; Issues to Consider focus on social issues that are central to abnormal psychology; and Abnormality across Cultures boxes illustrate the many different ways that disorders are diagnosed and treated in a variety of cultural settings. We have also used generous illustrations from popular culture to increase student awareness of how the various art forms in our culture, such as literature, popular song, and cinema, treat behavior.

Special Thanks

We find it impossible to acknowledge everyone who has helped with this project, but there are a number of people who deserve special mention. The most important have been our editors at Allyn and Bacon, John-Paul Lenney, Psychology Editor, and Tom Mancuso, Leslie Galton and Wendy Ritger, Developmental Editors, without whose assistance and dedication this book could not have been published. Quite simply, they were superb. We also wish to again thank Bill Barke, who helped us with direction and guidance in the initial formulation of this book.

We first want to thank all of those people whose influence we cannot specifically recount here. Several mentors and colleagues deserve special mention for their contributions to each of us that in turn aided our eventual production of this book: Norman Abeles, Curtis Barrett, Vytautas Bieliauskas, Ray Cattell, Herb Eber, Will Edgerton, Lucy Rau Ferguson, Ray Fowler, Jesse Harris, Phillip Johnson, Bertram Karon, Rhett Landis, Paul Lipsitt, Susan Matarese, Ken McNeil, Albert Rabin, Aaron Smith, Steven Smith, Harvey Tilker, Lee Winder, and Edwin Zolik. Excellent clerical and organizational help was provided by Sandy Hartz, Sharon Mills, Laura Abell, Mary Jane Cherry, Suzanne Paris, Steve Mill, Juanita Chatman, Janet Breckenridge, and Kathleen McDaniel.

Several readers critiqued the manuscript, or portions of it, and made invaluable suggestions for improvement. A special note of thanks is offered to them here. Juris Draguns, Diane Follingstad, Ted Friedberg, Mary Koss, Bill McReynolds, Irene Nolan, Alan Penn, Bob Perz, Dennis Saccuzzo, Joe Scalise, Robert Sommer, and Don Strassberg were all helpful in assisting us with earlier versions of the manuscript. We have tried to incorporate all of their suggestions whenever possible, and the book has gained much from their practical suggestions.

Finally, the following reviewers were helpful in refining more recent drafts of this manuscript; many thanks to them:

Ernest W. Dahl
American River College

Randal P. Quevillon
University of South Dakota

Thomas Cash
Old Dominion University

William Springer
Shippensburg University

Mary A. Rogers
Inver Hills Community College

Lawrence J. Lewandowski
Syracuse University

Lester A. Lefton
University of South Carolina

Don Devers
Northern Virginia Community College

Charles E. Joubert
University of North Alabama

Vern Haddick
California Institute of Integral Studies

Geoffrey L. Thorpe
University of Maine

Forrest Scogin
University of Alabama

Robert M. Gilligan
LaSalle University

Alexander R. Rich
Indiana University of PA

Debra F. Neff
Virginia Polytechnic Institute and State University

Professor Jack Kapchan
University of Miami

ABNORMAL PSYCHOLOGY

PART

I

Foundations

When I'm alone at night, I look out of my window, and it comes to me: we don't have to live great lives, we just have to understand the ones we've got.

Andre Dubus
Voices from the Moon (1984)

In *The Dresser*, Albert Finney portrays a Shakespearean actor performing the role of King Lear (with the constant companionship of his dresser, Tom Courtenay). Like Lear, Finney's character goes mad by the film's end. (The Museum of Modern Art/Film Stills Archive; © 1983 Columbia Pictures Industries, Inc.)

1

Abnormal Behavior: Historical and Scientific Issues

Abnormal behavior occurs in many forms. Though such behavior may be frightening or confusing to deal with, the study of abnormal behavior is fascinating to scientists, scholars, and students alike. People have attempted to study, change, or prevent abnormal behavior (also referred to as psychopathology) for thousands of years, but only in the past couple of centuries have we developed a controlled, scientific process for doing so. This chapter first considers the case of Jason, which will help to highlight the different issues and dimensions of abnormal behavior. We will then look at how attitudes, treatment techniques, and scientific methods of studying abnormal behavior have developed up to the present.

● The Case of Jason

Jason's father died when he was four, and he was raised by his mother in a small town in a Western state. He had always seemed "odd" to the people who knew him. By this, most people meant he occasionally seemed not to be paying attention to what was going on around him, would sometimes make comments that did not make much sense, and seemed to prefer being alone most of the time. But this behavior was tolerated, since Jason was generally a quiet child, seldom got into any trouble, and made at least passing grades in school. After graduating from high school, he became a cook in a local restaurant. He adjusted reasonably well. Then the restaurant in which he worked was bought by a national chain, which placed higher standards and expectancies on Jason's behavior. Shortly after this, Jason's mother died.

Jason's behavior now seemed bizarre, rather than simply different. He carried on conversations with invisible others. His work performance deteriorated rapidly, and he occasionally showed up for work dirty and disheveled. He admitted hearing voices that he thought were angels sent by his mother to help him. It was now almost impossible to keep up a rational conversation with him for more than a few minutes. Not surprisingly, Jason was fired from his job. He started crying in his supervisor's office, said a few things that made no sense whatsoever, and refused to leave the office. His uncle, who had been acting as his informal guardian, was called and took Jason to the local mental hospital, where he was admitted for diagnosis and treatment.

THE DIMENSIONS OF ABNORMALITY

Virtually anyone would agree that Jason was showing **abnormal** behavior, because "abnormal" simply means "away from the norm." However, more specific criteria are typically used to define the term abnormal in the study of psychology. Individuals can be "away from the norm" in several different ways or dimensions.

Statistical rarity.   Using this criterion, we label individuals as abnormal if they differ significantly from the average, or from what people agree is normal behavior. But **statistical rarity** can be a problematic criterion, since people who are geniuses, highly creative, or only eccentric would not be differentiated from people like Jason. In addition, the statistical rarity approach does not take into account the desirability of the norms of the particular society on which the judgment is based. So, a conscientious objector would be labeled as abnormal during a war seen by most of the society as desirable. Conversely, someone running a brutal concentration camp might be seen as normal in that same society.

An alternative form of the statistical rarity model is to set the criterion for judging at the "ideal" rather than the "average." Then, the farther away from the ideal, the more likely we are to be judged abnormal. The difficulty here is that most of us don't come anywhere near the ideal in many areas of our functioning. So there would be a tendency to see as abnormal many of us who are actually functioning adequately and are at least moderately content with our lot in life.

Individuals who vary from society's norms, such as Vincent van Gogh, exhibit talents—even genius—that are unrecognized in their own lifetimes.   (The Bettmann Archive)

Subjective discomfort.   An alternative criterion that is sometimes used is **subjective discomfort,** the individual's own judgment as to whether or not he or she is content with functioning and feelings. There are many people who seem on the surface to be psychologically healthy. They have interesting jobs, good family lives, and excellent achievements, but they seek psychological help because of reported inner turmoil. However, by itself, the subjective discomfort criterion is not a good basis for judgments of abnormality. Many alcoholics and most paranoids and criminals don't see themselves as having psychological problems. Jason would probably not have seen himself as psychologically disturbed. However, he was diagnosed as schizophrenic, a severe disorder characterized by thought disorder, interpersonal difficulties, persistent and unusual belief systems (delusions), and possibly seeing, hearing, or smelling things that are not there (hallucinations).

Maladaptive functioning. Using the criterion of **maladaptive functioning,** we judge people as abnormal if their thinking, feelings, or behavior interferes with their ability to function in their own lives and within society. This is probably the best standard of all. It incorporates the best aspects of both the statistical rarity and the subjective discomfort criteria. At the same time, it allows flexibility, since it focuses on functioning relative to one's life circumstances.

These criteria have been used to develop several general guidelines that are consistently relevant to the issue of abnormality throughout history and across most cultures (Kendler, 1987; Eaton, 1986; Waxler, 1984). These guidelines, described in detail in subsequent chapters, can be summarized as follows.

1. Some recurring behaviors that seem indicative of potential, developing, or existent mental disorder are: (a) an inability to inhibit self-destructive behaviors; (b) seeing or hearing things that others in the culture agree are not there; (c) sporadic and/or random outbursts of violence; (d) a consistent inability to deal interpersonally in an effective manner; (e) persistent academic and/or vocational failure; (f) anxiety and/or depression; and (g) an inability to conform to codes of behavior whether or not one verbalizes a desire to do so.

2. Using the factors listed above, the most consistent criteria for deciding whether or not a specific individual is abnormal are: (a) the deviance (or bizarreness) of behavior from the norms of that society; (b) the continuity and/or persistence of disordered behavior over time; and (c) the resulting degree of disruption in intrapersonal and/or interpersonal functioning.

Throughout this book we will use the following common terms to further define abnormality.

1. **Deviant** describes behavior that differs markedly from socially accepted standards of conduct. In many cases, the word has negative connotations, though it may also refer to those who are well above the norm, such as geniuses and the gifted.

2. **Different** also suggests behavior that varies significantly, at least statistically, from the accepted norm, but it usually has fewer negative connotations.

3. **Disordered** implies a lack of integration in behaviors; the result may be impairment of a person's ability to cope in various situations.

4. **Bizarre** suggests behavior that differs extremely from socially accepted norms. In addition, it connotes inadequate coping patterns and the

disintegration of behavior patterns. "Deranged" is sometimes used in place of bizarre, and they are quite similar in meaning.

5. **Mental disorder** refers to an observable pattern of significant maladaptive behavior and/or thinking that shows at least some persistence and consistency over time. "Mental illness" is sometimes used to designate such patterns, especially those that are thought to have a significant biological component as a cause of the disorder. The terms "mental illness," "mental disorder," and "emotional disorder" are used throughout the field of abnormal psychology; their meanings are so similar that they are virtually interchangeable.

RATES OF MENTAL DISORDERS

There have been many efforts over the past several decades to assess effectively the overall incidence rates of mental disorder. Earlier endeavors in this area provided some useful data, but all prior efforts pale in comparison to the landmark study developed by the National Institute of Mental Health (NIMH), which was initially reported in a series of six articles in the October, 1984, issue of the *Archives of General Psychiatry.*

The sheer scope of this study is unprecedented. More than 17,000 representative community residents (virtually a fivefold increase over the most exhaustive prior studies) were sampled at five sites (Baltimore; New Haven, Connecticut; North Carolina; St. Louis; and Los Angeles). These individuals were given a thorough and standardized structured interview, using the Diagnostic Interview Schedule, and were then followed up a year later with a reinterview. Unlike many earlier studies, this research was not restricted to reporting only on hospitalized mentally disordered persons, or only on prevalence of treatment, or on current symptoms or level of impairment. Instead, all 13 of the major disorder categories of the third edition of the *Diagnostic and Statistical Manual* (DSM-III), the generally accepted handbook of diagnostic categories at that time, were considered.

The researchers first measured these groups from the perspective of six-month prevalence rates, i.e., how many people show a particular disorder at some time in the six months during which the population is assessed. They found that about 19 percent of adults over age 18 suffer from at least one mental disorder during a given six-month period.

The types of problems reported include:

- Anxiety disorders (see Chapter 6), such as phobias, panic disorders, and obsessive-compulsive disorders. Afflicting about eight percent (that is, every eight out of 100 persons show this problem) of those surveyed, anxiety disorders appear to be the most common group of psychological problems—not depressive illnesses, as previously thought. These disorders include specific intense fears, such as fear of heights or animals, as well as agoraphobia, a fear of leaving the familiar setting of home.

- Abuse or dependence on drugs (see Chapter 11), afflicting an estimated six to seven percent of the population. About four fifths of the cases are linked to alcohol.

- Affective or mood disorders (see Chapter 9), such as major depression and manic-depression, which affected about six percent of the adults studied.

- Schizophrenia (see Chapter 7), probably the most severely disabling of mental illnesses. This was found in about one percent of the population. Another one percent are affected by antisocial personality disorders— deeply ingrained behavior patterns that bring a person into conflict with others, such as a low frustration level or an incapacity to feel guilt.

Somewhat different results are obtained if one takes the perspective of lifetime prevalence rates. To find this, the researchers assessed how often disorders occur in the lifetime of the people who are sampled. From this perspective (Robins and Helzer 1986), it would appear that the most common disorder pattern is substance abuse, at close to 20 percent (alcoholism, 13 percent; other drug abuse, 5.5 percent).

Drug and alcohol abuse is a common problem in modern society. An astonishing 80 percent of abuse cases involve alcohol.   (Rhoda Sidney/Leo de Wys, Inc.)

There was also a high rate for the anxiety disorders of 12 to 20 percent, and for the affective disorders of 8 to 9 percent. The variable estimates for the anxiety disorders reflects the fact that there was a much higher assessed rate of anxiety disorders in Baltimore than in the other sites. (Our hypothesis is that the study was conducted around the year the Colts football team left Baltimore for Indianapolis. The Baltimore Orioles didn't do all that well in baseball that year either.) The overall rate in these studies for schizophrenia was 1.0 to 1.5 percent, and the rate for the antisocial personality disorder was 2.5 percent.

Breaking down the anxiety disorder category, phobias were observed at about 10 percent, the panic disorders at 1.5 percent, and the obsessive-compulsive disorder at 2.5 percent. Breaking down the affective disorders, bipolar disorder was found at close to 1.0 percent, major depressions at about 5.5 percent, and dysthymic disorder (a milder form of depression) at 3 percent.

The NIMH project also looked at differences in rates of mental disorder among people who lived in urban central city areas, in suburbs, and in small towns or rural areas (Robins and Helzer, 1986). For schizophrenia, organic brain disorder, alcoholism, drug abuse, and the antisocial personality disorder, the rates were highest in the central city, at a middle level for suburban areas, and lowest in the rural/small town populations. Rates were relatively even throughout these three areas for major depressions and phobias, though somatization disorders, panic disorders, and some affective disorders were a bit higher in the rural/small town areas than in the other areas. The only disorder that was found to be higher in the suburbs was the obsessive-compulsive disorder. This study also examined data on the most frequent disorder patterns by age group; that data is presented in Chapter 16 (Psychological Disorders of Adolescence through Old Age).

Data, issues, and terms such as the above will appear throughout this book. For example, the next chapter looks at how different theoretical orientations may arrive at different perspectives on the same phenomenon. Chapter 3 addresses issues in, and methods of, assessing abnormality, and most of the later chapters examine the various categories of abnormal behavior. But first we present a brief review of Western trends in (and various cultural responses to) abnormality, to provide a context for understanding the various categories and theories relevant to the study of abnormal behavior.

This historical overview will highlight several themes, which have repercussions in the subject matter of this book.

1. Abnormality has been recognized throughout history. However, views about what types of behavior are abnormal may differ somewhat from society to society, and **cross-cultural research** of abnormal behavior provides evidence that the interpretation of similar behaviors can vary significantly across cultures (Waxler, 1984; Mezzich and Berganza, 1984). Comparing the traditions of other cultures through cross-cultural research highlights these differences.

2. Explanations of abnormality have evolved from superstition and demonology to science.

3. Explanations of abnormality have fluctuated between two main categories, physical causes and psychological causes.

4. Treatment of abnormality has evolved from cruelty to care.

Now let us turn to this historical overview.

RESEARCH PROFILE

On the Nature of Sanity

David Rosenhan began with a simple question: "If sanity and insanity exist, how shall we know them?" (1973, p. 250). In an intriguing study reported in *Science,* Rosenhan described the results of his efforts to determine whether psychiatric diagnostic characteristics are individual or environmental. The experiment was simple: eight normal subjects on twelve different occasions gained admission to psychiatric inpatient hospitals and submitted to diagnosis to determine whether or not they would be identified as sane. Rosenhan reasoned that psychiatrists' identification of these people as sane would provide compelling evidence that pathology reflected the characteristics of an individual's behavior, regardless of context.

Five of Rosenhan's pseudopatients (including himself) had backgrounds in psychology or psychiatry; the other three were a pediatrician, a housewife, and a painter. With one exception, the nature of the project was unknown to staff members at the various hospitals. Upon securing an appointment to seek hospital admission, all pseudopatients described symptom patterns consistent with existential crises and suggesting a condition—existential psychosis—that is completely undocumented in the research or clinical literature. The pseudopatients falsified names and current occupations, but provided accurate information about their personal history and upbringing. Following admission, they abruptly stopped simulating abnormal behavior and behaved as they normally would. Having been told that they would have to gain release by their own methods, all were motivated to behave in a most cooperative way (the majority wanted to be released immediately after admission).

None of the pseudopatients was detected, although all had anticipated exposure and, perhaps, humiliation. Each openly took extensive notes, yet none was questioned about it. All but one was admitted with a diagnosis of schizophrenia, and upon release each was given a diagnostic classification of "schizophrenia, in remission."

THE ANCIENT PEOPLES

The ancient peoples in most areas of the world believed abnormal behavior to be the result of direct supernatural action, the action of gods, demons, or other forces beyond nature. Very often this explanation incorporated a form of demonology, such as a belief in evil spirits who controlled or influenced human beings. For example, Saul, king of Israel in the eleventh century B.C.,

The experience, especially the strict segregation of staff from patients, left a powerful impression on Rosenhan and the other pseudopatients. This segregation resulted in very limited extended contact between the two groups. Those with the greatest control and power over patients—the medical staff—were the least available. More staff contact with patients might have led to greater awareness of the degrees of normality and abnormality present.

Segregation and isolation promoted feelings of powerlessness and depersonalization. Perfunctory interactions, absence of privacy, deprivation of personal possessions, and reliance on drugs as principal therapeutic agents contributed to such feelings.

For these and a variety of other reasons, Rosenhan's experience—and that of the other psuedopatients—was distinctly negative. He concluded that the fault did not lie with hospital staff, most of whom he was convinced were basically sensitive and caring people. Rather, he attributed many of the problems to unenlightened attitudes that promote ambivalence and avoidance, even among staff to whose care they are entrusted. The numerous manifestations of this attitude in psychiatric hospitals include custodial care, heavy reliance on psychotropic (i.e., generates psychological changes) medications as primary therapeutic agents, and rigid segregation of patients and staff. Rosenhan concluded that the detection of sanity in such places is unlikely. Given this probability, it is also likely that perceptions of persons who are truly psychologically troubled can be markedly distorted under the same circumstances. Moreover, the consequences of such hospitalization appear to be decidedly countertherapeutic. Less reliance on psychiatric labeling, a more pragmatic focus on solving personal problems, and creation of environments that promote health and well-being can do much to promote a realistic assessment of what is normal and what is not.

tried to kill his son Jonathan, and on another occasion stripped himself nude in public while in an obvious rage. His behavior was attributed to a demon, and attempts were made to exorcise the demon by prayers and ritual offerings. It is now believed that Saul suffered from a bipolar disorder (previously termed manic-depressive psychosis), a mental disorder marked by periods of depression alternating with occasional periods of mania (high energy and elation).

The peoples of other early civilizations also commonly attributed similar abnormal behavior to demon possession and supernatural influence. Yet, at the same time, there were isolated instances of an awareness that other variables, such as environmental events or physical causes, were involved in abnormal behavior. These more rational explanations were first thoroughly articulated and systematized in the early Greek and Roman cultures.

Greece

Portrayals of abnormal behavior were numerous in the mythology of ancient Greece. Greek plays and epic poetry display a rich source of knowledge about the human condition and about abnormality. Freud's hypothesis that a boy's incestuous feelings for his mother and jealous fear of his father cause psychological conflict was named the Oedipus complex after the events in Sophocles' play *Oedipus Rex*. In this play, Oedipus unknowingly kills his father and later unknowingly marries his mother. When he discovers what he has done, he blinds himself because of his anguish and distress. The Greek playwright Euripides (480–406 B.C.) also portrayed the range of human emotions and showed especially well how the normal can become abnormal. In his *Medea*, a mother's severe anger and jealousy, which in lesser degrees are at times a part of the emotional life of all parents, leads her to murder her children. In another play about Hercules, Euripides described in detail this hero's spells of frenzied activity, marked by loss of consciousness, frothing at the mouth, and occasional loss of control of voluntary muscle movements. During these episodes Hercules kills at least six people, including his best friend and his two children, and then destroys a flock of sheep for good measure. It is possible that Euripides was using the symptoms of psychomotor epilepsy, a relatively rare abnormality sometimes associated with homicidal outbursts, to describe Hercules.

Despite the perceptiveness of Greek writers, the prevailing belief was that abnormal behavior was a punishment from the gods. Consequently, people evincing such behavior were primarily under the care of priests, who also functioned as physicians, politicians, and masters of the occult. Treatment was generally a combination of warm interpersonal support, placebos, herbs, prayers, and rituals. Resistant patients were dealt with more harshly, with purgatives, beatings, restraints, and isolation. From this setting emerged one of the most influential physcians of all time, the priest Hippocrates.

Hippocrates and the rise of rationalism. Hippocrates (460–377 B.C.) was a Greek priest trained in exorcism as a way of controlling abnormal behavior. One of his primary contributions to a scientific understanding of abnormality was to challenge prevailing notions by attributing abnormality to natural causes, rather than to supernatural ones.

He did this in several ways. First, he asserted the **somatogenic** theory that disorder in the physical body (soma) causes psychological disorder. Second, Hippocrates focused on the brain. During his time, simple epilepsy was referred to as "the sacred disease" because it was believed to be the result of possession by a god. Hippocrates said, "If you cut open the head, you will find the brain humid, full of sweat and smelling badly. And in that way you see that it is not a god which injures the body, but a disease." He reached the right conclusion for the wrong reason. Epilepsy is indeed a brain disorder, but there is no evidence that there are gross and substantial lesions in the brains of epileptic patients, or that their brains sweat. Moreover, any brain that is cut open tends to smell after a while. Third, though he erred in some of his views, Hippocrates was well ahead of his time in emphasizing the importance of environmental and social stresses on human functioning (Kendler, 1987). And finally, Hippocrates placed great importance on taxonomy (the accurate observation and classification of phenomena), a necessary stage in the development of any science. Classification is still a major task in the field of abnormal psychology.

Despite his successes, Hippocrates consistently made a mistake in his thinking. He confused correlation with causation, a mistake still common today. **Correlation** (discussed in more detail later in this chapter) is the occurrence of events at the same time or place; **causation** is the act or process of one event affecting another. Hippocrates theorized, for example, that a sluggish or lazy temperament resulted from an excess of phlegm. It is true that persons afflicted with viral and bacterial disorders that generate phlegm are often slowed down temporarily in behavior, and it is tempting to see phlegm as a cause of sluggishness. But, in fact, it is only a correlate, something that occurs at the same time.

Rome

The Romans copied the Greeks in drama and philosophy but surpassed them in military organization, law, engineering, and medicine. The Romans were the first Europeans to build hospitals for civilians. The better hospitals had continuously flushing marble latrines, sewer systems, and drainage ditches. Surgical procedures were also quite advanced for the period and in crude form anticipated the first psychosurgery performed in modern times (in 1935, by a Portuguese physician named Egas Moniz) (Valenstein, 1986). The first caesarean section is said to have been performed at the birth of Julius Caesar. The most famous physician in Rome was Galen, who lived in the second century A.D. He came from Pergamum, the site of both a famous medical school and a shrine to Asclepius. Galen served as personal physician to the emperor Marcus Aurelius. He made a number of discoveries about the nervous system, and yet, in spite of his strong advocacy of the scientific method, he compiled a vast and highly influential encyclopedia of medical knowledge that he claimed to have received as revelations from Asclepius in dreams.

THE MIDDLE AGES

Rome copied the best aspects of Greek civilization, merged them with its own culture, and spread this influence throughout the Mediterranean basin. Eventually, however, the Roman Empire collapsed under its own weight. Historians usually cite 476 A.D., when a barbarian tribe sacked Rome, as the beginning of the Middle Ages, a period that lasted 1,000 years.

Individuals who exhibited abnormal behavior in the Middle Ages were assumed to be possessed by demonic spirts, who tormented the victim into acts of insanity.   (Historical Pictures Services, Chicago)

Medieval cures for abnormal behavior ranged from prolonged torture to burning. The "physician" shown here cures for patient's fantasies by fire.   (Historical Pictures Service, Chicago)

The Early Middle Ages: 500–1050

At the beginning of the medieval period, sometimes called the Dark Ages, Germanic tribes infiltrated the Roman Empire. Some broke through as warring bands, some were recruited as Roman mercenaries, and some settled peacefully within the empire. These movements resulted in the breakdown of Roman scholarship, education, science, and, most important for our purposes, medicine. The hospitals built by the Romans fell into ruin. Western civilization changed altogether.

The most significant change of the Early Middle Ages occurred in 496 when Clovis, king of the Franks, was converted to Christianity. His conversion meant that all of his subjects were also converted, and soon all the Germanic tribes renounced their paganism and embraced Christianity. The rise of Christianity, however, with its emphasis on virtue and good works, did not have a totally positive effect on the treatment of abnormal behavior. Medieval Christians tended to measure progress in spiritual rather than in here-and-now human terms. The mentally disordered either were left to roam aimlessly or were accused of being possessed by demonic spirits. The church equated some of the symptoms of abnormal behavior, such as depression or melancholy, with the sin of sloth or laziness, and people who suffered from these afflictions were sometimes considered to be possessed by the devil. No treatment was provided; instead, victims were cast out of society and left to associate with other misfits, such as the physically deformed and spastic.

Some abnormal behavior was considered curable, though the cures frequently were worse than the illness. Rest, sleep, and ointments rubbed on the side of the head were prescribed for the more fortunate. Those believed to be possessed by the devil had crosses shaved on their heads, or a cure was attempted by tying them to posts in churches.

Although few records remain from the early medieval period, some of the literature of the time describes the typical treatments for mental illness (Wright, 1939). In the old French romance, *Yvain*, the hero goes berserk when his "lady" (the term of that period for a noble woman) rejects him for failing to return to her after spending a year in tournaments (where he was wooing someone else's lady). Guilt, rage, and depression overcome him and he lives naked in the woods, where he survives on the flesh of wild animals. Another lady discovers him in the woods and turns him over to her damsel-in-waiting, who cures him by rubbing ointment on his temples and having him rest in a quiet place.

The High Middle Ages: 1050–1300

After the Dark Ages, universities were founded, and achievements and events of this period indirectly produced a positive effect on the treatment of mental disorder. One reason was the Crusades. On their travels to Asia Minor, the Christian knights rediscovered some of the Greek and Roman texts, including Galen's study of anatomy. Also, despite the emphasis on the supernatural, physicians began to thrive as a social class and developed effective treatments for certain physical diseases and some mental disorders. They understood, for example, that epilepsy is a brain disorder. Despite their high status, however, the church limited their function. Physicians were to provide relief; God would supply the cure.

Even in the High Middle Ages, there were no hospitals to care for the mentally disordered. Monasteries often served that function by providing quiet places of rest and retreat in which herbs and ointments were administered, along with prayers and spiritual counseling. If a nobleman chose not be a knight, he usually became a monk instead. Many monks rose to important positions, such as advisers to kings. Besides preserving the tradition of learning, monasteries provided care for the mentally disordered. Once again, the literature of the period provides an example of how people treated mental affliction. In Adam de la Halle's play *Le Jeu de la Feuillee*, a major character is described as a "madman" (today he would be described as paranoid), who is convinced that people are talking about him and that various forces are plotting to murder him. He distrusts even his father and threatens to strangle him. His father takes him to a monk who possesses relics of St. Alcair, who achieved sainthood by curing the mentally disturbed. The monk advises rest, prayer, and compassion, and in this play, the treatment was successful.

The Late Middle Ages: 1300–1500

The two major factors affecting the decline of the Middle Ages were the Hundred Years' War between France and England (1337–1453) and the onset of a devastating epidemic of bubonic plague, an infectuous disease of the lymph glands that killed nearly 20 million people.

One of the most interesting individual accounts of mental disorder during this period is that of the French king Charles VI, who ruled France during one phase of the Hundred Years' War. Charles was mentally disordered but was somehow able to remain on the throne. The result was chaos for France. En route to one of his military campaigns, the king was upset when he heard a loud clang. He immediately pulled his sword and killed several of his own knights before lapsing into a withdrawn state, probably a severe form of schizophrenia. He continued to rule despite similar intermittent attacks. He ran from his wife in terror and made rude and obscene gestures at her family's coat of arms. He often failed to recognize even his closest friends and was discovered on many occasions roaming the royal corridors mimicking a wolf. All attempts at treatment failed. One can imagine the effects if someone in King Charles' condition were ruling one of the superpowers today.

Some of the most fascinating accounts of abnormal behavior date from the fourteenth century, when the bubonic plague ravaged Europe. This devastating epidemic caused psychological side effects almost as severe as its physical effects. Historians sometimes describe these effects and this period as "mass madness" (Kendler, 1987).

The bubonic plague originated in central Asia and was carried by fleas and rats from ships that had visited Asian ports. It wiped out half the population of Europe between 1347 and the end of the century. The plague, or Black Death, derived its name from black swellings (buboes) about the size of eggs that appeared on the bodies of the afflicted. People died so fast (800 a day in Paris) that corpses were piled up in layers. The epidemic was especially terrible because people did not know its cause, or how it spread, and therefore had no remedies. It was generally viewed as a punishment by God for leading a sinful life. The abnormal behavior that resulted from the plague took several forms. Two of these were the flagellant movement and the phenomenon of the dancing mania, and they mark a step backward in the concept and care of abnormal behavior, before progress occurred once again at the time of the Renaissance.

The flagellant movement.   Because the plague was interpreted as divine chastisement, medieval people began to punish themselves. The flagellants were groups of men who wandered from town to town flogging themselves with leather whips tipped with iron spikes. Although these bands came from all parts of society, they particularly attracted the mentally disordered. Each band contained from 50 to 500 people and had a master to whom all the members swore allegiance. They marched for 33½ days at a time and followed strict rules. They were forbidden to speak to each other or to women and were beaten by the master if they did. When they arrived in a town, they formed a circle in front of a church and stripped to the waist. Each member, one by one, then threw himself facedown in the dirt, with arms outstretched in the form of a cross. Some lay in positions that symbolized their sins. Other members then struck them with their scourges. The master beat the ones who supposedly had the most sins. Then they all stood up and beat themselves. A classic motion picture, *The Seventh Seal,* directed by Ingmar Bergman, contains a flagellation scene and generally chronicles the mass psychological horror of the plague in late medieval Europe. The flagellant movement spread throughout Europe and rivaled the Crusades in the number of people it involved.

The dancing mania.   A movement similar to the flagellant movement was the dancing mania. The participants were convinced that they were possessed by demons. Like the flagellants, the dancing maniacs traveled in groups from town to town. The members danced vigorously in a great circle for hours and screamed the names of the demons they felt were tormenting them, then fell on the ground. Priests tried to rid them of the devils by exorcism, and wild party-like events often followed such exorcisms.

The sixteenth-century Flemish artist, Pieter Breughel, captured the struggle of St. Vitus Dance, in which participants gyrated and screamed maniacally, finally falling to the ground. It is now thought that St. Vitus Dance was produced by mass suggestion and facilitated by hysteric personality components.   (The Bettmann Archive)

According to historian Barbara Tuchman (1978), the period of the Black Death in Europe marks the end of medieval times. Survivors of the plague rejected the notion that it was the direct work of God, strove to improve their lives on earth, and prayed for an eternal life. Western civilization moved into a new era, and so did the treatment of mental disorder.

THE EARLY MODERN PERIOD

The Renaissance: 1500–1650

The word "renaissance" means rebirth, and the Renaissance in Europe is said to be the beginning of the modern age. In places like the Renaissance city–states of Italy, thinkers ignored the medieval past and looked for models of behavior back to the civilizations of Greece and Rome. Renaissance thinkers stressed individual accomplishment in this life, not in the hereafter. Not surprisingly, the Renaissance witnessed advances in the treatment of mental disorder. Renaissance thinkers suggested that abnormal behavior had natural causes. One such thinker was Johann Weyer (1515–1588), a physician and respected literary figure who was horrified by the scenes of exorcism and execution he had witnessed. In 1563 Weyer published a book asserting that most people who had been burned as witches were simply sick, either in mind or in body. Some church authorities denounced him, but several influential contemporary theologians and writers were impressed by his writings. St. Vincent de Paul (1576–1660) preached similar views, though not without heavy opposition. In England, at about the same time, Reginald Scot (1538–1599) wrote a well-reasoned and influential book called *The Discovery of Witchcraft* that attempted a straightforward and scientific interpretation of abnormal behavior. Theories of abnormality involving demonology, witchcraft, and supernatural intervention were beginning to yield to science and therefore to explanations based on reasoning, observation, and experimentation.

The Asylum Years

As views about the mentally disordered changed, their care shifted from monasteries to asylums and from priests to physicians. Asylums were at first quiet retreats from the world, reflecting the monastic model, and the treatment was simply adequate food and shelter, with a measure of human kindness. As we shall see, this concept has persisted until recent times.

It was not long before asylums became overcrowded and noisy; in time they became nothing more than long-term holding tanks for the mentally disordered. In fact, the word "bedlam" is a corrupted version of "Hospital of St. Mary of Bethlehem," which was a London asylum that in the late 1500s

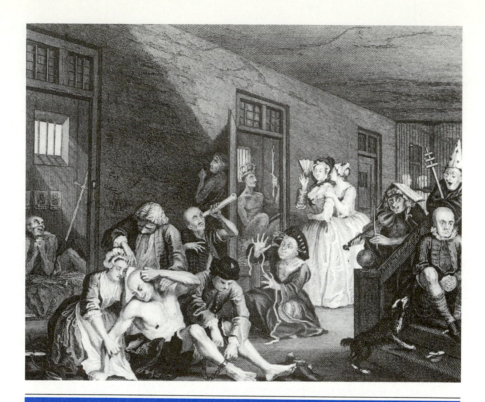

In his series of eighteenth-century engravings called *The Rake's Progress*, Hogarth showed members of London's upper class observing inmates of a mental asylum as a form of entertainment.   (Historical Pictures Service, Chicago)

became so overcrowded and chaotic that passersby were often startled by the screams from inside. Those who were more than routinely curious could view the violent patients for a penny. Similarly, the Lunatic's Tower, completed in Vienna in 1784, was constructed so that patients were restrained next to an outer wall, thus allowing observation by the local population. In other words, despite the growth of a rational point of view, the general population found abnormal behavior to be an unrelated, amusing curiosity and viewed it unsympathetically.

During the 1800s, reform of asylums occurred in Europe, England, and America. A historian (Spelling, 1940) has described conditions before reforms at La Bicêtre, a large asylum in Paris. The inmates were "shackled to the walls of their cells by iron collars which held them flat against the wall . . . they could not lie down at night . . . the food was usually mushy gruel . . . they were presumed to be animals . . . and not to care whether the food was good or bad" (p. 54). In 1793, Philippe Pinel (1745–1826) was put in charge of La Bicêtre. Despite much opposition, Pinel removed the chains from the inmates. He also initiated the practices of keeping case histories and records

---

EXHIBIT

Major Historical Developments Related to Mental Disorder

A. *Western Society*
   Early Greeks—Hippocrates (460–377 B.C.)—(a) focus on brain, (b) emphasis on life stressors
   Romans—Galen (2nd century A.D.)—(a) hospital as a treatment center, (b) thorough classification of disorders
   Age of Crusades—(a) physicians as higher status social class, (b) rediscovery of Greek and Roman texts, (c) contact with Near Eastern and Oriental influences
   Renaissance (1500–1650)—(a) beginning rejection of witchcraft, (b) naturalistic explanations of emotional disorder, (c) building of asylums
   Enlightenment (1700–1800)—(a) more humane care, (b) keeping of case histories and rudimentary statistics

B. *United States*
   Early colonial period—regression to witchcraft and demonology.
   1773—first hospital specifically for mental patients—Williamsburg, Virginia
   Late 1700s—"moral therapy" becomes popular
   Approximately 1850—hospital reform movement
   Late 1800s—medical model increases influence
   Early 1900s—Freudian model increases influence
   Early to mid 1900s—behavioral model increases influence
   1950s and 1960s—humanistic and cognitive models increase influence
   Early 1960s—community mental health care centers change care delivery structure
   1980s—"corporatization" of mental health care delivery. Those who pay for services (or their administrators—e.g., Preferred Provider Organizations [PPOs]) begin to capture system from those who deliver the services

---

and of talking to patients. Esquirol (1772–1840), Pinel's pupil and successor at La Bicêtre, continued the reforms. In the hope of determining potential causes for mental disorders, Esquirol also attempted a statistical correlation of conditions in patients' lives with the onset of illness.

During this period William Tuke established similar reforms in England at York Retreat, a humane Quaker institution. Some time after this, the efforts of Dorothea Dix (1802–1887) and others stimulated similar reforms in America.

TREATMENT OF MENTAL DISORDER IN THE UNITED STATES

Demonology persisted at least as long in New England as it did in Europe. There were numerous witch trials and executions. The most infamous occurred in 1693 in Salem, Massachusetts. Because of the frontier conditions and a religious system that did not leave room for psychological explanations

ABNORMALITY ACROSS CULTURES

Trance and Possession Phenomena

In August of 1837, a group of young girls, all members of a religious sect known as the Shakers, were attending a religious service near Albany, New York, when they began behaving in a most unusual manner. They shook and whirled, fell to the ground, and broke into spontaneous songs never before heard. Several reported seeing heavenly visions replete with angels, while others believed that they had seen an image of Mother Ann Lee, foundress of the Shaker movement. Within a year, there were reports of similar incidents in other Shaker communities on the east coast, all of which maintained close contact with one another.

These occurrences were conceptually similar to the situation that led to the Salem Witch Trials in 1692, when several young girls collectively displayed similar types of behavior. In Salem, however, the behavior was interpreted in decidedly negative terms, being deemed so unusual it was concluded that the children were possessed by the Devil. The afflicted girls began accusing other community members of being witches, creating a state of paranoia that eventually resulted in the deaths of 20 community members.

These events took place in communities (Salem and Albany) that had few basic values in common, which accounts in part for the diametrically opposed ways in which the behavior was interpreted. In the Shaker community, trances and states of possession were viewed positively, as manifestations of divine intervention. In Salem, the stern prevailing religious attitudes of the time judged harshly behavior that departed even marginally from the accepted norm. However, the substantial differences between the two communities should not obscure some characteristic patterns common to both situations that are of great interest to psychologists.

Trances and states in which people collectively report being possessed or overtaken by otherworldly forces have been reported in many communal organizations. The Greeks described such behavior as hysteria, a term derived from the Greek word for womb, and related the condition to a dysfunction of the female reproductive system. The relationship between hysteria and sexuality implied by the Greeks was later given added credence by Freud's view of such behavior as a manifestation of repressed sexual energies. Indeed, the episodes in both communities discussed here involved young women at or near the age of puberty, a time of difficult changes in physical and psychological makeup.

of abnormality, there were no mental hospitals in early Colonial times. Not until the eighteenth century were some hospitals founded, and the conditions in them were primitive. This was a time of violence and political unrest. With the passage of the Stamp Act in Britain, economic and political conditions so worsened that the mentally retarded and disturbed were left to wander in the countryside or were placed into primitive jails. But Virginia's Royal Governor Francis Fauquier persuaded (against much resistance) the Virginia House of Burgesses to build a hospital by playing upon the widespread belief that the

In the case of the Shakers, it was especially important that sexual energies be diverted effectively, because the Shakers were a celibate sect. Dynamic religious services provided an effective means of channeling adolescent energies into endeavors endorsed by the community. Visionary experiences, trances, and possession-like states were common and viewed in an extremely positive manner.

Is it sufficient to attribute such behavior only to a discharge of adolescent sexual energy? Indications are that the answer is No. From a psychological vantage point, other explanations are needed. Adolescents, for instance, place a great premium on allegiance to group behavior, and are likely to go to great lengths to imitate each others' behavior. This pattern of peer-group identification is clearly evident in the imitative behavior of girls in both communities. Their behavior, while clearly different from that of those who observed trance-like states, was apparently similar enough from girl to girl to suggest a strong imitative quality.

Sociological aspects also appear to be involved in behavior of this type. It has been noted that trance-like states and reports of "possession" are most common among persons with the least power in a community: specifically, women, economically disadvantaged men, and teenagers. The behavior attracts attention, and may even (as in the Shaker community) accord the individual enhanced status and prestige. It also serves as a pressure valve to divert excess energy that might otherwise disrupt normal social order. The Shaker's tolerance in this regard was likely motivated by this awareness. In Salem, the response involved a state bordering on paranoia, suggesting that community leaders were quite frightened of the potential for social disruption.

In considering the symptoms of "hysteria" as manifested in the Shaker and Salem communities, it is important to keep in mind that such behavior is not just silly or mindless. Rather, it appears to be intimately related to the strong, compelling forces underlying psychological and physical maturation during adolescence, and constitutes activity that community leaders are likely to try to suppress outright or else channel into directions compatible with the needs and goals of the larger social system.

Source: Foster, L. (1985) Shaker spiritualism and Salem witchcraft: Social perspectives on trance and possession phenomena. *Communal Societies* 5:176–193.

revolutionary unrest sweeping the colonies was a form of madness. However, it was not until after Fauquier's death that the first hospital intended primarily for mental patients finally opened, on October 12, 1773, in Williamsburg (Turkington, 1985). It burned down in 1885, but was recently reconstructed as part of Colonial Williamsburg. The first hospital in the United States, the Pennsylvania Hospital in Philadelphia, opened in 1751. Because of the encouragement of people like Benjamin Franklin, it did serve mental patients, but was not designed primarily to serve this group.

The Williamsburg hospital and other hospitals of that period were built with a much greater emphasis on security than treatment. In fact, the first keeper of Fauquier's hospital, James Galt, had been selected because of his experience as head of the public jail in Williamsburg. Conditions in hospitals of this period were barbaric, and treatment harsh. Inmates were often restrained or placed in dark cells that allowed little movement; their heads were shaved; and they were routinely bled or given strong purgatives to cleanse their supposedly diseased insides (Turkington, 1985). Even more extreme measures, such as beatings, were used with resistant inmates.

Several reformers attempted to develop a therapeutic approach that avoided supernatural explanations of abnormal behavior and that emphasized humane treatment and the possibility of recovery. Benjamin Rush (1745–1813), now known as the "father of American psychiatry," developed an approach that is the core of what was later termed "moral therapy." Moral therapy involves rest and supportive counseling, and, most importantly, responding to patients as normal persons who are having problems adjusting to life and who retain an ability to help themselves. The physical control of violent patients, however, remained a genuine problem, and some severe restraint devices were still in use. Rush is noted for devising a "tranquilizing chair," which restrained virtually all parts of the body. Though it did not tranquilize, the chair did help with security and control problems. Yet Rush, the attending physician at the Pennsylvania Hospital from 1783 to 1813 (and a signer of the Declaration of Independence), was generally progressive in his views of mental disorder, probably in part because his own son was a mental patient at the Pennsylvania Hospital.

Dorothea Dix and the Reformers

In the nineteenth century, Dorothea Dix (1802–1887), a Massachusetts schoolteacher who was probably the most effective lobbyist for mental health reform this nation has ever seen, initiated changes in the care of the emotionally disturbed. Others joined her, and together they compelled state legislatures to found new hospitals. New Jersey, in 1854 the first to do so, was followed by most states in the next three decades.

Ironically, these reforms had some negative effects. Several older institutions that had successfully followed the teachings of Benjamin Rush were transformed into large, centralized state hospitals and forced to handle many more patients. This increase in size reduced their effectiveness, and the promising moral therapy approaches fell into disuse. Moreover, the hospitals that were constructed in response to the reform movement were large, drab buildings located in sparsely settled rural areas. Their location reinforced the general belief that the mentally disordered were dangerous and needed to be isolated, which is inaccurate (Teplin, 1985). It also made the patients' transition back to their own homes abrupt and difficult.

Modern Trends

In about 1854 John Gray, superintendent of the Utica State Hospital in New York, became extremely influential in promoting the concept that mental disturbance is a result of physical disease and should therefore be treated with physical methods. This concept is known as the **medical (or organic) model.** Other theorists and practitioners supported him, and the medical model has been a major feature of American psychology and psychiatry ever since (Grob, 1983).

In 1912, Sigmund Freud delivered a series of lectures to a conference at Clark University in Worcester, Massachusetts (Evans and Koelsch, 1985), at which he introduced America to the psychological point of view. Freud lectured on emotional experiences as the origin of abnormal behavior, marking a break from the medical model. Freudian theory became well accepted in the United States, indeed, even more so than in Europe. From that time until the early twentieth century, American psychology and psychiatry were influenced primarily by the organic and Freudian positions.

Wilhelm Wundt (1832-1920), whose views formed the basis for behaviorism, established the first experimental psychology laboratory.   (The Bettmann Archive)

EXHIBIT

Mental Health Professionals

The label "mental health professional" is applied to a number of specific professional groups. Most have been trained in some form of psychotherapeutic intervention, though the duration of training is rather short in psychiatric nurses and social workers. Psychiatrists receive additional medical training, including instruction in the administration of medications. Clinical psychologists receive additional training in psychodiagnostic tests and in the design and evaluation of research studies.

Clinical Psychologists Have a master's degree and a Ph.D. in psychology (or in some cases, a Psy.D., which requires less research training), with specialized training in assessment techniques (including psychodiagnostic tests) and research skills.

Counseling Psychologists Have a Ph.D. (or sometimes a Psy.D.) in psychology. Typically work with adjustment problems (e.g., in student health or counseling centers) not involving severe emotional disorder.

Psychiatric Social Workers Have a master's degree in social work, sometimes a B.A., and very occasionally a Ph.D., with a specialized interest in mental health settings.

Psychiatrists Have an M.D. with a specialization in emotional disorders, just as other physicians might specialize in pediatrics or family medicine.

Psychoanalysts Have either an M.D. or Ph.D., with a training emphasis in some form of psychoanalytic therapy (see Chapter 2).

Psychiatric Nurses Have an R.N., sometimes with an M.A., with specialized training for work with psychiatric patients.

Adjunct mental health personnel Persons in the following categories don't deliver the primary services required by the mentally disturbed, yet they also have important roles in care and treatment programs.

Occupational therapists B.S. training in occupational therapy with extra training in helping the emotionally handicapped become more self-sufficient and effective.

Art or expressive therapists B.S. training, sometimes at the masters' level. Trained to help the emotionally disturbed express feelings and conflicts, and develop more life satisfaction through painting, sculpting, and other expressive modalities.

Pastoral counselors Ministerial degree with some additional training in counseling techniques, to help those clients whose emotional difficulties center on a religious or spiritual conflict.

Alcohol or drug abuse counselor Usually no higher than a bachelor's degree, and sometimes less than that, but with specific training to assist in the treatment of alcohol and drug abuse problems.

Community mental health worker Limited training, but assists in a variety of roles, usually in community mental health centers.

John B. Watson (1878-1958) advocated that psychologists limit their study to objective observation of external human behavior. (The Bettmann Archive)

A third position influential in twentieth-century America has been the behavioral view of abnormal behavior, which stresses the role of objective learning—rather than subjective emotional experience and organic disorder—in creating abnormal behavior. Ironically, Wilhelm Wundt, considered by many to be the father of modern experimental psychology (the basis for behaviorism), was also invited to address the Clark University conference, but declined because of his intense reluctance to travel. If he had attended, American psychology and psychiatry may not have been as strongly influenced by the Freudian position. The scientific behaviorism promoted in the United States by John Watson (1878–1958) in the early 1900s was first systematically applied to psychiatric therapy in 1924 by Mary Cover Jones. In more recent times, behaviorism has become a highly influential theoretical position, especially in the United States (O'Donnell, 1985).

The concept of prevention was given its first organized impetus in 1908, when Clifford Beers, a former mental patient, with the strong support of the famous psychologist William James and psychiatrist Adolf Meyer, published his classic treatise, *A Mind That Found Itself* (Grob, 1983). He later founded the American Mental Health Association, still one of our country's leading organizations for consumers and volunteers interested in improving mental health services. His ideas and efforts spurred people to think more directly of prevention of mental disorders, an idea that has grown slowly and still has far to go (Marx and Hillix, 1987).

THE SCIENTIFIC METHOD

Along with the evolution of attitudes toward the mentally disordered has come an evolution in methods used to study the phenomena of mental disorder and its treatment (Marx and Hillix, 1987). In early times, views of the cause and treatment of the emotionally disordered came from belief systems such as demonology. Later, there were attempts to solve the problems by reasoning. Today, we use the scientific method of direct systematic observation, correlational studies, and controlled experiments to study abnormal behavior. It was not until full development of the scientific method that knowledge in this field systematically developed.

The well-designed experiment is the result of this development. In the modern scientific method, initial insights and general ideas (hypotheses) eventually lead to experiments that help to generate full-blown models or paradigms of human behavior. The **model** is a systematic set of related facts and hypotheses (for example, the Freudian model, the behavioral model, and so on). The model is used to generate further experiments to validate the ideas that flow from the model. Thus, the following sequence: general ideas and insights; observations; hypothesis; operational definition; experiment; model or paradigm; new hypotheses; further experiments; new model or paradigm.

Observation. From the time of ancient civilizations, the personal observations of people who have studied the mentally ill have been a fruitful source of ideas. For these ideas to be scientifically validated, however, they have to be available for public observation and common agreement. That is, they have to be translated into a **hypothesis,** an idea that can be tested in the same manner by different scientists. Personal observation and rational thinking can lead to powerful hypotheses, but such methods are also subject to bias, or a dis-

EXHIBIT

Positive and Negative Aspects of Each Research Method

Method	Positive Aspects	Negative Aspects
Case study	a. Generates new theories b. Records rare situations c. Inexpensive and easy to carry out	a. Highly subject to selective and observer bias b. Can't generalize the results c. Can't determine any true cause
Natural event observation	a. Allows study of major event and overall cause b. Is not artificial	a. May introduce observer bias and/or disturb a natural event b. Can't repeat the event; difficult to generalize any results
Correlation	a. Allows quantification and replication b. Need not be artificial, though often is	a. Cannot define the specific cause
Experiment	a. May control, isolate, and define specific causes b. Allows manipulation of variables, repetition, and generalization	a. May become too focused, thus become artificial and miss the overall reality of the issue b. The control that is available is subject to unethical methods and abuse of subject rights
Model or paradigm	a. Provides new insights and hypotheses, and coherence between specific issues	a. Attachment to model may blind one to data that is contradictory

tortion of the truth. Until the possibility of this bias is eliminated, the results can never be considered scientifically valid.

There are a number of ways to eliminate bias. First, repeated observation establishes **reliability.** If the same observation is made over and over under similar circumstances, then that observation is probably reliable and not biased. Second, observations are made by people with different characteristics, so the observation is not biased by such variables as the sex, race, age, or intelligence of a single observer (Bausell, 1986). An older white male who observes two young black females in an argument might report the behaviors of this event in different terms than would a group of observers that included young and old, white and black, male and female.

Correlational methods and probability. Certain conditions cannot be measured by a true laboratory experiment. For example, the psychological effects of a tornado devastating a community cannot be studied under controlled laboratory conditions. Thus, at least some situations are amenable to study only by correlational techniques or by field study. Correlational techniques are means of assessing how often two phenomena occur together. For example, one could correlate the rate of mental hospital admissions with the stages of the moon. From that, we could say that the rates are higher at certain stages, but without more substantive information, it would still be incorrect to say one caused the other.

When using correlational methods, it is important to determine the degree of probability that the results of a specific experiment could occur by chance, that is, the **level of significance** of the experiment. If that particular correlation is determined to have a significance level of 0.001, it could have occurred by chance in only one out of a thousand times. The levels of significance that are typically used in psychology are the 0.05 or 0.01 level, which would mean that in only five cases out of a 100 or one case out of a 100, respectively, could the event have been caused by chance (Bausell, 1986).

The field study. The field study is used for rare events, for certain cross-cultural studies, or for events that are just very difficult to observe (Mezzich and Berganza, 1984). For example, after various natural catastrophes, such as tornados or volcanic explosions, scientists are quick to attempt to observe the effects on people in the affected areas. The critical issue in the field study is to avoid becoming a factor in the phenomena one is observing, but rather to be an unobtrusive observer who does not distort the phenomena either by (1) an interaction with the event or (2) perceptual bias. Perceptual bias can be controlled to a degree simply by having a number of individuals with different backgrounds and with different perspectives observe the same event.

The model. Initial experiments (as well as rational thinking) can in turn lead to a *model,* a systematic set of ideas describing or explaining the phenomenon that one is studying. Using a model makes it easier to derive subsequent hypotheses for study. For example, if your model of human behavior holds that humans learn by modeling the behavior of others, you could then more easily hypothesize that watching violent acts on television increases aggression in human beings. On the other hand, if you believe that fantasy participation in the behavior of others reduces the strength of the fantasied behavior, then you might hypothesize that watching violent acts on television acts as a kind of catharsis, or a way to lower the level of aggression, and thus lessens aggression in other situations.

The operational definition. Once a model has been formulated it is very important to describe it in terms that can be measured. This leads to the attempt to develop an **operational definition,** a set of specific behaviors or criteria that identifies a concept. For example, in a study of aggression you might define aggression as the actual number of times the person being studied physically strikes another in a certain setting. Since it may be difficult to observe any substantial number of people for a long period in this setting, you may restrict your observations to certain times, such as for half an hour every three hours for two days. In other words, you sample the behavior, and then infer, or assume, that the results apply to the whole period of two days.

The type of operational definition that you develop will in many ways determine the results that are obtained. It is important that other scientists who work in the same research area be able to understand the operational definitions used in a particular experiment so that they can attempt to validate your hypotheses by finding the same results. Hypotheses can also be validated using other definitions, and then seeing if the results that are obtained with one measure are also attained with another.

The single subject experiment. The case study (used extensively by Sigmund Freud) is simply a report of what occurred in a single situation, for example, an observation of people doing something or a psychotherapy case. It is a rich source of hypotheses, but per se it does not constitute a scientific experiment. When conditions with one subject are systematically manipulated and observed, for example, by giving a subject a drug for two weeks, taking the drug away for two weeks, giving the drug again for two weeks, and then observing the effects, it is referred to as the **single subject experiment.** It is a more refined approach than the simple case study method, but it also leads to information that should then be validated across a number of subjects, and in different studies by different experimenters, before being accepted as a scientific fact.

The controlled experiment. The **controlled experiment** is one in which the experimenter is able to exert control over the phenomena that he or she is interested in studying. One cannot exert control in a field study (studying the effects of a tornado), but in a controlled study (a study of the effects of drugs, for example), one does have control over many variables (which drug to use, the dosage, and so on).

Those variables of an experiment that are systematically manipulated by the scientist are referred to as **independent variables.** In a drug study, the different drugs or dosages of drugs are usually the independent variables. The effects of these variables are then assessed by measurement of the **dependent variables,** the results that change in response to the manipulations of the independent variables. In the drug study, those phenomena that are expected to change in the subject—level of depression, schizophrenia, and so on—are the dependent variables (Bausell, 1986). The power of the experiment derives in part from the fact that the scientist can compare an experimental group (a group that receives the independent variables) and a control group (essentially left untouched). For example, if you wish to study the varying effects of different dosages of a medication on a certain population, such as men over fifty, you might have three groups of such men. Those groups will receive three different dosages of the medication. You would also want to have a control group that receives a **placebo,** an inert substance that the group believes to be medication. If you wish to add to the study the effects of receiving the placebo, you would also have a group that was given nothing.

Research has consistently shown that expectancy effects, that is, the outcome or the effects in the direction that the experimenter believed would be the result, influence the experimental results (Kerlinger, 1985). For that reason, most modern experimental studies of the effects of treatment use the experimental procedure referred to as the **double-blind method** (Kerlinger, 1985). In a double-blind drug study, the individuals who actually carry out the study, those who administer the drugs, are kept unaware of the drug or dosage that each subject receives, and of the purpose or expected result of the study. The subject also does not know for sure which drug or dosage he or she is receiving. Specifically, if we are studying the effects of a certain type of medication, the physician (or agent of the experimenter) who is treating the patient is not aware whether the pill he or she is giving to the patient is a placebo. Similarly, the subjects may or may not receive actual medication, though they usually think they are. This controls the expectancy effects in both the experimenter and the subject.

The evolution of the scientific method has allowed the development of the information on which this book is based. The preceding survey of historical trends illustrates the fluidity and diversity of attempts to define and scientifically measure and study abnormal behavior. This diversity is very evident in the next chapter, which examines the major theoretical perspectives of abnormal behavior. The diversity of behavior and the various criteria for identifying and measuring abnormality are then explored further in Chapter 3.

CONCEPTS OF ABNORMALITY

In addition to the themes demonstrated in this historical overview, the following concepts will be developed in Chapters 2 and 3, and in the rest of this book.

1. The continuum of behavior ranges from clearly normal adjustment to definitely abnormal adjustment. Much behavior belongs in that middle area where decisions regarding abnormality are difficult to make.

2. A specific abnormal behavior pattern is seldom inherited genetically, but genetic factors may play a part in predisposing a person to abnormality of one sort or another.

3. The causes of any one abnormal behavior pattern are usually multiple.

4. Indicators of abnormality are not necessarily obvious. In many cases, the signs are uncommon and/or subtle.

5. Both long-term and transient social value systems affect judgments as to whether or not a person is abnormal.

6. Though there may be differences in how certain mental disorders are manifested within different cultures, most disorders are found in some form in most cultural groups. The differences are usually related to cultural traditions, expectancies, and ethics.

7. A psychological handicap often has a more negative effect on interpersonal relationships than does a physical handicap.

8. The label of psychological abnormality is a stigma that often remains with a person even after the disorder no longer exists. Such a label, resulting from the expectations and responses of others, may prolong the psychological disorder.

9. While some mentally disordered individuals are dangerous to other people, this percentage is not much different than the percentage of normal persons who are dangerous to others.

10. In most societies there is substantial overlap between judgments of mental abnormality and criminal behavior; the same specific behavior may receive either label, depending on who is doing the labeling.

CHAPTER REVIEW

1. There are numerous criteria (such as statistically different, ideal and maladaptive functioning, subjective discomfort, criminally insane, diseased, or socially deviant) by which one can evaluate behaviors and/or persons as abnormal.

2. Using six-month prevalence rates, the NIMH study of rates of mental disorder found an overall rate of 19 percent, and for specific disorders the following approximate rates were found: anxiety disorders, 8 percent; substance abuse, 7 percent; affective disorder, 6 percent; and schizophrenia, 1 percent. Using the perspective of lifetime prevalence rates, they found rates of substance abuse, 20 percent; anxiety disorders, 12 to 20 percent; affective disorders, 8 percent; schizophrenia, 1.0 to 1.5 percent; and antisocial personality, 2.5 percent.

3. Many of our current ideas about and approaches to abnormal behavior reflect our heritage from earlier civilizations.

4. Hippocrates played a critical role in changing conceptions of abnormality. He emphasized the accurate observation of behavior, study of the brain, and the significance of natural rather than supernatural causes in the genesis of abnormal behavior.

5. The distress generated in the Middle Ages by events such as the Hundred Years' War and the Black Death resulted in ineffective and destructive patterns, such as the flagellant movement and the dancing mania.

6. Much of the progress achieved in earlier times, such as the Romans' development of secular hospitals, collapsed in the Middle Ages but revived during the Renaissance and the Enlightenment.

7. Philippe Pinel's (1745–1826) removal of chains from many of the inmates of the La Bicêtre asylum initiated a trend toward a more humane and effective treatment of the mentally disturbed.

8. Although beliefs in witchcraft and punitive measures marked the approaches to abnormal behavior in the Colonial period in the United States, more enlightened views eventually gained acceptance due to the efforts of people such as Benjamin Rush, Dorothea Dix, and the early theorists in the organic, psychodynamic, behavioral, and humanistic traditions.

9. Early ideas on the causes of mental disorders came from belief systems and nonsystematic observation. Improvement came when reason and systematic observation were used, and in modern times correlational studies and controlled experiments are the accepted bases for established scientific information.

10. Correlation establishes only that two or more variables tend to occur together at a certain rate. To establish causation, i.e., that one variable in some way (possibly as yet unknown) causes another, we must use a series of controlled experiments.

TERMS TO REMEMBER

abnormal	cross-cultural research	operational definition
statistical rarity	somatogenic	single subject experiment
subjective discomfort	correlation	controlled experiment
maladaptive functioning	causation	independent variable
deviant	medical (or organic) model	dependent variable
different	model	placebo
disordered	hypothesis	double-blind method
bizarre	reliability	
mental disorder	level of significance	

FOR MORE INFORMATION

Eaton, W. (1986) *The sociology of mental disorders.* New York: Praeger. Surveys the ways in which sociological factors influence the occurrence and development of psychopathology

Fleming, M., and Manvell, R. (1985) *Images of madness: the portrayal of insanity in the feature film.* Rutherford, N.J.: Fairleigh Dickinson University Press. An interesting collection of ideas and photos on how abnormality is represented in feature films

Kendler, H. (1987) *A history of psychology.* Chicago: Dorsey. A good overview of the historical forces that have influenced modern clinical psychology, as well as psychology in general

Mezzich, J., and Berganza, C. (Eds.). (1984) *Culture and psychopathology.* New York: Columbia University Press. An extensive and interesting overview of the cross-cultural research related to abnormal psychology

Tuchman, B. (1978) *A distant mirror.* New York: Knopf. An interesting portrayal of events in the Middle Ages that still influence some of our views on mental disorders

Wright, E. (1939) Medieval attitudes toward mental illness. *Bulletin of the History of Medicine* 7:352–356. A fine summary of medieval attitudes toward mental disorder

Zilboorg, G., and Henry, G. (1941) *A history of medical psychology.* New York: Norton. An excellent overall account of historical conceptions and treatments of mental disorder

In the film version of W. Somerset Maugham's *The Razor's Edge*, Bill Murray searches for spiritual enlightenment in the tumultuous years following World War I. The self-actualization theory applies to Murray's attempt to cope with life's problems. (Museum of Modern Art/Film Stills Archive; © 1984 Columbia Pictures Industries, Inc.)

2

Theoretical Perspectives on Abnormal Behavior

The study of abnormal behavior can be approached from several vantage points, or perspectives (Marx and Hillix 1987). Each of the perspectives discussed in this chapter has made important theoretical contributions to the study of abnormal behavior. Just as significant is the fact that each perspective has also advanced the state of knowledge about normal behavior. The Freudian, behavioral, humanistic, systems, and cross-cultural perspectives have each attracted both theoreticians and practitioners interested in the interplay between forces shaping both normal and abnormal behavior.

● The Case of Ziggy

Ziggy, a college student, was arrested by campus police. He had been picketing a talk given by representatives of the local power company on the positive aspects of nuclear power. Shouting obscenities and gesturing wildly, Ziggy had refused to stop picketing and was charged with disturbing the peace and resisting arrest.

When questioned at police headquarters, Ziggy launched into a rambling tirade about a conspiracy involving the power company, the school board, and the university president. After listening to him for some time, the police took Ziggy to the local mental hospital for an evaluation. Let us suppose that while hospitalized, Ziggy was seen independently by advocates of psychodynamic, behavioral, and humanistic theories of behavior. Here is what each might have had to say about his condition.

Doctor 1: "In my opinion, Ziggy suffers from severe mental distress due to repressed rage at his father for deserting his mother. As a result, Ziggy experiences extreme tension and suppressed rage over authority figures, who represent substitute father figures. At the same time, Ziggy strongly desires to recover his father by identifying with these authority figures. To help him resolve these conflicting desires, I recommend extended psychoanalysis."

Doctor 2: "Clinical observation of Ziggy's behavior in a controlled environment reveals maladaptive behavior patterns. Ziggy has developed the habit of accosting strangers, then demanding that they interact with him on a personal level. He apparently has not learned some skills basic to social interactions, and as a result becomes frustrated whenever his largely inappropriate advances are not reciprocated. I recommend a therapy program that includes social skills and relaxation training."

Doctor 3: "Ziggy has been blocked in his strivings for self-actualization. He has grown up in a world that has posed one threat after another to survival and human development. These forces, which are largely beyond Ziggy's control, have conspired to frustrate his efforts to achieve a high level of individuality and productivity. Anxiety triggered by threats to self-actualization have mobilized Ziggy to lash out at those whom he perceives as standing in the way of his personal goals."

It might at first seem difficult to explain the differences among these three professional views on the facts of Ziggy's case. But a look at the recent history of approaches to abnormality, as discussed in Chapter 1, reminds us that there have been many different explanations for disordered behavior. This chapter describes four major theoretical perspectives that have influenced current views of abnormal behavior: the psychodynamic, behavioral, humanistic, and systems theories. Each reflects a distinctive viewpoint that has evolved through years of observation, study, and analysis of human behavior. Furthermore, each theory has contributed significantly to the understanding and treatment of abnormal behavior.

THE PSYCHODYNAMIC PERSPECTIVE

The work of Sigmund Freud (1856–1939) was a landmark in the origin and development of psychological theory (Lewis, 1981; Masling, 1982). Freud was a Viennese physician, orginally trained as a neurologist. However, as a result of contact with several eminent scientists, he was drawn increasingly to the study of the psychological aspects of behavior. Among these scientists was Charcot, whose strong interests in psychiatric phenomena led him to experiment with hypnosis in the treatment of hysterical disorders. Another significant influence on Freud's work was the Viennese physician Josef Breuer, who subsequently published a book on hysteria with Freud. Stimulated by the work of Charcot, Breuer, and others, Freud began his own study of the psychological determinants of behavior. Eventually, he developed a comprehensive theory of personality development that encompassed both normal and abnormal behavior, referred to as **psychodynamic theory.**

Psychodynamic theory is based on the doctrine of determinism, which holds that behavior is the product of specific causes. Freud's use of the term **psychic determinism** reflected his belief that psychic forces, or instincts, control behavior (Erdely, 1985). He suggested that these forces operate unconsciously, beyond the individual's awareness or control. If unchecked, these drives can lead to extremely self-centered, socially maladaptive behavior. Freud considered it the task of civilization to channel and regulate these forces so that the satisfaction of an individual's needs would not occur at the expense of society. He referred to the gradual process of harnessing instinctual drives and channeling them in socially sanctioned directions as socialization. The inevitable tensions between individual needs and social limitations are manifested in the release of excess psychic, or mental, energy. Examples include such things as vivid dreams full of self-indulgent fantasy, and the common occurrence of saying one thing while meaning something else (a "Freudian slip").

According to Freud, events such as these can be rationally explained if it is assumed they reflect a person's "true" (that is, unconscious) motives, which are often at odds with conscious intentions. No one is really free of such conflicts, and Freud spent considerable time discussing the irrational forces that seem to underly much so-called normal behavior. To Freud, the distinction between normal and abnormal reflected a difference of degree rather than kind. Psychologically healthy people, in his view, were those who managed to minimize the effects of intrapsychic conflicts through the development of effective coping strategies.

Psychosexual Development

Freud believed that human growth is guided by an overriding force known as the **pleasure principle,** the basic tendency to seek pleasure and avoid pain. Pleasurable sensations come in many forms, and during early development a variety of behaviors are directed toward this goal. Different parts of the body successively become channels for pleasure seeking. These parts are known as "erogenous zones," and serve as outlets for the biologically based energy termed **libido** by Freud. The particular region of the body charged with libido varies with age, beginning with the mouth and followed successively by the anal and genital areas. Each of these acquires intensely pleasurable associations during a specific phase of development. Freud named the corresponding developmental periods the oral (birth through age two), anal (age two through four), and phallic (age five through six) stages. These are followed by two additional stages, to complete the sequence of psychosexual development. The latency phase occurs during the early school years, and involves channeling the individual's energies into less overtly sexual, more socially oriented activities. Finally, the genital stage is reached with the onset of puberty, signaling the achievement of a capacity for mutually gratifying heterosexual behavior.

During the oral stage, the infant's behavior is governed largely by instinctual urges. Satisfaction centers on such basic needs as being fed and pacified; infants essentially relate to the world through their mouths. This stage is followed by the anal phase, a shift in pleasure seeking to the anal region and eliminative functions, during which children learn to control basic biological functions, and in so doing achieve a degree of autonomy not previously realized. Increasing autonomy is accompanied by feelings of power and accomplishment, and many infants seem to derive great pleasure from resisting parental efforts at toilet training.

During the third, or phallic, phase of development, the child's genitalia become the focus of curiosity and pleasure, much to the consternation of parents. Most children begin masturbating at this stage, a practice that is actively suppressed in some cultures. The phallic stage of development also marks the appearance of the **Oedipal conflict** for male children and the **Electra complex** for female children. These conflicts involve an intense, sexually-charged attraction to the parent of the opposite sex. The attraction, however, raises the possibility of discovery by the parent of the same sex as the child, a prospect that according to Freud creates substantial anxiety.

The resultant conflict between strong infantile sexual feelings on the one hand and intense anxiety on the other creates an extremely unpleasant state of affairs. The conflict is therefore repressed, and there follows a fourth phase of development, the latency period. During this period, the child's attention is directed away from the troublesome feelings aroused during the Oedipal stage toward more socially acceptable and safer channels of activity. Peer relationships and friendships with members of the same sex develop at this time. Academic, athletic, and other basic skills become the focus of attention. Children begin to be rewarded for their achievements in a variety of activities that promote self-development and social maturation.

It is interesting to note how the many accomplishments of the latency period reflected to Freud a means of dealing with underlying conflict—in this case, anxieties created during the phallic period. The theme of conflict-induced behavior is a common one in psychodynamic theory (Silverman, 1976). Conflict typically reflects the presence of competing motivational forces, as, for instance, when sexual attraction to a parent is accompanied by a strong negative sanction related to fear of the consequences. Conflict is present in much of what we do on a day-to-day basis, reflecting the fact that many of the things we deem pleasurable have associated costs or negative implications.

The process of *psychosexual development* is the navigation of each of the

RESEARCH PROFILE

An Experimental Evaluation of Jungian Theory

The psychodynamic theories have been justly criticized as depending on concepts that are difficult to test experimentally. The theories of Carl Jung, an early disciple of Freud's have been especially problematic in this regard. However, an interesting approach to experimental verification of Jungian theory was carried out by Cann and Donderi and reported in a 1986 issue of the *Journal of Personality and Social Psychology.*

Jung distinguished two types of dreams: the archetypal and the everyday. Archetypes are innate (that is, built into brain and cell structure) tendencies to structure experience in certain predetermined ways. Archetypal dreams arise from the collective unconscious, a primitive source of these innate patterns and memories that we share with other humans. Archetypal dreams deal with universal (rather than personal) themes, are frequently unusual or even bizarre, and are usually emotionally intense. Everyday dreams, by contrast, reflect subjective, personal matters and are relatively lifelike and routine.

Jung hypothesized that as we mature, we have fewer archetypal dreams because we both collect more and more personal memories and also more effectively use a variety of defense mechanisms to avoid the emotional impact of unconscious material. To test this hypothesis Cann and Donderi asked volunteers (primarily students at McGill University in Montreal) to take some personality tests and also to write down the earliest, most vivid, and most recent dreams they could remember. A smaller subgroup ($n = 30$) of this sample also kept a dream diary for three to four weeks. Dreams were than rated on a preset scale as to whether they were archetypal or everyday.

Consistent with Jung's hypothesis, the earliest dreams contained 59 percent archetypal dreams, the most vivid dreams 64 percent, and the most recent dreams 24 percent. As the estimated age of occurrence of these earliest dreams increased, the percentage of archetypal dreams increased.

The personality tests were scored on three Jungian dimensions: high and low neuroticism, extroversion–introversion, and sensation–intuition. More archetypal dreams were recalled by those on the intuitive and/or low neuroticism ends of the scales. This fits with Jungian theory, which would see intuitive and less neurotic persons as less caught up in everyday, personal conflicts and anxieties, and more in tune with universal archetypal conflicts. In summary, this research lends some empirical support to a basic concept of Jungian theory, and more importantly, suggests there may be ways to examine empirically at least some of the important hypotheses in the psychodynamic theories.

stages leading to heterosexual maturity. With each succeeding stage, libido is channeled either into different zones of the body or else into characteristic behavior patterns. It is a sequence marked along the way by conflict, chiefly as a result of strong sexual urges in competition with socially imposed sanctions that either deny gratification of basic drives or postpone their fulfillment.

The significant impact of early development on adult behavior was stressed repeatedly by Freud. This is a concept that has subsequently been validated in many empirical and theoretical analyses of human development. Freud believed that the foundations of personality traits are established early in life, largely as the result of significant experiences associated with each stage of psychosexual development. Evidence for this came in part from observing that, when encouraged to talk freely about their problems, Freud's patients almost invariably worked their way back to early childhood experiences. This tendency led Freud to propose that the origins of maladjusted behavior lay in the impact of unsettling experiences associated with early development. For example, being deprived of adequate gratification during the oral stage of development would cause an adult to orient much of his or her behavior toward the goal of oral stimulation. Excessive eating, drinking, and smoking are examples of behaviors commonly associated with this pattern of behavior.

This particular example illustrates the concept of **fixation,** in which inadequate gratification during a specific stage of development causes a person to become preoccupied with satisfying the unmet needs. As another example, consider an adult who is stingy, compulsive, and excessively orderly. These are features of what Freud referred to as an "anal" personality, and can be traced back to conflicts arising during the second phase of psychosexual development.

Such personality patterns by themselves are not necessarily presumed to be pathological in the sense of indicating highly disturbed behavior. That determination rests on assessing the extent to which the behavior actually proves to be maladaptive. Actually, Freud suggested that most people's behavior was "neurotic" to one degree or another. The term "neurosis" implies a condition of psychological discomfort stemming from chronic intrapsychic conflicts of the types mentioned earlier. Some individuals, such as those with "oral" or "anal" personality styles, possess sharply defined traits that make their behavior seem clearly disturbed. Yet nearly everyone, according to Freud, is troubled by conflicts stemming from early development, whether or not the conflicts are manifested in the crystallization of specific personality traits.

Personality Development

Freud's model of personality development is closely related to his sequence of psychosexual development. Central to personality development is the concept of the **ego,** which encompasses a variety of intrapsychic mechanisms that mediate the day-to-day interactions we have with our surroundings. The ego is not present at birth, but rather gradually develops during the first few years of life.

The behavior of infants is directed primarily toward satisfying basic biologic needs in a rather primitive way. According to Freud, this reflects the

Sigmund Freud (1856-1939), the founder of psychoanalytic psychology, boarded a plane in 1928 for his first air flight. (AP/Wide World Photos)

Id dominance: Freud proposed that infants behave largely by instinct; deriving pleasure through oral stimulation. (Terry Evans/Magnum)

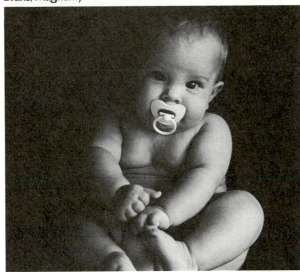

Ego maturation: As children grow, they begin to reason and learn to respond to the consequences of their actions. (Richard Kalvar/Magnum)

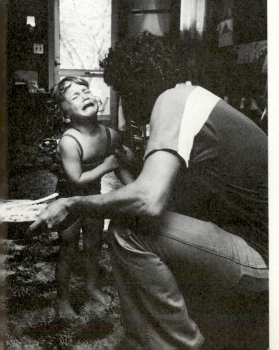

Superego development: As children mature, they develop a conscience and a set of values, learning to share and play with others. (Mimi Forsyth/Monkmeyer Press Photo Service)

dominance of the **id,** the most primitive personality structure. Behavior controlled by the id is almost entirely based on instinct and devoid of conscious control. The id functions without regard to practical matters, and the frustration of id-based drives is typically met with rage or aggression. Termed the "kingdom of the illogical" by Freud, the id is the only structure of the mature personality present at birth. Its presence is inferred from an infant's reflexive behaviors, which are oriented toward meeting such basic needs as food, warmth, and physical comfort.

The behavior of infants subsequently changes in important ways. The maturation of perceptual and cognitive capabilities during the early years gradually shifts the control of behavior away from reflexive mechanisms and toward conscious mediation. The emerging capacity of the young child to think and talk about things, even though in only a primitive way, signals the maturation of the ego.

The ego is that portion of one's personality that handles day-to-day concerns involving the real world. The ego has to balance internal needs expressed by the id against the availability of resources to meet those needs. Conflict frequently results when the id is denied gratification. One indication of early ego maturation, therefore, is evident in a child who has learned how to delay the gratification of pressing needs.

Ego functions are the mark of a maturing individual, one who is learning to balance inner needs and available resources in a realistic manner. As the ego matures, the child's behavior increasingly reflects the impact of conscious decisions rather than reflexive reactions.

As children mature, they become increasingly subject to the social customs and behavioral guidelines of their culture, many of which operate as constraints on behavior in the sense that they tend to specify and often limit a child's response options. During the first few years of life, most of these guidelines deal with immediate consequences of specific behaviors. Children are generally praised for good behavior and punished when they misbehave; so they learn very quickly what they must do in order to stay in their parents' good graces. This learning has far-reaching consequences, because the behavioral guidelines that children learn to conform to eventually become internalized so that they are capable of regulating behavior in the absence of direct involvement with parents or other adults.

This process of internalization signals the maturation of Freud's third personality structure, the **superego.** The superego may be thought of in part as analogous to one's conscience, and as such is the source of guilt feelings that are associated with wrongdoing. According to Freud, the onset and eventual resolution of the Oedipal complex marks a point of significant superego development. The Oedipal complex, you may recall, involved a complex web of feelings centering around a sexually-charged infatuation with the parent of the opposite sex. Ultimately, children recognize the inappropriateness of this attraction, and experience a painful combination of anxiety and guilt that causes the troublesome feelings to be repressed. The behavioral constraints that result from this process reveal the child's capacity to override the allure of a powerful impulse. It is this capability that Freud viewed as a major criterion of superego development.

The superego constrains more than the incestuous designs children allegedly have on their mothers and fathers. It provides a set of moral guidelines intended to govern behavior in many more mundane areas. Prohibitions against such things as lying, stealing, or disobeying people in positions of authority are associated with the superego.

There is another important role for the superego, one that is less concerned with restricting behavior. Freud introduced the concept of the **ego ideal** to explain the motivation evident in many people to strive toward high levels of achievement and self-fulfillment. The ego ideal, which might be thought of as embedded in the superego, embodies goals toward which one strives. The ego ideal may actually represent another person, as when young children imagine themselves becoming the prominent public figures associated with their personal interests. The ego ideal provides a reference point against which to assess the appropriateness of current behavior. The struggles, sacrifices, and self-discipline that frequently accompany the quest for the ego ideal attest to the power of the superego to regulate a child's behavior.

The fully formed personality, in Freud's scheme of things, reflects the integration of quite dissimilar structures. The impulse-ridden id and moralistic superego compete with one another, while the ego attempts to mediate the conflict, at the same time concerning itself with the day-to-day demands of the external environment. Conflicting needs and drives are virtually always present, even in "healthy" individuals. According to Freud, virtually everyone is "neurotic" (psychologically disturbed) to one degree or another. This assertion reflects his contention that the ego, a key personality structure, is conflict-ridden because of its role as mediator between id, superego, and the outer world. One of the chief manifestations of this concept is a form of psychological distress commonly called anxiety.

The Concept of Anxiety

Anxiety is a concept that pervades Freudian theory and is crucial for understanding many forms of abnormal behavior. The signs of anxiety are clear enough to most of us (Goodwin, 1986). Common physical sensations include muscle tension, queasiness, breathlessness, and a pounding heart. Psychological manifestations of anxiety may include such things as a feeling of impending doom or extreme apprehension. Freud considered anxiety an inevitable response to situations that created a state of vulnerability for the ego. Generally speaking, anxiety results from a generalized perception of danger, without regard to the specific situation. Freud contrasted the diffuse quality of anxiety with the concept of fear, which he believed occurred only in response to a specific threat. Anxiety is therefore a sort of "early warning system" likely to motivate the individual to escape from a situation that engenders fear (Shaw et al, 1987).

In seeking to locate the origins of anxiety, Freud proposed that certain events, beginning with the trauma of birth, evoke unpleasant sensations. These feelings are then generalized to other situations, to the point where their origin can no longer be readily identified.

The unpleasant feelings associated with anxiety motivate efforts to reduce the psychological distress; these efforts may take any of several forms. Freud used the term "defense mechanism" to describe the psychological techniques people use to minimize feelings of anxiety (Silverman, 1976). The purpose of defense mechanisms is to prevent unpleasant levels of anxiety from overwhelming the ego. Hence, they function as a sort of psychic shield. Since Freud believed that conflict and anxiety are unavoidable, the deployment of defense mechanisms is not in itself considered abnormal. For example, memories associated with having been physically abused during childhood tend to be driven from consciousness by a defense mechanism known as *repression*. If these memories were not repressed, they could cause unpleasant feelings that would soon affect many day-to-day situations. Contrary to popular understanding, defense mechanisms are generally healthy, if not used in such a way that one's grasp of reality is seriously distorted.

Defense mechanisms serve as a first line of defense against anxiety and do their job satisfactorily as long as the underlying anxiety is not too intense. If the individual suffers from chronic, unremitting anxiety, however, defense mechanisms may become exaggerated and unwieldy. At this point, symptomatic behavior indicative of marked psychological distress often results.

Sometimes, behavior designed to alleviate anxiety has symbolic connotations or special meanings that are not readily apparent to the naive observer. Consider for example the behavior of a compulsive handwasher who, on an average day, may make 30 to 40 trips to the sink. To an impartial observer this behavior may seem silly or even senseless. From a psychodynamic perspective, however, it makes sense if viewed as a means of coping with anxiety that threatens to become overwhelming. Compulsive handwashing is a form of *undoing*, by which a person attempts to negate some past event that is the cause of intense anxiety. The frequency with which the compulsion is acted out provides an indication of the severity of the underlying anxiety. A severe handwashing compulsion, such as the one described here, is characteristic of severe neurosis, to use Freud's general term in describing how people respond to intolerable psychological distress. People are considered neurotic to the extent that they become so psychologically constricted by their defenses that their ability to function effectively on a day-to-day basis is seriously impaired.

EXHIBIT

Defense Mechanisms

Defense mechanisms are protective responses to what would otherwise be overwhelming levels of anxiety (Silverman, 1976; Lewis, 1981). Thus, they function as natural therapeutic measures to reduce anxiety. Although the reduction of anxiety is normally an adaptive process, things can get out of hand if one's defenses distort things too much or become overly rigid. By themselves, defense mechanisms do not alter whatever conditions triggered the anxiety. Rather, they distort the perception of reality in a way that reduces anxiety. Some of the more common defense mechanisms are briefly described here.

Repression   Considered to be the predominant defense mechanism, repression is a process by which threatening feelings or thoughts are excluded from conscious awareness. Repression allows a person to avoid thinking about things that may be highly psychologically stressful, and it frequently serves to reduce the impact of traumatic experiences. Repression may also be applied to impulses associated with the id which, if allowed into consciousness, would trigger substantial anxiety. For example, strong feelings of sexual attraction toward a member of one's family are likely to be repressed because of the taboos against incest.

Projection   Projection is a defense mechanism in which the individual attributes personally unacceptable feelings to an external object or person. For example, a person who persists in attributing hostile impulses to others may be projecting his or her own angry feelings. Projection tends to make a person feel rather virtuous in comparison with those to whom the undesirable qualities are attributed. If carried to extremes, projection can cause a person to seriously misinterpret someone else's intentions and, as a result, lead to significant interpersonal problems.

Reaction formation   Freud noted a tendency for some patients to develop behavior patterns diametrically opposed to the expression of certain instinctual urges. Someone with a strong sex drive, for example, might behave in an excessively prudish, emotionally cold manner. An adolescent who has recurring violent fantasies may ultimately enter the law-enforcement profession. Both of these behavior patterns illustrate the defense mechanism that Freud referred to as reaction formation.

Denial   Denial is the act of ignoring potentially threatening events. A soldier about to embark on a dangerous patrol who characterizes the enemy as a dumb, ignorant sitting duck is, in all likelihood, engaging in denial. Denial provides a means of minimizing or even eliminating the impact of a significant threat to one's physical or psychological equilibrium.

Psychoanalysis

Freud developed a system of treatment known as psychoanalysis, sometimes referred to as the "talking cure." Fundamental to psychoanalysis is the process of *free association,* in which the patient is instructed to relate to the therapist anything that comes to mind. Freud discovered that the resulting monologue, over the course of numerous treatment sessions, would invariably come to focus on early childhood experiences. These, he believed, were at the root of most of the neurotic behavior exhibited by adults.

Free association occasionally was combined with other techniques, including dream analysis and hypnotherapy. The therapist (or "psychoanalyst") served as an impassive observer, taking notes of the client's free associations and offering occasional interpretive comments. The process of psychoanalysis was a lengthy affair, frequently requiring several years of sessions held several times per week. At the conclusion of therapy, the client was to have gained significant insight into the source of his or her psychological conflicts, and would also have experienced *catharsis,* a form of emotional relief associated with the attainment of insight.

Psychoanalysis, and the underlying theory of personality on which it was based, had a profound influence on modern concepts of therapy in several ways. First, it drew attention to psychic phenomena at a time in history when introspection was something quite novel. Because of Freud's focus on unconscious forces in the control of behavior, forms of psychotherapy developed that attempted to get behind the superficial aspects of problems to their roots.

Second, psychoanalysis helped promote greater understanding of the mentally ill by suggesting that there exists a continuum between psychological health and illness. Freud noted that conflict was an inevitable part of normal psychosexual development, and stressed the idea that everyone is neurotic to one degree or another. It thus became reasonable to treat abnormal behavior as an extension, or perhaps an exaggeration, of unimparied behavior in which normal defense mechanisms are not properly functioning.

Third, Freud's approach to treatment firmly established the one-to-one client/therapist relationship that has come to be a standard. Individual psychotherapy has proven to be the most widely practiced form of psychological intervention, although both group therapy and, more recently, family therapy have developed ardent supporters.

Finally, psychodynamic theory made people aware of developmental concepts and how they shape the destiny of the individual. The ideal that early experiences have a significant role in later behavior has had a powerful influence on modern theories of the genesis of both normal and abnormal behavior (Kohut, 1977; Masling, 1982).

THE BEHAVIORAL PERSPECTIVE

While Freud was developing his theories in Europe, other psychologists were forming an alternative model of human behavior, working independently in both the United States and the Soviet Union. This approach became known as *behaviorism*; it focused attention on factors that influence behavior that Freud left comparatively unexamined. Advocates of behaviorism contended that environmental influences, rather than intrapsychic forces, govern behavior. Much of their early research was concerned with demonstrating in laboratory settings how behavioral responses could be brought under the control of specific stimuli, a process referred to as *conditioning*. There was an emphasis on scientific rigor among the behaviorists, who felt that many of Freud's theoretical formulations were too imprecise to be investigated satisfactorily via laboratory experiments.

Behaviorism and psychodynamic theory have both remained highly influential in the evolving concepts of both normal and abnormal behavior. Psychoanalysis has remained influential because of the recognition that much of our behavior is too complex and at times irrational to be explained by conditioning procedures alone. On the other hand, behaviorism has attracted widespread support because it attempts to explain behavior through an empirical, rational analysis of conditioning procedures that have been clearly demonstrated to underlie many forms of learned behavior.

Several additional features of behaviorism make it an important model to discuss in any consideration of the factors underlying behavior patterns. First of all, behaviorists emphasize the necessity for empirical data when formulating principles of behavior. In addition, behaviorists make several important assumptions regarding the development of abnormal behavior (Price et al., 1978). First, to a behaviorist abnormality consists of patterns of *learned* maladaptive responses ill-suited to the individual's needs. By stressing the role in behavior of learning, behaviorists emphasize the capacity of a person to eliminate maladaptive behaviors and substitute more suitable and rewarding ones. Second, proponents of a behaviorist viewpoint argue that the criteria for deciding whether or not behavior should be considered abnormal is related to the way society metes out rewards and punishments. From this perspective, abnormal behavior is ultimately self-defeating because it deprives the individual of social approval and rewards. A third assumption underlying the behavioral perspective on abnormality is that therapy should focus primarily on overt behavior, rather than covert mental processes. For example, a client who complains of anxiety might well be able to trace the problem back to traumatic experiences in early childhood. Behavioral intervention, however, would focus on the current symptoms of anxiety, in an effort to provide relief. Rather than discuss the problem from a historical standpoint, the therapist would ask the client to identify in detail the specific behaviors associated with anxiety, and would then engage in a systematic program of behavior modification aimed at eradicating the symptoms. Behaviorists believe that treating the symptom directly will eliminate maladaptive behavior without undesirable side effects. In contrast, psychodynamic theorists believe that symptoms are indications of a significant, underlying stressor that needs to be treated for lasting relief to occur. It is their conviction that eliminating a single symptom will merely cause another to appear, a phenomenon termed **symptom substitution.**

Despite the fact that most behaviorists share the same basic assumptions, there are many different facets of behaviorism (Bellak et al., 1982). Five such approaches, discussed below, have at one time or another been identified with particular treatment techniques: classical (Pavlovian) conditioning, neobehaviorism, operant conditioning, social learning theory, and cognitive behaviorism.

Classical Conditioning

Classical conditioning is a form of learning that was extensively studied first by the Russian physiologist Ivan Pavlov (1849–1936). Pavlov was among the first psychologists to specifically address the issue of how learning actually occurs. He began by noting that certain events, which he termed **unconditioned stimuli,** could trigger automatic reactions, or **unconditioned responses.** These are reflexive patterns, and they occur without any prior training. Examples of reflexive responses are commonplace: campfire smoke causes one's eyes to become teary; touching a hot stove causes the hand to be reflexively withdrawn; and the sight (or smell) of food causes most people to salivate.

In all of these examples, the unconditioned responses are involuntary reactions to specific stimuli. Pavlov used these reflexive patterns as the basis for teaching other nonreflexive responses via a process termed **association.** The principle of association, fundamental to all learning theories, is that events that coincide in time tend to become linked with one another (Ferster and Culbertson, 1982). The links that are established may involve interconnections between mental, physical, or emotional factors. Pavlov put the principle of association to work in an experiment with dogs. First, he selected a reliable reflex pattern with an unconditioned stimulus (food) and an unconditioned response (salivation). Next, he paired a previously neutral stimulus—in this case the sound of a bell—with the unconditioned stimulus (food). He continued presenting the two together until the dog formed a strong association between the sound of the bell (the **conditioned stimulus**), and the food (unconditioned stimulus). Then on one trial, instead of presenting the food, he simply rang the bell. The dog salivated even though no food was actually present, a reaction known as a **conditioned response.** With this experiment Pavlov demonstrated a form of learning in which a reflexive response could gradually be brought under the control of previously neutral stimuli (see the Exhibit on classical conditioning).

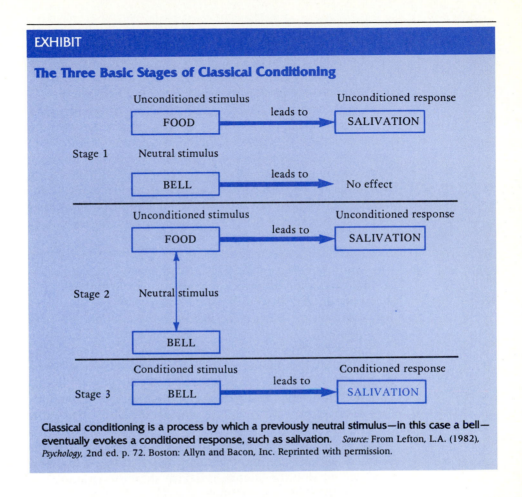

EXHIBIT

The Three Basic Stages of Classical Conditioning

Classical conditioning is a process by which a previously neutral stimulus—in this case a bell—eventually evokes a conditioned response, such as salivation.   *Source:* From Lefton, L.A. (1982), *Psychology,* 2nd ed. p. 72. Boston: Allyn and Bacon, Inc. Reprinted with permission.

Pavlov also studied other aspects of the conditioning process. For example, he discovered that conditioned responses begin to diminish when presented repeatedly without the unconditioned stimulus being present. After a sufficient number of trials the response can be eliminated entirely, an effect known as **extinction.**

Another conditioning procedure studied by Pavlov is referred to as *stimulus generalization.* Stimulus generalization is said to occur when stimuli similar to the original conditioned stimulus acquire the capacity to elicit conditioned responses. For example, Pavlov discovered that once a dog had been trained to salivate at the sound of a bell that rang at a particular frequency, bell tones similar to the original would also elicit salivation. Stimulus generalization occurs in many situations, and is a useful procedure for explaining certain clinical phenomena (Goldstein et al., 1979). For example, individuals with diffuse, generalized anxiety are often found to have started out being fearful of specific objects or situations. This fear gradually becomes associated with objects or events bearing some similarity to the source of the original fear, and can cause anxiety to spill over into many situations other than the one which originally provoked tension.

Principles derived from classical conditioning can help explain how symptoms are cured as well as why they develop. In the first systematic application of classical conditioning principles in a clinical situation, the behavioral psychologist Mary C. Jones conditioned a young child named Albert to fear a white rat, and then later demonstrated how the fear could be eliminated. Fear was conditioned by loudly striking a metal bar behind Albert's head whenever he approached the animal. The unpleasantly loud noise made by the bar constituted the unconditioned stimulus, which triggered a distressful response, the unconditioned response. Albert quickly became fearful of the rat (the conditioned stimulus) because of its association with the frightening noise, and he eventually cried at the sight of the rat alone. This response, the conditioned response, indicated that the unconditioned stimulus and the conditioned stimulus had become strongly associated. Subsequently, Albert was encouraged to gradually approach the animal once again without the bar being struck. Eventually, his fearfulness diminished to the point where it disappeared.

This straightforward application of classical conditioning clearly illustrates how fear, an emotional reaction, can become associated with a stimulus that by itself is not especially threatening. Classical conditioning has proven very helpful in explaining how emotional reactions such as fear and anxiety can be conditioned through an association with stimuli that trigger reflexive, distressful responses.

Mary Jones's work with little Albert marked the first of many applications of classical conditioning to human beings rather than laboratory animals. It was evident that the simple, reflexive stimulus–response chains of Pavlovian conditioning were not adequate to explain the role of mental processes in the association process (Akers et al., 1979).

Fear and anxiety are good examples of response patterns associated with both reflexive and mental (or "cognitive") factors. Reflexive physical responses to fear or anxiety include heart palpitations, profuse sweating, tremors, and muscle tension. These responses are triggered in response to danger and constitute an innate "fight or flight" mechanism. They can become associated with a variety of stimuli via Pavlovian conditioning. However, it is more difficult to explain the fact that a conditioned fear or anxiety response in turn leads to behavior aimed at avoiding the circumstances that gave rise to the problem in the first place. It appears that people tend to employ mental images of fearful experiences in ways that tend to inhibit their behavior. For example, someone who has had an auto accident on a certain road may come to avoid that road or even give up driving entirely. The extent of the behavioral inhibition that occurs is clearly related to thoughts and images that can become very frightening if allowed to develop unchecked (Lazarus, 1987).

A previous victim of violence, Bernhard Goetz may have turned to violence himself in part due to the availability of guns. The debate continues over whether weapons are a stimulus to violence. (AP/Wide World Photos)

Several clinical investigators have developed treatment procedures directed at the alleviation of both the reflexive physical and cognitive components of fear and anxiety (Goodwin, 1986). Although their techniques make use of Pavlovian principles to explain how conditioning occurs, they have all elaborated on the basic model in various ways to take into account the role of mental, as well as physical factors in the evolution of negative emotional reactions. The work of a number of these investigators, such as Joseph Wolpe, Thomas Stampfl, and others, is discussed in Chapter 4.

Operant Conditioning

The name perhaps most widely associated with the development of the behavioral perspective is that of B. F. Skinner. Among his contributions to the field of psychology is a detailed analysis of the many factors involved in basic learning processes. In particular, the principle of **operant conditioning** is attributed to Skinner, who developed his ideas on the basis of extensive work in both laboratory and applied settings. Operant conditioning describes a general model of learning in which behavior is governed by its consequences. A rat trained to press a bar will do so because the behavior has the favorable consequence of causing food to appear. The food is a positive reinforcer, an event that makes the behavior immediately preceding it more likely to occur in the future. Operant conditioning has been used to explain many behavior patterns in which the consequences of an act determine its future occurrence.

Central to Skinner's concepts of learning is a belief that the most valid method of analysis is to focus on observable events. Thus, terms such as "personality," "mind," or "consciousness" are meaningful only if defined in terms of observable behavior patterns. "Learning," for instance, is defined in terms of specific changes in behavior as the result of practice. Such a definition lends itself well to empirical investigation. Moreover, it is a concept of sufficient flexibility to encompass a wide range of both normal and abnormal behaviors. In

B.F. Skinner (1904-) analyzed the basic learning process and developed the principle of operant conditioning: certain behaviors leading to favorable outcomes increase the chance of future repetition of those behaviors. (UPI/Bettmann Newsphotos)

other words, when seen from this vantage point, virtually all behavior can be viewed as learned (Kanfer and Phillips, 1970). This reflects a somewhat optimistic attitude regarding explanations of both the origins and alleviation of psychological problems. The belief that these are essentially learned behaviors carries with it the conviction that new, more adaptive behaviors can be learned in place of the old ones.

It would be helpful at this point to consider an example of how a behaviorist would respond to a client in psychological distress. Consider briefly an individual diagnosed as having an "obsessive-compulsive disorder." In general terms, this is a disorder marked by repetitive thoughts and/or actions that the individual is powerless to control. A compulsive handwasher, for instance, might engage in more than 100 handwashings per day and have no voluntary control over the activity. From a psychoanalytic perspective, such behavior would be accounted for in terms of the negative impact of early experiences. Behaviorists such as Skinner, on the other hand, would be less interested in the origins of the disorder than in identifying the conditions that currently maintain the behavior. A behavioral analysis of the problem would generate a series of questions such as the following: What conditions immediately precede the behavior and might thereby trigger it? What sort of reward or reinforcement is associated with handwashing, given its high rate of occurrence? Under what conditions, and how frequently, does the behavior occur?

Using this information to define the problem, a Skinnerian would target for intervention those conditions in the person's environment that appear to be sustaining the problem behavior.

With regard to the handwasher, it might be found, for instance, that handwashing elicits attention from others that the individual finds gratifying. Getting others to pay less attention to the behavior might be proposed as a means of removing at least one source of reinforcement. Of course, consequences of behavior need not be observable to be effective. The handwasher might very well experience a sense of relief, or a belief that he or she is free of contamination, after handwashing. In this instance, a mental event—a thought—appears to constitute the reinforcement for a particular behavior. Although early behaviorists rejected the idea that thoughts could be defined clearly enough to permit empirical study, there is much current interest in the quantification and analysis of thought patterns as they pertain to behavior control. A number of so-called cognitive-behavioral psychologists, such as Donald Meichenbaum, Aaron Beck, and Albert Ellis, have all pursued this avenue vigorously. Their work is described more fully in Chapter 4.

Behavioral techniques are most effective when the individual is in a highly controlled environment. Not surprisingly, therefore, operant conditioning techniques have proven most successful in institutional settings where it is often possible to regulate environmental factors in a way that facilitates both gathering information about problem behavior and implementing effective treatment strategies.

EXHIBIT

Principles of Operant Conditioning

Extinction   If not rewarded, learned behavior patterns are gradually extinguished: the behavior decreases in frequency because it is no longer being reinforced. If the original reinforcer is reintroduced, either deliberately or inadvertently, the behavior will return in nearly full strength and subsequently become more resistant to extinction.

Punishment   Punishment involves presentation of an unpleasant (perhaps painful) consequence in response to an undesirable behavior (Ferster and Culbertson, 1982). The effects of punishment vary according to the conditions under which it is administered. One of the common effects of punishment is to suppress behavior rather than actually eliminate it. For example, a child who is punished for stealing candy will probably find that punishment does not eradicate the good taste of candy. The child will instead learn to avoid stealing it when there is a risk of being caught and punished. Punishment should be used sparingly and with recognition of the fact that it is often not effective in eliminating undesirable behaviors.

Reinforcement   This term is indelibly associated with behaviorism. Usually it conjures images of an experimenter doling out candy to expectant children or of laboratory rats pressing levers to receive food pellets. But there are many potential reinforcers other than candy and food pellets, both of which are termed positive reinforcers. Positive reinforcers increase the liklihood that the behavior immediately preceding will occur again. Positive reinforcers such as food, whose reward value is unlearned, are called primary reinforcers. Secondary reinforcers are not intrinsically rewarding but acquire reward properties. Compliments, money, and good grades are examples of secondary reinforcers that people learn to work for.

Shaping   This term describes the gradual process in which desired behaviors are created through the judicious application of reinforcers. Shaping is particularly useful in teaching complex behavior patterns that can be broken down into simple steps. The complex skills performed by animals such as seeing-eye dogs, pigeons that can play ping-pong, bears that ride bicycles, and even the family pooch who learns to retrieve the evening paper can all be taught with shaping techniques.

Social Learning Theory

In order to deal more realistically with principles of human development and learning, Albert Bandura has expanded the principles of behaviorism, which in the beginning were largely based on animal research. He is responsible for the development of social learning theory, which takes explicit account of the role of cognitive factors in human learning. We have already discussed the development of conditioning procedures for treating disorders such as anxiety that involve both physical and cognitive factors. Bandura is known for his work on the role of cognitive factors in early learning, using principles of social learning theory to help account for the rapid acquisition of knowledge characteristic of children.

Before Bandura, most behaviorists tended to view learning as the gradual acquisition of skills through shaping and systematic reinforcement. Bandura noted, however, that people learn a great deal simply by watching others perform and can often reproduce complex behavior patterns flawlessly without practice. Moreover, Bandura noted that because people often learn behavior patterns that they display only under certain circumstances, performance of a particular behavior cannot always be used as a criterion for learning. The capacity of people to (1) learn complex behavior patterns via observation and (2) be selective in their performance of them is the basis for Bandura's emphasis on cognitive factors in human learning.

It should be evident by now that the behavioral perspective of abnormal behavior does not exclude consideration of mental processes in discussions of either the origins or treatment of psychological disorders. Nowhere is this more evident than in the work of Martin Seligman, who has clearly described the role of cognitive factors in certain forms of depression. Seligman's development of the concept of *learned helplessness* has proven to have useful clinical implications. Learned helplessness is a behavior pattern in which a previously active, responsive organism acts passively because its behavior does not have beneficial consequences. In early studies, for example, Seligman found that animals subjected to inescapable electric shock became extremely passive. He concluded that a sense of helplessness results when there is no relation between one's efforts and the outcome of those efforts.

EXHIBIT

Observational Learning

Observational learning involves four distinct processes.

1. *Attentional process.*   This process ensures that observation actually occurs.
2. *Retention processes.*   In young children, retention processes are largely associated with the capacity to store *visual* images, since these are perhaps the most important source of observational information. As language skills develop, retention is aided by verbal cues and descriptions of observed behavior.
3. *Motor reproduction processes.*   Observational learning is manifested when the person translates the cognitive representation of the behavior into a motor pattern.
4. *Reinforcement processes.*   Exposure to models whose behavior leads to desirable consequences is most likely to result in imitation.

Martin Seligman's theory of learned helplessness helps explain why some people become depressed. Efforts to change their lives repeatedly have proven fruitless.   (David S. Strickler/Monkmeyer Press Photo Service)

When applied to clinical situations, learned helplessness helps explain why some people become depressed: According to Seligman, it is because their efforts to effect changes in their lives and have a positive impact on their surroundings have consistently failed. They develop feelings of learned helplessness because of a conviction that their behavior has little apparent impact on anything. Such feelings are typically accompanied by progressive withdrawal into a state of apathy and listlessness.

Other clinicians also have studied the effects of cognitive processes on behavior (Dryden and Golden, 1987). In subsequent chapters, we will discuss the work of a group of cognitive behaviorists who have made considerable inroads into effective treatment of anxiety, depression, stress, and many other mental disorders (Cautela and Kearney, 1986).

THE HUMANISTIC PERSPECTIVE

Humanistic psychology has attracted a number of important theoreticians and clinical practitioners (Pollio, 1982). It is based on the premise that people are basically good, and have within them the capacity to achieve high levels of personal fulfillment and achievement. The humanistic perspective is most commonly associated with the work of Abraham Maslow and Carl Rogers. However, a number of other psychologists have had significant roles in its definition, including Gordon Allport, Erich Fromm, and Erik Erikson. Collectively, these individuals stress the worth and dignity of all human beings, and tend to conceptualize psychological problems in terms of factors that interfere with personal growth.

Maslow and Self-Actualization

Abraham Maslow (1908–1970) made several important contributions to the humanistic perspective. Chief among them was the concept of **self-actualization,** which refers to a state of being in which a high level of personal fulfillment is achieved (Maslow, 1968). Personal fulfillment may take any of a variety of forms; there is no specific activity or form of endeavor uniquely characteristic of the self-actualized individual. Rather, the term is meant to refer more generally to the effective and harmonious integration of one's creative impulses, intellectual faculties, interpersonal skills, and biological energies. When effectively harnessed and directed, these forces can help the individual achieve the high level of personal integrity characteristic of the self-actualized individual.

Self-actualization presupposes that the individual has satisfactorily gratified a number of more basic, subsidiary needs. Maslow grouped these into a pyramid-like structure termed the "hierarchy of needs," with self-actualization at the top. At the base of the pyramid are such fundamental needs as those for food, warmth, and other biologic necessities. Further up are interpersonal needs such as emotional closeness, intimacy, and effective collaboration with other people. According to Maslow, although everyone has a need for self-actualization, most people struggle to have their needs met at lower levels on the pyramid and never attain the final step. As a result, they tend to be chronically frustrated in one way or another and fall prey to psychological disturbances such as anxiety and depression.

Maslow also believed that, although everyone has the potential to achieve a state of self-actualization, most people are frustrated in their efforts by the impact of interpersonal problems, cultural prohibitions, and social restrictions, which conspire against personal fulfillment. Maslow's position is consistent with that of many others, including Freud, who were aware that efforts to maintain social order with any culture necessarily imposes some constraints on the limits of individual behavior.

(a) Abraham Maslow (1908-1970) and (b) Carl Rogers developed the so-called self theories, which comprise a branch of the humanistic perspective.   (Both photos: The Bettmann Archive)

Clinicians partial to Maslow's ideas strive to help their clients achieve as full a state of self-actualization as possible. This often entails working within certain constraints imposed by personal, occupational, or other factors. The goal of therapy is to free the individual from unnecessary biological, interpersonal, and psychological constraints, and encourage greater latitude and diversity in behavior that ultimately may result in a state of higher personal fulfillment.

Rogers and the Self Theory

The "self" theory of Carl Rogers shares much in common with the ideas of Maslow. Carl Rogers developed a system of psychotherapy designed to help free individuals as much as possible from constraints that interfere with self-fulfillment. Rogers placed a great deal of emphasis on the importance of a positive self-concept. He believed that self-fulfillment depends on feelings of self-worth stemming from early experiences that foster competence and a positive regard for one's capabilities. He further postulated the existence of a universal need for **unconditional positive regard,** that is, a favorable evaluation of oneself by others.

As a therapist, Rogers attempted to alter the prevailing view of psychological problems as forms of illness. He spoke of clients, rather than patients. He avoided the use of medically oriented diagnostic terminology, believing that classifying individuals into preexisting diagnostic categories robs them of much of their individuality and dignity. His style as a therapist focused less on interpretive analysis than on constant efforts to understand the world from the client's standpoint (Rowan, 1983). This technique gave rise to use of the term **empathy,** the capacity to appreciate the world from the standpoint of another person. All of these characteristics contributed to a form of intervention known as **client-centered therapy,** which is based on the premise that most psychological problems stem from the constriction of personal growth. People in psychological distress, according to Rogers, are likely to have experienced efforts by others—parents, teachers, authority figures—to shape their development in ways that do not coincide with the individual's natural inclinations. The need for acceptance by others is so strong in most people that they will subjugate their personal needs to gain approval from others. Client-centered therapy attempts to provide an accepting atmosphere in which the client can feel free to explore new roles previously suppressed because they did not conform to the expectations of those who exerted significant influence over the client's early development. It is Roger's conviction that therapy can help clients be more attentive to their own needs and inclinations. Once this has begun to occur, the client's overt behavior will become more congruent with inner dictates. To promote this awareness, the therapist attempts to convey the quality of "unconditional positive regard," which involves an open acceptance of whatever feelings and ideas the client uncovers during therapy. Therapeutic success is measured in terms of how free the client feels to engage in self-expression, unencumbered by the denial or distortion of basic feelings.

THE SYSTEMS PERSPECTIVE

By now it should be evident that there are many ways to define and analyze abnormal behavior. Each of the perspectives discussed thus far—psychodynamic, behavioral, and humanistic—represents a unique approach to the characterization and treatment of abnormal behavior. All three perspectives, however, are characterized by a tendency to view individuals as the proper focus of attention.

Some of the attitudes inherent in approaches to the analysis of psychological problems reflect certain cultural and literary themes that have been popular in the past century. The struggle of man to master his environment and cope with the complexities of a high-technology society has encouraged a tendency to view conflict—psychological or otherwise—in terms of an individual's struggle to come to grips with life. This theme was effectively depicted in Charlie Chaplin's film *Modern Times,* which portrayed the funny and pathetic efforts of one man trying to cope with the impersonal qualities of a technical, asocial world. The theme of the individual against the world has been a popular one in Western culture, and particularly so in the United States, where a great deal of emphasis is placed on achievement and a competitive spirit. Not surprisingly, theories of abnormal behavior have leaned toward this viewpoint, and have opted for individualized, rather than collective, solutions to psychological problems.

More recently, an alternative approach to the study of abnormal behavior has gained widespread acceptance. According to this perspective, behavior needs to be examined in a social context to be meaningfully interpreted. Thus, it is difficult to understand the aggressive behavior of a young child without knowing something about the social context of that behavior. The behavior of clients with marital problems becomes especially meaningful when the couple is seen together, rather than just one person.

Basically, there are three major contexts for the study of both normal and abnormal behavior: the family, the community, and the culture. The determination of whether or not behavior is abnormal rests largely on determining how appropriate it is in these three contexts. From the standpoint of clinical work, the family context is the most practical level at which to intervene.

The Family Systems Model

Interest in the role of the family in causing and perpetuating abnormal behavior was stimulated by early theories of social organization. The sociologist George Meade, for example, wrote extensively about family relationships and role patterns. Gregory Bateson, an anthropologist, was among the first to associate psychopathology in children with the experience of growing up with seriously disturbed parents.

Relationships between family members were likened by some theorists to the interdependent way in which components of other systems interact (Bornstein and Bornstein, 1986). The field of **systems theory** eventually developed as a means of explaining relationships between members of an organized unit such as a family. Systems theory emphasizes the interdependence among members of a family or other social group. Such groups develop patterns of interaction governed by a state of equilibrium, in which each member's behavior comes to be reasonably predictable. Members of social systems learn to interpret cues from one another and use feedback effectively as a means of keeping things running smoothly (Karpel, 1986).

Principles derived from systems theory can be used in describing the development of abnormal behavior as well (Group for the Advancement of Psychiatry, 1986). The anthropologist Bateson developed the double-bind theory of schizophrenia, which states that children exposed to unending "damned if you do, damned if you don't" messages from their parents are prime candidates for severe psychopathology later in life. Such **schizophrenogenic parents,** as Bateson called them, set up a system of family interaction that causes children to experience endless futility and defeat. The result was that a child raised this way would develop abnormal behavior patterns as the only possible means of coping with a psychologically intolerable living situation.

Although research has not validated the concept of a "schizophrenogenic" parent, the idea has stimulated development of more sophisticated and comprehensive models of family interaction patterns (Jacob, 1987). It is now well established, for instance, that certain family situations clearly warrant analysis based on principles of systems theory. Framo (1979) identified several advantages to this approach. First, by evaluating entire families one can determine the function served by an individual member's symptoms in maintaining the family's equilibrium. Second, involvement of the entire family, even when the problem seems to involve only a single member, can help improve treatment motivation and lead to improvements in the social context that may have started the problem in the first place. Third, it is often easier to treat psychological problems when everyone in a family shares responsibility for them. By mobilizing an entire family in response to one member's drinking problem, for example, it is possible to promote therapeutic interactions within the family that continue long after the therapy session has ended.

These ideas are consistent with a basic assumption shared by advocates of a systems approach to abnormal behavior: a person's actions, thoughts, and feelings have little intrinsic meaning until they are viewed in the context of a social environment.

Mental Health and the Community

Moving to the next of the three social contexts described earlier brings us to the community as a potential source of factors contributing to patterns of abnormal behavior.

In 1963 President Kennedy signed into law the Community Mental Health (CMH) Act, which has had far-reaching effects. Before this law was passed, the care and treatment of the mentally ill was primarily the responsibility of large state institutions. People incarcerated in these hospital settings often languished for months or years without effective treatment. Institutions served primarily as containment centers, where people could be kept at little risk to themselves or others.

The CMH Act provided for five types of mental health services.

1. Inpatient hospitalization, generally short-term, for people experiencing acute psychological distress.

2. Outpatient clinical services oriented toward clients with less disruptive disturbances.

3. Partial hospitalization programs, in which clients could spend evenings or weekends as needed.

4. Emergency or crisis services, such as suicide prevention hot lines, aimed at helping people in crises find immediate relief.

5. Education and consultation services provided through community agencies, focusing on prevention, rather than treatment, of psychological disorders.

The goal of the last of these services—prevention of mental disorders—exemplifies the original intent of the CMH Act. Although considerable financial resources were allocated for treatment programs, it was hoped that in the long run it would be possible to bring about significant social and economic changes that would have the effect of reducing the incidence of mental illness.

In a discussion of the concept of prevention, Kelly (1970) identified three types of relevant services. The first is mental health consultation work, in which psychologists confer directly with authorities in community agencies such as schools and businesses to help program administrators become sensitive to the psychological needs of their personnel. Arranging for on-the-job counseling, developing drug-abuse screening procedures, and working to improve morale are all potential effects of mental health consultation. Such services help promote the attitude that the responsibility for preventing or alleviating psychological problems rests with those who have day-to-day contact with the individual.

A second aspect of prevention involves efforts to change the structure of organizations themselves to make them capable of responding to specific psychological needs. Typically, this involves training employees and staff members in crisis management techniques, to help members of an organization develop skills and flexibility in coping with problems as they arise.

Third, prevention can be effected through community planning. Community-based consultation may deal with social policy issues, political factors, and even such things as urban development planning. This level of intervention is the most far-reaching in its intent, which is to encourage community members to anticipate social needs and problems before they evolve into issues demanding immediate attention. For example, community-based consultation services could be requested regarding plans to develop low-cost housing in an inner-city ghetto. Such a plan would have as its intent the goal of improving living conditions, and, ultimately, contributing to a higher quality of life and a lower incidence of crime and psychological problems such as depression and drug abuse.

Each of these three levels of prevention provides an alternative way of looking at the problem of treatment. Concern for the individual client is replaced by a broader perspective encompassing social agencies and other components in the communal environment. The ultimate goal of community-oriented psychologists is nothing less than the eventual eradication of conditions that promote and sustain psychological maladjustment. This is an ideal many psychologists, whatever their orientation, would endorse. Hence, there is no basic incompatibility between community-based intervention and more traditional psychotherapy, even though the particular focus of interest is distinctly different in each case.

Perhaps the most important effect of the Community Mental Health Act was to increase awareness of mental health issues. It brought psychological problems out of remote inpatient hospitals and made them part of each community's responsibility. This was accomplished in several ways. There were established within many communities regional mental health centers designed to provide prompt attention to psychological problems. Unlike the older hospitals, these centers were located within the community, thereby making them an integral part of daily life. And by stressing mental *health* rather than mental *illness,* these programs subtly broadened the scope of psychological intervention techniques to encompass not only the treatment of mental disorders but also the promotion and maintenance of well-adjusted behavior.

ABNORMALITY ACROSS CULTURES

Padanaram Village

The quest for valid preventive measures for mental illness has led some visionaries to experiment with the concept of a mentally healthy community. Some have tried to create new communities, hoping to avoid many of the problems that plague modern society. Designed as conscious alternatives to the socioeconomic structure and competitive values of mainstream society, these utopian communities attempt to construct a healthier environment for their members, based upon principles of communal living.

One such community is Padanaram Village, located in rural Indiana, several miles from the nearest town. Founded by a charismatic minister named Daniel Wright, this community currently has more than 200 members. Its financial success rests on its operation of a thriving sawmill and lumber business. In this respect, Padanaram is exceptional, for many other nineteenth- and twentieth-century utopian communities have foundered due to lack of a sustaining economic base.

Like many earlier utopian communities, Padanaram operates upon principles of economic communism. All members of the community are expected to work at jobs commensurate with their capabilities. In return, they share equally in the profits of their joint enterprise. Costs for housing, food, recreation, and medical care are met from the common treasury. Members retain a basic nuclear family structure, and each family is allocated space in large, dormitory-style buildings. The division of labor within the community is traditional; men do most of the heavy work and dominate the lumber business, while women provide the majority of domestic services and are encouraged to raise children. Meals are taken in the communal dining hall, and frequent dances, films, picnics, and "rap" sessions reinforce members' sense of belonging to a close-knit, loving community.

To strengthen communal values further, particularly among the young, the community operates its own school. Although the curriculum emphasizes traditional subjects such as reading, math, and the natural sciences, the absence of grades and the preference for cooperative activities reflect the community's desire to foster an egalitarian, noncompetitive environment for its children.

A committee of seven elders make financial decisions and community policies. Rules are few, and the community relies on the closeness and common interests of its members to ensure behavior consistent with its values.

Communities such as Padanaram reflect the belief that economic inequality and our culture's undue emphasis on individualism account in large part for mental illness, crime, and violence. This perspective focuses on environmental factors in explaining human behavior and argues that a community founded upon equality and cooperation will produce happy, well-adjusted individuals.

CROSS-CULTURAL PERSPECTIVE

Many factors are involved in determining what constitutes abnormal behavior. The perspectives discussed so far have considered a broad range of contributory elements, ranging from subjective states of distress and the effects of family members' behavior on one another to the role of poverty and economic deprivation. However, many psychologists, anthropologists, and sociologists have convincingly argued that a thorough understanding of behavior also requires consideration of the cultural context in which it occurs.

The crosscultural society of the United States creates a blurry boundary between "abnormal" behavior and cultural habits.   (Richard Wood/Taurus Photos)

Not all behaviors have the same meaning across cultures. Depression, for example, is one of the oldest and most widespread psychological disorders known in Western societies. As a result, many ways of treating depression have evolved, and there is general agreement, at least within Western societies, about what are the core features of depression. Basically, it is a disorder characterized by sadness, a blue mood, self-defeating thoughts, and behavioral inertia. After reviewing considerable cross-cultural literature on the topic, Marsella (1980) concluded that the incidence of depression as defined here is comparatively low in non-Western society. Marsella noted that Westerners tend to analyze their experiences far more than do people in most other cultures. This tendency gives mental disorder a somewhat abstract, analytical quality. In contrast, many other cultures stress the subjective rather than the analytical aspects of experience, so that their descriptions of mental disorders tend to be more pragmatic and concrete.

Because definitions of abnormal behavior are in large measure culturally bound, it is difficult to make many generalizations about the prevalence of specific mental disorders. The widespread occurrence of depression in middle-class Americans, for example, does not mean that it is a universal phenomenon. This fact indicates the need for caution in drawing conclusions about the psychological needs of people in non-Western cultures. Many well-intentioned efforts to help such individuals have failed because they have not given adequate consideration to the cultural context of behavior.

Failure to appreciate the culture-related aspects of depression or any other mental disorder may have at least two unfortunate consequences. One is that behavior patterns may be mislabeled as abnormal when in fact they are entirely appropriate within the subject's cultural background. The other, and perhaps even more serious, consequence is that genuine psychological distress in someone with another cultural background may go unrecognized. According to Higginbotham (1976), professionals who develop mental health services for non-Western ethnic and cultural groups must do four things: (1) learn what types of behaviors are considered problematic within the culture; (2) become aware of existing norms that provide guidelines concerning normal development and adjustment; (3) establish good working relationships within the community at large, to ensure acceptance of the services and cooperation of community members; and (4) become aware of techniques already used within the culture to treat abnormal behavior. It is a common mistake to be overly critical of practices that appear archaic, irrational, or even foolish when those practices are viewed out of context. The wild gestures of an Indian medicine man over the inert form of a spiritually possessed tribe member, for example, are incomprehensible to an outsider. On the other hand, a non-Westerner might question the credibility of traditional psychoanalysis. Such an observer might describe this form of therapy as a procedure in which the client lies on a couch for an interminable time, talking about whatever comes to mind, while the therapist, out of view and nearly immobile, makes occasional comments. A tribe member would undoubtedly conclude that his own medicine man works a lot harder for his fee! Clearly, in both cases an understanding of the underlying beliefs and values of each culture is crucial before the therapeutic procedures begin to make sense.

Throughout this book we will discuss cross-cultural aspects of psychopathology. There are several reasons for doing this. First, it is important to be constantly aware of the role of cultural values in determining whether behavior is deemed abnormal. Second, diverse cultural views of abnormal behavior often provide new insights into the management of these conditions. All too often, culturally bound perceptions limit our way of approaching a particular condition. Another cultural perspective often provides a new and potentially effective means of understanding abnormal behavior. Third, emphasizing cross-cultural aspects of psychopathology illustrates the extent to which behavior is affected by the context in which it occurs. It becomes clear that, although nearly every culture can identify behavior patterns that appear deviant, comparatively few conditions appear to be manifested worldwide. Whereas biologically based disorders are likely to be unmodified by cultural factors, the majority of conditions discussed in this book appear to be shaped to varying degrees by experiences within one's environment. Finally, because the delivery of mental health services has become an increasingly complex task, students of abnormal behavior must broaden their focus to consider the psychological needs of persons with diverse cultural and ethnic backgrounds. In determining the best response to a universal need for understanding, it is critical that we appreciate the needs of all cultural groups.

CHAPTER REVIEW

1. Although many theories of abnormal behavior have been developed, the psychodynamic, behavioral, humanistic, systems, and cross-cultural perspectives have come to dominate current thinking about abnormality.

2. The psychodynamic perspective, developed by Freud, emphasized the power of unconscious forces in controlling behavior for good or ill.

3. Psychodynamic theory sees the motivating forces of behavior inside the individual; it is termed an intrapsychic theory.

4. Freud believed that the individual's personality is formed early in life; the three components of personality (the id, ego, and superego) evolve successively during the first years of life.

5. Conflict is a focal concept in psychodynamic theory. According to Freud, conflict is an inevitable part of life; how abnormal one's behavior appears depends on how effectively he or she manages conflict.

6. Anxiety results from conflict and may stem from any number of sources. Freud proposed defense mechanisms as a means of explaining how people guard against the discomfort of anxiety.

7. Behavioral psychologists focus on external, or environmental, factors in an effort to explain both normal and abnormal behavior.

8. According to the behavioral perspective, behavior is largely learned. Learning takes place in accordance with specific principles, which can also be used to modify or even eliminate certain behaviors.

9. Skinner and Pavlov, two important behaviorists, demonstrated in different ways the relationship between behavior and its control by environmental forces.

10. Humanistic psychologists, such as Maslow and Rogers, believe that many psychological problems result when people lack clear ideas about what they really want or need. The goal of therapy as practiced by humanistic psychologists is increased self-awareness and feelings of self-worth.

11. Systems views of behavior focus on the interrelationships between members of families and other social units. Abnormal behavior is interpreted as indicating improper communication patterns within the larger system.

12. Community-oriented mental health practitioners emphasize the need for careful community planning and for immediate responses to crises as means of preventing the development of serious psychopathology.

13. The broad vantage afforded by a cross-cultural perspective makes clearer the extent to which abnormal behavior is culturally bound. Most cultures have different psychological problems of varying degrees of severity, and different means of dealing with them.

TERMS TO REMEMBER

psychodynamic theory
psychic determinism
pleasure principle
libido
Oedipal conflict
Electra complex
fixation
ego
id

superego
ego ideal
symptom substitution
unconditioned stimulus
unconditioned response
association
conditioned stimulus
conditioned response
extinction

operant conditioning
self-actualization
unconditional positive regard
empathy
client-centered therapy
systems theory
schizophrenogenic parents

FOR MORE INFORMATION

Butcher, J., and Spielberger, C. (1986) *Advances in personality assessment.* Vol. 6. Hillsdale, N.J.: Erlbaum. An excellent source of information on the most up-to-date developments in various theories of personality and related research and in assessment issues

Craighead, W.E., Kazdin, A.E., and Mahoney, J.J. (1981) *Behavior modification principles, issues and applications,* 2nd ed. Boston: Houghton Mifflin. A comprehensive overview of the basic foundations of behavioral principles and their application to clinical problems

Drapela, V. (1987) *A review of personality theories.* Springfield, Ill.: Charles C Thomas. A concise and readable introduction to the personality theories that influence developments in the field of abnormal psychology

Erdely, M. (1985) *Psychoanalysis: Freud's cognitive psychology.* New York: Freeman. Written in a most interesting style, with cartoons, anecdotes, and case studies, this book is also a scholarly comparison of Freud's views with principles of modern cognitive psychology

Freud, S. (1965) *A general introduction to psychoanalysis.* New York: Washington Square Press. An extremely readable introduction to psychoanalytic theory that provides an excellent overview of Freud's original writings

Reppen, J. (Ed.). (1986) *Beyond Freud: A study of modern psychoanalytic theories.* Hillsdale, N.J.: The Analytic Press. A superb collection of writings on the various directions psychoanalytic and psychodynamic theories have taken in modern times

In Alfred Hitchcock's film *Spellbound*, Ingrid Bergman plays a psychoanalyst who tries to help Gregory Peck recover from amnesia through reliving traumatic experiences. (Museum of Modern Art/Film Stills Archive; © 1945 United Artists)

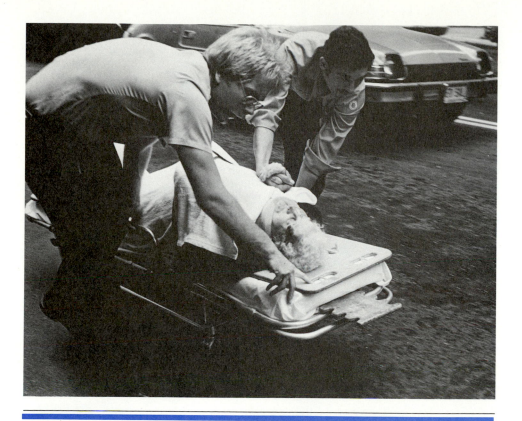

Causes of abnormal behavior may include physical trauma resulting from an accident. (David Hurn/Magnum)

cordial toward her colleagues at the law firm, Harriett was somewhat socially aloof. She did not enjoy social gatherings, believing them to be frivolous. What little free time she had was spent with her husband, a corporate executive. Married for 12 years, the couple had no children.

Following the accident, Harriett took three months of medical leave, during which she appeared to recover fully. Pronounced physically fit by her physician, she returned to the office, where it rapidly became apparent that she could not handle the demands of her job. She complained incessantly of headaches and dizziness, and found herself unable to concentrate because of the discomfort. She became irritable with her colleagues, one of whom she openly accused of trying to sabotage an important case. Previously blessed with almost total recall for the details of her cases, she now found it difficult to keep track of very basic information about her clients. During a briefing session with one of the senior partners, Harriett momentarily forgot his name, became flustered, and left the room in embarrassment. It was at this point

3

Assessment of Abnormal Behavior

Psychologists have approached the assessment of abnormal behavior from many different vantage points. Some have viewed abnormal behaviors much like physical diseases, which have specific causes and treatments. Others have looked into the complex web of cultural, social, and psychological forces that appears to shape behavior whether normal or not. This chapter provides a discussion of the issues involved in describing and classifying the many forms deviant behavior can take.

● The Case of Harriett

Harriett, an attorney, had an automobile accident while driving home from work one evening. She could not remember any details about the accident which had left her unconscious for nearly four hours. Neurologic tests at the time of the accident revealed mild, diffuse brain damage. In other respects her condition was good, and she appeared to make a rapid recovery.

Prior to the accident, Harriett had been a successful attorney in a prestigious law firm. As both a woman and the only child in her family to attend college, she was motivated to pursue an extremely high level of professional achievement. She had a reputation as a highly conscientious attorney who meticulously prepared her cases and zealously defended her clients. She did not tolerate opposition well, however, and behind her tough, businesslike facade she felt personally devastated when she lost a case. Although polite and that she contacted her physician, who referred her to a clinical psychologist specializing in neuropsychology, the study of brain-behavior relationships.

The neuropsychologist gave Harriett a battery of tests designed to assess the status of her general intelligence, language skills, memory ability, and perceptual capabilities. He obtained a detailed history of Harriett's life before the accident, and administered several measures of personality traits. Together with existing medical reports, this information enabled the neuropsychologist to provide a detailed analysis of Harriett's current mental and psychological status.

Among his pertinent findings was that, despite the mild nature of her physical injuries, Harriett had suffered an impairment in intellectual skills sufficient to interfere with her work. This conclusion was reached after comparing the IQ test given by the neuropsychologist with information taken from Harriett's academic and personal background. The evaluation also revealed a substantial memory deficit, impairing recall of both old and new information. This accounted for Harriett's difficulty in remembering such things as the names of her clients and colleagues. Third, an assessment of personality factors revealed that Harriett's behavior was historically characterized by perfectionistic tendencies, an intense fear of criticism, and social isolation.

The evaluation made it clear that Harriett could not be expected to resume her legal work as planned. The neuropsychologist estimated that recovery of psychological capabilities could continue for up to two years following the accident, at which time Harriett might still be left with some deficiencies. He also pointed out that her perfectionism and social isolation might make it more difficult to accept help and establish realistic goals for recovery.

The case of Harriett illustrates how a thorough psychological assessment can help evaluate the impact of traumatic injury on a patient. To all appearances, Harriett appeared to have recovered fully from her accident. Yet there was little doubt from the test results that the injury left her with residual problems, indicating that her brain had not fully recovered from the trauma. Assessments such as this are routinely conducted by clinical psychologists and neuropsychologists to aid in the description of a client's problems and to develop effective intervention plans.

This chapter surveys some of the techniques used by psychologists in the assessment of abnormal behavior. We first describe a pragmatic approach to the characterization of abnormal behavior. Next we discuss the principal current diagnostic and classification system of mental disorders, the *Diagnostic and Statistical Manual of Mental Disorders* (DSM). These general issues provide a context for consideration of the basic techniques employed by practicing clinicians: interviews, formal testing, inventories, and observations (Rabin, 1981; Turner and Hersen, 1984; Anastasi, 1987).

The Case of Carol

Carol, a music student and accomplished pianist, was troubled by severe performance anxiety. When required to play in recitals or group classes, she became acutely uncomfortable and on several occasions had been unable to perform. She reported symptoms that included rapid heart beat, tremors, muscle tension, and recurrent thoughts that she would forget her music and be ridiculed by the audience.

She described herself as always having been a bit nervous, but found the problem much worse since she had started college. Her teachers were perplexed by the problem; she was perceived as an intelligent, accomplished student with real musical aptitude.

The assessment procedure confirmed the presence of a form of anxiety known as social anxiety. The main feature of social anxiety is fear of being negatively evaluated by others, to the point that public appearances become extreme sources of tension. The evaluation also revealed several other important things about Carol. For one thing, she was troubled by a recurring thought that she had little musical talent, notwithstanding all evidence to the contrary. Second, she showed other signs of physical stress, including a pre-ulcer condition, a mild skin disorder, and frequent headaches. Finally, it was learned that she was a scholarship student from a small nearby town, the first student from her high school ever accepted into the university's conservatory. Her parents had opposed a career in music, and only grudgingly gave their approval when she was awarded the scholarship.

A consideration of these three factors made it evident that Carol was under extreme psychological pressure from a number of sources. The assessment documented evidence of negative self-statements, physical ailments, and social/familial pressures, which collectively led to extreme pressure and anxiety.

From the standpoint of a multimodal approach, Carol's situation was one in which several relatively independent factors—cognitive, physiological, and social—were all simultaneously contributing to her anxiety. It was recommended that Carol (1) have a brief series of therapy aimed at exploring the discrepancy between her perceived and actual abilities; (2) begin a program of biofeedback training to promote muscular relaxation and overall tension reduction; and (3) attend a group program for anxious musicians who performed for each other and provided one another with moral support.

Carol made rapid progress with this multimodal program. The assessment succeeded not only in identifying the disorder from which she suffered—social anxiety—but also provided information about the specific manifestations of the condition and the ways in which it could best be treated.

The case of Carol nicely illustrates how a single disorder can have multiple components, each of which requires intervention. The success of a multimodal approach in such cases is well documented (Lazarus, 1981; Meyer, 1983; Haynes, 1984), and its use is advocated throughout this book.

In assessing psychological problems such as those presented by Carol, psychologists gather information from many different sources, including interviews, structured psychological tests, personality inventories, and direct behavioral observation. Collectively analyzing this information for consistent patterns enables the clinician to characterize accurately the nature and severity of the client's condition. Thorough psychological assessments generally include the phases shown in the flowchart below.

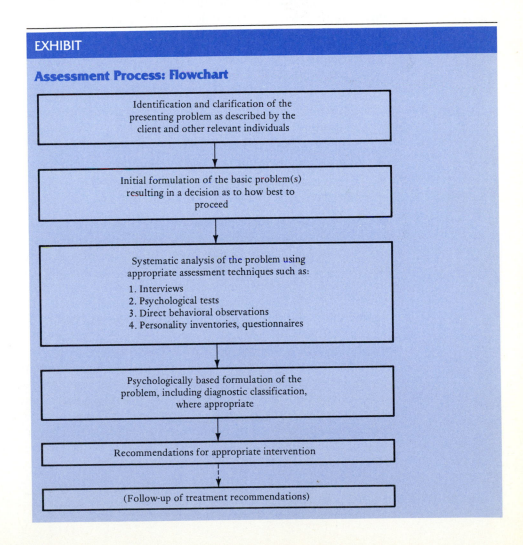

EXHIBIT

Assessment Process: Flowchart

Identification and clarification of the presenting problem as described by the client and other relevant individuals

↓

Initial formulation of the basic problem(s) resulting in a decision as to how best to proceed

↓

Systematic analysis of the problem using appropriate assessment techniques such as:

1. Interviews
2. Psychological tests
3. Direct behavioral observations
4. Personality inventories, questionnaires

↓

Psychologically based formulation of the problem, including diagnostic classification, where appropriate

↓

Recommendations for appropriate intervention

↓

(Follow-up of treatment recommendations)

Just how useful is this complex process? In return for the time and money invested, is it possible to assess mental disorders accurately? The answer is not simple. As in any scientific discipline, highly trained practitioners and dependable measurement techniques are a prerequisite to assessment rigor.

THE NATURE AND ASSESSMENT OF MENTAL DISORDERS

The view that abnormality is a disease that strikes passive victims, the so-called **disease model** of mental illness, dominated early conceptions of what abnormal behavior is. The following list summarizes the main features of a disease model of abnormal behavior.*

1. Diseases have a cause, a physical course of events consisting of an underlying state manifested in surface symptoms, and an outcome.

2. Psychological disorders are viewed in terms of an analogy with physical ailments. Therefore, it is assumed that an underlying state is manifested in outward signs, or symptoms. It is also assumed that eliminating symptoms will not necessarily cure the underlying disease.

3. It is assumed that people contract diseases through no fault of their own.

4. It is assumed that although diseases may have culturally distinct manifestations, the disease is essentially universal, not culturally specific.

This model, though popular during the early years of psychiatry, has been attacked by psychologists and psychiatrists alike (such as Szasz, 1961; 1987). Generally, such critics contend that use of a disease model does not necessarily increase our understanding of psychologically troubled people and may even misrepresent their condition. There are several reasons for this, two of which are discussed by Korchin. First, the disease model overemphasizes classification and disregards personal initiative and coping ability, which even people with serious psychological problems may possess. Second, it tends to encourage an attitude that psychological disorders, like most physical diseases, can be explained in terms of a straightforward cause-and-effect relationship.

In fact, searching for the underlying cause—or etiology—of a mental disorder is often unproductive for two reasons. First, relatively few mental disorders are caused by only one factor. Typically, a variety of events and conditions appear to contribute to the emergence of abnormal behavior. The lack of one-to-one correspondence between the characteristics of mental

*Adopted from Korchin, S.J. (1976) *Modern clinical psychology: Principles of intervention in the clinic and community.* New York: Basic Books. Reprinted with permission.

disorders and their underlying causes in turn makes it less likely that a particular pattern of abnormal behavior will yield to simple explanations. The situation is much different from the purely medical context, where knowing the cause of a disease helps physicians in both treating it and eliminating the conditions that gave rise to it in the first place.

Recognition of the difficulties inherent in attributing mental disorders to specific causes has gradually reduced the emphasis on etiological factors. Replacing it is a growing interest in accurate description of the behavior patterns that characterize mental disorders, including detailed analysis of the effect of these patterns on the individual's capability to function effectively on a day-to-day basis (Cone and Foster, 1982). Many clinical psychologists have recently adapted this viewpoint.

Certain abnormal conditions, such as the affective, or emotional, disorders and schizophrenia, can be described reasonably well by the medical or disease model. However, disorders involving anxiety or fear, and many developmental disorders, do not. In particular, the anxiety disorders (see Chapter 6) present a real challenge to the disease model, partly because they can stem from so many causes. Consequently, in our discussions of mental disorders we shall cite the disease model only when we consider it appropriate.

It is thus no accident that we use the term assessment rather than diagnosis in describing the process of evaluating mental disorders. **Assessment** is the process of gathering information about clients that helps the clinician make informed decisions (Korchin, 1976). It involves more than identifying disorders based on their symptoms, which is the essence of diagnosis. An assessment considers additional factors related to how the disorder is to be treated, such as general coping skills, motivation, available support systems, and other resources that may be brought into play on the client's behalf. Intervention strategies are developed with an awareness of these factors, as well as knowledge about any disorder present.

A client's problems are formulated in terms of a conceptualization that takes advantage of as many potential therapeutic resources as possible. In most instances, there is an attempt to coordinate the impact of these factors, so as to exert the maximum therapeutic "leverage" possible. Practically speaking, this means that a client's problems will be attacked on several fronts at once, an approach referred to as **multimodal,** or many-sided. The following case history illustrates how a multimodal evaluation would proceed.

THE DSM CLASSIFICATION OF ABNORMAL BEHAVIOR

Discussions of abnormal behavior have profited from recent efforts to develop comprehensive classification systems of mental disorders. Of the systems currently available, the most widely used is the *Diagnostic and Statistical Manual* (DSM), published by the American Psychiatric Association. Central to this classification system is the concept of a mental disorder. Mental disorders refer to behavior patterns associated with either substantial distress or impaired functioning in an important area of life. There are 17 categories of mental disorders in the DSM system, plus one additional category for conditions not attributable to a mental disorder that are nevertheless the focus of intervention (see Exhibit).

Because subsequent chapters of this book consistently refer to the DSM classification system, it is appropriate here to discuss briefly some of its important features.

Features of the DSM System

DSM is a **multiaxial classification system.** It employs five axes, or dimensions, each of which is used to evaluate a specific aspect of a client's psychological problems. Axes I and II are used to designate specific mental disorders in the DSM system. Axis III lists any medical problems that may be related to the mental disorders, while Axis IV specifies any social factors that may be involved. Axis V is used to determine how great a difference there is in the client's current functioning compared with prior levels of adjustment. Each of the five axes will now be described in greater detail.

The breakdown of the first two axes is as follows.

Axis I.   A. Clinical disorders
  B. Conditions not attributable to a mental disorder that are a focus of attention or treatment

Axis II.   A. Personality disorders
  B. Developmental disorders of childhood

Axes I and II are the dimensions used to record all of the mental disorders described in the DSM system. The distinction between Axis I and Axis II has to do with the types of disorders classified on each. Axis I disorders reflect relatively acute disturbances that are subjectively quite distressful. In most instances the onset of symptoms is readily apparent to the afflicted individual, who then tends to seek help. Axis II disorders are long-standing conditions having widespread effects on behavior. Persons with these disorders are less conscious of the condition because they have lived with it for so long.

Axis I is used to indicate the presence of mental disorders associated with symptoms such as anxiety, depression, and stress, and to record the presence of conditions not caused by mental disorders, but which may have a role in the client's problems. These include such things as school problems, marital conflict, and parent-child problems.

Two classes of disorders are listed on Axis II. The first, personality disorders, encompasses pervasive and enduring maladaptive patterns of behavior that impair social and work aspects of a person's life. The second group, developmental disorders of childhood, contains a number of biologically based disorders associated with childhood and early development.

Changes from R

EXHIBIT

DSM Diagnostic Categories

All on Axis I & II

1. Disorders usually first evident in infancy, childhood, or adolescence
2. Organic mental disorders   *Psychoactive*
3. Substance use disorders
4. Schizophrenic disorders +
5. ~~Paranoid disorders~~ - *Delusional Disorders*
6. Psychotic disorders not + elsewhere classified
7. ~~Affective disorders~~ *Mood disorders* S +
8. Anxiety disorders - +
9. Somatoform disorders S +
10. Dissociative disorders +

11. ~~Psychosexual disorders~~
12. Factitious disorders
13. Disorders of impulse control not elsewhere classified
14. Adjustment disorders S +
15. Psychological factors affecting S physical condition +
16. Personality disorders +
17. Conditions not attributable to a + mental disorder that are a focus of attention or treatment
18. Additional codes +

19. *Sleep Disorders*

Source: Diagnostic and Statistical Manual of Mental Disorders, 3rd ed., Revised. Washington, D.C., American Psychiatric Association, 1987.

children could be under any category.

If not 2, 45 & psychic has to be 6.

Axis III: Physical disorders and conditions.   There is a close association between psychological and physical health. This relationship is addressed by the DSM system on Axis III, which contains information about any physical illnesses contributing to the client's mental condition. The relationship between physical health and psychological status may be expressed in several ways. First of all, physical distress can cause some mental disorders. Certain neurologic diseases, for example, lead to dementia, a disorder with impaired thinking and memory skills. Second, physical disorders may arise in response to psychological factors. High levels of psychological stress, for instance, can lead to such physical impairments as ulcers, skin disorders, and even heart attacks. Finally, psychological disorders may be an indirect result of physical illness. A medical patient just informed of a serious medical illness, for example, may develop an anxiety disorder or depression in response to the news.

Axis IV: Severity of psychosocial stressors.   Social factors frequently contribute to the onset or maintenance of a mental disorder. Problems involving occupational status, marital relationships, and family life can create sufficient distress to cause mental disorders, and it is these factors that are specified on Axis IV. Many psychosocial stressors have only a mild or temporarily disruptive effect on an individual's functioning. The birth of a child, for example,

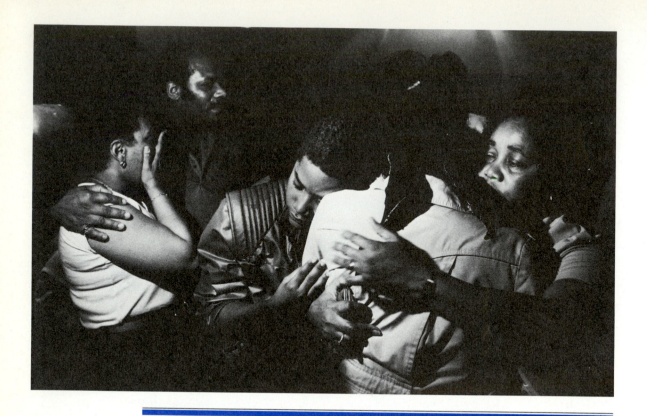

The psychological stress of losing a family member can result in severe depression or physical impairments such as headaches or skin disorders. (E.W. Faircloth/Magnum)

alters the structure of a family and may entail certain economic hardships, but does not usually cause lasting problems. Others are more disabling in their effects, such as the death of a close family member, divorce, or the loss of a job. The nature and severity of these psychosocial stress factors can have a significant bearing on the course and outcome of a mental disorder.

Axis V: Highest level of adaptive functioning. The final axis assesses the highest level of adaptive functioning during the year preceding the onset of problems. Axis V provides a baseline against which to measure the client's current condition. This helps the clinician evaluate both the severity of the disorder and the effectiveness of subsequent treatment. Axis V ratings also help in assessing the outlook, or prognosis, for a client; clearly, adequate adjustment during the year preceding the onset of a mental disorder suggests a better prognosis than when prior adjustment has been problematic.

Collectively, these axes provide a comprehensive overview of a client's condition at the time of assessment. The Exhibit on page 83 contains an example of an assessment based on the DSM multiaxial system.

82

Two additional features of the DSM system are equally important to note. First, it employs an approach to the classification of mental disorders that is descriptive, rather than theoretical, in nature. Discussion of the etiology, or origin, of these conditions is notably absent; instead, the emphasis is on comprehensive descriptions of behaviors associated with mental disorders. The intent is not to discredit the explanatory power of theoretical formulations, but rather to encourage the diagnostician to base explanations of mental disorders on theories that best suit the information obtained.

This descriptive approach has an important implication for intervention. Many theories of psychopathology encompass both disorders and their treatment, thereby implying that a specific treatment is dictated by the underlying theory. This is especially true regarding the psychoanalytic perspective, in which Freud's clinical work influenced the development of his theory, and vice versa. Yet the fact that clinicians of other theoretical persuasions have treated clients similar to Freud's suggests that there may be more than one way to treat a particular disorder. Deemphasizing theory in favor of concise descriptions of mental disorders therefore permits greater latitude in the choice of intervention strategies. Thus, a clinician may decide that a depressed client requires psychodynamically oriented therapy, but in addition would benefit from regular, rigorous physical activity to treat insomnia. There is no need to work within a particular theoretical framework in treating the client; the clinician is free to employ whatever interventions are needed. Second, the DSM acknowledges the vague boundaries of many mental disorders by employing somewhat flexible diagnostic criteria. It describes the various disorders in

---

EXHIBIT

Example of Diagnostic Classification Based on the DSM System

The following is an example of a diagnostic evaluation based on the DSM classification system. It concerns a 32-year-old computer programmer depressed by recent failure to secure a job promotion. Though competent enough when working with computers, this individual has a history of poor social relationships dating from childhood. Promotions of workers within the company, however, are awarded only to those who show managerial potential by exhibiting good interpersonal skills.

Axis I: Dysthmic disorder (depressive neurosis)
Axis II: Avoidant personality disorder
Axis III: Deferred (no known contributory physical disorder)
Axis IV: Severity of psychological stressors: moderate
      A.   Job promotion denied in favor of younger colleague
      B.   Forced by economic factors to move into an apartment with two roommates
Axis V: Highest level of adaptive functioning, past year: fair

terms of several criteria, not all of which need necessarily be present in every client. This approach makes it easier to evaluate conditions whose manifestations include one or two primary features along with other symptoms that occur either infrequently or inconsistently. It is, in effect, a way of recognizing that all individuals with schizophrenia (or any other condition) are not necessarily completely alike, and thus enables the clinician to identify the distinguishing features of a particular disorder as manifested in a particular client.

Here again is a clear implication for treatment: by responding to the characteristics of individual clients rather than to diagnostic labels, clinicians are able to tailor therapy to the client by using the multimodal approach.

DSM thus provides a comprehensive classification system that accommodates a wide range of mental disorders affecting both children and adults. Of course, subsequent clinical work and research may cause the diagnostic criteria for some mental disorders to change. For the present, however, the new system has shown considerable promise as an important assessment tool that accommodates both a wide range of mental disorders and the various therapeutic strategies employed by mental health professionals.

RELIABILITY AND VALIDITY OF PSYCHOLOGICAL ASSESSMENT TECHNIQUES

Assessments are used to gather information about four broad classes of data (Garfield, 1974). In the first group are measures of general abilities, such as intelligence, creativity, and overall social adjustment. Next are measures of more specific interests, aptitudes, and skills. Tests of reading, school achievement, vocational interests, and mechanical aptitude are all examples of measures from this second category. The third type of assessment data consists of measures used to assign people to diagnostic classification, of which the DSM system is a good example. Finally, other measures assess personality characteristics and social adjustment. Traits such as introversion or extraversion, dependency, and sociopathic tendencies can be evaluated with measures in this group.

In performing assessments, clinicians rely on four different categories of assessment techniques, including clinical interviews, structured psychological tests, personality inventories and questionnaires, and direct observations of behavior. A particular assessment problem may require the use of any or all of these procedures, depending on the nature and complexity of the issues involved. The theoretical orientation of the clinician also influences the types of techniques used. For example, behaviorally oriented clinicians rely extensively on behavioral observations and descriptions of current problems when conducting assessments, whereas more dynamically oriented diagnosticians routinely use psychological tests and inventories to help evaluate underlying personality traits and identify areas of conflict.

Regardless of the nature of the assessment problem or the theoretical orientation of the clinician, techniques should be selected on the basis of their proven ability to address particular issues. Yet the assessment techniques currently available vary widely both in terms of the issues they are designed to address and the rigor with which they carry out their roles. One way to evaluate their quality is to examine them with respect to two key statistical properties, reliability and validity (Anastasi, 1986).

Reliability refers to consistency of results of an assessment measure across different conditions. A ruler, for example, should measure the same distance whether you use it or someone else does. And its measurements should not not change from one occasion to another. The reliability of a particular assessment measure can be evaluated in three ways.

1. Split-half reliability concerns the internal consistency of assessment measures. If a test measure has this kind of reliability, dividing it into two groups of items (such as even and odd) will produce two test measures that give results virtually identical to each other.

2. Test-retest reliability concerns the extent to which an assessment measure gives the same results when administered to the same individuals more than once. If the test-retest reliability is high, the results will be the same or similar. If it is low, the results will differ. Generally, however, the longer the interval between tests, the lower the test-retest reliability.

3. Interrater reliability concerns the extent to which different individuals administering an assessment measure will come up with the same results. If a test measure has high interrater reliability, then the results obtained when Dr. A gives you the test will be very similar to those that Dr. B would get using the same test. If the interrater reliability is low, different administrators of the measure will come up with different results.

   For assessment measures that are well defined—such as multiple-choice questionnaires that have a history of consistent interpretation—interrater reliability tends to be high. For measures that are more loosely defined, such as interviews, the interrater reliability tends to be low. In other words, this type of reliability varies with the clarity of the assessment criteria. Interrater reliability also varies with the experience and training of those who interpret a given test. Marked differences in training or experience produce different results even though the assessment measure remains the same.

Validity is the degree to which an assessment technique measures what it is designed to measure. The validity of an assessment measure can be evaluated in the following four ways.

1. Content validity is the extent to which different items in the assessment measure the trait they were meant to. High levels of content validity indicate that test items accurately reflect the trait being measured. A questionnaire to assess anxiety, for example, would be high in content

validity if it included questions about known symptoms of anxiety such as muscle tension and a rapid pulse rate.

2. Concurrent validity reflects how well different measures of the same trait agree with one another. The concurrent validity of new test measures, for example, is often determined by comparing their results with the results of well-established measures. If a test possesses a high degree of concurrent validity, then it can be expected to give results very similar to other measures of the same characteristic.

3. Predictive validity is the ability of an assessment measure to predict someone's future behavior in a related, but different, situation. For example, SAT scores administered to high school seniors have been found to be fairly good predictors of success in college. An assessment measure with high predictive validity is capable of making accurate predictions of future behavior. Low predictive validity means that a measure is of little use in predicting a particular behavior.

4. Construct validity is the extent to which a theoretical construct such as a personality trait can be empirically defined. Traits are abstract concepts that are never really directly observed. Instead, they have to be inferred from the way people behave. For example, dependency is a trait that manifests itself in many ways. Dependent people rely heavily on other people, are anxious when left alone, and let others make decisions for them. An assessment measure designed to evaluate dependency would show a high level of construct validity if responses to items probing specific aspects of the trait showed a pattern consistent with the trait.

It is important that assessment techniques possess both validity and reliability. Meaningful discussion of disorders such as depression or childhood schizophrenia, for example, depends on the availability of accurate and dependable means of detecting them. The following discussion of commonly used psychological assessment techniques therefore includes an evaluation of their reliability and validity.

PSYCHOLOGICAL ASSESSMENT TECHNIQUES

Clinical Interviews

An interview is a meeting in which one (or more) people obtain information about a person for a specific purpose. Employers, for example, interview potential employees to evaluate their suitability for a particular job. Within the field of clinical psychology, the purpose of interviews varies widely. Common uses of interviews include clarifying the nature and severity of a client's

A clinical interview may be conducted by a participant observer, who engages the subject in dialogue and assesses the subject's behavior.   (Pozark/Gamma-Liaison)

problems, both at the time of the initial request for psychological services and later; increasing understanding of a client's problems by obtaining information about the person's history; systematically observing an individual behavior; or providing a format for conducting psychotherapy.

Whatever the purpose of an interview, the interviewer's behavior significantly affects the outcome. Effective interviewing is more than asking questions. Skilled interviewers are sensitive to the ebb and flow of the conversation and can judge when to question gently or indirectly, when to probe more deeply and directly, and when to remain silent. They are adept at putting their clients at ease at the outset of an interview, thus encouraging them to discuss their problems openly. It is also important that an interviewer possess an ability to see things from the client's viewpoint. If the interviewer can be open, accepting, and nonjudgmental toward the client, the client will in turn feel free to share intimate thoughts, knowing that the interviewer is genuinely interested in understanding him or her.

Sullivan (1954) characterized the interviewer as a **participant observer,** simultaneously capable of responding to clients' statements and making systematic observations of their behavior. Effective and productive interviewing requires skill and experience. Experienced interviewers are the first to admit that what their clients say can trigger in them all types of reactions; usually, these reactions are not shared with the client, as they might be in a nontherapeutic context. Instead, clinicians use their own reactions as a measure of what effects the client has on people in general. This latter information may be shared with the client to promote greater insight into his or her behavior. An interviewer may experience feelings of sympathy, anger, or perhaps even disgust in response to things clients say. Rather than acting directly on these feelings, well-trained interviewers use the information constructively to help the client.

Good interviewing skills demand more than openness and receptivity to another person. It is equally important for the interviewer to have some understanding of the client's background to determine how best to conduct the interview. This is particularly important when working with members of minority groups. Failure to be aware of such factors may jeopardize the success of the interview.

How reliable and valid are data gathered from an interview? A general answer is not easy to give because of the wide range of situations in which interviews are employed. Both the nature of the assessment problem and the experience of the interviewer influence the quality of information obtained. There is considerable evidence that interviewer and client influence each other's verbal behavior. This in turn significantly affects both the reliability and validity of the information obtained from the exchange. Krasner (1962), for example, has discussed the way in which the interviewer's smiles, gestures, and comments can subtly reinforce specific verbal behavior in the client. This feature may provide an indication of the client's susceptibility to social reinforcement, which is a legitimate diagnostic issue. However, unless this is actually an issue specifically being addressed, the effects of such reinforcement patterns may systematically distort clients' responses to questions. Few clinicians rely exclusively on interview data when conducting an assessment. When combined with results obtained through other measures, however, a skilled examiner's interview is often of great help in piecing together the details of a client's problems.

Psychological Tests

Psychological tests traditionally have been the clinician's basis for assessing behavior empirically. In the 1880s Sir Francis Galton established one of the first psychological laboratories, in which he measured and quantified many forms of human behavior. A major result of his efforts was to demonstrate the now well-known fact of individual differences, the fact that individual response patterns for most characteristics vary systematically. Intelligence quotient (IQ) scores are a good example of this sort of variability. Although the majority of IQ scores cluster around an average value of 100, individual scores range from less than 25 to more than 130.

The effect of Galton's work was twofold. First, it helped establish an empirical framework for studying human behavior. Second, it advanced the view that traits could be assessed through administration of specific tests. Before long, other researchers in the field began to devise specific tests to appraise many facets of behavior. Alfred Binet, for example, devised the first systematic test of mental abilities to evaluate the academic potential of Parisian school children. In its present form, the **Stanford-Binet Intelligence Scale** is widely used in the assessment of the intellectual abilities.

The early twentieth century saw the rapid development of many types of psychological tests, including the two types to be discussed here: the relatively structured tests of intellectual and mental skills, and the so-called projective tests, which soon gained wide acceptance in the assessment of personality traits (Rabin, 1981).

Contrary to popular belief, psychological test scores by themselves reveal very little about people. Few psychologists would administer an intelligence test for the sole purpose of determining IQ, because IQ scores alone may not have any particular relevance. Psychologists are more likely to use such tests as part of a more comprehensive assessment dealing with specific issues. For example, such a test might be administered to help determine whether an individual's intellectual skills are adequate for a particular job. Test results supply only a partial answer to such questions. Equally important to many clinicians is an analysis of how clients respond to particular tests. Along these lines, Graham has outlined a general strategy employed by clinical psychologists in the analysis of psychological test data (1978, pp. 319–320).

1. What was the test-taking attitude of the examinee, and how should this attitude be taken into account in interpreting the results of this test?

2. What was the general level of adjustment of the person who produced these responses?

3. What kinds of behaviors (symptoms, attitudes, defenses, and so on) can be inferred (or anticipated) about this person based on his or her performance on the test?

4. What set of psychological factors underlie this person's behaviors both during the assessment and on a day-to-day basis?

5. What are the most appropriate diagnostic labels for this person, based on the information obtained?

6. What are the implications for treatment based on this assessment?

These questions underscore the point that there is more to psychological assessment than computing test scores. Used by a well-trained clinician, psychological tests can add a wealth of descriptive and empirical information to the process of assessment.

Tests of intelligence. Intelligence tests traditionally have been included in psychological assessment batteries (Gregory, 1987). The Stanford-Binet, and the intelligence tests devised by David Wechsler (including the **Wechsler Adult Intelligence Scale-Revised,** or WAIS-R) are the most widely used measures of mental abilities in current clinical practice. The varying uses to which they have been put reflect several interesting assumptions about the nature of intelligence. First, it has generally been accepted that a comprehensive assessment of intellectual skills through an intelligence test constitutes a valid appraisal of an individual's ability to function in his or her day-to-day environment. This concept has been articulated most clearly by Wechsler, who emphasized a global concept of intelligence and avoided singling out any one ability as fundamental. These tests were thus designed to evaluate skills and abilities necessary for adaptation to one's cultural, social, and interpersonal environments. In actual practice, however, IQ scores correlate with a much more limited range of behaviors (Sternberg, 1985).

The IQ score derived from tests such as the Stanford-Binet and WAIS-R is a composite measure based on the subject's performance on a number of constituent measures. For example, Wechsler's scales comprise subtests that evaluate two broad areas known as "verbal" and "performance" factors. The verbal subtests assess such capabilities as vocabulary skills, abstract thought, awareness of social conventions, and so forth. The performance subtests focus on motor speed, visual organizational skills, and visuoperceptual abilities. When these various subtests are combined and converted into an IQ score, the resulting measure of intelligence is highly predictive of school achievement. In other words, IQ tests have high predictive validity for academic achievement (Matarazzo, 1972).

Clinicians can obtain several types of information by administering tests of intellectual abilities. First, they can compare the client's level of intellectual achievement with that of a comparable age group. The results provide at least a general indication of how well the individual can be expected to function on a day-to-day basis, particularly in an academic environment. In addition, the clinician often interprets qualitative features of test performance such as the subject's attitude toward testing, level of alertness, and relationship with the examiner. An analysis of such factors often aids in determining, say, why a child fails to perform at an expected level or why an employee is having difficulty getting along with other people at work.

Responses to individual items on intelligence tests provide yet another source of information for the clinician. For example, severe emotional disturbances—the psychoses—are frequently accompanied by impaired thought processes. The term **thought disorder** is often used to refer to this symptom. Thought disorders are often suspected in clients who give very vague or irrelevant responses, constantly wander off the topic, or even make up words that only they understand. If any of these characteristics are present, they will likely be manifested on test responses to measures of vocabulary or abstract thought. For example, a question such as "How are an orange and a peach alike?" typically elicits the response that both are fruits. Inappropriate

EXHIBIT

Summary Table: Correlates of IQ Scores

Correlate	Correlation Coefficient
IQ × mental retardation	0.90
IQ × educational attainment (years)	0.70
IQ × academic success (grade point)	0.50
IQ × occupational attainment	0.50
IQ × socioeconomic status	0.40
IQ × success on the job	0.20

Source: From Matarazzo, J.D. (1972) *Wechsler's measurement and appraisal of adult intelligence,* 5th ed. London: Oxford University Press, Inc. Reprinted with permission.

responses, such as "Both are shaped like stars," or the even more unintelligible "Peach fruits come pick winter" constitute evidence of a thought disorder that can then be further assessed through other measures. Thus, by evaluating the quality of responses to test items, the clinician is often able to form hypotheses about factors that may promote or inhibit the manifestation of intellectual skills.

Tests of intelligence such as the WAIS-R and the Stanford-Binet have undergone extensive refinement during the past 50 years. They have, nevertheless, come under considerable attack for several reasons. Their widespread use in determining school placement and vocational choices has led to a backlash of protest from people who feel that the tests do not provide valid data for making such decisions. There is often a tendency to attribute more predictive power to IQ tests than is really warranted. Part of the reason for doing so is a view of intelligence as a precisely measurable quantity like height or weight. Actually, intelligence is a theoretical construct that can only be approximated through the use of IQ test scores, which are subject to variability and error. However, theoretical debate on the nature of intelligence means little to the parents of children who have been excluded from academic programs in part because their IQ scores were "too low," or those whose children have been denied admission to compensatory academic programs because their IQ scores were "too high."

IQ tests do in fact predict certain kinds of behavior, including school performance, rather well (Matarazzo, 1972). In addition, the ability of IQ tests to provide hypotheses about behavior that can then be validated by other measures makes them an invaluable part of any assessment procedure. Much of the criticism of intelligence tests stems from their inappropriate application by untrained personnel. Given that the use of IQ tests has become widespread, this result may be inevitable.

RESEARCH PROFILE

The Stability of IQ Test Scores

Many people, including several eminent researchers, have argued that IQ scores are relatively permanent and unchanging. Whether because of effects of an impoverished environment, heritability, or both, young children who perform poorly on IQ tests are often presumed to be permanently handicapped. Belief in the stability of IQ scores is often accompanied by the conviction that early experiences unalterably shape an individual's destiny. According to this view, normal development depends on adequate early experience in the promotion of healthy growth.

Although in principle most psychologists would agree with the importance of early experience and the *relative* stability of IQ scores, a report by Jarmila Koluchovà (1976) reveals some interesting exceptions to this pattern. It concerns two identical Czechoslovakian twins who, severely maltreated and neglected in early life, subsequently manifested remarkable gains in a wide range of developmental areas.

P. M. and J. M. were born in September 1960 and placed in a children's home for 11 months. Their natural mother died in childbirth: their father subsequently remarried, and eventually took the twins into his new home. The events that followed came to light only several years later in court. Cumulative evidence indicated that the twins were grievously mistreated and neglected by their father and stepmother. They were confined to a small, barren room and were not seen outside the house for several years. Many neighbors did not even know of their existence. Occasionally they were locked in a closet for long periods. A few neighbors periodically heard cries and screams from the house, but these incidents were not investigated during the twins' early years. When an investigation was carried out, the father and stepmother were tried for criminal neglect and the twins removed to protective custody. After considerable time, they were placed in homes with foster parents.

When the twins were taken from their parents at age seven, they showed numerous signs of extreme deprivation and maltreatment. For example, they reacted to commonplace objects with fear and anxiety, indicating that they were totally unfamiliar with such things. They showed virtually none of the exploratory tendencies

Another recurrent conflict involving IQ tests concerns their validity when administered to persons whose cultural and/or ethnic background differs significantly from mainstream American cultures. A number of potential problems have been identified in this area. For one, the rapport between clinician and client is affected by the similarity of their cultural backgrounds. Marked discrepancies can interfere with testing results unless the clinician is especially adept at bridging cultural differences (Sattler, 1982). Motivational factors are related to cultural differences as well (Zigler and Butterfield, 1968). Middle-class American children are generally taught to do their best and to try to impress adults. Such traits are favorably viewed by most psychologists so characteristic of young children when confronted with unfamiliar objects. They were extremely distrustful of people, and evidenced no communicative language skills. At this time they were incapable of being tested in any formal way. On the basis of their behavior patterns, their mental capabilities were estimated to be at approximately a two- or three-year level.

From this point on, the twins made remarkable progress. Gradually they developed language skills and began to communicate with their caretakers. Eventually it was possible to test them with standardized instruments, and they were subsequently retested about once a year.

The results of testing revealed several interesting features. First, there was a striking overall increase in IQ scores: by age ten both twins were close to the average range. Second, despite the fact that the twins were identical, their IQ scores were not; this fact was corroborated by observations suggesting that they were highly individualistic. The initially wide gap between their scores narrowed considerably by the time they were 11, although differences remained. Finally, the greatest increases in IQ scores did not occur until *two years* after the twins had been removed from their original home. During this period they were developing social, linguistic, and other competencies that subsequently showed up in significantly higher IQ scores.

Follow-up studies of the twins indicated that they continued to make remarkably good adjustments despite their severe maltreatment during early childhood. One of the reasons for their success may have been the fact that they survived these years together, and at least had each other to rely on.

Whatever the basis for their recovery, their story is important for two reasons. First, it challenges the widely held belief that early experiences largely determine subsequent patterns of psychological adjustment. Were this the case, the twins would have been unlikely to change as rapidly and radically as they did. Second, the study dramatically emphasizes that IQ test scores are not necessarily permanent. Although the case of the twins is unusual, it does show that environmental factors can substantially affect both social and intellectual development.

who ascribe high motivation levels to these children. In some cultures, however, such behavior is considered in bad taste, and children are taught to be much more reserved around adults. If tested in a different cultural context, these children might mistakenly be perceived as less cooperative and more poorly motivated than their counterparts in the indigenous culture. Finally, the range of information assessed by IQ tests may or may not adequately assess the knowledge of people raised in other cultures.

The arguments for and against the use of intelligence tests with ethnic minority children have been summarized by Sattler (1982). The issue has generated considerable debate, but there are indications that important changes

Are IQ tests fair to children of all ethnic groups?   (Druakis/Taurus Photos)

in testing practices are forthcoming. One beneficial outcome is that IQ and other tests are being administered with much greater sensitivity to cultural factors than was previously the case. No longer is IQ considered a characteristic whose manifestations are the same across all cultures.

Projective tests are techniques for assessing personality by using ambiguous stimuli to reveal characteristic traits, attitudes, and conflicts. Projective tests for both children and adults have been developed (Rabin, 1986); those discussed here have all been employed with clients varying widely in age. Projective tests differ from IQ and related tests by being less highly structured and more open-ended. According to projective theory, in the absence of external structure people organize their responses to ambiguous stimuli according to the dictates of their own personalities. Thus, responses to the test stimuli show individual differences in style, organization, and perception. These differences in turn are associated with various aspects of personality, such as dominant traits, underlying motives, and areas of conflict. The most widely used projective tests are the **Rorschach Inkblot Test,** the **Thematic Apperception Test** (TAT), and the Draw-a-Person Test (DAP).

EXHIBIT

Use of IQ Tests to Assess Ethnic Minority Children

Arguments Favoring the Use of IQ Tests	Arguments Opposing the Use of IQ Tests
1. Test scores are useful indexes of present functioning.	1. Tests have a white, Anglo-Saxon, middle-class basis
2. Tests provide good indexes of future levels of academic success.	2. National norms are inappropriate.
3. Tests are useful in obtaining special services.	3. Ethnic minority children are deficient in test practice, reading, and exposure to the dominant culture. Thus they are handicapped in taking tests.
4. Tests serve to evaluate the outcomes of school or special programs.	4. Examiner–examinee report problems exist.
5. Tests help prevent misplacement of children.	5. Test results lead to the placement of ethnic minority children in inferior special-education classes and create negative expectancies in teachers.
6. Tests serve as a stimulus for change.	
7. Tests provide a universal standard of competence.	
8. Tests help reward individual efforts to learn	

Source: Adapted from Sattler, J.H. (1982) *Assessment of children's intelligence and special abilities,* 2nd ed. Boston: Allyn and Bacon. pp. 356, 364–365.

The Rorschach Inkblot Test. Developed by the Swiss psychologist Hermann Rorschach in the 1930s, the Rorschach consists of a series of 10 symmetric inkblots, some in color, and some printed in black and white. The client looks at each card in turn and is asked to tell the examiner what it looks like. Responses are evaluated according to a set of characteristics called **determinants,** features of the inkblots subjects use to organize their perceptions. Common determinants include color and form; other features are the appearance of movement, texture, or depth. Responses are evaluated according to the determinants employed, the portion of the blot selected, and the subject matter of the response. For example, a subject might say that a large region of one inkblot looks like a rocket because (1) the outline of the blot forms the shape, (2) red flames appear to be coming out the back, and (3) it looks like it's shooting into space. This response, using a prominent portion of the inkblot, is based on the determinants form ("the shape of the rocket"), color ("red flames"), and movement ("shooting into space").

There are other aspects of Rorschach responses that are routinely scored along with the determinants. These include the total number of responses per card, the amount of time taken before the first response to each card, and a rating of the relative popularity of each response.

The Rorschach possesses considerable clinical value for many psychologists. It has given rise to a number of scoring systems, which differ largely in terms of the relative importance they ascribe to the determinants and the subject matter of the responses. Despite these efforts, the Rorschach has been criticized on grounds of both poor reliability and questionable validity.

Efforts to rectify these problems have come from three sources. First, efforts have been made to develop more rigorous scoring and interpretive criteria than were previously employed. The best example of this approach is that of Exner (1986), who developed an interpretive system that can be scored on a computer. Second, more reliable ways to administer inkblot tests have been developed. A system developed by Holtzman (1968) uses a large set of cards and allows only one response per card, which helps overcome certain methodological problems associated with permitting more than one response per card. Third, cognitively oriented clinicians such as Fulkerson (1965) have suggested changing the interpretive framework of the Rorschach altogether. Instead of using it to infer underlying personality traits and conflicts, they advocate interpreting the Rorschach as a sampling of the client's thinking processes. Looking at inkblots, according to this perspective, tells you something about how an individual responds to ambiguity.

Continuing efforts to refine the scoring and interpretation of the Rorschach suggest that this assessment instrument will continue in wide use. It has fascinated clinicians and laypersons alike ever since its early development, and continues to stimulate new research and applications.

The Thematic Apperception Test (TAT).   The TAT is a projective test consisting of a series of two-tone, painting-like pictures about which the subject is asked to tell stories (Karon, 1981). Most of the pictures portray people in settings with some degree of ambiguity. As with the Rorschach, it is assumed that people respond to this ambiguity in terms of their own personality traits, motives, and needs. Psychologist Henry Murray developed the test initially to study fantasy activity (Morgan and Murray, 1935). However, subsequent research attempting to link fantasy with overt behavior, including an extensive longitudinal study by Skolnick (1966), has proven inconclusive. In actual clin-

EXHIBIT

Inkblot Facsimile

In a Rorschach test, an inkblot like this is shown to examinees; they are to respond in an open-ended way, telling the psychologist what the inkblots look like. From their descriptions, psychologists make inferences about underlying drives, motivations, and unconscious conflicts.

Source: From Lefton, L. E. (1982), *Psychology,* 2nd ed. Boston: Allyn and Bacon. p. 511. Reprinted with permission.

ical practice, most psychologists rely on the TAT less as a measure of fantasy activity and more as a means of eliciting themes involving social behavior. It is assumed that clients will identify with various figures portrayed in the cards and, by relating their imagined behavior, reveal something of their own behavior in similar situations. Four groups of 30 cards, intended respectively for boys, girls, men, and women, make it possible to tailor the test to certain basic client characteristics. A similar test exclusively for children, developed by Bellak (1975), is called the Children's Apperception Test (CAT).

Studies comparing the interpretive strategies of different clinicians reveal a lack of widely accepted scoring criteria for the TAT. Scoring consistency is highest when raters are trained in similar interpretive techniques (Kleinmuntz, 1967). However, lack of agreement is not necessarily a reason to abandon this or any other projective test, because many clinicians use these tests primarily as a valuable source of hypotheses about a client that may then be confirmed using more reliable test measures.

The TAT, like most projective tests, seems to possess at least some content validity despite problems with reliability. Efforts have been made to improve the rigor of the test by focusing less on vague concepts such as "fantasy life" and more on specific traits. The social psychologist David McClelland, for instance, used the TAT specifically to study what he termed **achievement motivation,** the strength of a person's desire to attain a set goal (McClelland, 1979). A number of TAT cards depict situations that can evoke themes related to achievement, such as one drawing of a young child dreamily contemplating a musical instrument. McClelland felt that, when asked to tell a story about scenes such as this, people would reveal something of their own achievement motivation. For example, a person who responded by saying the child was thinking about becoming a great concert artist would likely possess high achievement motivation. On the other hand, an individual who suggested that the child disliked practicing and preferred leisure activities would be viewed as less highly motivated.

Used in this fashion, the TAT has proven to be a useful assessment tool in obtaining what is termed an **analogue measure** of behavior. Analogue measures depict realistic situations to which a person's responses can be directly measured. McClelland used TAT responses as analogue measures of achievement motivation. He was then able to use this information to predict performance in school, business, and other endeavors where motivation is a prerequisite to success.

Figure drawings.   A third projective test warrents mention because of its widespread use. Figure drawings, of which the most popular is the Draw-a-Person (DAP) test, are widely used in clinical practice in the assessment of personality traits and areas of conflict. In the DAP test, the subject is simply asked to draw a picture of a person. Depending on certain characteristics of the resulting sketch, inferences are then made about the individual. For example, someone who draws a member of the opposite sex might be thought to have a conflict over sexual identification. Painstaking attention to irrelevant details of the drawing may suggest the orderly, highly controlled behavior of someone whose behavior is described as "obsessive–compulsive."

Despite the early promise of these techniques, subsequent research has not lent much support to their validity in personality assessment (Mischel, 1986). In an entirely different context, however, figure drawings may have some diagnostic utility, at least as screening measures. When viewed as samples of visuographic abilities, simple figure drawings may help in assessing brain damage. Warrington (1969) found that distinctive patterns of human figure drawings were associated with damage sustained by the left (or dominant) and right hemispheres of the brain. Patients with dominant hemisphere damage tend to produce relatively coherent but simple figures. Nondominant hemisphere impairment, by contrast, is associated with drawings that tend to look rather odd, as the accompanying Exhibit illustrates. Such figures typically appear fragmented because they lack proper spatial relationships among the various body parts. Warrington's study is one of several demonstrating that marked impairment of figure drawings—human or otherwise—is commonly associated with lesions of the nondominant hemisphere.

Projective tests such as the Rorschach, TAT, and DAP currently ly used, although not necessarily in ways intended by the people l-oped them. There has been a movement away from using projecti sts as measures of deep-seated traits, with more emphasis being placed or heir capacity to provide the clinician with samples of thought processes or analogue behavior measures. This trend away from the measurement of inferred traits toward a more descriptive approach to psychopathology has been extensively discussed by Mischel (1968) and others.

EXHIBIT

Figure Drawings: Assessment of Abnormal Behavior

A

B

Figure A. "Football Player." The eleven-year-old who drew this placed considerable emphasis on his athletic prowess. The impression created by the drawing, however, hints at the boy's underlying fears and anxieties, which were masked by his physically imposing appearance.

Figure B. "Family life." A seven-year-old child, handicapped by a perceptual problem, nonetheless graphically portrayed a family situation in which the members went about their daily activities in comparative isolation from one another.

Self-Report Inventories

Unlike projective tests, **personality inventories** pose specific questions and usually limit answers to simple yes/no responses; like projective tests, these inventories were designed to reveal an individual's characteristic traits, attitudes, and conflicts (Graham, 1987). Typically, clients are instructed to indicate which of a list of descriptive statements apply to them. Most contain items in a mixture of nonpathological and pathological content. An item such as "I regularly listen to news broadcasts" would fall in the first category, while "Strange thoughts are continually running through my mind" falls in the latter group. Of greatest use to clinicians are inventories that focus on symptoms of psychological disturbances such as anxiety, depression, or stress. The most widely used of all inventories, the Minnesota Multiphasic Personality Inven-

EXHIBIT

Figure Drawings Associated with Brain Damage

Examine the accompanying figures. Figure A was drawn by a patient who had sustained left hemisphere damage. Notice that the figure is recognizably human, though somewhat lacking in small details. Figure B, drawn by a patient with right-hemisphere impairment, lacks coherence and unity. Minute details, such as a plethora of buttons, are included, but the drawing lacks overall organization.

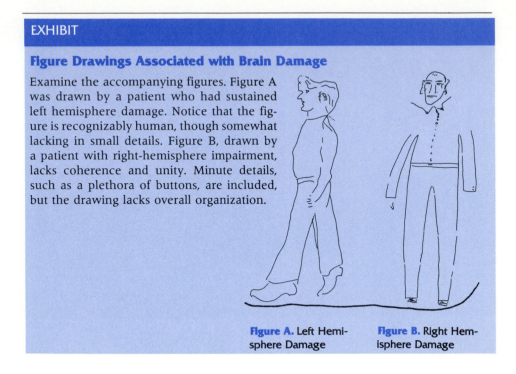

Figure A. Left Hemisphere Damage

Figure B. Right Hemisphere Damage

tory (MMPI), is designed to assess the presence of these and other symptoms in a wide range of clinical and social contexts (Dahlstrom et al., 1986; Butcher, 1987). The items comprising the MMPI and other inventories of this type are grouped into scales, each of which measures a different symptom. The test is easily scored, either by the clinician, or increasingly, by computer (Matarazzo, 1986; Butcher, 1987). The pattern produced when the scores on each scale are graphed is called a profile, which is used by the clinician for interpretive analysis.

Other commonly used self-report inventories include the Cattell 16 PF Personality Inventory, the California Personality Inventory, and the Millon Clinical Multiaxial Inventory (MCMI) (Meyer, 1983). Such tests are similar in format, if not specific content. Because the MMPI is the most commonly used of these, we shall discuss it in some detail.

The MMPI was initially developed to aid in the differential diagnosis of psychiatric patients (Hathaway and McKinley, 1943). The intent of its developers was to create a clerically scored inventory that would yield highly valid diagnostic information. The test contains 550 true-false items, selected because they produced the greatest differences in profile configurations between groups of psychiatric and nonpsychiatric subjects. MMPI test items are grouped into 10 scales, each measuring a different symptom. Referred to as the "clinical" scales, they include measures of depression, schizophrenia, anxiety, and other clinical symptoms. In addition, there are four scales comprised of items that help detect biased response patterns. Over- and underexaggeration of one's level of psychological disturbance are two common sources of bias that can be detected by these four scales, which are referred to as the "validity" scales.

When interpreting an MMPI profile, the clinician examines the scores of each validity and clinical scale. A high-scale score indicates the presence of symptoms measured by that scale. Moreover, the pattern of high- and low-scale scores is of interpretive significance as well, for there are many different profile patterns made up of combinations of two or more scale scores. The MMPI validity and clinical scales are listed in the accompanying exhibit, along with common interpretations of elevated scale scores (Meyer, 1983).

The MMPI has been extensively developed, refined, and applied to new assessment situations since 1948. In recent years, efforts have been made to improve its ability to analyze the specific symptoms of clinical disorders. As Kleinmuntz (1967) noted, whereas the MMPI can successfully distinguish normal from clinical populations, its ability to depict accurately the features of specific clinical disorders is not as well established. This problem has been addressed successfully by the development of interpretive strategies based on analyses of the client's two highest clinical scales (Lewandowski and Graham, 1972).

Currently, the MMPI enjoys widespread clinical use; next to projective techniques, it is perhaps the most frequently used test of personality. It is a convenient source of diagnostic information, which when used in conjunction with other assessment data can provide empirical validation of clinical impressions.

Direct Observation

Direct, systematic observation of behavior in natural settings is a powerful assessment tool (Cone and Foster, 1982; Nelson and Hayes, 1986). Seeing individuals in their accustomed setting often enables clinicians to identify situational factors associated with, and perhaps capable of eliciting, patterns of abnormal behavior. Adherents of behaviorism, who stress the role of environmental factors in the development and maintenance of behavior, strongly advocate direct observation of behavior (Ciminero et al., 1986). Many clinicians who are not ardent behaviorists also include observation in their assessment procedures (Corcoran and Fischer, 1987).

There are two basic types of observation techniques. The first, sometimes called **naturalistic observation,** involves viewing behavior in its natural setting. To learn more about a child's level of social development, for example, a clinician might observe the child at various times throughout the school day. Naturalistic observation involves minimal disruption of ongoing activities

EXHIBIT

MMPI Scales and Interpretations of Elevations

Scale Name	Interpretation of High Score
L	Trying to create a favorable impression by not being honest in responding to test items
F	May indicate invalid profile: severe pathology; moody; restless; dissatisfied
K	May indicate invalid profile; defensive; inhibited; intolerant; lacks insight
Hypochondriasis	Excessive bodily concern; somatic symptoms; narcissistic; pessimistic; demanding; critical; longstanding problems
Depression	Depressed; pessimistic; irritable; dissatisfied; lacks self-confidence; introverted; over-controlled
Hysteria	Physical symptoms of functional origin; lacks insight; self-centered; socially involved; demands attention and affection
Psychopathic Deviate	Asocial or antisocial; rebellious; impulsive; poor judgment; immature; creates good first impression; superficial relationships; aggressive; free of psychological turmoil
Masculinity–Femininity	Male: aesthetic interests; insecure in masculine role; creative; good judgment; sensitive; passive; dependent; good self-control Female: rejects traditional female role; masculine interests; assertive; competitive; self-confident; logical; unemotional
Paranoia	May exhibit frankly psychotic behavior; suspicious; sensitive; resentful; projects; rationalizes; moralistic; rigid
Psychasthenia	Anxious; worried; difficulties in concentrating; ruminative; obsessive; compulsive; insecure; lacks self-confidence; organized; persistent; problems in decision making
Schizophrenia	May have thinking disturbance; withdrawn; self-doubts; feels alienated and unaccepted; vague goals
Hypomania	Excessive activity; impulsive; lacks direction; unrealistic self-appraisal; low frustration tolerance; friendly; manipulative; episodes of depression
Social Introversion	Socially introverted; shy; sensitive; overcontrolled; conforming; problems in decision making

Source: Graham, J. R. (1978). The Minnesota Multiphasic Personality Inventory (MMPI). In: Wolman B. (Ed.). *Clinical Diagnosis of Mental Disorders.* New York: Plenum Press. pp. 316–317.

and aims at obtaining a realistic impression of behavior and the factors that influence it. Although the knowledge that they are being observed may cause people to change their behavior (Campbell and Stanley, 1963), most people eventually become accustomed to the presence of an observer and are not unduly affected by it (Haynes, 1984).

Structured observation is the second basic type of behavioral observation. In this the clinician can exert greater control over both the environment and the behaviors observed. A common application of structured observation involves having clients engage in role-playing activities having to do with situations that cause them difficulties in the outside world. The clinician can construct realistic scenarios in which he or she observes the client's behavior, and by employing a laboratory setting can arrange for systematic observations to be made via such things as one-way mirrors, videotape recordings, and other assistive devices. Gerald Patterson and his colleagues (Patterson, 1971) have made effective use of such structured behavioral observations in working with troubled families. Families are videotaped and observed during therapy sessions while they work on structured tasks provided by the therapist. Under such carefully controlled conditions, it is possible for the therapist to systematically observe interaction patterns among family members and to identify points where communications break down.

Both naturalistic and structured observation techniques can help reveal how people's accustomed surroundings affect their behavior. In addition, this assessment technique is particularly helpful to clinicians in at least three other ways. First, records based on systematic observation help clarify both the nature and severity of the problem. For example, detailed records kept by parents of a bedwetting child may tell the clinician that the problem occurs on an average of four times per week, only at night, and only when one of the parents is away on a business trip. Specific information of this type helps the clinician and parents gain a more complete understanding of the actual severity of the problem and of the conditions that tend to maintain it. Second, observation data can provide a baseline—normally collected during the assessment phase, before treatment begins—against which to compare the degree of behavioral change during and following therapy. Third, observational data often help the clinician formulate pragmatic solutions to problem behaviors. By its very nature, observation mitigates against theorizing without facts (often called "armchair theorizing").

It is comparatively easy to obtain high reliability on observations, provided the observers are adequately trained and the behaviors targeted for observation are clearly specified. Techniques for implementing the two types of observation emphasize the need for a careful, systematic approach if observations are to be meaningful. Following these principles, Sidney Bijou has provided guidelines for working with children (Bijou and Redd, 1975), and Ullman and Krasner (1965) have developed a comprehensive approach to abnormal behavior in both children and adults.

THE RELATIONSHIP BETWEEN ASSESSMENT AND INTERVENTION

The preceding discussion of assessment techniques demonstrates the wide range of information available to the clinician. A psychological assessment can use interviews, psychological tests, inventories, and direct observation of behavior singly or in combination. The accompanying Exhibit summarizes several of these techniques.

Eventually, this information must be organized to reflect accurately a client's problems and treatment needs. The specific techniques that clinicians employ and the manner in which they present their conclusions largely reflect their particular theoretical orientations. Staunch Freudians, for example, may rely almost entirely on interview data, particularly those dealing with the client's early development. Behaviorally oriented clinicians, on the other hand, will tend to emphasize the importance of observational data and perhaps questionnaire responses. If they conduct interviews or formal testing at all, they will probably treat the results primarily as samples of behavior without reference to the underlying personality traits these measures were designed to assess. Humanistically oriented practitioners may forgo the diagnostic process altogether, on the grounds that the processes of categorization and diagnostic labeling are dehumanizing. Yet they too may employ a wide range of less formal assessment techniques in an effort to focus on the distinct patterns of individuality that each of their clients manifests. Included among these would be such things as direct observation of the client's behavior and emotional status, and possibly some testing to help identify areas of concern for the patient.

From a pragmatic viewpoint, the key to assessment is the ability to collect the type and amount of information needed to make informed decisions regarding client's problems (Lazarus, 1985). Accordingly, many clinicians are beginning to view assessment as a problem-solving process that is relatively independent of traditional theoretical orientations. In addition, there is a growing awareness that both the reliability and validity of psychological assessment procedures are increased by the use of diversified measures, each designed to sample comparatively specific aspects of behavior. The time is past when a Rorschach test protocol or a human figure drawing would be viewed as the key to explaining someone's personality, and it is no longer appropriate to base decisions regarding school placement solely on the results of IQ tests. In short, psychological assessment is becoming more pragmatic, empirical, and more sensitive to the impact of social and cultural factors on manifest behavior (Meyer, 1983; Cone and Foster, 1982).

This trend is evident across virtually all mental health disciplines, as exemplified by the orientation of the DSM classification system. The features of

---

EXHIBIT

Representative Assessment Techniques

INTERVIEW
    Intake interview
    Mental status examination

PSYCHOLOGICAL TESTS
    A. Intellectual, mental abilities
          Stanford-Binet Intelligence Scale
          Wechsler Adult Intelligence Scale
    B. Projective Tests
          Rorschach Inkblot Test
          Holtzman Inkblot Test
          Thematic Apperception Test (TAT)
          Children's Apperception Test (CAT)

SELF-INVENTORIES AND QUESTIONNAIRES
    Minnesota Multiphasic Personality Inventory (MMPI)
    Cattell 16 PF Personality Inventory
    California Personality Inventory

BEHAVIORAL OBSERVATION TECHNIQUES
    Naturalistic Observation
    Structured Observation

---

mental disorders are increasingly based on specific diagnositic criteria and less on extensive reference to theoretical viewpoints, which traditionally focused on the cause of such conditions. As a result, assessment is becoming a more precise activity. Perhaps the greatest single benefit to be derived from this trend is in the area of planning specifically what to do for a client, which after all is the reason for conducting an assessment in the first place. As patterns of abnormal behavior are specified with increasing accuracy, appropriate intervention likewise becomes easier to develop, and its effectiveness easier to assess. The next chapter discusses the types of treatment that may be undertaken once the assessment process is complete.

CHAPTER REVIEW

1. Psychological assessment procedures help describe and classify patterns of abnormal behavior.

2. Mental disorders are often compared to physical illnesses, but the two types of conditions differ in a number of key respects.

3. Assessment is a process of gathering information about a client from a wide range of sources, then integrating this information into an effective intervention plan.

4. The DSM classification system employs multiple axes to record the characteristics, etiology, and prognosis of a wide range of mental disorders.

5. Assessment measures can be evaluated in terms of both reliability (consistency) and validity (accuracy in measuring a trait or characteristic).

6. The consistency of a test measure can be assessed through measures of split-half, test-retest, and interrater reliability. Content, concurrent, predictive, and construct validity are all ways of describing how authentic a measurement is.

7. Assessment procedures generally used by clinicians include interviews, formal tests, self-report measures, and behavioral observations.

8. Skillful interviewers combine objectivity and a sense of purpose with the ability to see things from the client's viewpoint.

9. Psychological tests are available to assess a wide range of skills. Among the most commonly used in clinical practice are structured IQ tests and more open-ended measures of personality known as projective tests.

10. Self-report inventories are often used to construct profiles of personality traits, patterns of psychopathology, and personal interests.

11. Good assessment procedures consider not only the client's answers to test questions, but such things as their test-taking attitude, overall level of adjustment, and needs as far as intervention is concerned.

12. Behavioral observation techniques provide a way to describe symptoms in precise numeric terms. Behavioral observations help determine how frequently target behaviors occur and what reinforcement contingencies affect them.

TERMS TO REMEMBER

disease model
assessment
multimodal approach
DSM system
multiaxial classification system
reliability
validity

participant observer
Stanford-Binet Intelligence Scale
Wechsler Adult Intelligence Scale
thought disorder
projective tests
Rorschach Inkblot Test
Thematic Apperception Test (TAT)

determinants
achievement motivation
analogue measures
personality inventory
naturalistic observation

FOR MORE INFORMATION

Anastasi, A. (1986) Evolving concepts of test validation. In: Rosenzweig, M., and Porter, L. (Eds.). *Annual review of psychology.* Vol. 37. Palo Alto, Calif.: Annual Reviews. Provides a comprehensive discussion of the issues involved in developing tests that are accurate and reliable

Ciminero, A., Calhoun, K., and Adams, H. (1986) *Handbook of behavioral assessment.* New York: John Wiley. A solid reference work on current assessment methodologies and their applications, presenting the latest theoretical formulations, techniques, and research findings for use with a broad range of specific disorders

Matarazzo, J. D. (1972) *Wechsler's measurement and appraisal of adult intelligence,* 5th ed. Baltimore: Williams and Wilkins. Perhaps the definitive work on the assessment of intelligence in adults, Matarazzo's book revises and updates many of Wechsler's ideas

Mischel, W.P. (1968) *Personality and assessment.* New York: John Wiley. A classic work on the relationship between personality structure and the assessment processes, Mischel's book provides an excellent overview of the critical, fundamental issues.

Rabin, A. (1986) *Projective techniques for adolescents and children.* New York: Springer. Authored by one of the major figures in this area, this is an excellent description of the research and applications of projective techniques for children.

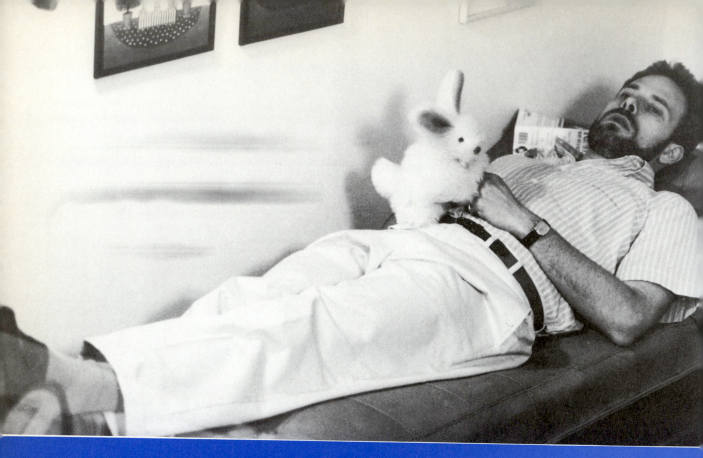

Though psychotherapy is a serious endeavor, the mystery and uncertainty that surround the process lend themselves to delightful and humorous portrayals as shown in the movie *Beyond Therapy*. (The Museum of Modern Art/Film Stills Archives)

4

Treatment Approaches

The term "psychotherapy" for many people evokes images of a client stretched out on a couch talking to a psychoanalyst. As this chapter will show, however, psychotherapy is practiced in many ways, and is but one of many potential intervention strategies. In keeping with the "multimodal" assessment model introduced in the previous chapter, our discussion of therapeutic strategies will focus on a diverse group of techniques and procedures for relieving the troubling manifestations of mental disorders.

● The Case of Dave

Dave, the youngest of four children, was his mother's favorite. Because of her doting protectiveness, he grew up sheltered from many of life's responsibilities. As a youngster Dave preferred to play in the house rather than with his peers. In nursery school he was initially inhibited and withdrawn, but eventually adjusted to the presence of other people. Periodically, he became fearful of going to school and would at these times feign illness to avoid having to go.

Despite these anxieties, Dave was a good student and considered by his teacher to be a model child. Because his older brother watched out for him, Dave was seldom teased by the other children, though secretly they made fun of him for being so timid and shy. In high school, he became involved in the student newspaper but otherwise kept a low profile.

The family celebrated when Dave received a partial scholarship in the premed program at the state university 150 miles away. However, when the time came for him to leave for school, his mother became depressed. She never told him of this, but he heard about it from his brothers. At school, Dave was confused and unhappy because nobody seemed to pay any attention to him. He was part of an entering class of over 500, and no one seemed to care whether or not he attended the huge lecture classes.

Dave made few friends and spent most of his free time taking long walks in the nearby woods. He began having trouble sleeping, awakening at times during the night in a state of near panic. His roommate, with whom he shared little about himself, tried to talk with Dave about his anxieties, but to no avail. Dave became increasingly withdrawn and reclusive. He became so anxious that he stopped attending most of his classes; being around so many strange people made him extremely tense. By the end of the first semester, he was failing in three of four subjects, and applied for an indefinite leave of absence.

Upon his return home, Dave's parents at first thought he was doing well. However, when his grades were released and it was evident he was failing, they conferred with the family physician, who referred Dave to a clinical psychologist.

TREATMENT ISSUES

Dave, like many college freshmen, was bewildered by how impersonal his first contact with the university was. Unlike many other freshmen, however, Dave came from a family background that made him especially vulnerable to the types of pressures that confront an individual on leaving home for the first time. He had grown accustomed to being the center of attention and having other people to call on whenever he had a problem. He had very few opportunities to develop independence as a child, as a result of which he was ill-equipped to deal with the competitive pressures of a college environment.

Because of his background, Dave would be considered a prime candidate for **psychotherapy**. Psychotherapy refers to a group of psychological treatment techniques designed to help people change distressful aspects of their behavior. Many therapeutic systems for promoting change have been devised over the years, and there are literally hundreds of self-styled therapists who lay claim to new and inventive techniques for making people feel good about themselves.

Despite this apparent diversity, the majority of psychotherapy systems stem from a relatively small number of theoretical viewpoints. Of these, the psychodynamic, behavioral, cognitive, humanistic, and systems perspectives already discussed have been the most influential. Each of these theories has given rise to psychological intervention procedures that have attracted devoted practitioners.

Aside from the limited number of theoretical heritages shared by most forms of psychotherapy, there are other factors that promote unity as well. The first concerns the underlying goal of therapy, which as already stated is to bring about changes in behavior. All systems of psychotherapy employ techniques specifically designed to help clients change their behavior. Second, there is unity in the general types of treatments currently practiced. Basically, these treatments can be divided into those that are physically oriented and those that are psychologically based. Medication is the best known form of physical intervention; it is commonly prescribed to relieve symptoms of anxiety, depression, and other disabling conditions. Psychological techniques—employed by the five perspectives just mentioned—are based on verbal interactions between client and therapist.

There is one additional important treatment factor related to medical and psychological intervention that bears mentioning—the **placebo effect**. Placebos are inert substances given in lieu of actual medication. They are used to test whether the drug itself or the client's expectations about the drug's curative powers are responsible for any changes that take place following ingestion. The placebo effect occurs when behavior changes associated with a particular treatment occur even though the client has actually been given a placebo. Placebo effects can also occur in psychological interventions. Many clients for example, improve because they believe strongly in effectiveness of therapy.

Psychological and physical treatment procedures may be employed either individually or in combination with one another. In Dave's case, for example, talking with a therapist could help him achieve insight into the origins of his chronic anxiety. He would also benefit from a group program designed to promote the development of social skills and to help make people feel comfortable around one another. To help control his high level of tension, Dave would profit from some instruction in deep breathing and muscle relaxation techniques. Finally, until he learns to employ these procedures effectively, Dave could be prescribed medication to quickly alleviate the disabling symptoms of anxiety.

Together, these four forms of treatment constitute a therapeutic intervention. The term "intervention" refers to the coordinated application of multiple therapeutic resources to a client's problems (Lazarus, 1985). Dave's proposed intervention program consists of insight therapy, group therapy, relaxation training, and medication. A program such as this can be implemented by a clinical psychologist or other qualified mental health professional, in conjunction with a psychiatrist to prescribe the medication.

Intervention strategies can be quite elaborate, depending on the nature of the client's problems that require attention. There are many different domains, or modalities, that may be the target of an intervention program. Arnold Lazarus (1981) has developed a systematic approach to intervention he and others have termed "multimodal therapy." Multimodal therapy is the general term for an intervention model that encompasses seven functional areas, collectively referred to by Lazarus as the **BASIC ID**. Each letter in this term refers to a different aspect of the client's make-up: *B* stands for "Behavior," and refers to the client's overt actions. *A* is "Affect," a term used to designate the individual's emotional state. *S*, or "Sensation," refers to a wide range of perceptual experiences involving sight, hearing, and the other sensory modalities. *I* stands for "Images," fantasies, dreams, and mental impressions people form about their world. *C* stands for "Cognition," and concerns thought patterns that regulate a great deal of overt behavior. The second *I* refers to "Interpersonal factors," and deals with the individual's pattern of social interactions. Finally, *D* ("Drugs") concerns physiological factors (including medications) that may be the focus of treatment. Together, these seven areas encompass a broad range of behavioral, mental, and physical phenomena, any of which may require therapeutic attention (Lazarus, 1985).

David's multimodal therapy intervention program focuses on three aspects of his "BASIC ID": (C) cognitions, or thought, concerning the way other people are supposed to respond to him; (I) interpersonal factors related to Dave's discomfort around people who do not pay attention to him; and (D) physical manifestations of anxiety that are treated through a combination of relaxation training and medication. A multimodal intervention program such as that proposed for Dave brings to bear multiple therapeutic resources on different aspects of a client's problems.

Throughout this text, the terms "intervention" and "multimodal therapy" will be emphasized. This is in keeping with the authors' conviction that therapy is most effective when it addresses more than one aspect of a client's functioning. In the same way that Dave's anxieties can be relieved through a combination of individual and group therapy plus medication, clients suffering from depression, stress, and all the other disorders in the DSM system benefit most from a coordinated blend of therapeutic agents.

Multimodal therapy is probably quite different in concept from the way most people think of psychotherapy. In Freud's time, it seemed simple: You lay on a couch, said whatever came to mind, and relied on the analyst to determine what was wrong with you. Multimodal therapy, in contrast, appears more complex. What accounts for the popularity of this intervention system? There are reasons that need to be discussed. First, by implementing more than one therapeutic procedure at a time, the clinician can ultimately shorten the duration of therapy. Multimodal therapy, therefore, represents a cost-effective approach to the treatment of psychological disturbances.

Second, because relatively few psychological problems can be conveniently traced to a single cause, it makes sense to design multifaceted intervention programs. Recall for a moment the case of Dave, which opened this chapter. Although it is clear enough that he suffers from intense anxiety, the cause of his anxiety cannot be readily traced to a single source. Certain unpleasant physical sensations, such as muscle tension and rapid heart beat, contribute to Dave's experience of anxiety. Being raised in an over-protective family undoubtedly led Dave to expect comparable treatment from others, and to feel anxious when it was not forthcoming. Finally, attending large lecture classes at college caused Dave to feel both alienated and anxious as a result of the impersonal quality of his surroundings. Each of these factors—physiologic, developmental, and environmental—contributed substantially to Dave's anxious condition. It stands to reason that an intervention program that addresses each of these factors is likely to be more effective than therapy that treats only one.

Multimodal therapy makes sense for yet another reason. When properly implemented, it comprises a therapeutic milieu, or atmosphere, that is conducive to change. Clients must contend with many forces outside the therapist's office that are counterproductive to change. Multimodal therapy is designed to neutralize as many of these factors as possible.

What are some of these negative factors? For one thing, old habits are difficult to change, no matter how maladaptive they seem. Pressures at work, school, or home can all help maintain old habits. Recall for a moment in the opening case how Dave took a step toward independence by leaving home for college. In response, his mother became depressed, a reaction that would tend to discourage subsequent efforts on his part to become more independent.

Another factor that can impede therapeutic progress concerns the underlying capabilities of clients to change. Some do not possess the necessary social, economic, or intellectual resources to alter their situation significantly. Multimodal therapy can work within such constraints by virtue of its flexibility, as it is essentially a general framework within which many different therapeutic techniques may be employed.

Factors such as these can impede progress in therapy irrespective of its theoretical orientation. Indeed, the different schools of therapy all have procedures explicitly designed to help overcome resistance to change. To some degree, the extent to which resistances can be overcome depends on how forceful, or compelling, treatment is.

Treatment Approach Dimensions

Treatment options for mental disorders can be divided into those that are physically based and those that are psychological in nature. Within each category, the available techniques can be organized according to how intrusive or compelling they are. A treatment is physically intrusive to the degree that some form of matter or energy enters the physical system to effect the desired change. Treatments are psychologically compelling to the degree that they do not require the client's conscious, voluntary choice to obtain the treatment effect. All physically intrusive therapies are also psychologically compelling, but there are many psychologically compelling therapies that are not physically intrusive. Hypnosis is a good example of a psychologically compelling therapy because of the control the therapist is able to exert over the client following induction of a deeply relaxed state. Of the physically intrusive therapies, procedures collectively referred to as **psychosurgery** top the list. Psychosurgical procedures are carried out on the brain and central nervous system, and are highly physically intrusive.

In the following discussion of therapeutic procedures, it will become evident that physical intrusiveness and psychological compulsion are useful concepts for evaluating therapeutic impact.

PHYSICAL THERAPIES

Chemotherapy

Chemotherapy refers to the therapeutic use of drugs in treating mental disorders (Persad, 1986). It may be used either alone or in combination with other therapies (Hersen and Breuning, 1986). Chemotherapy has been primarily used to treat anxiety, schizophrenia, mania, depression, alcoholism, and several childhood disorders. Anxiety is treated mainly with **tranquilizers**, which diminish physical arousal and alleviate psychological distress (Gabe and Williams, 1986). Schizophrenia is one of several severe mental disorders known as the psychoses, which are treated with **antipsychotic medication**. These powerful drugs have tranquilizing properties that inhibit highly disturbed behaviors such as aggression or self-injury. Moreover, they reduce abnormal perceptual experiences known as **hallucinations**, in which people report seeing or hearing things not physically present. Depression and mania are at opposite ends of the activity spectrum, and consequently each responds to a very different type of medication. **Tricyclic antidepressive medication** is a class of drugs used to combat the apathy and moodiness of depressed clients. Antidepressive medications have the opposite effect of tranquilizers; they increase physical activation and elevate the individual's mood. At the other extreme, the drug **lithium** is used to tone down the excitable, energetic behavior of clients suffering from mania. Some clients experience periodic mood swings that alternate between mania and depression, a condition known as **bipolar disorder**. Chemotherapy for this disorder may involve both tricyclic medication and lithium during different phases of the client's mood swings.

All of the above medications are prescribed to help alleviate symptoms of psychological distress. In the treatment of alcoholism, however, medication may be prescribed to *cause* discomfort. Certain drugs, when taken in conjunction with alcohol, produce feelings of nausea that discourage subsequent drinking because of the unpleasant association between the two.

EXHIBIT

Major Groups of Chemotherapeutic Agents

Effect Group	Chemical Group	Generic Name	Trade Name
Minor Tranquilizers	Propanediols	Meprobamate	Equanil Miltown
	Benzodiazepines	Clorazepate dipotassium Alprazolam Diazepam Lorazepam	Tranxene Xanax Valium Ativan
Neuroleptics (Antipsychotics)	Phenothiazines	Chlorpromazine Trifluoperazine Thioridazine	Thorazine Stelazine Mellaril
	Butyrophenones	Haloperidol	Haldol
	Thioxanthenes	Chlorprothixene	Taractan
Central Nervous System Stimulants	Oxazolidine	Pemoline	Cylert
	Amphetamines	Dextroamphetamine	Dexedrine
	Piperidyls	Methamphetamine	Desoxyn
		Methylphenidate	Ritalin
Antidepressants	Tricyclics	Doxepin hydrochloride (HCl)	Adapin Sinequan
		Amoxapine	Asendin
		Nortriptyline	Aventyl
		Trazodone	Desyrel
		Amitriptyline HCl	Elavil
		Imipramine	Janimine Tofranil
		Maprotiline HCl	Ludiomil
		Desipramine HCl	Norpramin
	Monoamine Oxidase Inhibitors (MAOs)	Phenelzine	Nardil
		Tranylcypromine	Parnate
		Isocarboxazid	Marplan

Of the childhood disorders treated with medication, perhaps the best known is hyperactivity. The excessive activity level of many children with this condition paradoxically diminishes when stimulant medication is administered. (The reasons for this are discussed in the chapter on childhood disorders.) Another common childhood disorder successfully treated with medication is enuresis, or bedwetting. This condition responds well to the drug **imipramine**, which has properties of a mild antianxiety agent.

The particular drugs used to treat each of these conditions are discussed, along with their benefits and side effects, in later chapters (also see the Exhibit on page 115).

Chemotherapy alone is a powerful therapeutic agent because of its ability to suppress rapidly the symptoms of certain mental disorders. It was originally employed, in fact, to control dangerous outbursts of psychotic patients. At that time, the only alternatives were constant physical restraint or an irreversible form of psychosurgery that rendered the client apathetic and unresponsive.

In terms of a multimodal intervention model, medication serves a much different purpose. When used in conjunction with other therapeutic resources, medication has much to offer. First of all, the immediate reduction of symptomatology brings relief and hope to clients, particularly those whose suffering has been chronic. Second, the alleviation of distress makes it easier for clients to make positive changes in their behavior. For example, the antianxiety medication recommended for Dave (described in the opening case) would enable him to learn how to interact with people without being overwhelmed by anxiety. Third, medication can hold symptoms in check until the client can learn how to control them voluntarily. Once Dave has learned some deep relaxation techniques, he will be able to achieve essentially the same effects as the medication induced.

Despite their obvious assets, drugs can have negative physical and psychological side effects as well. Some medications carry a risk of potential addiction when taken regularly. Others alleviate symptoms of one condition but cause another. A condition known as **tardive dyskinesia**, for example, is caused by long-term use of certain antipsychotic medications. Clients with tardive dyskinesia develop learning impairments and muscle control problems as a result of their antipsychotic treatment. Still other drugs create vulnerabilities to well-known physical ailments. A group of antianxiety drugs known as **beta blockers** and used by performers to control stage fright carry a high risk of heart attacks if long-term use is discontinued suddenly.

Negative side effects aside, many mental health clients feel that they are not receiving "real" treatment unless drugs are prescribed. So strong is their belief in the efficacy of medication that they often respond favorably to placebos. Both drugs and placebos are powerful therapeutic agents whose use needs to be carefully monitored. The dangers of drug use in general and of dependence on drugs as a means of combating mental disorders are discussed in more detail in Chapter 11.

Electroconvulsive Therapy (ECT)

In 1781 in England, W. Oliver, physician to King George III, accidentally overdosed a patient with camphor, causing a convulsion. In Oliver's opinion the patient's physical and psychological condition improved as a result. Much later, in 1938, after observing pigs being shocked to stun them before being slaughtered, Ugo Cerletti came up with the idea of using electric shock to induce convulsions. ECT was used initially in the treatment of schizophrenia, although it eventually found greatest favor as a means of treating severe depression.

Cerletti was not the first physician to propose electric shock as a therapeutic tool. Dioscorides, a Greek surgeon, first suggested electric shock as a cure for headaches. He used torpedo fish, capable of generating enough electricity to stun an adult, as the source of electric current. A live fish was clapped to the client's temples where it delivered its powerful shock (Harpe, 1979).

In modern-day psychiatric practice, convulsive states are normally induced with electric current, although a few psychiatrists rely on drugs (chiefly insulin). The term for this treatment is electroconvulsive therapy (ECT). ECT is administered by passing between 130 and 160 volts of electric current through

A patient is prepped for electro convulsive therapy at Duke University Medical Center. (Note the apparatus that prevents the subject from swallowing or biting her tongue.)   (Will McIntyre/Photo Researchers, Inc.)

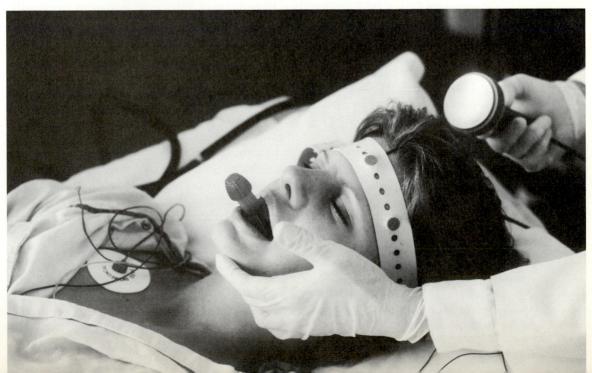

the brain for approximately one second. Current passes from the ECT apparatus through leads placed on either or both sides of the patient's forehead directly into brain tissue. Patients often undergo convulsive muscle spasms while current is passed through the brain, a condition that can generally be controlled with muscle-relaxant medication. Despite the involuntary grimaces and twitches that accompany ECT, the treatment is not painful. Patients awake a few minutes afterward, often in a mildly confused state.

There are innumerable theories as to how ECT works. It may bring about specific changes in the brain's electrical and chemical activity. Placebo effects may contribute to ECT's effectiveness. The combination of a patient desperate to be cured, a psychiatrist with unwavering faith in the treatment, and the impressive array of equipment used to administer ECT together create powerful expectancies for a beneficial, therapeutic effect. There is some research data to support this viewpoint. For example, Lambourn and Gill (1978) reported a study in which depressed patients who were judged appropriate candidates for ECT were divided into two groups. Half were administered ECT; the others went through the entire procedure but received no electric current. Lambourn and Gill found no differences in recovery rates from depression between the two groups.

Some researchers assert that ECT can cause brain damage, although advocates of ECT such as Fink (1979) and Blachly (1977) deny such effects. However, beginning with an early study by Janis (1950), evidence has steadily accumulated linking ECT with neurologic trauma. Carl Pribram, a highly respected neurophysiologist, has convincingly argued that brain tissue is easily damaged by sudden trauma, whether from electric shock or a physical blow. Pribram has stated, "I'd rather have a small lobotomy (surgical removal of brain tissue) than a series of electroconvulsive shocks. I just know what the brain looks like after a series of shocks, and it's not very pleasant to look at (1975, p. 23).

There is ample documentation of impaired learning following ECT (Squire and Chase, 1975; Squire et al., 1981), particularly after a series of treatments administered within a short time of each other. Memory deficits are common in the aftermath of both ECT and traumatic brain injury (as might be sustained in an automobile accident). In both instances, brain structures that regulate learning and memory appear to be damaged. In ECT, this effect appears to be due to the fact that the electrodes discharge current through the brain's two **temporal lobes**, which have a vital role in memory and learning (Goldman et al., 1972). The left temporal lobe stores memory traces of verbal, or linguistic information, while the right encodes information having to do with visually based information. When ECT electrodes are applied to both the right and left sides of the head, memory impairments for both language and visual information tend to follow.

To minimize the adverse effects of ECT on brain function, several procedural modifications have been employed. To avoid disrupting memory traces for vital linguistic capabilities, electrode placement is frequently confined to

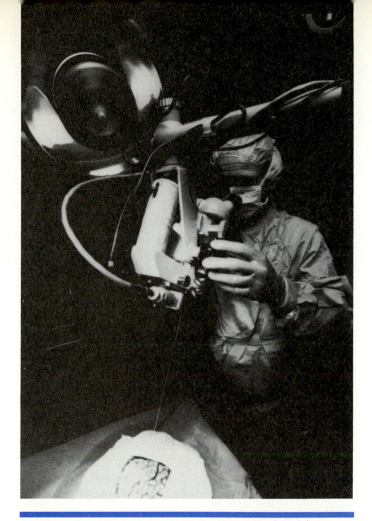

As a dramatic improvement over the drastic results of the lobotomy, modern laser surgery creates therapeutic lesions that leave surrounding tissue and blood vessels virtually unharmed. (A. Tsiaras/Science Source, Photo Researchers, Inc.)

the right side alone (thereby disrupting only nonverbal memory). Administration of oxygen during ECT has been found to help alleviate memory loss, but does not eliminate brain trauma caused by the high-voltage electric current (Friedberg, 1975, 1977).

Psychosurgery

Psychosurgery is a form of neurosurgery that alters behavior and emotions through the destruction of brain tissue. It usually arouses less controversy than ECT, for two reasons. First, it is less commonly used; the number of psychosurgical interventions—approximately 1,500 per year—is almost insignificant compared with the number of ECTs performed. Second, the effects of psychosurgery on the body and on behavior tend to be more predictable and precise.

The first modern psychosurgery in the United States was performed in the 1930s. The fashionable operation at that time was a procedure known as a lobotomy, used to control violent and aggressive behavior. Lobotomies were performed by cutting nerve fibers that connect the front-most part of the brain (the **frontal lobe**) to the other parts of the brain. In an intact brain, the frontal lobe is involved in controlling purposeful action. Deprived of this capacity, a lobotomized patient becomes docile and passive. Thousands of lobotomies were performed in subsequent decades, primarily because they constituted a crude but effective means of curtailing aggressive and destructive behavior. The technique was irreversible, and left its victims in a totally passive, dependent state for the remainder of their lives. By the 1950s, powerful medications were being developed to control undesirable behavior, and the days of the lobotomy were numbered. The technique eventually fell into disrepute and by 1960 was virtually abandoned as a therapeutic technique.

More recently, other psychosurgical techniques have been perfected. Modern laser and ultrasonic technology permits precisely controlled therapeutic lesions to be made in such a way that brain tissue and blood vessels surrounding the lesion are undisturbed.

As with ECT, this form of psychosurgery has proven most helpful in alleviating depression, although no one knows exactly how the effect occurs (Trotter, 1976). Psychosurgery creates lesions in those parts of the brain believed to control particular behavioral responses. However, widespread controversy persists as to whether specific brain structures really regulate discrete behaviors. Thus, even though it is possible to produce precise lesions in brain tissue, there is debate over just what the behavioral effects of these lesions are likely to be.

The lack of a clear cut association between specific brain structures and corresponding behavioral responses raises the possibility that psychosurgery, like ECT, may involve a significant placebo effect. Indeed, Trotter (1976) noted that many psychosurgery patients describe their recoveries in quasireligious terms and become fanatically devoted to their surgeons. Trotter rightfully concludes that, until brain–behavior relationships are mapped out with more precision, psychosurgery should be considered an experimental clinical procedure to be used only as a last resort.

Hemodialysis Therapy

Hemodialysis therapy, the use of an artificial kidney machine to remove toxic substances from the blood, is the traditional treatment for persons with kidney disease. Surprisingly, it has also been studied as a possible treatment for schizophrenia. In theory it could be applied to any mental disorder in which a toxic element in the blood is assumed to be a factor causing or maintaining the condition, and many researchers are convinced that schizophrenia is one such disorder.

ISSUE TO CONSIDER

Informed Consent

The issue of informed consent is important in any therapeutic procedure, but particularly so with ECT and psychosurgery. The first stage in the informed consent sequence is a cost–benefit analysis of the procedure being considered, and the first issue in that analysis is whether or not the procedure even works. There is general agreement that ECT is reasonably effective for acute, severe depression, but it is not the treatment of choice for schizophrenia, neurosis, or most other disorders. The major cost is probable cumulative brain damage.

These costs vary, depending on the individual's situation. One person who suffered an unexpected cost was the noted author Ernest Hemingway.

> *In December 1960, Hemingway underwent 11 shock treatments at the Mayo Clinic in Rochester, Minnesota. Three months later he was back for another series. His friend and biographer, A. E. Hotchner, described him at that time: "Ernest was even more infuriated with these treatments than the previous ones, registering even bitterer complaints about how his memory was wrecked and how he was ruined as a writer." Hotchner quotes Hemingway: "What these shock doctors don't know is about writers and such things as remorse and contrition and what they do to them. What is the sense of ruining my head and erasing my memory, which is my capital, and putting me out of business? It was a brilliant cure but we lost the patient." One month after the second series of ECT treatments, Hemingway killed himself. (Friedberg, 1975, pp. 25–26)*

Other problems can further complicate the issue of informed consent. When there is controversy over how a treatment works or what side effects occur, as with ECT and psychosurgery, what recourse does a damaged client have later? Unless there has been blatant abuse, professionals in most disciplines are reluctant to step forward and give the testimony necessary to restrict a colleague. This "conspiracy of silence" is common in traditional medicine as a defense against excessive malpractice suits.

Because the details of an informed consent as they were actually presented to the patient may be hard to establish later, there is an increasing push to use written and understandable informed consent forms. One proponent of ECT (Blachly, 1977) refers to these as "our grisly informed consent forms." Others, following a kind of Alice-in-Wonderland logic, assert that explanations of potential risk could make a patient decide not to undergo ECT treatment, and that this possibility is reason enough not to give any explanation. Given the risks involved in ECT, particularly the possibility of brain damage, a patient who fully understood the consequences would not seem unreasonable in declining treatment.

Although advocates of hemodialysis therapy have claimed high rates of success, there is no strong evidence from rigorous studies by unbiased observers to document these claims (Lewis et al., 1979; Schulz et al., 1981). The procedure is physically traumatic and time-consuming; over a period of several hours, the patient's blood is shunted out of the body and through a filtering system that removes impurities. Because of a high potential for resultant side effects, and in light of insubstantial research findings endorsing its therapeutic benefit, hemodialysis has not been widely employed.

Megavitamin Therapy

Megavitamin therapy is simply the administration of large dosages of specific vitamins, usually the B vitamin complex, in order to alleviate mental disorders. It appears that the origins of some mental disorders can be traced at least in part to biological problems caused by nutritional deficiencies. Nevertheless, only ardent proponents of megavitamin therapy have reported positive results, usually with extreme disorders such as schizophrenia and autism. These results have not been confirmed in systematic studies by unbiased observers (Ban et al., 1977; Bernheim and Lewine, 1979).

Sleep Therapies

Two techniques that primarily act to put the client to sleep have been used to treat such conditions as generalized stress disorders and anxiety. **Electrosleep therapy**, the first of these techniques, involves passing low-voltage current across the forehead. According to reports from the Soviet Union where the procedure has been most extensively developed, electrosleep therapy promotes feelings of tranquility and deep relaxation.

The second procedure, termed **continuous sleep therapy**, involves keeping the client asleep with medication for up to twenty hours a day, for periods ranging from several days to two weeks. The procedure is reminiscent of a technique used by healers in an African tribe, the Yoruba, for dealing with distressed tribespeople (Prince, 1980). Its effect is to interrupt maladaptive lifestyle patterns such as those in which people persist in making poor decisions in their lives over and over again. Other than the temporary interruption of such self-defeating behavior patterns, continuous sleep therapy offers no real therapeutic advantages; moreover its use has resulted in more than one death.

PSYCHOLOGICAL THERAPIES

Psychological therapies are basically derivatives of the "talking cure," a phrase originally used in reference to Freud's form of therapy, psychoanalysis. It is an apt description, for virtually all psychological therapies involve verbal exchanges between therapist and client. However, the nature of these interactions varies considerably depending on the clinician's theoretical orientation. In psychoanalysis, for example, the therapist responds with interpretive statements as the client free-associates. A behaviorally oriented therapist, on the other hand, engages the client in discussions about problematic behaviors, environmental forces that control them, and ways of developing more adaptive responses, under controlled learning conditions (Cattell, 1987).

Despite these differences, it is important to keep in mind the similarities between the different schools of psychological therapy discussed earlier in this chapter. Of these, the common goal of all therapies is paramount: helping clients change their behavior to improve day-to-day functioning.

Psychotherapy

Psychotherapy is a generic term referring to a broad range of psychological therapies. Systems of psychotherapy are powerful within their own right, but also constitute a useful adjunct to the physical therapies discussed earlier. In the broadest sense, the term psychotherapy can refer to almost any form of psychological therapy. In the narrower sense in which it is used in this text, psychotherapy refers to the involvement of the client and a qualified professional "in an interpersonal process designed to bring about modifications of feelings, conditions, attitudes, and behavior which have proven troublesome" (Strupp, 1978, p. 3). The direction of the discussion in a psychotherapy session depends on such factors as the particular problem involved, the client's ability to verbalize, the theoretical persuasion of the therapist, and the cultural context (Sue and Zane, 1987).

Most people agree that psychotherapy is at least somewhat effective, but a number of years ago Hans Eysenck triggered a lasting controversy by publishing data he claimed proved that up to 72 percent of psychologically distressed individuals improved significantly without psychotherapy, a phenomenon known as "spontaneous remission." In subsequent years, there were substantial criticisms of Eysenck's report. Bergin (1971) summarized a number of critical flaws in Eysenck's report and presented definitive evidence that in long-term follow-up studies of untreated, mentally disordered individuals, spontaneous remission occurs only about 30 percent of the time.

Many other researchers have presented evidence supporting the effectiveness of psychotherapy (Strupp and Hadley, 1979; Smith et al., 1980; Brenner, 1982; Landman and Dawes, 1982). In a particularly important study, Smith and Glass (1977) thoroughly reviewed all prior studies on psychotherapy, then selected a subgroup of 400 that employed rigorous research designs. Analysis of these studies yielded strong support for the benefits of psychotherapy. Smith and Glass' data indicate that the typical therapy client is better off than at least 75 percent of untreated persons with a comparable disorder. Subsequent work (Smith et al., 1980; Landman and Dawes, 1982) added further support to these conclusions, and present substantial evidence that psychotherapy, through rehabilitation and prevention, is effective in lessening the impact of predominantly physical problems.

The effectiveness of psychotherapy depends on a number of factors pertaining to both the client and the therapist (Leyber, 1988). Certain qualities in each have been found to increase the likelihood of positive change. Some of these qualities are discussed below.

The client. Most studies of therapy have indicated that a major predictor of change is the client's initial level of disturbance (Prochaska, 1979; Smith et al., 1980). Clients who are less disturbed at the outset of psychotherapy are more likely to improve than those who are seriously disturbed. In addition, clients who show a higher level of dissatisfaction with their personal functioning and a higher level of belief in the efficacy of therapy are most likely to make progress. This tendency may result simply from the fact that such clients tend to remain in therapy a long time (Prochaska, 1979).

The therapist. The therapist's level of expertise in a variety of psychother-apeutic techniques is a critical variable in treatment success (Brenner, 1982) because, as a rule, successful therapists are adept at matching therapeutic techniques with the needs of particular clients (Norcross, 1986). Consider, for example, an anxious client who accomplishes little and spends most of the time thinking about and analyzing his or her own behavior. Such an individual might respond better to behaviorally oriented, action therapy than to insight therapy, which would promote additional self-analysis. The needs of each client must be matched with an appropriate intervention program, a task that successful therapists handle skillfully (Seltzer, 1986).

Therapists vary considerably in terms of experience and expertise (Strupp, 1978; Brenner, 1982). Success as a therapist depends in part upon expectations toward one's clients: therapists who expect their clients to make progress have a higher rate of success than do therapists with low expectation levels.

Of course, a positive attitude toward therapeutic change does not guarantee success in psychotherapy. Therapists must also be extremely attentive to information provided by their clients as well as to their own psychological reactions to this information (Guy, 1987). Awareness of one's own reactions to another person is known as **objective self-awareness**, and it is a characteristic successful therapists have and use effectively. Objective self-awareness is what enables the therapist to function as a participant observer (see Chapter 3) in psychotherapy sessions. In this role, the therapist actively engages in a therapeutic relationship with the client but nonetheless retains a degree of objectivity.

Objective self-awareness is important therapeutically for two major reasons. First, by monitoring one's reactions to a client, a therapist can learn much about how others are likely to react. A client who, for example, arouses feelings of anger in the therapist is likely to provoke others as well. Awareness of such feelings can alert the therapist to the client's need to develop more appropriate social skills. Second, self-awareness helps the therapist keep track of how the therapy session is progressing. Most therapists set agendas for psychotherapy sessions, and a high degree of self-awareness helps the therapist stay on task.

Empathy, the ability to participate vicariously in another person's experiences, is strongly associated with Carl Rogers and nondirective therapy. According to Rogers, being able to appreciate the client's point of view is vital to successful therapy. Evidence suggests that therapists are differentially empathic with various types of clients (Brenner, 1982; Gladstein, 1987). Some seem to understand the inner world of schizophrenics, for example, while others show greatest empathy for clients with anxiety or stress-related disorders. In general, empathy is most pronounced when therapist and client have been effectively matched (Strupp and Hadley, 1979).

In a broad and thorough survey of the process of psychotherapy, Prochaska (1979) described four factors used by therapists in helping their clients change.

1. *Consciousness raising*, or helping clients acquire a heightened awareness of inner needs and conflicts. Consciousness raising is an essential component of group therapy, and is stressed in humanistic therapies as well.

2. *Catharsis*, the expression of emotions and feelings that have been suppressed or repressed, is particularly important in psychodynamic and Gestalt therapies.

3. *Choice*, through which clients come to take responsibility for the direction and consequences of their behavior. Therapies that employ confrontation tactics or emphasize existential issues stress the importance of decision-making as a mechanism of change and personal growth.

4. *Behavioral stimulus control* involves manipulating environmental settings and stimulus conditions to bring about changes in the client's behavior. Behavioral stimulus control is an essential component of virtually all forms of behavior therapy.

Either separately or in combination, these four factors help produce in the client two vital conditions for change: (1) the ability to *confront* and cope with feared stimuli and (2) the ability to *generalize* gains from psychotherapy to everyday life (Goldstein et al., 1979; Smith et al., 1980).

Psychodynamic Therapy

Psychodynamic therapy is based on psychoanalytic principles first enumerated by Freud. Included in this section are discussions of psychoanalysis as practiced by Freud, Jung, and Adler, as well as direct analysis and primal scream therapy. These therapies share a common emphasis on the importance of early experience in determining psychological adjustment in adulthood. The therapeutic techniques used by each variant of psychodynamic therapy are all aimed at promoting insight into the developmental antecedents of maladjusted behavior (Lewis, 1981).

Psychoanalysis, the name given by Freud to the system of psychotherapy he developed, is based on four concepts: free association, analysis of resistance, transference, and interpretation. Free association refers to the technique of having the client say whatever comes to mind without attempting to censor anything, even if the result is illogical or embarrassing. Most clients initially find free association difficult owing to the natural tendency to screen one's thoughts and communicate only those that appear meaningful. The procedure requires temporary suspension of rational thought processes, and indeed verbatim transcripts of a client's associations would seem to possess little apparent logic. Freud believed that free association provided a means of accessing unconscious drives and needs not under the control of rational faculties. The apparent illogical nature of free association was precisely the quality that provided clues about these hidden areas of conflict. Free association does not lead to these hidden recesses of one's personality either directly or quickly. Psychoanalysis as practiced by Freud was a long and arduous task, largely because of the convoluted paths taken by the client in the course of free association.

Therapeutic progress was also impeded by certain psychological obstacles referred to by Freud as areas of **resistance**. It might seem odd to speak of resistance in regard to voluntary clients, but the term does not refer to willful efforts to frustrate the therapist. Rather, resistance entails the involuntary activation of defense mechanisms as progressively deeper levels of the personality are accessed during free association. According to Freud, defense mechanisms protect the ego from threats emanating from both the environment and within the individual. Primitive drives and impulses from the unconscious are normally kept under tight control through repression. Techniques such as free association, which break through these defenses, meet with intrapsychic resistance. In other words, resistance serves to protect the client from confronting unconscious material that may prove highly threatening. In the context of psychoanalysis, resistances are patiently worked through so that the client can eventually confront the content of the unconscious.

Resistances are worked through in different ways. Sometimes the process of free association alone is sufficient to break an impasse. In other instances, the therapist makes interpretive statements aimed at clarifying the source of resistance.

The analysis of **transference** reactions is a critical feature of psychoanalysis, and one that is helpful in dissolving areas of resistance. In transference, the client acts out conflicts experienced in important early relationships, in effect carrying over or transferring past feelings and attitudes—both positive and negative—onto the relationship with the therapist. **Countertransference** refers to the same phenomenon in the therapist, who however has been trained to recognize it and prevent it from adversely effecting the therapeutic relationship.

Freud employed **dream interpretation** in the analysis of transference and when working to overcome resistance. He believed that dreams conveyed messages directly from the unconscious, which if interpreted correctly, contained important clues about underlying conflicts.

Psychoanalysis was a time-consuming procedure. Its goal was to promote insight into unconscious conflicts, which could take years to achieve. Most of Freud's clients were members of middle- and upper-class society, with both the financial resources and the time to undergo analysis. As noted in Chapter 3, psychoanalysis has been criticized for being too time-consuming and expensive and for presenting no clear evidence that it is more effective than other approaches.

In general, these are valid criticisms, but they should be considered in the context of two important points. First, whereas many therapy approaches attempt to return clients to a state of equilibrium by eliminating symptoms or conflicts, psychoanalysis aims for a large-scale change in overall personality structure, making the client far more able to deal with the vicissitudes of life than most other people. Second, the goal of psychoanalytic therapy is not necessarily happiness in the ordinary meaning of the word. Rather, the goal is a clearer awareness of the factors that need to be considered in making decisions about one's life. This state shares much in common with the experience of **enlightenment**, as discussed by many spiritual leaders. Parallels are evident between the outcome of psychoanalysis and the state of mind described by Buddha in the following words: "I obtained not the least thing from unexcelled, complete awakening, and for this very reason it is called unexcelled, complete awakening" (Watts, 1957, p. 126).

Jungian psychoanalysis.   Carl Jung was one of several analysts trained by Freud who eventually developed a modified form of psychoanalysis (Meier, 1986). He was one of a group of therapists known as Neo-analysts, who generally ascribe to Freudian theory but differ on certain key points. For one

Carl Jung (1875-1962) studied under Freud but eventually developed a modified form of psychoanalysis that focused less on sexuality as a behavioral factor.

thing, they focus far less than Freud did on sexuality as a motivator of behavior and source of conflict. Jung in particular felt that a component of personality he termed the **collective unconscious** held the key to much of conscious behavior. Jung believed the collective unconscious encompassed a set of inherited behavioral predispositions common to all mankind. It represented one of two components of what Freud called the unconscious, the other being an unconscious repository of personal traits. Manifestations of the collective unconscious are seen in works of art, symbolism, rituals, and ceremonies common to all cultures.

Jung believed that dreams and fantasies conveyed information about both the collective and personal subdivisions of the unconscious. His emphasis on the symbolic content of dreams continues a tradition of therapeutic dream analysis associated with Biblical stories, Greek sleep temples, and the rituals of many tribal cultures, including American Indians (Prince, 1980). Many interpretations have been ascribed to dreams, including messages from supernatural powers, symbolic enactments of intrapsychic conflicts, and fulfillments of wishes and needs. Jung's hypothesis that dreams could also tap content from the collective unconscious was a noteworthy contribution to dream analysis. In addition to his interest in dreams, Jung and his followers also focused extensively on the spiritual and mystical qualities of their clients' lives.

Adlerian psychoanalysis.   Alfred Adler, who broke with Freud in 1911, also followed Freudian principles but focused more on the social context of behavior than on intrapsychic forces. Freudian therapy is essentially *intrapersonal*, and based on the individual; Adlerian therapy in contrast is *interpersonally* oriented. Adlerian therapists concentrate less on the unconscious and on sexual conflicts and more on the need for meaning and the freedom to control one's future. This focus was influential in the thinking of several subsequent Neo-Freudians, including Heinz Kohut, who has written extensively on the need to develop what he terms "healthy narcissism."

Adlerian theory exerted little influence on mainstream psychology for many years. Recently, however, there has been an awakening of interest in several of Adler's ideas. His stress on the importance of making independent, self-fulfilling decisions while not ignoring the social context of behavior has found a sympathetic audience. In this regard, Adlerian theory is as close to the humanistic perspective as it is to the psychoanalytic.

Direct analysis.   Direct analysis, originated by John Rosen (1953) and developed further by Karon (1976) and others, is a unique modern psychodynamic therapy. Therapists who practice direct analysis offer interpretive statements without waiting for clients to achieve their own insights. The interpretations focus on "primitive conflict" areas such as infantile sexuality, fears of abandonment, and concern at being overwhelmed by impulses. By presenting interpretations graphically and vividly, often in coarse street language, therapists

Alfred Adler (1870-1937)
devised a technique of
psychotherapy that
focuses on interpersonal
relationships and
factors.   (Both photos:
The Bettmann Archive)

cut through complacency and defensiveness, thereby effecting rapid change. The colorful language of direct-analysis therapists enhances the content of their interpretations and makes it very graphic (Crits-Cristoph and Singer, 1981). Chapter 8 contains an example of such a therapist–client interaction.

Primal scream therapy.   Primal scream therapy was developed by Arthur Janov, who believed that primitive, gut-level releases of emotion could be highly therapeutic. Primal scream therapy works by inducing **catharsis**, a release of dammed-up emotion associated with earlier conflicts. Janov believed that the energy required to repress these strong emotions was psychologically damaging, and that their sudden, dramatic release in therapy was highly therapeutic.

Although the procedure has been endorsed by a number of clients, there is little research data available documenting the effectiveness of primal scream therapy.

Behavioral Therapies

Behaviorism encompasses a wide range of theories and techniques all based on the idea that behavior is essentially governed by its consequences. People persist in doing things for which they're rewarded, and avoid those that result in punishment. Learning is a key behavioral concept, and refers to the process of forming associations between behavior patterns and various consequences. Behaviorists contend that most behavior—whether normal or abnormal—is learned, and is thereby potentially amenable to modification. From Pavlov and Watson onward behaviorists have consistently argued that controlling behavior is largely a matter of manipulating its consequences. More recent research on cognitive processes has shown that thought patterns significantly affect how people perceive the consequences of their behavior. This refinement is reflected in "cognitive behavioral" (Lutzker and Martin, 1981; Dryden and Golden, 1987) techniques discussed in another section of this chapter.

Systematic desensitization (SDT).   First described in 1958 by the psychiatrist Joseph Wolpe, SDT has long been a mainstay technique of behavior therapists for the treatment of anxiety. SDT is based on the idea that if a client can maintain a state of relaxation when faced with anxiety-arousing stimuli, the stimuli will eventually lose their power to arouse anxiety. SDT works according to the principle of **reciprocal inhibition**, in which relaxation responses incompatible with anxiety are conditioned to occur in the presence of stimuli that previously evoked anxiety. Relaxation may be induced by a variety of means, including drugs, muscular relaxation training, mental imagery, and verbal cueing using words like "peaceful" or "calm." Of these options, mental imagery and verbal cueing have proven especially effective in promoting relaxation (Marks, 1978; Redd et al., 1979; Crits-Cristoph and Singer, 1981).

For relaxation to work in SDT, the client must practice it under conditions that previously elicited anxiety. Rather than direct confrontation with the feared object, SDT exposes clients to a graded series of images, described by the therapist, which are increasingly related to the object of anxiety. The graded series of images is termed a **hierarchy**, because it progresses from least to most anxiety provoking. A client with an intense fear of large dogs, for example, might construct a hierarchy that begins with the pleasant image of a child playing with a new puppy and progresses to the sight of a fierce Doberman pinscher.

As each step in the hierarchy is visualized, the client is instructed to relax. Only when a state of deep relaxation has been achieved is the next image in the hierarchy introduced. Once again, the client relaxes, creating a physical state incompatible with anxiety. Eventually, the client becomes able to envision the object of his or her fear while deeply relaxed.

There is some debate about whether an orderly and well-defined hierarchy is important, but the great majority of therapists employing SDT do construct one (Marks, 1978). A vast literature indicates that SDT is a significant therapeutic factor in the treatment of phobias, sexual problems, social fears, and school anxiety in children (Marks, 1978; Mathews, 1978; Lutzker and Martin, 1981).

Implosion therapy.   Implosion therapy is a behavioral technique that, like SDT, is used to treat anxiety disorders. However, rather than presenting anxiety-arousing cues in a gradual manner, implosion therapy uses intense imagery incorporating as many fearful cues as possible. Implosion therapy appears to work because the anxiety-arousing scenario depicted by the therapist is not followed by any real consequences. The anxiety is extinguished, and the client feels a great sense of relief. Chapter 6 describes an actual implosion therapy sequence.

Clients undergoing implosion therapy actively collaborate with the therapist. They are made fully aware of the procedure beforehand, and are instructed to visualize in great detail the therapist's scenario even though it may be very frightening. The concept of extinction is also explained, clarifying the reason for deliberately inducing anxious feelings (Chambless et al., 1979).

Implosion therapy is used not only for specific phobias, as is SDT, but also to uproot early, primitive fears, such as anxiety about being abandoned by one's mother. In this respect, implosion therapy possesses qualities of psychodynamic as well as behavioral approaches (Lutzker and Martin, 1981).

Aversion therapy.   Aversion therapy is a behavioral conditioning procedure especially suited for decreasing undesirable habits, such as excessive eating or smoking. In aversion therapy, the therapist arranges for an unpleasant event to occur simultaneously with the actual or imagined performance of the undesired behavior, in order to form an association between the two. Examples of such negative events include electric shock, nausea-inducing drugs, or self-generated imagery that elicits disgust. Although potentially an effective form of treatment, aversion therapy has some drawbacks. First, voluntary compliance is often difficult to secure owing to the unpleasant nature of the conditioning procedure. Second, aversion therapy appears to suppress symptoms rather than eliminate their cause, much as punishment does. Finally, aversion therapy can instill feelings of anxiety or hostility in clients who actually do comply with the regimen.

Aversion therapy is by no means a recent invention. The Romans, for example, discouraged excessive alcohol consumption by placing an eel in the wine cup of someone with a drinking problem, causing a scare no less aversive than the mild electric shocks often used in modern-day treatment.

Token economies.   The token economy, first thoroughly engineered by Ayllon and Azrin (1968), is fundamentally a microeconomic system normally

ABNORMALITY ACROSS CULTURES

Morita Therapy

In describing the tremendous diversity of existing psychotherapy techniques, Corsini's *Handbook of Innovative Psychotherapies* (1981) shows that Morita therapy, which originated and is still mainly practiced in Japan, has influenced Western therapy practices. Like Zen Buddhism—and, in some respects, psychoanalysis—Morita therapy is concerned primarily with the confrontation and acceptance of mental suffering rather than with generating happiness (Prince, 1980; Reynolds, 1980).

Morita (1874–1938) formulated his treatment techniques in the early 1920s primarily for a group of disorders he termed *shinkeishitsu* ("nervous ones"). These are similar to the DSM-III anxiety disorders and some of the stress-related disorders.

Morita therapy usually lasts four to eight weeks. Rather than focusing on sleep, the subconscious, or dreams as many Western therapies do, this therapy emphasizes isolation, solitude, and "psychological rest." The Morita therapist may also prescribe Zen Buddhist readings. Prince (1980) has listed the following stages as typical of most applications of Morita therapy.

1. Total isolation and rest for from four to 10 days—usually the person is not allowed to write, read, listen to the radio, and so on, and remains generally inactive.

2. During the next seven to 14 days the person starts a diary and does some light gardening, though no interpersonal contact is allowed.

3. During the next week or so, the person continues the diary, hears lectures from a therapist on self-control, and engages in heavier physical activities.

4. The person then phases back into his or her usual vocational and social life, but continues to hear lectures from the therapist and enters into group therapy—such as sessions with other Morita therapy patients.

Unlike Western therapies, Morita therapy does not ask the patient to seek personal fulfillment, or insightful understanding, nor even to focus on avoiding the disruptive behavior. Instead, the Morita patient is asked to confront and accept this behavior and to integrate it into his or her life in a more balanced and subordinate role that allows normal and productive behavior to proceed undisturbed. Morita therapy in Japan is quite effective with a variety of clients but is not of much help with the more severe disorders discussed in upcoming chapters.

established in an institution (such as a hospital ward or a prison) to reinforce behaviors considered by the staff to be socially appropriate and beneficial to the client. The concept is not a new one; it was described, for example, in Oliver Goldsmith's novel *The Vicar of Wakefield* (1843). One of the novel's characters, Dr. Primrose, institutes a system of "fines for the punishment of immorality and reward for peculiar industry" that resembles a modern token economy.

Behaviors considered important by the therapist, such as getting up and doing work assignments, or participating in different therapies, are periodically tallied and rewarded with tokens. At designated intervals clients who have accumulated some tokens can exchange them for things they find rewarding, such as cigarettes, a more pleasant room, or television time.

Research has found token economies to be very successful in modifying primitive or bizarre behaviors such as isolating tendencies and hallucinations. They are also quite effective in teaching basic social skills such as communicating effectively, holding a conversation, and learning to be assertive (Patterson, 1975; Hersen, 1981). Generally, the less fully functional and mature the client, the more effective a token economy is likely to be. Comparatively independent and intellectually competent clients generally have more complex motives for doing things and thus are more difficult to condition through a simple token economy system.

Behavioral contracting.   Behavioral contracting is the development and implementation of an agreement, usually in writing, between therapist and client. It specifies the behaviors expected of the client, along with the rewards for success and penalties for noncompliance. The following case history gives a good illustration of behavioral contracting.

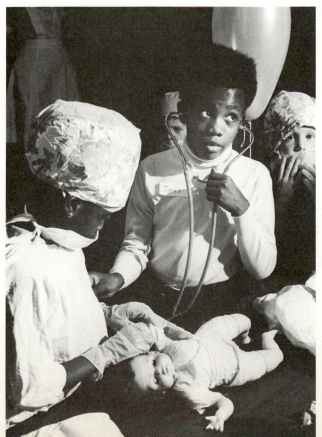

Modeling—aquiring a desired behavior through imitation—is a common form of learning therapy for children.   (Ellis Herwig/Taurus Photos)

The Case of Paul

Paul, a brilliant graduate student in biology, was also a chronic procrastinator. Although he always seemed busy, he had a chronic pattern of failing to meet deadlines for papers and laboratory assignments. His professors agreed that while he showed great promise as a scholar, his work habits might prevent him from attaining an advanced degree.

There were several facets to Paul's problem. For one, he consistently underestimated the amount of time needed to complete his assignments. Nor did he budget his time wisely. As a result, he was constantly rushing to meet deadlines, few of which he actually met.

A second aspect of the problem involved Paul's self-esteem. Though possessed of exceptional native intelligence, he had very little self-confidence. As a college student, he had always been able to get good grades without extended effort. He quickly grasped concepts and general ideas, but often failed to master detailed factual information. As a result, Paul felt that the high college grades misrepresented the actual depth of his knowledge. Feeling himself to be something of a charlatan, Paul delayed submitting assignments in part because he feared his lack of knowledge would be exposed.

After being informed that he was in danger of being dropped from his graduate program, Paul consulted with a clinical psychologist. After considering several options, the psychologist and Paul settled on a behavioral approach to the problem. Paul correctly concluded that an insight-oriented approach would simply play into his tendency to ruminate about things rather than getting them done. Besides, time was of the essence, and he had less than a semester to make substantial changes in his work habits.

Paul's intervention program was multimodal in form, and consisted of three components. The first entailed having him participate in an organization of biology students who shared their research ideas and skills. The idea was to help Paul gain a more realistic perspective on how much he knew relative to other students (he was more knowledgeable than he gave himself credit for). Second, Paul and his therapist developed a time-management system to budget his available time more effectively. Third, Paul agreed to a behavioral contract with the following provisions.

1. That he would designate three two-hour periods each day to work on class and lab assignments. Worrying about his lack of technical knowledge was to be confined to a single 15-minute period each day after lunch.

2. That he would bring a list of all assignments and responsibilities to the weekly therapy sessions for review and prioritization.

3. That he would devote three hours on Saturday afternoons to library research for the purpose of (a) rectifying knowledge deficiencies; and (b) beginning work on his master's thesis.

There were no specific rewards built into the contract; both Paul and the therapist felt that completing his assignments on time would be sufficiently gratifying. One cost penalty was included: Paul had to pay the therapist an additional $10.00 per week if any assignments were incomplete. To dramatize this penalty, the therapist told Paul that he would burn the bill with a cigarette lighter during the session.

Within eight weeks, Paul had begun to achieve control over his time and responsibilities. Eighty percent of his assignments were being submitted on time, thanks in part to the sacrifice of two $10.00 bills and a small amount of butane. Paul's professors were gratified by his progress and elected to keep him in the program, which he successfully completed the following year.

As is evident in Paul's case, behavioral contracts provide a concrete statement against which performance can be measured. Many clients in other forms of therapy finish sessions with promises to think or act differently in the future, only to forget by the time they return home. When bound by a contract concerning their behavior, they are better able to keep in touch with their resolutions (Bandura, 1969; 1981).

Paul's case is a good example of how a contractual agreement can effect compliance in changing behavior. Behavioral contracting has widespread applications, and is commonly used with families and couples (see Chapter 4), as well as with children having behavior problems in school. The only difficulties with this technique seem to involve weaning the client from expectations of specific rewards and creating a transition to situations where tangible rewards are not consistently given for specific behaviors.

Modeling. Our earlier discussion of social learning therapy (Chapter 2) stressed the importance of modeling and imitation in acquiring new behaviors or modifying old ones. As applied to clinical situations, modeling involves demonstrating to the client behaviors intended to replace self-destructive or problematic ones. This is typically done with either live or videotaped models. Modeling is commonly used with children (Bandura, 1969), but also works well with adults. Sometimes, after observing a model demonstrating the desired behavior, the client is asked to imitate the behavior during an interaction with the therapist. Group therapy also provides a good setting for practicing new behaviors: following observation of a model, clients can practice the new responses with each other. Such practice performance is known as **role playing**.

Because modeling is most effective when the client can easily identify with the model, the model should be as close in age to the client as possible, and of the same sex. There is also evidence that models who appear to be trying to cope, as opposed to those already showing mastery of behavior, produce more positive results. In addition to teaching new skills, such as how to be more assertive or a better conversationalist, modeling is effective in modifying existing behaviors or replacing them with new ones.

Assertiveness training. Assertiveness training is a set of procedures drawn from behavioral and cognitive approaches designed to help people effectively represent their own best interests. Examples of unassertive behavior abound in everyday life; people with breathing problems tolerate smokers rather than say something and create a scene; a spouse who desires children may quietly defer to one who does not; or a student may fail to question an exam grade for fear of seeming ignorant. In each of these examples, the individuals subordinate their own legitimate needs and are imposed on by other people.

Assertiveness training is used with people who are normally shy and inhibited to the point where they let others direct their behavior. The technique makes use of a number of procedures, including role playing, modeling, and behavioral contracting, combined with a number of cognitive techniques that are described in the next section.

Cognitive Therapy

Cognitive therapy is based on the premise that behavior is largely controlled by the individual's thought processes (Weiner, 1986). You may recall from the discussion in Chapter 2 that advocates of this viewpoint speak of **cognitive mediators**, which are thoughts that intercede between external stimuli and overt responses (Cautela and Kearney, 1986). When applied to clinical situations, cognitive theories assert that many mental disorders are either caused or exacerbated by problematic thinking (Dryden and Golden, 1987). Cognitive therapists work to help their clients develop more adaptive ways of thinking. Cognitive therapy techniques have been developed to deal with a wide range of psychological problems, including test anxiety (Meichenbaum, 1977), depression (Beck, 1976), and general adjustment (Kanfer, 1977). A number of rather diverse therapies have been developed that focus on thought patterns, including rational-emotive therapy (RET), paradoxical control therapy, thought stopping, and reality therapy (discussed in a later section). For the present, let us consider an application of cognitive therapy in the treatment of a depressed schoolteacher.

Rational-emotive therapy (RET). Rational-emotive therapy was developed almost exclusively by Albert Ellis (1973), who developed an approach to therapy that draws on cognitive, psychoanalytic, and humanistic theories (Ellis and Grieger, 1986). An interest in cognitive factors, beliefs, and attitudes is, however, central to RET. Ellis has, for example, enumerated a group of illogical assumptions he finds many clients make about the world and themselves. Included in his list are thoughts such as "Everyone I meet must like me," "My behavior is completely controlled by outside forces; there's no point in trying to change," and "I should be perfect in everything I try." Ellis and others have found that beliefs such as these promote many forms of maladjustment, for two major reasons. First, such beliefs are frequently phrased in absolute terms. Notice in the examples above how the words "must" and "should" convey a sense of inflexibility. Second, these beliefs are clear distortions of reality, and whereas each may contain an element of truth, none can suitably serve as principles to govern behavior.

Ellis contends that if people ascribe to beliefs such as these, they are very likely to be unhappy and spend much of their time trying to impose an unrealistic degree of control on the world. On the other hand, if people develop a rational view of the world and do not always feel a need to exercise self-control, they can influence those aspects of their lives that can be changed, and accept those that cannot. Ellis' system of therapy attempts to instill a rational view of life and the problems everyone is forced to confront.

Therapy sessions based on RET have a distinctive quality. Ellis and his colleagues constantly work to expose fallacies of their clients' thinking, and continually point out ways in which maladaptive thought patterns interfere with constructive behavior. This approach is evident in the following segment of a therapy transcript (Ellis, 1973, p. 186).

Client: "I don't know! I'm not thinking clearly at the moment. I'm too nervous! I'm sorry."

Therapist: "Well, but you *can* think clearly. Are you now saying 'Oh, it's hopeless! I can't think clearly. What a shit I am for not thinking clearly!'? You see: You're blaming yourself for that."

Client: (Visibly upset), can't seem to say anything; then nods.

Therapist: "No! You'll never get better unless you *think*. And you're saying 'Can't we do something *magical* to get me better?' And the answer is No!"

Paradoxical control therapy. Several therapists have observed that anxiety arising from anticipating the potential occurrence of an unwanted thought or behavior is critical in the development of obsessions, compulsions, stress and anxiety disorders, and habit disorders (Haley, 1959; 1973; Frankl, 1975; Lazarus, 1981; Schwartz, 1986). These therapists try to get clients to approach and perform the undesired thoughts and behaviors in a more controlled fashion, often by giving the clients apparently absurd directives. Frankl (1975), for

The Case of Nora

Nora, age 33, had taught elementary school for eight years. She was well liked by her students and colleagues, but had become increasingly despondent in recent months. She lacked energy, slept poorly, and occasionally started crying for no apparent reason. Unable to determine why this was happening, and unsuccessful in her attempts to cheer herself up, Nora sought treatment at a nearby clinic.

The therapist, a psychiatrist, initially prescribed a mild antidepressant to help improve Nora's mood and increase her energy level. As therapy progressed, however, the psychiatrist became impressed with the number of cognitive distortions that pervaded Nora's speech. Nora saw everything in black-and-white terms, and divided her students into groups who either loved or hated her. The word "should" cropped up everywhere in her conversation: "I *should* be a principal by now" and "I *should* get married soon before I'm too old" were two thoughts that Nora continually dwelled upon. Never one to push herself too hard, and coming from a privileged family background, Nora had grown up with the belief that the world owed her a living. As a result, she tended to expect others to recognize her talents and promote her on the basis of ability alone. As her professional career continued, however, it was becoming increasingly apparent that no one was paying much attention to her except to acknowledge what a nice person she was.

The therapist instituted a program of cognitive therapy to help combat some of these erroneous beliefs. First, she had Nora keep track of her daily activities on a schedule sheet. After a week of this, she had Nora rate each activity in terms of (1) her skill at performing it and (2) her level of interest. It turned out that Nora's competencies at work lay essentially in teaching math and computers, two activities she moreover enjoyed. The bulk of her time, however, was spent in classroom and administrative duties that she detested but performed ably enough. The results of this analysis suggested that Nora's time was being spent in activities holding little interest for her.

Further therapeutic exploration revealed some beliefs and assumptions that had caused Nora to fall far short of her potential. For instance, while growing up she was taught that girls *should* become teachers (if they work at all), and that scientific interests were for boys alone. She also harbored the belief that a woman in her early 30s without a family was a failure. The therapist worked with Nora to document decisions and behavior patterns that reflected these beliefs. Nora quickly began filling in the pattern. She recalled turning down a science scholarship in order to attend a local college with a boy she hoped to marry. She took her first teaching position because she was attracted to the school principal. The list went on, and it soon became apparent to Nora that much of her behavior was in fact governed by beliefs and attitudes that stifled her own true inclinations.

Eventually, Nora made some significant changes in her career. She helped develop a program of consultation services to schools employing computer-aided instruction and soon became its director. She discovered a latent talent for public relations work and became a research coordinator for the board of education, seeking funding from corporate sponsors.

These changes did not take place overnight, in part because even with therapeutic assistance, it is difficult to divest oneself of beliefs and attitudes acquired in childhood. But once Nora began to replace outmoded assumptions with new ones reflecting her personal beliefs, change was inevitable.

example, assumes that the undesired behavior is directly tied to a vicious circle of **anticipatory anxiety**. The more the person fears the repetitive symptom, the more intense the anxiety, which in turn generates more symptoms. Frankl paradoxically instructs clients to carry out or wish for that which they are currently resisting. For example, someone tormented by efforts to avoid unwanted thoughts might be instructed to generate as many unwanted thoughts as possible. A compulsive handwasher struggling to stop the habit might paradoxically be told to wash his hands 500 times a day. Jay Haley (1973) has been particularly successful in employing paradoxical directives, so called because they prescribe for clients the very behaviors they are trying to eliminate (Seltzer, 1986).

Why do paradoxical directives work? Much of their effect is due to the way they permit the therapist to take control of the client's symptoms. Haley and many other therapists tend to think of symptoms as "bargaining chips" that clients employ in power struggles with the therapist. It is generally assumed that clients are anxious to replace their symptoms with more adaptive behaviors. However, therapy for many clients and therapists becomes a battle of wills in which each tries to control the behavior of the other. Some clients, perhaps ineffectual in other social situations, may take pleasure in maintaining symptomatic behavior to frustrate the therapist. Their tactic is fundamentally to carry out the opposite of the therapist's recommendations. For such individuals, paradoxical directives work because of this tendency to do the opposite of what the therapist says. To return to one of the earlier examples, the compulsive handwasher, when instructed to wash his hands 500 times per day, may abruptly stop altogether.

Thought stopping.   Thought stopping resembles aversion therapy in that it ties an irritating or startling event to the emergence of an undesired thought or behavior in order to suppress the latter. But whereas aversion therapy is usually directed toward overt behaviors, thought stopping is intended to modify internal events. It is an appropriate means of treating obsessions or disruptive thought patterns commonly found in impulse disorders.

Thought stopping was used as early as 1938 by Alexander Bain in virtually the same form as it is today. More recently, the guru Rajneesh (1975) devoted a lengthy discussion to thought stopping as a useful technique in pursuing spiritual enlightenment.

In thought stopping, therapists tell their clients to let their obsessions flow and then, upon a cue, to shout "Stop!" This command usually serves to disrupt the train of obsessive thoughts. After a period of practice in the office, clients are encouraged to follow the same procedure at home when troubled by obsessive thoughts. They learn to vary the length of time before initiating the thought-stopping procedure, as well as to use subvocal, rather than audible, cues.

Humanistic Therapies

Humanistic therapies have evolved from the work of Carl Rogers and Abraham Maslow discussed in Chapter 2. The intent of humanistic therapy is to help clients determine the direction they want their lives to take (Rowan, 1983). Humanistic therapists strive to listen empathetically to their clients and encourage them to reveal their innermost needs without fear of being negatively evaluated. Four therapeutic models are associated with the humanistic approach: client-centered therapy, rational therapy, existential therapy, and gestalt therapy.

Client-centered therapy.

Client-centered therapy, the earliest embodiment of humanistic therapy, was developed by Carl Rogers (1951). Rogers was also the first to publish a full transcript of a therapy session, thus facilitating the scientific study of therapist–client interactions. Also known as nondirective therapy, his approach advocates a style of interaction in which the therapist neither attempts to influence the client directly by giving advice or reassurance, nor asks direct questions. Nondirective therapists instead believe that the greatest need clients have is for someone to understand them, which they attempt to do in a variety of ways. By listening empathetically, nondirective therapists attempt to understand things from the client's vantage point. They feed back the client's own feelings and statements to check whether they've understood them accurately. Finally, they take an active interest in their clients and convey as a result a sense of genuine concern for their welfare.

Nondirective therapy is especially well suited for college counseling centers, and indeed Rogers' first clients were primarily graduate psychology and theological students at the University of Chicago. Clients of this type have several distinctive characteristics: they are bright, well-educated, sophisticated in psychological jargon, and delighted to analyze introspectively their own (and others') psyches. Nondirective therapy is most effective with clients who have these qualities. It has been particularly influential in the practice of a great many therapists, irrespective of their avowed theoretical orientation.

Existential therapy. Existential therapy emphasizes the client's confrontation with the major issues of the human condition: finding meaning in life, risking commitment in relationships, attaining quality rather than quantity in life experiences, and confronting death. The existential therapist attempts to keep the client responding directly and "authentically," that is, with awareness and responsibility to these issues. The goal of existential psychotherapy is to increase awareness and choice in all areas of life, not simply eliminating psychological pain and distress. The extract from an RET therapy session given above reveals an existential component: Ellis forces the client to remain aware both of the desire to stop thinking about the problem and of the hope that there is an easy and quick cure for conflicts. American existential psychotherapists such as Rollo May and Eugene Gendlin are particularly concerned with the forces of determinism and depersonalization in modern life that can prevent people from realizing their full potential. Through discussion and confrontation of the issues, existential therapists try to help the client get in touch with experiential feelings that evolve from various psychological conflicts, and then to use these feelings to make informed decisions about life.

Existential therapy is often used with clients whose problems do not have a specific focus. It is most effective with the intelligent and verbal client, because it requires an ability to voice inner feelings, confront choices, and verbally communicate the resulting commitments.

Reality therapy. Reality therapy represents something of a simplification of existential therapy. Both reality therapy (Glasser and Zunin, 1973) and existential therapy hold that clients who perform negative or self-destructive behaviors must be made to accept the full consequences of those behaviors. Reality therapy acts to describe verbally avoidance of choice, to clarify the probable consequences of a choice, and then to hold the client to facing the consequences. Reality therapy can be a useful technique for a variety of disorders.

William Glasser, the originator of reality therapy, first developed the system while working with incarcerated delinquent girls in California. Many of these girls had developed lifestyles that allowed them to avoid the consequences of their behavior. As a result, they developed problematic behavior patterns characterized by irresponsibility and lack of forethought.

Gestalt therapy. Gestalt therapy, developed primarily by Fritz Perls (1958), reflects Perls' early training as a psychoanalyst but is primarily a humanistic-existential form of therapy. Perls' charm and charisma were as much responsible for the initial popularity of this approach as the new therapy itself (Harman, 1982). Gestalt therapy should not be confused with the gestalt theory of perception, which deals with the way visual and other sensory experiences are organized. Gestalt therapy and gestalt theories of perception are two completely separate theoretical areas.

Gestalt therapy resembles the psychodynamic theories in its emphasis on becoming aware of oneself and on attaining insight through catharsis. However, it rejects an emphasis on early experiences and focuses instead on the here and now. It has contributed several important techniques for helping clients gain awareness of their conflicts. One of these, the "empty chair" technique, is described in Chapter 12.

Gestalt therapy is particularly effective with clients who intellectualize their problems and talk about them without emotion (Perls, 1953; Harman, 1982). Intellectualization is a danger in all talking therapies, particularly in psychoanalysis, when the individual is generally free to continue without control by the therapist. The gestalt therapist immediately points out any intellectualization, forcing clients to confront their conflicts more directly and bringing them in touch with the emotional and physiological aspects of their concerns.

OTHER PSYCHOLOGICAL THERAPIES

There are several commonly used therapy techniques that have no connection with any particular therapeutic school. Three of these—hypnosis, biofeedback, and group therapy—are discussed here.

Hypnosis. Both Freud and Wolpe used hypnosis, a sleep-like state in which the client is willing to carry out suggestions. They both eventually abandoned it after it was discovered that only about 50 percent of people can be hypnotized using standard techniques.

Hypnosis was used in the sleep temples of the Egyptians and Greeks, where priests and other officials went to receive messages from the gods. It was not until the 1840s, however, that James Braide first used the term "hypnosis," adapted from the Greek word *hypnos* (sleep). In the same decade, James Esdaile, a Scottish physician practicing in India, used hypnosis to relieve the pain of surgery and collected the first data on its effectiveness. He found that hypnosis reduced the mortality rate of surgery patients from 50 percent to five percent, primarily because the reduction of pain and stress reduced the number of patients dying from shock.

Over the years hypnosis has been applied to a great variety of disorders, yet substantial controversy persists as to what it actually means to be hypnotized (Wadden and Anderton, 1982). People who are hypnotized show the same brain wave and physiologic responses that they do in a waking state. Most theoreticians now support the idea that hypnosis is an altered state of consciousness with analogies to role playing. (The issue of whether people can be compelled to commit acts against their will while under hypnosis is discussed in Chapter 5.) Hypnosis as a therapeutic tool typically takes two forms: direct suggestion and regression.

Direct suggestion uses the inherent passivity of the hypnotized subject both to make straightforward recommendations for new ways of thinking and to implant suggestions for posthypnotic behavior. The latter are referred to as **posthypnotic suggestions**. Direct suggestion is used primarily with the impulse disorders, such as overeating and tobacco addiction, but it has also proved useful in other problem areas (Meyer and Tilker, 1976).

In **regression hypnotherapy**, attempts are made to get clients in touch with early memories or feelings that have been either repressed or dissociated, but which are the source of current problems. In one case, a young woman who had recently been raped was hypnotized to alleviate the emotional trauma resulting from the event, all memory of which she had repressed. Hypnosis also helped her recall the license plate of her assailant's car, and this information led to his arrest and conviction. Under hypnosis she remembered the experience of the rape and also summoned up repressed memories of having been molested by her grandfather when she was eight. In therapy it was discovered that the fusion of these two incidents in her subconscious had compounded the guilt and anxiety she felt over the rape. After 10 sessions spent exploring these feelings under hypnosis, the client was able to admit them to consciousness to see and accept them. The emotional trauma they had previously caused then gradually dissipated.

Biofeedback. Many of the early researchers in biofeedback had worked previously in hypnosis. Hypnotized clients make a conscious decision to passively accept suggestions from a therapist; in biofeedback, clients receive signals from a machine that monitors their physical state while relaxed and passive, and then they use this information to change certain response patterns. Biofeedback is a general term for the procedure of monitoring inner physical states, particularly those involving activation of the autonomic nervous system. The information obtained from this monitoring process is then used to alter such variables as pulse rate, breathing rate, body temperature, and the production of certain brain waves. The premise of biofeedback is that controlling physiological processes can positively influence emotion and behavior (Hatch et al., 1986). Most people use biofeedback to learn how to relax, and by monitoring variables correlated with relaxation (such as pulse and respiration rate), can learn how to tell when they have reached a deeply relaxed state.

In biofeedback therapy it is important that the information obtained be converted into a form readily understood by the client (Schwartz, 1987). For

Biofeedback subjects receive signals from a machine that monitors
their physical state, and use this information to change and control
their physiological processes. (Robert Goldstein/Science Source,
Photo Researchers, Inc.)

example, few clients could gain any meaningful information from unprocessed
brain wave (EEG) tracings. By filtering, condensing, and displaying the information, biofeedback instruments provide much useful data. In the case
of brain activity, alpha waves are among the most common signals used in
biofeedback. Alpha waves occur at a frequency of between eight and 12 cycles
per second, and reflect a nonattentive state that facilitates relaxation. Using

an appropriate monitor, the client configures it so that whenever alpha waves are detected a tone or light will be triggered. The task is simply to keep this signal on as much of the time as possible. Through this technique almost any physiologic process for which measurement technology exists can be monitored and regulated. Because it is much easier to measure electric output from skeletal muscles than from, say, the intestinal tract or other inaccessible organs, electromyographic (EMG) feedback has proven to be the most efficient clinical feedback method (Hendrix and Meyer, 1976; Fuller, 1978). In EMG feedback, electrodes are placed on muscles where tension is focused, such as the muscles in the back of the neck, and the client then uses the resultant feedback to monitor and lower tension levels.

As effective as biofeedback procedures are, there is often a problem with generalization (Tursky, 1979). Some people learn to modify their responses while in the biofeedback lab but cannot achieve the same results in their everyday world. For successful transfer to occur, clients eventually have to learn the bodily cues associated with the desired change, rather than relying on the tone or light of a machine (Schwartz, 1987).

Group therapy.   Several forms of therapy, known as group therapy, involve more than one client per therapist. The overall effectiveness of group therapy is well documented (Meyer and Smith, 1977; Smith and Glass, 1977), and it is a cost-effective form of therapy. Positive outcomes from group therapy are most likely when the group is comprised of people who have at least moderately similar types of problems and degrees of personality disturbance.

Like individual therapists, group therapists differ in style. Some group therapists are content to take a background role, becoming just another group member, and let the group process take over. Others attempt to control group interactions in a low-key way by providing interpretations and only an occasional challenging comment. Still others, like Fritz Perls, the founder of gestalt therapy, set up one-to-one interactions with each group member, during which time the other members become observers.

Group therapy is ideally suited for problems that involve interpersonal and social disability, such as postdivorce adjustment (Bloch and Crouch, 1987). Groups can serve as a base of operations where clients try out new behaviors and ideas in front of other group members, who provide feedback and may suggest other response options. The social setting of group therapy facilitates generalization of any new behaviors to day-to-day situations (Yalom and Lieberman, 1971). The group setting also promotes self-esteem, since group members tend to be supportive of each other, particularly when they share common problems. Group settings also serve a monitoring function, in which members keep track of each other both during and outside therapy sessions.

Family and marital therapy.   Family and marital therapies (see Chapter 16) are forms of group therapy; they often rely on systems theory concepts (Framo,

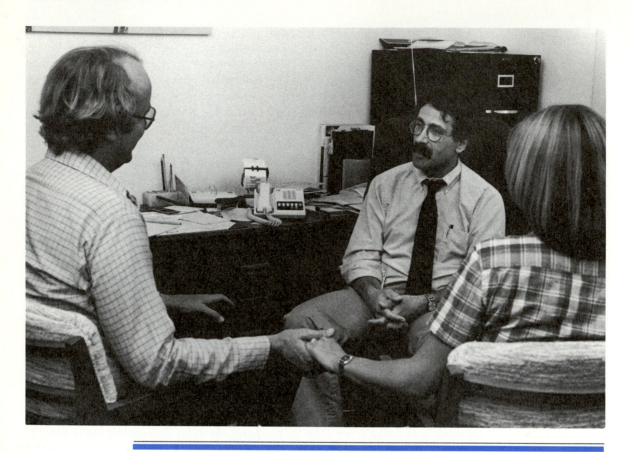

Family therapists attempt to correct dysfunctional communication patterns between family members.   (Mimi Forsyth/Monkmeyer Press Photos)

1979) such as those explained in Chapter 2. This is because families and couples have established habitual patterns of interactions prior to therapy, unlike members of therapy groups (Barker, 1986). There are also other points of contrast as well between group and family therapies. Group therapists tend to work with individuals who share similar types of problems. Indeed, groups are often constituted in terms of specific goals or programs. Thus, there are assertiveness training groups, phobia groups, consciousness raising groups, and so forth. As a result, therapeutic emphasis is typically on helping a group of individuals drawn together by a common problem. And although during therapy group therapists focus on interactions among group members, there usually is no compelling reason for the members to stay in contact outside the group itself. In contrast, therapy with married couples or families is typically undertaken with the realization that these individuals are in intimate contact with each other on an ongoing basis (Bornstein and Bornstein, 1986). The goals of therapy here typically center on alleviating dysfunctional communication patterns between family members, thus helping them to interact more effectively on a day-to-day basis (Piercy, et al., 1986).

Family therapists are often handicapped by a factor other group therapists seldom have to deal with. In traditional groups, members are usually voluntary participants, or are at least aware that they share problems in common with each other. In contrast, family therapists often must deal with family

---

EXHIBIT ^o

A Comparison of the Advantages and Disadvantages of Group and Individual Psychotherapy

Group versus Individual Psychotherapy	
Group therapy	Individual therapy
Extra people provide a fuller range of feedback.	Continuous one-on-one relationship allows more in-depth exploration of problems.
Some problems are especially responsive to the group process (through multiple feedback and/or confrontation) such as postdivorce adjustment problems and hypochondriasis.	Some problems are too embarrassing to the client to display to others or are upsetting to effective group process, such as sexual deviations or antisocial or paranoid disorders.
Group therapy is usually much cheaper per hour.	Individual therapy is cheaper in terms of cost per unit of time spent on a single individual's problems.
Everyone has a chance to be a helper as well as to receive help.	There is more chance to know the therapist as a person who has also experienced problems.
Group response is well suited to *interpersonal* aspects of problems.	Individual response allows fuller disclosure of *intrapsychic* aspects of problems.
There is a chance to break into new social systems and make new friends.	Confidentiality is more likely to be maintained.
If a therapist somehow gets on the wrong track or responds to a personal bias, at least one group member can often make a corrective comment.	Feedback from fellow group members who are biased or ignorant is not particularly valuable and wastes time.

members who are resistant to participating in therapy (Framo, 1979). Frequently, one particular family member is labeled, or "scapegoated," as sick. Family therapists are inclined to regard this as merely symptomatic of disruptive communications shared by all. The problem, however, lies in convincing other members of the family to share responsibility for these difficulties and collectively to participate in therapy (Barker, 1986).

Despite their differences, however, group and family therapies both tend to emphasize the importance of interpersonal factors in promoting adaptive behavior. Both family and group therapy programs have proven quite popular in recent years, indicating that there are strong needs for intervention techniques that provide an alternative approach to traditional individual therapy.

Milieu therapy. Milieu therapy attempts to establish an atmosphere on a ward or in a hospital that is highly supportive and therapeutic. Milieu therapy was first advocated in the moral therapy approach of the mid-nineteenth century, which called for pleasant surroundings, a concerned and supportive staff, meaningful activities, and minimal restrictions. Similarly, milieu therapy operates best when (1) the size of the unit is kept small, (2) staff is well trained in behavioral concepts, (3) staff has positive expectations about the potential success of its endeavors, and (4) staff and patients alike have as much input as possible in decision-making.

Certain institutions give lip service to milieu therapy, permitting clients little actual latitude in making decisions affecting the unit's policies. Moreover, the occupational, art, and activity therapies employed by some hospitals as a facet of milieu therapy often seem more oriented toward filling up time than toward preparing patients for a return to the real world.

Community therapy. A logical extension of group and milieu therapy is community intervention, which focuses a wide variety of community resources on the eradication and prevention of community-wide mental health problems. Community-wide intervention programs reach a wider audience than do either individual or group therapy, and their impact can be substantial. Community psychologists often must be as adept at political maneuvering and social activism as they are with traditional therapeutic skills, for they generally represent the needs of people who are economically, as well as psychologically, disadvantaged.

A TREATMENT PERSPECTIVE

Clearly, there are many different approaches to therapeutic intervention. Further variations exist in terms of the creativity and effectiveness with which therapists of many different orientations put the techniques to use (Valenstein,

1986). This abundance of techniques is desirable, since significant evidence exists to support what logic would suggest: certain types of therapy are more suited than others to certain types of problems. Evidence supports another logical assumption; a therapeutic approach is most relevant to the population for whom it was originally developed. Glasser, for example, formulated his ideas on reality therapy while working with institutionalized delinquent girls, and his procedures have proven helpful for clients who behave in an equally irresponsible, impulsive manner. Carl Rogers developed client-centered therapy while working with graduate students in theology and psychology. His techniques work best among clients who are bright and introspective and who take the initiative in formulating plans for their lives. Token economies were developed on institutionalized groups who were significantly impaired. Schizophrenics, brain-injured persons, and autistic children have all been helped by token economy systems, which are less effective with groups of bright, independent, and creative individuals. In any of these situations, compatibility between therapist and client, that is, the degree of rapport achieved, is an important element in effecting positive change no matter what form of therapy is employed (Strupp, 1978; Strupp and Hadley, 1979; Lazarus, 1981; Brenner, 1982).

The first four chapters have provided overviews of historical developments, theories, assessment procedures, and therapeutic techniques. The remaining chapters will discuss specific mental disorders.

CHAPTER REVIEW

1. Mental health professionals have a wide range of treatment techniques to choose from. At the broadest level, pharmacologic and psychological measures are the most commonly used techniques in working with a wide range of mental disorders.

2. Chemotherapy has proven useful in treating many biologically based disorders. At the very least, it tends to generate a positive expectancy; many people strongly believe that medical treatment is inevitably helpful.

3. Physical therapies other than chemotherapy (including ECT and psychosurgery) have found widest application in treating serious depression. Although ECT is still in moderately widespread use, psychosurgery is practiced on a much more restricted basis than was the case 40 or 50 years ago.

4. There is ample evidence that psychotherapy is helpful in alleviating the distress caused by mental disorders. Therapist skills are important; those correlated with positive outcome include (a) knowledge of multiple techniques; (b) objective self-awareness; and (c) empathy.

5. Psychotherapeutic effects tend to fall into four groups: (a) consciousness raising; (b) catharsis; (c) promoting decision-making; and (d) behavioral stimulus control.

6. Orthodox Freudian analysis was modified by Freud's followers, including Jung and Adler, and again later by theorist/clinicians such as Sullivan, Erikson, Klein, and Rosen. The system of psychotherapy they pioneered came to be known as the psychodynamic school.

7. Classic behavioral techniques for treating mental disorders, such as SDT, aversion therapy, modeling, and token economy programs, were developed more recently than psychodynamic procedures. They reflect a concern with scientific objectivity in an analysis of mental disorders; all have a strong empirical base.

8. Cognitive therapies, such as rational-emotive therapy (RET), cognitive behavior modification, and paradoxical control therapy, stress the extent to which thoughts control behavior. Maladaptive thoughts promote psychological maladjustment; taking a rational approach to one's situation can bring about adaptive changes in behavior.

9. The humanistic therapies, such as client-centered therapy, existential therapy, and gestalt therapy, focus primarily on helping clients develop a clear awareness of both their inner needs and the reality of their life situation.

10. Group and family therapies have both common features and differences. Both approaches offer a popular alternative to the individual client treatment model popularized by Freud.

TERMS TO REMEMBER

psychotherapy
placebo effect
BASIC ID
psychosurgery
tranquilizers
antipsychotic medication
hallucinations
tricyclic antidepressive medication
lithium
bipolar disorder
imipramine
tardive dyskinesia
beta blockers
temporal lobes
frontal lobe
electrosleep therapy
continuous sleep therapy

objective self-awareness
resistance
transference
countertransference
dream interpretation
enlightenment
collective unconscious
catharsis
reciprocal inhibition
hierarchy
role playing
cognitive mediators
anticipatory anxiety
direct suggestion
posthypnotic suggestions
regression hypnotherapy

FOR MORE INFORMATION

Brenner, D. (1981) *The effective psychotherapist*. New York: Pergamon. Does a good job of discussing and synthesizing the various factors that make an effective psychotherapist

Corsini, R. (Ed.). (1981) *Handbook of innovative psychotherapies*. New York: Wiley and Sons. A collection of more than sixty articles by major researchers and practitioners that describes a wide variety of therapeutic techniques

Hersen, M., and Breuning, S. (1986) *Pharmacological and behavioral treatment*. New York: John Wiley. Presents both the chemotherapeutic and behavioral techniques appropriate for a broad spectrum of psychological disorders

Prince, R. (1980) Variations in psychotherapeutic procedure. In: Triandis H., and Draguns J. (Eds.). *Handbook of cross-cultural psychology: Psychopathology*. Boston: Allyn and Bacon. Presents an excellent cross-cultural perspective on treatment techniques in general and the psychological therapies in particular.

Reynolds, D. (1986) *Even in summer the ice doesn't melt*. New York: Quill. Written by the foremost authority on non-Western therapy techniques, this book makes effective use of anecdotes, fables, case vignettes, and ancient sayings to explore two classic Japanese therapy techniques for promoting socialization and minimizing anxiety: Naikan therapy and Morita therapy.

PART

II

Stress and Anxiety Based Disorders

Early in life I was visited by the bluebird of anxiety.

Woody Allen

Woody Allen's character in *Hannah and Her Sisters* is the quintessential hypochondriac who complains of his various ailments to friends, lovers, and a series of doctors. (Museum of Modern Art/Film Stills Archive; © 1986 Orion Pictures)

5

The Stress, Somatoform, and Adjustment Disorders

The first group of disorders to be considered in this book are those in which psychological and physical factors intermingle. The term stress, our first topic of discussion, makes most people think in terms of both psychological and physical factors, and indeed there is ample research evidence to suggest that psychological factors can certainly have an impact on one's physical condition, if not actually bring about physical illness.

The second group of disorders covered in this chapter have in common physical complaints for which no clear-cut organic basis can be found. These are called somatoform disorders, and are widely believed to develop in people who tend to channel psychological conflicts into physical manifestations.

Adjustment disorders comprise the third group of stress-related conditions. These are characterized by abnormally high levels of psychological distress in response to stressors encountered in daily life, such as the loss of a job, divorce, or natural disasters.

● The Case of Ed

Ed is a 46-year-old mid-level manager in a company where he has worked for 20 years. On graduating from college, he had had wide-ranging interests and had felt a sense of excitement at the prospect of beginning his career. Now he feels trapped by the demands of both his family and job. The company offered him a promotion, but it meant moving to a distant small town. His family adamantly refused to move, leaving Ed to deal with demands for higher levels of productivity with little hope of promotion in his present job.

Shortly after he turned down the promotion, Ed had a falling out with his daughter, who was a student in a nearby college. He had always doted on her and was now surprised and hurt to find that she was deviating from the plan he had for her to be a biologist. She announced one day her intention of enrolling in a fine arts school and becoming an artist. Ed has little understanding of art, and moreover views artists as odd people. He became very critical of her plans; as a result, she began to distance herself from the family as much as possible.

These factors added emotional pressures to a marriage that Ed had become somewhat ambivalent about. Ed increasingly felt that his life consisted of too many demands and too few rewards and that no one really cared for him. Moreover, he began to experience stomach pains and severe headaches. Not being psychologically minded, Ed never considered the possibility that his physical symptoms might be related to emotional conflicts. However, he did mention them to his physician, who diagnosed a tension headache syndrome and a pre-ulcerous gastrointestinal condition. In addition, Ed's blood pressure was well above normal.

In part, Ed is the victim of a stress disorder. He shows a physical pattern characteristic of people who live with chronic stress that is not acknowledged or coped with.

What is stress? And how can it affect the body in such harmful ways? These are two of the questions posed by Ed's case. We will address these and other questions about stress disorders in the following sections.

STRESS AND STRESSORS

Stress is a state of mental and physical tension resulting from factors that are disrupting a person's normal equilibrium (Endler and Edwards, 1987). Being threatened by an angry dog as you walk home from the bus stop or being late for work can cause stress, a state in which your body tenses up and your mind feels the pressures of worry or concern. The external factors that disrupt an individual's equilibrium and make stressful demands on the individual are called *stressors.* There are different types of stressors: physical stressors, such as a car accident or tornado; psychological stressors, such as a threatening dog or a semester exam; and social stressors, such as overcrowded subways or racism. Stressors can range from everyday difficulties such as problems at work or with family members to catastrophic difficulties such as civilian disasters or war (Quick, et al., 1987).

Stress affects health. Research shows that even purely psychological stressors, such as chronic worrying, seem to make a person more vulnerable to disease. The fact that psychological stressors seem to increase illness illustrates an important relationship between mind and body, a relationship whose importance extends beyond the effects of stress. It is known, for example, that a positive or hopeful attitude can improve health (Bedrosian and Beck, 1979). When given a "medicine" with no actual medical benefit (a placebo), patients who believe the "medicine" will work often do show real improvement (the placebo effect). In the following section we shall examine more closely one portion of the relationship between mind and body: the relation between stress and physical disorders.

RELATION OF STRESS AND PHYSICAL DISORDERS

According to current thinking on the relation of mind and body, psychological stressors affect virtually all physical disorders to one degree or another (Harre, 1987). For that reason the DSM system does not use a separate category for physical disorders that derive from psychological problems, a category that previous editions called **psychosomatic disorders.** Asthma, ulcers, essential hypertension, headaches, and certain skin disorders were all considered specific psychosomatic disorders.

Physicians may diagnose patient complaints, such as stomach problems or headaches, as stress-related disorders.   (Richard Wood/Taurus Photos)

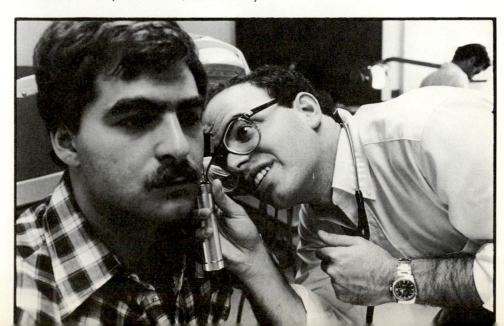

RESEARCH PROFILE

Psychosomatic Reactions and Family Stress

Conflict is a precursor to stress and anxiety. Conflict among family members can have especially telling consequences, particularly if successful resolution is not achieved. Children appear to be especially vulnerable to stress of this sort, and it is not uncommon for them to develop psychosomatic symptoms in the face of unremitting stress and conflict. Dr. Salvadore Minuchin and his colleagues at the Philadelphia Child Guidance Clinic have done significant research in demonstrating a clear physiological link between family conflict and subsequent stress reactions in children (Minuchin, 1977).

The subjects of the study were a group of diabetic children who had proved unresponsive to normal treatment. These children had suffered from recurring ketoacidosis, a disturbance of blood metabolism, for which no medical basis could be determined. The investigators noted that bouts of ketoacidosis ceased when the children were hospitalized, only to resume once they had returned home. The investigators hypothesized that the emotional climate at home might be causing these already vulnerable children to respond with this serious physical ailment.

Minuchin compared the stress reaction patterns of these "psychosomatic" diabetics with a group of normal diabetics and a control group of medically normal children with behavior problems.

The key to the investigation was knowledge that ketoacidosis is triggered by the release of free fatty acids (FFA) into the blood. FFA levels, in turn, are a sensitive index of emotional arousal, rising within minutes of exposure to stress. Accordingly, Minuchin and his colleagues designed a study to monitor FFA blood levels during a period of experimentally induced stress.

While the children watched from an observation room, an experimenter interviewed their parents for a few minutes, then told them to discuss a family problem and left the room. Returning shortly, the experimenter provoked added conflict by siding with one parent. This was followed by a period of interaction between parents and child, aimed at settling the conflict, and finally by a recovery period for the

The current DSM manual uses two axes to pinpoint combinations of physical and psychological factors. Axis I lists "Psychological Factors Affecting Physical Condition," henceforth abbreviated as PFAPC. Axis III is used to designate any contributory physical disorders or conditions that are presumed related to the Axis I diagnosis.

Disorders such as essential hypertension and ulcers are now diagnosed using these two axes. Previously, such disorders were identified by a number of different names, including "psychophysiological," "stress," and even "psychosomatic" disorders. In actuality, these terms appear to have referred to different conditions. "Psychophysiological disorder" refers to physical symptoms intensified by psychological factors, and is conceptually closest to DSM's PFAPC category. "Stress disorder" is a closely related condition, while "psychosomatic disorder" is a term used to emphasize primarily psychological entire family. Throughout the session, which was videotaped, the stress levels of all participants were monitored by devices drawing continuous, riskfree blood samples. The investigators determined FFA levels from the blood samples and evaluated their correspondence to the videotaped events.

Results indicated that not only did the children experience far higher levels of stress (as measured by FFA levels) during all phases of the experiment, but they also sustained elevated levels long after termination of actual stress. Perhaps even more significant, whereas most of the children's FFA levels increased dramatically when they entered the room and became involved in the ongoing conflict, the FFA levels of their parents simultaneously declined. It was as if the children absorbed or blunted their parents' stress responses, though at considerable personal cost.

The results yielded several important conclusions. First, and perhaps obvious, is the fact that family conflict is stressful. Second, children vary in their capacity to deal with, or absorb, stress. The seriously psychosomatically ill children appeared to be highly vulnerable to begin with, in the sense that they appeared physiologically more reactive than diabetic children without psychosomatic symptoms. It was further determined that these children came from families in which communication patterns promoted continual stress and tension. The combination of preexisting physical vulnerability and recurrent family conflict then triggered recurring bouts of ketoacidosis. At a broader level, Minuchin's study illustrates the extent to which illness—psychological or physical—in a child may be reflective of maladaptive behavior among other family members. In clinical practice it is not uncommon to find that children who are referred for psychological problems come from families in which stress, tension, and conflict are prevalent.

Intervention in such situations often involves working with other family members besides the person initially referred. As Minuchin noted, separating children and parents during bouts of ketoacidosis brings only temporary relief; his ultimate goal is effective treatment of not just the child, but the entire family.

aspects of an illness. For the sake of consistency, subsequent sections in this book will use the term "stress disorder" in referring to conditions in which both physical and psychological factors are intertwined.

The fact that a variety of terms has been used to characterize the pathological impact of stress attests to the variety of ways in which psychological and physical factors can interact. The issue is complicated further by the fact that in some cases physical symptoms appear to stem from psychological factors alone and do not correspond to any known disease process. For instance, someone may complain of numbness that does not and could not correspond with the pattern of nerve damage necessary to produce that numbness. In cases like this, psychological factors are presumed to affect physical condition to the extent that somatic symptoms are reported, yet there is no underlying physical disease. This is an example of what DSM terms a *somatization disorder*, a category we will discuss in detail at the end of this chapter. For now it is important only to recognize that the somatoform disorders and PFAPC differ to the extent that the latter always involves a diagnosed physical disorder while the former does not.

The relationship between stress and genuine physical disorders is neither completely understood nor precisely defined. Enough information exists to assume that the two are related (Stern et al., 1982). To what degree one correlates with the other varies from one physical disorder to another, though an overall correlation of about 0.3 appears to be reported fairly consistently. Theories on the relationship between stress and physical disorders concern such questions as: (1) How does stress affect the body? (2) What are the effects of different types and degrees of stress? (3) What factors increase a person's vulnerability to stress? In the paragraphs that follow we will discuss theories that attempt to answer these questions about the relation of stress and physical disorder. In the process we will also look at the larger question of how the mind and body relate to one another.

STRESS DISORDER THEORIES

Although it is hard to imagine people willingly subjecting themselves to stress, a great deal of theorizing regarding stress comes from studies done by Epstein and Fenz on volunteer parachute jumpers. As summarized by Fenz (1975), this research evaluated the cognitive and physiological responses of both novice and experienced parachutists. Cognitive factors were assessed by using word-association tests immediately before jumping and after landing. Physiological data included autonomic nervous system responsiveness. One major finding was that experienced parachutists showed somewhat greater anticipatory stress than did their novice counterparts, but that as the moment of the jump approached, the experienced parachutists became increasingly calm and the novice parachutists increasingly nervous. These differences were consistent as measured by both physiological responses and reactions to word-association tests.

Two basic interpretations of Epstein and Fenz' work seem possible. On one hand, it could be argued that repeated practice at parachute jumping causes a favorable change in one's physiological and psychological make-up, a change that enhances stress-handling capabilities (Kasl and Cooper, 1987). On the other hand, as suggested by Ursin, et al. (1978), it may simply be that the experienced parachutists were a highly select group who possessed good stress-coping capabilities to begin with and who were the only ones to complete training successfully.

Current theories about responses to stress contain elements of both ideas. There is a great deal written about learning to cope with stress and to manage tension effectively. However, it is equally common to read that some people are physically more vulnerable to the effects of stress, as if they had an inherited or developed susceptibility. In our discussion of stress disorders, it will become evident that there is an element of truth in both ideas, and that to understand the effects of stress, both behavior and vulnerability must be analyzed (King, 1987).

Objective Stress Theory

Hans Selye's objective stress theory states that stress activates the body's arousal system. He used the term **general adaptation syndrome** (GAS) to describe the body's mobilization of resources in response to stress. According to Selye, the GAS involves three distinct phases: alarm, resistance, and exhaustion. Selye noted that a wide range of factors could initiate GAS: physical threat, bodily trauma, even ingested foreign substances. There is increasing evidence as well (Stern et al., 1982) that psychological factors may be capable of triggering GAS responses.

Activation of the GAS produces a hormonal chain reaction (Kasl and Cooper, 1987). Overall, this chain reaction is carried out by the autonomic nervous systems (ANS), the branch of the nervous system that automatically regulates the body's response to environmental stress. The ANS, by connecting the central nervous system to internal organs and smooth muscles, regulates heartbeat, respiration, blood pressure, perspiration, pupillary dilation, and so on. During the alarm phase, external stimulation activates two brain structures, the thalamus and hypothalamus. These cause the pituitary gland to release a hormone known as ACTH (adrenocorticotrophic hormone), which stimulates the adrenal glands into activity. The adrenal glands, one atop each kidney, in turn secrete a number of hormones (including adrenalin and cortisol) that cause increases in respirations, heart rate, oxygen consumption, blood pressure, and muscle tension. In addition, the pupils of the eyes dilate, arteries constrict, and blood is diverted from the internal organs and digestive system to the skeletal muscles and brain. Mobilization to this degree draws heavily on the body's energy resources, and the basic metabolic rate increases markedly. In the second, resistance, stage the adrenal glands secrete other hormones that help rebuild any damage sustained during the alarm phase and that promote ongoing adjustment to stress. The third, or exhaustion, stage of the GAS occurs if the system is overwhelmed by unmanageable stress. Under these conditions, the arousal and resistance mechanisms break down, leading to any of a variety of disorders and possibly death.

Many people experience chronic stress that promotes persistent activation of the resistance phase of the GAS. Consider for a moment a day in the life of a hypothetical office worker. Driving to work, a near-accident triggers an intense physical reaction complete with pounding heart and sweating palms. A run-in with the supervisor over a missed deadline cues another reaction that

During the course of a typical day, an individual may be subjected to the frustration of rush-hour traffic and a boss's angry remonstrations. These situations, while commonplace, can add up to significant levels of stress.   (top: Ellis Herwig/Taurus Photos; bottom: Paul Fusco/Magnum)

RESEARCH PROFILE

Stress and Perceived Control

While significant stress can be destructive to us all, there are various factors that influence how a particular stressor affects any one person. The text mentions as one factor the biological predisposition of that individual, and the severity of the stress itself is obviously important. In addition, another factor that has been hypothesized as important is the degree of control the individual perceives himself or herself as having while in the midst of stress. An interesting attempt to verify this hypothesis was carried out by Kilminster and Jones (1986).

These researchers used the cold pressor test as a stressor. This involves putting and keeping one's hand into a bucket of extremely cold water. Kilminster and Jones took various physiological measures to see if the stressor was inducing stress; a test of persistence in and clarity of thinking was also administered. The 30 subjects in this experiment were randomly divided into two groups. Members of the first group, the perceived control group, were allowed the choice of which hand they wished to have immersed in the water, and were also told they could remove their hand at any time they wished, though they were encouraged to keep it in for the three-minute period that made up the test. The subjects in the second group, the no-perceived-control group, were simply asked to keep their hand submerged until the experimenter told them to remove it.

The physiological measures did indicate that stress was experienced, and the two groups differed significantly on both the motivational persistence and effectiveness of thinking measures. Perceived-control subjects showed higher levels of motivation as well as higher levels of effective and efficient thinking. This data, along with other data noted in this chapter (and also in the section on learned helplessness in Chapter 9), supports the contention that having a sense of predictability or control in the midst of stressful circumstances goes a long way toward generating more adaptive behavior and reducing potential negative effects.

leaves him visibly shaking. After work, a tiring drive home in rush-hour traffic is followed by an argument with his wife that ends in a shouting match. Even when the day is not punctuated with such graphic stressors, many people are subjected to a number of lesser stressors whose effects tend to be cumulative. With time, one's average level of physiological arousal can thereby increase, often imperceptibly, until the point where a major breakdown occurs. Not only does arousal become conditioned to recur with greater ease, but it also tends not to fully subside to the resting state, and so the body does not recover fully from the depletion of energy that has been expended. Under such conditions of unremitting stress, three structural changes may occur (Szabo, 1980). First, the adrenal glands become enlarged, reflecting a chronic state of activation. Second, the thymus, spleen, and lymph nodes deteriorate. These changes weaken the immune system and cause a decline in the efficiency with which worn blood cells are replaced. Third, the gastrointestinal tract becomes

EXHIBIT

Stress and Artistic Performance

"My courage sank, and with each succeeding minute it became less possible to resist this horror. My cue came, and on I went to that stage where I knew with grim certainty I would not be capable of remaining more than a few minutes. . . . I took one pace forward and stopped abruptly. My voice had started to fade, my throat closed up and the audience was beginning to go giddily round . . ."

The above words were written, not by a neophyte actor facing the stage for his first major performance, but by the world famous actor Sir Laurence Olivier, who was troubled by performance-related stress throughout much of his career. How does one account for this phenomenon?

There is increasing evidence that the performing arts, a source of pleasure and relaxation for members of the audience, carry with them both psychological and physical risks for the artists who appear on the stage night after night. Among musicians, frequent performance has been shown to result in what are termed "overuse" syndromes caused by excessive practice and playing. Cellists, guitarists, horn players, and keyboard players alike are vulnerable to such injuries, which frequently necessitate consultation with a neurologist.

In addition to physical stress syndromes, many performers are vulnerable to the psychological distress described by Sir Laurence Olivier. Often termed "performance anxiety," it is a symptom that has led more than one performer to leave the profession permanently. For many performers, the condition is essentially a stress, rather than an anxiety, disorder. This is because a chronic pattern develops in which bouts of severe tension at the time of performance are accompanied by less severe, but persistent, feelings of distress that frequently involve physical problems such as ulcers and possibly hypertension.

In writing about the subjective distress associated with performance conditions, Stephen Aaron has identified a number of sources of fear common to many stage performers, particularly actors. A common fear is that of being *looked* at by the audience. This may seem a bit surprising, as most people believe that actors and performers crave attention. But the tradition of fearing audiences goes back to the ancient Greeks, who wore masks as much to ward off the "evil eye" of spectators as they did to portray various characters and emotional states.

Fear of making mistakes is of course a major concern for performers of all types, who differ markedly in the extent to which they are able to recover and go on when an error occurs. Although some performers feel that developing contingency plans to cope with errors represents a form of negative thinking,

ulcerated. Up to a point, one can adapt physiologically to increasing levels of arousal. But there are limits to this adaptation capability, beyond which a stress-induced breakdown will almost inevitably occur.

Selye's objective stress theory proved moderately effective in making general predictions about vulnerability to stress disorders (Ursin et al., 1978). However, it was left to other researchers to define more specifically just what types of things should be considered stressful (King, 1987).

most veterans have developed tactics they employ to cope with such eventualities. For example, musicians who play from memory may practice intensively certain measures throughout a piece. That way, if a memory lapse occurs, they can return to one of these sections and go on without having to begin the piece again.

Some of the fears expressed by actors and musicians in advance of a performance often have a somewhat irrational quality, of which the individual is usually well aware. Fear of losing physical control, of having a heart attack or a seizure, or of doing something entirely out of character are all reported by people prone to performance-related stress. Sometimes these fears persist even after a series of successful performances, making it clear that they are not easily dispelled as a result of experience alone. The persistence of these and other irrational thoughts appears in part related to the uncertainty all performers must deal with. No matter how well prepared they may be, it is impossible to predict precisely how well things will go.

Psychological antidotes to performance stress may take any of several forms. In vivo performances before supportive and nonthreatening audiences appear to be quite helpful in aiding inexperienced performers overcome their trepidation. Many musicians and actors have found that relaxation training, meditation, and related procedures help diminish generalized tensions and make them more able to withstand the pressures associated with the performance itself. Recently, evidence has begun to accumulate suggesting that cognitive therapy may help reduce performance stress. Performers as a group tend to be highly self-critical and perfectionistic. As a result, they are often inclined to think about both themselves and their capabilities in negative terms. Cognitive therapy can help replace maladaptive attitudes toward performing with more appropriate responses. For example, the conviction that "I'll never be able to complete my piece without a mistake" may be replaced with a more tolerant attitude, as embodied in such self-statements as, "I'll prepare well, do my best, and not be overly concerned if I make a mistake."

Performance-related stressors constitute an occupational hazard for many musicians, actors, and actresses. Recent work by Aaron and others in this area has clearly demonstrated that psychological factors have a significant role in the evolution and maintenance of performance stress, and that techniques including relaxation training, in vivo desensitization, and cognitive therapy can all prove helpful in alleviating distress.

Source: Aaron, S. (1986) *Stage fright.* Chicago: University of Chicago Press.

A basic assumption made by researchers investigating the effects of stress is that any *change* in one's accustomed situation can be a stressor. The death of a loved one, or being terminated abruptly from one's job are obvious examples of such changes; but even everyday stressors, such as parking tickets and jammed candy machines can add up to significant stress. Researchers have assumed that vulnerability to stress is a function of the number and severity of such life changes within a given period of time. An important step in assessing this was taken by Holmes and Rahe (1967) when they developed an inventory of 43 life changes. Each event was assigned a score based on the degree of stress the respondents believed it to entail. Scores obtained for each event were totaled to determine the overall stress level. Holmes and Rahe suggested that individuals with scores between 150 and 300 had about a 0.50 probability of experiencing a moderate to serious illness within the following 24 months. The probability rose to 0.80 for scores in excess of 300.

This inventory was expanded by Woolfolk and Richardson (1978) into the Recent Life Change Questionnaire. It is interesting to look at some of the stressful life events on Woolfolk and Richardson's scale, which has achieved widespread acceptance. The most traumatic event listed is the death of a spouse (100 points); the least, minor legal violations (11 points). It is important to note that events such as vacation and the birth of a child, which are generally considered positive events, are assigned stress scores because they are changes in one's accustomed routine, and as such are considered stressful.

High scores on the Recent Life Change Questionnaire are positively correlated with incidence of physical illnesses. Viral disorders such as the flu, and even cancer (Sklar and Anisman, 1979) have been reported to be correlated with stress. Woolfolk and Richardson (1978) reported a study of flu-virus levels in the serum of women tested throughout the flu season. The amount of virus present had more to do with the amount of stress to which the women were exposed than to whether they had been exposed to the flu.

Cognitive influences.   Although research has proven its validity, the life-change model of stress is not without limitations. For one thing, degree of stress can be influenced by factors like culture, age, and sex (Barnett et al., 1987): For instance, going to a bank to borrow money is considered far more stressful in Japan than it is in the United States (Tseng and Hsu, 1980). A second, related criticism was offered by Woolfolk and Richardson: degree of stress can be influenced by personality and personal experience. The psychological impact of the loss of a spouse depends on the meaning the spouse and the marriage had for the survivor. People accustomed to being together—even in a relationship less than ideal—will find the loss harder to deal with than those accustomed to relatively independent lives.

As a result of such criticisms of the objective stress theory, increasing emphasis is being given to assessing the meaning events have to the individual (Hurst et al., 1978). This introduces a cognitive component into what has been predominantly a biologically based model of stress. In a study of highly stressed executives, Kobasa (1979) identified groups with high and low vulnerability to illness. Executives in the low-vulnerability group were found to have a clear sense of meaning in their lives, manifested in (1) a belief that they had some control over events in their world, (2) a view of their work as challenging but manageable, and (3) a strong commitment to long-term personal goals. In other words, under the same stressors, executives with more positive cognitions were less vulnerable to stress disorders. Generally speaking, events over which people feel they have little control are perceived as the most stressful (Stern et al., 1982).

Theories of Predisposition

Stress disorders take many different forms. Some people under stress experience physical disorders in a number of physical systems, as when someone develops both asthma and hypertension. For others, the vulnerability may appear to be confined to one, as in the case of a patient who is especially prone to ulcers. What is it that allows such variations? Are some people perhaps predisposed to greater susceptibility to one stress disorder? Research suggests that the answer is Yes (Kasl and Cooper, 1987).

Like many other syndromes, certain stress disorders (such as ulcers) tend to run in families. Although this fact does not rule out other causes, research indicates that heritability exerts a significant but variable influence on the development of ulcers, hypertension, and most other stress disorders (Emmelkamp, 1982). What appears to be inherited is a general predisposition to anxiety and tension (Reese, 1979); it is this predisposition that in turn increases the chance of developing specific stress disorders.

The variable impact of stress on different individuals could be a function of the differing physical vulnerabilities people have. One theory that involves an application of this principle is the so-called "organ-weakness" theory. It states that the body's weakest organ system (heart, lungs, or whatever) is most likely to break down under stress. A person may inherit weak lungs or may develop weakened lungs through illness or injury. In either case the respiratory system may become that person's weakest system. According to the organ-weakness theory, when that person experiences stress, the effects of stress are likely to show up in the respiratory system, perhaps as asthma. Another person may develop a weak circulatory system, perhaps through lack of exercise. In that person, stress may show up as hypertension.

Vulnerability to stress may even result from conditioning. Consider a child who experiences intense stress while preparing for school, manifested in a number of physical symptoms on a regular basis, such as shortness of breath or nausea. The child's mother is likely to respond to some symptoms with greater concern than to others. She may, for example, believe the nausea is more significant. Each time the child shows this symptom, the mother keeps the child home from school. When the child shows shortness of breath, the mother encourages the child to go to school. In this way the child learns to experience stomach disorders to avoid stress. Eventually, the child develops specific systemic or organ weaknesses that accompanies stress. The organ-weakness theory appears to make sense at an intuitive level, but lacks proof that specific organ weaknesses are highly predictive of subsequent breakdowns (Vaillant, 1977). Further criticism of the organ-weakness theory comes from longitudinal studies showing that as people age, stressors may affect different organ systems (Stearns et al., 1982).

EXHIBIT

Psychological Risk and Heart Surgery

Recent advances in heart surgery techniques have allowed many patients who would otherwise be incapacitated to resume useful, productive lives. Heart transplants have saved the lives of many individuals on the verge of death. Less dramatic and far more common are operations to restore an adequate supply of blood to the heart muscle itself. When the arteries supplying the heart become clogged or blocked, the risk of heart attacks increases substantially. Surgical procedures have been developed to either remove the blockage from these arteries or to graft veins taken from another area of the body onto the heart to carry a new supply of blood.

Heart surgery techniques have proven highly successful in alleviating the medical distress associated with coronary artery disease. However, patients with this and related conditions have been found to have significant psychological problems, which in some instances inhibit their recovery following surgery and prevent them from resuming a productive lifestyle. In a recent study dealing with the psychological risks associated with heart surgery, Pimm and Feist (1984) have provided a detailed description of the risks involved and effective psychological intervention techniques.

To begin with, patients at risk for coronary artery disease tend to show a history characterized by high stress coupled with poor general health habits. The classic "Type A" personality first described by Friedman and Roseman appears to be especially vulnerable to cardiac disease. Such individuals tend to be hard-driving, demanding of others, and under chronic stress and pressure. Many develop drinking or smoking habits, initially as a means of helping them control tension. In the long run, coupled with a generally unhealthy lifestyle, these factors combine to create a significant level of risk for both physical and psychological problems.

Such individuals do not react well to the prospect of physical illness. Most pride themselves on having felt relatively healthy for years, and seldom take time out from their work for relaxation or rest. Fitting the model of the stereotypic "workaholic," they are likely to become either depressed or anxious when deprived of the opportunity to maintain their breakneck pace.

Cardiac surgery carries with it certain physical and psychological risks, despite continuing refinements in operative procedures. Postoperative changes in neurological status and personality patterns have been reported in some patients, and there is a marked tendency for patients to become depressed in the immediate aftermath of surgery. Patients accustomed to high levels of activity preoperatively are often difficult to manage postoperatively because of their strong desire to resume an active lifestyle, despite the fact that it is this very lifestyle that has contributed to

Personality Pattern Theories

One group of theories about responses to stress assumes that greater susceptibility to stress occurs in individuals whose personality shows certain patterns of psychic conflict. In these personality pattern theories, it is assumed that susceptibility to stress develops as the result of psychic conflicts stemming from their illness. For this reason, coronary surgery patients are routinely referred into what are known as "cardiac rehabilitation" programs, which offer a set of structured group activities designed to promote gradual improvement in both a patient's medical and psychological status.

In the study reported by Pimm and Feist, a group of heart surgery patients were followed throughout the course of their surgery and recovery. Patients were randomly assigned to either a group receiving crisis intervention therapy or a control group that received no therapy. Patients receiving therapy met with a counselor on the day before surgery, and again postoperatively for eight weeks of supportive intervention. Results of the study provided clear documentation of the potential beneficial effects of this form of counseling. Basically, the investigators found that counseling (1) reduced the incidence of depression, anxiety, and suicidal thoughts evident three months following surgery; and (2) reduced the incidence of depression (as assessed by the patient's spouse) three years following surgery. Interestingly, the two groups did not differ in terms of the number of medical complications reported following surgery, suggesting that the effects of counseling were essentially confined to psychological, perhaps attitudinal, factors.

This study is important because it clearly documents the importance of effective pre- and postoperative attention to the psychological needs of cardiac surgery patients. This need stems from two key factors. First, these patients often have difficulty making appropriate adjustments in their lifestyles following surgery because their behavior patterns are so deeply engrained and have been reinforced for so many years. If left to their own devices, many would try to resume comparable activity levels without regard to the risk factors inherent in such behavior. Second, major surgery is a stressful event, despite the care with which it is performed and the sophistication of the techniques involved. Patients are abruptly confronted with their own mortality and the prospect of continuing vulnerability, as well as physical discomfort. The combination of these factors may contribute to the postoperative depression commonly reported by many patients. Those who take advantage of counseling programs of the sort described in this research study are likely to show a long-term recovery pattern in which depression and anxiety are minimized. Those whose recovery proceeds without the benefit of psychological intervention are more likely to be troubled with depression, as their customary coping mechanisms prove inadequate to the task.

Source: Pimm, J.B., and Feist, J.R. (1984) *Psychological risks of coronary bypass surgery.* New York: Plenum Press.

unresolved early phases of development. Furthermore, particular psychic conflicts are assumed to produce particular stress disorders. Bronchial asthma, a respiratory condition characterized by episodes of extremely labored breathing and diminished oxygenation in the bloodstream, for example, is assumed to occur in persons whose strong need for affection is matched by equally compelling fears of the intimacy necessary to obtain such affection. This pattern has been associated in particular with highly dependent children whose mothers were overly controlling. In a rather literal manner, the asthmatic symptoms are seen as a manifestation of psychological suffocation. Similar psychological analyses have been applied to other physical symptoms, such as ulcers, headaches, skin disorders, and the like. In each case, it is assumed that the disorder reflects a fundamental psychological conflict either within the individual or between the individual and others.

However, a general lack of empirical support for this theory diminished its impact. It was found, for example, that although emotional factors contribute to asthma attacks, the primary causes of the disorder involve the allergic and hormonal systems (Mikulich, 1979). There are two basic weaknesses with the personality pattern theories. First, relatively few people possess *all* the personality features assumed to accompany whatever disorder they have. For example, while an asthmatic child may appear highly dependent, it may be difficult to demonstrate the fear of intimacy that is presumed to lie at the root of the conflict. Second, stress disorders often depend more on the particular circumstances of a situation than on personality traits. Under stress, many people show signs of regressive or otherwise maladaptive behavior, but most of the time—when not under stress—they do not exhibit these traits.

One bright spot in the personality pattern theories comes from the work of Friedman and Rosenman (1959, 1974), who found that a higher incidence of coronary disease is associated with a distinct personality pattern they termed **Type A.** People who tend to be impatient and easily irritated, who perceive the demands of life as unfair, and who easily become competitive in relationships are Type A personalities. In contrast, the **Type B** personality is more relaxed and inclined to live one day at a time. These individuals were found to be less prone to heart disease and related physical problems. There is increasing evidence that the origins of Type A and B behavior patterns extend back to early childhood (Vega-Lahr and Field, 1986).

Essential Hypertension

The most common stress disorder is chronic high blood pressure that has no known organic cause. This condition is called **essential hypertension.** Ten to 15 percent of the population in the United States has high blood pressure. Most of these people, approximately 25 million in number, have essential hypertension (Meyer, 1981). About 1.67 million have high blood pressure due to physical causes such as kidney dysfunction or atherosclerosis, blocking of the arteries leading to the brain. Blood pressure is the amount of force exerted by the heart as it pushes blood through the circulatory system. Measurements of blood pressure are reported in terms of millimeters of mercury (mm Hg); they are measured as two values, the systolic and the diastolic. **Systolic pressure,** normally the higher of the two numbers, reflects the force exerted when the heart muscle contracts. It is more variable than diastolic pressure and changes with alterations in one's physical state. **Diastolic pressure** reflects cardiac output during the resting phase, that is, between contractions of the heart. It provides the best indication of the regular or long-term condition of the cardiovascular system. Normal blood pressure is approximately 120 mm Hg systolic and 80 mm Hg diastolic.

Causes. Essential hypertension seems to have multiple contributory factors. Seldom is it possible to point to one specific factor as the cause. Instead, the accumulative effects of a number of factors often create an underlying vulnerability. Genetic influences on structural components such as blood vessels and the autonomic nervous system play some part in causing essential hypertension. Diet may be significant as well. Diets high in salt and low in potassium significantly increase blood pressure, and there is evidence that high concentrations of saturated fats, cholesterol, and triglycerides do likewise. Trace mineral levels are yet another potential contributor to essential hypertension. Research has shown, for example, that excessive concentrations of cadmium, and deficient levels of selenium and silicon, can all lead to elevated blood pressure (Miall, 1961; Meyer, 1981). Smoking, excess weight, and lack of regular physical exercise contribute substantially to the risk of hypertension. Finally, hypertension may develop in part from conditioned anxiety or anger responses in much the same way that simple phobias develop.

Despite the acknowledged contribution of the above factors to essential hypertension, psychological stressors appear to be the most important single cause. Essential hypertension has been consistently found, for example, in persons undergoing significant changes in social, geographic, economic, or work-related aspects of their lives (Guthrie and Tanco, 1980). Employees who rotate their work shifts show much higher average blood pressure levels, as well as other stress symptoms, than do those who work only on one shift. In a quite different context, the high number of frustrating life experiences among the poor in areas such as Appalachia has been related to the development of essential hypertension. The equally frustrating experiences of blacks in our society may also explain why black males have higher average blood pressure levels than do white males. Genetic and dietary factors appear to influence this correlation. Furthermore, continuing prejudice coupled with mounting pressure to succeed despite the system's prejudice can create excessive stress in minority individuals.

Aside from environmental forces that tend to exacerbate stress levels, subjective responses to stress are important in determining the degree of dysfunction that takes place. For example, longitudinal research (Hokanson et al., 1971) has indicated that suppression of anger is associated with significantly elevated blood pressure (Meyer, 1981). Similarly, McClelland (1979) found that a tendency in early life to inhibit achievement motives and related forms of self-expression was a reliable predictor of high blood pressure two decades later.

In America, suppression of anger and other strong emotional reactions is strongly endorsed at a sociocultural level, despite apparent negative physiological consequences of such suppression. Woolfolk and Richardson (1978) assert that in fact there are few legally or socially sanctioned channels for the expression of anger. As a result, anger tends to be handled through either suppression or repression, or through the vicarious satisfaction derived from watching endless TV and movie violence and from spectatorship in many sporting events.

One unfortunate side effect of diverting strong emotional responses is a slight but perceptible increase in systolic blood pressure, known as the step-trend effect. These increments tend to be cumulative, and with time there is an increase in average blood pressure. Each time a person's blood pressure rises, a division of the ANS known as the **parasympathetic nervous system** (PNS) operates to bring it back to normal. However, if the increases occur too often, the PNS rebound effect is weakened. The result is a gradual structural accommodation to small increases in blood pressure. There are negative consequences to this accommodation process, however. Arteries, for example, can tolerate some increase in blood pressure but with an eventual loss in flexibility. This loss in turn increases the likelihood that any inherent arterial weakness may increase vulnerability to such common vascular traumas as stroke (Kasl and Cooper, 1987).

Intervention techniques. The large number of factors known to contribute to essential hypertension make it reasonable to base treatment on the multimodal principle. From a physical standpoint, diet and weight control are important first steps, and smoking is strongly discouraged. The intake of sodium, sugar, caffeine, saturated fats, potassium, and cadmium must be carefully monitored. The subjective contributions to essential hypertension are best handled via psychotherapy aimed at controlling psychological stressors. Stress associated with marriage, work, or other aspects of life can frequently be identified and alleviated through marital or individual therapy (Bagarozzi et al., 1982). Of course there are also stress factors endemic to society, such as unemployment and poverty, that do not lend themselves well to psychological intervention. Nonetheless, being able to talk about such problems can promote realistic coping skills.

Beyond supportive and traditional psychotherapies, more behaviorally oriented techniques can be very helpful in stress management. For example, for hypertension resulting from conditioned anxiety or anger responses, systematic desensitization may be helpful (Emmelkamp, 1982). Using a procedure analogous to constructing hierarchies of anxiety-arousing stimuli (see Chapter 4), the therapist and patient devise a sequence of images that elicit increasing levels of tension. The patient is then taught relaxation responses designed to counteract elevations in blood pressure and other signs of increasing stress.

Recently, Friedman and Rosenman (1986) reported on the successful treatment using behavioral techniques of army officers with Type A personalities who were susceptible to physical illness. Encouraging them to relax and engage in casual conversation after meals, moderate their work schedules, and maintain good health habits markedly reduced physical illnesses. An equally positive side effect was that many of the officers reevaluated their conception of leadership, and decided that a more relaxed, less authoritarian style created less stress for their men and, ultimately, for themselves.

Assertiveness training can be helpful for people whose inhibitions prevent them from appropriately expressing themselves. For hypertensive patients whose condition may reflect failure to control anger and other strong emotions, anger management is but one of several psychological techniques that can have beneficial effects on essential hypertension. Comparable programs aimed at either reducing or (more desirably) preventing hypertension have been found to lower overall disease and death rates (Lipowski, 1975).

Progressive relaxation and autogenic training are two effective relaxation procedures helpful in managing stress. Progressive relaxation involves learning to contract and relax in sequence the various muscle sets to alleviate feelings of tension. **Autogenic training** is a form of self-hypnosis accomplished through breathing and meditative activity (Jacobson, 1970). The effectiveness of these two techniques can often be enhanced when the client is trained to visualize particular images that connote active coping (Achterberg and Lawlis, 1980). Meditative techniques comprise an effective, long-range procedure for controlling hypertension (Shapiro and Giber, 1978; Carrington, 1984).

Considerable research has been carried out comparing the effectiveness of various relaxation and meditative techniques in reducing stress and tension. A recent study by Lehrer et al. (1983) is representative of work in this area. Lehrer et al. worked with subjects experiencing high levels of stress who were assigned to a relaxation, a meditation, or a no-treatment control group. Treatment consisted of five training sessions conducted in a group format of either progressive relaxation or meditation training. Following the training, subjects were asked to watch a movie with several graphically stressful scenes while muscle tension levels in the forearm and the forehead were monitored. Subjects were also given a series of paper-and-pencil tests to assess subjective levels of stress. Lehrer et al. reported that progressive relaxation resulted in consistently lower levels of muscle tension and a greater reduction in subjective symptoms than did either meditation training or no treatment. In general, training in either relaxation or meditation techniques was found to promote greater relaxation than did the no-treatment control condition.

Biofeedback (see Chapter 4) is yet another effective technique for dealing with stress, particularly when used in conjunction with meditation or general relaxation techniques (Frumkin et al., 1978). Biofeedback is generally considered to be most useful when stress is related to physiological factors that are directly accessible, such as headaches and muscle tension (Cox et al., 1975; Fuller, 1978; Schwartz, 1987).

In summary, all of these techniques have been shown to be effective in helping control essential hypertension. Unfortunately, many people discon-

Many therapists advocate yoga as a relaxing way of dealing with stress. (Charles Gatewood/Magnum)

tinue stress management programs once they have achieved the initial desired effect. Without consistent follow-through, the gains are easily lost (Forey et al., 1979). As is true with many disorders discussed in this book, a combination of techniques (a multimodal approach), consistently adhered to, will yield the most consistent results in effective control of hypertension.

Headaches

Headaches are another common response to stress. They generally meet the DSM criteria for PFAPC because the overwhelming majority of headaches are associated with psychological factors that clearly exacerbate the physical symptoms (Gaarder and Montgomery, 1981). Many victims of headaches report their onset during adolescence, and develop a pattern of chronic recurrence during times of stress. Early speculation linked headaches to personality patterns. Migraine victims, for example, were believed to be perfectionistic people with an excessive need for control. Subsequent work has failed to confirm this finding, though there is some indication that psychological adjustment problems (not personality traits) may be associated with tension headaches (Andrasik, 1982).

There are two common types of headaches for which psychological interventions are appropriate: muscle contraction and vascular headaches. A third, far less common type is due to inflammation of brain tissue or brain tumors and requires neurologic intervention.

Muscle contraction headaches are the most common type of stress-related headache. Frequently referred to as tension headaches, they result from sustained muscular contractions in the skeletal muscles of the shoulders, back of the neck, and head. Sensations include feelings of tightening on both sides of the head and neck.

Tension headaches tend to produce chronic, moderate discomfort that is often fairly constant. They develop when stressors cause muscles in the head and neck to contract and tighten. The resulting tension causes constriction in neighboring blood vessels, and the combination results in pain.

Tension headaches respond favorably to biofeedback training in which specific muscles in the neck can be isolated and relaxed (Hendrix and Meyer, 1976; Fuller, 1978). As with other forms of headaches, analgesic medication and muscle relaxing drugs may be used as well, particularly to help the patient obtain immediate relief.

Vascular headaches, the other major type of stress-related headache, are caused by excessive dilation of the cerebral arteries which in turn elevates localized intracranial pressure and causes uncomfortable feelings of intense pressure in a specific area, usually on one side of the head. **Migraine headaches** may last anywhere from a few hours to days at a time, during which some victims experience bearable discomfort while others are immobilized by pain. Migraines are the most common type of vascular headache, and may affect as many as 12 million people. Women are far more prone (by a 2:1 margin) to migraines than men.

Vascular headaches appear to be initiated when stress *constricts* blood vessels in the brain. Following cessation of the stressor, the cerebral arteries *dilate,* causing an overflow of blood to the brain at a rate in excess of what can comfortably be tolerated. The result is severe pain often accompanied by other physical disturbances, including dizziness, fainting, nausea, and vomiting.

In addition, some victims report that migraine attacks are preceded by auras or other perceptual alterations that suggest temporarily impaired neurologic functioning. In classic migraines, severe constriction of blood vessels can cause localized numbness, as well as affect vision, speech, and coordination. In its most common manifestation, however, a migraine headache is usually not accompanied by neurologic signs.

Psychological precursors of migraines have been identified as well: Adams et al. (1980) found that many migraine headaches stem from unpleasant thoughts and emotions associated with the anticipation of stressful events, including headaches themselves.

Migraines may be slow to respond to treatment. This is in part due to problems trying to control cerebral artery dilation. The problem is often compounded because the associated pain causes involuntary muscle tension leading to muscle contraction headaches (discussed above). Analgesics may help relieve the symptoms by reducing pain and promoting muscle relaxation.

Types of Major Headaches

Category of Major Headache	Triggering Stimuli	Symptoms	Causes	Common Remedies
Migraine	Fatigue; alcohol; bright or flashing lights; changes in altitude or weather; hormonal changes, particularly decreases in estrogen; use of birth control pills; excessive hunger, smoking, or stress; certain foods, such as aged cheese, smoked meats, vinegars, and caffeine	Flashing lights, blind spots, strange smells, or numbness in arm or leg can precede a classic migraine. Most migraines skip this warning. All produce mild to severe, often one-sided, throbbing pain; nausea and vomiting; sensitivity to sound and light; and dizziness. Roughly 70 percent of migraine sufferers are women.	Fluctuation of neurotransmitters such as serotonin and norepinephrine may affect the perception of head pain. Another possibility is that the constriction and subsequent swelling of blood vessels in the head impinges on nearby nerve endings.	Relaxation training and resting in a dark room; analgesics, such as aspirin, acetaminophen, or ibuprofen; ergot compounds; isometheptene mucate. *Preventive:* Relaxation training; biofeedback; beta blockers; serotonin inhibitors; antidepressants; calcium channel blockers
Muscle Contraction	Tension; stress; depression; holding the head or neck in certain postures (such as slouching in bed or looking down to read) for hours. Sometimes accompanied by aching shoulders and neck.	Consistent, dull ache frequently described as a band of pain encircling the head, or the feeling of having it squeezed in a large vise. Short muscle spasms may constrict local blood vessels, releasing pain-sensing substances.	Fluctuations in brain neurotransmitters or sustained contractions of head and neck muscles.	Muscle relaxants; analgesics; massage *Preventive:* Relaxation training; biofeedback; antidepressants

	Triggers	Symptoms	Cause	Treatment
Cluster	Seasonal and daily biological rhythms; cold wind or hot air blowing on the face; food containing nitrites and other compounds that dilate blood vessels; alcohol; heavy smoking; dream-filled sleep	Extreme pain, always centered on or near one eye. The eye turns red and tears profusely, the lid droops, and the pupil contracts. The pain is often described as an ice pick being driven through the head—so intense that sufferers rock compulsively. Attacks can occur daily for weeks or months, always at the same times, then disappear for months or years. Eighty-five percent of cluster sufferers are men.	Thought to be brought on by a disturbance in the central nervous system, possibly in a part of the brain called the hypothalamus, that can change levels of serotonin and other neurotransmitters. During headaches, arteries behind one eye are dilated and other blood vessels may spasm.	Pure oxygen; Ergot compounds *Preventive:* Lithium; steroids; beta blockers
Organic	Diseases, such as inflammation of arteries in the temples, herpes zoster, sinus infection, a brain tumor, or aneurysm	Abrupt severe head pain in someone previously free of headaches. Can be accompanied by nausea, double vision, or a rigid neck. Seizures or changes in personality, speech, gait, and coordination may indicate a tumor.	The triggering disorder.	Treatment of the triggering disorder
Posttraumatic	Tissue loss, damage, or scarring from injury or surgery	Similar to muscle contraction or migraine headache. Symptoms are frequent dizziness, insomnia, anxiety, or depression.	Damage to the muscles, blood vessels, or nerves of the scalp, or injury to the neck, vertebrae, spinal cord, or brain.	Same as muscle contraction or migraine headache

Source: Adapted from West, S. (1987) The Hell in My Head. *Hippocrates* 1:32–45.

Muscle-relaxant drugs and psychologically based relaxation procedures can be helpful as well. Skin temperature feedback, in particular, has proven helpful, an effect initially described in 1972 by Sargent et al. In skin temperature feedback, the subject is instructed to employ visual imagery in which parts of the body (usually the hands) are visualized as becoming progressively warmer. Warming is accomplished by increased blood flow to the area, redistributing the oversupply in the brain that is causing uncomfortable pressure.

Preventive measures for migraines are possible as well because certain chemicals are known to cause headaches by increasing cerebral artery dilation. These include sodium nitrate, present in hot dogs and other preserved meat; MSG, a flavor-enhancing agent used in Oriental foods; and tyramine, a chemical substance found in a variety of sources including wine and aged cheeses. Tyramine is chemically similar to epinephrine, and acts to elevate blood pressure.

Other Stress Disorders

A variety of disorders of the skin, respiratory tract, and gastrointestinal system are believed to result from chronic stress. Hives, rashes, and other forms of dermatitis are clearly associated with psychological stressors such as chronic worrying or conflict. Potential respiratory complications include such conditions as asthma, shortness of breath, and bronchial constriction (Kasl and Cooper, 1987).

Ulcers (lesions in the lining of the stomach or digestive tract) may be due to chronic stress, although hereditary predisposition and diet are important factors as well. For example, Pane (1977) demonstrated that unavoidable conflict and stress create a vulnerability to ulcers. Ulcers are not as common among high-level executives as they are in middle-management personnel because high-level executives can delegate much of the chronically stressful, day-to-day decision making to their subordinates, who can neither avoid nor pass on stress. Another study (Guthrie and Tanco, 1980) found a very high rate of ulcers in Northwest coastal American Indians who had major decision-making responsibilities and also had to live with chronic poverty and eroding tribal values.

Stress disorders, whether hypertension or hives, all share a common element. In every case, a documented physical disorder is accompanied by stress factors that may initially cause and later exacerbate the condition. These stress disorders are different from the second type of disorder discussed in this chapter: the somatoform disorders.

SOMATOFORM DISORDERS

Persons with somatoform disorders, like those with stress disorders, complain of physical problems. However, there is no evidence of a physical basis for their condition. It is presumed, therefore, that in cases of somatoform disorders there is a psychologically compelling basis to the condition. Yet people with somatoform disorders believe that their symptoms indicate a real physical disorder. In sum, *somatoform disorders* have no physical basis or course, but consist of physical symptoms that appear to mimic actual physical disorders in response to psychological conflicts. The symptoms appear involuntarily, which serves to differentiate them from the factitious disorders and malingering, discussed elsewhere. DSM acknowledges four categories of somatoform disorders: somatization disorder, conversion disorder, psychogenic pain disorder, and hypochondriasis.

Somatization Disorder

Somatization disorder is a somatoform disorder characterized by chronic complaints about numerous and varied physical symptoms for which the individual consults many physicians, sometimes concurrently (Swartz et al., 1987). The complaints are frequently vague, though accompanied by dramatic descriptions of symptoms. In addition, the patient is likely to be more preoccupied with specific symptoms than with the underlying disorder they may represent. To some degree, cultural values may encourage phrasing essentially psychological conflicts in physical terms. The Chinese, for example, view psychological disorders as signs of weakness, and somatization disorder is correspondingly more common (Sanua, 1980).

Somatization disorders typically begin in adolescence and are more common in women than men. Depressive symptoms are a common accompaniment of the disorder, in part because of the negative response that persons with somatization disorders tend to elicit from health care specialists. The tendency is to view this disorder as a sign of malingering, and to avoid spending much time with the patient getting to the root of the matter. Since an implicit goal of persons with somatization disorders is to attain support and caretaking from others, rebuffs are never treated lightly. Depression and drug abuse, or both, may evolve as a means of coping with rejection, and eventually may become the paramount symptoms. These new difficulties in turn tend to breed perceptions of other symptoms that encourage additional consultations for relief that never seems to occur.

In somatoform disorders it is presumed that the transformation of psychological conflicts into physical complaints at least aids in the suppression of anxiety that might otherwise be overwhelming. Because of this, hypnosis can be quite effective in unearthing conflicts and anxiety-provoking material that underly the physical complaints. The major obstacle to this form of treatment is the low rate of compliance. Patients with somatoform disorders tend to deny a need for psychological intervention, and in fact may even feel insulted by the mere suggestion of it.

Eliciting cooperation and dealing with the patient's anxieties are thus paramount to successful therapy. One reasonable way of proceeding is to focus on effective stress- and pain-management techniques without being overly concerned whether or not the discomfort is "real" (that is, medically documented). This can help pave the way for more insight-oriented discussions once the therapist has gained the patient's trust and the patient has become less defensive (Reid, 1984).

Conversion Disorder

Conversion disorder, formerly called hysteria, is a somatoform disorder characterized by loss or impairment of a motor or sensory function that does not correspond to any known pattern of underlying neurologic impairment. Commonly reported symptoms include partial or total blindness, deafness, paralysis, or loss of sensation. Some patients present with more bizarre symptoms, such as an inability to speak above a whisper or an apparent inability to swallow. As with the other somatoform disorders, the symptoms are involuntary and real to the patient but lack a clear physical or medical basis, and are presumed due to psychological conflicts.

For example, a 23-year-old woman presented with reports that the fingers on one hand were entirely numb. The numbness began at the middle joint of each finger and extended to the tip. A medical examination ruled out circulatory and neurologic problems. The patient had recently lost her job as an office worker, and had undergone the traumatic breakup of a relationship as well. The symptomatic numbness was abruptly reported for the first time three weeks later, preventing her from seeking new employment. She saw no connection between the symptoms and stress factors, and merely stated she wished to have the condition corrected so that she could resume job hunting.

Conversion disorder develops primarily in adolescence or early adulthood, and is primarily diagnosed in women. However, it is also found to a significant degree among men in combat.

Three basic symptoms are present in most cases of conversion disorder. The first concerns rapid onset of symptoms, often in the immediate aftermath of a clear psychological stressor. Second, the symptoms are selective, and often fail to correspond fully to medically based disorders. For example, patients who appear comatose following an apparent seizure will deflect their hand if it is held a few inches over their head and dropped. Seizures reflecting a conversion disorder seldom occur when the patient is alone.

Testing a patient with hysterical blindness will typically reveal discrimination performance that is *worse* than that of someone who is truly blind. For example, if asked to determine whether a light is on or off over a series of trials, a blind individual's random responses will be correct 50% of the time, whereas a person with conversion-based blindness is likely to err significantly more by deliberately choosing wrong answers.

The third key feature of conversion disorder is *la belle indifférence,* estimated to be present in about one third of all cases. Literally meaning "beautiful indifference," the term refers to the patient's tendency to be relatively unconcerned about their symptoms, even when they are as serious as paralysis. Unlike malingerers, who tend to be somewhat guarded in talking about their symptoms, patients with conversion disorder appear quite willing to talk about theirs. Their seeming indifference either to the consequences of their condition or to the possibility of having their symptoms exposed as psychologically based is characteristic of *'la belle indifference.'*

The reason for their apparent lack of worry has to do with the rewards associated with their symptoms. Primary gain results from the fact that the conversion symptoms help block awareness of psychological conflicts that would otherwise provoke intense anxiety. Secondary gain is apparent in the extent to which physical symptoms tend to elicit sympathy and caretaking reactions from others.

Although in many cases the striking nature of the physical symptoms clearly suggests conversion disorder, the condition can be difficult to diagnose accurately, especially in the rare instances when symptoms other than sensorimotor are present. In these cases, it is possible to confuse conversion disorder with PFAPC. Many conversion disorders are likely to go undetected because, although physical examination fails to reveal organic disease, the tendency of many physicians is to nonetheless attribute the patient's distress to medical causes.

On the other hand, it is important to note that what appear at the outset to be conversion symptoms in some cases are the beginnings of organic disease not yet clearly diagnosable (Keefe and Gil, 1987).

Treatment of conversion disorder is best conceived in terms of altering the patterns of primary and secondary gain discussed earlier. As originally described by Freud, conversion symptoms represent defenses against specific impulses, often having to do with sexuality or aggression. The symptom basically holds the impulse in check, as when paralysis of the hands might be viewed as a means of keeping the patient from strangling someone who had enraged him. From this vantage point, therapy would be aimed at helping uncover the source of the underlying impulses and gaining insight into more adaptive ways of dealing with them.

A behavioral perspective on the issue of primary gain would emphasize learning more adaptive coping responses without necessarily gaining insight into the reason for the blockage in the first place.

Because there is a tendency for clients with conversion disorder to be somewhat suggestible, it is sometimes useful to view their symptoms as the result of self-induced hypnosis, which can sometimes be undone via another hypnotic induction (Spiegel and Spiegel, 1978).

As far as dealing with secondary factors, the problem is one of lessening the need for sympathy while at the same time avoiding the implication that the patient's problems are purely psychological. For example, in one case apparent paralysis of a woman's lower right leg was clearly linked by the therapist to a need to elicit caretaking from her husband. Rather than confront the couple with a purely psychological explanation of the wife's problems, the therapist arranged for a rather grueling program of physical therapy that required the husband's collaboration. Within a few weeks the wife was walking again, having had a "grace period" during which the symptom disappeared, allegedly due to the physical therapy. During this same time the husband gradually began to pay more attention to her capabilities and stopped reinforcing her invalid behavior.

Psychogenic Pain Disorder

Psychogenic pain disorder is a somatoform disorder in which severe, localized pain is persistently present. The pain appears to have no physiological basis, or else may reflect the persistence of discomfort after signs of a physiological problem have diminished. People with psychogenic pain disorder tend to seek frequent medical consultations that tend not to corroborate their subjective reports of pain. Despite this, their reports of discomfort are often so convincing that they succeed in obtaining medicine and even surgery in hope of obtaining relief. As a result, they often end up with real physical impairments due to the often drastic treatment undertaken to alleviate their original complaint. The typical age of onset of psychogenic pain is most frequently in adolescence or later, and the disorder is more frequently diagnosed in women than men (Keefe and Gil, 1987).

Psychogenic pain is invariably associated with psychological factors, as are all the somatoform disorders. Typically, one particular complaint predominates, as in the case of patients with chronic lower back pain. This distinguishes patients with psychogenic pain disorder from those with somatization disorder, whose extensive litany of complaints has been facetiously labeled an "organ recital."

Case Example: A 45-year-old woman is seen with a complaint of chronic lower back pain that has troubled her for the preceding 10 years, since the birth of her last child. No organic basis for her complaint can be identified, though she is convinced that she suffered permanent injury at the time of the child's birth. She lives with her husband and child in a small, rural town after having grown up and worked in a large metropolitan area. Having little to do with her time and unable to find work, she broods about her physical health and takes frequent trips to neighboring towns seeking medical consultations. Finally referred for a psychological consultation, it is revealed that she is bored with her life, feels trapped in the small town, and has a deeply troubled marriage. The pain she experiences helps to keep her from thinking about the other problems too much. Moreover, she appears hopeful of eventually finding a cure for the pain, but holds little optimism that her social situation will improve significantly.

Psychogenic pain defies medical diagnosis. Sometimes it represents lingering discomfort from a prior illness, but may also appear without any apparent prior history. The distinction between psychogenic and organic pain can be difficult to make, though there have been some promising developments. Characteristic patterns of electrical brain wave activity detected with electroencephalograms (EEGs) may be used to differentiate the two. Chemical tests have been devised as well, based on evidence that certain substances in blood plasma are sensitive to general, organic disease. But with both of these measures, reliability is too low for a definitive determination of whether pain is psychogenically or organically based (Keefe and Gil, 1987).

The lack of a clear physical basis for psychogenic pain differentiates it from conditions such as headaches, which involve such organic changes as muscle tension and dilation of blood vessels. Psychogenic pain disorder can be discriminated from conversion disorder as well. Although in both cases the physical symptoms do not have a clear medical basis, psychogenic pain disorder is less likely to (1) have some symbolic connotations regarding the underlying psychological conflicts, (2) be accompanied by *la belle indifference,* (3) involve significant functional impairment, and (4) be chronic and unremitting.

Treatment of psychogenic pain disorder requires considerable clinical sensitivity. As with any somatoform disorder, issues of primary and secondary gain must be considered and will often be the focus of intervention. Quite often, physical pain and discomfort hides an unwillingness to face up to psychological conflicts. Part of the treatment, then, is to help the patient own up to responsibilities that are avoided because of physical distress. Teaching new coping skills can help improve feelings of confidence and lessen the tendency to adopt a patient role (Holzman and Turk, 1986). Family therapy techniques focusing on effective conflict resolution may reduce the threat posed by the prospect of a confrontation with spouse or child that has been avoided for too long. By focusing on these issues, attention is gradually drawn away from physical distress and refocused on issues that are psychologically troubling. Along these lines, it is interesting to note just how many patients with psychogenic pain visit a psychologist convinced they will be told that the pain is "all in their head." In reality, an effective technique is to reassure these patients that you take their word about the pain and do not wish to dispute its existence with them. Instead, it is proposed to the client that therapy will focus on surrounding factors (such as family relationships and work patterns) that may serve to intensify the physical discomfort. In this way, patients are allowed to "keep" their symptoms while at the same time making significant strides in the management of psychosocial conflicts.

Hypochondriasis

Hypochondriasis is a somatoform disorder characterized by an erroneous certainty that one is ill. Consequently, people with hypochondriasis exaggerate or otherwise distort physical sensations, and they take relatively unimportant changes in their physical state as indications of serious illness, maintaining such a belief in the face of expert medical opinion that there is no disease to worry about. Hypochondriacal individuals are highly vigilant, monitoring internal sensations and changes for indications of disease. Since in fact changes in physical status are constantly taking place in healthy people, these individuals can find plenty to worry about.

The essential feature of *hypochondriasis* is not a fear of being sick, but rather the certainty that one is ill. It is reasonably common beginning in adolescence and continues to be found well into advanced age, but is seen most frequently in people between the ages of thirty and fifty, with approximately equal proportions of men and women being affected (Meister, 1980). Meister believes there are also a substantial number of "closet" or quasi-hypochondriacs who, though not making the rounds of local physicians' offices, are constantly involved in health fads and who endlessly ventilate their health-related concerns to friends and family members.

Hypochondriasis resembles the other somatoform disorders in that it involves physical complaints without documented cause. Moreover, symptoms are involuntary. Hypochondriasis can readily be distinguished from the other somatoform disorders, however. Whereas persons with somatization disorder focus their attention primarily on *symptoms,* those with hypochondriacal tendencies worry about the underlying *disease.* Sincere in their complaints and anxieties, persons with hypochondriasis are not presumed to be malingering, as is sometimes suspected in cases of somatization disorder and psychogenic pain disorder. Their obvious concern with symptoms clearly differentiates this condition from *la belle indifference* so prominent in conversion disorder.

Moreover, persons with hypochondriasis are often scientific in their approach to symptoms. Some read medical journals and books to gain a clearer understanding of what their symptoms may signify, using this information to reinforce their belief that they are seriously ill.

Four predisposing factors have been observed in the development of hypochondriasis, and may be seen as creating a vulnerability for the disorder. The first is a background of growing up in an *atmosphere of illness* (Meister, 1980). Early exposure to invalidism or illness in the family can create such an atmosphere. Other predisposing events include such things as the death of a close family member at an impressionable time, or strong identification with someone who has marked hypochondriacal tendencies. Second is strongly *dependent relationships* with a parent or family member who cannot regularly express love or caring effectively, yet may do so when people are sick.

Third is *channeling* of psychological conflicts and needs for reassurance into hypochondriacal states. A person who cannot articulate, confront, and accept the realization of mortality, for example, may become unduly preoccupied with health-related issues, as if by doing so it might be possible to "beat the odds" of dying. In these circumstances, it is not surprising that reassurance from doctors or others has little effect, since the issue of fundamental concern—mortality—is not being addressed.

Fourth is the *reinforcement* of patterns that aid in avoiding the stresses and demands of daily life. Sometimes it is easier to become absorbed in matters of physical health than to confront major decisions. One such client was certain he would soon die from undiagnosed heart disease or cancer. In reality, he had never fully faced certain career choices, nor had he made a clear commitment in a longstanding relationship. By acting (really *not* acting) on the assumption that he was going to die soon, he rendered these issues irrelevant. Once he was able to confront them realistically with the help of a therapist, his intense feelings of physical vulnerability gradually subsided.

For hypochondriacs, taking their physical concerns seriously is an important first step in shifting their focus from the physical into the psychological realm. It is important for physicians to steer such individuals toward therapy in a sensitive manner, rather than treating them as chronic complainers or avoiding them. Once the psychotherapeutic process has been initiated, it involves empathizing with the concerns expressed by the client and with the anguish they cause, but not participating in the delusion of illness (Barrett, 1980). Sometimes, however, taking just the opposite tack may work, as when the therapist abruptly agrees with the hypochondriac's suspicions of imminent disease and death. The shock from this unexpected agreement often elicits the underlying psychological issues.

Family therapy can provide a means of getting others to stop inadvertently reinforcing the disorder (Bagarozzi et al., 1982). It also helps the hypochondriac to develop more honest and authentic ways of asking for needed affection and support.

ADJUSTMENT DISORDERS

The concept of healthy adjustment includes the ability to respond to a changing environment. When the environment changes radically or unexpectedly, as in the aftermath of a catastrophe like a tornado, an otherwise healthy person may evidence emotional disruption and occasionally reexperience the trauma through disturbing memories or nightmares (Perry and Lindell, 1987). If the changed behavior patterns persist beyond the situational disruption, in DSM-III terms they constitute a posttraumatic stress disorder (see Chapter 6). If the stressor is more within the normal range, such as divorce, or loss of a job, and if there is little reliving of the experience, the condition is diagnosed as an **adjustment disorder.** Usually the diagnosis is qualified by a phrase denoting the emotional direction of the response, such as "with depressed mood," "with mixed emotional features," "with disturbance of conduct." An adjustment disorder is not the exaggeration of a previous clear emotional disability, and it occurs in response to a clearly identifiable stressful event.

Stressors which give rise to adjustment disorders vary widely. They may range from psychosocial stressors, such as marital or family conflict, to conditions more widespread in their impact, such as civilian disasters.

Adjustment disorders are commonly diagnosed in people making transitions from one stage of life to another. Beginning school, finishing college, leaving home, starting a career, and retiring are all events which demand flexibility and psychological adaptation. All constitute changes in a person's accustomed lifestyle, and so in light of our previous discussion, are by definition stressful.

Overall, adjustment disorders are among the least severe of all major types of psychological disturbances. They are associated with a relatively favorable prognosis regarding such things as the need for hospitalization, the ability to resume work, and overall chronicity (Cooney and Gunderson, 1978).

Two rather dramatic instances of conditions which may prompt adjustment disorders are combat stress and the civilian disaster syndromes. Each involves the development of predictable symptoms in response to a clear form of psychosocial stress.

Combat Stress

Much of the early literature on adjustment disorders in adults dealt with disturbances caused by wartime stress and change. **Combat stress,** the combination of fatigue, uncertainty, and potential danger of combat, produced psychological demoralization, avoidant responses, anxiety, and long-term pathology (Belenky, 1987).

It is estimated that about 10 percent of those who fought in World War II were disabled by combat stress. The rate was about 7 percent in the early phases of the Korean War, dropping to less than 4 percent at the end of that conflict. In the Vietnam War, the rate was first thought to be only slightly more than 1 percent (Bourne, 1979), but it is now known to be higher.

A major reason for the decline in rates of combat exhaustion was the post-World War II practice of transferring personnel out of direct combat after about twelve months. Soldiers in Vietnam also gained a sense of respite because combat engagements tended to be sporadic, unlike the constant contact that characterized earlier wars (Figley, 1978, 1981). Better techniques of screening potentially vulnerable soldiers also helped lower the rates.

Treatment of Combat Stress

In World War II, soldiers who showed moderate to severe distress were usually taken out of the combat zone and shipped home. It was soon observed that the farther and longer they were away from combat, the more difficult it was for them to return. These and related observations led to the formulation of three basic principles of intervention: immediacy, proximity, and expectancy. These principles were applied with increasing effectiveness during the Korean and Vietnam conflicts.

1. *Immediacy* involves: (a) early detection, (b) prompt treatment, and (c) a speedy return to the conflict area. Afflicted soldiers are quickly taken to a nearby medical outpost, given a chance to discuss their fears, reassured, medicated to ensure a sound and restful sleep, and then returned to the combat area.

2. *Proximity* involves attempting intervention at a nearby outpost. If this is not effective, soldiers are given more extensive treatment at a division camp and usually returned to combat in a few days.

3. *Expectancy* that the soldier will soon return to combat is implied in the two previous principles.

Although the application of these intervention principles significantly lowers the rate of combat casualties and decreases long-term negative effects, exposure to combat (like chronically stressful civilian disasters) does take a long-term toll. Studies by the Veterans Administration have found that despite the effectiveness of intervention principles, significant problems plague combat veterans over time. Their rate of psychological symptoms is estimated to be much higher than that of noncombat veterans (Penk et al., 1981). Combat survivors also die earlier and show higher rates of physical disorder (Figley, 1978; Penk et al., 1981) than their noncombat counterparts.

Civilian Disaster Syndrome

People's reactions to disasters in civilian life (the aftermath of tornadoes and hurricanes, plane crashes, fires, and the like) have many parallels to the better-documented traumatic reactions in wartime (Raphael, 1986). The principles of immediacy, proximity, and expectancy are also effective in treating the **civilian disaster syndrome.** However, the unexpected nature of civilian disasters causes a different sequence of reactions than in combat. The typical civilian post-traumatic syndrome develops through the following stages:

1. *Shock period.* Victims are disoriented, dazed, and appear helpless. Initially victims may be emotionally flat, but they soon become highly suggestible to cues and influences from others. An immediate intervention to provide a supportive structure is very important.

2. *Denial period.* After the shock has worn off, many victims shift into a denial phase, even to the development of a spirit of quasi-celebration. For example, victims of a devastating tornado in 1974 in Louisville, Kentucky, banded together in a spirit of friendly solidarity that occasionally spilled over into partylike celebrations. In this way they effectively denied the devastation for a time.

3. *Reality phase.* When individuals eventually face the actual impact of the disaster, reality intrudes and delayed depression, anxiety, and phobic responses occur. For many years before the Louisville tornado, people had universally responded to radio and television reports of a possible tornado with bored indifference, joking that they didn't know the difference "between a watch, a warning, or a whatever." For many years afterward, those who had experienced the tornado knew exactly what the terms signified, and even minimal cues could send them scurrying into the southwest corner of their basements. Local therapists also re-

ported a heightened incidence of analogous psychopathology, such as thunderstorm phobias.

4. *Recovery period.* Finally the post-traumatic responses surface and must be dealt with. Even people not seriously affected have a continuing need to talk over the events. For several years after the tornado, Louisville taverns gave tornado parties on the anniversary date, and local newspapers and television reran stories and pictures of the disaster. Similar disasters, such as the eruption of the Mount St. Helen's volcano, have prompted similar responses in their aftermath.

Like combat veterans, most victims of civilian disaster experience no lasting disorders. The small minority who do are generally individuals (1) whose conditioned fears were not dealt with quickly or effectively or (2) who were in a relatively marginal state of adjustment at the time the major stress event occurred. Hence, their fears had time to generalize, crystallize, and amplify. Such events, along with a variety of other causes, can lead to the disorders discussed in the following chapters (Perry and Lindell, 1987).

CHAPTER REVIEW

1. Stress is a state of both mental and physical tension resulting from factors that overwhelm one's normal coping mechanisms.

2. Psychosomatic disorders are those in which physical conditions are made worse or intensified as a result of psychological stressors. Common psychosomatic disorders include asthma, ulcers, hypertension, and headaches.

3. The term "Psychological Factors Affecting Physical Condition" is used in the DSM system in place of "psychosomatic disorders," but the two terms have similar connotations.

4. The general adaptation syndrome refers to the body's natural system for coping with stress. The term was coined by Hans Selye, whose pioneering work on stress has added considerably to our knowledge of how stress affects health.

5. Recent work on the impact of stressful life events has led to the development of questionnaires and other assessment tools to gauge an individual's level of stress.

6. The "organ-weakness" theory of stress suggests that the body's most vulnerable organ system is the one most likely to break down under stress.

7. Personality theories of stress postulate that certain traits and early experiences make people vulnerable to certain kinds of stressors.

8. Essential hypertension is one of the most common stress-related disorders for which people seek treatment.

9. Stress-related headaches are of two types: muscle contraction headaches, and vascular headaches. A variant of vascular headaches, migraine headaches, is especially painful and debilitating.

10. Somatoform disorders are characterized by physical complaints in the absence of clear organic symptoms.

11. The DSM system differentiates four types of somatoform disorders: somatization disorder, conversion disorder, psychogenic pain disorder, and hypochondriasis.

12. Adjustment disorders reflect excessive psychological distress in response to stressful events encountered in everyday life.

TERMS TO REMEMBER

stress
psychosomatic disorder
general adaptation syndrome
Type A/B personality
essential hypertension
systolic/diastolic pressures
parasympathetic nervous system

autogenic training
migraine headache
somatization disorder
conversion disorder
psychogenic pain disorder
hypochondriasis
adjustment disorder

FOR MORE INFORMATION

Friedman, M. and Rosenman, R. (1974) *Type A behavior and your heart.* New York: Knopf. The classic study of an increasingly important syndrome in our fast-changing society

Holtzman, A., and Turk, D. (1986) *Pain management.* Elmsford, N.Y.: Pergamon. Not only discusses methods for treating and coping with chronic pain, but also discusses theories of pain and how it can be enhanced psychologically

Last, C. and Hersen, M. (1987) *Handbook of anxiety disorders.* Elmsford, N.Y.: Pergamon. Not only is this an excellent reference for the upcoming chapter on the anxiety disorders, but it is also a fine overview of physiological and psychological theories about how stress affects us physiologically and psychologically

Matthews, K., Weiss, S., Detre, T., Dembroski, T., et al. (1986) *Stress, reactivity, and cardiovascular disease.* New York: John Wiley. A comprehensive treatment of specific risk factors for cardiovascular disease and other stress-based disorders, this book examines key factors involved in treatment and prevention as well as theory and assessment

Raphael, B. (1986) *When disaster strikes.* New York: Basic Books. An interesting and readable portrayal of how individuals and communities respond to the stress and disruption of a disaster

Selye, H. (1975) *The stress of life.* New York: McGraw-Hill. This classic remains one of the finest surveys of the causes and physiology of stress disorders

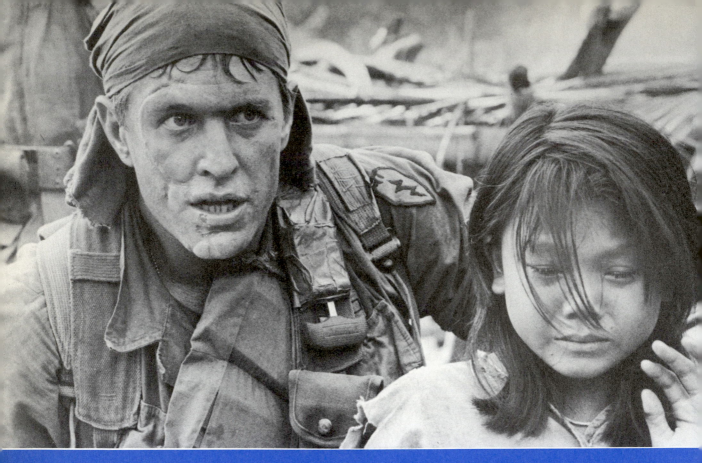

Tom Berenger in the 1986 film *Platoon*: post-traumatic stress disorder was a common aftereffect for Vietnam War veterans. (Museum of Modern Art/Film Stills Archive; © 1986 Orion Pictures)

ANXIETY

CLASSIFYING ANXIETY-RELATED DISORDERS

CHARACTERISTICS OF ANXIETY DISORDERS

ANXIETY STATES

> **Panic Disorder**
> **Generalized Anxiety Disorder**
> **Obsessive-Compulsive Disorder**

PHOBIC DISORDERS

> **Simple Phobias**
> **Agoraphobia**
> **Social Phobia**

POSTTRAUMATIC STRESS DISORDER

> **Relation to Other Disorders**

DISSOCIATIVE DISORDERS

> **Psychogenic Amnesia**
> **Psychogenic Fugue**
> **Depersonalization**
> **Multiple Personality**
> **Somnambulism**

6

The Anxiety and Dissociative Disorders

All of us have experienced anxiety at one time or another. Anxiety so intense or chronic that it constitutes an anxiety disorder affects at least 30 million people in the United States. The case of Larry introduces a classic anxiety disorder, the panic disorder, and points to some of the problems in defining, classifying, and categorizing anxiety, the first order of business in this chapter.

● The Case of Larry

Larry first began to feel vaguely uneasy in the middle of an important sales meeting. He next noticed his stomach becoming tight and "knotted" and a headache starting. Later he began to feel restless and panicky. His heart seemed as if it were racing, and he couldn't catch his breath, even though he was breathing rapidly.

Fearing that everyone was beginning to notice his upset and with a vague concern that he "might lose control of himself," Larry excused himself from the meeting. He then asked his secretary to tell everyone that he had received a message from his wife that his son had been hurt at school and that he was going home. He went home, but his physical upset continued and he became even more panicky. He called his family doctor who, on the basis of Larry's report, saw him immediately. After an examination, he reassured Larry that there was nothing physically wrong and gave him an injection and a prescription for tranquilizers.

It's interesting that everything had been going well in the sales meeting when this all occurred. Indeed, any outside observer would have judged that Larry had everything going his way, not only in his present life situation, but throughout his past history. Yet Larry had suffered four such attacks over the past two weeks, and he had also experienced tension and restlessness, along with occasional nausea on numerous occasions in the past.

His parents had always considered him to be "a nervous child," and Larry had had periods when he was afraid one or both of his parents would be killed and he would be left alone. As an adolescent there were times when he would become frantic and tense. Sometimes he would focus on a specific situation or event, for example, a feeling he had not done as well as he should have on a test. But more often than not, there was no reason or stimulus for the attack.

Periodically, Larry experienced intense fear and apprehension. He had adopted abnormal behavior to accommodate for these experiences, but this behavior also made life more difficult for him. What did Larry experience? What can psychology tell us about that experience and about Larry's reactions to it?

ANXIETY

In psychology, **anxiety** is classified as an emotional state that includes distressing feelings of fear and apprehension and an increased physiological arousal. The experience of anxiety may vary from mild to terrifying. It can occur as an attack or it can exist as an ongoing state (Wittchen and Semler, 1986; Turner et al., 1985). Anxiety differs from stress, even though the experiences of mental and physical tension are somewhat similar. Stress (see Chapter 5) results from external forces in the present. Anxiety, however, can occur without external forces and can be due to maladaptive learning in the past. Stress, by definition, is not part of a person's normal equilibrium, yet anxiety can become a regular part of a person's psychological makeup.

In general, the physiological arousal of anxiety prepares the body to face a threat. This preparation consists of stimulating the autonomic nervous system. A pounding heartbeat, "butterflies" or "knots" in the stomach, muscle tension, hyperventilation, perspiration, and cold hands and feet are typical physiological symptoms of anxiety. A person's movement is also affected: anything from slight trembling to severe shaking can take place during anxiety. In addition, an anxious person may show general restlessness, pacing, facial tics, fingernail biting, or other eccentric movements. The degree of physiological arousal varies with the degree of anxiety.

Physiologically, the amygdala, located in the limbic system, which is near the base of the brain, acts as a central relay point for anxiety (Beatty, 1987).

Anxiety can be manifested in many ways: nail biting, trembling, pacing, or a general restlessness that friends may try to soothe. (Michael Kagen/Monkmeyer Press Photo Service)

The amygdala is involved in memory and emotional processing, and virtually every neuropeptide (short chains of amino acids that alter emotions) is located in it. Rats conditioned to show startle responses no longer show the same startle responses after they receive even a small lesion to the central nucleus of the amygdala, and rats whose amygdalas are removed lose their innate fear of cats. Human beings react with feelings of anxiety when their amygdala is electronically stimulated.

The thoughts that accompany anxiety also vary with its intensity; thoughts vary from vague worries to the idea that death is imminent. Fear of suffocation and fear that falling asleep will cause death are typical preoccupations of persons experiencing anxiety. An anxious person will also experience a change in cognitive abilities, such as difficulty in making decisions or in concentrating.

The feelings of fear and apprehension may be accompanied by a sense of doom, that something terrible and unavoidable is about to happen, or a sense of dread, a great reluctance to face what is about to happen (Kendler et al., 1986). The emotional alarm that anxiety produces dominates the experience, whether the feeling adds up to full terror or merely distressful excitement.

Anxiety is not in itself abnormal. Everyone experiences anxiety in some form or degree. Anxiety about taking an examination or before skiing downhill for the first time is normal. In fact, in such cases it can be an adaptive response. Anxiety can mobilize a person to study or it can quicken the senses and reflexes of the first-time skier. Anxiety is abnormal when it is maladaptive either because of a paralyzing intensity or because of the ineffective or self-defeating behavior built up around it, as we see in Larry's inability to remain in a very important meeting. Maladaptive anxiety is the common ground of the anxiety-related disorders discussed in this chapter.

CLASSIFYING ANXIETY-RELATED DISORDERS

All anxiety-related disorders were classified originally as neurosis (Wittchen and Semler, 1986). It was Freud who adopted the term **neurosis** to mean any mental disorder caused by psychological or emotional factors. According to Freud (Freud, 1953), anxiety appears to let the ego know when a repressed desire or experience is attempting to become conscious. Neurotic behavior then develops, Freud said, either as a way to express this anxiety or as a defense against it. For Freud, anxiety was related either directly or indirectly to all psychological disorders (Rosenzweig, 1986).

Freud had taken the term neurosis (meaning a condition of the nervous system) from the work of William Cullen, a Scottish doctor who coined the term in 1769 to describe organic disorders occurring within the nervous system and causing bizarre behavior. Freud took Cullen's term, but not the biogenic meaning it had had for a hundred years. The psychogenic meaning Freud gave the term, and his classification of anxiety-related disorders as neuroses, has lasted for almost another hundred years. But in 1980 the DSM III proposed a new classification that has continued.

In DSM III, the term neurosis was discarded as too broad. Freud's use of anxiety as the common denominator of all psychological disorders has also been abandoned. Since anxiety is recognized as an experience of normal psychology and since some psychological disorders do not exhibit anxiety, the DSM has now narrowed the use of anxiety when classifying disorders. In place of Freud's classification the DSM separates the original anxiety-related disorders into three groups: anxiety disorders, somatoform disorders, and dissociative disorders.

Anxiety disorders are those in which a state of apprehension and fear is the dominant symptom. Somatoform disorders (discussed in Chapter 5) are those in which psychological conflicts appear as physical symptoms without a physical cause or basis. Dissociative disorders, discussed later in this chapter, are those in which consciousness, identity, or memory is involuntarily interrupted or altered. According to the DSM, somatoform and dissociative disorders are no longer anxiety-related disorders because they have distinctive behavior patterns that can be described without reference to anxiety.

(Contemporary psychoanalytic or Freudian perspective, however, still maintains that somatoform and dissociative disorders are related to anxiety, albeit indirectly, through involuntary mental or physical symptoms.)

Although according to the DSM the term neurosis no longer has a formal role in diagnosis, it is still used when paired with psychosis to distinguish mild from severe disorders. Disorders in which reality is greatly distorted or personality is disorganized are considered severe, or psychotic, disorders. Disorders in which self-defeating behavior, guilt, or anxiety render a person unhappy and ineffective are considered less severe, or neurotic, disorders (Wittchen and Semler, 1986).

CHARACTERISTICS OF ANXIETY DISORDERS

In general, anxiety is a powerful stimulus that tends to promote escape or avoidance behavior. **Anxiety disorders** are disorders in which anxiety is the predominant symptom and in which it is associated with maladaptive behavior. Within the category of anxiety disorders, the role of anxiety varies; this variation can be used to help distinguish the different types of anxiety disorders (see Exhibit).

Maladaptive anxiety can be either focused or free-floating, depending on the type of anxiety disorder. When specific objects or situations cause maladaptive anxiety, the anxiety is considered focused. The anxiety disorders that produce focused anxiety are the three phobias (extreme fears): simple phobias, social phobias, and agoraphobia. Simple phobias are fears of specific objects, such as snakes, or specific conditions, such as heights. Social phobias are incapacitating fears of certain social situations, such as public restrooms. Agoraphobia is fear of being out in the open and of being abandoned.

EXHIBIT

The Anxiety Disorders

A. Anxiety States *Free Floating*
    1. Panic disorder
    2. Generalized anxiety disorder
    3. Obsessive-compulsive disorder

B. Phobic Disorders *Focused*
    1. Simple phobia
    2. Social phobia
    3. Agoraphobia

C. Posttraumatic Stress Disorder

When maladaptive anxiety is free-floating or unfocused, that is, when it persists without identifiable causes, the anxiety disorder is referred to as one of the three anxiety states. With free-floating anxiety, people are unsure of the object of their intense fear and apprehension. This is clearer for the first two anxiety states, panic disorder and generalized anxiety disorder, than for the third, obsessive-compulsive disorder.

In a panic disorder, a person experiences unpredictable episodes of intense anxiety, usually accompanied by a sense of doom. In a generalized anxiety disorder, a person experiences chronic anxiety in a broad range of normally unthreatening situations. In an obsessive-compulsive disorder, a person experiences uncontrollable thoughts and actions whose presence produces considerable anxiety but whose absence produces even greater, free-floating anxiety.

When anxiety is caused by a traumatic event, the anxiety disorder is a posttraumatic stress disorder. Natural disasters, such as earthquakes or floods, or severe assaults, such as rape, can produce posttraumatic stress disorder. Anxiety is one symptom of this disorder, but symptoms such as depression, emotional numbness, a tendency to be startled, and impulsiveness are also pronounced. The anxiety of posttraumatic stress disorder differs from that of the other anxiety disorders we have described in that there is a real, external cause of the anxiety and in fact the anxiety is an understandable reaction to the trauma. The DSM acknowledges these differences but classifies posttraumatic stress disorder as the third type of anxiety disorder because anxiety is the primary symptom and because the behavior associated with the anxiety is still maladaptive.

Because of the large number of subcategories of anxiety disorders in DSM, the following discussion will be limited to the major disorders. Many of the subtypes have such an obvious meaning (for example, agoraphobia with or without panic attacks) that further discussion is unnecessary. On the other hand, we briefly discuss in this chapter some personality disorders that would otherwise be considered in Chapter 12. The reason is that two of these—the avoidant and compulsive personality disorders—share some features of phobias and obsessive-compulsive disorders, respectively. Each will be briefly discussed to illustrate the similarities and differences between disorders classified on axes I and II of the DSM (see Chapter 3).

ANXIETY STATES

As noted, the **anxiety states** are a subgroup of the anxiety disorders. They differ from the phobic disorders in that in the anxiety states the client's concern is directed toward a less specific concern. But there is still an intense experience of anxiety at some point in the evolution of the anxiety states.

Panic Disorder

Panic disorder, the diagnosis that would be appropriate for Larry, is an anxiety state characterized by random episodes of intense anxiety, usually accompanied by a sense of doom. These episodes of intense anxiety are called panic attacks. They appear suddenly and unpredictably; cold sweats, dizziness, trembling, sensations of fainting, and feelings of impending doom, such as going crazy or dying, are typical symptoms accompanying the intense anxiety. The anxiety of panic attacks is free-floating and has no apparent cause. Although panic attacks are separate incidents, they are not responses to a stimulus or to any event that is actually dangerous. Attacks usually last a few minutes, but may last for several hours. A DSM diagnosis requires the occurrence of several separate attacks as well as evidence of at least four temporary psychophysiological symptoms, such as heart pounding, feelings of fainting or trembling, or cold sweats. Between panic attacks, anxiety subsides to a relatively low level of tension. Central to panic disorders and other anxiety disorders, according to Albert Ellis (1979), is a "discomfort anxiety," the fear of being overwhelmed by the experience of anxiety.

The research of Norton et al. (1985) indicates that occasional panic attacks are not that unusual even in normal healthy adults. But, overall, approximately two percent of the population will, within their lifetime, suffer symptoms of enough severity to warrant clinical diagnosis of panic disorder. Reduction of panic attacks can be critical in some individuals; for example, men with panic attacks show higher death rates, especially from cardiovascular disorder and suicide, than men without panic attacks.

Generalized Anxiety Disorder

Generalized anxiety disorder is an anxiety state of chronic free-floating anxiety and hyperactivity of the ANS within a broad range of normally non-threatening situations. Its essence is conveyed in the following lines from William Wordsworth's poem "The Affliction of Margaret":

> *My apprehensions come in crowds,*
> *I dread the rustling of the grass.*
> *The very shadows of the clouds*
> *Have power to shake me as they pass.*

Although free-floating anxiety occurs in the generalized anxiety disorder, its essential feature is an overall physiological stress syndrome known as chronic ANS overactivity, characterized by sweating, heart palpitations, and the like. The DSM requires that the anxious mood be continuous for at least a month and that there be at least three of the following four symptoms: (1) apprehensive expectation, (2) easily elicited ANS responses, (3) hypervigilance, and (4) muscle tension. People suffering from generalized anxiety disorder are constantly watching for and expecting something terrible to happen,

The Case of Carleton

Carleton is the 33-year-old minister at a moderately fundamentalist church in a small midwestern community. Over the past three years he developed several odd behaviors that evolved into severe and disrupting obsessive-compulsive behaviors. When he left his house, he was overcome by thoughts that his wife might be dead when he returned. As he left the house, he felt compelled to check the contents of his briefcase three times, then go back three different times to check his bedroom to see if anything was amiss. On his way home from church, he felt compelled to memorize the license plates of all cars parked within a block of his house. After a time, he felt he also had to memorize the numbers of all moving cars that he saw in that block. This obviously requires unusual skills (and he, in fact, cultivated the ability to read license plates in the side and rearview mirrors as cars sped by). When he missed a plate or forgot a number, he felt compelled to return to the end of the block and start all over.

He also developed a compulsion to rub his chest in a circular motion whenever he thought of death, and ruminations about death became an increasing obsession. Because a minister has to deal consistently with the public and with issues related to death, this became a disabling symptom. Carleton knew that all these patterns were irrational but could not stop himself. Concerned about the embarrassment and distress these behaviors caused and their disruption of his life, he referred himself to a therapist.

although they cannot say what it is they are afraid of. Their heightened anxiety interferes with ordinary tasks such as eating, sleeping, or making decisions. In addition, they develop many physiological complaints, such as muscle aches, twitches, difficulty breathing, and the like. As a result, it is sometimes difficult to differentiate a panic disorder from a generalized anxiety disorder. However, Norton et al. (1985) find that panic-disorder clients show a wider variety of physical symptoms, higher anxiety levels, more expectations of disaster or catastrophe, and more disturbed childhoods.

Generalized anxiety disorder clients respond well to the minor tranquilizers, although panic disorders seem to respond better to antidepressants (Norton et al., 1985). Psychotherapy is used to help clients begin to articulate the fears and catastrophic expectations that underlie this disorder. Anxiety may be lessened through such techniques as systematic desensitization, carbon dioxide inhalation therapy, or flooding (Wolpe, 1987) or by mastery of psychologically induced relaxation responses (Emmelkamp, 1982).

Obsessive-Compulsive Disorder

Carleton, described in the accompanying box, suffers from an **obsessive-compulsive disorder**, an anxiety state characterized by either persistent uncontrollable thoughts, an irresistible impulse to perform certain actions repeatedly, or both. Obsessions are thoughts that are persistent and unwanted and that the person feels unable to stop. Compulsions are similar, but they are actual behaviors, not thoughts. Although the obsessive-compulsive disorder is listed in the DSM as an anxiety disorder, the direct experience of anxiety is not as evident as in the other anxiety disorders. People with the obsessive-compulsive disorder see their patterns of behavior and thoughts as irrational and distressing, but usually do not experience panic.

People such as Carleton know that their thoughts or behaviors are absurd, or at best irrelevant and time-consuming. They are often embarrassed about these behaviors and may take extreme measures to hide them from the scrutiny of others. At least initially, such people may experience a high level of distress. However, similar to some clients with the other anxiety disorders, obsessive-compulsive clients are often reluctant to give up their symptoms. Although the symptoms are upsetting, they allow avoidance of concerns that are potentially even more threatening. The following extract from Joseph

---

EXHIBIT

Clinical Cases of Obsessions and Compulsions

Obsessions

Case 1. Though very cordial, and mild-mannered, a 20-year-old male is consistently concerned with thoughts of killing, butchering, and eating people close to him.

Case 2. A 40-year-old female speculates and ruminates constantly about whether she was molested by her father and other males who were close to her during childhood. She cannot recall any such event, but her fears that it could have happened are causing her psychological problems.

Compulsions

Case 1. A 33-year-old female has a need to recheck at least five times the work she does as an accountant. Although she is precise, she is far too inefficient because of the time she spends rechecking. She is also disturbed if anything gets "out of its place" in her office, and easily loses her temper if things are misplaced by her secretary or the janitor.

Case 2. A 58-year-old male has a classic handwashing compulsion. He feels the need to wash his hands at least four times whenever he shakes hands with or touches someone; otherwise he feels as if he has been "contaminated." He will wash only with a special soap that he carries with him all the time.

Heller's novel *Something Happened* (1966) may slightly overstate the condition, but conveys the essential experience.

> *I do indeed know what morbid compulsion feels like. Fungus, erosion, disease. . . . A sinking heart, silence, taut limbs, a festering invasion from within . . . it starts like a fleeting whim, an airy, frivolous notion, but it doesn't go; it stays; it sticks; it enlarges in space and force like a somber, inhuman form from whatever lightless pit inside you it abides in . . . an obscure, untouchable, implacable, domineering, vile presence disguising itself treacherously in your own identity, a double agent—it is debilitating and sickening. It foreshadows no joy—and takes charge (pp. 489–490).*

Obsessive-compulsive disorders are rarer than other anxiety disorders, occurring in only one percent of the population (Turner et al., 1985). However,

Obsessive behavior ranges from clock-watching to persistent thoughts of cannibalising one's family and friends.   (Dave Schaefer/Monkmeyer Press Photo Service)

the very low reported incidence may be in part a function of the sufferers' embarrassment at talking about their affliction. Many people willing to admit to phobic anxiety are not willing to say they think and act in ways they can't control, the hallmark of the obsessive-compulsive client. Of those treated for this disorder, more than half show full-blown symptoms by age 25 (Rachman, 1980), with the age of onset generally occurring in adolescence or early adulthood.

Certain personality disorders (see Chapter 12) initially appear to be very similar to various other forms of psychopathology. The **obsessive-compulsive personality disorder**, for example, is analogous to the obsessive-compulsive disorder. As in the case of other personality disorders, people with the obsessive-compulsive personality disorder do not view their symptoms as **ego-alien**, that is, as out of their control. Rather, they are emotionally controlled, distant, conforming, overly concerned with details, interpersonally dominant, and highly oriented to efficiency and productivity (Kozak et al., 1987).

The obsessive-compulsive anxiety disorders seem to be linked to cultural factors. Less complex and less technologically advanced societies, such as rural African, South American, and Asian tribal groups, show low rates of obsessive-compulsive disorder (but higher rates of conversion disorders; see Chapter 5) (Draguns, 1980). Interestingly enough, while in most Western cultures people with the obsessive-compulsive disorder show a much lower than average marriage rate (probably reflecting their general social maladaption and sexual inhibitions), in India they show a higher than average marriage rate. This fact likely results from the obsessive-compulsive's inclination to be very conforming to social rituals and mores, combined with a continued emphasis on formal courtships and arranged marriages in India (Turner et al., 1985).

In the United States the incidence of obsessive-compulsive disorder is proportionately higher in middle- and upper-class individuals. As noted in Chapter 1, obsessive-compulsive disorder is the only disorder that is more common, per capita, in the suburbs than in rural or urban areas. Obsessive-compulsive clients tend to be brighter than those with other anxiety disorders, which seems appropriate, as obsessions in particular are an intellectual coping strategy for anxiety (Rachman, 1980).

This disorder does not include compulsions to perform behaviors that many people find inherently pleasurable, such as overeating or overindulgence in alcohol. Although many people may not be able to control these latter behaviors, they do not find them foreign or intrusive; and although they may be leery of the consequences (obesity or alcoholism), they feel no discomfort about the specific behaviors themselves.

Etiology. Various explanations of the causes of the obsessive-compulsive disorder have been offered. Turner et al. (1985) note that there are a variety of indicators for a biologically predisposed state of physiological over-

arousal in obsessive-compulsive clients, especially when the disorder is severe and is accompanied by depression. They hypothesize that people with
the obsessive-compulsive disorder adopt their ritual-like behaviors as a way
of controlling this overarousal. Studies of twins have found the occurrence
of the disorder in both twins to be higher in monozygotic (identical—same
genetic structure) twins than in dizygotic (fraternal—different genetic structure) twins, thus suggesting a genetic component. There is evidence also that
obsessive-compulsive clients may have higher rates of brain abnormalities, and
chronically higher levels of organismic arousal than do normal people. Obsessions and compulsions are coping patterns to arousal, and this arousal can
be generated by stress, emotional conflict, physiological dysfunction, or some
combination of the three (Turner et al., 1985; Mavissakalian et al., 1985).

Freud viewed obsessive-compulsive people as people whose concerns
and level of functioning are still at the anal-sadistic stage of development
(Adams, 1985). Their concern about bowel functions leads them to express
hostility by soiling others, either literally or figuratively. Freud's notion has
face validity (that is, it initially appears to be valid, though not from any clear
or empirical evidence), as people with this disorder often have obsessions
about avoiding dirt, along with the related handwashing compulsions. Cawley
(1974), however, points out that no strong evidence yet supports this as a
consistently valid explanation.

Psychodynamic theorists postulate a variety of defense mechanisms employed by obsessive-compulsive clients. **Intellectualization**, the tendency to
talk or think about a problem while avoiding any emotional impact and not
really doing anything to cope with the problem, is a common pattern (Adams,
1985). This is not surprising, given that obsessive-compulsive clients tend to
be bright, well educated, and from the middle or upper socioeconomic strata
(Kozak et al., 1987).

From a cognitive perspective, it is clear that obsessive-compulsive clients
are often highly oriented to control. Most of us find uncertainty and ambiguity
uncomfortable. But obsessive-compulsive clients are very threatened in these
situations. Their obsessive thoughts and compulsive behaviors help them
regain a sense of control. As a result, it should not be surprising that they
are often perfectionistic and strongly oriented to regularity and punctuality.

The **learning-avoidance theory** of obsessions and compulsions provides
a thoroughly researched explanation for the genesis of many cases of anxiety
disorder. In 1927, Pavlov created an "experimental neurosis" in dogs that were
restrained and subjected to electric shocks over which they had no control.
That work, extended to humans by Gantt, Masserman, and others, led to
the view of anxiety as a response to unpredictable or uncontrollable forces
in one's environment. Under such conditions both human and nonhuman
organisms tend to develop repetitive behavior that is ineffective in alleviating
the underlying anxiety. Kozak et al. (1987) and Rachman (1980) offer further
support for this concept, which implies that symptoms are evolved (though

inefficient) methods for controlling anxiety, even if a biological disorder of some sort is the original cause of the anxiety. Interestingly enough, when the individual is taught more effective ways of coping, such psychological change in turn affects the person's physiology, so physiological indicators of anxiety may be present in an individual either as a cause or result (Bandura et al., 1985).

Treatment.   The obsessive-compulsive disorder is one of the most difficult anxiety disorders to treat, probably because a number of defensive patterns contribute to avoidance of the anxiety and of underlying concerns. Medication has not been markedly effective in the treatment of most obsessive-compulsive disorders (Marks, 1978; Mavissakalian et al., 1985), nor has psychoanalysis (Cawley, 1974). However, in the more severe cases, and especially where there is an accompanying depressive component, chemotherapy with clomipramine (Turner et al., 1985) or imipramine (Telch et al., 1985) is helpful. Psychosurgery, usually involving severing some of the connections between the frontal area of the cerebral cortex (the part of the brain usually associated with planning and organizing behavior) and the limbic system (associated with the general arousal of the organism) has been effective in some severe cases. But it is often not effective, and the irreversibility of the procedure and the strong possibility of severe side effects indicate that this is seldom if ever the treatment of choice (Turner et al., 1985; Rachman, 1980). In fact, no technique has been overwhelmingly successful.

Any technique that prevents the disordered response from occurring is important in the treatment of the obsessive-compulsive disorder (Rachman, 1980). Thought stopping (see Chapter 4) has the value of demonstrating to the client that the obsessions can actually be controlled. It has proven effective in a multimodal treatment program designed to teach a variety of competency skills. In vivo exposure to the actual feared situations or modeling of more-adaptive coping strategies can also be helpful (Rachman, 1980).

Treatment of Carleton's compulsions included some of the paradoxical control procedures (see Chapter 4) developed by Jay Haley (1959; 1973; Seltzer, 1986). Haley's focus on the power struggles that often arise between the therapist and client reflects his primary training in communications theory, and the outcome of Carleton's therapy confirms the persistence of that power dynamic. One of Haley's preferred tasks is to take control of the client's symptoms by turning the tables and actually performing them, often in slightly modified form. Haley feels that clients are often motivated to resist or disobey their therapist's directives, and would go to any length—even giving up their symptomatic behavior—as a means of "defeating" the therapist. Toward this end, the therapist asked Carleton to go through his checking routine five times instead of three, had him memorize license plate numbers backwards instead of forwards, and made minor variations in a number of other compulsions. Carleton at first wondered if the therapist might also be disturbed, though

The Case of Leslie

Leslie was blessed with loving and devoted parents, and grew up in a pleasant upper-middle-class community on Long Island in New York. She was a good student, and had many good friends. The only psychological problem of any significance she ever experienced was a fear of snakes. Her mother shared this fear, and though a fun-loving and high-spirited woman, would show a visible shudder and give a cry of disgust even at the sight of a snake in a movie or a magazine. Leslie's father thought this fear was sort of charming in the two most beloved women in his life, though he would never tolerate such behavior in his son.

Fortunately, Leslie's fear of snakes had never resulted in any disruption of her life, as she could play comfortably in the woods, and even enjoyed going to zoos, though she would never venture near the reptile exhibit. The only real upset that seemed to result from her fear occurred when her older brother, out of the ambivalence of sibling love, would put a rubber snake in her bed, or shriek "snake" when they were walking in the woods.

Leslie married at age 22, and reports having a generally satisfactory marriage. She has raised two healthy and happy children, and has been moderately successful in her part-time occupation as an interior designer. However, Leslie is now 44 years old, and her long-standing fear of snakes has intensified gradually over the past two years.

Things first worsened when Leslie received a painful spider bite while on a family vacation in Florida. She was physically ill from the bite, and also became so anxious about the possibility of another bite that she talked the family into cutting the vacation short and returning home.

Though the bite healed without leaving more than a tiny scar, Leslie's fears were increasing, and also generalizing into fears about related objects. As Leslie put it, "I really can't even stand the sight of spiders or snakes, or even any kind of little crawly things." A waterbug scurrying across the bathroom floor could send her into a mild panic.

Leslie was a believer in meeting any crisis head-on with "willpower." She decided she simply wouldn't be afraid of these things anymore. She was a little better in responding without panic to such things as waterbugs. However, she then encountered a spider on the headboard of her bed as she awakened one morning, and, as she put it, "I lost it." She ran downstairs screaming and would not go upstairs until the exterminators she had called reported they could find no evidence of more than the one spider. Her anxiety about "crawly things" of all types again intensified. She talked to her physician about her fears, and she referred Leslie to a private clinic for therapy. As is often the case with the simple phobias, of which Leslie's pattern is a classic example, therapy was successful within a reasonably short period of time, in this case two months.

he carried out the requests. In the ensuing weeks the therapist altered the number of variations requested, sometimes lowering the requested rate below the initial level, sometimes raising it. In effect, the therapist began to take control of the symptom, a fact that was not lost on Carleton. Perhaps more importantly, he gradually came to the realization that the symptom, not the therapist, was ultimately what was constraining his own behavior. When Carleton left treatment after 22 weeks, he had given up all but one small, nondisruptive compulsion—a token link, perhaps, with his prior self-identity.

PHOBIC DISORDERS

Phobic disorders are patterns in which chronic avoidance behaviors occur in conjunction with an irrational fear of a particular object or situation.

A **phobia** is an intense, persistent, and disproportionate fear. What the phobic person fears may not actually present a danger at all; or the danger it presents may be much less than the phobic person believes. To qualify as a phobia, the intensity of the fear must be severe. Fear of the dark is normal and may produce some apprehension; fear of the dark that produces severe anxiety is a phobia (Wittchen and Semler, 1986). A *phobic disorder* is a disorder in which a phobia produces avoidance behavior that is disruptive and disabling to the phobic person. Persons with phobic disorders generally are aware of how irrational their fears are and may even acknowledge that their anxiety is distressing to a disproportionate degree. A classic phobia is marked by "Disproportionate, Disturbing, and Disabling responses to a Discrete stimulus."

Simple Phobias

The **simple phobias**, of which the accompanying case of Leslie is a good example, are those that involve fears of specific objects or situations. Leslie has developed a set of related simple phobias. Her long-standing fear of snakes, shared by many persons in our culture, was not initially disruptive, and thus would not have been formally labeled a phobia. The addition of related phobias, however, so markedly restricted her feeling of freedom and her actual mobility that a diagnosis of simple phobias became appropriate. Simple phobias may have had an evolutionary value for the human species; fears of snakes, darkness, heights, eating rotten foods, and so on, may have helped protect the species. The objects of such phobias may still—even at this stage of our evolution—have a specific effect on us. Hugdahl and Ohman (1977) conditioned students to fear either snakes and spiders or houses and faces by pairing each conditioned stimulus with shock. As the electrodes were being removed at the end of the conditioning, the subjects were told that they would no longer receive any shocks. Though the fear of houses and faces was almost immediately extinguished, the fear of snakes and spiders remained in

No treatment or etiology

Just Diagnosis & Characteristics

EXHIBIT

Types of Simple Phobias

Acrophobia—fear of heights

Astraphobia—fear of storms, lightning, and thunder

Claustrophobia—fear of closed rooms and areas

Hematophobia—fear of blood

Hydrophobia—fear of water

Mysophobia—fear of germs and contamination

Nyctophobia—fear of the dark

Ochlophobia—fear of crowds

Phobophobia—fear of phobias

Thanatophobia—fear of death

Xenophobia—fear of strangers

Zoophobia—fear of a type of animal or animals in general

---

full force, perhaps indicating a natural **preparedness** for fear-conditioning with these objects. In general, persons with simple phobias are less disturbed and emotionally reactive than those who tend toward more encompassing phobias such as agoraphobia (Wolpe, 1987).

Etiology. From a biological perspective, certain individuals are more likely to develop phobias and other anxiety disorders because of a genetic predisposition toward high lability of the autonomic nervous system (Foa and Kozak, 1986; Kendler et al., 1986; Turner et al., 1985). Labile individuals are biologically predisposed to respond more quickly, more strongly, more lastingly to stressful stimuli with such symptoms as rapid heartbeat, high blood pressure, sweating, muscle tension, trembling, and restlessness. They are consistently more "edgy" or "jumpy," and are more easily startled by a novel stimulus. This high-level reactivity and lability of the autonomic nervous system is often referred to as neuroticism, and it is consistent with a tendency to become more anxious under pressure. It is best thought of as a general predisposition to various disorders, but especially the anxiety disorders. The occurrence of a specific disorder in a specific person is then determined by behavioral and cognitive variables.

From a strictly behavioral perspective, the development of a phobia is clearly reinforced by the reduction in anxiety that results whenever the individual employs the phobic pattern to avoid the feared stimulus. This is an example of operant conditioning. Experiments in classical conditioning have also produced phobias. The classic case is that of John Watson's conditioning Little Albert to fear the white rat. Campbell et al.'s well-known but ethically controversial study in 1964 graphically demonstrated how classical conditioning can quickly produce a strong phobia. Five alcoholic patients were given scoline, a drug that paralyzes all the skeletal muscles. This makes breathing extremely difficult, causing extreme anxiety to the point of terror and panic. The onset of effects of only one administration of scoline was paired with a tone, and the tone alone then produced the fear. Most importantly, the tone still produced strong fear after 100 extinction trials (trials with the tone but no scoline). Classical conditioning is often a major component of an overall pattern of phobia development, called direct experience learning, to be discussed shortly.

Combining both the behavioral and cognitive perspectives, the two major ways in which phobias seem to develop are via (1) **modeling** and (2) **direct experience learning** (Foa and Kozak, 1986; Kendler et al., 1986; Mineka and Cook, 1986; Mineka et al., 1984). Leslie's case is a good demonstration of how modeling can generate a phobia. As is true of most people, her fear of snakes was not based on an actual unpleasant encounter with a reptile; that is, there was no direct experience learning. Rather, Leslie became aware that her mother was extremely fearful of snakes and reacted with revulsion at the sight of them when visiting the zoo with Leslie. As a result, Leslie simply incorporated her mother's reaction. By doing so, she acquired a fear of reptiles in an indirect, or vicarious fashion. It should be pointed out that, in a wide variety of circumstances, modeling is a powerful tool of learning. Adults who model culturally approved behaviors save their children from the inefficiency and, sometimes, the risks associated with trial-and-error learning. Unfortunately, sometimes these modeled patterns promote maladaptive behavior, as in a phobia (Mineka et al., 1984; Emmelkamp, 1982). In a well-controlled study, Mineka and her colleagues (1984) demonstrated that young monkeys raised by parents who had a fear of snakes and who showed some evidence of fear in an actual encounter with a snake later developed such fears themselves. Young monkeys raised by parents without such fears (or who had the fears but were never observed by the young monkeys in an encounter with a snake) did not develop a fear of snakes.

Leslie's subsequent encounter with the spider is an example of how people develop phobias by direct experience learning. She had a strong negative behavioral experience with the actual stimulus itself. From her fear of snakes, Leslie generalized to the more disabling phobia of insects and "crawly things." Cognitive generalization occurs from repetitive thinking (or rumination) about a traumatic event. This rumination generates cognitive expectancies of further negative events in the future. As a result, a higher level of arousal develops out of this apprehension, providing a fertile ground for at least a continuance and probably an increase of anxiety disorder patterns (Kendler et al., 1986).

RESEARCH PROFILE

To Be or Not to Be—Phobic: A Parent's Prerogative

The text presents the research by Mineka et al. (1984) and others on how modeling may influence the development of phobias. An interesting follow-up study by Mineka and Cook (1986) shows how modeling may not only create phobias, but also protect against their development as well.

In the first stage of this experiment three groups of lab-reared rhesus monkeys (eight per group) from the University of Wisconsin Primate Lab were given one of three different pretreatments. The first group, the immunization group (IM), spent six sessions watching another lab-reared monkey behave nonfearfully while in close proximity to snakes. A second group, a latent inhibition group (LI), spent six sessions by themselves behaving nonfearfully in close proximity to snakes, with the total exposure time to snakes being equal to that for the immunization group. A third group, a pseudo-immunization group (PI), a type of control group, spent an equal amount of time watching another monkey behave nonfearfully with some neutral objects, actually some wooden blocks.

In the second stage of the experiment, all three groups spent a similar amount of time watching another monkey (in this case, a wild monkey from India who had acquired a fear of snakes) respond with fear (leaping to the back of the cage, flattening against the cage, screeching, shaking the bars, and so on) when brought into proximity to the snake.

After watching this, all monkeys in the three groups were individually brought into proximity to a snake to assess their response. Both the PI and the LI groups now showed significant fear responses, with the PI group's response being somewhat stronger than the LI group's. It is also of interest that there was no slackening of this fear when these monkeys were reassessed three months later. But, six of the eight monkeys in the IM group showed no fear, and the other two in the IM group showed relatively mild responses.

Such experiments indicate that observational learning can rather quickly generate a phobia, and, alternatively, that nonfear or mastery responses can help to prevent the development of later phobias. Thus, while the genetic predisposition to easily develop stress and anxiety responses will facilitate or dampen the effect, the behavior of parents and other significant models in a child's early years will in large part predict the amount and content of later phobias.

Leslie's phobias were also associated with considerable secondary gain. Secondary gain is the behavioral reinforcement that comes as an indirect benefit from the phobic behavior. It is important in maintaining most severe phobias, even though modeling and direct experience learning are usually primary in generating them. An existential theorist (see Chapter 4) could point out that Leslie's phobias provide secondary gain in dealing with the anxieties in her life. Two years ago Leslie was facing the anxiety of a decision about whether or not to go back to work now that her children were becoming less dependent upon her parenting—the classic ambivalence of the "empty nest" syndrome (Rubin, 1980). During the vacation, her oldest son had been allowed to remain home with friends instead of going on the vacation, and his obvious thrust toward independence increased her anxiety. Because of the spider bite and her phobic reaction, her family let her return home early from the vacation. In this way, her phobia allowed her the secondary gain of reasserting her parental role over the son who had stayed home.

Treatment. The **systematic desensitization technique** (SDT), described in Chapter 4, is the most commonly used and most effective technique for treating specific phobic symptoms (Emmelkamp, 1982). Using SDT, Leslie's therapist first trained her in relaxation and then worked with her to construct a hierarchy of anxiety-arousing stimuli. Eventually they devised three hierarchies: one on spiders, one on insects in general, and one on "crawly things," including snakes. Leslie was asked to describe the most anxiety-producing situation she could in each category, and that scene was assigned a score of 100. The situation evoking little or no anxiety received a 0. The accompanying Exhibit shows the hierarchy for situations involving spiders.

EXHIBIT

Phobia Treatment with Imagined Stimuli

Hierarchy of Scenes for Treating Leslie's Spider Phobia, Using Imagined Stimuli

Response level	Imagined stimuli
100 (Highest—most anxiety arousing)	Thinking of spiders crawling in and out of my body orifices Thinking of lying down with a spider crawling over my stomach Letting a spider walk in my lap Touching a still spider
50	Seeing a spider across a room Seeing a spider ahead of me in a woods Being told by someone that there are spiders in this general region Just walking in a woods Seeing a spider in a movie Seeing a picture of a spider
0 (Lowest)	Hearing an instructor mention the word *spider* in a lecture

In 10 sessions, Leslie received relaxation training and was then taken through the hierarchies she had helped devise, confronting her fears one step at a time. The results of these procedures generalized so well that she was eventually able to go comfortably about her normal activities while in a room containing spiders and snakes. Through confronting the images of her fears, Leslie was finally able to confront snakes and spiders. Confrontation with the feared stimuli is the critical factor in the cure, as so aptly described by G. Gordon Liddy (*Playboy*, October, 1980), one of the main perpetrators of the Watergate break-in that eventually led to Richard M. Nixon's resignation as President.

For example, to conquer my fear of thunder, I waited for a big storm and then sneaked out of the house and climbed up a seventy-five foot oak tree and latched myself to the trunk with my belt. As the storm hit and chaos roared around me and the sky was rent with thunder and lightening, I shook my fist at the rolling black clouds and screamed, "Kill me! go ahead and try! I don't care! I don't care!" As the storm subsided, I heard my father ordering me to come down. As I lowered myself to the ground, he shook his head and said, "I just don't understand you." "I know," I said.

I repeated this kind of confrontation over a period of years, mastering one fear after another. I was afraid of electricity, so I scraped off an electrical wire and let ten volts course through me; I feared heights so I scaled buildings with one of my friends. (p. 208)

In clinical practice, SDT alone is often sufficient to deal with simple phobias (Emmelkamp, 1982). More complex or multiphobic situations may require multimodal intervention. Simultaneous use of such techniques as chemotherapy, assertiveness training, modeling, or group therapy helps repair social deficits that have resulted from phobic withdrawal or avoidance (Kahn et al., 1986; Telch et al., 1985). Newer medications (such as buspirone hydrochloride) don't seem to have as many side effects as the traditionally used benzodiazepines (such as Valium and Xanax). Meditation also appears to be useful for teaching skills to prevent a recurrence (Shapiro and Giber, 1978). In terms of preventive techniques, there is evidence that general training in relaxation techniques and cognitive self-talk techniques (see Chapter 4) may be helpful in impeding the development of phobias (Danish and D'Angelli, 1980).

Agoraphobia

Agoraphobia (literally translated as a "fear of the marketplace") is a complex phobic disorder centering on an intense fear of being alone or of finding oneself in public places without access to the help one anticipates needing. It is fear of fear itself. Such individuals can become housebound, breaking their loneliness with manipulative behaviors toward spouse and children and spending long hours talking on the telephone. Unfortunately, such defenses are seldom effective because they ultimately alienate those from whom help is sought. Thus isolated, many agoraphobic people become depressed as well, and in some cases, a biological predisposition may facilitate a pattern that combines agoraphobia and severe depression (Breier et al., 1984). Many use alcohol and other drugs to dilute their anxiety, which may in turn lead to an overlay pattern of addiction and further complicate treatment.

Graduation phobia, an interesting variation of agoraphobia, is the fear of graduating from school and taking on adult responsibilities. It is especially common in Japan, reflecting the high level of dependence developed in most Japanese children, the long period of adolescent freedom from adult responsibilities, and the high performance levels required for success in adulthood (Tseng and Hsu, 1980).

Etiology.   Typically, full-blown agoraphobia is preceded by a series of panic attacks. Agoraphobics have a sense of helplessness, anticipating that these panic attacks may occur at any time without advance warning. Their ultimate fear is of being psychologically abandoned and forced to confront the possibility of panic that will occur and overwhelm them (Fisher and Wilson, 1985; Chambless et al., 1984a). Agoraphobics have a very low threshold of panic because they fear that they will be overwhelmed by fear and anxiety (Chambless et al., 1984a). There is research evidence to indicate that this different threshold for panic may be related to individual physiologic differences. In a model of what stress does to the body physiologically, Liebowitz and his colleagues (1985a) administered sodium lactate to 43 people with agoraphobia and panic attacks and to 20 normal controls. None of the 20 controls showed any response to the sodium lactate, while 31 of those who had already shown agoraphobia-panic attack responses panicked. These researchers note that taking in carbon dioxide appears to have the same effect as sodium lactate. Both work as chemoreceptors that monitor blood acidity and, like a smoke alarm, set off a panic response that tells the body something is wrong physiologically. Essentially, this response would have survival value, but those susceptible to panic attacks respond too quickly and too often.

Those who did panic in Liebowitz's study were those who had significantly higher heart rates and blood pressures (classic signs of anxiety) to start with. This indicates that clinical panic attacks, often either a precursor or an accompaniment to agoraphobia, may provide both a predisposition to respond as well as a stimulus that acts as a catalyst for the response. It's also worthy of note that the predisposition toward panic attacks can be heightened not only by thoughts and temperament as transmitted genetically, but also by something as simple as caffeine (Veleber and Templer, 1984).

Treatment.   Agoraphobic clients (in contrast to those with a simple phobia) typically require well-coordinated, multimodal intervention. A combination of psychotherapy, assertiveness training, social skills training, and chemotherapy

ABNORMALITY ACROSS CULTURES

Alternate Perspectives on Overcoming Phobias

The text describes a number of modern approaches to the treatment and prevention of phobia and fears. Early North American Indian tribes took a much different approach, as described in the following quote, often using rituals involving endurance of pain, fatigue, and fear. The techniques were efficient for those who "passed" them; they often showed lifelong traits of courage and fearlessness, and occasionally cruelty as well. Those who failed them often became outcasts, or, in some tribes, were required to don the garb of a squaw and remain in the village doing a squaw's duties. The following quote concerns William Tall Bull, a man who "passed."

A Cheyenne Indian named William Tall Bull describes a 1947 vision quest he undertook to rid himself of his fear of thunder. He went up into the back hills accompanied by his mother and a shaman named Whistling Elk. After complex ritual preparations involving sage, a buffalo head, a sweat lodge, and the like, Whistling Elk pierced the flesh of Tall Bull's chest with a knife and ran tent pegs through the two sets of wounds; the tent pegs were attached by ropes to a tree, around which Tall Bull then danced, the pegs pulling agonizingly as he leaned his weight back. "It seemed like here was a thing I had to go on with. I couldn't give up."

He smoked a sacred pipe, chanted, and prayed as he danced. A kind of transcendental power seemed to take over, as the night wore on. "I thought of my people, my relatives, the Cheyenne people in general . . . I wasn't in pain. The tiredest part of me was the small of my back." The dancing went on till dawn, when Alex Brady, Whistling Elk's assistant, came and cut Tall Bull loose. "I was just as happy as could be. When you talk of something of such joy, you spoil it . . . I was walking on air . . . I wanted to touch everything." More complicated prayers and sweats followed the ceremony; Tall Bull never panicked at the sound of thunder again, and became, instead of a nervous, unimpressive sort of fellow, a real Cheyenne Mensch.

Schulter, R. (1985) *Bone games.* New York: Fromm International Publishing. pp.57–58.

on occasion, may be necessary to reverse the allied social and interpersonal problems that often accompany agoraphobia. Modification of a significant component of depression may also be necessary (Breier et al., 1984). In addition, systematic desensitization (SDT) and **implosion therapy** (or flooding) (see Chapter 4) are often used to deal with the high anxiety and phobic aspects of agoraphobia (Chambless et al., 1984a; Emmelkamp, 1982).

Implosion therapists typically ask the client to imagine variations of the feared stimulus. For convenience, the feared stimuli are seldom presented **in vivo** (an actual, real stimulus or situation), even though doing so might be just as effective or even more so. So, the anxiety arousing stimuli are presented verbally and processed in the imagination, as in the following excerpt from an actual implosion session.

> *Therapist:* Your mother and sister have now left you in that old abandoned cabin . . . you have no car, no phone . . . you're in a wilderness . . . the clouds are dark and ominous . . . you can hear your mother's voice. "We don't want to see you anymore, leave us alone," . . . See all this very clearly, you're very alone.

> *Client:* Oh, God, I don't want to. (starts crying)

> *Therapist:* Don't stop the images now. You're so alone . . . it's cold and gray and ugly out . . . you imagine hearing the vague voices of your mother and father talking just after you were born. "I wish we'd never had this one . . . it's too much trouble, maybe we could just abandon it somewhere, or give it up for adoption."

The technique is decidedly unpleasant and may even seem cruel; yet Chambless found that without the experience of strong anxiety there may be little improvement. One group of agoraphobics was treated with a standard implosion technique, but a second group received Brevital, a relaxant, during implosion therapy so that they would not experience the anxiety the images suggested. The first group improved, and the other did not.

Social Phobia

Social phobia is persistent anxiety about negative scrutiny of one's behavior by others. People with social phobia are often acutely fearful of making public presentations of any sort. Even eating at a center table in a restaurant may cause anxiety. The most common manifestation of social phobia in adults is a severe fear of any public speaking, leading to a classic vicious cycle. First, social phobics experience anxiety about a public performance. If they attempt to go through with the performance, their anxiety interferes, possibly causing them to shake visibly or twitch. Their prophecy that they will be inadequate is then fulfilled, and anxiety about any similar situation is heightened (Liebowitz et al., 1985b). Operationally, people with social phobia experience disruptive and irrational fear, and high anticipatory anxiety, but they do recognize the inappropriateness of their anxiety. Some people with social phobia use alcohol to reduce anxiety; if this is a persistent pattern they are at risk for alcoholism. Once again a multimodal approach to treatment is warranted, as is the case for agoraphobia. Many people with social phobia recall that their parents used shaming as a primary and consistent disciplinary technique. The disorder is slightly more common in males and usually first appears in midadolescence, when conflicts generated by puberty provide an easy focus for fears of being publicly embarrassed.

EXHIBIT

Factors in Various Phobia Patterns

Factors	Simple Phobias	Animal Phobias	Social Phobia	Agoraphobia
Frequency	Common	Fairly rare	Not uncommon	Common
Level of distress	Generally low	Low	Moderate	High
Point of onset	No specific point— anytime	Usually in childhood	Usually adoles- cence or later	Usually early adult- hood or later
Other associated symptomatology	Few or more if only one phobia; anxiety, moderate depres- sion if multiple phobias	Few or none	Few, though some do show allied depres- sion, panic, or alcohol patterns	Several are prob- able—anxiety, de- pression, with- drawal, alcohol or drug abuse
Physiological responsibility	Usually average if one phobia; higher if multiple phobias	Average	Above average to high	Usually high
Response to treatment	Good if one phobia; moderate if multi- ple phobias	Good	Moderate	Poor—though some recover, it is diffi- cult to treat

In particular, SDT, implosion therapy, and social skills training are useful in dealing with social phobia (Emmelkamp, 1982). The traditional medications for anxiety, the benzodiazepines (e.g., Valium) and the MAO inhibiters (see Chapter 9), are not helpful here. The beta-adrenergic blockers, which in part reduce cardiovascular responsivity, can be of some help (Liebowitz et al., 1985b).

Agoraphobia or social phobia may initially be confused with the avoidant personality disorder. The avoidant personality shows a heightened sensitivity to social rejection, a lack of personal initiative and of self-assertive behaviors, and as a result may appear to be homebound or socially phobic. But avoidant personalities, like those with other personality disorders (see Chapter 12), differ from people with anxiety disorders in three important ways: (1) their behavior causes them little anxiety; (2) the origins of their problems can be traced back to childhood; and (3) their specific symptoms do not feel foreign (or "ego-alien") to their overall personality, at least until distress in dealing with significant others leads to situationally generated anxiety.

POSTTRAUMATIC STRESS DISORDER

Posttraumatic stress disorder is an anxiety disorder in which a traumatic event, such as combat or a natural disaster, produces disabling psychological reactions, in particular emotional numbing (Pearce et al., 1985). The common sequence is as follows.

Traumatic Stressor Events	Common Psychological Effects	Common Physical Consequences of Reactions
combat natural disasters man-made disasters (car accidents torture kidnapping hijacking assaults rape	emotional numbing depression guilt over survival flashbacks and night-mares obsessive thoughts about the traumas anxiety tendency to be startled inability to relax problem in memory and concentration impulsiveness	diminished sex drive insomnia hypertension tension headaches stomach and intestinal disorders excessive fatigue heart palpitations

To apply the diagnosis of posttraumatic stress disorder, there must be evidence of a substantial stressor that would seriously disturb most people, such as being raped or being in an airplane crash, and reexperiencing of the stressful event, as indicated by at least one of the following: (1) recurrent related dreams; (2) déjà vu about the event; or (3) persistent memories of the event. As a result, there is a distancing from the external world, as evidenced by at least one of the following: (1) lessened emotional responses; (2) lowered interest in at least one usual interest or activity; or (3) detachment from others.

In addition, two of the following behaviors must exist, though not present before the stress: (1) sleep disruption; (2) hyperalertness; (3) guilt over survival; (4) memory or attention disruptions; (5) intensified upset if reexposed to the stressor; or (6) avoidance of any stimuli for recall of the stressor.

The severity of the posttraumatic stress disorder varies in relation to several factors that are external to the individual. Not surprisingly, the more similar the present conditions are to the original traumatic event, the more severe the present reactions. Also, subsequent reactions are typically more severe to the degree that the original trauma was directly produced by human action (Pearce et al., 1985; Kelly, 1985).

Posttraumatic stress disorder, known in other wars as shell shock or combat fatigue, plagued many Vietnam vets long after their return home.   (AP/Wide World Photos)

Relation to Other Disorders

The posttraumatic stress disorder differs from common stress responses (see Chapter 5) in that in the posttraumatic disorder the trauma is more severe, unusual, abrupt, and specific. Also, in an adjustment disorder the stressor is less severe and more within the realm of common experience. It differs from the civilian disaster syndrome (see Chapter 5) in that the initial symptoms in the disaster syndrome are not as severe, there are seldom any severe long-term symptoms, and there is some evidence of progress toward cessation of symptoms. In contrast, the posttraumatic stress disorder is marked by the presence of long-term symptoms. Indeed, in some cases, the response is delayed, but the symptoms are severe and resistant to treatment when they do appear.

The posttraumatic stress disorder differs from the other anxiety disorders because for the posttraumatic disorder the external stimulus is by itself a convincing explanation as to why the disorder occurred, even though it is true that many people exposed to the same trauma do not develop the disorder (Boulanger and Kadushin, 1986).

Etiology.   In a study of Vietnam veterans, Foy et al. (1984) found that those who had had trouble adjusting to military life were especially prone to developing a posttraumatic stress disorder. However, the adequacy of their psychological adjustment to life prior to entering the service did not predict whether or not they developed the disorder. The only other major factor that determined whether or not they developed it was the ongoing level of autonomic arousal. Those with higher levels were more vulnerable. Thus, persons with any tendency toward a generalized anxiety disorder (discussed above) would also be prone to developing a posttraumatic stress disorder when encountering a specific and severe trauma. Thus, a posttraumatic stress disorder is not a normal reaction to the stressor (the sequence described in the civilian disaster syndrome would be considered more normal—see Chapter 5); yet given the severity of the trauma, the posttraumatic stress disorder is an understandable reaction and is not that uncommon.

Treatment.   The principles of crisis intervention (immediacy, proximity, and expectancy) provide an excellent framework within which to treat posttraumatic stress syndrome. *Immediacy* is the early detection and treatment of the disorder, with an emphasis on returning individuals to their normal life situations as quickly as possible. *Proximity* emphasizes the need to treat them in their ongoing world by avoiding hospitalization. Lastly, *expectancy* is the communication of the therapist that while the client's reaction is quite normal, it does not excuse him or her from functioning adequately.

Within this framework, a specific case can be treated using a variety of methods. For example, an individual may be taught a controlled relaxation response (through progressive relaxation, autogenic training, or any other form of systematized relaxation training—see Chapter 4), in order to treat both acute panic attacks and a chronic state of autonomic arousal. In the case of the latter, use of biofeedback has also proven helpful (Schwartz, 1987). In some cases, prescribing tranquilizers to be taken "as needed" serves to give the individual a feeling of control while learning other techniques, though any indications of potential for substance abuse place limitations on this practice. If clients with posttraumatic stress disorder can be convinced to work on the relaxation training in a group setting, they become aware that others share the problem, and they may also begin to discuss the problems in a fashion similar to group therapy. This discussion facilitates later entry into actual group therapy.

Group therapy is ideal for the posttraumatic stress disorder, not only because it allows expression of feelings but also, just as important, because there is a sense of support and sharing with other victims (Kelly, 1985). Psychodrama is a form of group therapy developed in Vienna in the early 1920s by Jacob Moreno, the first therapist to use the term group therapy (see Chapter 4). Psychodrama uses techniques of unrehearsed acting and dramatic play to facilitate the spontaneous expression of emotions. Persons with posttraumatic stress disorder can replay, in this mini-theater format, the events of the trauma, even taking the positions (running, falling, crouching, and so on) that they were in at the time. This allows feelings to dissipate and a greater sense of mastery to emerge.

An overall supportive atmosphere of warmth, understanding, and empathy is also critical. Since the environment to which these individuals return should be similarly supportive, sessions with family and friends can be beneficial in helping them to understand the nature of the problem and the role they can play in successful readjustment (Foy et al., 1984).

DISSOCIATIVE DISORDERS

Dissociative disorders are syndromes characterized by a splitting, or fragmenting, of consciousness or identity. The effect is to isolate psychologically distressing memories in such a way that they do not intrude into conscious awareness. This may involve a loss of memory, a multiple personality, or an experience of unreality about one's self. Though this splitting is almost always temporary, it may wax and wane.

On rare occasions, behavior resembling a dissociative disorder stems from an organic condition, such as tumor or epilepsy. Therefore, initial screening of symptoms should include standard neurological tests, such as a brain scan or an EEG, along with psychological tests. Dissociative disorders must also be distinguished from culturally approved, temporary dissociative states in such groups as the cultures of Bali, the Palau Islands in Pacific Micronesia, and some tribal groups of Africa and Southeast Asia. For example, chanting, dancing, drugs, and the like produce ritualistically controlled dissociative states that are a temporary therapeutic escape from conflict (Prince, 1980).

There are four dissociative disorders: psychogenic amnesia, psychogenic fugue, depersonalization, and multiple personality. No specific data is available to assess the overall rates of these disorders, though most experts agree that none of the patterns occurs very often (except at times of great disaster, when they are more common), relative to other forms of psychopathology (Winer, 1978; Thigpen and Cleckley, 1984; Eaton, 1986).

Psychogenic Amnesia

The common meaning of the term **amnesia**—a temporary loss of ability to recall past experiences—conveys the essence of this category. Psychogenic amnesia, however, refers to sudden amnesia generated by psychological trauma, such as the abrupt loss of a job or an important relationship, rather than by an organic cause such as a blow to the head. The information that is lost may refer to something that happened in the immediate or distant past, or to a certain topic. Only in rare cases is memory of all prior events lost, as it can be in certain organic cases.

There are four patterns of recall disorder in psychogenic amnesia. In the most common type, localized amnesia, there is an inability to recall all events during a specific time period, usually the first several hours after a deeply disturbing event, such as an auto accident in which a loved one is killed. Selective amnesia, which occurs somewhat less often than localized amnesia, is a failure to recollect some, though not all, of the events that occurred during a specific time period. For example, a woman might remember an ambulance coming to the scene of an accident she was in, but not remember riding in it to the hospital. The least common types of amnesia are continuous amnesia, in which a person cannot recall events after a specific time or event up to and including the present, and generalized amnesia, in which there is a failure to recall throughout one's entire life.

Interestingly enough, in any of the amnesias, basic learned patterns, preferences, habits, and abilities do not change during the amnesia. People who disliked pizza will continue to dislike it during the amnesia. Also, they will retain their abilities to ride a bike, type, work with tools they are familiar with, and the like. At the same time, they are not likely to recognize friends or family or remember aspects of their personal identity such as their name, address, or occupation. For example, while they might still work skillfully with plumbing tools, they probably won't remember much about the plumbing company they work for.

In cases of psychogenic amnesia the recovery of memory is usually sudden, either a day or several years later, whereas in organic conditions accompanied by amnesia, recovery, if it occurs at all, is gradual. The alcohol amnestic syndrome specifically differs from psychogenic amnesia in that the person is able to recall information for only a few minutes because the ability to transfer information into long-term memory has been lost. Loss of long-term memory also occurs in some persons who have had numerous electroconvulsive therapy (ECT) treatments.

Psychogenic Fugue

Psychogenic fugue can be considered a specific form of psychogenic amnesia in which people are unable to recall their prior identity, suddenly leave where they live, and assume an entirely new identity. Recovery is usually complete, but people seldom recall events experienced during the psychogenic fugue state. This syndrome typically occurs in response to a severe psychosocial stressor. Excessive use of alcohol or drugs can help induce psychogenic fugue through the dissociation inherent in such users' states of consciousness (Vaillant, 1983). A respected middle-level executive, for example, disappeared for two weeks and was found working as a short-order cook at a "greasy spoon," a stark contrast to his previous position. It turned out that two days before his fugue episode his wife had told him that she was leaving him for another man. From his perspective, there was no apparent reason for her to do so. He had been extremely dependent on her and simply dissociated from the severe stress he anticipated would occur when she left him.

Depersonalization Disorder

Depersonalization disorder involves experiencing the self as unreal or as drastically altered. It is not a true dissociative disorder, because consciousness is never truly split. But there seems to be no better place for it in the DSM, and an emerging dissociation is seemingly involved. People with a depersonalization disorder feel separated from their normal consciousness as if they were separate observers of themselves. They report feeling that the reality of the external world has been altered, but there is no break in consciousness or memory.

All people experience minor reactions like these, and modern gurus, such as Krishnamurti, even assert that such experiences are necessary if one is to attain enlightenment. A disorder arises when a person feels a lack of control during or in anticipation of such occurrences. Many people fear that the depersonalization experience predicts more aberrant behavior. It then becomes conditioned to anticipatory anxiety, and a vicious cycle can develop, reinforcing the belief of going crazy.

Munich (1977) describes the case of an adolescent girl who developed a depersonalization response to her feelings of anger toward her mother and her incestuous thoughts about her father. A previous mild delirium experienced when she was stung by a bee may have served as a model for the experience. Psychotherapy proved effective, as it usually is with depersonalization disorders.

Multiple Personality

According to DSM, the essential feature of the **multiple personality** disorder is the existence in one individual of two or more distinct personalities. These personalities are distinctly dissociated from each other. Each incorporates a complete identity, with a consistent and individual set of behavioral and social patterns, and the transition between personalities is sudden (Kluft, 1987).

Most studies that attempt to study and document the multiple personality find it to be extremely rare. For example, in one of the earliest thorough reviews, Taylor and Martin (1944) found only 76 cases prior to 1945; Winer (1978) found that only about 200 cases have been clearly documented in the literature up through 1978; Greaves (1980) reports a count of 50 cases between 1970 and 1980. However, there have been more reports in recent years (Bliss and Jeppsen, 1985). Several factors may be involved in such an increase, for example, a multiple personality may be confused with other disorders, such as schizophrenia. Also, Thigpen and Cleckley, as well as Winer (1978) and Gruenewald (1984), note that several secondary gain factors (both for the client and for the therapist) may generate a case of multiple personality, or expand the number of personalities in one of the rare true cases. They point out that:

1. Clients with hysteria conditions or certain personality disorders may be motivated by a desire to seem special, and the glamour and drama of the multiple personality may help them unconsciously produce a false appearance of multiple personality.

2. Clients who are in legal trouble may produce a multiple personality facade in order to escape responsibility for their behaviors.

3. Therapists are likely to find alluring the prestige attached to treating multiple personalities, and thus help to produce false cases. Thigpen and Cleckley (1984) assert that "unfortunately, there also appears to be a competition among some therapists to see who can have the greatest number of multiple personality cases" (p.64).

The multiple personalities popularized in the movie "The Three Faces of Eve" (Sizemore and Pittillo, 1977) and the book *Sybil* (Schreiber, 1974) may have been iatrogenically (that is, caused by the treatment itself) induced in this fashion.

One of the most famous cases of multiple personality involved Chris Sizemore, whose story was dramatized in the 1957 film "The Three Faces of Eve." Mrs. Sizemore eventually developed 22 distinct personalities.   (AP/Wide World Photos)

The mass media has commonly associated multiple personality with schizophrenia (Confer and Ables, 1982). But multiple personalities are not psychotic, and thus not schizophrenic. Although there may sometimes be a delusional quality to their thinking, there are typically no real delusions about the external world and no disturbance of perceptual and cognitive processes. Because no actual loss of contact with reality occurs, no psychosis is involved (Kluft, 1987).

Etiology. Psychodynamic theorists have traditionally viewed the multiple personality as the successive awakening of a person's repressed ego states (Rosenzweig, 1986; Osgood et al., 1976). A more explanatory theory emphasizes the effects of psychological trauma in combination with prior mild dissociative experiences (such as alcohol intoxication) and/or experience in role playing (as an actor, perhaps) (Winer, 1978; Gruenewald, 1984). The dissociation typically follows a severe emotional shock that the original personality cannot cope with or integrate. From this perspective, the dissociation is a purposeful, though subconscious, emotional attempt to maintain psychological survival in the face of potential disruption. In that sense, the person develops a separate personality in a process that is similar to self-hypnosis, and indeed, Bliss and Jeppsen (1985) found that multiple personality patients showed exceptionally high scores on the Stanford hypnotic susceptibility scale.

The social–psychological perspective goes a step further to assert that certain people learn to take the role of the multiple personality. Personality traits, such as suggestibility, proneness to fantasizing, and histrionic traits, interact with a sociocultural milieu and situational demands to prompt people to take on the role of a multiple personality (Spanos et al., 1985). Certain therapists may help elicit such behavior, and in turn provide official validation for these "personalities" (Thigpen and Cleckley, 1984). While the social-psychological approach does not assert that people showing multiple personalities have consciously concocted these personalities (though some people do; for example, to escape criminal prosecution), it does suggest that these other personalities are "less real," that is, they are situationally generated and maintained rather than supported by separate physical or long-term personality structures.

Spanos et al. (1985) provide added experimental support for this position. Forty-eight college students were asked to play the role of an accused murderer, and they were then to be interviewed by a psychiatrist as part of a pre-trial examination. They were then randomly assigned to three treatments that varied as to how much the treatments included cues for symptoms of multiple personality. The most suggestive condition included a hypnotic-like interview. Most of the students displayed the major signs of multiple personality (spontaneous posthypnotic amnesia, adoption of a different name, and so on). In a later session, the students who showed the characteristics of a multiple personality performed quite differently on various psychological tests (sentence completion tests, the semantic differential) than they had originally. Those who had failed to produce multiple personality symptoms performed similarly at both testings. These findings are consistent with those of other researchers (Winer, 1978; Thigpen and Cleckley, 1984; Gruenewald, 1984) in explaining multiple personality as a gradual development from early role-playing and fantasizing in certain persons predisposed to such behavior, to the point where the roles take on a "real" quality to the person, and in turn serve a number of interpersonal goals and obtain a variety of reinforcements from others.

Not surprisingly, the new personalities often incorporate traits that are opposite from the original personality (Confer and Ables, 1982) and that demonstrate behaviors that the person had previously found it difficult to express. The original personality tends to be relatively conservative and socially constricted, and flamboyant personal styles with sexual acting-out find an outlet in the newer roles.

In the case of Nancy described by Winer (1978), a somewhat different aspect of the personality was first dissociated and later reemerged as an alternate personality called Kitty. Nancy had a very traumatic history that included being molested by her great-grandfather, witnessing violent fights between her mother and father, and being raped by her mother's boyfriend at age thirteen while her mother lay next to them in a drunken stupor. In the same year she had also come home to find her mother in bed with Nancy's first boyfriend. Shortly after this, Nancy showed her first minor dissociative pattern. She married to escape, only to find her husband abusive, alcoholic, and unfaithful. Her mother openly flirted with and eventually seduced him. When Nancy became upset about this, her mother became abusive and threatened her with a knife. Nancy had always been forced to suppress any angry or assertive feelings, and had usually been quiet and mildly perfectionistic. Not surprisingly, Kitty, her alternate personality, was very aggressive, hostile to men, and yet at the same time constantly flirtatious toward them.

Persons who (1) are under significant stress, (2) have somewhat contradictory personality factors, (3) have been abused as children, (4) have experienced maternal rejection, (5) tend toward overdramatic behaviors, and (6) have unrealistically high standards of performance are especially susceptible to developing a multiple personality (Gruenewald, 1984; Greaves, 1980).

Treatment. Traditional psychotherapy, usually oriented toward psychodynamic theory and supplemented by hypnosis, has been the typical treatment for multiple personalities (Kluft, 1987; Gruenewald, 1984; Winer, 1978). Use of hypnosis, however, requires caution because of the dissociative quality of the hypnotic experience itself. Successful treatment usually results in a "fusion" of some split or dissociated parts of the personality, but full reintegration may take several years.

Somnambulism

Somnambulism, or sleepwalking, has traditionally been classified as a dissociative reaction but is now listed separately in the DSM because it does not consistently involve psychologically generated dissociation. Rather, it is most often nondistressing learned behavior that was not quelled at its onset. We discuss it here because it offers an interesting contrast to the true dissociative reactions.

True dissociative reactions are commonly treated with psychotherapy and/or hypnosis. For somnambulism, however, a straightforward aversive technique is most effective. Treatment is often sought because of the annoyance the behavior causes to others. Occasionally, the problem is more acute. One man was referred to the senior author for treatment two nights after he had stood in front of his wife's bed in a somnambulistic sleep state and pointed a loaded shotgun at her. The first step in treatment was not an exotic form of therapy, but simply getting the man to promise that he would remove the guns from the house. Next, his wife was instructed to buy a police whistle. They moved their single beds together against a wall, and because the beds' footboards were high he had to crawl over her to get up to sleepwalk, thus awakening her. At that point, she would blow the whistle in his ear, a truly aversive stimulus. It was sufficiently aversive that the man attempted to sleepwalk and was abruptly awakened only twice; three years afterward he had not again walked in his sleep.

CHAPTER REVIEW

1. The anxiety disorders comprise the phobic disorders and anxiety states. In phobic disorders the focus of concern is somewhat more specific than in anxiety states.

2. Panic disorder, the most severe anxiety disorder, is marked by episodic anxiety attacks and a sustained high level of psychological tension. Generalized anxiety disorder has a more physiologic symptomatology, including chronic autonomic hyperactivity. Posttraumatic stress disorder is characterized by less evident physiologic distress, a clearer external stressor, and a more vivid reexperiencing of the stressful event.

3. Anxiety is not as clearly evident in the obsessive-compulsive disorder as in other anxiety states. Yet the behaviors are ego-alien, as opposed to the ego-syntonic patterns of the obsessive-compulsive personality disorder.

4. Psychodynamic theorists cite intellectualization as an important defense mechanism in the obsessive-compulsive disorder. Behaviorists and social learning theorists view learning-avoidance responses and an extension of superstitious behaviors as crucial elements in this disorder. A variety of treatments have been used, but with only moderate success.

5. Phobic disorders are marked by chronic avoidance behaviors and irrational fears that are disproportionate, disturbing, disabling, and marked by a response to a relatively discrete stimulus.

6. Phobias typically develop from (a) modeling, which may be vicarious, or (b) direct experience learning. Secondary gain is important in maintaining most phobias.

7. Agoraphobia is an extreme fear of being alone or finding oneself in public places without access to the help one anticipates needing. It is the most severe phobia and is often preceded by panic attacks. Implosion therapy or systematic desensitization (SDT) are often

used to treat the specific phobic patterns in this and most other phobias.

8. Social phobia involves persistent anxiety about scrutiny by others, such as during any public presentations. It differs from the avoidant personality disorder, in which the behaviors are chronic and not ego-alien.

9. The dissociative disorders are marked by a splitting of consciousness. Amnesia and psychogenic fugue are characterized by memory loss, the rare multiple personality by sepa-

rately conscious personalities, and the depersonalization disorder by a sense of unreality about one's self.

10. Most of the dissociative disorders reflect an inability to accept or integrate psychological conflict or trauma or unacceptable impulses. A previous experience with a dissociative state (perhaps under the influence of alcohol or during fever-induced delirium) is common.

TERMS TO REMEMBER

anxiety
neurosis
anxiety disorders
anxiety states
panic disorder
generalized anxiety disorder
obsessive-compulsive disorder
obsessive-compulsive personality
  disorder
ego-alien
intellectualization

learning-avoidance theory
phobic disorders
phobia
simple phobia
preparedness
modeling
direct experience learning
systematic desensitization
  technique
agoraphobia
implosion therapy

in vivo
social phobia
posttraumatic stress disorder
dissociative disorders
amnesia
psychogenic fugue
depersonalization disorder
multiple personality
somnambulism

FOR MORE INFORMATION

Aaron, S. (1987) *Stage fright.* Chicago: University of Chicago Press. One of the few good sources of material on this common form of social phobia

Boulanger, G., and Kadushin, C. (Eds.). (1986) *The Vietnam veteran defined.* Hillsdale, N.J.: Lawrence Erlbaum. A good overview of situations that generated the posttraumatic stress disorder

Crabtree, A. (1985) *Multiple man: Explorations in possession and multiple personality.* New York: Prager. Presents numerous cases of possession and multiple personality, with the perspective that these experiences, rather than being bizarre anomalies, are closer than has been thought to normal experiences

Hand, I., and Wittchen, H. (Eds.). (1986) *Panic and phobias.* Berlin: Springer-Verlag. An excellent examination of the empirical evidence supporting the various models of the development of these disorders

Lewis, H. (1981) *Freud and modern society.* Vol.1. New York: Plenum. An excellent updating of the psychodynamic views on a variety of disorders that has a special focus on anxiety, phobias, and the obsessive-compulsive disorder

May, R. (1977) *The meaning of anxiety.* New York: Norton. A well-written treatise on issues in anxiety by one of the leading existential humanist theorists

Osgood, C., Luria, A., Jeans, R., and Smith, A. (1976) The three faces of Evelyn: A case report. *Journal of Abnormal Psychology* 85:247–286. A series of articles that explores all aspects of the multiple personality, but especially the critical issue of how one can judge whether there is true separateness among the various personalities.

Rachman, S. (1980) *Obsessions and compulsions.* Englewood Cliffs, N.J.: Prentice-Hall. An important treatise on the causes and treatment of the obsessions and compulsions

III

Disorders Involving Psychosis

In a real dark night of the soul it is always three o'clock in the morning.

F. Scott Fitzgerald
The Crack-Up

Jack Nicholson portrays a schizophrenic turned violent murderer in *The Shining*. (IMP/GEH Stills Collection; © 1980 Warner Brothers)

DIAGNOSIS

ETIOLOGY

TREATMENT

7

The Schizophrenic Disorders

This chapter, along with the following two chapters (Paranoid Disorders and Affective Disorders), discusses disorders that warrant the label psychosis. The hallmark of the **psychosis** is a lack of contact with reality, which means that the disorder significantly, persistently, and consistently interferes with a person's **reality testing**. Reality testing is our ability to get a clear and accurate picture of the world by interacting effectively with the world, by observing accurately how other people interact with the world, and by then processing that information in our brains without significantly distorting the information. Schizophrenia, the topic of this chapter, is arguably the most severe form of psychosis, and the upcoming case of Lena documents the severe symptoms that typically occur in schizophrenia. Because this disorder so often requires hospitalization, we will discuss the problems of being placed in a mental hospital—that oft-dreaded symbol of "craziness"—and the negative effects of being institutionalized.

● The Case of Lena

Lena was brought by her husband to the admission office of a private psychiatric hospital. For the first week or two in the hospital, she would simply stare into space, and if someone moved her limbs into a different posture, she might remain in that position for hours. After a while, these symptoms disappeared, and she became simply quiet and withdrawn, occasionally mur-

muring odd phrases or sentences to herself. She hardly responded to anyone, shuffled from place to place, and would not answer questions.

Her husband reported that she had been acting strangely for the past year or two. He had observed her talking as if there were others present, but she would deny she had done so. She also had become much more distant from their family acquaintances and seemed content to spend long hours doing little or nothing.

The social history that was completed later revealed that Lena had manifested mild episodes of hyperactivity in early childhood and periods of odd behavior in late childhood and adolescence. Lena's mother had been diagnosed as schizophrenic and had died under questionable circumstances (a possible suicide) while in a mental hospital, when Lena was two years old. Her father remarried when Lena was four. Though aware of her atypical behavior, Lena's father and stepmother avoided seeking help or even openly acknowledging her problems, probably out of fear that Lena would be disturbed as her mother was. Because of their conflicted feelings, Lena experienced parenting that alternated inconsistently between affection and emotional avoidance. Lena's teachers also viewed her as odd, although Lena got good grades and enjoyed studying. She was shunned by her peers and seldom made friendships that lasted for any significant length of time.

She seldom dated, and married after only a short courtship. Her husband, a quiet individual who avoided stress of any sort, was actually attracted to Lena because he found her quiet and docile. He was not fully aware that these qualities were associated with deeper pathological tendencies toward withdrawal and extreme passivity. Gradually, however, Lena's emotional isolation and inner fantasy life so increased that it became evident she had truly lost touch with reality.

Lena shows the essential feature, loss of reality contact, of a psychosis, as well as the symptoms of the specific subcategory of psychosis called **schizophrenia.** Schizophrenia is a disturbance in accurately receiving and processing information, with attendant problems in emotional responses in interpersonal and vocational life, and accompanied by hallucinations or delusions. Of course, most people undergo temporary periods when emotional stress or fatigue may cause them to become slightly confused. Schizophrenics, however, show these symptoms along with significant thought impairment for substantial periods of time.

DIAGNOSIS

Incidence

Schizophrenia is the most severe psychosis in terms of severity of overall disturbance, prognosis, speed of recovery, emotional and physical cost to the client, and emotional and financial cost to family and society. One of every

This painting is typical of artwork produced by schizophrenics. (Collection de l'Art Brut, Lausanne, Switzerland)

one hundred people in the United States will be diagnosed as schizophrenic at least once, and a one percent rate has been consistent across cultures and across the years within our culture (Myers et al., 1984). A schizophrenic patient released after a first hospitalization has only about a 50 percent chance of staying out of the hospital for two years. The incidence of schizophrenia is believed to be approximately equal among males and females, although recent statistics suggest that males are more commonly afflicted (Lewine, 1981).

The DSM Criteria

The DSM cites thought disorder, hallucinations, and/or delusions as the essential features of schizophrenia, though each may occasionally be noted in other disorders (Levin, 1987; Sommers, 1985). **Thought disorder** includes delusional thinking, gaps in logic, and loose associations (see the Exhibit on Disordered Verbal Patterns in Schizophrenia later in the chapter). **Hallucinations** are sensory experiences in the absence of appropriate stimuli; for example, seeing something that is not there. One client stated that his mother constantly spoke to him, telling him to do various things. The fact that he believed she really was speaking to him, and that it was not just his imagination or a dream, made it a hallucination. It is possible to hallucinate in any

ABNORMALITY ACROSS CULTURES

Schizophrenic Symptom Differences in Rural and Urban Turkey

As noted in the text, it is generally clear from the literature that schizophrenia occurs at about a one percent rate across most cultures, and it is also clear that the symptoms vary somewhat from culture to culture. Several researchers (Chu et al.), writing in *The International Journal of Social Psychiatry* (1986, 32(3)) compared the symptomatology shown by rural and urban schizophrenic patients in a well-defined cultural area, in and around the city of Istanbul, Turkey.

Patients were included in the study only if they were of full Turkish ancestry, and were at least second-generation residents of the country of Turkey. Two thirds had been life residents of the specific geographic area they now lived in, and only four percent had lived in that area for less than five years.

Data was collected through extensive personal interviews with both the patients and their families. Symptoms at admission were rated on two well-validated symptom scales, the Brief Psychiatric Rating Scale and the Itil-Keskiner Psychopathological Rating Scale. Statistical agreement was high among all interviewers and raters.

The urban schizophrenic patients were more frequently anxious and tense, and were more depressed than the rural patients. The urban patients also showed more thought and speech "pressure," that is, they talked very fast, almost as if they were manic, and were not responsive to social cues to slow down or to wait for the responses of listeners. On the other hand, the rural patients were more withdrawn interpersonally, showed much less interest in communicating with others, and generally showed more bizarre behaviors than did urban patients. The rural patients evidenced more hallucinations, more interruptions in the flow of thoughts and consciousness, and seemed more disoriented to time and place.

In general, the differences between rural and urban schizophrenics in Turkey were much greater than has traditionally been found between rural and urban schizophrenics in the United States. This supports two basic conclusions. First, the idea that symptoms of schizophrenia are influenced by cultural factors. Second, within a given culture, manifestations of psychopathology can vary widely from one setting to another. A common cultural heritage does not negate the impact of other environmental factors or behavior. Contrasting influences of urban versus rural settings on psychopathology have been documented elsewhere, and they appear especially pronounced in modern-day Turkish society.

of the senses, but auditory hallucinations (hearing things that are not there) are the most common type found in schizophrenia. **Delusions** are inaccurate beliefs about the world, which persist despite information to the contrary. A person who believes he is Jesus Christ is delusional. A man who believes he is being followed may be delusional, though some investigation might be necessary to clarify whether or not he actually is being followed. It is very likely that impaired information processing in schizophrenia accounts in part for the maintenance of delusional thinking. Delusions, which are the essential characteristics of paranoia, will be discussed in the next chapter.

The DSM requires that the disordered pattern be chronic, though not always active, for at least six months before schizophrenia is diagnosed. As in Lena's case, the person's condition need not be documented by a clinician's direct observation throughout this period. The requirement that symptoms be observed for six months makes sense given that fatigue, overindulgence in alcohol, a variety of drugs, and even disturbances of calcium and phosphorus levels in the blood can trigger brief episodes resembling schizophrenic disorder (Carman and Wyatt, 1979).

Characteristics

Although evidence of hallucinations, delusions, or thought disorder are considered essential to the diagnosis of schizophrenia, other features may be found as well. Eugen Bleuler (1930) introduced the term schizophrenia as a replacement for the earlier "dementia praecox," a Latin term meaning mental deterioration at an early age used by the German psychiatrist Emil Kraeplin to designate a set of conditions that had this common feature of early and continuing severe mental disorder. Bleuler then listed what he considered to be the common characteristics of the disorder, historically referred to as the four A's: autism (similar to depersonalization), affect (a person's mood or feeling state), ambivalence, and disturbances of association. Used in this context, autism refers to a progressive inability to differentiate between oneself and the surrounding environment, as if one's very identity gradually dissipates. This is usually accompanied by withdrawal from others. Ambivalence refers to conflicting feelings that disturb interpersonal relationships. Disturbance of association refers to difficulties in making logical connections between ideas, which is basic to the thought disorder of schizophrenia (Berenbaum et al., 1985). For example, one hospitalized schizophrenic man said to his therapist, "I watched the ball game last night . . . the queen went to the ball. No, I'm not a queen, a queen of the ball." Disturbed affect primarily entails extremes of either an absence of or a variability—often referred to as "lability" by psychologists—in emotional response. Though not an inclusive or detailed description, Bleuler's four A's were an excellent first step in the classification of schizophrenic behavior. The characteristics psychologists now look for have been broadened somewhat; the following are considered essential.

Disturbance of affect.   This is usually manifested as either inappropriate or absent emotional responses in those situations that would normally generate an emotional response. In inappropriate affect, there is a disparity between what people say and the corresponding emotion which is conveyed (Miklowitz et al., 1986). For example, one schizophrenic woman continually giggled while describing her mother's long and painful death from a blood disorder. Flatness (or absence) of affect would have been noted instead if during her description the patient had expressed no emotion at all. Affective flattening is noted in most schizophrenics and in some chronically depressed patients.

Depersonalization. A common feature of schizophrenia, **depersonalization** is often associated with flattened affect and is similar to Bleuler's concept of autism. Sometimes referred to as a "loss of ego boundaries," depersonalization may lead to hallucinatory experiences. As people find it increasingly difficult to differentiate between self and nonself experiences, they hear their own thoughts and inner voices as if from the outside. The larynx of a schizophrenic sometimes moves at the time the person "hears" a voice (McGuigan, 1970), suggesting that auditory hallucinations are in essence subvocalizations of their inner thoughts and fears.

Consistent with depersonalization, schizophrenics withdraw from involvement with other people. They also show *thought disorder* (similar to Bleuler's disturbance of association) in coping with environmental stimulation, in part because of the odd and loose associations that characterize their thinking processes. There is often a related problem in controlling reactions to events, so that schizophrenics are often overwhelmed by even minimal levels of stimulation. Psychologists refer to this control as *gating*. One schizophrenic would go to a movie only if there were very few people there. It wasn't a phobia about being in a crowd. She simply couldn't attend effectively to the movie if there were other people near her, as they immediately distracted her. Withdrawal from people, particularly from groups of people, can thus serve as a defense against overstimulation, just as it apparently does for some elderly individuals.

Even in the early stages of schizophrenia, there are reductions in motor behavior, though they occasionally are interspersed with episodes of vigorous, repetitive movements. As the disorder progresses, however, such outbursts become less and less frequent. As a result, the major task facing those who work with chronic schizophrenic patients is to get them active—no easy task. One attendant on a ward with schizophrenics described his job as "a daily struggle against a great mass of inertia." This often entails overcoming the effects of medications, which tend to treat the outward symptoms of the disorder and decrease body movement. It may come as a surprise to learn that most inpatient units in which schizophrenics are hospitalized are actually quiet, sedate places, despite impressions conveyed in books and films to the contrary.

DSM Diagnostic Subtypes

An important study by the World Health Organization (1979) demonstrated the reliability of the overall diagnostic concept of schizophrenia in a variety of sociocultural settings. Schizophrenia is found across all cultures, affecting approximately one percent of the population worldwide. However, there are variations in how the diagnosis is made in different cultures. For example, British diagnosticians tend to view symptoms that border on both schizophrenia and affective disorder (see Chapter 9) as manifestations of an affective

---

EXHIBIT

Disordered Verbal Patterns in Schizophrenia

Several odd verbal patterns occur in schizophrenia. *Echolalia* is fairly common. Here the person repeats words of the question itself or even parrots the whole question, as in this example of an interaction between Lena and her therapist the day after she was admitted.

Therapist: Well, how are you feeling today?

Lena: I am feeling today, feeling the feelings today.

Therapist: Are you still hearing the voices?

Lena: Am I still hearing the voices, voices?

Therapist: Do you feel like you want to talk today?

Lena: I don't know if the feelings can talk today.

In addition, schizophrenics (as well as scientists, advertising agencies, and poets) are noted for developing *neologisms*, literally "new words." Schizophrenics often construct new words that link disparate ideas with a sort of internal logic known only to themselves. Because most people have little interest in deciphering these often bizarre association patterns, the result is further social distancing. One schizophrenic client who often used the mord *miltherove* had deep feelings of having been rejected by his mother, and it became apparent that this word symbolized an entire constellation of feelings. As best as could be determined, it was a combination of *milk* and *mother's love.* Schizophrenics occasionally run various loosely associated thoughts, neologisms, mispronunciations, and the like into odd and confusing verbal combinations referred to as word salad.

---

disorder. American diagnosticians, on the other hand, are more likely to regard them as indicative of schizophrenia (Draguns, 1980). No one is certain why this is so. However, most believe it is because American psychiatrists are a bit more optimistic about treating schizophrenia, and thus are more willing to make that diagnosis.

It is difficult to establish accurate subclassifications of schizophrenia because schizophrenia is a disorder with variable manifestations—really, a group of loosely related disorders with certain traits and patterns in common.

Symptoms of more than one DSM subclassification of schizophrenia may co-exist in one person at the same time; symptoms may wax and wane; some symptoms (together with specific subdiagnoses) may disappear altogether, while others emerge. Research on the DSM categories is not yet complete. However, clinicians do find the DSM subcategories useful, as do others who come in contact with the mental health system (including teachers, lawyers, and police). The complex nature of the disorder should be kept in mind as you consider the following phenomenologic (that is, descriptive rather than explanatory) subtypes.

Disorganized (hebephrenic) schizophrenic disorder. The **disorganized schizophrenic** (termed hebephrenic in earlier DSM classifications) displays disrupted or incoherent speech and markedly inappropriate affect, often in the form of random giggling. "Silly" is an apt way of describing this behavior. Delusions or hallucinations are present, but usually show no coherence or pattern. Disorganized schizophrenics usually evolve chronic, more apathetic patterns over time. The likelihood of significant, long-term recovery is low.

Catatonic schizophrenic disorder. There are two categories of catatonic schizophrenia, stuporous and agitated. Lena, whose case was described at the beginning of this chapter, showed **catatonic** symptoms early in the course of her schizophrenia. She was brought to the hospital after her husband found her sitting in a very odd posture on the floor. She stared into space and would not respond to him at all. If he moved her arm or body in any way, she retained the new position indefinitely. Lena manifested a type of catatonic schizophrenia known as stuporous catatonia, characterized by reduced movement, and in some cases "waxy flexibility," a condition in which the body is passively receptive to movement. The severe degree of disturbance associated with stuporous catatonia is manifested primarily as extreme lethargy and psychomotor slowing. Dealing physically with stuporous catatonics is much like moving store mannequins through a range of motions.

Agitated catatonia, in contrast, is marked by uncontrollable motor and verbal behavior. Patients in this state are difficult to manage, and can be quite dangerous to themselves or to others. This is not so much due to any personally directed hostility, as it is a tendency to see other people simply as objects to be thrown about or destroyed. Before the use of potent drugs that suppress virtually all activity, agitated catatonics were sometimes put in padded cells where they occasionally exhausted themselves to the point of stupor and even death.

Catatonic schizophrenia typically follows one of two courses. In the periodic catatonia type, an abrupt onset is followed by alternating periods of stupor and agitation. A good recovery is typical, although recurrences are possible. Periodic catatonics are particularly dangerous during the shift from stupor to agitation, mainly because there is usually no prior warning as to when the shift will occur.

There is also a chronic form of this disorder, characterized by uninterrupted stupor. The onset is gradual, and recovery is unlikely. Like disorganized schizophrenics, chronic catatonic patients often eventually develop undifferentiated or residual schizophrenic patterns.

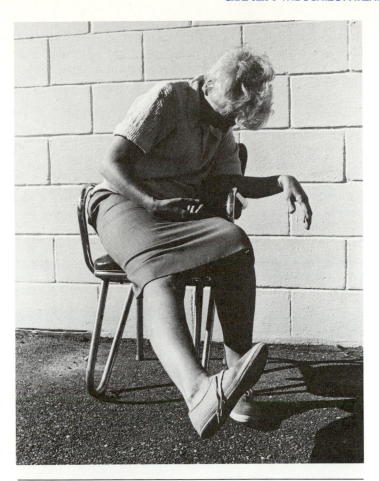

With bent arm and twisted leg, this catatonic schizophrenic may maintain an uncomfortable position for hours, even days, seemingly oblivious to her surroundings. (Grunnitus/Monkmeyer Press Photo Service)

Paranoid schizophrenic disorder.   Paranoid schizophrenia is denoted by persecutory or grandiose delusions or delusional jealousy, often accompanied by related hallucinations. The delusions are more disorganized than those of the other paranoid disorders. This interesting syndrome is discussed in detail in the next chapter.

Schizoaffective disorder.   **Schizoaffective** disorder stands as a totally separate category in DSM. As its name implies, it occupies a functional midpoint between schizophrenia and the affective disorders. People with this fairly common disorder show both severe affective (usually depressive) and schizophrenic (usually thought disorder and withdrawal) symptoms. Compared with schizophrenics, schizoaffective patients tend to have a shorter course of their disease, leave the hospital sooner, have less chance of remission, and are less likely to have other family members with a true schizophrenic disorder.

Undifferentiated schizophrenic disorder.

This common catchall category is used when the schizophrenic client shows prominent signs of schizophrenia (such as thought disorder or disorganized behavior) without the clear, dominant signs of any one of the syndromes described above. The longer a person remains schizophrenic, the more likely he or she is to show this general pattern of symptoms. Thus, in terms of number, it is by far the most common schizophrenic pattern.

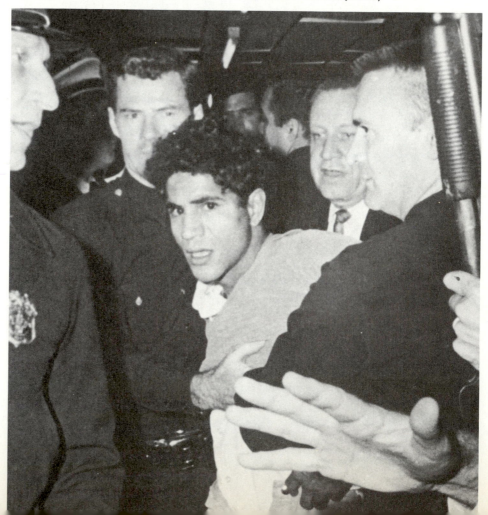

Sirhan B. Sirhan, shown here moments after he assassinated Robert F. Kennedy, was later diagnosed as a chronic paranoid schizophrenic. (UPI/Bettman Newsphotos)

Residual schizophrenic disorder.   Residual schizophrenic disorder is diagnosed when the person has already manifested a clear schizophrenic episode fitting one of the subtypes described above, but the symptoms have subsequently lessened. It is often applied to formerly hospitalized schizophrenic patients. The client may still show signs of social withdrawal, emotional flatness, or even mild delusions or hallucinations, but the symptoms are no longer prominent enough to disable reality testing (the ability to reasonably assess and use information from the environment). The obvious difficulty with making this diagnosis is that a judgment as to whether symptoms are prominent is necessarily subjective. The diagnosis is further complicated by the potency of chemotherapy in masking behaviors.

Related Disorder Patterns

The DSM includes several other disorders related in some way to schizophrenia. The term *schizophreniform disorder,* for example, refers to a person who shows schizophrenic behavior, but for less than six months and more than one week. If such behavior occurs for less than a week and there is a clear provoking trauma, such as a death in the family, it is called a *brief reactive psychosis.* Both categories commonly reflect either (1) breakdowns in marginally adjusted individuals (see the schizotypal personality disorder, discussed below), (2) the effect of severe but transitory physiologic and psychological disruptions, or (3) reactions to acute stressors, such as the sudden and unexpected loss of one's job. The extreme severity of disturbance in these disorders justifies the psychotic label.

Persons with the schizoaffective disorder show some schizophrenic symptoms. However, though schizoaffective disorder is a psychosis, it is not a schizophrenia. The crucial diagnostic criterion is whether the affective disorder occurs before or after the schizophrenic component; if it occurs first, it is a schizoaffective disorder; if it occurs afterward, a schizophrenic label is appropriate.

There are also two DSM personality disorders (see Chapter 12) that resemble schizophrenia, the *schizoid personality disorder* and the *schizotypal personality disorder.* People with a schizoid personality disorder manifest the severe problems in social relationships characteristic of schizophrenia, but they show no thought disorder or disorganized behavior. These individuals are solitary in their interests and habits, and their odd behavior often gives them a reputation as an eccentric or a recluse.

The schizotypal individual is more obviously disturbed that the schizoid personality. Although schizotypal persons do not always show severe avoidance in interpersonal relationships, they do show odd behavior or mannerisms and peculiar speech and languages usage. A mild example of this last syndrome is the comical pronunciations of Inspector Clouseau, the bumbling French detective immortalized by Peter Sellers in the still-popular Pink Panther movies.

EXHIBIT

Manifestation of Schizophrenia

Self-Concept Symptoms	Interpersonal Symptoms	Physical and Behavioral Symptoms
• Unable to separate self from outside environment (loss of ego boundaries)	• Withdrawn	• Hallucinations
	• Cannot relate to others	• Delusions
• Disturbed body image and loss of identity	• Loss of interest in self, others, and environment	• Increased motor activities (in agitated catatonia); impulsive
• Unkempt physical appearance and poor personal hygiene	• Suspicious	• Decreased motor activities (in catatonic stupor)
	• Litigious	
• Bizzare behaviors, i.e., grimacing, odd mannerisms, stereotyped postures	• Argumentative	• Poor muscle tone due to a lack of desire to be active
	• Violent or aggressive	• Sleep pattern disturbances
	• Negativistic	• Poor eating habits, i.e., may become obese or undernourished
• Excessive preoccupation with sex, religion, identity, and somatic complaints	• Assaultive	
	• No emotional involvement with others; indifferent to environment	• Speech: confused, illogical, incoherent, repetitive, circumstantial, mutism, flight of ideas, autism, neologism
• Fearful and avoidant	• Cannot relate to others; uncomfortable with relationships	
• Apathetic		
• Ambivalent	• Negative to suggestions	
• Guilt feelings	• Few problem-solving skills	
• Inappropriate emotional responses		
• Lack of motivation		

One reason for differentiating between these two syndromes is the difference in their prognoses. Schizotypal personalities, who may show odd thought patterns or some paranoia, are much more likely to have occasional brief psychotic episodes. Schizoid personalities tend to develop increasingly isolated and eccentric lifestyles.

Alternative Classification Systems

There are conceptions and continuums other than the DSM that have been developed to classify schizophrenic behavior. One early well-researched scheme (Lorr et al., 1963) has identified 10 clusters of psychotic symptoms, including hostile belligerence, paranoid projection, and motor disturbances. Though sophisticated methodologically, Lorr's system does not enjoy the official sanctioning of DSM-III, and, as a result, has not been integrated into the work of practicing clinicians.

The paranoid-nonparanoid continuum has received much attention in the literature (Mirsky and Duncan, 1986; Bernheim and Lewine, 1979); there is good evidence that it reflects genuine differences in functioning and even in etiology. This system receives full consideration in the next chapter.

The acute-chronic dimension suggests that length of illness could be a factor in predicting remission. Generally, the longer people have been schizophrenic, the more likely they are to be in a hospital, to remain in a hospital, to return quickly if released, and to remain schizophrenic for life.

A more elaborate version of the acute-chronic continuum is the process-reactive dimension. It expands the simple time concept of acute-chronic into a number of other variables that suggest a schizophrenic process marked by slowly developing evolutionary factors (process) versus an abrupt schizophrenic reaction in which a major component is environmental conflict and stress (reactive). Females are slightly more likely than males to show reactive rather than process schizophrenia (Lewine, 1981). The reactive schizophrenic client shows a more sudden onset, and it is often possible to identify a specific stressor (such as a death in the family or marital separation). Process schizophrenia shows a more gradual development and a greater probability of birth trauma, introversion, hyperactivity, and school maladjustment—symptoms that are usually noticeable in early childhood—with biological factors that are more likely to be causal. The probability of recovery is much higher for a reactive than for a process schizophrenic.

Somewhat related to the process-reactive dimension is a conceptualization of the symptoms of schizophrenia as positive or negative. This is an idea first put forth by J. Hughlings Jackson in the late 1800s, and reintroduced by Strauss and his colleagues in 1974 (Sommers, 1985; Strauss, 1985). Positive signs are those likely to respond to chemotherapy and are more common in acute than chronic schizophrenia. There is some difference of opinion as to which symptoms are "negative." But, in general, negative symptoms are those that are less responsive to chemotherapy and are more likely to reflect structural abnormality rather than psychological or biochemical disorders. They are more likely to be seen in chronic or process schizophrenia.

Difficulty in Diagnosis

Confused thoughts, especially those that are not persistent or recurring, take place in disorders other than schizophrenia, occasionally making it difficult to differentiate among them (Berenbaum et al., 1985). Disorders frequently confused with schizophrenia include certain brain disorders, drug overdoses, mental retardation, multiple personality, and severe affective disorders. Because many organic conditions (brain tumors, toxins) can cause hallucina-

---

EXHIBIT

Premorbid Factors in Schizophrenia

Premorbid factors, or factors associated with (not necessarily causal to) the later development of schizophrenia, provide an even broader focus than the process-reactive dimension. Only a few of the factors listed below may be noted in any one case, but they are common across cases.

Premorbid predictors

1. A schizophrenic parent or parents or—a less potent variable—the presence of other schizophrenic blood relatives. For sons, separation from even a disturbed mother seems to be more damaging than it is for daughters. For daughters, the earlier a mother becomes schizophrenic, the greater the likelihood they will too.

2. A history of prenatal (pregnancy) disruption or birth problems.

3. Slowed reaction times in perception (such as slowness in becoming aware of a stimulus) or very rapid recovery rate of the autonomic nervous system after some stress or novel stimulus.

4. Hyperactivity, signs of central nervous system dysfunction (such as convulsive disorder), or evidence of enlarged cerebral ventricles (the spaces between brain tissue).

5. Low birth weight and/or low IQ relative to siblings.

6. Early role as odd member of family or scapegoat.

7. Parenting marked by inconsistency and by emotionally extreme (both positive and negative) responses and double messages; parental rejection, particularly when one parent's negative effect is not countered by corrective attention and care from the other parent.

8. Rejection by peers in childhood or adolescence; being perceived by both teachers and peers as more irritable and more unstable than other children.

---

tions, delusions, or thought disorder, neurologic screening is important in confirming a diagnosis. The use of certain drugs can also result in symptoms resembling schizophrenia. For example, toxic doses of amphetamines or phencyclidine (see Chapter 11) administered for as little as a week can produce symptoms closely resembling schizophrenia, and the effects can continue for a substantial time after their use has been stopped.

Lysergic acid diethylamide (LSD) can also produce symptoms resembling psychosis. Because LSD predominantly affects the visual system, visual hallucinations are common, but these usually do not last beyond the period of drug intake. Detection of psychosis caused by prolonged amphetamine, alcohol, or drug abuse may require a lengthy drying-out period.

Mental retardation, when associated with flat affect, odd behavior, and

social isolation can also be confused with schizophrenia. If a valid intelligence test and sociobehavioral history indicates retardation, a diagnosis of schizophrenia should be made only when there is a clear indication of hallucinations and delusions or other severe distortions in thinking and perception.

The diagnostic distinctions between paranoid schizophrenia and the other paranoid disorders and between schizophrenia and the affective disorders are discussed in Chapters 8 and 9, respectively.

ETIOLOGY

The DSM treats schizophrenia as a phenomenologic label, meaning that it is a cluster of related disorders that often have similar outward manifestations but which may have different causes, patterns of development, and outcomes. The possible causes for schizophrenia are called **generic variables,** which are those general causes from which any one case of schizophrenia may originate. These result in **mediating variables,** the secondary but more obvious manifestations of the disorder. Mediating variables are symptoms directly associated with the critical marker (or defining variable) of schizophrenia, an attention and information processing deficit that we refer to as the **common channel** for the disorder. **Maintenance variables** are the external variables that serve to sustain and amplify the disorder once its development is well under way.

A number of generic (not necessarily genetic) causes have been proposed. Several different generic causes can eventually lead to the manifest behaviors of schizophrenia. Some theories have more support than others, but it is clear that in any one schizophrenic person, many factors may combine to form the behavioral patterns observed.

EXHIBIT

Hypothesized Factors in Schizophrenia

Generic Factors	Mediating Factors	The Common Channel	Maintenance Factors
Genetic	Hallucinogen	Attentional and informational processing deficit	Social isolation
Birth and/or prenatal disorder	Transmethylation		Scapegoating
Viral	Dopamine		Labeling
Social learning	Auditory or visual processing deficit		Impression management
Psychodynamic-regression			Learned helplessness

EXHIBIT

An Exploration of Genetic Theories on Schizophrenia

As the text suggests, most research on schizophrenia points to biological, rather than psychological, factors as the original or generic cause of the disorder. More specifically, some recent studies seem to indicate that schizophrenia is indeed genetically based.

In 1987, Drs. Steven Matthyse and Phillip Holzman of McLean Hospital in Massachusetts discovered that a majority of the schizophrenic patients in their study—and approximately 50 percent of their healthy relatives—have a subtle, though distinctive defect in their ability to track a moving target with their eyes. This disorder, similar to some of the other information-processing defects cited in the text as "the common channel" of schizophrenia, is believed to reflect a single underlying brain defect that has not, as yet, been clearly identified.

Although the eye tracking defect is subtle, researchers are able to measure it using an instrument, worn like a headset with glasses, that records the eyes' movements as they follow a dot on a video screen. While normal subjects are able to easily and smoothly follow the dot, those with poor eye tracking exhibit a series of erratic, jumpy eye movements. In doing so, it is believed that they lose bits of information available to them and, over time, may be unable to solve problems accurately or record stimuli in the environment.

As the text notes, however, such possible biological links are not the only factor in the cause of schizophrenia. For example, ongoing studies in Finland involving children given up for adoption by schizophrenic mothers, have found that schizophrenia develops more often among those whose adoptive parents are characterized as disturbed, as compared to those whose adoptive parents appear normal. This finding suggests that the onset of schizophrenia is influenced both by original, biologically generated defects and a disturbed, facilitative environment, that is, one with the mediating and maintenance variables noted in the text.

Other variables may be seen as mediating factors. There is much literature supporting the idea that schizophrenics have perceptual and other neurologically based processing deficits. As a result, they are more easily distracted by irrelevant aspects of stimuli and may use odd and/or idiosyncratic logic systems in their thinking (Hartmann et al., 1985). Their reaction times to simple stimuli, such as a tone, are much more variable than normal. Also, schizophrenic patients consistently come up with different conclusions than other people about what seems to be the same data from the environment. Not surprisingly, many schizophrenics report a sense of operating in a "fog" or complain of "too much stuff (stimuli) to deal with" (Miklowitz et al., 1986; Bernheim and Lewine, 1979). The consequent attention and information processing deficits are best seen as the common channel between earlier generic and mediational factors and later consequent patterns, such as rejection by others, withdrawal, or poor vocational performance.

As the text and the studies on eye tracking indicate, schizophrenia appears to have a close genetic link, but much more research needs to be done on this debilitating disorder.

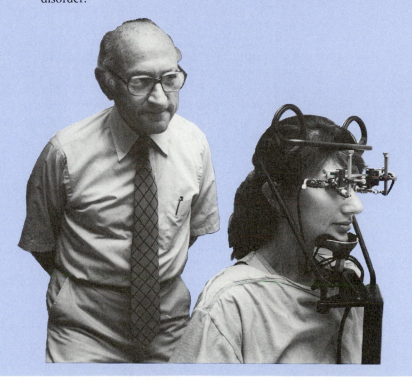

Maintenance variables provide a means of explaining why schizophrenia tends to be chronic. For example, the label "schizophrenic" has negative interpersonal consequences that strenghten and perpetuate the person's schizophrenic status (Goldstein and Strochan, 1987).

The accompanying Exhibit tabulates the various major generic, mediating, and maintenance factors that theorists have listed as contributing to an eventual diagnosis of schizophrenia. The status of some of these variables is occasionally disputed. For example, Ullmann and Krasner (1975) would probably label attentional deficit as a generic variable, but most other theorists would view it as a mediating factor.

Generic Factors

The genetic view.   The past decade has witnessed increasing acceptance of the idea that genetic variables have a significant role in the development of schizophrenia (Beatty, 1987; Berenbaum et al., 1985). The first evidence supporting this claim came from observations that schizophrenia tends to run in families. While the incidence of schizophrenia is about one percent in the general population, in parents of schizophrenics it is around five percent, and in children and siblings of schizophrenics about 10 percent. Although these statistics are consistent with a genetic cause of schizophrenia, environmentally based factors, such as modeling and commonality of parenting technique, could effectively explain such findings. Efforts to devise more sophisticated research that could clarify the issue led to twin studies and adoption studies.

Twin studies. As early as 1946, Kallman found a higher incidence of schizophrenia among monozygotic (identical) twins than in dizygotic (fraternal) twins. Ullman and Krasner (1975), however, demonstrated significant weaknesses in Kallman's methodology. More recent studies have overcome some of those difficulties, but several issues continue to plague researchers. For example, when an identical twin becomes schizophrenic, it is most often the twin whose birth was more difficult and/or who weighed less at birth; thus, a good case can be made of including prenatal environmental and birth trauma factors in explanations supporting the genetic theory. There is also good reason to believe that identical twins are treated by parents and others more similarly than fraternal twins; hence, environmental commonalities could also be a factor. As a result of these problems, researchers have turned to adoption studies to find definitive support for the genetic view.

Adoption studies. Denmark is a country that keeps excellent centralized health records. Its small size makes it easy to trace people, so it has been the site of many studies of adoptees who were placed in normal homes, but whose natural parent or parents later became schizophrenic. A smaller number of normal children who came from normal parents, but whose adoptive parents turned out to be schizophrenic, have also been studied. Researchers such as Kety and Mednick have used this population to support the idea that genetic factors are important in schizophrenia (Kety, 1975; Mednick and Christiansen, 1977).

Most theorists now agree that there is a significant genetic component in the development of schizophrenia, with four important qualifications.

1. At most, genetic factors do not appear to account for much more than 50 percent of all factors causing schizophrenia, even in identical twins (Kety, 1975).

2. Rates of schizophrenia in identical twins and in cases noted in adoption studies are highest "for severe chronic schizophrenia" (Kety, 1975, p.14). In the acute and reactive forms of schizophrenia—the mild and/or short-term standard diagnostic categories—the evidence is that the genetic component is less important.

3. Data from genetic studies do not indicate the mode of transmission of the genetic factors in schizophrenia. It is unclear whether transmission

EXHIBIT

Family History of a Typical Schizophrenic Person

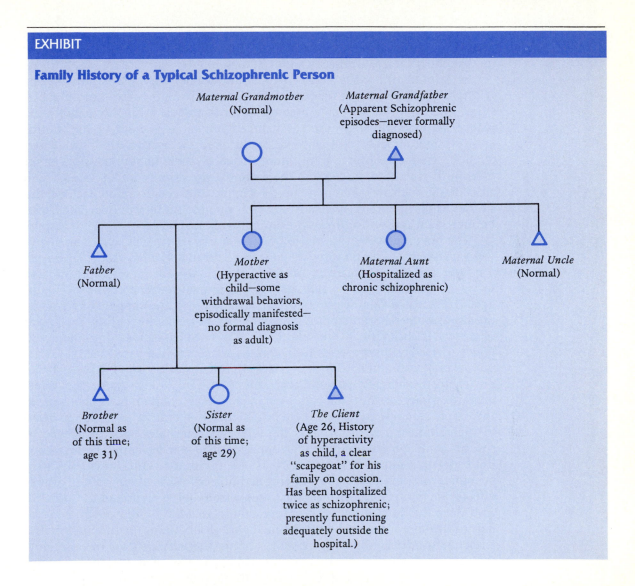

occurs through nerve and/or blood chemistry factors, brainstem dysfunction, or some other mode.

4. The genetic factors do not operate directly, as a gene for hair color would; they operate only as a predisposition. Two persons may have the same genetic predisposition, but because of other factors (such as family or modeling) one may become schizophrenic while the other does not.

High-risk studies. The existence of a genetic component in schizophrenia suggests that certain people are born with predisposing vulnerability. As noted earlier, the incidence of schizophrenia in the normal population is about one percent, but for people with one schizophrenic parent it is almost 10 percent. For those rare situations where there are two schizophrenic parents, the likelihood of occurrence is about 35 percent.

In a long-term study referred to as the Israeli high-risk study, Nagler (1985) and his associates followed four groups of subjects for more than 16 years. The high-risk groups are comprised of subjects with a schizophrenic parent. Normal individuals used as matched pair subjects made up the control groups. Environmental influence was controlled for by two groups matched to these groups. Subjects were either raised in their family of origin or in a kibbutz environment. Hence, there were four groups (of 25 each): high risk–family, high risk–kibbutz, control–family, and control–kibbutz. Because of the insularity of Israeli society, attrition rate for these groups is negligible, an important reason for doing the study there.

The children were assessed by blind examiners (that is, examiners who were unaware of whether the subjects were normal or high-risk children) on a number of clinical scales for preschizophrenic trends, for example, anxiety level and irritability, at 11 and again (by different examiners) at 16 years of age. There was a significant effect for most of the scales, implicating genetic predisposition as a predictor for schizophrenia. In the kibbutz group the family effect was nonsignificant for almost all of the scales, as was the interaction effect. These results were confirmed again at the 16-year assessment.

Several researchers (Garmezy, 1978; Hartmann et al., 1984; Nagler, 1985) are trying to identify persons who are at risk to study them from birth onward. Many of the concepts discussed in this chapter have come from this important research. But there is a significant ethical problem involved in such studies, namely, what is the effect of being identified as a child at risk for schizophrenia? Since schizophrenia may not be apparent for years, these persons must be followed well into adulthood, and, inevitably, they become aware of the reason for being scrutinized. What, then, are the overall effects on children and their parents simply from being identified as "at risk?" And does this long process of observation alter what would have been the natural results, without the added factor of observation? In this regard, the Heisenberg principle in physics states that in the very process of observing, the nature of what is observed itself is changed. Also, is it reasonable to put a person with one schizophrenic parent through potential worry and upset if there is only a one-in-10 chance of becoming schizophrenic? The issue is a cost–benefit one. The primary costs are worry, hassle, and implicit labeling as disordered. The benefits are knowledge that could help other schizophrenics and, more importantly to the individual being studied, the likelihood that with an early identification of risk, a degree of prevention through family therapy and remedial-skills training is possible (Garmezy, 1978; Hartmann et al., 1984). These researchers argue that the possibility of prevention is the benefit to the individual that tips the balance in favor of benefits over costs.

Diagram of Brain's Major Sections

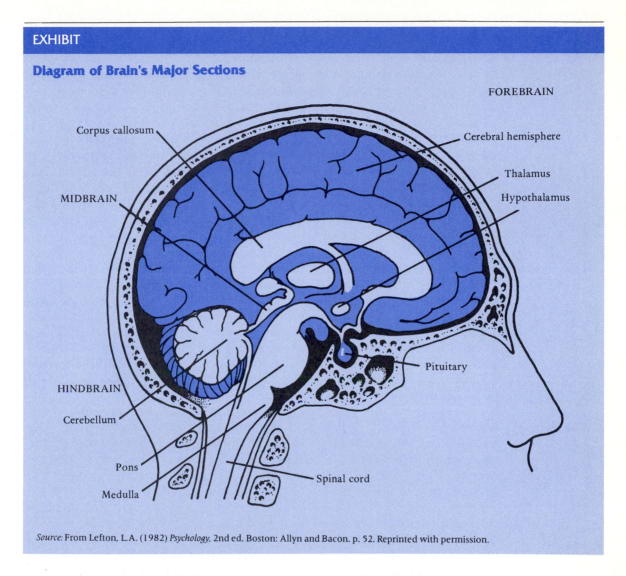

Source: From Lefton, L.A. (1982) *Psychology,* 2nd ed. Boston: Allyn and Bacon. p. 52. Reprinted with permission.

Neurological processing deficits.   The schizophrenic shows a wide range of problems in gathering accurate information from the environment and using it effectively. One hypothesis that accounts for such a variety of deficits is that schizophrenics simply may not hear and/or see as well as normal people and that this deficiency has not yet been detected. The schizophrenic thus has less social leeway than a person with a clearly labeled vision or hearing problem. For people known to be hard of hearing, allowances are made for occasional misinterpretations or failures to respond in a conversation. If not so labeled, others begin to think of them as odd, hostile, or uninterested, and begin to distance themselves interpersonally (Curran et al., 1982).

A slightly higher than normal percentage of schizophrenics do have obvious deficits in hearing and vision, but not enough to account for the overall incidence of schizophrenia. However, evidence is emerging that schizophrenics differ from normal people in subcortical auditory and visual processing pathways, particularly in the hippocampus and reticular activating system regions. Thus, although they generally hear sounds as accurately as others, they do not process and integrate them as efficiently. Because standard auditory examinations do not record this type of deficit, the subjects receive no "impaired hearing" label. Nevertheless, both schizophrenic patients and those around them are likely to find other labels to explain the behavior, usually derogatory ones. Even tags such as "odd" or "uninterested" have a negative connotation and lead to both distancing and loss of self-esteem.

There is also research evidence that schizophrenics visually process information differently than normal people (Regan, 1987; Pritchard, 1986). For example, Place and Gilmore (1980) investigated whether schizophrenics used the visual perception principles of proximity and similarity in the same way normal people do. They presented a line-counting task for approximately 20 milliseconds under three grouping conditions: (1) *homogeneous,* all lines were of one orientation; (2) *heterogeneous/adjacent,* both line orientations, but lines of the same orientation in an uninterrupted sequence; and (3) *heterogeneous/nonadjacent,* both line orientations, but no two adjacent lines were of the same orientation.

As Place and Gilmore (1980) predicted, the most accurate line count for normal subjects occurred in the homogeneous condition. They did less well in the heterogeneous/adjacent condition, and even worse in the heterogeneous/nonadjacent condition. On the other hand, schizophrenics showed little variation across conditions. And, most importantly from the perspective of research methodology, these results were replicated by Wells and Leventhal (1984) using different conditions. These data indicate that schizophrenics are less effective in information processing because they do not engage in an initial global analysis of stimuli, as do normal people, but instead rely almost exclusively on a detailed local analysis. Wells and Leventhal note that schizophrenic patients also use this same ineffective style in the recognition of human faces and even pain, causing obvious social problems. Researchers agree that the most probable explanation for this deficiency is cerebral dysfunction.

Evidence for these deficits has emerged in studies of cortical evoked potentials (Regan, 1987; Pritchard, 1986; Zuercher, 1980). In this type of research, a series of clicks (auditory) or blips (visual) is delivered to the subject at varying rates while EEG measurements are taken from different parts of the brain, such as the cortex, midbrain, and brainstem, to measure the speed and adequacy of immediate brain response in each area. This approach is quite sensitive to both voluntary and involuntary response patterns. In fact, evoked potentials may well be a part of lie-detector examinations someday.

Zuercher's finding (directly supported by Braff and Saccuzzo, 1985, and Hayashida et al., 1986) that schizophrenic patients respond inadequately at subcortical levels suggests that even though they hear it, they process information inefficiently, leading to a poor response to auditory information, particularly when there are many competing stimuli. Other researchers have noted especially poor performance in schizophrenics during high auditory or visual stimulus conditions (Regan, 1987).

While psychopaths (a subgroup of the antisocial personality disorders, see Chapter 12) are stimulation-seeking (for example, they love crowded and noisy beaches at spring break or the infield at the Kentucky Derby), schizophrenics are **stimulation-avoidant** (they prefer small quiet groups, if they socialize at all). Interpersonal withdrawal is an effective stimulus-avoidance behavior; unfortunately, it feeds into a cycle of person avoidance–peer labeling, peer rejection–negative self-labeling. Garmezy (1978) found early peer avoidance and subsequent rejection to be an important predictor of later schizophrenia in children at risk.

Birth disorder theories.   How might this central auditory or visual processing deficit occur? Genetic defect is one possibility. Another compelling theory is that prenatal and/or birth difficulties cause temporary asphyxiation, leading to brain damage (Zuercher, 1980; Schulsinger et al., 1984; Regan, 1987). **Asphyxia,** a combination of anoxia (a loss of oxygen to brain tissue) and increased carbon dioxide tension in the blood and tissues, leads to an acidic metabolic condition that results in tissue damage.

The traditional view has been that a short period of asphyxiation in newborns does no lasting damage. It is now clear, however, that asphyxiation, for even a period of minutes, causes damage (Beatty, 1987; Towbin, 1978). Because newborns have weak pulmonary systems, recovery from asphyxiation is difficult; a child with weaknesses in other body systems (such as circulation) can be damaged in an even shorter time. Thus, even very brief periods of asphyxiation may cause minimal (and therefore hard to detect) damage.

Towbin's work suggests that there is a high incidence of anoxia in premature infants, but that resulting cell loss may sometimes be hard to detect. He states that "with diffuse cortical hypoxic neuronal loss, the cellular depopulation may be lightly and evenly spread as to escape detection microscopically. A depletion of neurons up to 30 percent may go unrecognized even by experienced neuropathologists" (p. 630). The site most vulnerable to this kind of damage is the brainstem, particularly the cochlear nuclei (Zuercher, 1980), which are critical in the processing and integration of auditory information. Zuercher's research suggests that schizophrenics have poorer evoked-response performance to auditory stimuli at the brainstem level.

Neurocirculatory dysfunction.   Another specific variation of the neurologic deficit theory is the idea that problems in blood circulation in the brain (possibly genetically based, or possibly from early viral infections) are a central factor in schizophrenia. For example, Gur and her colleagues (Gur et al., 1985) measured blood flow in various regions of the brains of 19 unmedicated schizophrenics and 19 matched controls. These researchers found that in the schizophrenic patients, blood flow was significantly higher in the left hemisphere, while blood flow was approximately equal in both hemispheres in the controls. This disparity was even greater for the more severely disturbed schizophrenics. Together, these results suggest that overactivation of the left hemisphere may be an important factor, and in line with that view, some of the chemotherapies appear to eliminate this left-right difference, thus regulating the behavioral pattern as well.

In a similar study, Silverton et al. (1985) used 27 subjects from a Danish longitudinal study (mean age, 31.5 years) on whom they had good measures of birth patterns. Enlargement of the ventricles (the spaces between brain tissue), implicated in certain neurologically based theories of schizophrenia, was found significantly more often in schizophrenics than in controls. Enlargement was proportionately greater in those subjects with a low birth weight and height, and with a history of a difficult birth, as rated by the attending midwife. Silverton et al. believe this could reflect insults, possibly of a viral origin, experienced either in utero or in the birthing process.

Social learning theory.   There is a general agreement that the factors cited by social learning theorists are very important in facilitating the development of schizophrenic behavior (Sarbin and Mancuso, 1980; Levin, 1987). Somewhat more controversial is the assertion of Ullman and Krasner (1975) that these factors *cause* schizophrenia. In their view, schizophrenics do not attend to stimuli in a normal way because from early in their lives they have not received adequate reinforcement for such behavior. According to this perspective, the attention problems central to schizophrenia are a direct product of parenting and environment, rather than being related to genetic, viral, or birth trauma factors. Although good evidence indicates that social learning variables are critical in the sequential development and maintenance of schizophrenia, there is no clear evidence that they play a causal role. Indeed, providing such evidence would be extremely difficult; social learning theorists could neither practically nor ethically take infants and make them schizophrenic through learning procedures. Even if schizophrenia occurred as predicted, it would not clearly prove the point. For example, administration of high levels of amphetamines also causes schizophrenic-like behavior, but it cannot then be argued that schizophrenia necessarily develops because of a high intake of amphetamines.

Psychodynamic theory.   Psychoanalysts see regression to an earlier, more primitive level of adjustment as an essential cause of schizophrenia. In their view, the severely disturbed schizophrenic regresses to the oral-passive period,

Therapists hypothesize that severely disturbed schizophrenics regress to the oral-passive phase of development where hallucinations may replace an unacceptable reality.   (Terry Cooke/Photo Researchers, Inc.)

when infants are just beginning to discriminate their own self-boundaries. Some consider paranoid schizophrenics (who are often verbally—or orally— aggressive toward other people) to have regressed to a slightly higher period, the oral-sadistic stage, when children like to bite and use their mouths to explore just about everything.

The schizophrenic's regression is thought to occur because of a significant increase in id demands (aggressive or sexual impulses) or because disapproval by the super-ego (such as guilt over sexual indulgence) results in overwhelming anxiety. Hallucinations and delusions constitute an attempt to substitute a different reality from one that is too threatening. The illogical thought processes and odd speech patterns are thought to be components of personality organization that existed before the development of ego control and logical thought. The difficulty with these hypotheses is that they are almost impossible to validate empirically (Miklowitz et al., 1986).

The schizophrenogenic mother theory and the double-bind concept, both of which are variations of psychoanalytic theory, have received modest support. According to the first of these (Meyer and Karon, 1967; Karon, 1976), the schizophrenogenic mother unconsciously uses the child to satisfy her emotional needs, while normal mothers tend to interact with their children in ways that promote the best interests of both parties. For example, a schizophrenogenic mother may spend much time attending to her child in public in order to get praise for her role as mother, and then in private ignore or even punish any of the child's demands. A major methodologic problem with this theory is that parent-child combinations are almost always studied after the child has been labeled as schizophrenic. Thus, it is extremely difficult to tell if the mother's behavior is a cause of or a reaction to the schizophrenia.

The double-bind theory of schizophrenia was first proposed by an anthropologist named Gregory Bateson. Later refined by Jay Haley and other advocates of a family-systems approach to psychopathology, the double-bind theory has received moderate support from empirical research (Miklowitz et al., 1986). Basically, double binds are established when parents issue a strong negative injunction to a child (for example, "Don't you dare bring home friends I don't approve of!"), which they then manage to implicitly contradict. To use this example, the parent might then encourage the child to invite a playmate, friend, or date over whom the child knows full well has been "blacklisted." The child must then decide which of these two incompatible messages to obey, but likely as not will be punished for selecting either one!

A logical solution would be to opt for neither alternative, and perhaps confront the parent with the inconsistency implicit in his or her demands. Unfortunately, children victimized by double binds are locked into dysfunctional family systems that do not permit such options. Instead, when persistently confronted with such no-win situations, such children tend to develop bizarre responses and mannerisms indicative of the severe underlying conflicts created by their parents' contradictory messages. Such behavior, of course, does comprise an alternative to the choices offered by the parent, and may forestall the punishment that would otherwise be sure to follow. Thus, secondary gain factors appear to be operating; avoidance of punishment becomes a powerful reinforcer of the child's bizarre behavior. The cost to the child, however, in terms of conflict and emotional trauma is incalculable. One schizophrenic teenager, for example, took to reciting nursury-like rhymes in a dream-like, sing-song fashion when confronted with any decision process whatsoever. It turned out that for years her mother had literally forced her to dress in a sexually provocative manner, only to publicly criticize her as a promiscuous simpleton, unable to choose as dates men with any redeeming social qualities. The negative injunction in this instance was the command, "Don't date men your parents wouldn't be proud of."

As with social learning theory, the explanations offered by proponents of psychodynamic and systems theories are relevant in the development of some schizophrenics, but there is no convincing evidence that they are initial causes. More convincing is the evidence that the disorder develops from genetic defects or from birth disorders and is probably mediated biochemically.

Mediating Factors

Mediating factors are not original causes, but are the secondary and more easily observable manifestations that are seen once the schizophrenic process starts to develop. Problems in perceptually processing and then effectively attending to various stimuli are critical mediating factors in schizophrenia. We now examine some theories about how they are manifested at the biochemical level.

Hallucinogenic model.   For many decades researchers have hoped to find a single and simple physical variable, such as a disordered component in the blood, as a consistent explanation for schizophrenia. Experience with hallucinogenic substances like LSD, and observing the effects of long-term amphetamine use, continues to fuel this hope, but research has not yet supported the idea that these substances either cause schizophrenia or are even consistently associated with it.

Transmethylation hypothesis.   The **transmethylation hypothesis** is a more complex and sophisticated version of the hallucinogenic model. In 1962, Osmond and Smythies noticed the similarity between the chemical structures of norepinephrine and mescaline (a natural hallucinogen). They theorized that the biochemical transmethylation (change of molecular structure) of norepinephrine might in turn produce a hallucinogen that could cause schizophrenia. Other researchers thought schizophrenics might consistently show different levels of serotonin than normal individuals, but a review by Matthyse (1978) found no significant support for any of these theories.

Two emerging technologic developments, computer data analysis and better processing of brain tissue at autopsy, could reinvigorate these approaches. "Brain banks" (where brains are stored for further use, as in organ or blood banks) would permit a more thorough study of brain chemistry, replacing the traditional dependence on less direct measures such as EEG or blood and urine samples. Computer-based data analysis of theories that postulate complex interactions now supersede the single-agent theories that predominated in the past. However, complex models of this sort are not without drawbacks. For example, when a theory becomes so complex that only a computer can deal with it, the researcher is reduced to taking the word of the computer that the theory has been proved.

RESEARCH PROFILE

Biochemical Aspects of Schizophrenia: The Dopamine Theory

Cumulative evidence suggests that people with schizophrenia may have biochemical abnormalities of the central nervous system. One such abnormality may be an excess of the chemical dopamine.

Electrical impulses traveling throughout the nervous system cross many nerve endings on their way to and from the brain, and in doing so must span the small intervening gaps known as synapses. This bridging occurs when electrical nerve potentials trigger the release of chemicals called *neurotransmitters,* which cross the synapses. One of these neurotransmitters, dopamine, has been implicated as a contributory factor in schizophrenia. One source of evidence demonstrates that excessive dosages of chemicals that stimulate dopamine production in the brain (such as amphetamines, or "uppers") can produce behavior patterns virtually indistinguishable from schizophrenia. Another is the successful use of drugs that deactivate dopamine in treating some of the more florid features of schizophrenia (Bernheim and Lewine, 1979). A third strand of evidence comes from research on patients with Parkinson's disease (a neurologic condition in which the patient is afflicted with uncontrollable tremors). These cases are usually treated with L-Dopa, a chemical that increases the amount of dopamine in the brain. Excessive dosages of L-Dopa sometimes trigger psychotic-like behavior in patients with Parkinson's disease who have prior psychiatric histories (Davis et al., 1978).

Collectively, these findings strongly suggest that excessive levels of dopamine in the brain may underlie schizophrenia. However, the fact that certain drugs under specific conditions can mimic the symptoms of schizophrenia does not conclusively prove that dopamine—or any other chemical—actually causes schizophrenia. In fact there is only tentative evidence to support a direct link between the levels of dopamine secreted in the brain and the presence of schizophrenia (Carlson, 1980).

Results such as those obtained in a study by Crow et al. (1978) suggest that differences between schizophrenic and nonschizophrenic persons may depend on the actual number of dopamine receptors in the brain rather than on the amount of dopamine secreted. Nerve synapses contain *receptor sites* that absorb dopamine and other chemicals. Certain drugs, upon binding to these receptor sites, inhibit the transmission of dopamine. One such drug, haloperidol (Haldol), is commonly used as an antipsychotic medication. In studying brain samples taken from deceased normal and schizophrenic individuals to determine whether they differed in chemical composition, Crow et al. used a drug chemically very similar to haloperidol that was specially treated to make it mildly radioactive. Using a device similar to a geiger counter, they measured the amount of this chemical absorbed at synaptic receptor sites in the brain samples. The results showed that, on the average, there was greater binding of the radioactive drug in the brains of schizophrenic subjects. The researchers have interpreted this finding as an indication that there are more receptors for dopamine (or chemicals that inhibit dopamine) in the brains of schizophrenic patients.

These results, though not conclusive, provide additional clues regarding the nature of biochemical processes in schizophrenia. Although dopamine is clearly related to schizophrenia in some way, the exact nature of that relationship has yet to be determined.

● "Benito Sereno," by Aloïse, born in 1886 in Switzerland. At the outbreak of World War I, she proclaimed her pacifism and humanitarian ideas so exaltedly that she was confined in 1918 to an asylum, where she spent the rest of her life. Soon she began writing and drawing, producing most of her work after 1941 until her death in 1964. (Collection de l'Art Brut, Lausanne, Switzerland)

● "Rinôcêrôse," by Gaston Duf, born in 1920 in a mining town. His father was a brutal drunkard and Gaston had a miserable childhood. He was sickly, illiterate, a drinker, and suicidal. Gaston was dismissed from a series of jobs and eventually confined to a psychiatric hospital. He worked for six years on drawings of an ever-increasing size, after which he stopped altogether. His favorite subject was a strange beast he described as a rhinoceros. (Collection de l'Art Brut, Lausanne, Switzerland)

• "Monstre Ailé a Queue de Poisson," by Augustin Forestier, a victim of a 1914 train derailment who was afterwards confined to a psychiatric hospital for life. He arranged a small workshop for himself where he sculpted dolls with a paring knife, adding scraps he picked out of rubbish bins. (Collection de l'Art Brut, Lausanne, Switzerland)

• "Monsieur Oui Oui," by Raymond Oui. Suffering from severe psychological impairment all his life, Oui was admitted to a French psychiatric institution around 1948. During ordinary conversation, Oui continuously interjects the word "oui," and repeatedly includes the word in his artwork. (Collection de l'Art Brut, Lausanne, Switzerland)

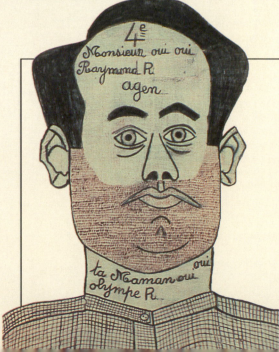

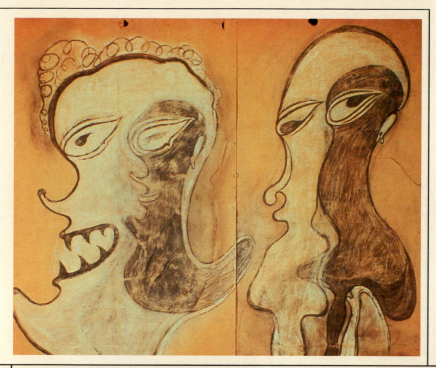

- "Deux Visages," by Heinrich Anton Müller, who invented an ingenious pruning machine around 1903. His idea was stolen and exploited by others, which led to severe mental troubles, eventually causing his confinement in a psychiatric hospital. His psychiatrists said Müller suffered from grandeur and persecution mania. (Collection de l'Art Brut, Lausanne, Switzerland)

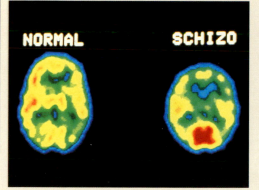

- PET scans of a normal human brain and the brain of a person with schizophrenia show dramatic differences. The large area of blue and yellow show that the schizophrenic brain consumes lower levels of glucose, an indicator of lessened brain activity. (NIH/Science Source, Photo Researchers, Inc.)

- "Le Provence—Dessin Animé," by Guillaume Pujolle, the son of an overprotective mother and an ineffectual father. At 31, Pujolle showed signs of a morbid jealousy, which led to violent tantrums. His suicidal melancholy alternated with notions that he was persecuted by his wife and her imaginary lover. He was eventually confined in a psychiatric hospital, where he produced a series of drawings with undulating, problematical outlines. (Collection de l'Art Brut, Lausanne, Switzerland)

• "La Grande, Grande Princesse Zegga St. Gothard," by Adolf Wölfli, who was working as a goatherd by age 8 due to his family's extreme poverty. At 25 he showed an abnormal inclination for young girls, which led to several arrests and imprisonment. He became so violent, he was put in almost continuous solitary confinement for 20 years. About 1899, at 35, he began to compose music, to write, and to draw, working from morning to night. So far, no one has been able to decipher his musical scores. (Collection de l'Art Brut, Lausanne, Switzerland)

• "Jeune Fille a la Robe Jaune," by Johann Hauser. (Collection de l'Art Brut, Lausanne, Switzerland)

1) *Excess Dopamine in Schizophrenia*

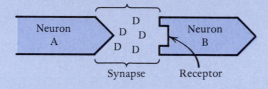

2) *Action of Phenothiazines*

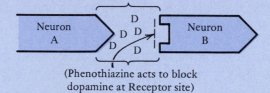

(Phenothiazine acts to block
dopamine at Receptor site)

3) *Normal*

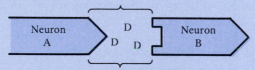

Normal amount of dopamine
release & reuptake

4) *Low Dopamine in Parkinson's Disease*

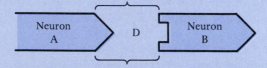

5) *L Dopa acts to increase dopamines in
Parkinson's Disease to normal level*

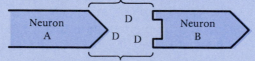

The Dopamine Hypothesis. Like the transmethylation and hallucinogenic models, the dopamine hypothesis is a biochemical theory that explains schizophrenic behavior at the molecular or biologic level (Miklowitz et al., 1986). **Dopamine** is a neurotransmitter, a hormone-like chemical that communicates signals between nerve cells. Dopamine deficiency has been shown to occur in Parkinson's disease as a result of the destruction of several subcortical brain structures, including the substantia nigra and corpus striatum. In contrast, an excess of dopamine is implicated in severe schizophrenia.

Most theorists believe that a faulty mechanism, as yet undetermined, in schizophrenic patients causes excess dopamine and deficient norepinephrine when the neurons of the brain are relaying signals to each other (Mirsky and Duncan, 1986). The success of dopamine-depleting drugs, such as chlorpromazine (Thorazine), in controlling some schizophrenic symptoms has provided the strongest evidence for the theory. However, not all dopamine depletors work with schizophrenia, and there is some evidence that these drugs are also useful in the treatment of affective disorders, contrary to the theorists' claim that, if excess dopamine causes only schizophrenia, the drugs should cure only schizophrenia.

Neurologic defect. As already noted, there is strong evidence that schizophrenics may inadequately process auditory or visual information at a subcortical level. This defect could be a result of imbalances in brain chemistry. But the defect could just as easily occur as a result of genetic, birth-trauma-related, viral, or other disease process factors, and would thus act as a mediating variable.

The Common Channel

Whatever generic cause the various theorists support, most (Garmezy, 1978; Schulsinger et al., 1984; Berenbaum et al., 1985; Goldstein et al., 1986) agree that general deficits in the ability to attend to and effectively use information are central to schizophrenia. These deficits together are the critical marker for schizophrenia, and are referred to as the common channel of the schizophrenic process. These deficits have been thoroughly established in long-term research by Dennis Saccuzzo and his colleagues (Braff and Saccuzzo, 1985). Nearly as critical in schizophrenia is the presence of affective (or mood or emotional) disorder, manifested in absent or ineffective emotional responses to situations. Collectively, these deficits comprise a common channel leading from causation and mediating factors to the commonly observed features of schizophrenia once it is fully developed and is evident to others. This channel creates a "vulnerability" in certain individuals, predisposing them to develop the behaviors characteristic of schizophrenia.

Onset of schizophrenia. The first clear signs of schizophrenia usually occur in late adolescence, although earlier significant psychological disturbance of

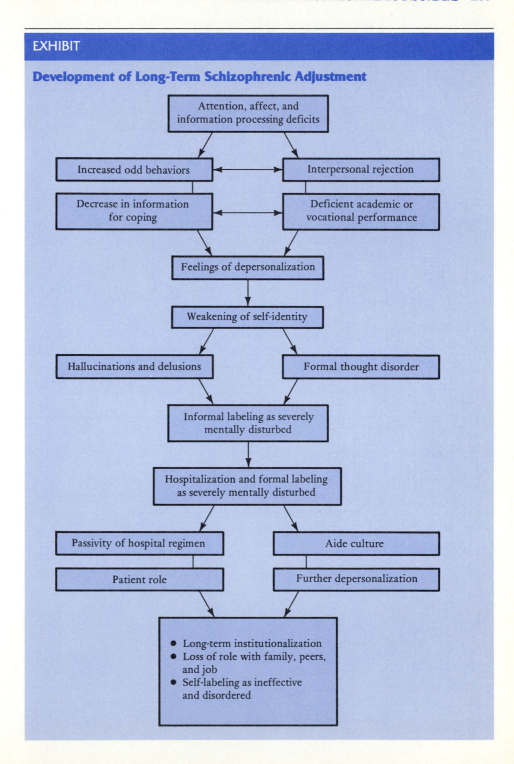

EXHIBIT

Development of Long-Term Schizophrenic Adjustment

The Case of Steve

Steve had many early markers for schizophrenia. His paternal grandfather and his father's brother had both been diagnosed with schizophrenia. Steve had few friends during childhood and adolescence, and never really dated. The few friends he had during those years admitted Steve was "a bit of a nerd"; others less kindly referred to his as "strange" and conferred on him the nickname of "Dr. Bizzarro." But Steve made it through school with acceptable grades, developed a high level of skill with computers, and had neither been in trouble nor been pushed toward any kind of counseling or psychotherapy.

His father died when Steve was 17, and Steve continued to live with his mother into adulthood. However, when Steve was 28, she suffered a major stroke, and was thereafter confined to a nursing home. The demands of living alone were too great for Steve. His neighbors lodged a variety of complaints with the police about him. The most common one was that Steve wandered through their yards at night, though there was no indication of intent to steal, hurt anyone, or peep into windows. At this time his attendance and performance on the job also became erratic, and he was fired. He began wearing odd clothes, usually wandered in a section of town frequented by derelicts and drunks, and now even introduced himself as Dr. Bizzarro. His sister, who lived in the same town, finally became concerned enough to take him to the state mental hospital in a nearby city where he was quickly admitted, and quickly medicated.

During the first week on the ward, Steve refused to go to most of the activities, and kept insisting they bring him his computer. This request was consistently refused, and Steve would stay in his room whenever possible. He was diagnosed as also having depression, and electroconvulsive therapy (ECT) was prescribed. After the sixth treatment Steve started to come out of his room more often and stopped asking for his computer. He was now more placid, but he also showed some memory lapses; he participated in activities when ordered to do so, but without any initiative or enthusiasm.

After three months, Steve was released, and referred to an outpatient program. He participated for a couple of weeks, during which time he looked for a job, but without success. He then disappeared for about five months, and, when he returned, moved back into the derelict atmosphere he had been in before. He would now talk out loud, in apparent response to some hallucinated voices, as he walked along. One day, the police officer on that beat asked Steve how he was doing, and Steve simply gave her a shove, causing her to stumble backwards over a trash can. Rather than pressing charges, she drove him back to the hospital, where he was again quickly admitted. Unfortunately, this pattern has continued for Steve, the only difference being that his stays in the hospital are now longer and the time between hospitalizations shorter.

some sort (such as hyperactivity or peer rejection) may have been observed earlier. It is not surprising that schizophrenia, like most mental disorders, first appears clearly in adolescence. Children in our society are protected from responsibility, both socially and physically Then, during adolescence, they encounter familial and peer demands for identity development, affluence, and mobility, and a lessening of influence from traditional socializing groups, such as the church and the extended family. The result is stress, a lack of coherent structure for the changes demanded, and, for vulnerable persons, personality breakdown.

As we will see in Chapter 16, personality breakdown under stress can result in various types of abnormal behavior, depending upon the unique vulnerabilities of the individual, level of stress, age, type of family structure, and so on. For those who are vulnerable to developing schizophrenia, the breakdown is marked by those symptoms associated with the common channel of schizophrenia, that is, deficits in attention, affect, and information processing. Once these deficits come into operation, a developmental sequence of symptoms and problems usually takes place.

A Developmental Sequence in Schizophrenia

Problems in (1) attention, affect, and information processing naturally lead to (2) an increase in odd interpersonal and speech behaviors, a decrease in information helpful in effective coping, and greater interpersonal distancing. As these occur over time, (3) interpersonal rejection by peers and family members increases. Concomitantly, (4) academic and vocational performance declines.

Operating out of a restricted social and information base, the person experiences (5) feelings of depersonalization. There is also (6) a loss in self-identity, or, in psychodynamic terms, a weakening of ego boundaries.

At this point, (7) hallucinations or delusions are likely, signaling a breakdown in the sense of self and in standard coping behaviors. (8) Formal thought disorder, increased depersonalization, and more disorganized behaviors also occur as allied patterns. The person may now be informally labeled by family, peers, and co-workers as "mentally ill" or "crazy." Any significant continuance usually leads to (9) hospitalization. Health professionals, who function as agents of society as well as treaters, now formally label and stigmatize the person as schizophrenic and thus out of touch with reality.

This sequence is common, though not inflexible; hospitalization may occur earlier in the sequence, other factors later. One feature, however, is constant: In Western cultures the label of schizophrenia is difficult to discard even when the person manages to behave normally (Sarbin and Mancuso, 1980). In cultural groups where there is little or no stigma attached to being schizophrenic (for example, the aborigines and the Chinese living in Taiwan), the prognosis for a return to full functioning is much better (Sanua, 1980).

Maintenance Variables

Maintenance variables sustain and even amplify a disorder once the development of the disorder is well under way. Several such processes can help to maintain schizophrenic patterns. The informal labeling that occurs as schizophrenia develops further isolates the individual. Now, not only does the individual have problems processing information, he or she is getting less information, as well as less social feedback and support. The isolation is furthered, as is the loss of self-esteem because of this perceived social rejection (Goldstein and Strachan, 1987).

Institutionalization is a process of adaptation to a specific environment whose demands differ markedly from those of a normal environment; most schizophrenics are institutionalized at one time or another. The "aide culture" (Ullman and Krasner, 1975; Szasz, 1986) of the hospital operates against assertive, creative, or productive behavior styles. Although the therapist has legal responsibility and ultimate decision-making power, those persons lowest in training and commitment to a therapeutic model, the aides and nurses' assistants, have the most contact with, and control over, the patient's world. What they reinforce is what the patient or inmate learns. In an efficient ward, initiative, independence, or even happiness are not strongly encouraged, and in many instances are suppressed (Curran et al., 1982). For example, the hero of the novel *One Flew Over the Cuckoo's Nest* could not overcome the constant pressure to act in a passive and acquiescent manner.

A specific refinement of institutionalization is the patient role. Passive acquiescence in the routine of the hospital is a pervasive ethic. People in hospitals tend to be referred to as "patients," rather than "clients." Enforced passivity leads to iatrogenic behaviors (new or amplified patterns that stem from the treatment itself) that are nonfunctional in the real world (Sarbin and Mancuso, 1980). In the hospital, inmates are told when to get up, when to eat, and when to go to bed (usually with a sleeping pill), and are occasionally asked to engage in the type of activities suited to a minimally active retirement. When they leave the hospital, reinstituting self-initiative behaviors is the biggest problem they must deal with. Also, the rather high dosages of medication that are administered in the hospital (and sometimes outside of it) may

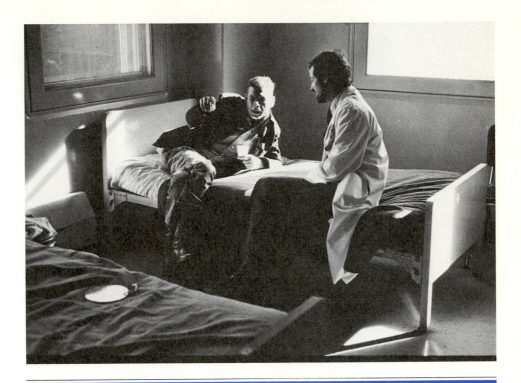

Institutionalization of the schizophrenic is a crucial phase in the potential "cure" of the patient. Often, patients cannot adjust to life outside the institution, where their days were closely controlled by drugs, aides and doctors.   (Michael O'Brien/Archive Pictures)

cause memory difficulties which in turn are then seen by observers as further evidence of deteriorating functioning (Frith, 1984).

It is becoming increasingly clear that the high rate of failure to adjust when released from the hospital is not necessarily a function of the original severity of the disorder. Rather, the hospital-appropriate behaviors have been too thoroughly learned. Besides depersonalizing the individual, the hospital regimen promotes additional affective disorder through the development of learned helplessness. Price and his colleagues found that as a result of institutionalization the level of depression in many hospitalized but nondepressed schizophrenic clients reached that of originally depressed patients. These people came to believe that they could do little to deal effectively with their world, and as a result were inclined to avoid positive action, assuming ahead of time that they would fail.

As formal labeling continues, hospitalized psychiatric cases are more and more inclined to label themselves as "crazy," "psycho," "schizo," or even to apply formal labels to themselves. These labels and the allied assumptions about what kinds of behaviors are probable become integrated into their

EXHIBIT

Political and Economic Factors in Schizophrenia

Braginsky and Braginsky (1976), who studied impression management, have found evidence to support the concept that the labeling and processing of schizophrenics constitutes a political move by their family and by society: hospitalization occurs because for some reason the person is not liked, rather than because of a primary desire to cure the disorder. Thomas Szasz (1974; 1986) and Ronald Laing (1979), in-house critics of the psychiatric establishment, have often made the same point. There is no doubt that in some instances individuals have been persecuted by others, even by those closest to them, and have been maliciously incarcerated in mental institutions. But to claim that deliberate persecution accounts for the hospitalization of the vast majority of schizophrenics is to go far beyond the data.

As mentioned earlier in this book, evidence does show that low socioeconomic status is associated with high incidence rates of psychosis (Hollingshead and Redlich, 1958), and this is specifically true for schizophrenia. Research has also demonstrated that admissions to psychiatric hospitals increase as economic conditions worsen, though the specific incidence rates for schizophrenia do not rise, probably because many of the common indicators for schizophrenia (apathy, withdrawal, and so on) are also the common psychological consequences of economic hard times in an individual's life (Mirsky and Duncan, 1986).

Two factors are thought to account for the higher incidence of schizophrenia in the lower socioeconomic classes. First, people of low socioeconomic status have fewer means available either for initially coping with stress (which facilitates the emergence of schizophrenia in those predisposed to schizophrenia) or for rehabilitation. Poverty both promotes stress and renders inaccessible many of the ways to overcome it. In a related vein, Sanua (1980) notes a high rate of schizophrenia among male Mexican-Americans and attributes it to the ethnic discrimination they often face, combined with the devaluing of machismo (a culturally conditioned emphasis on flamboyant masculinity) in the American culture. Second, as people become disturbed, they drift downward in socioeconomic status and again have less access to means of coping. Since genetic problems are often a factor, the family of the schizophrenic has probably dropped over the years on any sociobehavioral scale. The socioeconomic factors are undeniably important contributing causes to the development and maintenance of schizophrenia (Strauss et al., 1986), but they are unlikely to play a major causal role in individual cases.

identity. Meichenbaum (1977) has thoroughly demonstrated how pervasively and self-destructively people develop and use such labels in "self-talk."

These patterns lead some people to fear leaving the hospital even after they acquire the necessary coping skills. Consequently, these individuals may exaggerate their symptoms in order to remain institutionalized, a pattern that has been termed "impression management" (Braginsky and Braginsky, 1976). At the same time, others expect former patients to be at least obnoxious to be around (which they may be sometimes, as are many other people) and probably dangerous (which they are not, at least not any more so than normal people; Teplin, 1985). Thus, self-labeling, learned helplessness, loss of initiative behaviors, and interpersonal passivity combine with the original attentional deficit and other allied patterns to maintain and amplify the schizophrenic pattern and to make a full return to adequate functioning difficult to generate.

TREATMENT

The developmental progression of schizophrenia is difficult to reverse, let alone totally cure. The complexity of the disorder, with possible contributions from genetic and biochemical disorders, attention deficit, disturbed interpersonal relationships, iatrogenic behaviors, and losses in self-identity, indicates that truly effective treatments must be multimodal (Strauss et al., 1986; Curran et al., 1982). Unfortunately, in most cases treatment consists only of medication (chemotherapy), occasional short conferences with a therapist (sometimes euphemistically referred to as supportive therapy), and standard psychiatric hospital care, as described earlier in this chapter.

Physical Techniques

Chemotherapy.   The antipsychotic drugs, often referred to as the major tranquilizers, have proven effective in allaying many of the more severe symptoms in a majority of more disturbed schizophrenics (Goldstein et al., 1986). They are more likely to be beneficial in low-competence, severely disturbed patients. These drugs are thought to block the dopamine receptors and thus effectively reduce and filter out stimuli from the environment. This in turn decreases symptomatology and induces a calming effect. The primary positive effect is a decrease in hallucinations, delusions, and thought disorder; thus, tranquilizers are especially helpful in both the hospital and outpatient management of the disorder's more bizarre aspects. **Chemotherapy,** a managed program of medication, also reduces—but seldom eliminates—attention and information processing disturbances. Interpersonal and psychological vulnerabilities usually persist.

The discovery of a specific antipsychotic effect was really an unexpected outcome of research dealing with an entirely different issue. Field testing of **chlorpromazine** (with the trade name Thorazine) as both an anesthetic and a sedative in France in the early 1950s included some mental patients as subjects. To everyone's surprise, their symptoms substantially diminished. Subsequent research focused more directly on this effect, and in 1955 chlorpromazine was first marketed in the United States as an antipsychotic agent (Goldstein et al., 1986).

EXHIBIT

Prognostic Indicators for Schizophrenia

Just as there are factors that predict occurrence, several variables (independent of the type of treatment) may predict adequate remission once schizophrenia is diagnosed. These variables are correlates rather than explicit causes in any positive change.

Positive prognostic signs in schizophrenia

1. Sexual-marital status: married, or at least a prior history of stable sexual-social adjustment
2. A family history of affective rather than schizophrenic disorder
3. Presence of an affective response (elation or depression) in the acute stage of the disorder
4. Abrupt onset of the disorder; reactive rather than process schizophrenia
5. Onset later than early childhood
6. Minor or no paranoid trends in the disorder
7. Higher socioeconomic status
8. Adequate premorbid vocational adjustment
9. Premorbid competence in interpersonal relationships
10. Short length of stay in hospital
11. No history of ECT treatment
12. Tendency to be stimulation-receptive rather than stimulation-avoidant
13. Clear precipitating factors at the onset of disturbance

Although there is now available a wide array of generic antipsychotic drugs (see chart in Chapter 4), chlorpromazine is still prescribed most often. Chlorpromazine is in the phenothiazine family of drugs; other major families are the butyrophenomes (Haldol) and the thioxanthenes (Proxlin). Although Proxlin creates problems with side effects and overall effectiveness, it can be administered in a long-acting form. This feature allows more control in patients who, because of confusion or lack of motivation, do not take medication as prescribed. However, in general, there are no great differences among these generic drugs.

All these drugs share drawbacks as well as advantages. First, they seem to be of little benefit to a sizable minority of schizophrenics. Second, in many schizophrenics the effect is variable, and over-medication easily occurs. It is also clear that some physicians use these drugs inappropriately. Davis (1976) points out that megadoses are too often used, and as general rule "megadoses produce no better results" (p. 41). Hesbacher (1976), in studying the records of a group of family physicians, found that less than one percent of their patients with allied mental problems showed schizophrenic behavior, yet 21 percent of the medications administered were potent antipsychotic medications.

The third and major drawback concerns side effects, which may be substantial since these medications are potent to begin with and are often administered in high dosages. The problem is made worse by the probability that a majority of schizophrenics will need this type of medication for many years, perhaps even for life.

Side effects of chemotherapy.   About 35 percent of patients on antipsychotic medication experience muscular disturbances and alternating feelings of restlessness and lethargy. After a couple of years on these drugs approximately five percent of patients (but 40 percent of the elderly) develop tardive dyskinesia. **Tardive dyskinesia** is a usually irreversible syndrome that involves involuntary head and neck movements, grimacing, and lip-smacking, all of which obviously hinder recovery in the interpersonal area. Even more insidious is the fact that tardive dyskinesia is associated with the deterioration of brain centers—collectively called the basal ganglia—that mediate new learning and other cognitive processes. Damage to these structures may thus further deplete the adaptive capabilities of schizophrenic clients, which are typically at a low level to begin with. In recognition of such adverse side effects, many physicians have made it a practice to periodically withdraw antipsychotic medications. Unfortunately, evidence indicates that this practice can make the problem even worse (Goldstein et al., 1986). The most promising development in the prevention of tardive dyskinesia involves techniques that replace brain acetylcholine, which is apparently depleted by antipsychotic medications.

Smaller numbers of patients experience side effects in the form of sexual dysfunction, cardiac complications, and dystonia, or extreme rigidity in the head and neck area. The phenothiazines tend to suppress the gag reflex, and a significant number of deaths due to aspiration asphyxiation have been reported.

We have already noted the occurrence of Parkinson-like symptoms (tremors, facial-muscle rigidity, and shuffling gait), which are conservatively estimated to occur in at least 10 percent of all cases. But Mason et al. (1977) studied the drug prescription patterns of four mental hospitals and found that over 40 percent of drug orders were for medication to combat these symptoms. They also noted that at least 75 percent of patients were on heavy multimedication schedules.

Possibly the most disturbing side effect is the loss of creativity, spontaneity, and initiative reported even by those who "recover" from schizophrenia, which is confounded by memory loss (Frith, 1984). This effect is amplified by the maintenance factors discussed earlier, such as institutionalization and the patient role. Even a strong advocate of chemotherapy has acknowledged that "not every schizophrenic should be initially treated with antipsychotic drugs. They should be psychologically supported for several weeks to see if they do recover without drugs" (Davis, 1976, p. 37).

We used the term "recover" here, but the fact is that few schizophrenics ever return to fully normal and healthy functioning. Most have some residual problems that recur throughout their lives; many have to take medication off and on for the rest of their lives.

ECT (electroconvulsive therapy) and psychosurgery.

In addition to chemotherapy, two physical techniques that have traditionally been used for schizophrenia are ECT and psychosurgery. A pioneer in **convulsive therapy,** a Hungarian named Ladislaus von Meduna, observed (inaccurately) that epileptics rarely if ever manifested schizophrenia. So, in the 1930s he induced convulsions in schizophrenics with a camphor derivative on the assumption that the convulsive state would somehow drive out the schizophrenia. This technique failed, and his successors who use electric shock (electroconvulsive) therapy to induce convulsions have never shown anything approximating impressive positive results. Although there has been modest success with severe catatonics, even advocates of ECT therapy admit that evidence supporting its use with most schizophrenics is equivocal at best (Valenstein, 1986). Critics of the technique point to the lack of success, the short-term psychological disruption and confusion, and the risk of memory deficit and brain-tissue destruction when a significant number of treatments are administered (Valenstein, 1986; Squire and Chase, 1975).

The major predictive criterion of successful treatment of a mental disorder with psychosurgery (the cutting of some portion of the brain) is the presence of a severe depressive component (Valenstein, 1986). If a person is diagnosed as schizophrenic and is also significantly depressed, psychosurgery could be useful as a last resort to alleviate the depression, although it does little for the allied symptoms. As a result, under standard diagnostic criteria, such a person might be diagnosed as having a schizoaffective disorder prior to surgery and schizophrenia afterward.

Biofeedback, dialysis, and megavitamins.

Biofeedback has not been used extensively with schizophrenics, but its success in helping normal persons increase their attention span suggests that it could be useful in comparable training with schizophrenics. It could also be effective as a adjunct technique to decrease excitability or to deal with motor side effects, such as tardive dyskinesia (Hatch et al., 1986).

Renal dialysis is a process of running all of the blood out of the body, through a set of filters, and then back into the body. Since dialysis does the work of the kidneys, it is normally used to treat patients with kidney diseases, but it has also been used to treat schizophrenia. Studies of this application, however, assert that there is little evidence to support its usefulness (Goldstein et al., 1986; Valenstein, 1986). Many persons who have been accepted for dialysis treatment have been more histrionic than schizophrenic; this type of client responds well to any dramatic placebo, which is what dialysis could be functioning as in such cases.

Biochemical hypotheses also suggest a possible role for vitamins and nutrition. There is anecdotal clinical evidence that megavitamins, primarily the B vitamins, are helpful in treating schizophrenia. Certainly good nutrition, which would include an adequate supply of vitamins and minerals, can aid a schizophrenic in recovering, as it does for almost any disorder. But a well-controlled study (Ban et al., 1977) found megavitamins to be less effective than a placebo in the actual treatment of schizophrenia. Wurtman et al. (1979), studying other nutritional factors in the treatment of schizophrenia, found that the administration of lecithin and choline enhances the effects of the standard chemotherapies even though these nutritional factors by themselves have no positive effect.

Psychological Methods

Psychotherapy. Psychotherapy, as it is usually thought of, an ongoing verbal analysis of the client's emotional and interpersonal life, may be a part of the treatment plan for schizophrenia at various points in the course of the disorder. It is not usually as constant a feature of the treatment as is chemotherapy. For example, the psychodynamic and Rogerian models have had considerable influence on existing one-on-one therapeutic techniques, yet neither originally evolved from work with schizophrenics, and few therapists who use either approach have many schizophrenic clients.

The variation of psychoanalytic psychotherapy called direct analysis (Rosen, 1953; Karon, 1976) holds faulty parenting to be a critical causative element in the development of schizophrenia. The technique has proven to be of some use with schizophrenics, and we shall discuss it further in the next chapter, in the context of paranoid schizophrenia.

Supportive psychotherapy is usually part of any total treatment program for schizophrenics, especially when they are at the point of entering or leaving the hospital. This may entail no more than a discussion of how they are doing in their environment (inpatient, group home, family), their reactions to medications, their fears, and their future plans. It also includes encouragement toward new initiative behaviors, reassurance about fears and concerns, and help on adjusting back into family or social networks; in that regard it is often supplemental to family counseling (Goldstein and Strachan, 1987).

Token economies and milieu therapy. Research has proven token economies to be quite successful in modifying a wide range of behaviors—including bizarre variants—and promoting the development of social skills (Strauss et al.,

1986; Goldstein et al., 1986). In general, token economies have been very effective as part of an overall treatment plan for schizophrenia, particularly in counteracting the major deficits in social skills that most hospitalized schizophrenics have. Their effectiveness, relative simplicity in initial design, and lack of negative side effects suggest that token economies should be an integral part of any hospital milieu for schizophrenics. Unfortunately, they often are not, as many psychiatrists place too great a reliance on chemotherapy and the general hospital environment. The reinforcement system provided by token economies works best if it gradually approximates the real world, so as to help the person make the transition back into normalcy.

The supportive environment provided in milieu therapy (see Chapter 4) has also proved successful in the treatment of hospitalized schizophrenic patients. It gives a sense of support, helps to counter the effects of negative labeling, and encourages thinking of oneself as a person rather than a patient.

A Total Treatment Approach

Most mental health experts rightly assert the superior efficiency of prevention over treatment in a variety of mental disorders. There are initial signs of the value of prevention in working with children at risk for schizophrenia (Garmezy, 1978). Usually this is a program to teach better attention skills, ways of dealing with specific deficits, and attempts to teach behaviors that make them more likely to be accepted by peers. However, as yet these programs reach only a small number of those people who will eventually become schizophrenic.

Medication is probably not the initial treatment of choice in the early stages of schizophrenia, and outpatient treatment may be all that is required in numerous cases (Goldstein et al., 1986). Because of the problems that follow from institutionalization, the patient role, and labeling, hospitalization should not be as quickly resorted to as it currently is. However, it will be hard to change this pattern, especially since psychiatrists make much more money per unit of time spent with a person when the person is seen in the hospital rather than the office.

For both outpatients and inpatients, adjunct therapies such as biofeedback, environmental and nutritional planning, and family or group therapy have been used for various facets of schizophrenic disorder. For clients who require hospitalization, a token economy, supportive therapy, plus art and relevant vocational therapies can all be used (Strauss et al., 1986). Chemotherapy is very important in most cases that require hospitalization. Cognitive retraining is useful in changing the negative self-talk and self-perceptions that are inevitable in persons who go through the schizophrenic sequence described earlier.

Helping a person to recover in the hospital is a difficult task; helping the client make a smooth transition from the hospital back into community is also difficult, and just as critical (Curran et al., 1982). It makes little sense to expend significant efforts and monies on persons while they are in a hospital (or any other institution, for that matter) and then to provide only a minimum of effective follow-up care when they leave. Family and/or group therapy can help mend the family and interpersonal patterns disrupted by institutionalization. This assistance during transition is especially relevant for schizophrenics, whose social problems are almost certain to be increased by the hospital experience (Hartmann et al., 1984).

Efforts at primary prevention at the community level emphasize identification of factors that facilitate the development of schizophrenia. Such efforts include high-risk studies of the sort mentioned earlier (Nagler, 1985; Garmezy, 1978) and a detection of the social systems that facilitate schizophrenia (Strauss et al., 1986). Secondary prevention, the early identification of mild forms of disorder, is aided by educational programs for people in school and work settings. Once they know the relevant symptoms, it becomes possible to refer people at an early stage of the disorder, and treatment in an early stage is more likely to be effective for any disorder.

CHAPTER REVIEW

1. Schizophrenia is the most severe psychosis in terms of overall cost to person, family, and society, and it occurs across most cultures at a rate of about one in every one hundred people. It is best considered as a cluster of related disorders rather than as a disorder with one specific cause, course, and treatment.

2. Like all psychoses, schizophrenia is characterized by a lack of contact with reality. Schizophrenia is marked by significant and consistent thought disorder, often manifest in delusions or hallucinations.

3. Other characteristics commonly noted in schizophrenia are withdrawal, disturbance of affect, depersonalization, reduction in motor behavior, and odd verbal patterns, such as echolalia and neologisms.

4. The five major types of schizophrenia are disorganized, catatonic (agitated or stuporous), paranoid, undifferentiated, and residual. Alternative classification systems focus on such continuums as acute-chronic and process-reactive.

5. Several factors predict but do not necessarily cause schizophrenia. These include a schizophrenic parent or parents and early rejection by peers. Positive prognostic factors include sexual-marital status and abrupt onset of disorder.

6. The three types of etiological factors in schizophrenia are: (a) generic, such as genetics or birth disorder; (b) mediating, such as transmethylation or dopamine processes; and (c) maintenance, such as scapegoating or la-

beling. The common channel is an attention and information processing deficit that leads to a typical developmental sequence in the life of the schizophrenic.

7. It is generally agreed that genetic factors are at least a predisposing variable in most schizophrenics. Attention and information processing deficit is reflective of neurologic disorder, and has been related to asphyxiation during pregnancy and to birth disorders.

8. Maintenance factors, such as the side effects of institutionalization and the stigma from the label of schizophrenia, serve to sustain and even amplify the disorder.

9. Chemotherapy has been quite effective in controlling many of the schizophrenic's symptoms, especially for low-competence hospital-prone cases. Significant side effects, such as tardive dyskinesia, are important considerations.

10. A multimodal program of therapy is useful in addressing the multifaceted symptomatology of schizophrenia. Token economies, aversive techniques, psychotherapy, family therapy and other approaches can all be helpful.

TERMS TO REMEMBER

psychosis
reality testing
schizophrenia
thought disorder
hallucinations
delusions
depersonalization
disorganized (hebephrenic)
catatonic
schizoaffective
premorbid
generic variables

mediating variables
common channel
maintenance variables
stimulation-avoidant
asphyxia
transmethylation hypothesis
dopamine
institutionalization
chemotherapy
chlorpromazine
tardive dyskinesia
convulsive therapy

FOR MORE INFORMATION

Kaplan, B. (Ed). (1964) *The inner world of mental illness.* New York: Harper and Row. Presents first-person accounts of the various mental disorders; the cases on the experience of schizophrenia are especially good

Reynolds, D., and Farberow, H. (1981) *The family shadow: Sources of suicide and schizophrenia.* Berkeley: University of California Press. Provides an interesting perspective on family issues in the development and treatment of schizophrenia

Menuck, M., and Seeman, M. (1985) *New perspectives in schizophrenia.* New York: Macmillan. An excellent summary of the various theories of schizophrenic development

Strauss, J., Boker, W., and Brenner, H. (1986) *Psychosocial treatment of schizophrenia.* Lewiston, N.Y.: Hogrefe. An excellent overview of psychological methods of treatment appropriate for schizophrenia

Torrey, E. (1979) *Schizophrenia and civilization.* New York: Jason Aronson. Discusses the cross-cultural issues in schizophrenia and presents the historical evolution of views as to what constitutes schizophrenia

In *The Mosquito Coast*, Harrison Ford plays Allie Fox, a man who frequently suffers paranoid reactions to civilization's "evils" and attempts to escape by building his own world. (Museum of Modern Art/Film Stills Archive; © 1986 Warner Brothers)

PARANOID (DELUSIONAL) DISORDER
THE DSM PARANOID DISORDERS
Paranoia
Shared Paranoid Disorder (Folie à Deux)
Acute Paranoid Disorder
OTHER PARANOID DISORDERS
Paranoid Schizophrenia
Paranoid Personality Disorder
Capgras Syndrome
Graves Disease
ETIOLOGY
Physical Theories
Psychological Theories
Stages of Paranoid Development
Diagnostic Indicators
TREATMENT
"Crashing-Through" Techniques
"End-Around" Techniques
Other Approaches

8

The Paranoid Disorders

A mild initial distrust or alertness in interpersonal relationships is functional in our fast-paced society. However, when such attitudes increase to an inappropriate suspiciousness or hypersensitivity to criticism, the behavior is labeled as paranoid. An extreme belief in one's own abilities or self-importance is referred to as grandiosity, and is the primary marker of a few paranoid individuals. Thus, paranoid means thinking characterized by irrational suspiciousness and fear of persecution, irrational jealousy, or by thoughts and feelings of being exceedingly important or powerful (both the noun paranoid and the adjective paranoid are used for a person who has any one of the paranoid disorders). Terms such as "paranoia" and "paranoid schizophrenia" refer to more specific patterns.

● The Case of Phil

At the insistence of his wife, Phil, a successful engineer and until recently a pleasant and conscientious husband and father, admitted himself for evaluation to a small private psychiatric hospital. In the hospital he provided a stark contrast to the other patients because he always showed appropriate emotional responses, was considerate of others, and talked logically and coherently in everyday conversation.

There was only one area in which Phil showed unusual thought patterns. He was convinced that his wife was conducting an affair behind his back, and was actively developing plans with her lover to take his money and leave him. For evidence, he cited a number of everyday occurrences (such as an anonymous phone call and an odd odor that he was convinced was cigar smoke). When presented with reasonable explanations for these, he rationalized away their applicability to the present circumstances.

His accusations, both implied and direct, had caused his wife considerable distress during the past year. Even more upsetting were other more recent behaviors. Occasionally he would take a day off from work, park the car down the street, and observe his house with binoculars. Eventually, he was seen by neighbors, which caused his family acute embarrassment. At home he bugged the phones by connecting them to recorders he had hidden in the basement. He also adapted a technique from a James Bond movie: he attached pieces of thread from the bedposts to the floor on the theory that if his wife had a lover, their passion would shake the bed and dislodge the threads.

After numerous discussions with his therapist, Phil agreed to discontinue his surveillance behaviors. Six months later, however, he reverted to the behavioral pattern of suspicion and distrust that expressed his unfounded belief in his wife's infidelity. As a result, his wife divorced him a year after his discharge from the hospital.

PARANOID (DELUSIONAL) DISORDER

All available evidence indicated that Phil's belief that his wife was unfaithful was totally unfounded. Such an irrational belief, which is held persistently in spite of evidence to the contrary, is termed a **delusion.** A delusion is referred to as systematized when it is held consistently and has good internal logic. That is, though the initial premise (for example, Phil's premise that his wife was interested in seeking another man) may be incorrect and out of touch with reality, much of his consequent thinking and behavior (he ought to get more information, she may already have a lover, and so on) was then logical.

Persecutory delusions (ideas that other people or forces are against one), grandiose thinking (such as beliefs that one is superior or perhaps supernatural), and irrational jealousy are common in paranoid disorders. Even normal people occasionally may feel misunderstood or mistreated. The paranoid person, however, feels misunderstood and/or persecuted on a chronic basis (Karson and Bigelow, 1986). Indeed, the distorted beliefs of paranoids may in some cases contain a grain of truth, reflecting real aspects of their situation (Lewis, 1985). But it is the significant exaggeration or distortion that clearly defines a disorder as paranoid. LaRusso (1978) has found paranoid persons to be more sensitive and accurate than normal persons in picking up certain nonverbal interpersonal cues. Unfortunately, though they are more alert to these cues, they then proceed to misinterpret the meaning of the cues, furthering the paranoid system. Another major feature of paranoid thinking, cited in causation theories (Colby, 1977; Heilbrun et al., 1985), is the projection of thoughts away from the self onto other people or events. This projection allows the self to view negative thoughts, and thus anxiety-arousing conflicts, as if from an external source.

Swanson et al. (1970) credit Hippocrates with first introducing the term "paranoid," which in Greek means "besides oneself." Paranoid thinking occurs as a predominant feature in conditions that range, on a continuum of how systematized the delusions are, from paranoia, the psychotic disorder shown by Phil, to the nonpsychotic paranoid personality disorder, where there are only the beginnings of thought patterns that could be considered delusions. We will use the general term "paranoid" to refer to all such patterns in this chapter.

Paranoid patients typically exhibit feelings of persecution and distrust of others.   (Globe Photos)

In the DSM, the term **paranoid disorder,** also termed delusional disorder, was traditionally limited to three psychotic disorders—paranoia, shared paranoid disorder, and acute paranoid disorder. Recent revisions of the DSM have downplayed or eliminated the shared paranoid disorder, but since it still exists as a clinical phenomenon, and was first given significant attention in the DSM system, we will include it here. This chapter also discusses several other paranoid disorders, including paranoid schizophrenia and the paranoid personality disorder. As the accompanying Exhibit shows, paranoid disorders can also be ranked according to the degree of personality disorganization involved. The nonpsychotic paranoid personality disorder is the least disturbed in functioning, the psychotic category of paranoid schizophrenia the most disturbed. The wide scope, fragmentation, and severity of disorder of the paranoid schizophrenic is humorously described in the following quote from the novel *Mulligan Stew* by Gilbert Sorrentino.

If God be with us, who can be against us? Strategic Air Command, New York Yankees, First Marine Division . . . Army of Northern Virginia, the Administration, Japanese Marines . . . 82nd Airborne Division, Viet Cong, Zeros, Pittsburgh Pirates, Army of the Potomac, Adolf Hitler Division, Apaches, the times, Internal Revenue Service, Camp Pickett, diseased whores, Crazy Horse, Nelson Rockefeller, book reviewers, Stukas, 2nd Army, People's Republic of China, KP, pushers, the customers, bookmakers, Geheime Staatspolizei, CIA, Platoon sergeants, the odds, Fort Hood, San Francisco Giants, narcotics dealers, the past, Joint Chiefs of Staff, the rich, the future, landlords, and the advertising business. Others on request.

EXHIBIT
Range of Disturbance in the Paranoid Disorders

Psychotic				Nonpsychotic
Paranoid schizophrenia	Paranoia	Shared paranoid disorder	Acute paranoid disorder	Paranoid personality disorder
Most disturbed				Least disturbed

THE DSM PARANOID DISORDERS

The DSM traditionally lists three subcategories of psychotic paranoid disorder: paranoia, shared paranoid disorder, and acute paranoid disorder. Paranoid disorders as described in the DSM are psychotic conditions marked by persistent persecutory feelings, jealousy, or delusions of grandeur. Although severe impairment in daily functioning is uncommon, marital and social functioning is often disturbed.

Paranoia (Delusional Disorder)

Paranoia, though somewhat rare, is a clearly defined syndrome as documented by current research (Oltmanns and Maher, 1988; Turkat, 1985; Kembler, 1980). Phil exhibited the classic symptoms of paranoia, that is, an internally consistent delusional system based on feelings of persecution or jealousy; generally normal thoughts, behaviors, and emotional responses except for the manifestations of the delusional system; the delusions being impervious to change in the face of contrary evidence; and a use of projection of unacceptable thoughts and feelings to protect one's self-image.

Despite his delusional beliefs, Phil's other moods and manners seemed appropriate, and his thinking clear and coherent. Coherence of thought is an important feature, since in most cases of paranoia, once the first premise is accepted, logic makes the conclusions seem inescapable and almost reasonable. Usually, however, the paranoid's initial premise is based on minimal circumstantial data. Furthermore, people with this disorder are especially resistant to changing their erroneous beliefs (Rutter, 1987). As Phil's case reveals, a verbalized willingness to change misconceptions is often used to appease critics or skeptics, but the underlying delusions are maintained.

The delusional systems of most paranoid persons reflect practical concerns in their lives. Phil's paranoid belief system focused on the loss of his wife and his money because he was struggling with occasional impotence and with a cessation of growth in his business. Subconsciously, he feared that these factors would cause his wife to stop loving him and even turn against him.

Shared Paranoid Disorder (Folie À Deux)

When two people share a delusional system, they participate in a "folly of two." In this "folie à deux" or **shared paranoid disorder,** the person originally diagnosed as being psychotic (usually paranoid rather than paranoid schizophrenia) finds someone to control, as this allows them to see their belief system as valid. The receiver incorporates the other person's psychosis into his or her own belief system, mimicking the beliefs and behaviors of the controller. As noted earlier, the shared paranoid disorder has been downplayed

The People's Temple cult, led by Jim Jones, are an extreme example of a shared paranoid disorder. In November 1978, Jones convinced some 900 followers to participate in mass suicide by drinking from a vat of cyanide-laced Kool-Aid.   (UPI/Bettmann Newsphotos)

or eliminated in recent DSM revisions, but it was traditionally included, and is still an important clinical phenomenon, so it is dealt with here.

In most instances, the controlling person and the receiver have been involved in a close and intimate relationship. Often the receiver has exhibited a history of psychological dependence on the controlling person. Thus, it is primarily the receiver who is diagnosed as having a shared paranoid disorder and who receives the primary therapeutic focus (see the accompanying Exhibit).

Acute Paranoid Disorder

Acute paranoid disorder refers to persecutory delusions or delusions of jealousy that are present for a short period of time, e.g., not longer than six months. Unlike the other paranoid disorders, this disorder usually appears quite suddenly.

Acute paranoid disorder usually affects people who have experienced abrupt or radical changes in their personal lives. Thus, prisoners of war, refugees, and people who have left home for the first time are prime candidates for the acute paranoid disorder. Initial therapeutic techniques, including education about the new culture and the development of support systems, help such people adapt to their new environments.

ISSUE TO CONSIDER

Cults and the Shared Paranoid Disorder

The DSM traditionally defined the shared paranoid disorder as a system of persecutory delusions that evolves in a relationship with another person who already manifests a delusional disorder (usually diagnosed as paranoia). Typically, if the relationship ceases, the person with the shared paranoid disorder (the "receiver") soon drops the beliefs. The DSM also asserts that only rarely are more than two persons involved. However, descriptions of cult behavior (Kaslow and Sussman, 1982) suggest that the behavior and beliefs found among the followers in these groups often fit the description of shared paranoid disorder. Although only a small percentage of cult leaders show the paranoid belief system characteristic of the dominant individual in a shared paranoid disorder, many show psychopathic components (see Chapter 12).

Like shared paranoid disorder "receivers," cult members typically accept the new beliefs rather abruptly, and the belief tends to dissipate upon separation from the belief source. Acceptance of the new belief commonly represents an attempt to solve a painful life crisis. Very often this acceptance does in fact reduce the implicated anxiety or depression. The costs of reduced distress include the necessity of accepting many personally superfluous aspects of the cult, diminished flexibility in future adaptations, and increased dependency needs. People who later regain strength and independence and no longer want or need the cult may find it difficult psychologically to distance themselves and sever connections with it. In some cases, other cult members coerce people to remain in the cult. There is evidence of such coercion of at least some of the cult members who died in the Jonestown, Guyana, tragedy a number of years ago.

Although separation from the dominant person or the cult decreases acceptance of the previously shared beliefs, dependency traits, a sense of personal inadequacy, and a wide variety of other psychopathology may remain to be dealt with. A supportive and nonpunitive network of family or friends is especially helpful in facilitating adjustment (Kaslow and Sussman, 1982).

The Case of Sue

Sue, now 44 years old, made good grades in high school and received a partial scholarship to college. While a sophomore in college, she fell in love with a boy she had met in one of her classes. Sue had been raised by strict moralistic parents who were staunchly opposed to premarital sex. Despite such indoctrination, she eventually had sexual intercourse with her boyfriend. Unfortunately, despite the use of spermicidal foam and a misinformed application of the rhythm system, she became pregnant. Although both Sue and her boyfriend were ambivalent about going through with the pregnancy, they married, had the child, and eventually had four children, the last born as a "blessed surprise" when Sue was 42.

For a year or so before her schizophrenic break, Sue showed increasingly odd beliefs. She worried constantly that her youngest child might have various fatal diseases, and gradually developed the notion that the candy one of the neighbors was giving the child was coated with nausea drugs and laxatives. She continued to attend church every Sunday and occasional weekday services, but began claiming that her minister was persecuting her children.

One weekday while this minister was conducting a service, Sue stepped over the alter rail, chased him with a butcher knife, and inflicted a minor wound before being subdued. She was taken to a psychiatric hospital in a severe delusional state. She unleashed a tirade against "a secret conspiracy of ministers, rabbis, and priests" that God had ordained her to war against, then abruptly shifted her attention to a "sickness–laser-ray machine" she believed neighbors were beaming at her via the television antenna. She expressed a variety of other, similar beliefs whose specific focus of concern shifted from day to day. While hospitalized, she became convinced that her laser-beaming neighbors had infiltrated the hospital disguised as old people. Believing herself to be in imminent danger and wishing to frustrate an attack, she one night placed lighted matches under the sheets of some bedridden elderly patients. An alert nurse prevented what could have been a holocaust.

OTHER PARANOID DISORDERS

Four additional paranoid disorders—paranoid schizophrenia, paranoid personality disorder, Capgras syndrome, and Graves disease—are not included in the DSM's specific category of paranoid disorders but are related in terms of symptoms. Of the four, Graves disease alone is known to have a purely physical cause; however, all are characterized by the delusional and distorted beliefs typical of paranoid thinking.

Estimates vary as to the incidence rates of the various paranoid disorders. After a thorough review of the studies in this area, Turkat (1985) concludes that (1) paranoid disorder represents one to four percent of all psychiatric admissions; (2) approximately 25 percent of all schizophrenic persons have a severe paranoid component; and (3) within the personality disorders, approximately five percent are paranoid personality disorders.

Paranoid Schizophrenia

Like other paranoid disorders, **paranoid schizophrenia** manifests itself in distorted beliefs, including persecutory and/or grandios delusions. The case of Sue describes the behavior pattern of a paranoid schizophrenic.

Paranoid schizophrenia is classified as a schizophrenic disorder, because it involves hallucinations and disorganized associations in thought processes. As such, it has many features in common with both the other paranoid and other schizophrenic disorders. As the following breakdown indicates, it also contrasts with these disorders (Swanson etal., 1970; Meissner, 1978; Lazar and Harrow, 1985; Turkat, 1985; Levin, 1987).

Paranoid Schizophrenia	**Other Paranoid Disorders**
Delusional system is poorly organized, and may contain a number of delusions that change over time	Irrational beliefs may not be so severe as to constitute a delusion, there tend to be few of them, and they don't often change
Schizophrenia and the belief system disorder are both fundamental to the abnormality	Belief system disorder is the fundamental abnormality
Presents a generally bizarre appearance and attitude	Appears normal
Problems in reality contact	Relatively good reality contact
Delusions are wide-ranging, including persecution, jealousy, grandiosity, irrelevant thoughts	Delusions are of persecution or delusional jealousy
Often develops later in life	Shows more consistent relation to early developmental patterns
Biological factors may be significant contributing causes	Psychological factors are generally the primary causes

Just as paranoid schizophrenia can be contrasted with the other paranoid disorders, it can likewise be contrasted with the other schizophrenic disorders.

Paranoid Schizophrenia	Other Schizophrenic Disorders
Depression not that common	More often show depression or other mood disorder
Develops later in life	Shows first manifestations in adolescence or late adolescence
More common in males	Approximately equal incidence in males and females
Often shows some reasonably normal appearing outward behaviors	Appears disoriented or withdrawn
Higher intellectual ability than other schizophrenics	Often of lower than average intelligence
Seldom occurs in many rural non-Western cultures	Approximately equal occurrence rate across cultures
Proportionately shorter hospital stays	Tends toward long periods of hospitalization
More often tend to be mesomorphic (the body of the powerful athlete)	Average body build

Studies have also found that paranoid schizophrenics usually show less impaired judgment (Gillis and Blevins, 1978) and that they make fewer errors in performing a variety of cognitive tasks (Bernheim and Lewine, 1979; Lazar and Harrow, 1985). Indeed, Magero (1980) asserts that paranoid schizophrenics react differently to their external environment: nonparanoid schizophrenics have a perceptual bias in that they are stimulus-bound, that is, they are too highly influenced by immediate or distracting stimuli; paranoid schizophrenics, on the other hand, have a conceptual bias. Their thinking is dominated by inner, bizarre conceptions and beliefs, and they too easily tune out stimuli and information from the environment (Oltmanns and Maher, 1988).

Finally, a biosocial component appears to play a role. For example, as noted, paranoid schizophrenia is more common in males, whereas depression is more common in females. Lewis (1985) attributes this to innate differences that are later accentuated by society's pull for females to be more comfortable with dependency and males to be more oriented to violence. The innate differences Lewis particularly notes are that newborn girls spend more time in reflex smiling (a smile in appearance only—that is, it is only a physical response to changes in the body or to movement in the environment, and is not a response to people) than boys, as well as in social smiling (an actual response to people that appears at approximately three months of age). At the same time, newborn boys show more "startle" responses in both waking and sleeping states, a forerunner to greater irritability in boys, both of which predispose to paranoid responses (Meissner, 1978; Lewis, 1985).

How does paranoid schizophrenia fit into the process-reactive continuum discussed in Chapter 7? Heilbrun and his colleagues (Heilbrun et al., 1985) have found, through a series of studies, that there are differences in the way paranoid beliefs develop in process schizophrenia versus reactive schizophrenia. They used techniques such as (1) a standardized procedure for normal and paranoid persons to report their introspective thinking processes on certain tasks; (2) responses to a word association task and other psychological tests; and (3) responses to a series of positive, negative, and neutral behavioral adjectives as to whether they were "more characteristic of me" or "more characteristic of my peers." They found that the delusional content of reactive paranoid schizophrenics is significantly more concerned with the environment, particularly the negative features of the environment, than the more disturbed process paranoid schizophrenics, who were more preoccupied with their self than the environment. Since reactive paranoids are more likely to use social comparisons, they are, not surprisingly, more likely to use projection as a defense. Thus they show more delusions concerned with persecution than process schizophrenics. On the other hand, process paranoid schizophrenics are more likely to show delusions that evolve out of the unusual thinking characteristic of preoccupation with self.

Although some experts allege that Adolf Hitler was a paranoid schizophrenic, his organized thought patterns and behavior make it more likely he was a paranoid personality.   (Historical Picture Service, Chicago)

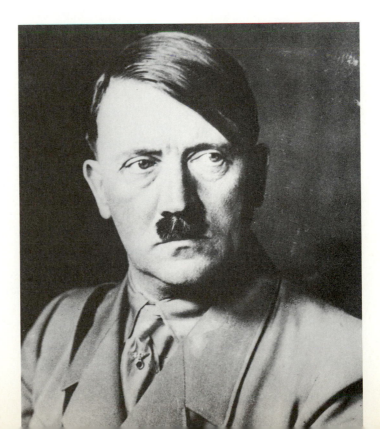

The Case of Jeff

Jeff's parents spent a lot of time with him when he was a youngster, though they put down a lot of rules and were not particularly loving or demonstrative. When he misbehaved his parents would try to shame him and inculcate guilt rather than using physical punishment. From an overall perspective, he was taught that the world is harsh and retaliatory. He had many friends in school and was elected to several campus offices in high school and college, but he never developed any friendships that involved exchanging deep confidences and vulnerabilities. After a short courtship he married a meek and passive woman and fathered a child. But the marriage seemed to both of them to be based more on emotionless routine than on love.

Jeff and his family became increasingly isolated in the neighborhood, primarily because of frequent arguments between Jeff and the neighbors that usually involved his berating neighbors whose lifestyle he disliked or shouting at kids he thought were trying to bother him. Moreover, he was involved in two civil suits. One was against a painter, who, Jeff claimed, had not painted his fence the color agreed upon. The other, against a neighbor, was for "pain and psychic damages" caused when Jeff's son fell off a swing while playing with the neighbor's children in the neighbor's yard. He also was interested in political groups whose efforts were primarily directed at controlling "subversives" or "intruders" of one sort or another. He never gave any apparent thought to changing his behavior patterns, and was never in contact with any mental health personnel. This is common, as such individuals never see any need for psychological treatment, and only end up in therapy because of pressure from others. Jeff's wife was too passive to force this, though she believed it was needed. So, his history is known only through information from neighbors and his wife's colleagues.

Paranoid Personality Disorder

There was always some truth (though it was somewhat distorted) to the concerns shown by Jeff (see accompanying Case), as he never lost contact with reality. In addition, he remained only suspicious and distrustful, rather than developing well-formed delusions. Thus, he shows neither the significant thought disorder of the paranoid schizophrenic nor the well-formed delusional belief system of paranoia. His disorder is not a psychotic condition, and is included in the DSM system as a personality disorder rather than a paranoid disorder. Nevertheless, general paranoid thinking and feelings of persecution are central to Jeff's disorder, as they are to other paranoid disorders. Like other personality disorders (see Chapter 12), Jeff's is a chronic and inflexible pattern of suspicion that developed in childhood and was distinctly recognizable in

---

ISSUE TO CONSIDER

Violence, Paranoia, and the Television Addict

Fisher (1982), in reporting on the continuing work of George Gerbner and his associates at the University of Pennsylvania's Annenberg School of Communications, notes that 17 percent of prime-time programs have a violent theme or actually portray violence. Of characters portrayed as mentally disturbed, 73 percent are shown as violent (compared with 44 percent of normal characters), and 81 percent as victims of violence (compared with 44 percent of normal characters).

Yet the actual rate of violence among the mentally ill is approximately the same as in the rest of the population (see Chapter 12). Also, many of these portrayals suggest that the mental disorder is a result of irrational evil forces or sin. Because the mentally disordered are unlikely to band together to oppose this distortion, it will probably continue.

Such portrayals, combined with a high incidence of violence and deception on television, create a "mean world syndrome" in heavy consumers of television (Fisher, 1982). Such viewers (1) have an exaggerated expectancy of becoming a victim of assault, (2) overestimate the occurrence of crime, and (3) believe the mentally disturbed are far more violent than they actually are. The concern and anxiety that these distorted beliefs generate leads viewers to be more accepting of a violence-as-retribution political atmosphere; as a result, the cycle of violence is enlarged. As in the case of increased suicide rates (see Chapter 9) as a result of media publicity, the media have yet to acknowledge and respond to their responsibilities in this area.

The actual effects of TV viewing, of course, are difficult to document due to the general lack of available feedback from viewers. One researcher, however, found a way around this problem and was able to assess the impact of television on viewers' moods and attitudes. Robert Kubey (*APA Monitor*, April 1987, p. 28) selected a random sample of more than 100 TV viewers, men and women aged 18 to 63 years, who were employed full-time in five Chicago-area companies. Each subject carried a radio pager that went off approximately eight times per day. At the sound of the paging unit, the subjects stopped whatever they were doing and filled out a brief questionnaire assessing their emotional state at the time. Kubey found that subjects who watched a great deal of TV were consistently more irritable and suspicious than those who did not. He also discovered that television viewing engenders a craving for excitement and stimulation, particularly that which is portrayed in television violence.

adolescence. Imitation of parental or sibling behavior of suspiciousness is more frequent in this disorder than in the psychotic paranoid conditions.

Jeff displays the common features of the **paranoid personality disorder.** Though superficially competent in interpersonal relationships, he seldom lets anyone, even his wife, see his vulnerabilities or emotions. He is **litigious** (prone to undertake lawsuits against others for minor reasons), suspicious, and is always watching for intrusions into his world. Everyday occurrences and normal errors are magnified and seen as personal affronts. Yet, while his behavior is aberrant, it is not bizarre, there is no undue anxiety or depression, and he would appear quite normal in most circumstances. Like the other personality disorders, the paranoid personality disorder is composed of long-standing, inflexible personality patterns manifested in varying but lesser degrees in normal individuals.

Capgras Syndrome

Capgras syndrome is similar to paranoia, except that it involves the specific delusion that the important people in one's life are imposters. Though named for the French psychiatrist who supposedly first described the syndrome, it is now clear that the German psychiatrist Kahlbaum had accurately detailed it 57 years earlier, in 1866 (Nikolouski and Fernandez, 1978).

Lesions in the parietal and temporal lobes of the brain have been found in some people with Capgras syndrome who acted with violence against the subjects of their false beliefs (Nikolouski and Fernandez, 1978). While such lesions are not usually considered to be the cause of the Capgras syndrome, animal research has supported the idea that lesions in these brain areas can cause a loss of impulse control.

As with the classic paranoid disorders, there is evidence that most clients with Capgras syndrome develop their delusional beliefs as a defense against unacceptable feelings. Rather than accept and acknowledge the hatred they feel toward loved ones on whom they are too dependent, they define the target person as an impostor and thus render the hate less threatening to themselves. For example, one young woman began to believe her father was not really her father. It turned out that he had recently made sexual overtures toward her. She could not deal with either her anger or her guilt from her own reciprocal sexual feelings toward him that later became evident to her during psychotherapy. As a defense against these feelings, she developed Capgras syndrome. Her symptoms also achieved a secondary gain: when she developed them, her father stopped making sexual overtures.

Graves Disease

Graves disease was first described in the early nineteenth century by Robert Graves, an Irish physician. In this hyperthyroid condition, an oversecretion of thyroxin by the thyroid gland acts directly to speed up the metabolic process. Persons with Graves disease show a high level of apprehension and anxiety that commonly results in paranoid and confused thoughts and hallucinations. Development of this disorder is rapid. Several surgical and chemical treatments for the thyroid disorder are effective in curing the condition.

ETIOLOGY

Most psychopathological patterns are exaggerations or distortions of normal behavior, and the paranoid patterns are no exception. Certainly it is normal and even healthy to be alert to changes in our environment, to occasionally be suspicious of persons and situations, and to think well of ourselves. Paranoid disorders are severe exaggerations of these normal adaptations.

Most theorists agree that various psychological factors (defenses against unacceptable sexuality or hostility, coping with feelings of inadequacy, and so on) underlie paranoid behavior (Meissner, 1978; Heilbrun et al., 1985; Turkat, 1985; Levin, 1987). These factors are particularly evident in paranoid disorders that lack a schizophrenic component. In certain cases, besides that of Graves disease, toxic or chemical substances or other biologic disorders generate or significantly contribute to a paranoid disorder (Bridgeman, 1988).

Physical Theories

Chemical agents. Toxic or chemical substances may occasionally be causal factors in the development of paranoid syndromes other than Graves disease (Cornelius et al., 1984; Currie and Ramsdale, 1984). Evidence suggests that heavy-metal poisoning eventually caused the patterns of paranoia and extreme irritability that Sir Isaac Newton exhibited later in life. Newton's diaries reveal that he routinely tasted the ingredients of his chemical experiments, including lead, mercury, and other heavy metals. Also, he often slept in his lab at night near where the metals were stored, making exposure to fumes very possible. Analysis of locks of his hair willed to some of his descendants suggests that mercury was the probable cause of the symptoms he developed.

Commonly available drugs may also on occasion generate paranoid symptoms. For example, Cornelius et al. (1984) described a woman who developed paranoid symptoms, which eventually led to her stabbing her mother, after digesting a high amount (approximately 900 mg) of cough syrup containing phenylpropanolamine, also a common diet-aid ingredient. The paranoid symptoms subsided later while she was hospitalized. Then, to confirm the role of phenylpropanolamine in producing paranoid symptoms, the woman's informed consent was obtained and she was given a small dose (50 mg) of the chemical. Within three hours she became paranoid and slightly confused. These symptoms subsided within the next six hours.

A number of other chemical agents can induce, at least temporarily, psychotic paranoid behavior patterns (Johnson and Anger, 1982). Many of these compounds, such as toluene and methylene chloride, are commonly encountered in the environment, especially in industrial settings. Workers who have had significant contact with such chemicals are at risk for a wide variety of physical and psychological disorders, including paranoia. Other drugs may also induce paranoid thinking. People who take "angel dust" (phencyclidine hydrochloride), cocaine, LSD, or amphetamines are at risk for paranoia as well as other manifestations of psychosis (Currie and Ramsdale, 1984). The paranoid symptoms are usually reduced or eliminated after cessation of chemical intake, but in a small percentage of cases the paranoid effects persist.

There are various hypotheses to explain how chemical agents generate paranoia. Interference with the brain's own chemical functioning is the probable hypothesis. Some theorists view paranoia as a coping behavior that the organism selects whenever sensory and perceptual abilities are altered. The paranoid thinking operates to explain these changes to the self. Industrial workers suffering from chemically induced paranoid patterns, and at a loss to explain a decrease of energy or efficiency on the job, may blame others (such as the company or the supervisor) to avoid self-devaluation.

Biochemical disorder.   As noted in Chapter 7, biochemical imbalances can induce various forms of psychotic behavior, including paranoia (Raisanen et al., 1984). Birth trauma, disease, or genetic causes may alter levels of serotonin or other brain chemicals and generate paranoid behavior (Lazar and Harrow, 1985; Cornelius et al., 1984; Currie and Ramsdale, 1984). Paranoid schizophrenia is the one paranoid disorder that seems particularly likely to be generated by biochemical disorder. Some physical disorders, such as Graves disease, may feature paranoia among their symptoms.

Psychological Theories

Although physical causes can certainly lead to paranoia, most theorists agree that in most cases unaccompanied by schizophrenia, psychological causes are usually primary (Oltmanns and Maher, 1988). Throughout the following discussion of various theories, and from an overall perspective, it appears that the following general schema (Turkat, 1985) operates to reinforce the development of paranoid patterns.

> *"Others are against me" (anxiety is elevated);*
> *"There is something wrong with me" (anxiety is further elevated);*
> *"There is something different about me; I'm better than others" (anxiety is reduced).*

The Freudian theory.   The oldest theory of a psychological source of paranoid disorders is the one first articulated in Freud's early writings and still popular in the media and in many modern psychodynamic theories. Freud postulated that homosexual impulses, because they were felt to be unacceptable, were unconsciously transferred from the self to the target of the impulses, a process known as **projection.** Rather than face one's own feelings of attraction to a person of the same sex, the paranoid person turns the situation around and imagines the other person as having the homosexual attraction. In this way the paranoid person would not have to see himself or herself as unacceptable.

Later theorists agree that most paranoids use projection (the denial and attribution of unacceptable personal attributes) as a defense, not just for unacceptable homosexual impulses, as was central to Freud's theory, but for unacceptable feelings in general (Heilbrun et al., 1985). For Freud, the feeling "I love (*someone of the same sex*)," is unacceptable to the paranoid's unconscious self-image. The paranoid then transforms the thought into "I hate him/her," which also causes self-image conflicts, because there is no adequate consciously available reason for the hate. Final transformation into "He/she hates me" allows avoidance of the guilt and anxiety associated with the prior beliefs. For the grandiose paranoid the unacceptable "I love him/her" is translated into "I don't love anyone." However, since psychic energy must be attached to something or someone, that person's reality concept becomes "I love only me," the basis of delusions of grandeur.

The Schreber Case. Much of Freud's early theorizing about paranoia (which in turn influenced so many later theories) developed out of his analysis of the now famous case of Daniel Paul Schreber. Schreber, a distinguished attorney and politician in Germany, was born in 1842. Schreber's career was interrupted occasionally when he was hospitalized, and he spent most of the late 1890s and early 1900s in a mental hospital. He wrote his *Memoirs* during 1900–1902 in the hospital. Freud later analyzed and then published them in 1911, just after Schreber's death, though Freud never actually met Schreber (Meissner, 1978).

Schreber had a number of delusions. The most persistent was that he was being transformed into a female by the power of God, as a result of which his genitalia was changing into women's genitalia and he was growing breasts. He felt that God's calling him toward femaleness made him a special agent of God, and that his first treating physician, a famous neuropsychiatrist of the time named Flechsig, was trying to commit "soul murder" on him. God, symbolized by the sun in Schreber's fantasies, was viewed by Freud as symbolizing Schreber's hate–love relationship with his father, and the acceptance of God would be marked by a willingness to be castrated, which was in turn related to unconscious homosexual wishes based on a frustrated longing for the father. Some years later, Freud added (1) the notion of projection, and (2) the concept that delusional jealously is a classic form of paranoia and reflects the paranoid's perception of the partner's impulses toward infidelity. These ideas, along with Freud's view that paranoia in females stemmed from the fear of being killed by the mother, set the stage for Melanie Klein's (a later psychodynamic theorist) subsequent emphasis on hostility alone as the primary factor in paranoia.

Cases in the clinical literature offer some support for Freudian theories of paranoia, yet there is clear evidence that these defense sequences are neither common nor critical (Lazar and Harrow, 1985). For one thing, a variety of other conflicts have been found to be central to the development of paranoid systems, such as any type of shame or humiliation experience. For another, numerous paranoids have been overtly homosexual, and without any apparent psychological conflict over their homosexuality.

Hostility theory. Hostility theory, primarily generated by Melanie Klein, omits the initial premise "I love him/her" but otherwise follows the phases of belief development of the early Freudian theory. Although hostility probably has the advantage of including as causal more potential conflict areas than sexuality, the theory is vague in explaining why those conflicts don't lead to paranoid patterns in most people. Most important, it does not explain why the person became hostile in the first place.

The learning theory view. According to this theory, modeling of another's behavior and the unique pattern of environmental reinforcement in a particular individual's world have an important role in the establishment of the paranoid personality disorder, just as they do in virtually all of the personality disorders. The theory states that modeling and conflict-generated behaviors are held to be of equal importance in creating psychotic paranoid disturbances. The major difficulty with this theory is that it does not specify what environmental contingencies generate paranoid behavior.

Social learning theory. The social learning position developed out of several related theories, including learning theory. Advocates of this theory, such as Cameron and Lemert, as reported by Ullman and Krasner (1975), have postulated that paranoids are part of a **paranoid pseudocommunity.** This pseudocommunity is composed of those people whom the paranoid believes are against him or her. It is a *fantasied* conspiracy, as it infers similar intentions and even communication among persons who actually have neither the persecutory intentions nor often even any relationship whatsoever with each other.

At the same time paranoids learn at an early age to behave in ways that tend to isolate them from any consistent interpersonal support and feedback, and, via modeling, to blame others for whatever goes wrong (Rutter, 1987). They did not learn to share responsibility or to be open to constructive feedback from others. When normal stressors occur, they therefore isolate themselves. They cannot share their vulnerability and thus cannot dissipate their anxiety. They freely alter this perception of reality rather than change their false, basic beliefs. If this new "reality" does not possess the dimensions of a clear delusional system (that is, a highly systemetized and/or a consistent and specific focus of persecutory delusions), it reflects a paranoid personality disorder. If the person does define a systematic "them," and a true delusional system evolves, as in both Sue and Phil's cases, they are psychotic paranoid disorders.

The evidence in most cases (and one generally accepted by most psychological theorists) is that if the feeling of being persecuted has any reality at all, it is a result rather than a cause of the paranoid behaviors (Lazar and Harrow, 1985). Jeff's and Phil's behaviors, for example, were so disruptive that people eventually turned against them.

Shame-humiliation theory. This theory, which evolved from the social learning position, has such a general structure that it allows incorporation of all the other psychological explanations of the causes of paranoid disorders. The **shame-humiliation theory** is an information-processing theory that assumes that all people have a symbolic mental model of themselves that they attempt to maintain in the face of anticipated or actual assault on the ego, but that the paranoid's mental model is more inflexible and farther away from reality than the normal person's. Their model provides paranoid people

During the 1972 Chess Olympiad, Russian Boris Spassky insisted that mysterious forces caused him to lose concentration, and thus the match. His insistence was interpreted as a paranoid attempt to avoid humiliation at the hands of American Bobby Fisher. (UPI/Bettmann Newsphotos)

RESEARCH PROFILE

Colby's Shame-Humiliation Theory of Paranoia

In 1972, American chess master Bobby Fischer confronted Boris Spassky, the Soviet world champion, for a championship match in Iceland. A great deal of national prestige was at stake, particularly for the Soviets, who had been undefeated world champions for the preceding 24 years. As the match progressed, it became evident that Spassky was facing a humiliating defeat. As this became imminent, the Soviets claimed that Spassky was being adversely influenced by illegal means (such as chemicals or electronic devices) and requested a search of the hall where the match was being played. Although the search failed to reveal anything clandestine, Spassky maintained to the very end that his concentration had been disrupted by mysteriously unexplained forces.

Kenneth Colby used the Fischer-Spassky match to illustrate his theory of paranoid thought processes. Colby explains paranoia as an attempt to reduce or avoid the unpleasant experience of being shamed or humiliated. In this example, Spassky was on the verge of relinquishing a championship that his country had retained for years to a challenger who was generally considered somewhat eccentric and inexperienced in international competition. To lose under such circumstances would undeniably be humiliating, and according to Colby, Spassky's situation was precisely the sort in which paranoid behavior would be likely to occur.

Spassky lost the match, but the impact of his defeat was tempered somewhat by his persisting allegations of having been adversely influenced by forces outside his control. Spassky's complaints had a semblance of credibility because they were backed up by representatives of the Soviet Union and because he was a chess player of considerable repute. Yet there was also a pathological element in the way he constantly peered at the overhead lighting during the match and complained about the vaguely defined forces that conspired to impair his concentration. Outside the context of the world championship competition, such comments would surely be construed as indications of paranoid thinking.

In clinical work with paranoid patients Colby advocates exploring their history

with a means of absorbing potentially shattering losses they believe they could somehow have prevented (as in Phil's case). If paranoids were to believe that the ego assault occurs because of an unchangeable aspect of their self, they would become depressed. According to Kenneth Mark Colby, the originator of the shame-humiliation theory, "When a belief in the self's inadequacy is activated by relevant input, the paranoid mode uses symbol-processing procedures to forestall a threatened unpleasant affect experience of humiliation, detected as shame signals. . . . In preventing humiliation, the procedures use a strategy of blaming others for wronging the self" (1977, p. 56).

This set to respond, even when no data is yet available, was found in paranoids in an early experiment by Abroms et al. (1966). These researchers for evidence of experiences that engendered shame or humiliation. It is not so much that these patients have deeply experienced the pain of being humiliated, but rather that they have developed compensatory strategies to avoid such experiences. This is done by first denying any personal shortcomings or inadequacies and then blaming others when things do not go well. Paranoid thought develops as a means of reducing the impact of a potentially humiliating event, and hence involves an element of anticipation. It is noteworthy, for example, that the investigation was demanded by Spassky at a point when defeat appeared imminent. Early in the match, perhaps confident of winning, Spassky presumably did not foresee any threats to his self-esteem or competence. After he had lost several games, though, the prospect of being humiliated loomed larger and larger. To avoid confronting the full impact of this defeat, Spassky and the Soviet team instigated an investigation rather than accept personal responsibility for losing the match.

The validity of Colby's theory has yet to be proved conclusively, but in the meantime it provides the clinician with clues to the kinds of experiences that may contribute to the development of paranoid thought processes. According to Colby, suspiciousness and deep mistrust frequently reflect a background in which experiences of shame and humiliation were distorted to the point that personal problems were seen as the fault of other people.

To the extent that shaming, if not outright humiliation, is a common practice in childrearing, many people are likely to experience mildly paranoid thought patterns at one time or another. (Few cannot remember being chastised by a parent with the words "You should be ashamed of yourself!") Such experiences, repeated continually, perhaps with mild variations, would almost necessarily result in the development of thought processes that distorted and reduced their hurtful effect. Colby has suggested that paranoid ideation is less prevalent in cultures where shaming is not incorporated into normal childrearing practices. Subsequent crosscultural research may confirm this interesting possibility.

hypothesized that in a standard gestalt figure completion task, paranoids would try to put together more components that would in actuality not fit together. Administering the gestalt perceptual tests and a modified MMPI in order to measure the personality traits (see Chapter 3) they found that the tendency to overassimilate increased with the severity of the paranoid personality trait.

The shame-humiliation theory not only provides a comprehensive framework for other psychological theories, but it also allows predictions that are more easily tested by objective experiments. A study of Kipper and Ginot (1979) also supports Colby's explanation of the paranoid's strategy. They found that persons who tended toward paranoid functioning were able to protect their self-imaging by distorting even very clear and unambiguous information presented in a videotape of their behavior. Also, since sexual dysfunction especially tends to cause shame in many males, one would predict an increased rate of paranoid thinking when sexual dysfunction occurs, and this indeed is the case (Rakic and Ignjatonic, 1983).

Stages of Paranoid Development

Several developmental factors are common in the evolution of paranoid thought and behavior. Foremost are parental behaviors. Parents who use projection as a defense and use intense shaming (as seen in Jeff's case) as a discipline in childrearing contribute heavily. Environmental experiences such as social isolation, language differences, false arrest, or the loss of physical powers (such as impotence or progressive loss of hearing) can be catalytic agents in persons predisposed to paranoid patterns. The disorder commonly evolves in the following sequence (Meissner, 1978; Heilbrun et al., 1985; Turkat, 1985; Rutter, 1987; Oltmanns and Maher, 1988).

1. *General distancing.* Shaming during childhood, child abuse, or other environmental trauma creates an emotional distancing from others. Parents usually communicate the messages "You are different from others" and "You should be very careful about making mistakes." Thus, the child accepts a basic concept that he or she is different and that other's evaluations are important and are often negative.

2. *Distrust.* Lacking the emotional and interpersonal feedback available in normal relationships, the paranoid develops an attitude of distrust toward others and the world in general.

3. *Selective perception and thinking.* Distrust often brings about a more selective filtering in the perception of information and the thought processing of that information. This adds to further distancing and distortion in the paranoid's relationship with the world.

4. *Anxiety and anger.* The person suppresses anxiety and uncertainty by viewing others as the source of problems. A hostile orientation toward the world easily flares into anger and suspiciousness toward specific others. Interpersonal patterns that maintain an emotional distance soon develop, and in turn, others tend to avoid the paranoid person, possibly making them the butt of social jokes or negative nicknames.

5. *Distorted insight.* As distancing and hostility become more focused, the person develops a sense of "seeing it all clearly now," sometimes referred to as a "paranoid illumination." Targets for hostility become specific, and the paranoid's reasons for the behavior are accepted as fact by the paranoid.

6. *Deterioration.* Specification of targets and acceptance provoke a break from reality, resulting in delusions. There is also a loss of some or all of

the few supportive interpersonal relationships still available. The paranoid is now truly isolated emotionally and cognitively, and becomes even more dependent on the erroneous beliefs and systems that have been generated. From this point on, the disorder becomes self-perpetuating.

Diagnostic Indicators

In addition to diagnosis through interviews and psychological tests, various physiological factors have been studied as markers of paranoid traits. One of best attempts in this regard was by Raisanen et al. (1984), in their study of bufotenin. Bufotenin, a normal component of human urine, is a hallucinogenic derivative of serotinin, and is a biogenic amine, as are the amphetamines.

The urine of 48 male violent offenders from a locked forensic ward were examined for bufotenin, as was the urine of a control group of 23 laboratory personnel. Some of the offenders were diagnosed along the DSM guidelines, through a blind analysis of their written records. Seventeen had intermittent explosive disorder (see Chapter 12), ten had paranoid personality disorder traits, and six had traits of paranoia, paranoid personality disorder, or paranoid schizophrenia. Thirty-five had histories of alcohol abuse, but they had had no alcohol for many months.

Levels of bufotenin were higher in the 48 offenders than in the 23 laboratory personnel; the 16 patients with paranoid symptoms had the highest levels. Among the 11 who had committed violent acts against close relations, the level of bufotenin was especially high. Bufotenin excretion did not significantly correlate with alcohol abuse, psychiatric drug use, or diagnosis of intermittent explosive disorder. Thus, there may be a connection between bufotenin excretion levels and paranoid thinking and, in some cases, the resultant family violence. If this result were to stand up in future research, bufotenin could be a valuable diagnostic marker for paranoia.

TREATMENT

Treatment of paranoid disorders is especially difficult (Curran et al., 1982), because paranoids are constantly on guard against intrusions and assaults on their vulnerability. They reasonably interpret therapy as a situation that will force them to confront deficits and vulnerabilities in themselves, and as a result seldom seek treatment (Lazar and Harrow, 1985). As in the cases described earlier, persons with a paranoid disorder typically are forced into treatment by people who become increasingly intolerant of their behavior.

When therapeutic encounters become inevitable, paranoids often find methods of reducing their impact. Phil, the opening case of this chapter, was in the hospital for a couple of weeks, but during that time he never acknowledged his behavior as a cause of his difficulties. By the time paranoids reach a therapist they have had long experinece in effectively avoiding any real confrontation with their basic fears. Also, most therapists have had little experience or training in working with paranoids. Thus, treatment of the paranoid disorders is often not very effective, and treatments that do offer some success are usually long term.

If the delusional system is not well established, behavioral techniques can sometimes be useful. This usually includes removal of reinforcement when the paranoid beliefs are stated, or even giving an aversive response at such times. However, if not done skillfully, such techniques can further the interpersonal isolation in the paranoid's life that feeds the delusions. More effective approaches are those that attempt to directly break into the paranoid system ("crashing-through" techniques) or those that emphasize gradually gaining the paranoid's trust and confidence in order to more indirectly defuse the paranoid beliefs ("end-around" techniques).

"Crashing-Through" Techniques

One therapy approach that has proved effective with severely disturbed paranoids (Rosen, 1953; Karon, 1976) attempts directly and forcefully to cut through the habits and defenses used to avoid facing basic concerns. Rosen developed "direct analysis" (see Chapter 4) primarily to treat schizophrenic disorders, but his technique seems particularly well suited to paranoid schizophrenics and other severely disturbed and withdrawn clients, particularly in the initial stages of therapy. Karon has independently produced some experimental evidence supporting the value of this approach.

Direct analysis, because it is based on psychoanalytic theory, emphasizes the interpretation of what are considered to be the paranoid's primitive conflict areas, often centering on sexuality. The following actual therapist–client interaction is fairly typical.

Therapist: You don't want to talk to me at all, do you?

Client: You're just one of those people that . . . I know you have a mind-reading ray.

Therapist: You're afraid I know about those thoughts—the ones where you want to screw your mother.

Client: I never think bad thoughts! (screams) You just want to put those in my mind.

Therapist: You know I'm right. You want to fuck your mother.

Client: (screams) I don't think that! I don't think that!

As in many other cases of paranoid disorder, there was a grain of truth in this client's delusions, though it had been distorted and exaggerated. For example, although the therapist obviously did not have a mind-reading ray, he was trained to recognize behavior patterns and conflicts, and in that limited sense was indeed reading the client's mind.

The therapist's interpretation of a desire for intercourse with one's mother reflects the theories of Freud, and more specific to paranoids, those of later British psychanalysts like Melanie Klein and Anna Freud (Sigmund Freud's daughter). Many critics argue that such hypotheses may not be accurate, yet they acknowledge that direct analysis does get the patient to respond emotionally—not always an easy task with a paranoid. By substituting conflicts other than sexuality, some implosion therapists, or therapists who support Colby's shame-humiliation theory, have adapted this technique successfully for their work with paranoid clients.

"End-Around" Techniques

Rather than crashing through the conflicts before the paranoid can avoid them, the majority of therapists advocate using various psychotherapies to try to help the paranoid understand the meaning embedded in his or her delusions (Colby, 1977; Barrett, 1980, 1981). These "end-around" techniques seek to minimize avoidance but at the same time seek to generate a degree of trust. Thus, the first goal in this approach is comparable to systematic desensitization (SDT) (see the discussion of SDT in Chapters 4 and 6): Topics of concern are approached cautiously, and then, only when the patient is fairly comfortable, more sensitive issues are brought up. In general, end-around techniques are useful because they help the paranoid to develop more truthful and consistent relationships (the set of relationship skills the paranoid has never had or has lost from disuse) (Goldstein and Myers, 1985).

The initial critical feat is to gain the trust of an individual who is chronically untrusting. First, the therapist has to avoid labeling the paranoid's logic as "crazy" or "preposterous," which requires a lot of emotional discipline. At the same time the therapist must maintain his or her integrity by accepting, sometimes confronting, but never participating in the paranoid's delusional system (Barrett, 1980, 1981; Shemberg and Leventhal, 1984).

Inevitably, paranoid persons ask if their theories are unreasonable. The response recommended in end-around techniques is to point out that it is impossible to unequivocally prove a negative, such as that the phone is not tapped or that one's spouse is not unfaithful. The therapist at the same time communicates that he or she understands how frightening it must be to feel that those things might be true, and provides a simple straightforward explanation for the phenomena the paranoid is interpreting (Shemberg and Leventhal, 1984). Therapists can also point out to paranoids that immense physical resources would be necessary to actually accomplish what they fear is occurring. It is important for the paranoid at some point to grasp how unlikely it is that someone could influence so many facets of the world without leaving any clearly documented evidence.

Finally, Barrett suggests that therapists verbalize similarities between their own life and the paranoid's. Doing this provides both a new frame of reference and a model for coping with life's stresses and frustration. Through humor and discussion of the therapist's own personal worries and coping techniques, the paranoid can perhaps learn to consider other perspectives on relevant issues. This approach is not always successful, but making it the central feature of a treatment plan improves the chances of positive change.

Other Approaches

Once any degree of trust or willingness to cooperate develops, various techniques (for example, relaxation training) are used to lower the anxiety level. This is followed up by social skills training, which is very important in teaching the paranoid how to act in a more normal fashion and in how to develop more positive interpersonal relationships. Both steps are crucial if any long-term change is to occur (Turkat, 1985; Goldstein and Myers, 1985).

Antipsychotic drugs are useful in controlling the more disturbed aspects of a paranoid schizophrenic's behavior, as they are with other schizophrenics. Also, the major tranquilizers can be helpful in treating the development of paranoid delusions in elderly clients. Group therapy has been attempted with the full range of paranoid disorders, but because such clients resist meaningful involvement, it is helpful only if a reasonable degree of trust has already been developed through other approaches. Electroconvulsive therapy (ECT) and psychosurgery have been used with some of the more severe forms of paranoid behavior. ECT disrupts the delusions of the paranoid and in that sense allows the therapist an entry through the defenses. But the intrusiveness of ECT and the cognitive confusion it often produces are likely to increase a sense of vulnerability, and thus to increase the paranoid's defenses. Psychosurgery can have similar problematic consequences, although newer techniques that involve less tissue damage (see Chapter 4) could lessen this effect.

Hospitalization can help by removing the person from stimuli generating the paranoid beliefs (Colby, 1977; Cornelius et al., 1984). However, the effects of institutionalization may increase paranoid feelings by stimulating the paranoid's fear of being formally and publicly labeled "crazy" (Meissner, 1978).

Like the schizophrenic and paranoid disorders, the upcoming affective disorders can also be severe, though there is often wide variation in the level of disorder displayed.

CHAPTER REVIEW

1. Paranoid patterns of disorder range from the severe, psychotic, extremely disorganized delusions of paranoid schizophrenia through the psychotic, but better organized DSM paranoid disorders, to the nonpsychotic but chronic paranoid personality disorder.

2. In many cases there is a grain of truth to the paranoid's concerns or fantasies; it is the overreaction, projection, and closed system of thinking that define the belief as paranoid.

3. Paranoid schizophrenia differs in several respects from the other schizophrenias; for example, it typically occurs later in life and in more intelligent people. Yet, overall adjustment is worse than in other paranoid disorders, reflecting the significant disruption in many areas of functioning that is found in most schizophrenics.

4. Certain rare physiological conditions, such as heavy-metal poisoning or thyroid disease, may cause paranoid patterns, but in most cases psychological factors are considered to be the primary causes.

5. The shame-humiliation theory, which includes many important concepts of other theories (such as projection), views paranoid behaviors as attempts to avoid anticipated ego assault from shame and humiliation experiences.

6. Several developmental factors, such as modeling from parents, and environmental experiences, such as social isolation, are usually observed in the evolution of paranoid behavior. General distancing, distrust, selective perception and thinking, anxiety and anger, distorted insight, and deterioration are commonly noted stages in paranoids.

7. The paranoid can be treated by cutting through the belief system or by more subtle, "end-around," techniques that involve supportive questioning and feedback of data contradictory to the paranoid beliefs. The latter are more commonly used and appear more useful for the majority of paranoid clients.

TERMS TO REMEMBER

delusion
paranoid disorder
paranoia
shared paranoid disorder
  (*folie à deux*)

acute paranoid disorder
paranoid schizophrenia
paranoid personality
  disorder
litigious

Capgras syndrome
Graves disease
projection
paranoid pseudocommunity
shame-humiliation theory

FOR MORE INFORMATION

Colby, K. (1977) Appraisal of four theories of paranoid phenomenon. *Journal of Abnormal Psychology* 86:54–59. An excellent analysis of four major theories of how paranoia develops; it also gives references to some of the major historical works in paranoia

Keiser, T., and Keiser, J. (1987) *The anatomy of illusion,* Springfield, Ill.: Charles C Thomas. This book goes far toward dispelling the confusion and mystique surrounding the shared paranoid and cult experiences, including the risks and legal implications of coercive deprogramming.

Meissner, W. (1986 & 1978) *Psychotherapy and the paranoid process* or *The paranoid process.* New York: Jason Aronson. Definitive works on the paranoid disorders

Merriam, K. (1976) The experience of schizophrenia. In: Magaro P. (Ed.). *The construction of madness.* New York: Pergamon. An articulate and insightful account of the inner experience of paranoid schizophrenia, written by a person who was himself a paranoid schizophrenic.

Meyer, R., and Osborne, Y. (1987) *Case studies in abnormal behavior.* Boston: Allyn and Bacon. This collection of case studies and analyses of paranoid schizophrenia and the paranoid disorders includes the case of General Grigorenko, a Soviet dissident who was diagnosed as a paranoid schizophrenic in his homeland but found to be normal by a team of American diagnosticians.

By the end of the film *'night, Mother*, Sissy Spacek's character, Jessie, who has struggled to gain control of her life, attains her goal by committing suicide. (Museum of Modern Art/Film Stills Archive; © 1986 Universal City Studios, Inc.)

MANIA
Symptoms
Etiology
Treatment

DEPRESSION
Symptoms
Incidence of Depression
Cross-Cultural Variables
Age Variables
Sex Variables
Dimensions
Assessment
Etiology
Treatment

SUICIDE
Incidence
Genuine versus Manipulative Suicides
Causes and Prediction
Prevention

CHAPTER

9

The Affective Disorders and Suicide

Affective disorder refers to disordered patterns of mood or affect. **Affect** is the subjective experience of emotion, whereas **mood** is a consistent or pervasive emotion that influences our view of the world as well as ourselves. The term affective disorder encompasses disturbances that range from manic episodes (as in the upcoming case of Kurt), marked by hyperactive speech and behaviors and significant euphoria (often spiced with irritability whenever "interference" is perceived) to severe depression marked by sadness, slowed behavior, and a sense of hopelessness. There are four major categories of affective disorders in the DSM: (1) major depression, (2) dysthymic disorder, (3) the bipolar disorders, and (4) the cyclothymic disorder. This chapter also discusses suicide because it is more closely linked with depression than with any other disorder.

● The Case of Kurt

Kurt is a professor of fine arts at a small West Coast university. His colleagues and students perceive him as "creative," "energetic," and "disorganized." He is known as a hard worker and intense person, but also as someone who has never achieved at a level that others (or even he) thought he would.

However, on occasion, Kurt's already high energy level would dramatically increase. He would start a variety of major projects, frenetically jump from one to the other, give sporadic attention to each, but seldom finish any of them. In the midst of one episode, he was simultaneously working on 10 paintings and six sculptures at his office studio, and about 10 other paintings at home. Only two were ever completed.

During these episodes, he seemed to be both "in high gear" and "on a high." He was continually moving and talking, sometimes skipping sleep at night, and seldom sleeping more than a few hours at a time. At times, he talked so fast, almost as if the ideas were zipping through his brain at breakneck speed, that the students weren't sure whether he was a genius they couldn't understand, or just crazy. For example, when commenting on a student's painting, he once bellowed, "That perspective, it's reflective. Those colors are infecting. They're infecting that perspective." The student just sat, perplexed, as Kurt strode away.

He would burst into an angry tantrum when something frustrated him, but generally was elated and enthusiastic, just as if he was on an "upper." Even though he had apparently boundless energy, he could neither organize it nor focus it. As a result, both his personal and work worlds would become disrupted. His students, who had always liked him, would now avoid him, as it was almost impossible to deal effectively with him. They usually went away from conversations with him not really understanding what he had said or wanted, yet they could not point to anything clearly absurd or illogical in his statements. Just as it is nerve-wracking and exhausting to interact for long periods of time with a hyperactive child, it is likewise disturbing to try to have any consistent relationship with someone in a manic episode. Kurt's wife, who, by her own account, was being "worn to a frazzle" by these episodes, finally forced him to go to their family doctor, who then referred Kurt to a psychiatrist who instituted successful treatment with lithium.

MANIA

Symptoms

The three cardinal features of **mania** (all of which we see in Kurt) are: (1) hyperactive motor behavior; (2) labile euphoria, or irritability, and (3) flight of ideas (Endicott et al., 1985; NIMH Staff, 1977).

1. *Hyperactive motor behavior.* The manic has seemingly inexhaustible energy, although attention span may be short. Fast and seemingly pressured speech is also typical. Behavior is often frantic, but more purposeful

and organized than that of the schizophrenic. Many grandiose projects are undertaken; few, if any, are ever finished. Bright people with a mild and periodic mania can be effective if they have co-workers who can organize and complete the many projects they generate.

2. *Labile euphoria or irritability.* The affect of the manic is not consistently joyful, but it is intense. Euphoria is usually more evident in those phases when grandiose plans are being made. When plans lie unfulfilled, euphoria often changes to irritability and complaints. Because the change of affect is usually rather abrupt, it is designated "labile."

3. *Flight of ideas.* **Flight of ideas** denotes rapid progression from one thought pattern to another, and at certain times, classic thought disorder is noted (Marengo and Harrow, 1985). The speech pattern seems odd because the manic person uses far fewer conjunctions in speech than a normal person does (NIMH Staff, 1977). The choice of words is not peculiar, but it seems as if the manic's mind skips and links between thoughts; the standard verbal steps just are not there. Thus, the confusion Kurt's students experienced after talking to him is not surprising. Flight of ideas is often accompanied by a grandiose view of the self; these two features, when combined and uncontrolled, result in delusions of grandeur or power.

Behaviorally, mania is to an adult what hyperactivity is to a child, though there is no clear causal link between the two. Mania is evident in behaviors such as restlessness, energetic movements, increased talking and gestures, increased sexuality, a reduced need for sleep, and euphoria and/or irritability. Yet, contrary to popular opinion, as we have noted, manic persons are not necessarily always euphoric or happy during the manic episode. When not in the midst of an episode of mania, the manic person often desires to be rid of this behavior.

Disorders including a clear manic component account for only about five percent of psychiatric hospital admissions, whereas the diagnosis of unipolar depression (depression without mania) is common. **Bipolar disorder** is the DSM term for a severe level of disorder (often psychotic) that includes both mania and depression. The incidence of severe bipolar affective disorder (including both mania and depression) is about 300 per 100,000 people, or 0.3 percent (Berger, 1978). This rate, however, is increasing. One reason for the increase may be that there is now a reasonably effective and straightforward cure for bipolar disorder, whereas schizophrenia, with which it is occasionally confused, is less easily treated. Clinicians apparently put borderline cases into the more hopeful category.

Mania and depression.   Depression and mania designate the extremes of an activity spectrum, and both have been recorded since ancient times. Hippocrates attributed depression (or melancholy) to an excess of black bile (melan, "black"; choler, "bile"), and mania to one of yellow bile. Aretaeus of Cappadocia was the first to note a relationship between manic and depressive episodes. This linkage is described adequately on a variety of "normal" dimensions, such as depression-joy or depression-contentment.

Although some theorists, including ourselves, would disagree, the DSM asserts that manic episodes always occur in relation to some degree of depression, past or present. Consequently, the bipolar disorder category (mixed, manic, or depressed) includes both manic and depressive elements and is now the DSM label for the traditional DSM-II category of manic-depressive psychosis. **Cyclothymic disorder** also combines manic and depressive components, but at more moderate levels, and it is not a psychotic disorder. Though it is far less intense, it is more chronic and is not even diagnosed unless the recurrent mood cycles of moderate mania and depression occur for as long as two years. Kurt would likely receive the diagnosis of bipolar disorder: manic, as depressive components are not significant in his case.

Differentiating mania and schizophrenia.   While affective disorder is primarily a disturbance of emotion, schizophrenia and paranoia (the subjects of the previous two chapters) are primarily disorders of thinking. Thus, in most cases the thought disorder and flat affect typical of schizophrenia make confusion with mania unlikely. For cases that resemble both categories, several characteristics are useful in arriving at the correct diagnosis.

1.   Although both schizophrenic and manic persons are distractible, schizophrenics are distracted by internal thoughts and ruminations; manics are distracted by external stimuli that often go unnoticed by others.

2.   Whereas schizophrenics usually avoid relationships with others, manics are profoundly open to contact (albeit superficial contact for the most part) with other people (NIMH Staff, 1977).

3.   Whereas the thought disorder of manics is one of inappropriate combinations of unrelated thoughts that are often accompanied by humor, flippancy, and playfulness, the thought disorder of schizophrenics is composed of disorganized and confused thought combinations marked by peculiar, though usually bland, words or phrases (Solovay et al., 1987).

4.   On the average, schizophrenics show a smaller degree of response in their cortical evoked brain potentials (the immediate electrophysiologic

EXHIBIT

Manic and Depressed TAT Stories

The stories below were told by the same person, but on two different occasions, in response to Card 14 of the specific projective test called the Thematic Apperception Test (see Chapter 3) (Karon, 1981). The first story was told when this 20-year-old female college student was in a manic phase; the other while she was in a depressed phase. Card 14, which is often assumed to elicit suicidal thoughts, shows the silhouette of a man gazing out of a high window. Whereas the depressed story is orderly, not bizarre, very short, and indicative of guilt, the manic story shows the lack of organization generated by a flight of ideas, a grandiose view of the self, and a mild paranoid theme.

Manic phase response

He's up there, feeling like he's boss of it all, I'm pretending he's talking to some workers there, just came off of a strike, they had too many money problems so they gave up the strike. He likes being boss, gets to do what he wants, gets to do lots of things he likes, has money to go out a lot—he likes to disco. He has to move fast—some people are jealous of him, his power—but he deserves it—he's usually the best at what he does—a really good athlete. He can take care of the worker problem but he has to be tough with them—keep them in their place.

Depressed phase response

He's just thinking about his childhood—his life. He doesn't feel he's made much out of it. He's thinking a lot of people he's hurt. He wants to jump, but is thinking whether he'll only get hurt bad instead of killed.

response of the brain to a sound or light stimulus) than do manics, and do not show the supersensitivity to light that is characteristic of many manics (Lewy et al., 1985). (See Chapter 7 for a further discussion of cortical evoked brain potentials.) Also, manics tend to have higher levels of cortisol, noradrenaline, and thyroxine, but lower levels of testosterone than do schizophrenics.

At a somewhat more experimental level, newly developed brain-scanning techniques appear to be effective in differentiating between mania and schizophrenia. An x-raylike technique called positron-emission tomography (PET)—alternatively known as positron-emission transaxial tomography (PETT)—was first used on human beings in 1976. It reveals abnormal patterns of glucose (a simple sugar) metabolism (breakdown) in the brain, and there is evidence of some difference in these patterns between manic and schizophrenic persons. Some manics show increased glucose activity in the right temporal region if they are in the midst of an attack, whereas most schizophrenics tend to show decreased glucose metabolism in the frontal cortex. The drawbacks of the PET technique are: (1) this diagnostic differentiation can be made more easily in other ways; (2) when the behavior patterns are very similar, PET does not consistently make the differentiation; (3) it is expensive; (4) it requires the introduction of a catheter into a blood vessel, a small but distinct risk; and (5) the introduction of radioactive material into the brain may pose long-term risks that are not yet fully understood.

Etiology

There are fewer theories about the psychological causes of mania than there are about many other disorders. Behaviorists contend that certain manic behaviors reflect basic patterns of high reinforcement and the extinction of inhibition. Psychoanalysts have generally viewed mania as either a relief from depression, or the denial of the underlying depression as central factors (Lewis, 1981).

However, nearly all theorists, including behaviorists and psychoanalysts, have now accepted the idea that a biological disorder is most often the major contributory factor in primary mania (Endicott et al., 1985), and as the accompanying Exhibit indicates, mania is also a secondary reaction to a variety of physical substances and events (Stasiek and Zetin, 1985). Support for this view is drawn from several sources. First, there is evidence of higher levels of bipolar disorder and of cyclothymia (significant, though not so severe as to be psychotic, mood swings) in blood relatives of persons with bipolar disorder than in normal persons or persons with other types of emotional disorder (Klein et al., 1985). Second, the specific and dramatic effect of the chemical lithium on mania is well documented (NIMH Staff, 1977; Prien et al., 1984; Endicott et al., 1985). Third, there is evidence that a genetically based abnormality in the ease and speed with which lithium and sodium transfer between certain brain cells plays a part in affective disorders with a manic component. Finally, the shift from mania to depression is marked by increased blood levels of calcium and phosphorus. The same phenomenon has been noted when some withdrawn depressed persons move toward agitation (Prien et al., 1984).

There are impressive data that whatever the exact biological mechanism that causes mania, a genetic factor is of major importance (NIMH Staff, 1977; Klein et al., 1985; Lewy et al., 1985; Beatty, 1987). The evidence is less clear about what this brain process might be in mania, as distinct from depressive

EXHIBIT

Causes of Secondary Manic Reactions

Drugs

Isoniazid
Procarbazine
Levodopa
Bromide
Decongestants
Bronchodilators
Procyclidine
Calcium replacement
Phencyclidine
Metoclopramide
Corticosteroids
Amphetamines

Metabolic disturbance

Postoperative state
Hemodialysis
Vitamin B_{12} deficiency
After-effects of weaning
Dialysis dementia
Hyperthyroidism

Seizures and degenerative and vascular diseases

Right temporal seizure focus
Multiple sclerosis
Right hemisphere damage

Infection

Influenza
Q fever
Neurosyphilis
Post-St. Louis type A encephalitis
Benign herpes simplex encephalitis

Neoplasm (tumors)

Parasagittal meningioma
Diencephalic glioma
Suprasellar diencephalic tumor
Benign spheno-occipital tumor
Right intraventricular meningioma
Right temporoparietal-occipital metastases
Tumor of floor of fourth ventricle

Adapted from Stasiek and Zetin, 1985.

disorders. Most theorists believe that it is generally the opposite process from that which causes depression, or indeed, simply an even more severe form of the biological process in severe endogenous depression (Tsuang et al., 1985) described in detail later in this chapter.

According to Kestenbaum (1979), children are at risk for later bipolar disorder with a clear manic component if (1) they have a family history of bipolar disorder; (2) they have shown affect problems, particularly hyperexcitability; (3) they show significantly higher ability on the verbally based items (rather than those depending on visual-motor performance) on the Wechsler Intelligence Scale for Children (WISC-R); and (4) there is evidence of EEG irregularity in the frontal lobes of the brain.

Treatment

Prior to the use of lithium, a wide array of treatments received anecdotal support as useful for mania. Hopes were high for each, but empirically valid data confirming their effectiveness were never forthcoming. A major reason is that spontaneous remission is common in mania. Thus, therapists who

---

EXHIBIT

Creativity, Poetry, and the Bipolar Disorder

The concept that creativity is positively correlated with psychopathology is hardly new, and is a persistent theme of certain authors such as Arthur Koestler. But new research, such as that reported in the book *Manic-Depressive Illness* (1986) by Goodwin and Jamison, offers evidence that this is true for the bipolar disorder (manic-depressive disorder), and especially for certain artistic endeavors (Leo, J. (1985) The ups and downs of creativity. *Time* 124(15):76).

The list of first-rank artists who appear to have also suffered a bipolar disorder is impressive: Poet-painter Dante Gabriel Rosetti, playwright Eugene O'Neill; writers F. Scott Fitzgerald, Ernest Hemingway, Virginia Woolf, John Ruskin, and Honore de Balzac; and composers Robert Schumann, Hector Berlioz, and George Frederick Handel. Indeed, Handel wrote *The Messiah* in a frenetic 24 days during a manic high.

But it is poets who are most often bipolars. Byron, Coleridge, Shelley, Poe, and Gerald Manley Hopkins all suffered from bipolar disorder, as did many of the major American poets like Hart Crane, Robert Lowell, Anne Sexton, Theodore Roethke, Sylvia Plath, and John Berryman.

Some might argue that poets tend to be bipolars because poetry often celebrates the inner turbulence of one's psyche. But even in the 18th century, a time in which poetry did not really focus on inner upset and complexity, a high proportion of accomplished poets also appear to have been bipolars. So, the relationship of poetry and bipolar disorder may more directly result from the fact that frenetic but sporadic effort is more effectively productive in poetry than other areas, and because the imagery inherent in poetry is more like the primitive thought found in severe emotional disruption. Perhaps the depressions of the bipolar mood swing provide the fuel of emotional depth to the productivity of the manic high.

Some afflicted artists avoid therapy out of a fear that successful treatment would curb their creativity. It appears that in some cases they may be correct. What do you think?

coincidentally happened to do something unaccustomed (such as bring up a new topic, give a new drug, or even fall asleep) at the same time one or two of their manic clients spontaneously remitted would infer that the new method was responsible for the cure. If they were sufficiently ambitious to publish a clinical report, the new technique would become the focus of attention until someone else discovered another presumed cure.

Lithium is a chemical element first isolated in 1817 by John Arfwedson, a young Swedish chemistry student. He named it lithium because he found it in stone (lithos in Greek). John Cade, an Australian psychiatrist, discovered the positive effect of lithium on mania by chance in the 1940s (Lipton, 1979), while studying whether an excess of uric acid might be the cause of manic-depressive episodes. Cade injected humans with urea from the urine of guinea pigs. Expecting to learn that uric acid (a compound containing urea) increased the toxicity of urea, he added the most soluble salt of uric acid, lithium urate, and was surprised to find instead that the urea was less toxic as a result. Further experiments isolating lithium indicated its curative properties (Lipton, 1979; Prien et al., 1984).

Lithium is usually administered as lithium carbonate, a chemically convenient form that also contains a high percentage of lithium per weight. Lithium therapy is a bit more demanding than other chemotherapies. Because the kidneys absorb lithium rapidly, it must be taken in divided dosages to avoid kidney damage. Educating clients about its use is most important; they must, for example, take it continually and on schedule even though they may feel well (and manics feel quite well at times). Cochran (1984) found that a series of six sessions with a therapist, specifically designed to enhance compliance with the prescribed medication regimen, resulted in better general functioning, including less likelihood of being rehospitalized.

However, lithium does have numerous probable long-term side effects, including hand tremor, weight gain, and frequent urination. Because lithium suppresses thyroxin secretion, goiter and related thyroid problems can occur. Kidney failure is also possible.

There has been surprisingly little research on lithium, while more exotic, less widely available compounds have received much attention. Two explanations for this seem plausible. First, there was warranted concern about the significant side effects of lithium. Second, since lithium is a naturally occurring element it cannot be patented. Drug companies are much more interested in researching new synthetic compounds that they can patent, so that they can control the market and gain substantial profits.

Lithium reverses the symptoms of mania in 70 to 80 percent of cases (NIMH Staff, 1977; Endicott et al., 1985), and is most effective with clients with more severe manic patterns and those whose last episode was a manic one rather than a depressive episode (Prien et al., 1984). Hollon and Beck (1978) have demonstrated that combining lithium therapy with psychotherapy and specific behavior therapies is more effective than using lithium therapy alone.

The Case of Ann

Ann had completed her divorce proceedings eight months before calling a psychologist for an emergency appointment. Her marriage of 12 years had rarely been better than average, and the final three years had been marked by constant verbal abuse of her by her husband. She had mixed feelings about staying in the marriage, and did not seek a divorce even though her husband had beaten her severely on several occasions during this period. When she finally sought a divorce, he at first refused to give her one. But when he saw how definite she was in her intent, he cooperated. A month after the decree was signed, he quit his job and left town.

Ann had always enjoyed both her job as a teacher and her two children, ages four and seven. Although she had anticipated feeling good after the divorce, she became increasingly depressed in the five weeks before her self-referral. For the last of those weeks she had trouble getting to sleep every night, had little appetite, felt very fatigued, and showed no interest in her usual activities. She stayed home from school for two days because she "just didn't feel like going in." Though she loved her children very much, she found herself unable to handle some of the required tasks of childrearing, which added to her depression. Late one afternoon she went straight to bed, leaving her children to fend for themselves. Then, the night before calling for an appointment, she took five sleeping tablets and a couple of stiff drinks and went into a stuporous sleep, sleeping through her alarm. As she said, "I don't think I wanted to kill myself; I just wanted to forget everything for awhile."

In therapy, Ann revealed that she had been feeling increasingly helpless in dealing with the demands of her world. She now consistently described herself as a failure at work and a bad mother. She was surprised that she had not been happy with her freedom after her bad marriage, a feeling she expressed in the following poem:

> The cold grip of nowhere
> The heavy load of no-thing
> The freedom

Ann eventually responded well to therapy. It then became clear she was not comfortable with handling the demands of single parenting, even though her depression had lifted. She enrolled for several parent training courses, and gradually developed a reasonable sense of mastery in this area.

DEPRESSION

Depression has been termed the "common cold" of psychopathology. However, this phrase refers only to its high incidence; it does not express the intensity or duration of the disorder. To be severely depressed is to be emotionally frozen. Initiative disappears. Most depressed persons remain aware of their world, but, as in Ann's case, they lose their desire to continue to interact with it. Their sense of self is diminished; the past carries guilt and reproach; the present seems oppressively forever; and the future is bleak.

And there is pain. The pain is as real as any physical pain, and likewise commands one's complete attention. Charles Darwin noted in his diary that his bouts of depression made him "inexpressibly gloomy and miserable." Winston Churchill pungently termed depression his "black dog." As Albert Camus described the experience, "The living do not suffice to people my world and dispel my boredom." Thus, depression affects the entire organism. Although anxiety was often the primary concern in earlier eras, most experts now see *depression* as the predominant form of psychopathology (Arieti and Bemporad, 1978; Steinbrueck et al., 1983; Levin, 1987).

Major depression is subdivided into single episode or recurrent, and there must be significant symptomatology for at least two weeks before any depression is labeled as an episode. Ann would receive a diagnosis of major depression, single episode. The DSM allows the clinician to diagnose depressive episode as psychotic only when there are hallucinations, delusions, or "depressive stupor," that is, the client is mute and unresponsive. The **dysthymic disorder** (which replaced the traditional DSM-II term depressive neurosis) requires a consistent though not constant manifestation of depressive symptomatology over a two-year period (one year for children and adolescents). It is a more moderate level of disorder, and does not reach psychotic proportions. It is more common than major depression. Also, like the cyclothymic disorder (moderate mania *and* depression), it is only diagnosed if the episodes persist over a two-year period.

Symptoms

Many people experience mild or transient depressions at various points in their lives. Short depressions as a reaction to losses (death, job, money) or separations (divorce, geographic move, graduation) are normal.

Depression is manifested in one or more primary symptoms.

1. Dysphoria (feeling bad) and/or apathetic mood
2. A loss of usual sources of reinforcement in the environment (stimulus void)
3. Chronic inability to experience pleasure, that is, anhedonia

The normal depression experienced by a college student overwhelmed with work can be sharply contrasted to the severe depression of a suicide attempt. (top: Cornell Capa/Magnum; bottom. AP/Wide World Photos)

Depression is also often associated with a number of secondary symptoms.

1. Withdrawal from contact with others.
2. Rumination about suicide and/or death
3. A sense of hopelessness
4. Sleep disturbance, particularly early-morning awakening
5. Psychomotor agitation or retardation
6. Disruption and/or decrease in eating behaviors
7. Self-blame; a sense of worthlessness; feelings of guilt with no solid reason for them
8. Lack of decisiveness; slowed thinking; lack of concentration
9. Increased alcohol or drug use
10. Crying for no apparent reason

Incidence of Depression

It is estimated that 20 to 40 million persons in the United States have experienced a serious depression of some type. This is an approximate rate of 12 to 13 percent, which has remained stable for several decades (Murphy et al., 1985). At least 200,000 people are hospitalized for depression each year. It is also estimated that up to one fourth of the office practice of physicians who focus on physical disorders is actually concerned with depression-based symptomatology: about 85 percent of the psychotropic medication dispensed for depression is prescribed by nonpsychiatrists, primarily internists, gynecologists, and family practitioners.

Cross-Cultural Variables

Depression is not diagnosed as often in certain cultures. For example, both French Canadians and the Japanese show low rates. The low rate of *clinically diagnosed* depression in Japan may reflect a greater acceptance of that type of experience. Indeed, the Japanese word for "sad" (kanashi) can also mean beautiful or affectionate (Marsella, 1980).

Age Variables

Whereas manic disorders and depressions with a manic component usually begin before age 30, depressive disorders can begin at any age (Clarke-Stewart et al., 1988). Separation anxiety and school phobia may be manifestations of underlying depression in young children. Adults who have had one major severe depression have about a 50 percent chance of experiencing another episode, and those who have had several episodes are more likely to shift into a chronic bipolar disorder (manic-depressive) than are those who have only had a single episode.

Sex Variables

Prior to adolescence, symptoms of depression are equally common in males and females. From that time on, females are more likely than males to be depressed, and this divergence persists throughout adulthood. Brown and Harris (1979) found that at least two thirds of adults treated for depression are females, often of lower socioeconomic status. They are more likely to have accepted the traditional or stereotypic passive female role, as passivity facilitates depression. Several researchers assert that, regardless of socioeconomic status, there is an actual higher base level of depression in females (Chevron et al., 1978; Brown and Harris, 1979). However, traditional sex roles still exert a critical influence on this disparity. Males, who are much more likely to be trained to channel their problems into assertive and action-externalizing behaviors, show higher rates of aggressive disorders, disruptive behaviors in school, and drug and alcohol disorders. Females are more prone to passive disorders, that is, they have a learned susceptibility to behavior patterns that facilitate depression.

Chevron et al. (1978) studied the content of the depressive experience in females and males. They found that depressions in females were more likely to be "anaclitic," or dependency oriented, reflecting a loss of satisfaction in relationships. The depressive experiences of males, on the other hand, focused on self-criticism, a perceived failure to live up to competency and goal expectations (Chevron et al., 1978; Blatt et al., 1982).

There are other reasons why females may be diagnosed as depressive more often than males. First, they are simply more willing to admit to feeling depressed, whereas males often deny feelings suggesting vulnerability. For example, it is noteworthy that an infant wrapped in a blue blanket, and believed by nurses and other caretakers to be a boy, will be held less frequently and for a shorter time than an infant in a pink blanket, regardless of the actual sex of the child. Second, the majority of mental health professionals who make diagnoses are male. It is possible that through the bias of sex-role stereotyping they are more likely to view a series of behaviors as "depressed" in women, yet to give the same behavior in males a different label, such as "adjustment reaction" (Brown and Harris, 1979; Sarbin and Mancuso, 1980).

Premenstrual syndrome. The idea of a specific disorder related to negative mood changes premenstrually was first proposed by Frankin in 1931. It was later labeled **premenstrual syndrome** (PMS), and is also termed late luteal dysphoric disorder. There is much controversy as to whether this pattern should be considered a psychiatric (or psychological) diagnosis—certain feminists have argued strongly against this—and there is also wide disagreement about its incidence, cause, and treatment (Clare, 1985). The most generally accepted theory is that PMS reflects a sequence of hormonal imbalances, primarily involving estrogen, progesterone, and prolactin. Treatments include drugs to regulate hormones and diuretics to control water retention and bloating. Also, increased exercise (as women who are physically active tend to suffer less from PMS) and dietary changes are advised. Reduction of nicotine and caffeine helps reduce irritability and anxiety, and reduction of alcohol lessens depressive feelings. Cutting down on sodium reduces water retention, and eating small, frequent meals stabilizes blood sugar levels, which in turn steadies the estrogen-linked increases in insulin production that are believed to increase PMS symptoms.

Dimensions

There are a number of ways to conceptualize differences in depression. We have just noted one, the anaclitic versus self-criticism model (Blatt et al., 1982). A number of other meaningful dimensions have also received attention in clinical practice and research.

1. *Normal-inappropriate.* Reaction to grief, an occasional period of the "blues," and other temporary depressive responses are normal. When they persist and do not lead to any coping behaviors, or when the focus of concern changes from the problem to the self (all of which were noted in Ann), they reach abnormal dimensions (Fabry, 1980).

2. *Acute-chronic.* This dimension is useful in almost all areas of psychopathology. As with chronic schizophrenia, people who develop chronic depression are less likely to recover fully.

3. *Agitated-slow.* Whereas some depressive persons display anxiety and agitation, others manifest a slowing of behavior. The agitated depressive is more likely to reflect an acute situational reaction. In this sense the agitation is positive, for it reflects a continuing attempt to struggle with the problem at hand.

4. *Neurotic-psychotic.* This continuum is still used by practitioners even though the DSM no longer directly recognizes the label "neurotic." It is essentially a measure of severity that can be applied to various depressive behaviors (Solovay et al., 1987).

5. *Primary-secondary.* Depressions can be the primary disorder or they can be secondary to other mental disorder syndromes (such as schizophrenia), or to severe physical illness and chronic pain.

6. *Unipolar-bipolar.*   These terms simply discriminate between depressions associated with manic episodes (bipolar) and those without (unipolar). Depue et al. (1981) found two major differences between bipolar and unipolar depressions: unipolar depressives tend to show more agitated motor behavior and sleep disruption; while bipolars show more psychomotor retardation and hypersomnia—that is, they tend to get two or more hours of sleep per night more than normal persons, and even then take frequent naps.

7. *Endogenous-exogenous.*   This popular classification system attempts to categorize depressions by cause. **Endogenous** depressions are assumed to originate from internal psychic and physical causes (such as hormonal disruption); **exogenous** depressions from external causes (such as personal loss) (Wierzbicki, 1987). The four traditional behavioral indications of a significant endogenous depression are (1) slowed response patterns, (2) early-morning sleep disruption, (3) more severe mood problems, and (4) significant weight loss without dieting.

Assessment

Standard psychological tests, such as the Rorschach Ink Blot Test, Thematic Apperception Test, and the MMPI, are often used to assess affective disorders. The MMPI contains separate scales for depression and mania, but the results of the MMPI depression scale taken in isolation have not always proved to be reliable (Graham, 1987). Several other short tests, each containing about 20 questions, are designed specifically to measure depression. Most notable among these are the Zung Self-Rating Depression Scale and the Beck Depression Inventory. Below are several condensed items from the Beck Scale (Beck, 1967).

> *I feel sad.*
> *I feel I have nothing to look forward to.*
> *I feel guilty a good part of the time.*
> *I have lost most of my interest in other people.*
> *I don't sleep as well as I used to.*
> *My appetite is not as good as it used to be.*

Physiological measures have also been used to assess depression, but an efficient measurement of the brain substances thought to cause depression can be difficult without surgery. EEGs and urinalyses are not accurate enough, but blood tests can be helpful. The extraction of cerebrospinal fluid via a spinal tap is another way in which this can be carried out. As noted earlier, the dexamethasone suppression test is generally effective in discriminating endogenous from exogenous depression. In this laboratory test of endocrine function, the abnormal response is an early cessation of internal cortical pro-

EXHIBIT

Types of Depression

It has long been hypothesized that various types of depression may be generated in different ways. Lewis and Winokur (1983) combined their own research with a thorough review of other relevant research to develop subclassifications of unipolar depressive disorder that suggest three different types of and causes for depression.

1. *Sporadic Depressive Disease (SDD):* No family history of alcoholism, antisocial patterns, or depression; clearly exogenous depression.
2. *Familial Pure Depression Disease (FPDD):* A family history of depression only—the endogenous group.
3. *Depressive Spectrum Disease (DSD):* Marked by first-degree family members with alcoholism and/or antisocial personality problems. There may or may not be a family history of depression; a mixed group.

The important differences between these groups are (1) the mean age for the first depressive episode is much later (41.3 years) for the SDD group than the DSD (34.6) or FPDD (33.4) groups; (2) the FPDD group is more likely to show an abrupt or acute onset of depression and more total episodes; (3) the DSD group shows a much higher rate of interpersonal (sexual and marital problems) and legal difficulties; and most importantly, (4) the FPDD group shows a much higher incidence of nonsuppression of serum cortisol in the dexamethasone suppression test (a test wherein the most clearly and severely depressed individuals show a different physiological reaction to the drug dexamethasone), much higher rates of insensitivity to insulin in the recovery phase of depression, and a higher rate of EEG abnormalities during sleep. These results suggest that the family pure depressive disease group (FPDD) is a distinct entity, whose depression is related to neurobiological dysfunction probably derived from a genetically based disorder in the regulation of the hypothalamic-pituitary-adrenal systems. On the other hand, SDD is primarily derived from situational problems and inadequate coping methods, while DSD derives from multiple causes.

duction due to suppression by the orally administered drug dexamethasone. Unfortunately, there are a number of false-positive results with this test, that is, substantial numbers of exogenous depressives, schizophrenics, and some normal individuals can show an abnormal response (Peselow et al., 1987).

Etiology

Darwin hypothesized that depressive behaviors evolved because, in a temporary form, they have a value for the survival of the species: they alert the social group to danger. Disorder occurs when depression is intense and lasts a significant time (Lewinsohn and Hoberman, 1982). Most theories on the causes of significant depressive disorder have developed from four major theoretical positions: physiological, psychodynamic, behavioral, and cognitive.

Physiological theories. According to the **catecholamine theory,** depression reflects an alteration in the level of brain neurotransmitters (norepinephrine, serotonin, and histamine—chemicals that facilitate transmission of nerve impulses to the brain) (McNeal and Cimbolic, 1986; Bandura et al., 1985). Such disorder could be generated in a number of ways, for example, by genetic disorder, trauma, infection, or ingestion of chemicals or drugs (Wierzbicki, 1987). Most adherents to this theory attribute the major depressions to a deficiency in the neurotransmitter norepinephrine. According to the ongoing research of Jay Weiss and his colleagues (Turkington, 1982), cognitive stress causes a rise in the rate of norepinephrine release in the brainstem. This apparently stimulates certain neurons to absorb unused norepinephrine faster than it is released. This ultimately results in a depletion of norepinephrine, which in turn causes depression. Tyrosine hydroxylase, an enzyme that synthesizes the needed norepinephrine, has proven an effective curative agent. Tyrosine hydroxylase is generated in the locus ceruleus area of the brain by the natural recovery processes of the body (in normal persons), by certain drugs, and by electroconvulsive therapy (ECT).

In a related fashion, the monoamine oxidase (MAO) inhibiting drugs used to treat depression disrupt the action of the enzyme that metabolizes (or breaks down) norepinephrine. Other antidepressant drugs, the tricyclics, are thought to inhibit the reabsorption of norepinephrine into the neuronal synapses (McNeal and Cimbolic, 1986).

Some researchers (McNeal and Cimbolic, 1986; Kety, 1975) believe that a second group of neurochemicals, the indoleamines (such as serotonin; see Chapter 7), may be the causative factor in depression. This is not necessarily contradictory to the norepinephrine theory since various indoleamine transport systems go through the locus ceruleus in the brain, which in turn influences norepinephrine levels.

So, it appears reasonable to consider the possibility of two different physiologically generated depressions. (1) A norepinephrine-based depression, characterized by low levels of 3-methoxyl-4-hydroxyphenolglycol (MPHG) (the principal metabolite, or by-product, of the breakdown of norepinephrine) and high levels of 5-hydroxyindolacetic acid (5-HIAA) (the principal metabolite of serotonin). This norepinephrine based depression is more likely to result in suicidal behavior, and responds better to the tricyclic drug imipramine. (2) A serotonin-based depression, with high MPHG and low 5-HIAA, which responds better to the tricyclic drug amitriptyline (Lobel, 1984; Lyons et al., 1985).

The interactions between the neurotransmitters and the body's hormones may also be significant. For example, melatonin, a hormone secreted by the pineal gland, has a molecular structure that is very similar to that of serotonin. The secretion of melatonin is triggered by low-light conditions, which may help to explain the common phenomenon of sleep disturbance in depressives, as well as the phenomenon of *seasonal affective disorder,* the heightened incidence of depression in the winter (Lobel, 1984). Some mild depressions that are apparently caused by winter have even been alleviated by several hours' exposure to bright (four times brighter than ordinary room light) light over several days.

Other evidence suggests that a disturbance in the cells in the brain's nerve system that especially respond to histamine may also be an important variable. In fact, the antidepressants are often 100 to 1,000 times more potent than antihistamines in blocking the histamine receptors (Kolata, 1980), suggesting that antihistamine action may comprise the antidepressant effect.

Genetic theory. Significant data indicates that genetic variables play a part in both severe depression and bipolar affective disorder (Winokur, 1979; Klein et al., 1985; Wierzbicki, 1987), perhaps through genetically produced differences in the ability of an individual's brain to quickly and easily pass histamine, or lithium and sodium, between the brain cells. But other data (Winokur, 1979; Lewinsohn and Hoberman, 1982; Lyons et al., 1985; Bandura et al., 1985) suggest that genetic factors are not the major variables in most depressions. Situationally generated stress, prolonged inactivity, or even a high intake of caffeine can cause the substantial physiological changes that produce depression, including a change in levels of norepinephrine or neurotransmitter-related enzymes (Bandura et al., 1985; Veleber and Templer, 1984). Also, medications for other disorders, for example, the beta-blockers used to treat hypertension, can increase depressive feelings. Like schizophrenia, depression embraces several separate syndromes (Lewis and Winokur, 1983), and any one case commonly includes several contributory factors. So, while genetic variables probably contribute to many cases of depression, only a minority of depressives, at best, are compellingly predisposed genetically to depression.

Psychodynamic theories. Since Karl Abraham's classic paper early in this century (Abraham, 1916), psychoanalysts have seen frustrated unconscious aggression as the cause of depression. The hypothesized defense mechanism is primitive oral eroticism, manifested in outbursts of verbal hostility or in eating disorders, which is followed by guilt and a need for punishment. Thus, by assuaging this guilt, there is relief from the depression. Several psychoanalysts have asserted that this is why ECT is helpful with depression: the patient lessens the depression by experiencing electroconvulsive shocks as deserved punishment.

Freud also considered **ego loss** to be a cause of depression (Lewis, 1981). In a typical hypothesized sequence, a person reacts to an actual loss (such as a death in the family) by incorporating aspects of the lost other into his or her own personality or ego. At the same time, the person feels unconscious hate toward the lost other because of the abandonment implied in the loss. This hate is then turned against the incorporated aspects of the other that are now a part of the self. Freud also hypothesized that societal sexual repression contributes to depression, but data have clearly disproved this theory. Even in an age marked by sexual liberation, there has been no decrease in the incidence of depression.

Silvano Arieti and Jules Bemporad (1978) provide an updated version of the traditional psychodynamic view. They regard the depressed person as one who suffered great loss in childhood, such as a first child who experienced "paradise lost" when a new sibling near in age stole the heretofore undivided attention of the mother. The loss could come in other ways, including parental death or abandonment or even a sudden parental decision to prohibit certain types of childish behavior and to insist that the child now act "grown-up."

According to Arieti and Bemporad, the person strives to regain "paradise" by trying to please others, particularly "dominant others." The person adopts a lifestyle designed to "achieve greatness" in order to please the dominant other. These self-generated expectancies often exceed the person's capabilities; thus, failure follows, self-blame and reproach increase, and various forms of self-destructive behavior may occur, most notably suicide (Fawcett et al., 1987).

One client of a Jungian therapist relived this "loss of paradise" in a dream state. The client saw himself on the lawn next to the house where he had lived until age six. He saw his mother as she must have been as a girl, slim and beautiful. She was seated on a multicolored blanket that they had always used on picnics when he was a young child. As he saw himself running freely and joyfully in tandem with his dog "Mikey" in the bright sun through shimmering green grass, he suddenly and intensely experienced the thought: "I can't ever have that again." He awoke sobbing and cried deeply for an hour. Yet this was a positive turning point for the client not only in terms of handling relationships with his parents and his own child, but in helping him to decrease the demanding expectations he had imposed on himself as well.

A relatively recent attempt to validate empirically the psychodynamic approach was carried out by Barnes and Prosen (1985). The Centre for Epidemiological Studies Depression Scale was administered to a sample of 1,250 patients in general practitioner's offices in the province of Manitoba, Canada. These persons were asked to indicate whether they had lost a father or mother by death and their own age when the loss occurred. Interestingly, there was no significant correlation of depression with loss of a mother, while those who lost a father while in the 0 to 6 and 10 to 15 age ranges reported the highest depression levels. These results, if replicated (especially in a sample of clearly clinically depressed clients, and using observational rather than self-report data) would require some major revisions of most psychodynamic theories, as well as the upcoming behavioral theories.

In general, the psychodynamic theories of depression have not produced a significant amount of clearly supportive empirical data. Nevertheless, numerous practicing clinicians consider these ideas useful, and psychodynamic views have always been a fertile ground for the development of new theories. In fact, the psychodynamic views of depression are not very different from some of the cognitive theories, except for the unverified emphasis in psychodynamic theory on both early experience and the unconscious nature of conflicts.

Behavioral theories.   The major premise of the behavioral position, first thoroughly articulated by Ferster (1965), is that depression occurs when the individual is deprived of accustomed positive reinforcements. This claim does not differ much in form from Freud's proposal that the early loss of a loved object (usually the mother) causes an oral dependency pattern, which in turn makes the person overly vulnerable to the loss of external emotional support. For the behaviorists, though, "oral dependency" is a useless intermediate descriptor, and the first loss need not have occurred in infancy or even childhood.

Building on Ferster's work, the behaviorists have come to the viewpoint that depression can result from either of two processes (Ferster, 1965; Ferster and Culberston, 1982; Lyons et al., 1985). In one, an environmental change (such as a death in the family or the loss of a job) curtails the level of incoming reinforcement. Persons who rely on one or two principal sources of reinforcement are particularly vulnerable to depression stemming from curtailed reinforcement, referred to as a **stimulus void.** Ferster uses the example of two spinster sisters who had lived, and bickered, together for a long time, in comparative isolation from others. When one died, the other suffered a severe depression. The predominant source of reinforcement (even if it was only negative attention gained from bickering and nagging) was gone, leaving a stimulus void in the behavioral repertoire. It is a loss of stimuli, not a loss of love, that is important. This was also evident in the earlier case describing Ann. Ann reacted to the stimulus void created by her divorce and the disappearance of her husband. Many of her behavior patterns were dependent on interactions with her husband, even though the relationship no longer included much love. Thus, the loss need not involve a loved one, it need only be a person or even an object with a high stimulus value; one that is central to the person's activities.

A second behavioral perspective views depression in terms of avoidance behavior, in other words, depression occurs when a person's attempts to avoid aversive circumstances have become so strong that they preempt behaviors that bring reinforcement (Lewinsohn and Hoberman, 1982). Social withdrawal from anxiety-generating stimuli may be so great (as in agoraphobia—see Chapter 6) that the person loses most social reinforcement contacts, and depression ensues. Subsequent experiences increase and maintain the depression, even though for a time, the depressed person may obtain sympathy from others (a secondary gain). Eventually, even those who were initially sympathetic can become hostile and/or depressed after interacting with a depressed person (Doerfler and Chaplin, 1985). When they then withdraw, either physically or emotionally, the social isolation of the depressed person becomes almost total.

Although the behavioral model has been effective in clarifying processes in the development of depression, it suffers the same problems as the "counting of events" approach to stress (see Chapter 5); both fail to deal with the differences in people's reactions to similar events.

Cognitive theories. *The cognitive distortion model.* The cognitive distortion model tries to account for the fact that similar environmental stimuli can have different effects on various individuals. This model, as detailed by Aaron Beck (1967), has been particularly influential among contemporary behavior therapists who see no inherent conflict between behavioral and cognitive theories. The cognitive approach owes much to George Kelly's work on personal constructs (1955, 1977) and to Albert Ellis (1973). Yet as early as 1602, Felix Platter expressed virtually the same view when he described depression as resting "upon a foundation of false conceptions."

Beck believes that traumatic early events (such as the death of a parent, a father's shooting a pet dog in front of a child, or perhaps even a "paradise lost") sensitize and predispose an individual to depression. Through vicarious modeling and self-labeling, depressed clients develop a cognitive style marked by several of the following distorted thinking patterns. They simultaneously (1) *minimize* any positive achievements and (2) *magnify* any problems into "catastrophic expectations"; they also tend to (3) *polarize* (view things in extreme terms) and easily (4) *over-generalize* from one or two isolated events. As a result of these cognitive distortions, depressed persons develop a negative view of themselves, their surroundings, and the future (Vestre, 1984). Albert Ellis (1973) has shown that such irrational but persuasive beliefs as "I need everyone to love me" and "I have to be competent in everything I undertake" easily lead to depressive responses in anyone, and that these beliefs are characteristic of the clinically depressed individual.

Most people talk to themselves in some fashion. The self-verbalizations of depressives are likely to focus on negative comments about the activities they engage in and about their own self-identify. This occurs even when there is evidence that their performance on a given task is as adequate as that of normal persons (Lobitz and Post, 1979). In general, as depressed clients improve, they talk more positively about themselves, develop more active coping strategies, and are both more active and positive interpersonally (Billings and Moos, 1985).

Learned helplessness. The **learned helplessness** (LH) theory of depression is in many ways analogous to cognitive theory, except that it also incorporates some learning theory principles. The syndrome called "Tawatl ye sni" of the Sioux Indians of North America, especially those whose lifestyle alternatives are restricted by life on a reservation, resembles learned helplessness in that it is marked by feelings of total discouragement and the sense that one can do nothing to change what is happening (Marsella, 1980).

EXHIBIT

Features of Learned Helplessness and Depression

Depression	Learned Helplessness
Nonresponsive	Nonresponsive
Generally apathetic	Passive in certain situations
Sense of helplessness and hopelessness	Sense of helplessness
Persists or recurs	Decreases with time
Avoidance of situations that could change attitude	Changes in response to new situations
Reflects long-term experience variables, often in conjunction with physiological predispositions	Evolves primarily from cognitive evaluation of recent experiences
Sees the world as negative	Sees reinforcement in the world as randomly related to one's behavior
Inclined to be suicidal	Usually not inclined to be suicidal
Often harbors unexpressed hostility	Inner hostility not usually a major element

The LH theory was originally based on the animal research of Overmeir and Seligman (1967). They administered painful electric shocks in two different situations. In the first phase of the experiment, some dogs were placed in a cage with electric grids in the floor; they could not do anything to escape the shocks. This group was then grouped with dogs who had not had the shock experience. In the second phase, all the dogs were placed in a similar shock cage, but in this cage the dogs could avoid the shock by jumping over a slat as soon as they heard a warning buzzer. Those dogs who had never had the inescapable shock experience soon learned to jump over the slat. But those who had had the shock showed some initial distress and then simply laid down and passively accepted the shocks.

When the LH theory was first elaborated into a theory of human depression, a major difference from cognitive theories was obvious; LH predicted only that people would develop a feeling of lack of control from similar experiences, whereas cognitive theory and most clinical observers additionally predicted the self-blame that clearly exists in most depressions. As a result Abramson et al. (1978), in a major reformulation, added **attribution theory** to the original LH concepts. Its essential point is that when people experience failure or a loss of control, they attribute it to some cause. If they attribute it to fate or nonrecurring external causes, there is no loss of self-esteem and only a minor lessening of activity. But if they attribute the failure to a stable, internal characteristic (such as "I'm stupid" or "I'm no fun to be with"), both self-esteem and level of activity are reduced, resulting in depression (Sweeney et al., 1986). Research indicates that treatments that reduce the sense of LH also reduce depression (Klee and Meyer, 1981).

Though any of the above causes may be primary in any one case of depression, external and internal factors usually combine in varying degrees in most cases of depression in the following self-perpetuating sequence.

1. Negative environmental condition + possible biological predisposition, leading to the first manifestation of depression; then
2. Social withdrawal + lowered information processing;
3. Inadequate social behaviors + guilt and self-blame;
4. Further self-devaluation + social withdrawal;
5. Actual biological change that facilitates further depression.

Treatment

Psychological and biological techniques in various combinations have proved effective in curing some depressions (McNeal and Cimbolic, 1986; Lyons et al., 1985; Steinbrueck et al., 1983). Indeed, even a simple program to increase the amount of vigorous physical exercise may, in some cases, be helpful (Tomporowski and Ellis, 1986; Thompson et al., 1982). However, relapse back into depression, after some response from any of the following treatments, can occur, and long-term treatment effects are not strikingly positive in much more than 50 percent of those persons who are significantly depressed (Hersen et al., 1984).

Gonzales et al. (1985) thoroughly evaluated 125 people who had been diagnosed as significantly depressed and who had been participants in treatment programs at the University of Oregon Depression Research Unit. Each person was rated by interviewers, and given several psychological tests. Most of the interviewers were graduate students in psychology and undergraduate majors who had been thoroughly trained in diagnostic interviewing through a quarter-long course in conducting interviews. Gonzales et al. found that the people who were most likely to *relapse* back into depression showed (1) a greater number of previous episodes of depression, (2) a higher depression level at the entry point into the study, (3) a family history of depression, especially with a history of depression in first-degree relatives, (4) poor physical health, (5) a higher level of dissatisfaction with their major life roles, and (6) were younger in age. Most of these factors are consistent with prior studies, with the exception of the higher probability of relapse for younger clients, which is a controversial finding.

EXHIBIT				
Various Characteristic Attributions of Students Who Do Poorly on a Critical Exam				
	External		Internal	
	Stable	*Unstable*	*Stable*	*Unstable*
G L O B A L	Essay tests are all unfair	It was an unlucky day, you know, Friday the Thirteenth	I'm not very smart	I'm just exhausted
S P E C I F I C	This professor always gives unfair multiple-choice questions	My copy of the test was blurred, so some of the key words must have been missing	I've never been able to do well in this subject	I drank too much last night; I just can't work with numbers when I do that

Chemotherapy.   Chemotherapy for depression is not a new approach; in Homer's *Odyssey*, Penelope used a drug to ease her grief for her long-lost husband. In the modern pharmacopoeia, the two major subcategories of the antidepressants are the MAO inhibitors and the tricyclics, both introduced in the 1950s. Lithium (discussed earier in the section on mania) can also be helpful with some depressions.

Interestingly, the antidepressant effects of both the tricyclics and the MAO inhibitors were discovered serendipitously. The first tricyclic, imipramine, was discovered while looking for a more effective antipsychotic drug, and the function of the MAOs came to light while studying iproniazid, a drug used to treat tuberculosis (Lobel, 1984). Both the MAO inhibiters and the tricyclics have traditionally been understood to exert a therapeutic effect by increasing neural transmission and, as noted earlier, different depressions respond better to different tricyclics (Lobel, 1984). Research by Lyons et al. (1985) indicates that all of these drugs, when they are effective, act primarily by increasing the frequency of activity-related behaviors, and only indirectly and inconsistently change interpersonal and cognitive components. Both the MAO inhibitors and the tricyclics usually require from several days to one or two weeks to take effect, and trial-and-error adjustment on dosage (titration) is often necessary.

For Marilyn Monroe, a chronically depressed patient, drug therapy became a dependence that compounded her already severe emotional problems. (AP/Wide World Photos)

Also, resarchers have found that people metabolize certain medications at different rates, depending on race. Compared with whites, for example, Asians generally require lower doses of drugs for either depression or schizophrenia, and Hispanics often need lower doses for depression (Beatty, 1987; Lyons et al., 1985).

Use of MAO inhibitors has declined for two reasons: They have not proved significantly effective in curing many depressions (Fabry, 1980), and they have significant side effects, including toxic reactions in the liver and cardiovascular systems and problematic interactions with certain foods.

Tricyclics also have significant side effects, such as dizziness, heart palpitations, and gastrointestinal disorder, and as a result, some 30 to 70 percent of patients who have been prescribed the drug will stop taking it (Hersen et al., 1984). Also, they tend to be effective only for clients with endogenous depression, where their rate of effectiveness is about 40 to 60 percent (McNeal and Cimbolic, 1986; Lyons et al., 1985).

As a result of these problems, interest is turning to newer drugs, such as trazodone HCl, maprotilene, nomifensine, mianserin, and bupropion, which are neither MAOs nor tricyclics, and which so far don't show many of the same problematic side effects (McNeal and Cimbolic, 1986; Lobel, 1984).

ECT and psychosurgery.   As noted in Chapter 4, ECT and psychosurgery have been found to be effective in treating disorders with a depressive component. ECT, and possibly some forms of psychosurgery, may lessen depression by releasing tyrosine hydroxylase, an enzyme that in turn acts to normalize the depleted norepinephrine levels that are hypothesized to cause depression. For seriously suicidal patients, ECT is less radical than psychosurgery and works more quickly than drugs or psychological therapies. However, the clinician must consider the potentially costly side effects of these techniques.

Psychotherapy.   Most forms of psychotherapy are useful with depression. Indeed, a review of 56 outcome studies on the treatment of depression by Steinbrueck et al. (1983) found that the psychotherapies in general were superior in effectiveness to the drug therapies, a result echoed by Hersen et al. (1984) and others (*Behavior Today,* 1986; Gotlib and Colby, 1987). An especially appropriate form of therapy for depression is cognitive behavior modification.

Cognitive behavior modification.   Cognitive behavior modification combines cognitive and behavioral techniques into various treatment packages. Certain **cognitive behavior modification** techniques have been developed in particular detail for depression.

The graded-task approach. The initial objective with depressed clients is to get them active again. The graded-task approach breaks down goals or activities into subgoals or smaller behavior sets to make them less overwhelming. For example, depressed students may be asked to read only three pages of an assigned text at a time instead of an entire chapter. The purpose is to make the task simple enough so that the client completes it and gains the reinforcement of success. As therapy progresses, the tasks are increased in duration and complexity (Bandura et al., 1985).

Inducing incompatible affect and behavior. The therapist can act to elicit affective responses such as humor and anger, since these are incompatible with the despondency characteristic of depression, and interrupt its continuity (Gotlib and Colby, 1987). This procedure is analogous to the manner in which SDT therapists promote relaxation, which is incompatible with anxiety. For example, aides on a ward could harass depressed clients until they become angry, then reinforce the anger response by acceptance (Redd et al., 1979). Also, exercise seems effective in combating depression, or, to paraphrase *Spenser's Second Law* from the private detective character in Robert Parker's book and the television show "Spenser for Hire," "When in doubt, work out."

Moving from unpleasurable to pleasurable activities. The activity levels of depressed clients tend to be relatively low to begin with. What activities they do engage in, moreover, appear to bring little pleasure. Their everyday activity pattern is often a passive skeleton of routine behaviors. They are also inclined to associate with other depressed people, a tendency that increases the depression in all concerned. Because depressives respond negatively to almost all new suggestions, strong encouragement and concrete (often written) contracts are often necessary to get them to even begin to participate in more pleasurable endeavors (Lewinsohn and Hoberman, 1982). The therapist asks clients not to judge any specified activity until they have engaged in it for a set period. This allows them time to get involved and begin to enjoy it.

Changing self-verbalizations. Eliminating negative subvocal self-verbalizations such as "I'm no good" or "I can't do it" is useful in treating depressives (Meichenbaum, 1985). In the initial period of self-monitoring, clients compile a list of negative self-statements they tend to use, and usually a second list of potentially offsetting positive statements. The therapist instructs the client to purposely say the positive statements at various times, possibly aloud but usually subvocally. The therapist should agree with the inevitable protest that the client will not believe the statement when saying it. The therapist and client devise a contract in which the client agrees to say them anyway, and the therapist assures the client that repeating the statements will eventually be helpful. The difficulty is to get the client to persist with the new behaviors outside the therapy session and perform them with some consistency.

Use of the **Premack principle** can help here. The Premack principle states that high-probability behaviors (those that a person performs often) will reinforce and increase the occurrence of the low-probability behaviors (such as positive self-statements) that they are paired with. For example, clients could be asked to say "I'm a good person and I'm feeling much better" every time they start their car or open the door of their house. Other appropriate statements can be paired with other high-probability behaviors. As clients persist in them, depression subsides.

Imagery-based techniques. Lazarus (1987; 1981) has used an interesting variation of the systematic desensitization technique that he calls "time projection with routine reinforcement." He asks depressed clients to fantasize that they are in the future and are engaged in previously pleasant activities. He then asks them to return to the present while maintaining the positive feelings and the images of future pleasure. This is similar to the unpleasurable-to-pleasurable technique just noted, except that it is carried out by controlling the imagination rather than by overt behaviors. By using images of pleasurable activities paired with perceptions of the future, the time-projection strategy promotes positive expectations and thus generates hope, a cognitive set conspicuously lacking in depressives.

Changing negative views and increasing interpersonal skills. Initial steps to challenge and change the depressed client's general negative view of the world typically use Ellis' rational-emotive therapy, Beck's cognitive therapy, or a similar approach (Vestre, 1984). Later, such therapy can be combined with assertiveness training, interpersonal skills training, or other techniques that allow the client to reexperience the sense of coping and competence necessary for any true cure (Gotlib and Colby, 1987; Billings and Moos, 1985).

SUICIDE

Just as I shall select my ship when I am about to go on a voyage, or my house when I propose to take a residence, so shall I choose my death when I am ready to depart from life (Seneca, Epistulae ad Lucilium, No. 70 II).

The Roman philosopher Seneca's description of a rational decision to commit **suicide** demonstrates that suicide is not necessarily a pathological act. In fact, the modern existentialist Albert Camus began his essay on the myth of Sisyphus with the assertion "There is but one serious philosophic problem and that is suicide." However, far more people who are clinically diagnosed as depressed are likely to kill themselves than are normal persons or those with any other type of mental disorder (Fawcett et al., 1987).

The writer Ernest Hemingway and his wife outside their Sun Valley, California home. Discouraged by unsuccessful shock therapy to curb his bouts of depression, Hemingway finally committed suicide.   (The Bettmann Archive)

For most people raised in the Judeo-Christian tradition, suicide is a religious rather than a philosophic issue. Yet neither the Old nor New Testament directly forbids suicide. The early church elders labeled suicide as sinful to deter the zeal of the faithful, whose desire for martyrdom was accompanied by a penchant for suicide; in 693 the Council of Toledo proclaimed that a person who attempted suicide was to be excommunicated (Shneidman, 1985). The stigmas of sin and crime attached to suicide by the Judeo-Christian tradition now seem to be waning. In fact, various religious groups have recently published pamphlets on how to kill oneself efficiently and painlessly!

In some Western countries, legal sanctions against suicide persist as reflections of religious tradition. As late as 1961, suicide was still a crime in England, where the typically practical English response to a suicide attempt was to hang the individual if he or she survived. This punishment superseded a more flamboyant one of driving a stake through the heart of the person who attempted suicide.

Incidence

About 25,000 suicides are reported each year in the United States, and there is some evidence that the former rate of 10 to 12 per 100,000 population may now be increasing. Several European countries, including Switzerland and Sweden, report rates of about 18 to 25 per 100,000 population. Traditionally, suicide rates in nonwesternized nations have been thought to be lower: rates of 3.5 and 7 per 100,000 have been reported for Thailand and Uganda, respectively. However, rates as high as 43 and 37 per 100,000 have been found in Mandurai, India and Tikapia in the Western Pacific, respectively (Tseng and Hsu, 1980)

There is a long list of famous suicides, including Ernest Hemingway, Marilyn Monroe, Jack London, Amadeo Modigliani, Virginia Woolf, Adolf Hitler, Samson, and Cleopatra. But in general, the typical person who attempts suicide is most often an unmarried white female who had an unstable childhood, has a history of past and recent stressful events and who now has few social supports and lacks a close friend to confide in. The typical person who successfully commits suicide is most often an unmarried, divorced, or widowed white male who is over 45, lives alone, has a history of significant physical or emotional disorder, and likely abuses alcohol (Lobel, 1984; Warren and Tomlinson-Keasey, 1987). At the same time, suicide is the second highest cause of death in the United States for white males aged 15 to 19 (88 per 100,000), though it still ranks far behind the highest cause, accidents (627 per 100,000). About three times as many women as men attempt suicide, but three times as many men actually kill themselves (Shneidman, 1985; Lobel, 1984). In an interesting cross-cultural parallel, Germans have a high ratio of actual suicides to attempts, the Japanese a low one (Marsella, 1980).

Such statistics, however, often underestimate actual rates. Because suicide still has the taint of sin and crime, coroners and police officers are reluc-

EXHIBIT

Facts and Fables about Suicide

Numerous false beliefs persist about suicide. The following list is compiled from numerous sources, but especially from the continuing work of the two most noted names in suicide research, Edwin Shneidman and Norman Farberow.

Fable (myths)	Fact
1. Suicide happens without warning.	1. Suicidal individuals give many clues; 80 percent have to some degree discussed with others their intent to commit suicide.
2. Once people become suicidal, they remain so.	2. Suicidal persons remain so for limited periods; thus the value of restraint.
3. Suicide occurs almost exclusively among affluent or very poor individuals.	3. Suicide tends to occur proportionately in all economic levels of society.
4. Virtually all suicidal individuals are mentally ill.	4. As already noted, this is not so.
5. Suicide is inherited or runs in families.	5. There is no evidence for a direct genetic factor.
6. Suicide does not occur in primitive cultures.	6. Suicide occurs in almost all societies and cultures.
7. Ritual suicide is common in Japan.	7. Ritual suicide is rare in modern Japan; the most common method is barbiturate overdose.
8. The high suicide rate in Sweden is caused by the high level of social welfare programs, which take away a sense of individual initiative.	8. The suicide rate in Sweden today is about as high as it was in 1910, before the advent of its social welfare programs.
9. Writers and artists have the highest suicide rates because they are "a bit crazy to begin with."	9. Physicians and police officers have the highest suicide rates; they have access to the most lethal means, and their work involves a high level of frustration.
10. Once a person starts to come out of a depression, the risk of suicide dissipates.	10. The risk of suicide is highest in the initial phase of an upswing from the depth of depression.
11. People who attempt suicide fully intend to die.	11. People who attempt suicide have a diversity of motives.

Hungary
↑
36/100,000 —overall

3x—more suicides
By men.
More women attempt
men use guns.
women—drugs.

Schizophrenia—
wierd—cocacola +
closk.

tant to cite it as a cause of death. Moreover, many individuals who commit suicide try to make it look like an accident so their survivors are spared any stigma and can collect on life insurance. Most experts believe that actual rates are two to ten times as high as official figures.

Genuine versus Manipulative Suicides

Clinicians have found the distinction between genuine and manipulative suicides a meaningful one (Landis and Meyer, 1988; Shneidman, 1985) (see Research Profile). Genuinely suicidal people truly want to die and are prevented from doing so only by miscalculation or fate. People who attempt a manipulative suicide do not really want to kill themselves; their act is a controlled attempt to manipulate others.

One example of the latter type known to us firsthand was the father of a grade school classmate. This man periodically climbed to the top of the local water tower and threatened to jump off; the townfolk would arrive on the scene, as would his wife (as soon as she could be located, since she was involved in numerous affairs). He would shout accusations at her; she would get upset; they would tearfully make up; he would come down (to the relief of most of the onlookers), and their situation would be outwardly calm for another year or so, when he would again make an ascent on the tower.

Several cases from the files of a prison clinic demonstrate both ends of the genuine-manipulative continuum. Fred had told his cellmate that he intended to kill himself, and the cellmate quickly reported this to the prison clinic head nurse. When confronted, Fred said his life had caused pain to everyone around him and he had few prospects for happiness (not a totally unrealistic perspective). Because it was clear that he was serious about killing himself, he was immediately placed in a control cell that contained only a very small locker and a toilet embedded in concrete. Personnel observed him during meals so that he would not use eating utensils against himself, and he was issued light tearaway clothes.

Late that evening he was found dead, hanging in the locker. He had torn strips off his clothes and braided a noose, attached it to a hook in the small locker, squeezed into the locker, doubled his legs up behind him, and fallen forward. Fred's death was clearly a genuine suicide.

Doug, another inmate, enjoyed getting high and also liked the attention he had received in a previous mild suicide attempt that involved cutting his wrists. This time he tried to combine both goals. Reasoning that he might be able to maximize the kick he got from cigarettes, he boiled out the essence of several and injected it. Only after he became very sick did Doug tell the staff physician what he had done. When told that his injection would be fatal and that nothing more could be done for him, it was clear from Doug's scream and the anguish on his face that he had not really intended to kill himself.

RESEARCH PROFILE

Suicide in Gifted Women

The first chapter of this book discussed various research techniques, such as the case study. An interesting study that was essentially a survey of case studies evaluated the causes of suicide in a sample of gifted women. The data was drawn from the Genetic Study of Genius, a longitudinal study of 1528 gifted persons (857 males, 671 females), with a mean I.Q. of 135. The study was begun in 1922 by Lewis M. Terman, and assessments every five years have continued up to the present, gaining information on the subject's early childhood, education, personality, physical and mental health, careers, families, life satisfaction, and so on.

The focus of this study, by Warren and Tomlinson-Keasey (1987), is eight documented female suicides (with a mean I.Q. of 143 for these eight) from the Terman gifted group. The massive amount of data on these eight women was sifted by the researchers to see if there were any common themes, and then contrasted to data from an earlier study by noted suicidologist E. Shneidman on the males from the Terman group who had commited suicide. Warren and Tomlinson-Keasey found that, similar to the males, the female suicides showed a life marked by unstable emotional and personal lives, anxiety, depression, and prior threats of suicide. Two other factors found in the men, a history of drug abuse and homosexuality, were not found in the women.

This long-term data survey, however, revealed some consistent patterns in these women that were different from the men. One clear factor was the strong role their mothers had played in their lives, in most cases up to the time of their death. Yet their fathers were psychologically and emotionally absent, though not separated from them by divorce, as was true of a number of the male suicides. Another consistent finding was a general sense of intellectual and vocational failure. The women felt they had never accomplished as much in these areas as they had the potential for, and in most cases this perception had at least a grain of truth to it. Many of them felt their major accomplishments came as part of their "derived identity", those areas of recognition and lifestyle accrued through marriage.

One another less consistent finding is worthy of note. Three of the eight women had experienced the suicide of a significant other, for example, a father or a loved uncle. As with most other studies (Shneidman, 1985), it's becoming clear that anyone who commits suicide risks leaving a tragic legacy for those that follow.

Just as chance events can prevent the consummation of a genuine suicide attempt, so a miscalculation can transform a manipulative attempt into an unplanned fatality. Many suicide attempts combine both genuine and manipulative elements in varying degrees. The preceding cases demonstrate that, just as in sexual deviations (see Chapter 10), the type of attempt is restricted only by one's imagination. Indeed, an elderly California man tried to kill himself by driving nails into his head with a nail gun. He survived the attempt. But before he could stop the bleeding, his wife attempted to kill him with a knife; an incredible story to tell to one's grandchildren.

[Handwritten marginal notes:]

Behavioral - ?.
Change in Reinforcement loss of job, Bad health - not enough reinforcement. Death is rewarding - removes pain

3.
Sociological - suicide is an act of individual within society.
· A sudden change in the society - stock market crash - earthquakes.

Schizoid or avoidant
3. not integrated - loner - High on list of suicide

Altruistic - suicide done because it is valued - Kamikazes

EXHIBIT

Types of Suicide

1.	*Realistic*	These are suicides precipitated by such conditions as the prospect of great pain preceding a sure death.
2.	*Altruistic*	The person's behavior is subservient to a group ethic that mandates or at least approves suicidal behavior, like kamikaze pilots in World War II.
3.	*Inadvertent*	The person makes a suicide *gesture* in order to influence or manipulate someone else, but a misjudgment leads to an unexpected fatality.
4.	*Spite*	Like the inadvertent suicide, the focus is on someone else, but the intention to kill oneself is genuine, with the idea that the other person will suffer greatly from consequent guilt.
5.	*Bizarre*	The person commits suicide as a result of a hallucination (such as voices ordering the suicide) or delusions (such as a belief the suicide will change the world).
6.	*Anomic*	An abrupt instability in economic or social conditions (such as sudden financial loss in the Great Depression) markedly changes a person's life situation. Unable to cope, the person commits suicide.
7.	*Negative self*	Chronic depression and a sense of chronic failure or inadequacy combine to produce repetitive suicide attempts eventually leading to a fatality.

Causes and Prediction

Since Freud, psychoanalysts have viewed most suicidal individuals as classic depressives, that is, as persons with high aggression turned toward the self (Menninger, 1938). Freud's concept of death instinct, Thanatos, has also been invoked, but it has never satisfactorily explained why one individual comes to have a more compelling death instinct than another. The diversity of people who attempt suicide makes prediction in terms of a single or even a few discrete personality types impossible. It seems more useful to focus instead on various factors associated with high rates of suicide (Warren and Tomlinson-Keasey, 1987).

Emile Durkheim (1951) pioneered an emphasis on sociological factors contributing to suicide. He hypothesized that as a society goes through rapid change, certain subgroups lose cohesiveness, members feel alienated (such as the stockbrokers in the Great Depression), become depressed, and are then more likely to commit suicide. His typology of suicidals (anomic—under conditions of normlessness; egoistic—lack of group ties; altruistic—suicide for the good of some cause) is still influential, as the accompanying Exhibit indicates. Evidence generally supports Durkheim's ideas. But his theory does not explain why a specific individual in a subgroup commits suicide while others do not, or why a person in a subgroup experiencing little change nevertheless commits suicide.

There also appear to be cross-cultural differences in what prompts a suicide attempt, even within a relatively small geographic area. In Sweden, for example, the majority of suicides appear to involve people who consider themselves failures, in response to that culture's high performance expectancies from parents and peers. On the other hand, Norwegians, on the average, seem more likely to commit suicide in response to a moral conflict, and Danes in response to a loss of a dependency relationship (Tseng and Hsu, 1980). Of these three Scandinavian countries, Norway has the lowest suicide rate, possibly reflecting the lower emphasis there on competition and guilt-oriented childrearing techniques (Sanua, 1980).

ABNORMALITY ACROSS CULTURES

Cross-Culture Shock: A Study of Immigration and Suicide in Canada

The accompanying section in your text on types of suicide points out how rapid culture change has been linked with suicide. An excellent empirical study of this notion was published in *The International Journal of Social Psychiatry* (32(3)). Frank Trovato (1986), a Canadian sociologist, applied a complicated statistical procedure, a multiple regression technique (which consecutively compares each set of data to each and every other set to find the highest correlations), to data taken from published Vital Statistics and Census tabulations from Statistics Canada.

Dr. Trovato focused on two variables that have traditionally been viewed as important in generating an increase in the suicide rate: transnational immigration and unemployment. He found that, contrary to traditional expectations, these variables did not produce a particularly strong effect (as indicated by relevant correlations) across all age groups.

However, the effect for both variables was strong for one subgroup: young adult males, aged 15 to 34, in which either a high rate of unemployment or a high rate of migration from another country produced a much higher suicide rate. Within this group, the significant loss of one's ties to one's kin and community from a migration and economic and ego loss from unemployment take a direct toll by generating more suicides. Trovato argues that the effect from migration is not as strong now, and thus does not so seriously effect all age groups, because Canadian immigration policy has become more stringent and selective. Currently, incoming immigrants are better educated and have better emotional and economic resources than immigrants of prior years. As a result, they are better able to cope with the shocks and stresses associated with the immigration experience.

Psychological tests and psychiatric interviews have historically proven poor at predicting suicidal potential. However, more complex analyses have been showing increasingly better predictive validity for psychological test data (Maltsberger, 1986; Exner, 1978). Other related data can also be useful, such as the content and affect of suicide notes. Shneidman and Farberow (1957) (and Shneidman, 1985) found that notes written by genuinely suicidal individuals were concrete and matter-of-fact. Ironically, those written by manipulative suicidals were emotional and flamboyant, more like the sort of note most people would expect to reflect a genuine intention.

In adults, a number of primary behavioral clues appear to predispose an individual to successful suicide attempts.

1. Previous suicide attempts; in this context, the first axiom of psychology could well be "Behavior predicts behavior." The second axiom would be "Behavior without intervention predicts behavior."

2. Statements of a wish to die, especially statements of a wish to commit suicide.

3. Certain *consistent* life patterns of leaving crises rather than facing them: in relationships, "You can't walk out on me, I'm leaving you," or in jobs, "You can't fire me because I quit."

4. Suicide attempts by an important identity figure, be it a parent or a hero.

5. Feelings of failure, together with a loved spouse who is competitive or self-absorbed.

6. Early family instability and parental rejection of one's identity.

7. A recent severe life stress, or the presence of a chronic debilitating illness.

Several factors can then increase this potential.

1. A cognitive state of "constriction"—that is, an inability to perceive any options or a way out of a situation that is generating intense psychological suffering.

2. Easy access to a lethal means; drug overdose, for example, is the prevailing form of suicide among physicians (Pitts et al., 1979).

3. Absence of an accessible support system (family and good friends).

4. Life stresses that connote irrevocable loss (whether of status or of persons), such as the relatively recent death of a favored parent. This factor is particularly important if the person at risk is unable to mourn the loss overtly.

5. High physiologic responsiveness—cyclical moods and a high need for stimulation-seeking in spite of suicide thoughts (Mehrabian and Weinstein, 1985).

6. Serious sleep disruption and abuse of alcohol or drugs.

7. Depression, particularly when combined with a sense of hopelessness, loss of pleasure in activities, or loss of a sense of continuity with the past or present (Fawcett et al., 1987). As noted earlier, depressions marked by low levels of 5-HIAA, as well as high levels of cortisol and a high ratio of adrenaline to noradrenaline, increase the probability of suicide attempts (Lobel, 1984).

Prevention

Suicide prevention techniques have been developed at both the societal and individual level, but implementing them is not always easy. The following dialogue from the old television show "Mary Hartman, Mary Hartman" shows the difficulty most people have in responding effectively to a potential suicide's questions.

> *Heather (Mary's twelve-year-old daughter):*   I have nothing to live for.
>
> *Mary:*   Sure you do.
>
> *Heather:*   Like what?
>
> *Mary:*   Well . . . wait and see.

Societal prevention.   Several things can be done on a societal level to lower the incidence of suicide (Long, 1986; Shneidman, 1985). Educating the public on the myths and facts of suicide is an important first step. Second, there is evidence that suicide-prevention telephone hotlines and centers can slightly decrease the suicide rate, although one study reported an increased rate of suicide in areas after a suicide prevention center was started (Hankoff and Einsidler, 1979). At the very least, suicide-prevention hotlines become general community information lines; some callers feign thoughts about suicide only to come out later with matter-of-fact requests, such as whom to call about a lost welfare check. Thus, in many cities, crisis centers developed in response to calls to a suicide-prevention center, when it became clear that this kind of community need was not being met.

A third step in suicide prevention may involve some restriction on media publicity about suicides. Phillips (1974; 1986) documents the correlation between a rise and fall in suicide rates and the amount of newspaper publicity given to suicides in that locality. Such self-imposed restriction is a thorny ethical issue for newspapers and television, especially because rates of all externally directed violence (murder, rape) may also be increased by publicity about similar incidents (Phillips, 1986; Rubinstein, 1981). Balancing free speech and the public's right to information with a responsibility for not increasing self- and other-directed violence presents a real dilemma for media policymakers, one that few have confronted directly.

Just as in the control of the violence toward others, control of access to commonly used methods (for example, guns or drugs) can lower the incidence of suicide, as indirectly portrayed in Ernest Hemingway's (1937) novel *To Have and Have Not.*

> *Some made the long drop from the apartment or the office window; some took it quietly in two-car garages with the motor running; some used the native tradition of the Colt or Smith and Wesson; those well-constructed implements that end insomnia, terminate remorse, cure cancer, avoid bankruptcy, and blast an exit from intolerable positions by the pressure of a finger; those admirable American instruments so easily carried, so sure of effect, so well-designed to end the American dream when it becomes a nightmare, their only drawback the mess they leave for relatives to clean up (p. 238).*

Individual prevention.   Several precautions can be taken at the individual level.

1. Attend seriously to people who voice a desire to kill themselves or "just go to sleep and forget it all." About two thirds of those people who actually kill themselves have talked about it beforehand in some detail with family, friends, or others (Lobel, 1984).

2. Attend especially to depressed individuals who speak of losing hope (Fawcett et al., 1987).

3. To the degree possible, keep lethal means (guns, large prescriptions of sedatives) away from suicidal individuals.

4. Generate a personal concern toward a suicidal person; a suicide attempt is most often a cry for help. Suicidal individuals need a temporary "champion" who can point them toward new resources, suggest new options, and at least in a small way can diminish the sense of hopelessness.

5. Try to get the person to perform some of the following behaviors: (a) engage in regular physical exercise, (b) start a diary, (c) follow a normal routine, (d) do something in which he or she has already demonstrated competence, (e) confide inner feelings to someone, (f) cry it out. Try to get the person to avoid self-medication and other people inclined toward depression.

6. Make every effort to guarantee that a suicidal person reaches professional help. Making an appointment is a good first step; getting the person to the appointment is the crucial step.

The focus of this and the past two chapters has been on disorders that may involve a bizarre component and/or loss of contact with reality, with much intrapsychic conflict or distress. The next three chapters focus on disorders that often include acting-out behavior, that is, behavior that conflicts with social standards. These are the sexual variations, drug abuse patterns, and the personality and impulse disorders.

CHAPTER REVIEW

1. Depression and mania are the two extreme manifestations of affective disorder. The DSM includes mania in its category of bipolar disorder; it does not allow for the presence of mania without some indication of depression as well.

2. The three major symptoms of mania are hyperactive motor behavior, labile euphoria or irritability, and flight of ideas.

3. Most theorists agree that mania is primarily a biologically based disorder. One strong piece of evidence for their claim is the general effectiveness of chemotherapy with lithium.

4. Depression, the most widespread affective disorder, is usually manifested in one or more primary symptoms: (a) dysphoria or apathetic mood, (b) loss of caring about people or things previously important, and (c) chronic inability to experience pleasure.

5. More females than males report, and probably experience, depression. Traditional sex-role programming, social reinforcement, and the predominance of males in diagnostic roles are possible generic factors.

6. Endogenous depressions are marked by slowed response patterns, early-morning sleep disruption, mood problems, and significant weight loss without dieting. Depressions associated with mania are more often marked by psychomotor retardation, rather than agitation, and hypersomnia rather than insomnia.

7. Among the physiologic explanations for depression, the catecholamine theories have received the most support. The corresponding chemotherapies most commonly used are the monoamine oxidase inhibitors and the tricyclics.

8. Psychodynamic theorists emphasize ego loss as a cause of depression. The depressed individual tries to please "dominant others" as well as internalized images, a virtually impossible task, thus leading to increased depression.

9. Of the psychological theories explaining depression, the cognitive distortion and learned helplessness models have recently received increasing attention. Their therapeutic approaches attempt to get the depressed person to resume an active role and to increase positive self-talk and the amount of time spent in pleasurable activities.

10. The diversity of personality patterns and external factors involved in suicides and the persistence of myths about suicide make prevention efforts at both the individual and societal level important.

TERMS TO REMEMBER

affect
mood
mania
flight of ideas
bipolar disorder
cyclothymic disorder
lithium
major depression
dysthymic disorder
premenstrual syndrome

endogenous
exogenous
catecholamine theory
ego loss
stimulus void
learned helplessness
attribution theory
cognitive behavior modification
Premack principle
suicide

FOR MORE INFORMATION

Depue, R., Slater, J., Wolfstetter-Kausch, H., Klein, D., Goplerud, E., and Farr, D. (1981) A behavioral paradigm for identifying persons at risk for bipolar depressive disorder: a conceptual framework and five validation studies. *Journal of Abnormal Psychology* 90:381–438. Not only a primary source for information on bipolar disorders, but also an excellent portrayal of methodological issues in researching most patterns of psychopathology

Farberow, N. (1975) *Suicide in different cultures.* Baltimore: University Park Press. Like the other excellent books on suicide by E. Shneidman and N. Farberow, this gives an in-depth view of relevant cross-cultural research

Gotlib, I. and Colby, C. (1987) *Treatment of depression.* New York: Pergamon. An excellent overview of all forms of treatment for depression, including information on lithium and its applicability to both unipolar and bipolar depression

Maltsberger, J. (1986) *Suicide risk.* New York: New York University Press. A definitive work on assessing suicide risk, this book examines factors that predict suicide, as well as methods that are useful in prevention.

McNeal, E., and Cimbolic, P. (1986) Antidepressants and biochemical theories of depression. *Psychological Bulletin* 99:361–374. The most thorough and lucid presentation of a most complex area, i.e., how biological factors can produce depression, and how antidepressant chemotherapies act to lessen the depression

Phillips, D. (1986) The effects of mass media violence on suicide and homicide. *Newsletter of the American Academy of Psychiatry and the Law* 11:29–31. A short but excellent summary of how greater media visibility of cases of suicide and homicide may in turn produce higher rates of both patterns, and the difficulties in researching this issue

PART

IV

Social and Personality Disorders

If you drink very much from a bottle marked "poison" it is almost certain to disagree with you sooner or later.

Lewis Carroll
Alice in Wonderland

Dennis Hopper gives a convincing portrayal of a sadistic sexual deviant in *Blue Velvet.* The chief target of his amorous attentions is Isabella Rossellini. (Museum of Modern Art/Film Stills Archive; © 1986 DEG)

10

Sexual Variations; Dysfunctions and Disorders

As in evident from the following case, the range of sexual behavior is restricted only by the imagination. This potential for variation is a theme that runs through the three sub-areas of this chapter: the sexual dysfunctions, the gender disorders, and the paraphilias (or the sexual deviations). The sexual dysfunctions refer to those disorders (impotence, frigidity, premature ejaculation, and vaginismus) in which a person is dissatisfied with his or her ability to achieve sexual satisfaction with a partner. The gender disorders are patterns in which the person feels a basic disparity between his or her psychological gender identity and the actual sexual anatomy, and as a result, may seek to change their anatomical sex by surgery. The paraphilias (traditionally referred to as the sexual deviations) are those sexual variations that have either (1) an antisocial component, for example, exhibitionism or pedophilia or (2) a sexual pattern that hinders sexuality in an interpersonal context (fetishism, zoophilia). In the following case, you will note that Chris shows elements of both the sexual dysfunctions and the paraphilias. Other aspects of sexual disorder that are specific to the conflicts and challenges of adulthood are discussed in Chapter 16. Because rape is often more a crime of aggression than of sexuality, it is discussed in Chapter 12.

● The Case of Chris the Casket Man

To satisfy his unusual sexual desires, Chris, the 27-year-old bachelor son of a wealthy industrialist, routinely performed the following ritual. First, he took a girlfriend or a prostitute out to an elegant and sumptuous dinner. Upon returning home, he put on a modified suit of knight's armor, asked the woman to put on a dress of the same period (without underwear), then requested her to urinate and then masturbate as he watched.

When he became extremely aroused he went into another room and asked her to wait until he called her in. Soon he did so, and she walked into a huge room decorated like a throne room for the days of King Arthur and the Knights of the Round Table. A black and gold casket rested where the throne would normally be, and Chris was lying in it, masturbating. The woman usually responded with at least a small scream at the sight, whereupon Chris ejaculated. Chris had tried normal sexual intercourse with women on several occasions, but was always impotent unless he could carry out this particular ritual.

Later he would ask the woman if she knew a friend or another prostitute who might be willing to participate, but asked her not to disclose what happened in the "throne room." Many prostitutes in that metropolitan area in turn took part in these events, each giving a grand shriek, and at least acting naive, because Chris paid generously for the privilege.

Diversity of sexual behavior is common not only among individuals, such as Chris, but also across cultures. In a landmark survey, Clellan Ford and Frank Beach (1951) noted such wide variance in sexual practices among cultures that no one society could be considered truly representative of normative human sexual behavior. Some groups encouraged sexual exploration by their children but imposed severe restrictions on adults. Certain groups repressed female sexuality while condoning variation for males; others did the opposite. Some societies followed their stated sexual mores; others did not. Thus, only variation in behavior was, and still is the rule (Allgeier and Allgeier, 1988). Certainly variation, as well as elements of both the sexual dysfunctions and the paraphilia, are evident in Chris.

HISTORICAL CONSIDERATIONS

The Judeo-Christian tradition has influenced all areas of thought and behavior in our society, including sexuality. Long before the birth of Christ, the Jews developed a simple code that forbade certain practices, such as temple prostitution. Yet, they were not much concerned about deviation, and merely discouraged excessive sexuality. From about 600 B.C. to 65 A.D., however, sexuality became a pervasive concern. Sex was believed to be a form of Satanic temptation, and those who yielded to sexual impulses were considered weak and sinful. Later, Jewish law again became more permissive. But Christianity had already incorporated the older views (Bullough, 1976).

Several major themes persisted in the new Christian religion. Pleasure was considered a secondary by-product of procreative sex. Procreation itself was

EXHIBIT

The Cheese-Hat Fetishist

The following spoof of a "bizarre but true" sexual case history was written by Gerald Sussman and published in the *National Lampoon* in 1974. We reprinted it here as a companion piece to the actual case of Chris to show that real cases are often just as strange as imaginary ones. Despite the humor in this satire, it is important to remember that pain and conflict often accompany the variations and disorders described throughout this chapter.

The Case of the Cheese-Hat Fetishist

A certain 'D.' from Leipzig, age 57. Testicles square in shape. Claims he can abstain from urinating for days, evinces great fear of birds, no matter how small. Both parents died in a tannery explosion when he was six. He was adopted by an aunt who was poor at mathematics and he had ringworm.

The only way the subject can achieve ejaculation is to put a great amount of creamy cheese under his hat and have a heavy object dropped on the hat, crushing it, causing the cheese to stream down his face.

Upon further examination, D. revealed that his aunt made him wear three hats, one over the other, when he was a boy, fearing that any exposure of his head to the elements would result in sickness. One day his aunt made him a fresh cream cheese sandwich for his school lunch. D. tucked it under his hats so that his nemesis, the local bully, would not steal it. On his way to school, he was hit on the head by a small safe that was accidentally dropped out of the window of a commercial building. Luckily, his hats and the cheese sandwich absorbed much of the blow, saving him from certain death. Before losing consciousness D. remembers getting a violent erection, ejaculating copiously, and experiencing indescribable pleasure.

As he grew into manhood, he tried to duplicate this experience by pounding cheese-filled hats down over his face with his fists. But it did not give him the same pleasure. For complete gratification he had to pay someone to drop a large heavy object on his head from a great height. He experimented with many styles of hats—bowlers from London, Borsolinos from Italy. His preferences settled on fine opera hats from Vienna and the creamy ricotta cheese of Italy. The opera hats were made to be flattened and could withstand abuse. The thought of normal coitus with women was abhorrent to him. Women interested him only as hat crushers. He seemed to be incapable of grasping the immorality of his disgusting perversion and continues to do it despite frequent migraine attacks. Claims to have a collection of over 570 hats.

encouraged to the extent that even sterility and failure to marry bordered on the sinful, or were at least causes for social disapproval. Masturbation, homosexuality, prostitution, and any deviation from standard intercourse during marriage were explicitly forbidden.

Our more permissive culture of today (Coles and Stokes, 1985) is somewhat closer in spirit to that of ancient Greece, whose influence had waned

Paolo Veronese's *Leda and the Swan* represents the common mythological theme of zoophilia, or human sexual contact with animals. Zoophilia is rare in life, especially when human sexual outlets are available.   (The Bettmann Archive)

by the time of Christ but subsequently revived in the Middle Ages. Appreciation of beauty and joy in sex figured prominently in the cultural ideals of the Greeks. The state did little to suppress sexual expression, which flourished in a variety of forms. Homosexuality was widely practiced, pederasty (the sexual initiation of young boys by older men) accepted, and nudity in public places common. Zeus, the chief god in the Greek mythology, was fabled to have had numerous ardent sexual affairs with both mortals and immortals, men as well as women (Kosovich, 1978).

The ambivalence created by these two major cultural influences, ancient Greek and the Judeo-Christian traditions, has resulted in a number of interesting coping patterns in subgroups and individuals in Western society today (Luria et al., 1986; Boswell, 1980). One persistent concept is that the acknowledgment and direct expression of sexual impulses is wrong. Five major patterns reflecting this notion helped generate and now influence most of the classic deviation disorders discussed later in this chapter.

1. *Devaluing the sexual stimulus.* One inevitable outcome of male-dominated overt attitudes in a culture is widespread misogyny, or woman-hating. Misogynists' major coping strategy is to convince themselves that women are disgusting, so as to lessen a woman's sexual attractiveness. This tendency found expression as early as the fourth century A.D. in an undoubtedly unwelcome letter of advice from Saint John Chrysostom to a friend who had just fallen in love: "The groundwork of her bodily beauty is phlegm and blood and yellow bile and black bile, and the fluid of masticated food." In the sixth century, the Roman philosopher Boethius voiced a similar opinion: "Woman is a temple built upon a sewer." Distorted sexual patterns naturally result from such beliefs.

2. *Rendering the mechanism nonfunctional.* Certain early Christians took literally Christ's words "There be eunuchs which have made themselves eunuchs for the kingdom of heaven's sake." Thus, for some time self-castration was a mark of holiness, though the church eventually forbade it. Temporary measures for sexual abstinence include cold showers and prolonged exercise (and putting saltpeter into mashed potatoes). True self-mutilation of the sexual organs still occasionally occurs, usually during a psychotic delusion. Certain forms of inhibited sexual functioning are a psychological way of rendering the mechanism nonfunctional.

3. *Stopping short.* Stopping intercourse short of orgasm or engaging in fondling without actual intercourse became acceptable and even admirable in many subcultures. In certain medieval courts, *amor purus,* or prolonged but unconsummated foreplay, was considered superior to normal intercourse. The poet Dante's pure, distant, and lifelong adoration of Beatrice (though he also had a wife and several mistresses) is another example. The Oneida community in New York State decreed a system of "complex marriage" that permitted adults relatively free sexual access to one another. To deal with the obvious problem of birth control, however, males were not permitted to ejaculate inside females unless sanctioned by the community to father a child. This practice was known as male continence.

4. *Avoiding sexual practice.* Much preparation for sexual intercourse and intimacy takes place in fantasy, especially during masturbation. Although most modern experts agree that masturbation is both harmless and universal, sexual myth has alleged a variety of dire effects, ranging from acne to brain tumors. Saint Thomas Aquinas regarded masturbation as more sinful than fornication. The claim that masturbation leads to other variations has some truth; masturbatory fantasies do influence the intensity and the target of sexual impulses (LoPiccolo, 1985). Yet people can also use such fantasies to direct themselves back into more traditionally acceptable patterns. The crucial element is the content of the fantasy.

5. *Combining sex with pain.* Many people apparently come to believe that experiencing pain during sexual relations makes the accompanying pleasure more acceptable. The ultimate coping patterns that form this belief are sexual sadism and masochism.

SEXUAL DYSFUNCTIONS

The sexual dysfunctions include those disorders, such as impotence, frigidity, inhibited sexuality, premature ejaculation, and vaginismus, in which a person is dissatisfied with their ability to achieve sexual satisfaction with a partner. Concerns about sexual dysfunction are found to some degree in most societies. Welch and Kartub (1978) studied the incidence of psychosexual dysfunction in numerous societies and found that the higher the sexual restrictiveness of the society, the higher the incidence of dysfunction. The incidence is even higher when a restrictive society is just beginning to shift to more liberal value systems. Freud's words on the subject in 1912 still hold largely true: "If a practicing psychoanalyst asks himself on account of what disorder people most often come to him for help he is bound to reply—disregarding the many forms of anxiety—that it is sexual impotence" (Strachey, 1957, p. 179).

Psychosexual Arousal Dysfunction in Males

In males, **psychosexual arousal dysfunction** (PAD-M) (the pattern we see in Will) is the inability to retain erection long enough to achieve orgasm, or to provide sexual gratification to a partner, although in many males, a flaccid or nonerect penis will ejaculate if it receives enough stimulation. (The commonly used term "impotence" is not really accurate because it often connotes a general personality inadequacy, just as frigidity inappropriately designates dysfunction in females—note that both terms are the opposite of traditional role expectations, i.e., strength for males, warmth for females.) Our designation PAD-M covers the DSM categories Inhibited Sexual Excitement and Inhibited Male Orgasm. The former refers to inability to maintain erection, the latter to a problem in attaining orgasm once erection occurs. As we see in the case of Will, both are often observed in the same person, and there are many similarities in their etiology and treatment.

Incidence. Masters and Johnson (1970) consider this dysfunction a clinical problem if there are failures in 25 percent of attempts at intercourse, so it is evident that the criteria for clinically labeling such behaviors can be quite arbitrary. However, it is estimated that more than half of all males have experienced occasional transient episodes of PAD-M, and there appears to be no correlation with race or socioeconomic status. Ard (1977) studied 161 couples

EXHIBIT

Changes in Attitudes Toward Sexual Dysfunctions

Over the years, there have been several revolutions in the thinking about what are the causes of sexual dysfunction. While Stages 1 and 3 are no longer that influential, the other stages should be seen as cumulative, that is, in any one individual case, many or all of the later insights can be relevant. The approximate year(s) when this idea became an influence is also listed.

1. *Moral degeneracy (an ancient belief).* Masturbation, or virtually any sexual play, in one's early years and/or prior to marriage is seen as a degenerate pattern that leads to later sexual dysfunction, as well as brain damage and a wide variety of other diseases. A more sophisticated version of this is the "You only have so many bullets in your gun," which is still prevalent in certain cultural subgroups.

2. *Physiologic dysfunction (a traditional view).* Sexual dysfunction is a result of low hormone production, physiologic disruption, or anatomic dysfunction.

3. *Arrested psychosexual development (early 1900s).* Primarily reflecting the theories of Freud, it leads to the conception that long-term psychotherapy is necessary to move one from an earlier stage (allegedly the phallic stage in women who only have clitoral orgasms) to greater maturity, a side-effect of which will hopefully be adequate sexual functioning.

4. *Phobic-like anxiety (1950s).* Reflects the work of Masters and Johnson, who talked of "sensate focus" and "performance anxiety," which were refinements of the work of the early behaviorists, but most importantly, also saw good sexuality as involving a set of skills, which, if deficient, resulted in sexual problems

5. *Cognitions about sex (1960s).* Reflecting the work of the cognitive behaviorists, the sets of thoughts around possible sexual failure, sometimes referred to as "catastrophizing," are critical to sexual dysfunction. This is an evolutionary step up from the phobic-like anxiety theory.

6. *System maintenance (1970s).* No matter the original cause of the dysfunction, it presently has a function in maintaining the couple or family as stable. Reflects sex therapists' experience that as the dysfunctional partner becomes functional, the relationship often comes under great stress, and if this is not attended to, the improvement will disappear or the relationship may collapse.

who had experienced a single, long-term (more than 20 years), satisfactory marriage. The mean age of the males was 47, and 36 percent reported having experienced PAD-M at some time. Ard also found that satisfactory sex is not crucial to the happiness of a marriage, and, conversely, that many marriages are unsatisfactory even though the couple's sexual relationship is excellent. The increase in PAD-M with age may be due partly to expectancy, but it is also related to the physiologic changes characteristic of aging (Silney, 1980). Even so, estimates are that eight out of 10 males retain the ability to have erection and orgasm until age 70.

The Case of Will

Will, who is 25 years old, referred himself to a therapist after experiencing erectile dysfunction for 15 months. Before that, his sexual performance had been adequate. The problem started late one night after a party where he had been drinking heavily. His girlfriend asked him to take her home, where they quickly moved into heavy petting. As he put it, "she got real hot—she wanted it bad, and it just didn't come up at all." Will also mentioned that she made her disappointment very apparent. Humiliated, he did not try intercourse again until a month later, this time with another woman. He admitted to high anxiety at the time, and he had achieved only a momentary erection. After two more unsuccessful efforts in the next month, Will gave up all sexual encounters until he referred himself. During these 15 months he had no difficulty attaining an erection and orgasm through masturbation.

Psychosexual Arousal Dysfunction in Males

Etiology. Psychological factors, either alone or combined with physical causes, are estimated to account for 70 percent of sexual dysfunction cases. People with severe diabetes commonly experience PAD-M, but it is hard to tell in an individual case whether expectancy or a circulatory system problem plays the crucial role. Physical factors such as general stress and fatigue (even heavy smoking or the use of certain drugs, for example, antihistamines) can be contributory, particularly in combination with heavy alcohol use. Alcohol disrupts arousal in males more than it does in females (Snyder and Karacan, 1981).

The medical examination. Anyone with any of the sexual dysfunctions should have a medical examination to rule out physical causes (circulatory problems, tumors, and so on) that could be a factor. However, most urologists and gynecologists are not trained to examine thoroughly for physical causes of PAD. There are institutes and laboratories that specialize in such exams, and though they are expensive, they are much more likely to come up with an accurate diagnosis (LoPiccolo, 1985; LoPiccolo and Stock, 1986). For example, over and above the usual exam, such labs will take precise measures of blood flow into the male's penis, speed of emptying, and the reactivity of the penile nervous system to stimulation, among other things.

One factor that has been used to differentiate biologically generated dysfunction from PAD-M is the occurrence of nocturnal penile tumescence (NPT), or erection during sleep (Thase et al., 1987). Most males experience several NPTs a night, just as females show clitoral arousal while asleep. The general theory has been that males experiencing psychosexual arousal dysfunction usually show no decrease in NPTs, whereas those with biologically based dysfunction have few or none (Fisher et al., 1979). Because it is often difficult to find volunteers to stay awake all night to watch, many clinicians simply have the client lightly tape a strip of postage-stamp-like paper around his penis before going to bed on several successive nights. If the tape is broken each morning, it is thought to be indicative of NPTs. However, LoPiccolo (1985) and Thase et al. (1987) (see Research Profile) found NPTs to be an

---

RESEARCH PROFILE

Psychological Factors in Male Erectile Dysfunction

The text points out that, in addition to physical factors, psychological factors such as performance anxiety can interfere with a male's ability to achieve and hold an erection. Clinicians have long been aware that acute trauma-based depressions can cause temporary erectile dysfunction. Men coming out of upsetting and depressing divorces commonly report a period of time when they have trouble gaining erections, which usually passes in a short time. But research by Thase et al. (1987) found that major depression can also be a factor to a degree that can mimic organically based erectile dysfunction.

They measured nocturnal penile tumescence (NPT), or erections while sleeping, over two or three consecutive nights in 10 men who were diagnosed as having major depression and 10 healthy age-matched control subjects. Taken as part of an EEG study of sleep patterns, NPTs were measured by two mercury-filled strain gauges, one placed at the base and one at the tip of the penis. These are devices that encircle the penis and respond to any erection with a consistent increase of pressure in the mercury tube. This has an advantage over the standard method of encircling the penis with postage-stamp-like paper and then seeing if it breaks overnight in that the strain gauge not only measures the fact that erection did occur, but also incidates how often erections occurred, how long they lasted, and how "hard" the erection was. For example, men with physiologically generated erection difficulties that are caused by problems with their veins, rather than arteries, as is typically assumed by urologists, have only minimal problems achieving erections, but they are seldom very strong erections. The postage-stamp paper would not allow this discrimination.

Overall, the depressed subjects showed about the same number of NPTs as the controls, but the duration of the NPT episodes was shorter. Most important, three of the depressed subjects showed such an absence of erections that they would normally be diagnosed as having an organic based erection problem, and possibly even be referred for surgery. However, follow-up evaluations discovered that when the depressions lifted, the erection problems diminished.

ABNORMALITY ACROSS CULTURES

Koro **and Sexual Dysfunction**

Koro, a specific form of panic over sexual dysfunction, is relatively common among males in southern China and also occurs occasionally among Chinese people elsewhere. This is somewhat analogous to the Western fear (which is inaccurate) that sexual potency is related to the size of the penis. The basic belief leading to *koro* is that excessive indulgence in sexuality is harmful and results in shrinkage of the penis, which may ultimately retract into the abdomen and cause death (Tseng and Hsu, 1980).

Victims of *koro* usually have a history of previous emotional instability, specifically associated with overdependence on their mothers and lack of identification with their fathers. In this sense they resemble people described by psychoanalysts as having difficulty resolving an Oedipus complex, with attendant castration anxiety (see Chapter 2 and Silverman, 1976). *Koro* is simply another disorder in which the basic fear is loss of the penis.

A related sexual fear, found primarily in southern China, northern India, and Malaya, is that males are physically weakened by excessive semen loss. Given a traditional Indian belief that it takes 40 drops of blood and 40 days to form one drop of semen, it is understandable that anxiety about semen depletion would often lead to inability to have intercourse. There is some evidence that this fear still exists to some degree in Western cultures. A humorous portrayal was found in the movie *Dr. Strangelove,* in which a paranoid general fears sexual contact with women because he believes they will rob him of "essential body fluids."

unreliable indicator. Although there is a statistical difference (between the mean or average number of NPTs) between those with psychologically based and biologically based dysfunction, there is too much overlap, i.e., some cases with a psychological cause show very few NPTs, and some biologically caused cases show some NPTs.

Most experts (Luria et al., 1986; Masters and Johnson, 1970) agree that the major mediating variable for PAD-M is **performance anxiety.** Performance anxiety means that unrealistic expectancies about performance generate fears about not meeting these standards, a condition seen in Will's case. A posture of "spectatoring" develops, in which the person detaches from the natural flow of the sexual act and instead focuses on outcome.

Various theories have evolved to explain why performance anxiety occurs. Certainly modern Western value systems that emphasize the importance of constant pleasure can foster an apprehension that one will get too little, or be left out entirely. Freudian theory contends that castration anxiety arising from the Oedipal conflict (usually occurring in the third to fifth year of life) in turn causes fear of the sexual act (Strachey, 1957).

Although much has been written about castration anxiety, few substantive empirical data exist to support this idea. Welch and Kartub's (1978) solid data point out that external factors are more likely to be the causes. It is true that in some couples one partner (either male or female) may perform a symbolically castrating role by being critical, demeaning, hard to please, and by showing little true regard for the needs of the other person. The perception of this symbolic castration may be accurate or may only reflect the dysfunctional partner's distorted belief systems (Masters et al., 1982). Certainly in Will's case, his fatigue and high alcohol intake undoubtedly interfered with erection, and his partner's apparent demands and expressed disappointment further sapped his self-esteem. Even though his later sexual partners were supportive and understanding, the performance anxiety pattern was already established, in a cycle of (1) failure, (2) self-blame, (3) heightened anxiety, (4) avoidance behaviors, and (5) repeated failure.

Treatment. A variety of chemical, physical, and psychological techniques have been used to treat PAD-M. Ancient cultures employed a wide array of herbals and drugs. Ginseng, a favorite of the Chinese for centuries, is gaining wide acceptance in Western countries, but its effectiveness has yet to be empirically proven. Testosterone derivatives are helpful if the client has a deficiency of this hormone, but ancillary psychological therapy is also usually needed. In most cases of PAD-M, a hormone deficiency is not the problem.

There is some support for the effectiveness of certain drugs. Of these, a combination of the drugs papaverine and phentolamine, which apparently act to dilate the blood vessels of the penis, has proven to be the most effective so far, at approximately a 75 percent success rate. Most clients who don't respond are over 70 years of age, or have severe circulatory disorders (Silber, 1987). One downside to this approach is that the client must give himself an injection of these drugs directly into the penis every time intercourse is desired. Also, the drugs are expensive, there are occasional occurrences of "priapism," or persistent painful erection, and there may be some as yet unknown side effects of consistently using these injections over a long period of time.

Revascularization surgery, which restores blood flow to the penis rather like a coronary bypass restores blood flow to the heart, is effective, especially where erectile dysfunction occurs because of acute trauma. Also, several prosthetic devices have been developed to treat male sexual dysfunction. But these are usually considered advisable only for cases involving significant physical factors. In one technique, a penile prosthesis made of a silicone sponge is surgically implanted in the corpora cavernosa, the two parts of the penis that normally fill with blood during an erection. This device has three major problems. First, it causes permanent erection, which can cause discomfort and embarrassment. Second, although intercourse can take place, orgasm does not always occur. Third, perpetual erection makes a number of urologic diagnostic procedures difficult or impossible.

A hydraulic system operates another type of prosthesis. Compression of a rubber bulb implanted in the scrotum or abdomen inflates sacs in the corpora cavernosa. A second compression of the bulb deflates the erection. Although this mechanism avoids many of the problems of the silicone prosthesis, it is expensive, and there are the potential problems (such as breakdowns, infections, or tissue rejections) that can occur with any implanted mechanical device.

Note that the idea of a prosthesis is not necessarily a modern scientific invention, as is documented by R. O'Hanlon in his book *Into the Heart of Borneo* (1984).

> *"But Leon, when do you have it done? When do you have the hole bored through your dick?"*
>
> *"When you twenty-five. When you no good any more. When you too old. When your wife she feds up with you. Then you go down to the river very early in the mornings and you sit in it until your spear is smalls. The tatoo man he comes and pushes a nail through your spear, round and round. And then you put a pin there, a pin from the outboard motor. Sometimes you get a big spots, very painfuls, a boil. And then you die."*
>
> *"Jesus!"*
>
> *"My best friend—you must be very careful. You must go down to the river and sit in it once a month until your spear so cold you can't feel it; and then you loosen the pin and push it in and out; or it will stick in your spear and you never move it and it makes a pebble with your water and you die."*
>
> *"But Leon," I said, holding my knees together and holding my shock with my right hand, "do your have one?"*
>
> *"I far too young!" said Leon, much annoyed; and then, grinning his broad Iban grin as a thought discharged itself: "But you need one Redmon! And Jams—he so old and serious, he need two!" (p. 82–83).*

The great majority of psychological treatments for PAD-M are based on the work of Masters and Johnson (1970). A common goal in these approaches is to get clients focused on the process of experiencing pleasure rather than on achieving orgasm, a technique known as **sensate focus.** By doing so, the client begins to give up the passive, spectator role characterized by being anxiously on the lookout for signs of imminent orgasm. In initial sessions, the label "client" is applied collectively to both the referred person and the partner. In an approach similar to paradoxical control therapy (see Chapter 4), the couple is instructed to practice the sensate focus techniques and to avoid orgasm, thereby calling attention to pleasuring, facilitating arousal, and helping to avoid anxiety (Masters et al., 1982). It is additionally helpful to use a program of directed masturbation to increase familiarity with sexual sensations (LoPiccolo and Stock, 1986). Therapy may also include systematic desensitization for specific phobias (such as vaginal odor). In conjunction with sex education and counseling with the couple, such techniques result in cure in about 80 percent of cases. There is evidence that males who do not respond

William Masters and Virginia Johnson, renowned sex researchers and therapists, concluded that approximately 50 percent of married couples in the United States suffer some sort of sexual dysfunction. (AP/Wide World Photos)

to this general approach tend to be compulsive and narcissistic and to harbor strong feelings of hostility toward women (Jacobs, 1977), factors that may mandate individual psychotherapy before the standard technique can be of help. Therapy for sexual dysfunction is usually not effective with people who are (1) marginal in their emotional adjustment, that is, liable to degenerate into psychosis, especially if they are being treated for the psychosis with phenothiazines, which themselves inhibit erection; (2) significantly depressed; (3) severe substance abusers—indeed, older chronic alcoholic males may have permanently lost the ability to maintain erection; and (4) couples who are so severely distressed in other areas of the relationship that they are liable to break up (Allgeier and Allgeier, 1988; Lo Piccolo and Stock, 1986).

One problem with the specific Masters and Johnson approach is that it requires the person to have a partner. The laws of a few states would probably allow the use of sexual surrogates, but most define this as a form

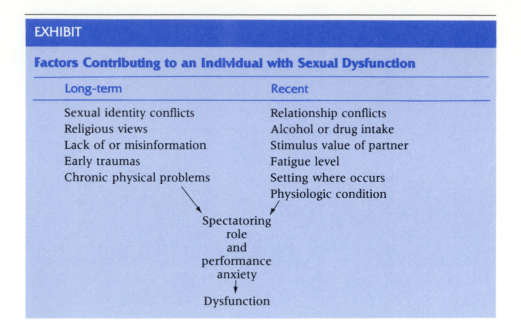

EXHIBIT

Factors Contributing to an Individual with Sexual Dysfunction

Long-term	Recent
Sexual identity conflicts	Relationship conflicts
Religious views	Alcohol or drug intake
Lack of or misinformation	Stimulus value of partner
Early traumas	Fatigue level
Chronic physical problems	Setting where occurs
	Physiologic condition

Spectatoring
role
and
performance
anxiety

Dysfunction

of prostitution. Moreover, treatment via a surrogate is not as effective as treatment involving a partner who has already been intimate with the client and who will usually be the client's primary partner after therapy is completed.

Psychosexual Arousal Dysfunction in Females

Our term psychosexual arousal dysfunction in females (PAD-F) designates the two major DSM categories, Inhibited Sexual Excitement and Inhibited Female Orgasm. Inhibited sexual excitement in females (often inappropriately termed frigidity) refers to an inability to attain or maintain the swelling and lubrication responses of sexual excitement long enough to allow completion of sexual intercourse. Although aging slows these physiologic responses, most elderly women remain able to participate satisfactorily in intercourse (Silney, 1980). Inhibited female orgasm refers to an inability to achieve orgasm even though there is sufficient sexual excitement. In a number of women both conditions coexist but are manifested on different occasions. The etiology and treatment for the two conditions are often quite similar.

Just as with males, there is a plethysmograph (an instrument that measures blood flow) for females, a small tampon with a light at the outside tip. The amount of blood flowing in the vaginal walls, which is directly related to the degree of arousal, changes the light that is reflected through the tip.

Etiology. Three factors differentiate PAD-F from psychosexual dysfunction in males. The first two—the fear of pregnancy and the traditional female expectation of a passive sexual role—have had smaller roles in recent years as a result of the wide availability of effective contraceptive measures, abortions, and the rise of the women's liberation movement. The third factor concerns the difference in physical system responses: whereas females can actively cooperate in intercourse without arousal, males cannot. But although arousal dysfunction has inevitably more far-reaching consequences for males, PAD-F is also distressing to women who experience it.

Performance anxiety can eventually promote psychosexual dysfunction in females as it does in males. Various motivations, both conscious and subconscious, appear to provoke the performance anxiety. Two basic factors that occur in many cases of apparent PAD-F are (1) the woman's belief that she ought to experience orgasm during intercourse even if she receives no manual stimulation of the clitoris or (2) the belief that orgasm is less "real" if attained in that way. These cases usually require only couple counseling and information that more clitoral stimulation is necessary (Masters et al., 1982). In cases of true PAD-F, there may be additional complications. Such things as unresolved anger toward males, unconscious beliefs that sexuality is sinful or dirty, negative experiences with sex, and ambivalence about the specific relationship in which the sexual problem occurs can all contribute to arousal dysfunction. Clients who harbor such feelings usually require moderately extensive psychotherapy in addition to a specific program to develop an orgasmic response (Teyber, 1988).

Treatment. The program for developing orgasmic responses in females is similar to that used with males. Most therapists follow Masters and Johnson (1970) in having the couple adopt the sensate focus tactic, with its emphasis on nonorgasmic pleasuring. When the client regularly attains a state of arousal, intercourse is allowed as long as there is no sense that orgasm is expected or demanded. There is no purposeful effort to achieve orgasm—the emphasis is on letting it happen.

The treatment of inhibited sexual excitement usually also includes masturbatory practice associated with fantasies of penile penetration and stimulation, later supplemented by penetration and stimulation with a dildo (artificial penis), with the male partner present throughout. Later he participates, first by holding the dildo and then in intercourse. Thus, through conditioning, arousal value is transferred from finger stimulation to the dildo, then to the partner. This approach accords well with general theories of sexual preference development (Brody, 1985) and improves upon the already excellent cure rate of approximately 70 percent obtained with the original Masters and Johnson technique.

Psychotherapy may be necessary to deal with pervasive beliefs or conflicts that perpetuate PAD-F, whereas systematic desensitization can deal with relevant specific phobias. Hypnotherapy has occasionally been used successfully to explore deep-seated conflicts that impede orgasmic response. Most PAD-F clients also need to increase significantly their ability to be clear and more open about their sexual feelings.

The pubococcygeus muscle, located in the pelvic region, is related to a woman's control of orgasm. Because this muscle is thought to be much weaker in nonorgasmic women, exercises to strengthen it are usually an effective adjunct to treatment (Jayne, 1984), though some studies do not find these exercises to be helpful (Chambless et al., 1984b). In the standard set of exercises, the woman contracts her muscle by acting as if she were trying hard not to urinate. In some cases a perineometer, a cylindrical diaphragm, is inserted and squeezed in order to train and exercise the pubococcygeus muscle.

Inhibited Sexual Desire

This DSM category refers to an absence of desire to initiate a sexual encounter. Since humans are "hard-wired" for sex, in other words, the drive is physically operative in reasonably healthy people, the disorder usually reflects a conflict over continuance of the couple's relationship (see Chapter 16). The client's statement that there is a low sex drive is often a cover for other feelings that the person either cannot or does not want to come to terms with. For example, they may fear becoming emotionally needy on others, or may be so obsessional that they have no real sense of what pleasure is. Also, they may have a much higher need for space and freedom than the partner, and a low rate of sexual involvement helps actualize this need by providing emotional distance. In some cases the low-drive person may be both homoerotic (having sexual impulses toward the same sex) and homophobic (very negative toward acting out those impulses).

The most effective treatment techniques for low sexual drive include training the person to be more comfortable with sexual imagery (assuming the above-mentioned conflict areas have also been resolved) and increasing the sex drive by some combination of (1) hormone treatments, if necessary; (2) learning how to more effectively and consistently express physical affection; (3) training in "sensate focus"; and (4) learning to use erotica to increase sexual fantasies. Unfortunately, clients with a low sexual drive also usually have a low drive for sex therapy, and even when they do enter and persist in therapy, they are still one of the more difficult sexual dysfunction groups to gain success with.

Premature Ejaculation

Premature Ejaculation (ejaculation praecox) is an inability to exercise control over the ejaculatory reflex, so that, once they are sexually aroused, premature ejaculators reach orgasm very quickly and before they wish to. Unlike

A couple engaging in a normal pattern of heterosexual affection.
(Ed Lettau/Photo Researchers, Inc.)

males, females experience no following refractory period during which the sexual organs are unable to function in a sexual act, so premature ejaculation is usually considered a problem only in males. Masters and Johnson, though acknowledging that the meaning of "very quickly" varies according to individual judgment, define premature ejaculation as a clinical problem if it occurs before the partner's orgasm 50 percent of the time. Individual expectations are important to assess here. One client who would engage in intercourse for 15 to 20 minutes before ejaculating felt he was a premature ejaculator because his wife wanted him to continue for up to an hour. Since for most couples the duration of actual intercourse is 4 to 7 minutes (LoPiccolo, 1985), he was certainly not premature by any statistical standard.

Etiology.   Premature ejaculation occurs in males of all ages and socioeconomic levels, but it is most common in young males. Levine (1979) reports that 36 percent of a sample of happily married men reported occasional experiences of premature ejaculation. There is no consistent correlation between premature ejaculation and deep-seated conflicts about sexuality or other general forms of psychopathology. Physical conditions such as prostatitis or spinal cord tumor can cause this disorder, though physical causes are rare. Two major patterns, labeled "primary" and "secondary," account for nearly all cases of premature ejaculation.

Primary premature ejaculation, the more common pattern, is diagnosed when the problem has existed since the person's first attempt at intercourse. An initial failure to learn control is the preeminent cause, often accompanied by sexual inexperience, unarticulated fears of intimacy, and typically by a high level of anxiety. The anxiety interacts with inexperience, high arousal, and a lower stimulation threshold for ejaculating to produce quick ejaculation (Spiess et al., 1984; Masters et al., 1982).

Cases of secondary premature ejaculation, in which there is a previous history of normal sexual functioning, commonly stem from deterioration in a relationship, usually compounded by one or more of the factors just noted. Such cases are often an indirect expression of rejection and hostility.

Treatment.   Treatment of the primary pattern usually begins by having the client increase his frequency of masturbation or intercourse to reduce the high arousal. The first step in treating the secondary pattern is to clarify and resolve the problem relationships. Then, in either case, therapy can proceed to specific techniques that promote ejaculatory control, and to control of the level of sexual arousal, since research shows that premature ejaculators appear to ejaculate at lower levels of sexual arousal (Spiess et al., 1984). The following procedures have been found to be effective in close to 100 percent of cases of primary premature ejaculation, and in secondary cases once the conflicts in the relationship have been resolved (Masters et al., 1982; Spiess et al., 1984; LoPiccolo and Stock, 1986). Usually only a few sessions are needed, and there is no indication of any significant relapse over time.

Consistent with the general technique of sensate focus, the client should:

1. Concentrate totally on the physical sensations during any sex play.
2. Allow his partner to gradually increase the amount of genital stimulation without attempting intercourse.

Then, more specific to this problem:

3. Let his partner know if he is coming close to orgasm; she then ceases stimulation and uses the "squeeze technique," a quick, moderately hard squeeze just below the rim of the head of the penis that interrupts the muscle spasm cycle or preejaculation.
4. Enjoy and experience fully all orgasm sensations if orgasm does occur spontaneously.
5. Don't attempt orgasm in intercourse until some sense of control has emerged.

6. When first trying intercourse, allow the penis to remain in the vagina for a time without thrusting.

Vaginismus and Dyspareunia

Vaginismus refers to intense involuntary spasms of the vaginal masculature, primarily the bulbocavernosus and leviator ani muscles (Silney, 1980). The result is **dyspareunia,** a condition in which intercourse is extremely painful or impossible. Vaginismus is not necessarily associated with sexual inhibition or orgasm problems; many women with vaginismus enjoy sex and assert a strong desire for intercourse. In some cases an overlay phobia of penile penetration and intercourse may develop secondarily to the pain and upset. In other cases the phobia comes first, and it in turn promotes the vaginismus (Masters et al., 1982).

Etiology.   Historically, vaginismus was considered to be a hysterical conversion disorder symptom that symbolized a desire to castrate men. In this view, the primary cause was envy and hostility toward men. This view may have some general relevance to LoPiccolo's (1985) observation that a significant number of women with long-term vaginismus were sexually molested as children or have been raped. Most theorists do not deny that in certain women such feelings do contribute to the disorder, but most agree that for the majority of women a true conditioned response is central. Masters and Johnson (1970) found that in any one case a variety of factors contribute to such conditioning. These include, for example, a strict religious upbringing, sexual guilt, or the husband's impotence, as well as any prior experiences with molestation, assault, or rape. Physical causes are not common, though previous pelvic disease or traumatic pelvic examinations can contribute initially by causing conditioned pain and anxiety responses. LoPiccolo (1985) notes that the more specific the locus of pain is in dyspareunia, the more likely it is to be psychologically based.

Treatment.   Specific phobias about intercourse and penile penetration are usually treated with systematic desensitization or implosion therapy. As with premature ejaculation, therapy may have to first address any conflicts or interpersonal problems before dealing with the specific features of vaginismus. One simple and commonly used technique is to insert successively larger catheters into the vagina (Schover et al., 1982). The first catheter may be as thin as a pencil. When the client can keep this in comfortably, a larger one is substituted, and the process is continued until the client can tolerate a catheter the size of an erect penis.

Masters and Johnson (1970) recommend that the client's partner both participate in the insertion of the catheters and witness the pelvic examination. This helps to dispel any irrational concerns or fears that the partner may have developed. For example, it reassures the partner that the vaginismus is neither a voluntary response nor one that is specific to his efforts at intercourse. Masters and Johnson report a success rate of nearly 100 percent with vaginismus. Others using these techniques have obtained lower rates, though in general still quite high. Differences from the way that Masters and Johnson's define cure and their somewhat biased samples (highly preselected) probably explain the difference in cure rates for this and other disorders.

THE GENDER DISORDERS

We are filled with terror. All those afternoons we went skinny-dipping, the curiosity about what each other looked like—is something terrible going on? . . . Once, at the river, Jim made his pecker talk, moving its tiny lips as he said, "Hi, my name's Pete. I live in my pants." Now it doesn't seem funny at all. If it's not wrong, why were we worried somebody would come along and see?
Garrison Keillor
Lake Wobegon Days (1985)

The **gender disorders** involve a basic incongruence between gender identity and a deeply felt conviction, usually firmly established by age 18, that one is female or male. The DSM subcategories are Transsexualism and Gender Identity Disorder of Childhood.

Transsexualism

Transsexuals are individuals who persistently and strongly identify with the opposite sex. This is manifest in (1) cross-sex dressing without the goal of sexual excitement and (2) a desire for a change of sexual apparatus through hormone therapy and surgery. The strong identity with the opposite sex and the desire for a gender change are what primarily differentiate transsexualism from transvestism (cross-sex dressing for arousal) (Barnett et al., 1987; Brody, 1985).

The first sex-change operation occurred in 1930 in Europe and came to popular notice in 1953 with the case of Christine Jorgensen. Since then thousands have undergone such a change, most frequently from male to female (Blanchard et al., 1985). There are several probable reasons for this. For one thing, surgery for the reverse procedure is difficult and often unsuccessful. Also, Money and Weideking (1980) believe that because, genetically, maleness is "femaleness repressed" (in males an extra Y chromosome modifies the basic genetic structure), males are more vulnerable to gender problems.

Imperato-McGinley et al. (1979) studied pseudohermaphrodites, people with substantial levels of the male hormone testosterone who, because of a prenatal defect, also have female sex organs. They found that 19 pseudo-hermaphrodites who were raised as girls began to think of themselves as male

ual. In the rare cases resulting from a hormone deficiency, hormone therapy should precede other treatment measures. Otherwise, the therapist can attempt to return the client to a nontranssexual orientation through a combination of psychosocial conditioning and sexual reorientation training (discussed later in this chapter) (Luria et al., 1986; LoPiccolo, 1985).

It has been argued that sex-change surgery is unnecessary, that with time and counseling the transsexual will revert to normalcy. But the weight of evidence indicates that surgery is generally worthwhile for many transsexuals (Pauly, 1968; Blanchard et al., 1985; Abramowitz, 1986) although technically it is a form of rehabilitation rather than cure. In evaluating the results of 121 male-to-female reassignments, Pauly (1968) found that successful cases outnumbered unsuccessful ones tenfold; later research, however, reports lower levels of success (Money and Weideking, 1980). These lower success rates could reflect the use of less thorough psychological selection techniques in screening out applicants for surgery who have inappropriate motivation and/or psychopathology. As any new procedure for any disorder becomes more widely available and commonly used, there is a danger that candidate selection will not be as thorough as it was when the procedure was experimental. For example, some schizophrenics have a delusional belief that they are really members of the opposite sex. They and others with psychological disorders can easily view a sex-change operation as a magical cure, thus avoiding confronting the actual focus of their problems. A sex change in such cases does not solve the essential problems and in fact usually worsens them.

Surgery is preceded by hormone therapy and a period when the client attempts to live fully and publicly as the opposite sex. This trial period provides an opportunity to consider the decision fully in light of experiences likely to be encountered after surgery. While the change from male to female is a relatively simple, single operation, using skin from the penis and scrotum to make a blind vaginal pouch, the change from female to male usually entails three separate operations. In the first, breasts and internal sex organs are removed, a scrotum is derived from labial tissue, and plastic testicles are enclosed. A penis is developed in two stages: a skin graft from the abdominal wall is formed into a tube that encloses an artificial urethra; additional tissue is engrafted later. Since the clitoris is embedded in the artificial penis, the capacity for orgasm is sometimes retained. The success rate (that is, various measures of client satisfaction) of the female-to-male change is only about 50 percent, much lower than that for the reverse operation.

Gynemimesis.   There is a subgroup of people who cross-dress, show a high level of identification with the opposite sex, often take hormones to change their body structure, but whom are content to live with their original genitalia and never get to the point of seeking transsexual surgery. This phenomenon, which is far more common in males, is termed **gynemimesis,** or "woman-miming" (Money and Lamacz, 1984). These individuals thus fall between transsexualism and transvestism. Such individuals often make a living as erotic dancers and prostitutes (either catering to very specialized tastes—i.e., a gynemimetophilic, or providing a true surprise to their clients). Money and Lamacz assert that there is a large gynemimetic community in the United States, and note that there are culturally accepted parallels in the cultures of India and Oman. In India the gynemimetic group is called "hijra," and they are members of a special caste and partially a religious order. The caste has its own specialists to perform castrations on those who choose to have this done. The penis, testicles, and scrotum are removed without the benefit of anesthetic. The age of onset is around puberty, and they have the role of performing and providing sexual stimulation. In Oman, the status of the gynemimetic is not that of a man or of a woman, but something in between called a "xanith," with specifically prescribed dress and mannerisms. The incidence is approximately two percent of the male population of Oman.

Gender Identity Disorder of Childhood

Gender identity disorder of childhood refers to a condition in which the child prefers the company, activities, clothes, and toys of the other sex and in some ways indicates dissatisfaction with present sexual anatomy. The child favors fantasy characters of the other sex, expresses a desire to be a person of the other sex, and rejects standard same-sex activities. Approximately 75 percent of males who eventually cross-dress begin to do so before age four; the average age of onset for females is only slightly later. The pattern in females commonly takes less severe forms (such as tomboyism); in males it tends to be chronic and more severe. Most children occasionally manifest aspects of this syndrome. Only when such behaviors persist for months is concern warranted.

Except in very rare cases, there is little evidence that abnormalities of the sex organs or sexual hormone levels are involved in cases of gender disorder, and little evidence of genetic disorder (Blanchard et al., 1985). In contrast, overt physical characteristics appear to play important contributory roles. Females who adopt the male pattern tend to be physically stronger than their peers, and males who adopt female patterns have often been described as attractive in a feminine way (Rekers, 1977). In general, the factors that predispose to transsexualism also operate in the gender disorder of childhood, especially any powerful environmental and/or parental influence in initially conditioning the child toward atypical gender role behavior.

Green (1985) studied two groups of males, initially in boyhood and later in adolescence, using a multiple-choice questionnaire and a standardized interview. The first group was composed of 66 clinically referred boys who showed behaviors such as an interest in cross-dressing, preference for playing with females and with dolls, and expressing an interest in being a girl. The other group, of 56 boys, while occasionally showing some of these behaviors, did not have them in combination or frequently enough to warrant a clinical di-

EXHIBIT

Internal and External Disruption in Abnormal Behavior Patterns

All disorders studied in this book exact high costs (psychologically, physically, and financially) from both the person suffering the disorder and the people affected by that person. However, we can consider the pathology, and in that sense the major cost, as being primarily directed either in toward the self or acted out toward society (hence, the term "acting out" commonly used by clinicians for these latter patterns). Up to this point in our book (through the sexual dysfunctions and with the exception of paranoia), the patterns of abnormal behavior studied have been primarily marked by a disruption of the self. Conversely, in most of the disorders studied in the last part of this chapter, the sexual deviations (or paraphilias), and in the next two chapters (substance abuse, personality and impulse disorders, violence), the disruption is primarily directed outward toward others such as family and society.

This diagram indicates how people move away from well-adjusted, contented levels of functioning into patterns of abnormal behavior that either disrupt the self, or instead "act out" the disruption toward others.

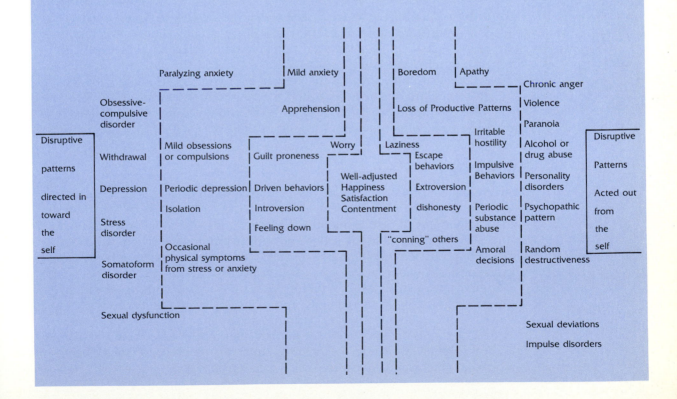

agnosis. Two thirds of each group (44 and 34, respectively) were reevaluated by means of interviews and rating scales in late adolescence and early adulthood. Thirty of the 44 from the first group (those with cross-sex interests), and none of the 34 in the comparison group, were then found to be bisexually or homosexually oriented.

Treatment.   Treatment of gender identity or role disorder in children is usually effective, and the children's long-term adjustment is markedly superior to that of similar children who have received no therapy (Schaefer, 1988; Rosen et al., 1978). Family therapy is commonly employed. Vicarious modeling and behavior management counseling have also been helpful in controlling the social learning variables that have fostered the pattern, particularly if therapy begins early (Rekers, 1977; Rosen et al., 1978; Blanchard et al., 1985). Although aversive treatment of specific behavior patterns is theoretically feasible, it is not advised. Using shock techniques with children involves serious ethical issues, and the other, less extreme techniques have been effective (Teyber, 1988).

THE PARAPHILIAS

Paraphilia is the DSM term for sexual deviations; in this section we use the two terms interchangeably. These deviations are usually marked by one or more of the following three features: (1) violation of a legal, public health, or accepted morality standard; (2) a gross impairment in the capacity for affectionate sexual responses with adult human partners; and (3) acknowledged subjective emotional distress regarding the source of sexual arousal. We include both the disorders listed in DSM (even though some occur relatively rarely) and some other deviations not listed there.

Transvestism

Transvestism, sometimes referred to as transvestic fetishism, involves cross-sex dressing and behavior typical of the opposite sex. Although it includes some components of gender identity disorder, transvestism is closer in most respects to the paraphilias, as it does not involve any personal identification with the opposite sex (Blanchard et al., 1985). The DSM unrealistically focuses this diagnosis on males; in fact transvestism occurs in both sexes.

Transvestites usually seek sexual arousal by wearing clothing of the opposite sex, often next to the genitals. Just as in fetishism, the next paraphilia we discuss, an inanimate object is the initiating stimulus in transvestism; there may be little or no dependence on a human relationship for sexual gratification. Transvestites may have masochistic fantasies, which sometimes lead to masochistic heterosexual or homosexual relationships.

Psychodynamic theories of male transvestism (dressing as a female) emphasize a disturbed mother-child relationship and identification with an aggressive mother as a means of denying fear of castration; identification with a powerful, threatening, and strict father is considered generic in female transvestism. Behavior theories, on the other hand, emphasize the role of generalized reinforcers, such as attention for being "cute" when wearing clothes of the opposite sex in the formative years. The pattern solidifies when there is an eventual pairing (often accidentally at first) of orgasm and the dressing-up behavior.

As in most sexual deviations, behavioral change through conditioning techniques is a frequent and effective form of treatment (Sandler, 1985; Redd et al., 1979). Concurrent use of psychotherapy may help clients deal with the significant social problems (such as rejection by peers or parents) that most transvestites experience.

Fetishism

The DSM defines **fetishism** as a condition wherein nonliving objects are used as the exclusive or consistently preferred method of stimulating sexual arousal. To a degree, mild fetishism is socially condoned, as evidenced by the widespread acceptance of objects such as perfumes, seductive clothes, and mementos with strong sexual connotations. Usually the fetishist obtains sexual excitation by kissing, tasting, fondling, or smelling the object. Most fetishists are male, and most use the object while masturbating alone, but in some cases it is used as a necessary preliminary to intercourse.

Traditionally the term fetishism has also included attraction to specific parts of the body, and in that sense, behavior theory suggests that some fetishistic behavior is commonly associated with intercourse (McConaghy, 1982). Normal foreplay involves attention to sexually arousing objects or parts of the body, with consequent arousal and eventual progression to coitus. In fetishism, however, the fetish takes primacy over intercourse as a means of obtaining orgasm, possibly as a result of an earlier accidental association of the object with orgasm (Allgeier and Allgeier, 1988).

Bemporad (1977) describes a case that demonstrates this process of accidental association and at the same time re-emphasizes the wide range of deviation that can occur in all the paraphilias, and especially in the fetishes. An eight-year-old boy showed a variety of bizarre behaviors in school, including an odd interest in other people's feet. Upon questioning, his mother finally admitted to school personnel that when he was a one-year-old, she would fondle him with her foot. Later, he would often play with her feet, even kissing and mouthing her toes. When he was five or six, he would get erections when they played. The mother downplayed the importance of this. But later, when he gave up this play while he was at camp, she then bribed him with money to start doing it again. When she was questioned about all this, she replied, "It's harmless," and tried to insist that there was no problem here.

Shoes, bras, and panties are the most common objects in fetishism, and psychodynamic theory emphasizes their symbolic value. According to Freud, the chosen object is a substitute for the penis the child believes his mother once had.

Odors can be important in the development of fetishes, just as they can be important in normal sexual stimulation, which may explain Emperor Napoleon Bonaparte's letter upon returning from battle to Josephine, "Ne te lave pas, Je reviens," meaning "Don't wash, I'm coming home." Psychodynamic theory asserts, for example, that the odors from shoes constitute the primary appeal to fetishists and indicate a regression to an anal level of development. Behaviorists note that the smell of a chosen object may simply have become the discriminative cue for sexual arousal.

Occasionally a fetishist commits an act of breaking and entering in search of women's used bras or panties. Frequently, the excitement of the illegal behavior itself increases the sexual arousal. In other instances, the problem becomes defined as a clinical disorder only when the fetishist requests treatment.

In 1956, Raymond found only three successfully treated cases of fetishism reported in the literature. Since then, however, behavior theorists have had success with aversive conditioning treatment (McConaghy, 1982; Sandler, 1985). Both nausea-inducing drugs and mild electric shock have proved effective in conditioning procedures in which the object of the fetish, or a fantasy of it, is paired with the aversive stimulus, thus decreasing its arousal value (Barlow et al., 1979; Sandler, 1985).

Zoophilia

Whereas **bestiality** specifically refers to sexual intercourse with animals, **zoophilia** includes all forms of sexual experience with animals. Zoophilia is a very rare condition in which a person uses animals as the exclusive or preferred method of sexual stimulation. It becomes clinically significant when the person prefers the animal even when other forms of sexual outlet become available.

The incidence of zoophilia is related to access. Thus, it is most common in rural areas. Zoophilia is practiced primarily by preadolescent males. Persistence of the behavior beyond this age is usually an indication of severe disorder.

Most theorists claim that zoophilia is functionally similar to fetishism. In both patterns anxiety about engaging in human sexual relationships with the related possibility of intimate, personal encounters is eliminated. Latent zoophilia has been associated with the behavior of adolescents who develop a fixation on horses and of adults who dote excessively upon their cats or dogs.

Wayne Williams, who molested and murdered an unknown number of Atlanta children in the early 1980s, personifies an extreme case of pedophilia.   (UPI/Bettmann Newsphotos)

"Little Red Riding Hood was my first love. I felt that if I could have married Little Red Riding Hood, I should have known perfect bliss"

Charles Dickens
(p. 90 of Creative Storytelling by J. Maquire (1985).

Pedophilia

The DSM defines **pedophilia** (literally "love of children") as a preference for sexual experience with sexually immature persons. It may involve overt force or more subtle coercion. As in many rape patterns, aggression is an important component—at times the predominant one—in pedophilia (Calhoun and Atkeson, 1987). Rape is discussed in Chapter 12, as many experts feel it is at least as much an aggressive and impulsive disorder as it is a sexual one. For a clinical diagnosis of pedophilia, the DSM usually requires that the behavior be repeated. It also arbitrarily requires an age difference of 10 years between the pedophile and the victim, unless the pedophile is a late adolescent. Pedophilia is extremely rare in females.

EXHIBIT

Myths about Sexuality

For the past three decades, Western culture has witnessed a transition from sexual conservatism to sexual liberalism. The myths listed below reflect these changing attitudes. Myths are crystallizations of the beliefs of a society. Although they may have functional value to the persons who hold them, they do not often reflect facts.

Traditional Myth	Modern Myth
The development of a happy marriage is not related to the development of an active and satisfactory sex life.	Developing an active and innovative sex life is crucial in creating a happy marriage.
Female orgasm rarely occurs and indicates perversity.	The female orgasm is a cataclysmic event that affects a woman's entire outlook on life.
Clitoral orgasms are less fulfilling than vaginal orgasms.	There is no difference at all between clitoral orgasms and vaginal orgasms.
Sexual disorders are difficult to cure and require long and in-depth therapies.	All sexual disorders can now be cured by simple techniques in a short time.
Love is required for a satisfying sexual experience.	Love is irrelevant to satisfying sex. Technical skill and a willingness to experiment are the essential factors.
Women have little interest in sex.	Women are so sexually aggressive and needful that men will never satisfy them.
Elderly people have little interest in sex.	There is no loss of sexual ability or interest with age.
The psychologically healthy young person is chaste.	All adolescents are promiscuous.
Masturbation is harmful psychologically and physically.	Masturbation is always a more satisfying experience than intercourse.
Homesexuals are inherently unhappy people.	Homosexuals are more sexually fulfilled than heterosexuals.
Homosexuality is seldom "cured."	Homosexuals should never try to change their sexual orientation; they should work to change the repressive society around them.
Exhibitionists, voyeurs, and "degenerates" are out to entice innocent women and children into a life of sexual perversion.	Exhibitionists and voyeurs are passive individuals who never seduce children or become aggressive toward anyone.
The sexual organs may shrink in size (a popular belief in Southeast Asia called koro) or become distorted, causing a change in sexual identity.	Sexual identity is directly related to size of the breasts or penis.
Incest is rare and reflects a deeply perverted mind.	Incest is common and may help in developing healthy adult sexual patterns.
Pornography is the first step to a life of perversion and sexual aggression.	Pornography is totally harmless.
Women who are raped usually have stimulated the rapist by acting seductively.	Rape is solely a crime of aggression.
Sexual fantasies are sinful and indicate a weak will.	Sexual fantasies are harmless and do not lead to changes in behavior.
Masochism is healthier than sadism.	Sadism is healthier than masochism.
We now know most of the essential facts about human sexuality.	We now know most of the essential facts about human sexuality.

There are significant differences between homosexually and heterosexually oriented pedophiliac males. Homosexual pedophiles are less likely to be married, and they prefer a slightly older target, age 12 to 14; heterosexual pedophiles prefer seven- to 10-years-olds. Heterosexual pedophiles are more likely to know their victims, are more inclined to look and touch rather than proceed to orgasm, and show a better prognosis for cure. Many heterosexual male pedophiles are impotent. When ejaculation does occur, it is usually achieved through exhibitionistic-voyeuristic masturbation. Attempted intercourse with the child is likely to be traumatic and painful for the victim and increases the probability that the incident will be reported to the police (Calhoun and Atkeson, 1987).

In the largest study of pedophiles ever undertaken, an analysis of 571 cases (Becker, 1987), several interesting facts emerged: (1) boys are far more likely to be victims of sex abuse than previously believed, with two out of every three victims molested outside the home being boys; (2) boys are more likely to be victims of "hands-on" abuse incidents, often with physical abuse being involved, whereas girls are more likely to be victims of "hands-off" incidents such as voyeurism and exhibitionism; (3) offenders who admitted to one to four incidents to probation officers admitted to an average of 75 crimes each when guaranteed anonymity—those who molested young boys admitted to an average of 281 offenses, those who violated young girls admitted to an average of 23 incidents, whereas adult rapists admit to seven incidents each; and (4) molesters typically engage in a wide variety of sexually deviant behaviors, and typically start molesting by at least age 15 and often younger.

Etiology. Though many pedophiles and child molesters are antisocial psychopaths (Doren, 1987), others are primarily responding to feelings of inadequacy about their sexuality, especially in dealing with adult women. This second type of pedophile may specifically focus on the size of his penis, or he may be obsessed with his incapacity to maintain an erection. Contact and/or comparison with a sexually immature child alleviates the anxiety associated with the intimacy of a mature sexual encounter. There is also a narcissistic component in identifying with a youthful and attractive sexual target.

Marital distress and alcohol abuse are common catalysts for pedophiliac behavior. Virkunen (1976) has noted that in cases involving a schizophrenic or mentally subnormal pedophile, the victim has often initiated the contact. Nevertheless, this fact should not be considered reason to shift moral or legal responsibility to the children involved. Finkelhor (1985) observed that an unusually high percentage of sexually victimized children came from households from which the mother was absent before they were sixteen. They may have missed a subtle, even unconscious, modeling of behaviors that would have enabled them to avoid or reject this type of sexual approach.

Some believe that there is a familial transmission (not necessarily genetic—possibly by modeling) for pedophilia, and Gaffney et al. (1984) carried out a naturalistic, double-blind study which provided support for this idea.

They compared the incidence of pedophilia and nonpedophilic paraphilia in relatives of male pedophiles and nonpedophiles. Their data came from the records of inpatients at the Johns Hopkins Biosexual Psychohormonal Clinic (a unit specializing in the treatment of sexual deviancy) from 1980 to 1983. Blind to the individual family history, a diagnosis was made applying DSM criteria to the historical data. As a third comparison group, a hospitalized psychiatric population was used, 33 male inpatients from the same age range meeting the DSM criteria for depression.

In a comparison of morbidity risk (likelihood of developing the disorder), the highest morbidity risk in pedophilic families was for pedophilia; the highest in the nonpedophilic families was for a nonpedophilic paraphilia. These differences were statistically significant. The morbidity risk for men was much higher than that for women; most relatives with paraphilias were men. The depressives' families had, as expected, a low familial rate of paraphilia (3 percent vs. 18.5 percent in the paraphilic families).

These findings indicate that sexual deviancy in the broad sense is not familial. However, a specific syndrome, in this case pedophilia, can be familially transmitted. Further research would be needed to define whether the specific mode of transmission was behavioral (for example, via modeling and reinforcement) or genetic.

Treatment.   The standard aversive conditioning techniques are helpful in some cases of pedophilia (Julien, 1985). Some therapists have used **antiandrogens** (suppressors of hormones) such as medroxyprogesterone acetate or cyproterone acetate to limit the sexual libidos of male pedophiles, exhibitionists, and rapists (Walker, 1978; Walker and Meyer, 1981). These drugs reduce or eliminate sexual arousal by dramatically reducing serum testosterone levels. Treatment with antiandrogens has shown moderate success, particularly when combined with psychotherapy. As a rule, however, pedophiles are usually not inclined to change their behavior until legal coercion occurs or is anticipated.

Forgione (1976) treated pedophiliac clients by having them reenact their pedophiliac behaviors in response to a childlike mannequin, filming the episode, and having the clients watch the replay. Viewing their own behavior proved aversive, and the clients' behavior decreased. Pairing shock with selected slides of such behavior could further increase the aversive response. Jack Higgins described an aversion technique adapted to pedophilia in his novel *Day of Judgment* (1979):

> *In the other room, a picture appeared on a screen. A young girl—very young and extremely pretty. Suddenly the shadowy figure in the chair bucked, straining against the straps, and from the sound box above the window there issued a cry of agony. . . . "One of the techniques we try here. The subject has a long history of rape, and he prefers them young. We show him suitable pictures, which naturally arouse him,*

then administer severe electric shock. If he is a bad boy, he gets hurt, you see. Childish, but extremely effective. The trouble is, it takes rather a long time." "My God," Klein said. [p 62]

Incest

Incest, though not traditionally a formal DSM category, is a pattern that deserves attention as a specific subcategory of pedophilia. Incest refers to socially prohibited sexual interactions between close family members. There is evidence that the breakdown of traditional institutions and the "future shock" of change and mobility have decreased the sense of family bonding, thus diminishing the taboo against incest and increasing its incidence (Blair and Justice, 1979). Freud first postulated that many forms of psychopathology stem from the repression of actual incest (Lewis, 1981). He later modified this claim, stating that usually only fantasized incest is involved.

Incest is extremely rare between mother and child but relatively common between brother and sister. Father-daughter incest is the usual target of legal and public health authorities (Frazier and Borgida, 1985). The strength of this last taboo is evident even in a prison subculture, where inmates are likely to socially isolate and physically abuse those incarcerated for incest.

Most experts believe there are good reasons for the taboo, and that society would be severely disrupted without it. One widely accepted theory is that genetic inbreeding eventually produces an inferior genetic strain (Bridgeman, 1988). Another, Freud's "primal horde" theory, states that if such basic taboos were broken, chaos would soon reign. Freud's is a mythological version of the axiom that society can flourish only if there is trust in relationships.

Several situational factors increase the probability of incest. These include geographic isolation of the family, long periods of separation between father and daughter, a family pattern of going nude or seminude in the house, the mother's consistent absence from the house, and alcohol abuse. Male children who have been the target of father-son incest or who have had a long period of brother-sister incest are more likely to repeat the pattern in their own families (Blair and Justice, 1979; Becker et al., 1982).

There are three basic subpatterns in father-daughter incest (Swanson and Biaggio, 1985; Blair and Justice, 1979):

1. *Pedophilic incest.* A psychosexually immature and inadequate father who is functionally a pedophile has incestuous contacts with his sons, his daughters, and other children.

2. *Psychopathic incest.* A psychopathic (see Chapter 12) father relates to most people as objects, shows little or no guilt about his behavior, and is usually promiscuous with adults and children, both in and out of the home (Doren, 1987). At times, such behavior may be close to legal rape (Frazier and Borgida, 1985) (also see the discussion of rape in Chapter 12).

3. *Family-generated incest.* The father is passive and the mother has a personality disorder (see Chapter12). The marriage is shaky, and the child who is the target of the incest, most commonly the eldest daughter, takes on more than just a sexual function. She becomes a mistress in all meanings of that word. The mother is likely to be aware of the incest but helps keep it a family secret, believing that the family will fully disintegrate if the incest ceases (Calhoun and Atkeson, 1987).

Family therapy is commonly used with family-generated incest, though in some cases such intervention will further the disintegration of that family. For pedophilic incest, aversive training techniques, often combined with family therapy, have proved effective. However, Swanson and Biaggio (1985) find that adult victims of father-daughter incest eventually have to be able to verbalize the fact that it occurred and discuss their feelings with someone other than a therapist before any full cure is obtained. So far, therapists have had little success in changing those who commit psychopathic incest (Becker et al., 1982).

Exhibitionism

Exhibitionism is the exposure of one's genitals to a stranger in order to become sexually aroused. The exposure is unexpected by the victim, arousal in the exhibitionist occurs immediately or shortly afterward, and the act of exposure is usually the only sexual encounter sought. Onset is usually in adolescence, with peak incidence in the middle to late twenties. Exhibitionists are almost always male (though there are exceptions; Grob, 1985), perhaps because there are a number of acceptable outlets for exhibitionism available to women, such as exotic dancing. Even when female exhibitionism occurs in an unusual place or situation, males seldom react negatively and are unlikely to report it to authorities. This social attitude, together with society's continuing reinforcement of an aggressive sexual behavior role for males, is the major reason many of the paraphilias are primarily male disorders.

Exhibitionists constitute about one third of all sex offenders and show the highest rate of recidivism—about 25 percent. A wide range of personality types with a diversity of motivations may engage in exhibitionist behavior (Grob, 1985; Levin, 1987).

1. *Impulsive.* Obsessional, tense, and sexually confused individuals whose exhibitionism is an impulsive response to intrapsychic distress.

2. *Inadequate.* For people who are not only obsessional but also shy, introverted, and lacking in adequate social relationships, exhibitionism is an ambivalent combination of an anger response and an attempt at both ego affirmation and socialization.

3. *Unaware.* For some, exhibitionism is a secondary result of mental retardation, organic brain disorder, or extreme alcohol intoxication.

4. *Assaultive.* For people influenced by a strong element of anger and hostility, exhibitionism achieves sexual arousal, but the shock response of the victim is the primary reinforcement, and there is little guilt over the behavior.

Except for those in the third category, many exhibitionists have a history of an absent or ineffective father combined with a domineering mother. Also, there is often a covertly sexualized mother–son relationship, though the stated attitudes in the household tend to have been puritanical. Psychoanalytic theorists would carry this one step further to assert that the exhibitionism is a crude attempt to overcome castration anxiety generated by an expectancy of a father figure's retaliation for the sexualized mother–son relationship (Grob, 1985). In any case, the ensuing struggle over dependence-dominance often carries over into the exhibitionist's adult relationships with women and men. Exhibitionists are not usually dangerous, particularly those in the first three categories. However, the characterological exhibitionist occasionally moves into aggressive pedophiliac behavior or even rape and assault on adults.

The multimodal treatment program for exhibitionism described in the accompanying box demonstrates a number of techniques that can be useful with exhibitionists. But many exhibitionists do not respond to standard techniques. One technique that has been helpful with constantly repeating exhibitionists who are at least willing to try to change is aversive behavior rehearsal (Wickramsekera, 1976). Not unlike the technique for pedophilia (Forgione, 1976) described earlier in this chapter, aversive behavior rehearsal has the exhibitionist perform their usual exhibitionistic pattern in front of both an audience and a mirror. It is best if the audience can both respond authentically (for example, laughter and comments such as "It isn't all that big, is it?") and at the same time keep questioning and talking to the exhibitionist so that he does not indulge in the reinforcing fantasies that usually accompany his behavior (Simon, 1987). Most, but not all, exhibitionists experience marked anxiety during such sessions, and this anxiety facilitates the therapeutic effect. In persons who do not experience much anxiety, it could theoretically be increased by bringing people into the sessions who are emotionally close to the exhibitionist, or by chemically increasing anxiety by injections of sodium lactate prior to the sessions (Liebowitz et al., 1985). Also, videotapes of the person's actual victims saying how he was silly or unimpressive can be effective. In any case, with virtually any technique, booster sessions at some point are necessary to maintain the withdrawal from exhibitionistic urges and behavior (Wickramsekera, 1976; Simon, 1987).

Everything that is stripped has always impressed me.
Joan Miro
Painter and Sculptor

EXHIBIT

Multimodal Treatment for Exhibitionism

Hendrix and Meyer (1976) successfully used the following program to treat Roger, a 24-year-old exhibitionist who had exhibited himself for seven years on an estimated 600 to 700 occasions. His diagnosis would typically be exhibitionism, associated with a passive-aggressive personality disorder. Hendrix and Meyers's multimodal treatment plan incorporated techniques from a variety of therapy approaches. Most of the techniques used to treat Roger are potentially useful with any of the paraphilias.

1. Roger was taught a relaxation technique to lower his tension-anger pattern.
2. Cassette tapes of the relaxation instructions were provided for home practice.
3. Autogenic training, a fantasy relaxation technique, was given to increase relaxation and to provide a control fantasy to supplant the exhibitionistic fantasies.
4. Psychodynamic psychotherapy clarified Roger's anger toward his mother and his fears of approaching females appropriately.
5. Systematic desensitization (SDT) was used to reduce Roger's phobic fear of being rebuffed in his efforts to meet females.
6. Supplemental positive coping imagery (vicarious modeling) helped him initiate and maintain satisfactory relations with females.
7. Hendrix accompanied Roger to the campus snack shop, was introduced as a friend if necessary, and monitored and later counseled him on his improving social behaviors.
8. Roger was asked to monitor closely and log the situations that seemed to set off his exhibiting behavior.

Voyeurism

A voyeur repeatedly seeks opportunities to look at unsuspecting individuals who are naked, taking off their clothes, or engaging in sexual activity. In **voyeurism,** the act of looking serves as the chief stimulus for arousal and orgasm. In our society, voyeurs are almost always males, approximately one third are married, and onset is usually in the late twenties. Many voyeurs have a history of other types of juvenile offenses. Parents of voyeurs usually manifest much marital discord, and as youngsters few voyeurs have had close and affectionate relationships with sisters or other girls. Voyeurs are seldom dangerous to the victim. Those who are dangerous (1) are more likely to enter a building to do their peeping, and (2) intentionally draw attention to themselves while in the act (Smith, 1976).

9. Behavioral contracts for a hierarchy of exhibitionistic behaviors, culminating in those that posed a high arrest risk, were negotiated and kept.

10. Roger was taught control of masturbatory fantasy to increase the arousal value of appropriate sexual behavior. In this procedure, the client deliberately thinks of the target fantasy at the time of orgasm. This association, by increasing the arousal value of the fantasy, helps to channel thought toward later appropriate sexual encounters.

11. Assertiveness training was used to help Roger appropriately channel his anger toward his controlling mother and to reduce in general his fear of being dominated by women.

12. Training in positive self-talk (Meichenbaum, 1977) was used to increase his self-esteem and confidence.

13. When Roger did initiate several heterosexual relationships, sexual counseling along the lines of Masters and Johnson (1970) helped him to maintain the relationships successfully.

14. When occasional discouragement set in, sections of earlier tapes were played in which Roger had expressed happiness about his steady progress. The cognitive behavior modification technique helped remove the limitations on his unchallenged beliefs that had led to depression and tension (Beck, 1967, 1976).

After 32 sessions in a six-month period, Roger was free of exhibitionistic behavior and at several follow-up sessions throughout the next three years showed no sign of resuming it. Roger objected to the use of aversive conditioning techniques; otherwise, these could also have been used.

Psychodynamic theorists consider reassurance against castration anxiety to be the paramount motivation, with repressed sadism generating the voyeurs' patronizing attitude toward their unaware targets. Behaviorists point out that a certain degree of voyeurism is intrinsic even in healthy sexual activity and becomes problematic only when the process becomes the sole stimulus for arousal and climax. Triolism (the sharing of a sexual partner while being watched), for example, is a major reinforcement in group sex experiences and is not classified by the DSM as voyeurism.

Aversion therapy has been moderately successful with voyeurism, but the technique must be adapted to the particular client. One voyeur was administered shock upon being shown slides of nude bodies inside a window—the hypothesized arousal stimuli. But treatment was ineffective until the shock was paired with slides of open windows as viewed from about 30 feet away.

Open windows with vague figures had become the initial discriminative stimulus (the catalyst) for the voyeur's arousal. Only when the latter slides were paired with shock did the voyeurism cease.

Sexual Sadism and Sexual Masochism

Sexual **sadism** and **masochism** are obviously interdependent patterns. People engaging in these deviations often pair up to satisfy each other, and in some persons both patterns coexist (Luria et al., 1986). Sexual masochism is the intentional acceptance of pain or humiliation in order to produce sexual excitement. The term itself, coined by Kraft-Ebbing in 1886, is derived from Leopold von Sacher-Masoch (1836–1895), whose novels focused on masochistic men subjected to sadistic women. Sacher-Masoch himself lived out the concept, obtaining excitement from the fantasy that his wife was flagrantly unfaithful. Freud believed that masochism arose from a fixation on or regression to infantile sexuality and centered on anger turned in toward the self. Most theorists agree that guilt feelings about sex can be a factor; the masochist seeks suffering as a way to atone for guilt over obtaining pleasure (Masters et al., 1982). Interpersonal theorists regard masochism as a way of promoting sympathy and intimacy. If it becomes a compelling interpersonal manipulation, masochism can serve as a passive-aggressive mechanism (see Chapter 12). Masochism, though relatively rare, nevertheless occurs a bit more frequently than sadism, and more frequently in females than in males.

In a rare pattern that was thought to be a form of sexual masochism and occurred usually in men, known as "terminal sex," a man hangs himself by the neck with a noose to increase his sexual pleasure while masturbating. Releasing the noose just before unconsciousness allegedly increases the pleasure, probably by developing an oxygen debt that facilitates the orgasm. This practice of eroticized hanging is more likely to occur among adolescents and young adults. It is estimated that this practice may cause as many as 150 deaths in the United States each year. In an analogous process, some women can only reach orgasm if they are mildly strangled when they get sexually aroused (LoPiccolo, 1985).

The term sadism derives from the Marquis de Sade, whose writings focused on sexual pleasure gained through inflicting pain and even death on others. Clinical diagnosis requires the real or simulated infliction of pain or humiliation in order to produce sexual excitement.

Siomopoulos and Goldsmith (1976) describe a variety of paths leading to sexual sadism, the only central behavioral factor being the fusion of sadism, usually through beating, and erotic pleasure. According to existential theorists, the major reinforcement is the attainment of a sense of complete control over another.

Frotteurism

Frotteurism has received increasing official recognition as a separate pattern of sexual deviation, that is, one that is not always associated in an actual case with another sexual deviation such as exhibitionism. **Frotteurism** is generally defined as touching and rubbing up against the body of a stranger in order to attain sexual arousal and even orgasm. The great majority of frotteurs are males, and the most common sexual target is the buttocks, though as the case of Fred in the accompanying Exhibit indicates, attempts to touch other body parts also occur. The act is usually done in a crowded public place like a bus or subway or crowded dance floor. Also inherent to the frotteur's pattern is a system of cover-up plans, and ways to avoid the embarrassment of being caught and publicly humiliated. Most of the ideas on the causes and treatments of both fetishism and exhibitionism, discussed earlier in this chapter, apply to frotteurism as well, as there are significant elements of both of these paraphilias in frotteurism.

Other Sexual Deviations

The DSM does not cover all known sexual deviations, merely those for which people most often seek or receive treatment. We mention two somewhat rare but related deviations to indicate the existence of a still larger sample. In coprolalia, arousal is obtained by using crude and vulgar language descriptive of excrement. It is a kind of verbal exhibitionism and is a common factor in obscene phone calls. Coprolalia should be discriminated from Ganser syndrome, in which the obscene language appears to be uncontrollable. Another deviation is saliromania, which is the desire to damage or soil the body of another person, often with excrement.

Pornography and the Sexual Deviations

Many people are concerned that easy access to pornography may spur the acting-out of some of the more aggressive sexual deviations, particularly toward children. Early studies on this topic found that pornography actually reduced anxiety in some people and/or stimulated a renewed interest in sexual contact within marriages. Wilson (1978) also noted that adults who show "deviant sexual behavior" have had, on the average, much less exposure to pornography in adolescence than have normal individuals. On the other hand, some studies have found that use of pornography by individuals may in some instances increase sexual acting-out and/or more unusual forms of sexual expression (Luria et al., 1986; Levin, 1987). For example, White (1979) found that pornography that a person views as positive may lessen aggression, whereas erotica that focuses on aggression or bizarre or sadistic sexual behavior in-

The Case of Fred

Fred and Kathy came to a psychologist seeking help with their marriage. The marriage had always been "rocky." But it had really started to deteriorate when, during a discussion of their problems with sex, Fred admitted some sexual preferences that horrified Kathy, and resulted in her insistence that they seek help.

Further exploration with the psychologist revealed that Fred had a well-developed pattern, termed frotteurism. It had started accidentally in early adolescence. He would ride home at night with his mother on a bus from the after-school center where she picked him up after she finished work. The bus was crowded and he found himself bunched up against an attractive, well-dressed, and well-developed older woman. He soon became aroused. At first he was embarrassed because the swaying of the bus caused his penis to rub up against her buttocks, and he was sure she felt it. However, she made no effort to change her position, and once even turned to smile at him. It wasn't long before he ejaculated profusely, and he was well on his way to a second climax when he came to his stop. When he was home he immediately went to his room and masturbated while thinking about all of this.

Ever since then Fred would periodically try to replicate this experience, purposefully seeking out crowded buses or subways, usually during rush hours. He would position himself next to a woman he found attractive, fantasize about how she would look in the nude, and let the natural movements during the ride cause enough friction to bring him to orgasm. Oftentimes he would, in his words, "try to cop a feel" by touching her on the breasts or in the genital area, again trying to make this appear accidental.

The pattern then broadened in two ways. First, he would try to sexually touch several women as he made his approach to the woman he would eventually position himself against. Secondly, he began trying the touching while swimming underwater at a crowded swimming pool. But he never developed this second pattern very extensively, probably because he felt so much more vulnerable to being caught. In all of these patterns, most women seemed unaware of what was going on, a few even passively participated, and a few became obviously upset and moved away. Yet, though he had done this hundreds and hundreds of time, he had never been reported.

As the extent of these endeavors became apparent, and because Fred had not yet entirely ceased these activities, Kathy became even more distant in the marriage. In spite of the therapist's best efforts, Kathy decided she could no longer respect Fred. She dropped out of therapy, moved to her own apartment, and instituted divorce proceedings. Fred did attend therapy for four more sessions, but these were interspersed with two last-minute cancellations and one "no-show," as his motivation to change was obviously lessening. He never did come back after the fourth session, saying and seemingly believing that he could stay away from the frotteurism on his own volition. It is almost certain that he returned to the pattern rather quickly, and would some day be apprehended for it.

creases the potential for acting-out. Since sexually explicit films account for at least 10 percent of the videocassette market, and at least 20 million Americans buy sex-related or "adult" magazines every month, it is clear that pornography does not stimulate criminal or grossly deviant sexual behavior in the great majority of users. At the same time, users of pornography do seem to become desensitized to the implications of the themes of the particular pornography they are viewing, for example, demeaning and subjugating women and directly violent themes (Allgeier and Allgeier, 1988). Also, there is a very small subgroup of people for whom pornography acts as a catalyst for various antisocial behaviors (Luria et al., 1986; Levin, 1987). The difficulty for society is balancing the rights of free speech and privacy against the need to control pornography's antisocial effects in certain individuals.

We now turn to an increasingly publicized sexual variation in modern Western society, which most experts do not consider a deviation.

HOMOSEXUALITY

Homosexuality has been a controversial topic in the United States, especially in recent years (Levin, 1987; Coles and Stokes, 1985; Masters et al., 1982). Gay rights groups have clashed head on with others who see homosexuality as sinful, a sign of emotional disorder, or detrimental to the optimal development of society.

Ego-Dystonic Homosexuality

The DSM-I classified homosexuality as a sociopathic personality disorder, and in the DSM-II it was listed as a personality disorder (see Chapter12). Yet, in 1974 the American Psychiatric Association voted 5,854 to 3,810 to exclude it as a DSM-II disorder. However, they devised a new term, sexual-orientation disorder, to designate people who felt distress because of their homosexual

---

EXHIBIT

AIDS: Cruise Control on Promiscuous Heterosexuality and Homosexuality

Acquired immune deficiency syndrome (AIDS) has been termed the "modern plague." It is a very serious disease that affects the immune system. Patients with AIDS become susceptible to a variety of infections and malignancies, which ultimately cause their death. It is a frightening disease because it is transmissible, has no cure, and has a long incubation period—from six months to more than 10 years—so that infected individuals may not manifest the disease for a long time. Renee Blinder, writing in the *American Journal of Psychiatry* in 1987 (144; 176–181), notes that although first reported in 1981, AIDS has occurred in the United States since 1978. The causative virus, human T-lymphotrophic virus-type III (HTLV-III) was discovered in 1984, and a test for AIDS was discovered in 1985. Subsequent follow-up of groups of homosexual men (at high risk for AIDS) indicates that about five to 20 percent of persons with detectable HTLV-III antibodies go on to develop AIDS.

Though the use of a condom, from start to finish of the sexual act, is effective in preventing the spread of AIDS, no one asserts it is a sure method. The only sure method is knowing that your partner is AIDS-free.

As a result of education about the spread of AIDS, evidence indicates that homosexual men have already dramatically altered their behavior, for example, by condoms, avoiding anal intercourse, and most importantly, cutting down on the number of partners. Cruising for anonymous partners has been especially reduced, as it is extremely risky.

Heterosexuals of both sexes are now showing the first signs of "cruise control." As education and awareness about AIDS increases, further changes in heterosexual patterns will occur, and none too soon.

A disease that was once considered the curse of homosexuals is now being found increasingly among heterosexuals, with sobering implications. One physician friend recently described a case of his, a retarded though physically attractive young woman of 19, who was diagnosed as having AIDS. As far as can be deciphered so far, she had at least 200 different sexual contacts in the prior year.

---

behavior. The DSM-III replaced this with yet another term, **ego-dystonic** (unacceptable to the conscious self) **homosexuality,** and then in 1986 simply dropped this label from the DSM, though there is a continuing controversy as to whether or not it should be put back in.

In any case, people who feel concern about their homosexuality simply because of situational constraints, such as fear about the loss of a job or fear of AIDS, did not warrant the label of ego-dystonic homosexuality; there had to be some distress resulting from internalized conflict about being a homosexual.

Homosexuality is found in almost all societies and is considered acceptable in many (Ford and Beach, 1952; Masters and Johnson, 1979; Luria et al., 1986). Boswell (1980) notes that the term gay preceded the term homosexual by several centuries, deriving from the old Provençal word gai. Ford and

Beach found that 64 percent of the 76 societies they surveyed considered homosexuality normal, though these were generally more primitive societies than those found in Western culture. Many people in our own society have had a homosexual experience (Kinsey et al., 1948, 1953; Coles and Stokes, 1985).

In an elegant and scholarly book, Boswell (1980) documents the extent to which urban societies that tolerate religious diversity generally accept considerable sexual variation, including homosexuality, without fuss. Even during certain periods of the Middle Ages, homosexuality was openly accepted, applauded in erotic poetry, and practiced by monks, archbishops, and saints. Saint Ethelred, a twelfth-century abbot in England, practiced homosexuality and prescribed that his monks be allowed to hold hands in public (Boswell, 1980). Freud himself did not take a uniformly negative view of homosexuals. The following excerpt is from a letter he sent to a woman who had asked for advice about her homosexual son.

The 1980s, the "coming out" decade for many lesbians and homosexuals, were filled with gay pride marches and gay community events. However, the sweeping AIDS epidemic cast a pall over gays' newfound acceptance and self-esteem. (Bettye Lane/Photo Researchers, Inc.)

Dear Mrs. . . .

I gather from your letter that your son is a homosexual. I am most impressed by the fact that you do not mention this term yourself in your information about him. May I question you, why you avoid it? Homosexuality is assuredly no advantage, but it is nothing to be ashamed of, no vice, no degradation. It cannot be classified as an illness. . . . Many highly respectable individuals of ancient and modern times have been homosexuals, several of the greatest men among them (Plato, Michelangelo, Leonardo da Vinci, etc.). It is a great injustice to persecute homosexuality as a crime, and it is cruelty too. . . . [Friedman and Rosenman, 1959, pp. 606–607]

Incidence

In a study of more than 5,000 males, the Kinsey group (1948) found that 40 percent reported at least one homosexual orgasm between late adolescence and old age. Their data on females showed a lower incidence of homosexual behavior. Because these data were collected when most people were reluctant to admit to homosexual behavior, these estimates are undoubtedly low for both males and females. Subsequent surveys and reviews (Coles and Stokes, 1985; Masters and Johnson, 1979) have reported varying rates, but all agree that homosexuality is relatively widespread.

Masters and Johnson intensively studied 94 homosexual men and 82 homosexual women. All but 16 women composed "committed couples" who had an established, stable relationship for at least one year. The remaining 16 women were assigned same-sex partners for the laboratory studies carried out from 1964 to 1968. There were extensive follow-ups, even up to the point of publication of their data.

From a research methodology perspective, the Masters and Johnson study has been justly criticized for using unclear assessment procedures and for having a biased sample. Not only was there a preponderance of committed couples, but the subjects, especially the homosexual couples, were above average in intelligence and education and were predominantly from large urban areas and academic centers. Exclusive homosexuals—that is, those with little or no heterosexual experience—were also underrepresented. These biases invalidate some conclusions more than others. For example, the conclusion that homosexual couples get more pleasure from lovemaking—even without intercourse—than do heterosexual ones is unwarranted. Other results are less tainted by this methodological bias. One is that fantasy patterns of heterosexuals and homosexuals are not significantly different: both groups do appear to indulge in a relatively high percentage of "cross-preference fantasy" as well as in fantasies consistent with their usual sexual orientation. This finding indicates that the traditional concept of a latent homosexuality, which is based on the assumption that cross-preference fantasy is rare, is neither meaningful nor predictive to pathology. The study also found that homosexuals are about as responsive as heterosexuals to treatment for sexual inadequacy. Finally, Masters and Johnson found that physicians, like most other people, operate from "a quagmire of misconceptions" about homosexuality and sexuality in general.

Male and Female Homosexuality

Until recently most research on homosexuality has focused on males. However, gay women's groups have always insisted that female homosexual patterns are different, and there is increasing evidence to support their claim. Works such as Simone de Beauvoir's *The Second Sex* have helped to counter the cultural stereotype of the lesbian (named for the Greek island of Lesbos where the homosexual poetess Sappho lived) as masculine and unattractive in appearance and obnoxiously aggressive in demeanor.

There *are* behavioral differences between male and female homosexuals. Male homosexuals tend to be more promiscuous and to have more one-night encounters, though these patterns have been significantly curtailed by the fear of AIDS. Many do form stable, monogamous relationships. Male homosexuals are also likely to have masturbated earlier and more frequently, to have engaged in more oral-genital sex, and to have engaged in homosexual experiences earlier than females (Masters et al., 1982; Tripp, 1976).

Etiology

Physical theories. The traditional view has been that homosexuality is caused by a genetic predisposition and/or a deficiency in the hormone systems. The genetic theory was particularly stimulated by Kallmann's (1952) finding of a 100 percent concordance rate for homosexuality in certain monozygotic twins, with only an average rate for dizygotic twins. Later studies, however, have found evidence that clearly contradicts this view (Meyer and Freeman, 1977; Masters and Johnson, 1979).

The notion that hormonal differences dictate sexual preference has superficial validity, but empirical results have not significantly supported this idea. Loraine et al. (1979) found higher testosterone levels in heterosexual males than in homosexuals, but Hatfield et al. (1975) found the opposite. Others have summarized similarly conflicting results in both males and females (Masters and Johnson, 1979; Marmor, 1980). It is generally agreed that low testosterone levels are more likely to cause an overall lack of sexual arousal than to increase homosexual behavior (Walker, 1978, Walker and Meyer, 1981). It is now clear that the great majority of homosexuals do not have abnormal hormonal levels. Yet it does seem reasonable that a deficiency in the hormones predominant for their sex might influence (not compel) at least some homosexuals in their sexual orientation (Loraine et al., 1970).

Psychological theories. As in many other areas, the two major psychological causation theories are the psychodynamic and the learning models. The learning theory model applies fairly equally to both sexes, the psychodynamic model focuses on male homosexuality.

Freud suggested that all persons are initially bisexual and that homosexuality represents a regression to this undifferentiated state. The major factor in this regression is the homosexual's problematic relationship with his father, aggravated by a dependency-generating and seductive mother. The castration anxiety that develops as a result can be understood more broadly as a fear of any type of intimacy with females (Lewis, 1981). Major support for the psychodynamic position comes from the work of Bieber et al. (1962) who had 77 psychoanalysts conduct in-depth interviews of homosexual clients to obtain 106 case studies. The common parental features found were a cold and distant father and a seductive mother. The researchers agreed that the primary causal role was the father's behavior, on the grounds that a warm and positive father would override the influence of a rejecting mother. The methodology of this study is heavily flawed by the fact that people already predisposed toward the theory did the interviewing. Moreover, there is evidence that not all homosexuals have this background and that many heterosexuals do (Marmor, 1980). Although Bieber's results have received some support from others (Silverman, 1976, Socarides, 1976), evidence for the social learning theory formulation is apparently stronger (Masters and Johnson, 1979; Brody, 1985).

Female homosexuals also have a variety of parental backgrounds. Some have had a pattern similar to that considered typical of male homosexuals; others have had intense, seductive relationships with their fathers and detached relationships with narcissistic mothers. Rivalry with male siblings, combined with a perception that the parents would have preferred a male child, has had an important role in the development of some female homosexuals; still others have had normal parental backgrounds (Marmor, 1980; Masters et al., 1982).

Learning theory maintains that reinforcement of differing sex role behaviors establishes a person's sexual orientation. This view does not deny the importance of specific parental behavior. But it broadens the perspective to include such potentially critical influences as peer influence, fantasy behavior, and specific positive reinforcement in early sexual experiences (Simon and Gagnon, 1970; Coles and Stokes, 1985; Brody, 1985). The essential points are (1) that homosexual adjustment (in either sex) is a complex social phenomenon composed of many individual and social behaviors, and (2) that the sexual preference response develops similarly in homosexual and heterosexual adjustment.

Changing a Homosexual Orientation Voluntarily

Because most mental health professionals no longer consider homosexuality to be pathological, and because there is good evidence to show that many homosexuals are well adjusted (Masters and Johnson, 1979; Luria et al.,

1986), it is inappropriate to speak of curing homosexuality. However, some homosexuals desire to change to a heterosexual orientation for reasons of personal advantage (perhaps because of job problems or because they would like to have children) or conscience. As Freud and others point out, in our culture a homosexual orientation often has disadvantages.

Traditional psychotherapies have not been notably successful in changing a homosexual orientation, a failure recognized in the following poem by A. E. Housman, himself a homosexual. He penned these lines when he read of the suicide of a homosexual cadet of his acquaintance (Graves, 1980).*

Shot? so quick, so clean an ending?
  Oh that was right, lad, that was brave:
Yours was not an ill for mending
  Twas best to take it the grave

But more recently, the behavioral therapies (Meyer and Freeman, 1977; McConaghy, 1982; Brody, 1985) and the approach of Masters and Johnson have proved successful in changing a homosexual orientation. Masters, Johnson, and Kolodny use techniques similar to those used for sexual dysfunctions (psychotherapy and actual controlled practice of new behaviors) and report a success rate of about 65 percent. Behavioral therapies have been just as effective. Meyer and Freeman (1977; 1975) report long-term success in 11 of 13 cases, which included several exclusive homosexuals. Even the two who had returned to homosexuality had already made significant changes toward heterosexuality. One of these had a woman with vaginismus as his first heterosexual lover (certainly a situation that could provide aversive suppression of any newly developing heterosexual behaviors), and the other was invited back into a homosexual relationship by his boss.

Two behavioral techniques in particular have proven successful in altering sexual orientation: aversive conditioning and masturbatory conditioning. As with many other disorders (such as alcoholism), treatment is effective only when the client has made a strong and clear decision to change. Masturbatory conditioning involves pairing fantasy with sexual arousal (particularly with orgasm), to increase the erotic value of that fantasy. The individual's predominant masturbatory fantasies determine which stimuli have increasing arousal value, and thus the direction of the individual's sexual orientation. During sexual reorientation training, the therapist works with the client to change the masturbatory fantasy, thus promoting a change in sexual orientation (LoPiccolo and Stock, 1986).

Like sexual variations, the abuse of various substances (such as alcohol) can be a focus of societal concern and, occasionally, restraint. These drug-use patterns, especially those that result in disorder, are the subject of the next chapter.

---

* A. E. Housman, as quoted in Graves, R.P. (1980) A.E. Housman: The Scholar-Poet. New York: Charles Scribner's Sons. Reprinted with permission of Charles Scribner's Sons and of Routledge & Kegan Paul Ltd.

CHAPTER REVIEW

1. Although physical factors can promote psychosexual arousal dysfunction in males and females, the causes are usually psychological. The major cause is loss of contact with the natural course of the sexual act, known as "spectatoring."

2. Treatments for psychosexual arousal dysfunction include surgery, chemotherapy, improving communication, sensate focus training, psychotherapy, and masturbatory training.

3. Most cases of premature ejaculation reflect anxiety, fears of intimacy, and/or high arousal combined with inexperience in controlling sexual arousal. Anxiety conditioned by a traumatic event is the most frequent cause of vaginismus. Sensate focusing and the "squeeze" technique are used to treat premature ejaculation; graduated catheters and relaxation training are used to treat vaginismus.

4. The gender disorders reflect a basic conflict between one's sexual self-image or identity, and one's actual anatomic sex. Transsexual patterns can be influenced by hormones and appearance, but parenting and conditioning factors appear to be predominant.

5. Treatment of a gender disorder via psychotherapy, specific behavioral approaches, and/or family therapy is usually successful if the pattern is not firmly established and the client (or parents if the client is a child) truly wants to effect a change. In clients where the pattern is more established, treatment usually includes surgery and hormone therapy along with psychological therapies.

6. Paraphilias, the DSM term for the sexual deviations, reflect social mores and legal codes.

7. In fetishism, nonliving objects are used as the consistently preferred method of stimulating sexual arousal. Many of the other paraphilias are specific forms of fetishism, for example, in the wearing of clothing of the opposite sex in order to obtain sexual arousal, the clothes take on a fetishistic function.

8. Zoophilia is the use of animals for sexual gratification even when other outlets are available.

9. Pedophilia, a consistent preference for sexual experience with children, usually reflects strong feelings of sexual and personal inadequacy. When directed toward a child who is a close relative, it is termed incest.

10. Exhibitionism and voyeurism are common paraphilias and show high recidivism rates. Most exhibitionists and voyeurs do not pose any real danger to their targets.

11. Frotteurism involves touching and rubbing up against the body (often the buttocks) of a stranger in order to attain sexual arousal and even orgasm. It has received increasing recognition as a separate and specific paraphilia.

12. Although homosexuality has traditionally been regarded as a deviation or disorder in our society, the great majority of experts now reflect this view. The term *ego-dystonic homosexuality* was used in the prior DSM-III to describe those who are uncomfortable with their homosexuality because of internal motivations (not situational constraints).

TERMS TO REMEMBER

psychosexual arousal dysfunction
performance anxiety
sensate focus
premature ejaculation

vaginismus
dyspareunia
gender disorder
transsexual

gynemimesis
paraphilia
transvestism
fetishism

bestiality   incest   masochism
zoophilia   exhibitionism   frotteurism
pedophilia   voyeurism   homosexuality
antiandrogens   sadism   ego-dystonic homosexuality

FOR MORE INFORMATION

Boswell, J. (1980) *Christianity, social tolerance, and homosexuality.* Chicago: University of Chicago Press. A beautifully written and thoroughly documented study of the evolution of societal attitudes toward homosexuality

Bullough, V. (1976) *Sexual variance in society and history.* New York: John Wiley. An encyclopedic and well-written classic source book on all the sexual deviations that also provides a broad overview of the evolution of sexual patterns in general

Cleveland, D. (1986) *Incest: The story of three women.* Lexington, Mass.: Lexington. An interesting and detailed account of the effects of incest on three victims, as well as a good overview of the topic.

Cox, D., and Daitzman, R. (1980) *Exhibitionism.* New York: Garland. An in-depth analysis of one of the most common paraphilias that includes an interesting discussion of the relevant legal issues; most of the points made apply to the majority of paraphilias

Kiell, N. (1976) *Varieties of sexual experience.* New York: International Universities Press. An intriguing analysis of the sexual variations as they are portrayed in various literary works

Luria, Z., Freidman, S., and Rose, M. (1986) *Human sexuality.* New York: John Wiley. Provides a good background and overview of sexuality, both normal and abnormal patterns

Masters, W., Johnson, V., and Koldony, R. (1982) *Human sexuality.* Boston: Little, Brown. An overall perspective on human sexual development that includes detailed discussion of the sexual dysfunctions

Money, J. (1986) *Lovemaps.* New York: Irvington. An interesting and very readable portrayal of the gender disorders and some of the paraphilias by one of the leading researchers in this area

Wilson, G., and Gosselin, C. (1981) *Sexual variations: Fetishism, sadomasochism, and transvestism.* New York: Simon & Schuster. In addition to discussing in detail the patterns mentioned in the title, the authors comment on most of the sexual variations

Sean Penn's character is a cocaine addict in the 1985 film *The Falcon and the Snowman*. (IMP/GEH Stills Collection; © 1985 Orion Pictures)

11

The Substance Use Disorders

Drugs are popular in our culture for a number of reasons. First and foremost, drugs often generate their effects rapidly and intensively, so the reinforcement effect is immediate and strong. Also, we commonly see advertising that implies that taking a pill or a drink can be a quick solution to any problem (Helman, 1981; Donovan, 1986). In addition, we expect some kind of individual response from our physicians, and that quick response is all too often a prescription for pills. Many physicians find writing a prescription quicker and easier than giving explanations and reassurance. Writing the prescription is a clear signal to the patient that the time with the doctor is up, and it is more financially efficient, and therefore reinforcing, for the physician. It is also no coincidence that the same drug industry that promotes a pill to cure every problem also provides heavy financial support to the medical profession by intensive advertising in medical journals. Support of the common use of the drug prescription has helped physicians gain a significant measure of economic and political control over the health-care industry (Helman, 1981; Blackwell, 1979).

The choice of a drug by a potential abuser often depends on media exposure, parental modeling, and peer subculture influences (Blane and Leonard, 1987; Orford, 1985). In addition, reinforcement properties in the drugs themselves may lead certain individuals to choose them. Alcohol, tranquilizers, and depressants primarily dull anxiety and release inhibitions (a clear motivation in the upcoming case of Butch). Opiates and other narcotics reduce aggression, pain, sexual desire, and negative ruminative fantasy. Amphetamines and other stimulants reduce hunger, fatigue, and depression and increase motor activity. Hallucinogens intensify fantasy activity (Julien, 1985; Bertinetti, 1980).

Butch is a good example of alcohol abuse. Since alcohol is by far the most commonly abused drug in our society, we will go into some detail on the causes of and treatments for alcoholism. This discussion serves as the model for most abuse patterns. In our discussions of prescription drug abuse, opiates (heroin), and amphetamines, we mention issues specific to these drugs. The discussion of opiates provides the model for drugs that function as physiologic depressants, and the discussion of amphetamines for drugs that are physiologic stimulants.

● The Case of Butch

Butch remembers his childhood as generally happy. Though his father was frequently quite strict and demanding, he could at times be very warm toward Butch and his sister. Butch's mother was attentive to her children. She set many standards, but she seldom enforced them firmly.

For as long as Butch can remember, his parents forbade drinking alcohol. Neither of them drank, and they often commented that his Uncle Ken was a "lush" who couldn't hold his liquor. However, Butch always enjoyed time spent with his Uncle Ken. Butch had his first experience with alcohol when he was 12. He and three buddies spent an afternoon sampling the contents of the liquor cabinet at a friend's house. Later, Butch's mother saw him falling down when he tried to walk up the front steps and noticed his slurred speech. She sent him to his room, where he promptly fell asleep. His father administered a severe spanking later that night, after Butch had sobered up.

Butch drank only sporadically during adolescence. When he did drink, he usually did so until he lost control. His social and academic performance in high school was average, and he joined the army after graduation. He was soon assigned a tour of combat duty in Vietnam. During his first two months of service he drank moderately; later, like many of his friends, his drinking increased markedly.

After returning home, Butch married and started working as a low-level manager in a manufacturing company. Until he was 38, he tended to drink socially but avoided uncontrolled drinking. Then his father died and his eldest daughter became involved in a series of shoplifting incidents. Butch's criticism of his daughter's behavior resulted in shouting matches or times when they did not talk at all. Butch thought his wife was emotionally more supportive of their daughter than of him, and he became increasingly distant from his family. He experienced occasional sexual impotence and began staying away from home and drinking himself into unconsciousness. He was picked up twice by the police and brought home drunk. On one occasion he started a fight with the officers. Butch insisted that he was not really an alcoholic, because he did not drink every day and could stop when he wanted to. Finally, his wife threatened to leave him unless he got help, and he agreed.

Alcohol has a long and colorful history, beginning centuries before Hogarth engraved "Gin Lane" in 1751. Today, alcohol abuse still poses a threat to drinkers and non-drinkers alike.   (The Bettmann Archive)

ALCOHOLISM

Butch shows a classic pattern of alcohol abuse; the various types of alcohol abuse that show any consistency in an individual's functioning are referred to as **alcoholism**. Alcoholism is the most prevalent substance abuse pattern in our culture. **Substance abuse** is commonly defined by:

1. Use of the substance for at least one month.
2. Complications from use, such as legal difficulties (arrests for intoxication) or social or vocational problems (arguments with family or missed work).

Substance dependence requires fulfillment of the above criteria for substance abuse, plus either psychological dependence or a pathological pattern of use. Psychological dependence refers to a compelling desire to use a substance and an inability to inhibit that desire. Pathological use refers primarily to episodic out-of-control use patterns, as seen in Butch's case. Also required is an additional factor of either tolerance or withdrawal. Tolerance means that more and more of the drug is required to attain the same effect. Withdrawal simply means that a specific syndrome (most commonly, a set of flu-like symptoms) accompanies reduced use of the substance. Because there is no clear evidence that Butch either required increasing doses of alcohol to obtain the same effect or experienced specific symptoms when he stopped drinking, and because he fits the three substance abuse criteria, he would receive a diagnosis of alcohol abuse rather than alcohol dependence.

Alcohol has been used—and abused—since prehistoric times. Mead, an alcoholic beverage produced from honey, was drunk in the Paleolithic period, about 8000 B.C. Berry wine and beer were used at least as early as 6400 B.C.,

---

EXHIBIT

Common (and Inaccurate) Myths about Alcohol Use

1. Alcohol helps people to sleep better
2. Drinking only beer or wine does not lead to alcoholism
3. People who never lose control while drinking can never be alcoholics
4. Alcohol is less destructive or habituating than marijuana
5. Alcoholics can never learn to drink in moderation
6. Alcohol leads to better sex
7. Drinking coffee or exercise counteracts the perceptual and sensory problems of a drinking binge
8. Alcohol is a stimulant
9. Experienced drinkers can take in a lot before their sensory-perceptual systems are affected
10. Alcohol is not truly addicting
11. It is harder to break a heroin addiction than an alcohol addiction
12. A 12-ounce can of beer has less alcohol than one ounce of 86-proof liquor
13. You can always tell a person has been drinking from body tremors or liquor on the breath
14. Alcoholics are better able to judge their amount of alcohol intake than social drinkers or nondrinkers
15. Alcohol abuse does not cause any long-term physiologic damage
16. An alcohol user is aware of when their judgment and sensory-perceptual reactions are impaired
17. Liver damage in alcoholics is caused by diet deficiencies, not the alcohol itself

and grape wine dates from about 4000 B.C. Today, more than 100 million Americans drink alcohol at least occasionally, and one in eight is on the way to having a significant alcohol problem, that is, alcoholism. The costs of alcohol abuse in terms of personal distress and societal disruption are enormous (Blane and Leonard, 1987). Alcoholics live approximately 19 years fewer than the norm. Alcohol-related accidents are a leading cause of death among 15- to 25-year-olds, taking close to 10,000 lives in that age range yearly. Drivers with severe drinking problems are responsible for at least half of all traffic fatalities, and alcohol is a factor in almost half of all suicides, homicides, and other violent crimes. And statistics cannot describe the sadness and deterioration of the alcoholic's personal life.

The increasing use of alcohol is not unique to the United States. The World Health Organization (1979) reports that in this century alcohol intake and alcohol-related disorders have been constantly increasing in most countries, and intervention seldom occurs as early as it did in Butch's case.

Categories of Alcoholism

Several DSM categories denote organic factors that further complicate a person's dependence on, or abuse of, alcohol.

Alcohol intoxication refers to the neurologic and psychological signs (such as slurred speech, lack of coordination, labile mood) that occur when anyone becomes very drunk. When these effects are noted in a person who actually has had little to drink—the stereotypical "easy drunk"—the diagnosis is alcohol idiosyncratic intoxication (pathologic intoxication). Such individuals are often shy or mild-mannered persons who under the influence of alcohol may become assertive and aggressive.

Alcohol withdrawal is a diagnosis often applied to the person who is withdrawing from a period of several days or more of drinking. Stomach problems, muscle tremor, signs of autonomic nervous system hyperactivity such as elevated blood pressure, anxiety, and transitory hallucinations are common. If the hallucinations persist, a diagnosis of the rarer disorder alcoholic hallucinosis is appropriate. Cessation of alcohol use after five or more years of episodic abuse may set off an alcoholic withdrawal delirium, that is, **delirium tremens**, commonly known as the DTs. This pattern is interestingly termed "manniporchia" in parts of northern Maryland, from the Latin "mania a potu," meaning craziness from drink. Delirium is an acute organic brain disorder (see Chapter 13) marked by confusion and disorientation, often accompanied by visual or auditory hallucinations. Autonomic nervous system hyperactivity is also common in such cases. Delirium tremens occurs in less than five percent of people withdrawing from alcohol. Also, if an individual has been drinking heavily and expects the DTs to happen, they are indeed more likely to be experienced by that individual; expectancy facilitates the occurrence of DTs.

EXHIBIT

Alcohol Intake and Behavioral Effects

Intake amount (in drinks*)	Appropriate** percent of alcohol in blood	Time (in hours) required for alcohol to leave blood	Effects
1	0.025–0.03	1	Slight, appears normal
2–3	0.06–0.10	2–4	Mild relaxation and loss of inhibitions; modest decrease in mental efficiency. Could be legally drunk, depending on body size, etc.
4–5	0.10–0.15	10	Further loss of inhibitions and mental efficiency. Unsteady gait, clumsiness, legally drunk in most states
8	0.25	10–12	Severe disruption in all areas; staggering, tremors
10	0.30	12+	Nonfunctional, probably stuporous, minimal comprehension of any information

* 1 drink = 1 bottle of regular beer, 5½ oz. ordinary wine, or 1 cocktail or highball
** Percent of blood alcohol will vary with body weight, metabolism rate, other foods ingested, rate of alcohol intake, and so on.

Wernicke's syndrome, a neurologic disease marked by confusion, ataxia, and ophthalmoplegia, indicates a thiamine deficiency and responds to megadose therapy. The alcoholic's usually inadequate diet can be a factor. However, since heavy consumption of alcohol disrupts absorption of vitamins, the disorder can occur even when the diet is adequate. If untreated, Wernicke's syndrome progresses to the alcohol amnestic syndrome traditionally known as Korsakoff's syndrome, which seldom responds substantially to treatment. This irreversible deficit for specific memories usually follows many years of heavy drinking and thus rarely occurs in individuals under age 35 (Zucker, 1986).

The last DSM subcategory associated with alcoholism is dementia. Dementia refers to problems and a deterioration in memory and perception, a common pattern in chronic alcoholics that in some cases may be revealed only by sophisticated psychological testing techniques. Both alcohol and inadequate diet are causal factors in dementia. Skills and abilities are often affected only subtly, and the person can therefore deny the detrimental effects. We evaluated a dentist who had been a chronic alcoholic for many years but had continued to practice dentistry. He had always categorically denied that his heavy drinking had affected him negatively. This denial was shattered by his performance on a psychological test (Benton Visual Retention Test) with simple requirements. He was asked first to draw a figure that was placed before him, and he did this reasonably well. However, when asked to wait 10 seconds after all cues were removed before reproducing another figure that he had just seen, he was unable to start the figure. He burst into tears and sobbed when he realized how profoundly his alcohol dependence had affected his functioning.

The Effects of Alcohol

Alcohol is not digested. It is absorbed through the stomach and intestinal walls and then broken down by oxidation, primarily in the liver (Seixas, 1981). In oxidation, alcohol is converted into acetaldehyde, then to acetic acid (vinegar), and finally to carbon dioxide and water, which are passed out of the body. Because the liver can break down only about one ounce of 100-proof whiskey or its equivalent per hour, any excess remains in the bloodstream and affects the brain, causing intoxication.

Pharmacologically, alcohol acts as a depressant. It inhibits first the functions of higher brain centers and then the lower centers. As a result, behavioral tendencies normally censored are no longer suppressed. This releasing effect on external behavior, which undoubtedly accounted for Butch's fighting with the police when arrested, is what leads to the mistaken belief that alcohol is a stimulant (Bridgeman, 1988).

With continued alcohol intake, there is a loss of the more complex perceptual and cognitive functions, followed by disturbance of even simple memory and perception processes and motor coordination (Seixas, 1981). Part of the effect depends on whether the drinker is in the process of getting drunk or is sobering up. Those who are getting high perform worse on short-term memory and perception tasks than those with the same blood level of alcohol who are sobering up.

Simply believing that alcohol has been consumed can apparently cause loss of inhibitions (Blane and Leonard, 1987). Researchers such as Alan Marlatt and Terence Wilson have demonstrated that this belief is often more important than whether alcohol has actually been ingested. In one study (Lang et al., 1975), half the subjects were led to believe that they would be drinking alcohol (vodka and tonic) and half that they would be drinking only tonic water. In each group, half of the subjects actually received alcohol and half were given tonic. After the drinking, an assistant deliberately provoked and insulted half of the subjects, and had a neutral interaction with the other half. The aggressiveness of all subjects was then measured by placing each in the

Some alcoholics hit rock bottom—losing their careers, their homes, and their families. (Charles Harbutt/Archive Pictures)

role of a "teacher" who could vary the duration and intensity of shock administered to another subject, allegedly to change the latter's behavior. The only significant determinant of the amount of aggression expressed was the subjects' belief that they had consumed alcohol, not their actual consumption. Those who thought they had drunk alcohol were significantly more aggressive. Amount of alcohol ingested does add to this effect, but the belief factor is preeminent (Brown, 1985a).

It is a common belief that alcohol facilitates sexual arousal in both sexes (Wilsnack and Wilsnack, 1986). In fact, some alcohol does promote physiologic arousal for most females, but it physiologically inhibits arousal in males. And chronic alcoholism causes consistent psychosexual arousal dysfunction (see Chapter 10) (Allgeier and Allgeier, 1988). Thus, for males, the words of Shakespeare's *Macbeth* are especially apt: "It provokes the desire, but takes away the performance."

As already noted in cases of Korsakoff's syndrome and dementia, chronic alcoholism results in brain dysfunction. Hill and Mikhael (1979) have found atrophy of the brain in alcoholics, and damage to the frontal lobes of the brain in both chronic alcohol and heroin users. Fine and Steel (1979) have presented substantial evidence of significant brain damage with long-term alcoholism, especially in alcoholics who continue moderate drinking (as opposed to total abstinence) and in older alcoholics. That is, five years of alcoholism causes more neurologic damage to a person over 40 than an equal amount of abuse by a person under 40. These brain deficits do not always show up clearly on standard intelligence tests. But they can become evident on highly sensitive tests of specific neuropsychological abilities (Reitan and Wolfson, 1986) (see Chapter 13).

Liver damage through fat accumulation, another common effect of chronic alcoholism, was traditionally thought to result from poor nutrition. Now that the alcohol itself is known to be the major cause, blood chemistry analysis of liver function can be used to identify alcoholics who are denying their alcoholism and who refuse to undergo psychological testing. Ulcers, cardiovascular problems, and the increased probability of fetal abnormalities in pregnant alcoholics commonly accompany alcohol dependence. Also, the incidence of oral cancers is markedly increased if alcohol abuse is combined with smoking or the heavy use of other drugs.

Stages of Dependence on Alcohol

Dependence on alcohol typically develops in stages (Donovan, 1986; Morey et al., 1984). The sequence of behaviors and symptoms listed below is not necessarily inevitable. For example, many so-called social drinkers never move into the second stage and become alcoholics. Nonetheless, this progression is fairly common.

1. *Prealcoholic phase.* (a) Social drinking and an occasional weekend drink are the major symptoms. (b) Both tolerance and frequency of drinking increase, usually slowly. (c) Alcohol use serves primarily as an escape from anxiety, mild depression, or boredom.

2. *Initial alcoholism.* (a) Tolerance, frequency, solitary use, and abuse increase. (b) More is drunk per swallow; often there is a shift to more potent drinks. (c) Depression increases, along with loss of self-esteem over drinking patterns. (d) Occasional blackouts occur.

3. *Chronic stage.* (a) True loss-of-control patterns (such as drinking throughout the day and using any source of alcohol) predominate. (b) Inadequate nutrition affects functioning and physical health. (c) Signs of impaired thinking, hallucinations, paranoid thoughts, and tremors emerge.

ABNORMALITY ACROSS CULTURES

Patterns in the Inheritability of Alcoholism

The text notes that there is good evidence that a predisposition to alcoholism can be inherited (Vaillant, 1983). There are clear individual differences in how individuals respond to a drink of alcohol. Indeed, there is evidence that some genetic strains of rats prefer alcohol virtually undiluted, some prefer it diluted, some prefer either to water, and some will totally avoid alcohol. Similarly, some people react very sensitively to a small amount of alcohol, with an increase in pulse rate, respiration, and skin temperature, often accompanied by marked facial flushing. Others can ingest a drink or two without noticeable effect, but quickly "feel drunk" if they drink more, while still others can take in huge amounts and appear relatively normal (Heath, 1986; Donovan, 1986). Unfortunately, in this latter group, motor and perceptual processes have been markedly disrupted, and since they also may perceive themselves as "normal" they can put themselves and others at great risk, for example, by driving.

Since there are marked individual differences within any cultural group to alcohol, based on genetic factors, it's not surprising that there are differences across cultural and racial groups. The text notes how psychological expectancies can influence such differences, but there are primary differences in how alcohol is metabolized. For example, a high proportion of people from the Asian based races (including Eskimos and most Native American groups) show the sensitivity reactions (flushing, etc.) to small amounts of alcohol. This innate aversive response acts as a block to developing alcoholism. Only three to six percent of Caucasians show this response.

This contrast reflects genetic differences that are manifested at the molecular biological level. For example, Caucasians and Orientals show differences in two different enzymes that are critical to the metabolism of alcohol: alcohol dehydrogenase (ADH) and acetaldehyde hyrdrogenase (ADLH—also referred to as acetaldehyde in the section in this chapter on metabolism of alcohol). Some individuals have lower rates of these enzymes or show a variant form of ADH or ADLH. This causes pure acetaldehyde (not ADLH) to accumulate in the body, causing the sensitivity reaction, a process parallel to that generated by Antabuse, as described in the aversion therapies section of this chapter.

There are a variety of other possible "sites" for genetic differences that generate different responses to alcohol, for example, speed of neurotransmitter processing systems, differences in brain nerve-cell membrane permeability as a response to alcohol, and so on. Nevertheless, whatever the site, it is clear that genetic differences do affect an individual's response to alcohol.

Etiology

Biological Theories: The Disease Model. Nearly two centuries ago, Edinburgh physician Thomas Trotter theorized that drunkenness is a disease. Since then, others have put forth genetic disorders as the cause of alcoholism. Though the quest for a single ultimate physiologic cause continues today, the disease model of alcoholism promoted in the 1950s by theorists such as Jellinek, is now widely accepted in legal, medical, and lay definitions (Heath, 1986; Morey et al., 1984).

The disease model emphasizes the physiologic effects of alcohol abuse and implicitly (or sometimes explicitly) downplays the roles of choice and psychological dependence. There are two fundamental assumptions in the disease model of alcoholism. The first is that because of an as-yet-unknown physical or psychological malfunction, alcoholics cannot control their intake of alcohol. The second is a logical corollary of the first: although alcoholics may learn to abstain, they can never use alcohol without completing the full sequence of intoxication (Vaillant, 1983).

Several studies indicate that at least a minority of alcoholics have a genetic predisposition for problem drinking (Goodwin et al., 1973; Vaillant, 1983; Cadoret et al., 1985; 1987). One aspect that may be important genetically is simply the ability to tolerate large amounts of alcohol. Certain ethnic groups, such as some Orientals, experience physiologic upset from even small amounts of alcohol, which seems to serve as a natural barrier to alcoholism. Other studies have indicated that people who drink heavily for a significant period eventually begin to metabolize alcohol in the liver differently. They show a higher acetaldehyde level than normal social drinkers (Seixas, 1981). This finding is consistent with the disease model. However, there is little evidence that this change occurs until late in the sequence, nor is there evidence that a higher acetaldehyde level in turn compels further drinking. In fact, a high acetaldehyde level is one of the therapeutic control aspects of Antabuse, which we will discuss shortly. Moreover, some researchers contend that some alcoholics may be able, through self-discipline or treatment, to return to moderate social drinking without relapse (Lovibond and Caddy, 1970; Peele, 1984). Indeed, in a long-term study by a proponent of the disease model, Vaillant (1983) was eventually forced to *discard* such axioms of that model as (1) alcoholism inevitably worsens without treatment, (2) alcoholism is a clearly demarcated variety of alcohol abuse, and (3) alcoholics cannot ever again drink without endangering their sobriety.

The disease concept of alcoholism does have the advantage of eliminating the connotations of sinfulness that have been tied to alcohol for centuries. But is has replaced the requirement for total self-change that was implied by the "sinful" label with the passivity of a patient role. Finally, the great majority of variables in alcoholism do not stem from genetic or other biologic dysfunctions (Blane and Leonard, 1987); most physical symptoms are effects rather than causes.

Psychological Theories. Freud viewed alcoholics as fixated at the oral dependent stage (Wurmser, 1981). This theory has some surface validity, for alcohol is taken orally and many alcoholics are also heavy smokers. As with so many other aspects of psychodynamic theory, though, few hard data exist to support this claim. Psychodynamic theorists also have commented, in part facetiously, that the superego dissolves nicely in alcohol (Wurmser, 1981). This view would fit well with physiologic concepts; that is, alcohol, by inhibiting the higher brain centers, gives free play to the impulses of the id-dominated lower brain center.

Not only does alcohol dissolve the superego, it dilutes fear as well. In a landmark study, John Conger (1964) first exposed animals to shock as they approached to feed in a certain place, such as a classic approach-avoidance situation, and the animals soon developed intense fear responses. He then injected alcohol into half of them, and these animals were able to overcome their fears and approach the food.

Other psychodynamic theorists have asserted that ambivalence toward dependency relationships, associated with pathological narcissism, is a primary cause of alcoholism (Adams, 1978). In support of this view, Orford (1985) presented evidence that alcoholic males view their wives as far more dominant than their wives view themselves, whereas normal couples usually show no significant discrepancy in their perceptions of each partner's actual relative dominance. A cross-cultural study by Bacon (1974) yielded similar results. Bacon looked for an association between psychological factors and alcoholism rates in a subsample of 38 preliterate societies. Bacon's careful analysis consistently found three factors in societies that showed problems in controlling the use of alcohol: (1) lower levels of parental nurturing, which effectively limits indulgence or dependency; (2) high demands for achievement in childhood; and (3) suppression of dependent behavior in adulthood. These findings also support Adams' claim that ambivalence about dependency plays a large role in alcoholism. The concept is applicable in Butch's case: when he began to feel distanced from the support of his family, his drinking increased markedly.

Various studies (Blane and Leonard, 1987; Heath, 1986; Seixas, 1981) indicate that alcohol's physiologic depressant effect is reinforcing to most people. It follows, then, that alcoholics have developed a need to attain this altered state of consciousness more often and/or more intensely than others do. Why these people in particular develop this need, however, is still far from clear.

Modeling plays a large role in alcoholism, as in other disorders. Indeed, it accounts for the significantly higher rates of alcoholism in children of alcoholics as plausibly as the genetic theories do. Laboratory studies have shown that modeling also can strongly influence how much a person drinks (Blane and Leonard, 1987). The concept of behavioral reinforcement is as important for alcoholics as for normal drinkers. Alcohol permits one to bypass anxiety, depression, guilt, feelings of self-recrimination, and many other negative emotional responses. Unfortunately, this effect is short-lived, and drinking may actually then increase the person's level of anxiety and/or guilt (Cadoret et al., 1987). Initially, the alcoholic repeats the behavior because of its short-term reinforcement effect. As tolerance increases, the person needs more alcohol to attain the effect. Support of family and friends erodes, causing more anxiety and depression, and the negative cycle becomes self-perpetuating (Gorski and Miller, 1986). This cycle is typical not only of alcoholism, but also of most other drug abuse patterns.

Jones (1971) found that while male alcoholics were impulsive, female alcoholics were somewhat more likely to be passive and socially avoidant, a result supported by Wilsnack and Wilsnack (1986). Jones's sample of alcoholics also had a disproportionately high percentage of individuals whose family backgrounds were characterized by either heavy drinking (Butch's Uncle Ken) or total abstinence (Butch's parents).

Treatment

Numerous treatment approaches have been tried with alcoholism, and as we will see, a combination of several approaches is needed in each case. Two of the most commonly used approaches are Alcoholics Anonymous and aversion therapy.

Alcoholics Anonymous.   The primary treatment mode for alcoholism in recent years has been Alcoholics Anonymous (AA), founded in 1935 by two recovered alcoholics, Bill Wilson and a man known only as Dr. B. AA clearly accepts a disease model but has tried, not always successfully, to reject the "sick role." The organization's requirement of total abstinence for a recovered alcoholic often acts to bind the person to AA for the rest of his or her life.

Four elements of AA seem particularly useful in helping people overcome alcoholism: (1) the requirement that they clearly self-label themselves as alcoholic by admitting to themselves and to others that they need help, (2) the quasi-group therapy structure of AA meetings, (3) the availability of consistent rituals to respond to crises in their lives, and (4) the chance for social contacts with nondrinkers (Blane and Leonard, 1987; Brown, 1985b).

There is no question that AA has been effective with many alcoholics, and is critical to those who are group dependent and in the chronic stage of alcoholism. However, AA's success rate is not quite as high as the organization often claims (Brandsma, 1979). For one thing, AA usually does not quite count people who find that the meetings are not useful for them and eventually leave.

In addition to its biased outcome data and its commitment to the axiom that total abstinence is required of all recovered alcoholics, some criticize AA's religious fundamentalism.

In the AA literature, Bill Wilson, one of the founders, has written

We aim to cause a crisis, to cause him to "hit bottom" as AA's say. . . . Once he has accepted the fact that . . . he is powerless to recover unaided, the battle is half won . . . he is hooked.

This exchange of one dependency for another is not conducive to self-esteem. The perception that one cannot control the use of alcohol through will power alone is a central feature of the disease model (Peele, 1984). Yet even with these limitations, AA remains one of the most effective approaches for many alcoholics.

Aversion Therapies. A young couple and a friend on their way home from a Saturday matinee movie stopped off at a tavern for a drink. Soon afterward the couple suffered similar symptoms: a tingling in the arms, a swelling of the hands, a hot flush on the face and neck, a metallic aftertaste, a rapid heartbeat, and then severe nausea and vomiting. The friend, who had consumed only a soft drink, experienced no symptoms and drove them to a hospital, where they told the attending physician they had been given bad vodka.

Fortunately, the attending physician asked them what they had eaten during the past few days. All three friends had shared a meal the night before that included freshly gathered mushrooms. Most of the mushrooms were *Coprinus atramentarius*, one of the family of common mushrooms known as the "inky caps" because they gradually dissolve into a black liquid when picked. These mushrooms contain coprine, which interacts with alcohol to cause the symptoms the couple experienced.

A similar drug, disulfiram (Antabuse), is often administered to alcoholics so that if they drink, they experience the same undesirable symptoms. Both disulfiram and coprine contain a chemical structure that binds molybdenum, a trace mineral necessary for the liver to detoxify alcohol. With molybdenum unavailable, the ethanol breakdown is halted at the acetaldehyde stage. This excess acetaldehyde, through a reaction of the autonomic nervous system, generates the unpleasant symptoms (Lincoff and Mitchell, 1977).

At one time, Antabuse was hailed as the long-awaited cure for alcoholics. One pill a day (effective for 24 to 48 hours) was prescribed on the assumption that the prospect of the painful reaction would make the person abstain from alcohol. There were several problems with this approach. First, some people failed to respond to Antabuse. Second, those who wanted to drink simply stopped taking the Antabuse and started drinking. Third, because alcoholics are prone to chronic denial of their problem, most of them stop taking the pills after a few days, leaving them defenseless against the impulse to drink. A surgical implant of a time-release capsule of Antabuse (Wilson et al., 1984), or some technique that forces them to come in for the Antabuse (Barrett, 1986a) can be effective. However, some alcoholics continue to drink anyway, and heavy alcohol use with Antabuse carries a risk of fatality similar to some drug overdoses.

Other aversive techniques have been used to treat alcoholism (Sandler, 1985). One approach pairs electric shock with specific segments of the drinking behavior, such as picking up the drink and taking a sip. This technique has worked effectively to suppress some of the alcoholic's behavior, but seldom generalizes beyond the treatment situation. It is, however, useful as one part of a multimodal treatment.

A Multimodal Treatment Approach for Alcoholism.   Alcoholism is produced and maintained by many variables specific to the individual's case, including anxiety, depression, or a social phobia. These factors require treatment, and various approaches that have proved effective for these disorders are covered elsewhere. For the problems shared by most alcoholics, several of the following techniques can be employed in various combinations, depending on the individual client (Brandsma, 1979; Peele, 1984; Brown, 1985b; Heath, 1986).

1. *Detoxification.* Many alcoholics need an initial phase of hospitalization to "dry out." This allows their systems to readjust to a lack of alcohol, and hospital supervision controls the impulse to return to alcohol.

2. *Antabuse.* Antabuse is of help to alcoholics who want to change but are likely to give in to a temporary impulse to drink. As noted, the drug is of little use as the sole or predominant treatment technique.

3. *Aversion therapy.* Aversion therapy can be helpful in controlling specific problem behaviors unique to the client (Sandler, 1985).

4. *Biofeedback.* Just as obese individuals are usually unaware of how much and how fast they eat, alcoholics are often surprisingly less competent than normal drinkers in judging their blood alcohol levels. Biofeedback of blood alcohol level is useful in teaching the alcoholic to discriminate cues to the degree of intoxication (Lovibond and Caddy, 1970).

5. *Alcoholics Anonymous.* Involvement with AA or a similar group provides the advantages noted earlier, especially the opportunity for consistent associations with nondrinkers (Donovan, 1986; Mathew et al., 1979). But when the alcoholic has been coerced into treatment, AA is less effective than other techniques (Brandsma, 1979).

6. *Family and/or marital therapy* (see Chapter 16). Because alcoholism is extremely disruptive to family life, family and/or marital therapy to repair the damaged relationships is necessary (Jacob, 1986). Such therapy not only helps provide the supportive atmosphere essential to anyone recovering from an emotional disorder, but also helps reduce or eliminate any unconscious reinforcement of the alcoholism by the spouse or family (Donovan, 1986).

7. *Psychotherapy.* Alcoholics commonly experience conflicts, anxiety, and self-esteem problems. For these, a variety of psychotherapy techniques (such as rational-emotive therapy or traditional insight therapy) can be of help (Brown, 1985b; Brandsma, 1979). Brandsma found that persons receiving either type of treatment had higher recovery rates than those who received only standard care, although they tended to relapse at 12-month follow-up. Thus, long-term monitoring and therapy may be necessary even when alcoholics appear to have recovered. Because alcoholics are likely to give distorted reports of their alcohol intake, it is also important to obtain information about possible relapse from others such as family members (Gorski and Miller, 1986).

EXHIBIT

Preventing Relapse in the Alcoholic

Despite progress in understanding alcoholism, only a minority of treated alcoholics remain abstinent for as much as a year. Most "relapse"; that is, they resume drinking and are re-hospitalized.

Relapse prevention begins with the recognition that prolonged use of alcohol results in biological, psychological, sociological, and spiritual changes. At the beginning of the recovery process, biological factors have priority over other factors. Quite simply, the alcoholic's brain is damaged, does not work very well, and will not work well for about nine to 15 months of abstinence. Problems with memory, sleep, depression, concentration, irritability, and dealing with abstract information plague the alcoholic during the very time that he or she is trying to learn to live without alcohol. Stresses that alcohol insulated the person from, or that were dealt with by alcohol, often build up. Alcohol dilutes stress, just as it does guilt, but brings on worse distress later.

Gorski and Miller (1986) and Barrett (1986a) agree that the first year after a client enters treatment is critical. They focus much of their effort on this period, and all advise attendance at support groups such as AA. Gorski and Miller systematically teach clients about the "relapse process" and emphasize that resumption of drinking does not occur suddenly. This counters the myth that alcoholics are "suddenly taken by drink." They teach the "warning signs" of relapse that are unique to that person and prepare him or her for appropriate action when the warning signs appear. The use of fairly simple, repetitive procedures and slogans, for example, "One day at a time" and "You slip in slippery places" are particularly valuable to one suffering from neuropsychologic impairment.

Though the above methods can be helpful, treatment with alcoholics is often unsuccessful, especially if the alcoholic has not made a clear decision to change, and/or if the alcoholism has been severe and chronic. Indeed, Vaillant (1983), who worked with many such clients, using detoxification, inpatient treatment, compulsory AA attendance, and an active follow-up program, demonstrated results after two and eight years that were no better than the natural history of the disorder.

In light of many of the issues presented in this chapter, it should not be surprising that children of alcoholics show greater than average problems of adjustment, even into adulthood (Vaillant, 1983; Cadoret et al, 1985), such as:

1. They fear they are likely to become alcoholic. This fear is, of course, not entirely groundless. Although having had an alcoholic parent does not compel one into alcoholism, it does increase the probability.

2. If they have avoided alcoholism or antisocial patterns, they tend to (a) overreact to minor life changes, and have difficulty judging what

Barrett proposes also that it is necessary to "use a chemical to fight a chemical." Since the therapists' task is to have the client abstinent long enough for biological functions to return to normal, clients are required to come to the hospital for disulfiram (Antabuse) daily for one year. Unfortunately, many alcoholics strongly resist both medications and psychological treatments that interfere with their opportunity to use alcohol. Therefore, Barrett has devised a number of strategies to influence alcoholics to comply with his disulfiram based program, for example, having employees contract with their employers so that the latter are to be notified if the client does not show up for daily medication and therapy.

Central to these strategies is the recognition that above all else, alcoholics act to protect their opportunity to drink alcohol again if they choose to do so. Alcoholics assume that alcohol will be *needed* at some future time. So, there must be an exceptionally strong incentive for an alcoholic to allow any action that will interfere with this potential choice, both now and in the future, to drink. Few incentives can be present at every minute of the alcoholic's life to prevent a relapse event. However, disulfiram exerts a constant presence, and, in Barrett's view, achieving compliance with prescribed use of disulfiram has the highest priority in preventing relapse. With this component effectively in place, the other standard treatments are brought to bear on preventing a relapse. Of course relapse can occur after a year's abstinence, but the one year mark seems to be a breakpoint. Most alcoholics who make it past the one-year mark are well on the road to recovery, but it is a road they have to stay on the rest of their lives.

is "normal"—stemming from the unstable patterns they lived with as children and (b) become overstrict in judging themselves, continuing the natural tendency of children to blame themselves for whatever goes bad in their world.

Psychotherapy, especially group therapy with other people who have encountered these same problems, can be of help, but an even more important issue for all concerned is prevention.

Prevention

The difficulty of successfully treating alcoholism once the pattern has been established stresses the immense value of prevention. The following steps are recommended in any prevention effort.

1. If children are to be allowed to drink alcohol at all in later life, introduce it to them relatively early, and, of course, in moderation.

2. Associate the use of alcohol with food and initially allow its use only on special occasions; de-emphasize its value in controlling feeling states.

3. Provide a consistent model of low-to-moderate drinking, and use beverages such as beer and wine that have low alcohol content, rather than hard liquor.

4. Make sure there is a thorough understanding and agreement on what is and is not allowed about drinking.

5. Never associate drinking with the attainment of adulthood or other identity accomplishments.

6. Label excess drinking behavior as stupid and in bad taste rather than as stylish or "cool."

7. Label help-seeking behaviors in people who have an alcohol problem as evidence of strength rather then weakness.

8. Encourage alcoholism education programs and public health measures such as a restriction on the use of alcohol in certain settings and age groups.

POLYDRUG ABUSE

Mr. E.—Elvis Presley—exemplifies a pattern that is increasingly evident in our society, **polydrug abuse**. The pattern is not surprising, given society's general acceptance of multiple drug use (see the accompanying Exhibit and

The Case of Mr. E.

Mr. E. died from an apparent heart attack in August 1977. An autopsy confirmed a reported pattern of long-term polydrug abuse, which probably contributed significantly to the heart attack. Most of the drugs had been obtained by prescription. Mr. E.'s blood and tissues were found to contain toxic levels of the sedative methaqualone (Quaaludes), 10 times more codeine than would be needed for any therapeutic purpose, and residual amounts of at least 10 other drugs, including Valium, barbiturates, and various stimulants and opiates.

the list in the section on prescription drug abuse, below) and the emphasis in many teenage peer subcultures on recreational drug use (Mash and Terdah, 1988). This last factor is ironic, since Elvis was such a powerful role model for teenagers in the 1950s and early 1960s. Polydrug abusers may or may not include prescription drugs in their abuse patterns. Motivations and treatments are generally similar to those for alcoholism, except that the abusers are usually younger (most are adolescents) and more psychologically disturbed. Treatments are accordingly tailored to the client's age, degree of disturbance, and the specific features of the predominant drug involved.

EXHIBIT

Commonly Abused Drugs

The following list shows the volume of mood-changing drugs obtained either by prescription or illegally in the United States in one year, from May 1976 through April 1977. The data were gathered by the National Institute of Drug Abuse (NIDA) and the National Prescription Audit of NIDA (Bertinetti, 1980). The overall rate of drug usage is probably as high or even higher today, despite the increase or decrease in popularity of individual substances. Thus, although the rate of prescription abuse of amphetamines should now be lower as a result of greater federal and state controls, the number of users of cocaine, narcotics, and marijuana is probably higher.

Narcotics—552,000 users; 2,345,000 prescriptions/refills

Analgesics—34 million prescriptions/refills

Barbiturates and related sedatives—1,060,000 users; 19,416,000 prescriptions/refills

Minor tranquilizers—1,360,000 users; 98,495,000 prescriptions/refills

Major tranquilizers—11,936,000 prescriptions/refills

Inhalants—375,000 users

Amphetamines/stimulants—1,780,000 users; 5.5 million prescriptions/refills

Cocaine—1,640,000 users

Cannabis—16,210,000 users

Nicotine—64,570,000 users

Hallucinogens—7,140,000 users

The extent of caffeine use in the United States—the major ingredient in coffee, tea, most soft drinks, and many over-the-counter medications—is impossible to determine. Coffee consumption alone is estimated at 16 pounds per adult per year.

In the United States today, drug abuse and dependence, particularly of prescription drugs, though secondary to alcoholism in terms of numbers of abusers, is still a very problematic substance use disorder. The remainder of this chapter discusses prescription and nonprescription addiction and abuse.

PRESCRIPTION DRUG ABUSE

Our culture has a long history of intensive use of legally available drugs, many of which are available only by prescription. Before 1914, a significant proportion of the U.S. population was pharmacologically and psychologically dependent on legally obtainable patent medicines, often marketed in combination with alcohol, whose other main ingredients were opium compounds, morphine (a derivative of opium), heroin (a semisynthetic opiate), or barbiturates. The Harrison Drug Act of 1914 made most of these compounds illegal and unavailable, except by prescription.

Several factors have contributed to prescription drug abuse in the United States: (1) a cultural tradition that emphasizes large-scale use of drugs, (2) intensive promotion of drugs to physicians by drug companies, (3) the availability by prescription of many mood-altering drugs, and (4) strong cultural acceptance of the idea that most disorders can be remedied by a quick cure such as a pill (Blackwell, 1979; Wurmser, 1981). Another factor intensifying prescription drug abuse is the shift in physicians' behavior from a personal to a production-line approach, accompanied by use of the prescription as cure, placebo, pacifier, and end-of-session cue. This change undoubtedly increases the number of physician-patient contacts per day. Yet Mellinger et al. (1978) found that patients with ill-defined symptoms (about 70 percent of most family practitioners' clients) benefited just as much if their family physician gave them attention and discussion time and told them they were essentially well and needed no medication. In 1972 the average consultation time during an office visit with a physician was 17 minutes (Chowka, 1979); today it is even less.

Drug companies, physicians, and patients must all share the blame for prescription drug abuse and dependence. Blackwell (1979) notes that for many years more than two billion diazepam (Valium) tablets were prescribed annually in the United States (diazepam is only one drug in the benzodiazepine family). Evidence from a variety of sources (including Chowka, 1979; Bertinetti, 1980; and Helman, 1981) relates directly to this problem.

1. Every 24 to 36 hours, 50 to 70 percent of all adults in the United States take at least one medically prescribed drug.

2. More than 5,000 drugs are available by prescription (thus, the dependence of physicians on drug salespeople for information is understandable).

3. For the past 15 years, drug-industry profits (as a percentage of sales and net worth) have typically exceeded those of most other manufacturing industries on the nation's stock exchange.

4. At least 20 percent of all television advertising is for drugs (including alcohol and caffeine). Larger pharmaceutical firms budget 15 to 30 percent of their annual sales for advertising, almost 10 times what nondrug manufacturers normally spend.

5. The *Journal of the American Medical Association* has carried up to 5,000 pages of pharmaceutical advertising per year. Drug ads in the American Medical Association's journals typically provide at least 20 percent of the AMA's total annual revenue.

6. In 1973 the AMA invested almost 40 percent of its retirement fund in drug-related company stocks, and this trend has generally continued.

7. Drug companies have spent up to $3,000 a year in promotional funds on every U.S. physician to pay for free drugs and office equipment, sponsorship of seminars and vacation trips, "unbiased" educational cassettes and speakers, and office items.

The rest of this section details the abuse patterns for the most commonly prescribed drugs.

The Minor Tranquilizers

Diazepam (Valium) is the most commonly prescribed drug in the United States today. Like all **benzodiazepines,** it causes muscle relaxation and reduces anxiety. Typical side effects are skin rash, nausea, and impairment of sexual functioning. Meprobamate, developed in 1954, is functionally similar to the benzodiazepines but differs chemically and usually produces a more severe withdrawal after prolonged use. The traditional assumption was that many of the minor tranquilizers had little addiction potential. However, all of them easily generate psychological dependence (Helman, 1981; Julien, 1985).

Physicians who do not specialize in psychological problems may underestimate this potential (Wurmser, 1981). Yet these physicians issue more than 90 percent of the prescriptions for mood-altering drugs, the majority of them to women. The benzodiazepines are also often prescribed for alcoholics, to reduce the anxiety and upset of withdrawal. However, Schuckit and Morrissey (1979), in a study of a large sample of alcoholic women, found that one third abused the tranquilizers prescribed for their disorder.

There are three other risks involved in prescribing benzodiazepines for alcohol problems: (1) potential dependence on both the benzodiazepines and the alcohol; (2) the synergistic effect of benzodiazepines on alcohol—that is, the increased potency of each when abused together—which significantly increases the risk of death by overdose if they are abused together; and (3) the danger of psychotic reactions in people who have a blood sensitivity to benzodiazepines. This last risk indicates that therapists should perform a blood chemistry analysis before administering benzodiazepines.

Barbiturates

Barbiturates are another class of drugs that has consistently been abused. Though traditionally thought of as tranquilizers, barbiturates actually function as sedatives or hypnotics. The first barbiturate, Verinol, was introduced in 1903. Since then, barbiturates have been commonly used to induce sleep and to calm very agitated (not hyperactive) children.

Like the minor tranquilizers, barbiturates quickly produce dependency. They also produce a withdrawal syndrome similar to alcohol, but often more intense. They are commonly implicated in drug overdose; a lethal dose is usually only 10 times the dose to which the user has developed tolerance. Physicians have become more aware of the dangers of barbiturates, and drug companies are promoting other (newer and more expensive) compounds. Consequently, the legal use of barbiturates has declined in the past 10 years. Nevertheless, barbiturate abuse is common today among 35- to 55-year-olds, and is becoming increasingly popular among teenagers.

Amphetamines

Another commonly used group of prescribed medications is the **amphetamines.** Though first synthesized in 1887, amphetamines did not come into wide use until Benzedrine inhalers for nasal congestion were marketed in 1931 (Morgan, 1981). For many decades before that, an isolated alkaloid derived from a desert shrub, ephedrine, had been used for asthma relief and as a stimulant. As Weil (1972) has noted, once a drug is isolated and synthesized, it is particularly likely to be abused.

During World War II, amphetamines were used to combat fatigue in American servicemen, and the Japanese used them to help kamikaze pilots complete their suicide missions. Amphetamines were also heavily used in Japan for a short period after the war. During that nation's massive social and economic reconstruction, ads for amphetamines contained slogans such as "Get rid of slumber and be full of energy." As social reconstruction neared completion, popular opinion turned against excessive use of amphetamines, and the problem diminished (Tseng and Hsu, 1980). Somewhat paradoxically, amphetamines have commonly been used to treat hyperactive children. Their stimulant effect is believed to cause arousal in brain centers that normally appear to inhibit excessive behavior. Students, truckers, and athletes often resort to amphetamines to fight fatigue.

Amphetamines produce euphoria in some people, irritability and anxiety in others. An initial prescription for diet control is often the first step to dependence. Those who develop an abuse pattern combine these relatively normal starting patterns (such as a diet aid or a source of extra energy) with an abnormal need for stimulation seeking or an inability to cope with underlying feelings of depression and inadequacy. Symbolically, the person is saying, "I'm strong, but vulnerable" (Quay, 1965; Zuckerman et al., 1980; Wurmser, 1981). Because tolerance to and psychological dependence on amphetamines increase rather rapidly, persons abusing them quickly increase their intake (Morgan, 1981). Continuation of this pattern may lead to a binge, followed by a crash, when fatigue catches up and the person needs to sleep for the better part of several days. Continuation of this "speeding" causes paranoid and psychotic symptoms that may continue for some time after the drug is discontinued.

The methamphetamines, more potent versions of the amphetamines, are even more dangerous (Morgan, 1981). Because they are relatively inexpensive and easy to obtain, they are commonly included in street-source drugs, particularly street LSD.

Treatment of amphetamine abuse usually involves tricyclic antidepressants (see Chapter 9), administered for one to three weeks to ward off a crash from stopping the use of stimulants too abruptly (Morgan, 1981). This therapy may be continued in order to alleviate the client's underlying depression; however, the psychological treatments for depression are preferable to replacing one form of chemical dependence with another. Certain stimulant abusers may need to be directed into more appropriate methods for coping with obesity and/or a need for extra stimulation (see Chapter 12).

NONPRESCRIPTION DRUG ABUSE

Cocaine

Coca leaves, from which the alkaloid **cocaine** is derived, were chewed by the Aztecs and are still used by at least four million Indians in Peru and Bolivia. Cocaine, the fad drug of recent years and seemingly a favorite drug of abuse for sports and media personalities, first attained importance in 1860 when Gaedecke and Niemian discovered its effectiveness in alleviating pain. Cocaine is a stimulant, and in some people it provides a sense of euphoria (Washton, 1987; Spotts and Shontz, 1984).

Such diverse notables as Sigmund Freud, John Philip Sousa, and Conan Doyle's character Sherlock Holmes have sung the praises of cocaine. In the late 1800s, John Pemberton, an Atlanta druggist, combined cocaine, sugar, and kola nut extract to produce Coca-Cola, so the shortened trademark Coke is not inaccurate, and indeed it was at one time "the real thing." Though early ads called it "the ideal brain tonic," the Pure Food and Drug Law of 1906 forbade the use of cocaine, so caffeine is now the drink's main stimulant ingredient.

The Case of Cassie

Cassie excelled in school, from grade school through the M.B.A. she earned at age 22. She had never been in any significant trouble as she grew up, though, as her parents put it, "she studied hard, played hard, and partied hard." She was competent in most sports, and excelled in several. She was captain of her high school and college tennis teams, and for a couple of years after college was ranked as high as fourth as an amateur in the large Southeastern state she was born and raised in. In an interview her college coach said "she wins because she is pretty quick, works like a dog, and is a vicious competitor."

After she received her M.B.A., she accepted a position with an investment firm in Atlanta. She was a hard worker, and most people in the firm thought she did a good job. She liked to party with her fellow workers, and started using cocaine once or twice a month with them. Cassie had smoked about 1/2 a pack of cigarettes a day since she was a senior in high school, and occasionally smoked marijuana. Cassie had little trouble controlling her use of cocaine for about two years. But she began to feel increasingly frustrated at what she saw as a lack of progress in her career. Two people who came into the management training program with Cassie were promoted. Though several others at the same level with Cassie were not promoted, Cassie was upset. She began working even longer hours, and now started to use cocaine as an escape from work pressures, and as an antidepressant. Then the boyfriend she had been going with for the past couple of years broke up with her. He told her she was "just too intense" for him. Cassie was now using cocaine once every two or three days, was still getting more depressed, and was having sleep problems. Not surprisingly, the quality and quantity of her work went down. Her supervisor suspected a cocaine abuse problem, probably because of reports from her co-workers. She was referred to a drug abuse counselor, and for six months or so seemed to have the problem licked. Unfortunately, Cassie made the mistake of thinking she could again occasionally use cocaine. It was almost as if she wanted to prove she could gain control over it. She failed. The firm did not give her another chance. After being fired, Cassie began using cocaine daily. She became very depressed, and either accidentally or purposely walked in front of a car and was killed. Cassie fits many of the characteristics of the typical cocaine abuser noted in this book. Unfortunately, she didn't put the effort and persistence into the first treatment attempt that she put into sports and work.

Refined cocaine is sniffed in small amounts or taken orally with heroin or morphine (a "speedball"). Most of what passes for cocaine is not pure ("free base") cocaine but cocaine hydrochloride, a salt that is approximately 85 percent cocaine by weight. Pure cocaine is sometimes smoked, a far more dangerous psychophysiological process than sniffing.

Cocaine was a favored drug until the 1930s, when the cheaper and longer-lasting amphetamines became available. Recognition of the negative side effects of amphetamine use and of cocaine's low tolerance and withdrawal characteristics have brought cocaine back to a high usage level. The use of purer forms of cocaine is still somewhat restricted by the expense. Comedian Richard Pryor expressed it this way; "Cocaine is God's way of telling you that you make too much money." Yet the data from the 1985 President's Commission on Organized Crime and the National Institute on Drug Abuse indicates that in the U.S. (1) 20 to 24 million people have tried some form of cocaine, (2) about 30 percent of all college students will have tried cocaine by their senior year, and (3) there are about five million regular users of cocaine (i.e., using it once a month or more).

It's debatable whether or not cocaine is classically addicting (requires more and more of the drug to get an effect, and withdrawal generates definite physiologic symptoms). However, it is clear that cocaine is highly habituating in that it creates a tenacious dependence (Washton, 1987), marked by (1) compulsive use, (2) loss of control over its use, and (3) continued use despite its destructive consequences. It is also dangerous, and not only when it is free-based, as Richard Pryor discovered when he was close to dying from an explosion that occurred while refining (or free-basing) cocaine. Bozarth and Wise (1985) implanted tubes in the necks of 23 rats so that each rat could press a lever in its cage to self-administer a set dose of either heroin or cocaine into its bloodstream. The rats were divided into two groups, one for each drug. After 30 days, 11 of the 12 cocaine-using rats were dead, a mortality rate of more than 90 percent, compared with only four of the 11 heroin-using rats, a 36 percent rate. Overall, cocaine-using rats lost more weight and suffered a more marked decline in health. In humans, long-term use can result in numerous debilitating physical side effects, including cardiac problems and even death (Washton, 1987).

For cocaine users, the most important effect of the drug is the euphoria created by disruption of communication between brain cells, which interact by means of chemical messengers called neurotransmitters.

After a brain cell receives a chemical message, it sends the neurotransmitter back so that it can be used again. Most investigators now think that cocaine both stimulates the synthesis of neurotransmitters—particularly one called dopamine—and blocks their return.

Dopamine and other neurotransmitters then accumulate in abnormally high quantities at the receiving cells, overstimulating them. This flooding is thought to produce the euphoria associated with cocaine use.

At the turn of this century, cocaine was the ingredient in Coca-Cola that put "vim and go into tired brain and bodies." By the 1980s, cocaine's resurgence in popularity claimed the lives and careers of users such as Len Bias, who died of an overdose while celebrating his draft into the NBA champion Boston Celtics team.   (left: Historical Picture Service; below: UPI/Bettmann Newsphotos)

Because of the overproduction of neurotransmitters, however, the brain eventually runs out of the chemicals from which they are made. Cocaine users then become depressed and develop a strong craving for the drug. If they get high again, the depletion of neurotransmitters is redoubled, and the craving and depression are worse the next time the user comes down.

Spotts and Shontz (1984) did an in-depth analysis of middle-class male cocaine users, age 21 to 44, using extensive interviews and a variety of psychological tests. They concluded that consistent users in this subgroup, when they are not simply peer-stimulated users (going along with the group, as a party experience), were intense, achievement-oriented persons, who maintain acquaintanceships and family relationships but strongly avoid intimacy and vulnerability in relationships. They are often struggling against underlying feelings of depression and use the drug as a "booster" in competition to achieve.

To be effective, psychotherapy needs to focus on the cocaine user's avoidance of dependency and unresolved spiritual and intimacy-betrayal crises, and needs to take into account their feelings of both intense anger and despairing depression. Also, certain medications, such as imipramine, typically employed as an antidepressant, can be useful in lowering the reinforcing properties of cocaine, as it binds to the same site in the brain that cocaine does. Once some progress is attained here, a group therapy modeled on AA principles can be of use (Ehrlich and McGeehan, 1985).

Marijuana and Derivatives

The Chinese emperor Shen Nung wrote the first pharmacological text, called *Psen Tsao,* or the The Great Herbalist, in 2737 B.C. In it, he described an extract of hemp as the "delight giver." The plant it was extracted from, *Cannabis sativa,* is more commonly known as **marijuana** and has been an important part of American culture since the 1960s.

Marijuana is usually smoked, during which only 50 percent of the active component, tetrahydrocannabinol (THC), is inhaled. In high dosages, THC closely mimics the hallucinogenic properties of LSD. Hashish, a concentrated derivative of marijuana, is produced by compacting the crude resin of the cannabis plant into a brick. Marijuana deteriorates rapidly in potency and must be refrigerated to retard this process. Yet even when its real potency is minimal, marijuana has a strong culturally induced placebo effect (Julien, 1985).

Recently there has been a steep rise in the potency of the marijuana available to the American public; it is now about five times as potent as that available to most buyers in the mid 1970s. As a result, its effects are considerably greater for naive subjects, and a higher dependency may occur than in the past (Orford, 1985). Surveys show that at least 80 percent of college students in 1981 had smoked marijuana, compared with 55 percent in 1974, 32 percent in 1969, and five percent in early 1967. The only reverse trend is that many students appear to be giving up marijuana to return to alcohol.

Marijuana derivatives in the blood are metabolized in the liver in much the same way as alcohol. The main physiologic effects are lowered blood pressure, reddened flesh around the eye, and dry mouth. Standard dosages produce minor changes in brain physiology, and there is less impairment of muscle control than is experienced with alcohol in comparable dosages.

The psychological effects in experienced users are sleepiness and mild euphoria, usually lasting one to three hours, and an increase in suggestibility. There is little evidence that psychological disorder occurs directly as a result of moderate marijuana use. Marijuana and its derivatives have been used effectively to control glaucoma and to lessen pain in cancer patients.

Opiates

According to archaeologists and historians, the first users of the opium poppy were primitive Neolithic farmers in the mountainous areas of western Asia Minor. Clay tablets from the Sumerian civilization, over 6,000 years old, refer

EXHIBIT

Commonly Abused Drug Types and Their Effects

Drug	Usual effects	Effects of acute abuse (overdose)	Effects of chronic abuse
STIMULANTS			
Amphetamines *Cocaine* *Caffeine* *Nicotine*	Increased motor behaviors; sense of agitation or euphoria; greater alertness; increased blood pressure, pulse rate, and sweating	Agitation; imsomnia; increased pulse, blood pressure, sweating; possible cardiac arrhythmias; speeded-up and rambling thoughts (with cocaine and amphetamines, probable paranoia, possible hallucinations, and even death if severe overdose)	Numerous physical side effects, e.g., cardiac and lung disorders with nicotine; restlessness and agitation; paranoid responses likely; cyclic anxiety and depression; increased tolerance and physical dependence; physical withdrawal primarily with caffeine and nicotine
DEPRESSANTS			
Alcohol	Reduction of tension; loss of inhibitions; increasing loss of coordination; slowing of motor behavior; and cognitive confusion	Cognitive confusion, perceptual disorientation, and loss of motor coordination; at very high levels, stupor, unconsciousness, even death, especially in combination with certain other drugs	Definite psychological and physical dependence; probable liver and neurologic damage; social and emotional disruption
Tranquilizers *Barbiturates*	Reduction of tension; mild "high," in some cases; slowed reflexes and motor behaviors; sleepiness	Rapid and weak or erratic pulse; dilated pupils; sweating; chills; anxiety; possible coma and even death, especially when taken with alcohol	Physical dependence, especially with the barbiturates; high psychological dependency; possible kidney or liver disruption; withdrawal symptoms

to opium as the "plant of joy" (Bertinetti, 1980). The Roman physician Galen prescribed it for epilepsy, snake bite, melancholia, and virtually any other disorder he could think of. The **opiates** mimic the body's natural reaction to pain. When severe physical trauma occurs, cells in the hypothalamus and pituitary gland release peptide hormones called endorphins, which attach themselves to the surfaces of the cells responsible for the pain and, like opium, suppress the perception of pain (Simon, 1981).

Three events spurred the use of opiates in western European culture. The first was the isolation of morphine early in the nineteenth century, fol-

Drug	Usual effects	Effects of chronic abuse	Effects of acute abuse (overdose)
NARCOTICS *Heroin* *Morphine* *Opium* *Demerol* *Dilaudid*	Pleasant sense of tension reduction, warmth, and detachment; sleepiness; slowed physical responses	Nausea; sweating; anxiety; "pinpoint pupil" response; if severe, coma and/or convulsion, even death	Extreme psychological and physical dependence; rapidly developed tolerance; variable physical withdrawal symptoms
MARIJUANA	Mild or no symptoms in some naive subjects; usually euphoria, sleepiness (occasionally anxious agitation), and reduction of inhibitions; increased appetite; some cognitive confusion and motor and perceptual disorientation	Significant cognitive confusion and perceptual and motor disorientation; sleepiness and torpor (feeling as if one can move only slowly, if one even wants to)	Mild physical dependence and moderate to high psychological dependence; apathy; nasal and lung problems if smoked
HALLUCINOGENS *LSD* *PCP* *Natural hallucinogens such as peyote*	Perceptual and time distortions; hallucinations; delusions and disruptions in reality contact in some individuals	Vivid hallucinations with LSD and natural hallucinogens; manic responses with PCP (significant anxiety and/or paranoia in some individuals)	Moderate psychological dependence; little physiological dependence with LSD, moderate with PCP

lowed about 50 years later by Alexander Wood's perfection of a more efficient method of administering drugs—the hypodermic needle. Morphine, which is 10 times stronger than opium, quickly became popular as a painkiller (Bertinetti, 1980) and was included in many patent medicines. The third event, near the end of the nineteenth century, was Wright's discovery of **heroin,** a semisynthetic opiate. Heroin was once widely used to cure morphine addiction, just as another addicting drug, methadone, is now used to treat heroin addiction.

Heroin is a narcotic. It induces a warm, almost sensual euphoria, usually followed by lethargy and sleepiness. The user rapidly develops tolerance and needs higher doses. Some seven to 12 hours after the injection, however, withdrawal symptoms begin. The severity of these symptoms increase in proportion to the amount of heroin used, but they are rarely as severe as the mad ravings portrayed in the media. Most addicts describe withdrawal as similar to flu symptoms.

Heroin abuse appeared to decline in the 1970s, but two factors have caused a resurgence: the increasing use of heroin by people of middle and upper socioeconomic status, and the greater availability of extraordinarily pure heroin (primarily from Iran, Pakistan, and Afghanistan)—up to 90 percent pure, compared with earlier varieties containing as little as four percent.

There is little valid evidence of severe psychological damage from a low to moderate level of consistent heroin use. Chronic heroin abusers show less emotional disturbance than chronic abusers of amphetamines or barbiturates (Penk et al., 1981). Cultural attitudes are important in producing this emotional disturbance. In Laos, where opium is a cash crop, an opium abuser is subject to only limited social hostility. Most abusers continue to function (though not optimally) within their family and society and seldom show criminal patterns (Tseng and Hsu, 1980). However, there is evidence that children born to narcotic-addicted mothers show much higher rates of both psychological and physical disorder, from birth onward (Householder et al., 1982).

Etiology.   As with drug abuse, denial and avoidance of conflict are central to abuse of opiates (Wurmser, 1981), and modeling from significant peers is a crucial factor (Huba et al., 1979). In general, the same personality factors that contribute to alcoholism also promote heroin addiction; sociological factors subsequently determine the path a particular individual takes. Yet the fact that there are specific opiate receptors in the brains of all vertebrates, from hagfish to humans, suggests that evolution has provided a built-in reinforcement pattern (Simon, 1981). As for the psychological reinforcement provided by opiates, perhaps the French humanist and poet Jean Cocteau expressed it most graphically:

> Everything we do in life, including love, is done in an express train traveling towards death. To smoke opium is to leave the train while in motion; it is to be interested in something other than life and death [Jarvik, 1967, p. 52].

Treatment.   As with alcoholism, treatment of heroin addiction has never been markedly successful for several reasons. Addicts enjoy the effects. Few have much prospect of finding a satisfactory replacement for heroin, and many know only a lifestyle shaped by the addict subculture (Wurmser, 1981; Zucker, 1986). Moreover, the wide variety of therapies available have had only limited success. Many feel that the best chance of success for dealing with drug addicts in general,, and with heroin addicts specifically, lies with group confrontation techniques, first used in the therapeutic communities.

Opiates such as opium and heroin continue to be widely used due to their ability to induce feelings of euphoria and well-being.   (Ian Berry/Magnum)

Therapeutic communities. Synanon, Daytop Village, Odyssey House, and Phoenix House are some of the more well-known therapeutic communities, most of which are run by ex-addicts. Synanon was begun in a run-down Santa Monica storefront in 1958 by Charles Dederich and several colleagues. Early hopes for its success soon dissipated as word got out that Synanon was evolving into an authoritarian regime (Deitch and Zweben, 1981).

Most addict-led drug treatment groups have resisted including professionally trained staff, even in the planning and evaluation of programs. This policy is somewhat misguided, for although the communities have a rich asset in the ex-addict staff's experience with drugs, they lack objectivity, awareness of a wide range of treatment techniques, and general sophistication in the various forms of psychopathology.

Despite these problems, such groups have successfully treated a significant number of addicts. They are effective both in breaking down the addict's common delusion of not really being addicted and in providing a peer system that can help initiate more positive behaviors and prevent backsliding into addiction. Outpatient groups such as Narcotics Antagonists (similar to AA) can be helpful as the person moves back into normal society.

Like Alcoholics Anonymous, most of the therapeutic communities claim high cure rates, though methodologically sound data are again hard to get (Deitch and Zweben, 1981). Dropout rates are usually high (up to 50 percent and higher, compared with 20 percent for methadone programs).

Methadone. Methadone is a synthetic narcotic that first received significant use around 1965. Since the 1970s it has been the primary agent in federal programs aimed at treating heroin addiction (Lowinson, 1981). Although methadone also is addicting, it has the following advantages over heroin. It can be taken orally. It is legal and cheap. It lasts about 24 hours, so it can be taken once a day (compared with two to three times a day for heroin). And it rarely produces the euphoria associated with heroin and the synthetic narcotics, such as Demerol.

Three criticisms of methadone are fully justified: (1) chronic use produces substantial negative side effects; (2) it is often traded on the black market to other addicts; (3) methadone treatments are simply substitutions of one addiction for another. Nevertheless, methadone does help wean a significant proportion of addicts off drugs altogether, and few treatments now used for drug addiction can make a better claim. Programs using newer drugs, such as naltrexone (O'Brien and Greenstein, 1981), offer some promise of decreasing drug dependence without creating a secondary addiction.

Hallucinogens

LSD (lysergic acid diethylamide), mescaline, and psilocybin are popular psychotomimetic drugs. As **hallucinogens** they cause hallucinations and delusions of varying intensity. Mescaline, the active alkaloid of the peyote cactus, has long been used by Southwestern and Mexican Indians in ceremonial rites. Psilocybin comes in a crystalline powder and is isolated from various mushrooms that grow in the United States (Julien, 1985). LSD was synthesized by the Swiss chemist Albert Hoffman in 1938. It was first used in the United States in the early 1950s and was popularized by cultural "gurus" such as ex-Harvard psychologist Timothy Leary.

Hoffman discovered the hallucinogenic properties of LSD accidentally when he ingested a small amount in 1943 and went into a "delirium" in which "an uninterrupted stream of fantastic pictures of extraordinary plasticity with intense kaleidoscope like play of colors surged in on me" (Hoffman, 1979, p. 58). LSD is the most potent of the three hallucinogens. The usual dose of about 250 micrograms is comparable to a dose of about 400,000 micrograms of mescaline or 30,000 micrograms of psilocybin. The direct effects of psilocybin usually last about six hours, those of LSD and mescaline about 10 hours. The natural source of LSD is ergot (used to treat migraine), a purple fungus that infects rye plants. It is possible that some of the mass hysterias of past centuries occurred as a result of eating bread made with infected grain (see Chapter 1). Other cultures have used LSD-like substances in a more positive manner. Ahahuasca, a vine containing an LSD-like substance, is central to an effective psychotherapy ritual in Inquitos, a city on the Amazon in northeastern Peru (Prince, 1980).

In the United States, experiments have been conducted to see if LSD has any beneficial effect on mental patients, prisoners, and cancer patients, three groups that have a weak political constituency to protect them from such experimentation. Certain individuals have had positive "enlightenment" experiences that helped them, but for the most part no special benefits were found.

Many people taking these and other drugs have had "bad trips" and, later, "flashbacks" when they were no longer on the drug. The bad trips are not surprising, given the odd assortment of ingredients found in purportedly pure street drugs and the marginal adjustment of many individuals when taking the drug. Although flashbacks are usually attributed to the drug itself, they are more accurately conceptualized and effectively treated as severe anxiety responses (see Chapter 6). The anxiety comes from the loss of control experienced under the drug and is then cognitively conditioned to thoughts first stimulated by the actual drug experience.

An interesting variation on the therapeutic use of hallucinogenics was developed by Walter Pahnke and Stanislav Grof (Pahnke, 1963; Grof, 1986). In one study, 20 theology students were given psilocybin and 20 an active placebo (nicotinic acid, which produces some similar initial effects, such as tingling of the skin), followed by an elaborate two and one-half hour religious service, on Good Friday no less. The spiritual and religious experiences were reported by the psilocybin group to be much deeper. Later, a group of mental health professionals were administered a strong dose of LSD in a controlled setting (selected music piped in through earphones, blindfolds to restrict visual stimulation, etc.). In the first sessions, people reported "sound and light shows" (vivid perceptual phenomena) followed by very strong personal images, for example, of a visual tie between one's child and one's parents and grandparents, and then into symbolic images (misty forests) of one's ancestors. However, in most who went through a second session, the images became extremely abstract. One participant drew several of his images from his LSD session, only later to find out that they were almost exact replicas of ancient Sanskrit religious symbols that he had never seen before.

A psychotomimetic drug that also has some stimulant qualities similar to the amphetamines is phencyclidine hydrochloride, known by the street names PCP and "angel dust." PCP was first compounded and used legally as an animal tranquilizer and then, in the 1950s, as a surgical anesthetic for humans. It produced such bizarre side effects that its use with humans was stopped immediately. Rather than the visual hallucinations common to LSD or the paranoid and schizophrenic symptoms common to amphetamine abuse, PCP often produces either a psychotic manic pattern or psychotic behavior that resembles standard schizophrenic symptoms (Luisada, 1981). Unfortunately, it is easily compounded in large quantities in relatively unsophisticated laboratories, and is being increasingly abused by adolescents.

Various other herbs and weeds can also cause hallucinations, but many of these, such as juniper berries (a major ingredient in gin), are quite toxic. Even high dosages of nutmeg can cause hallucinations, but it also is toxic.

For centuries the common weed *Datura stramonium,* also known as jimson-weed or thorn apple, has been chewed for its hallucinogenic properties. In the 1970s, Don Juan (the Mexican Indian guru to writer Carlos Castaneda, not the lover) made the drug famous. Recently, some adolescents have taken to chewing the seeds of the plant, a practice that is sometimes fatal.

Inhalants

Inhalants are often abused by adolescents because of their wide availability and because few adolescents are aware of the dangerous effects. The abused inhalants include: (1) anesthetics such as nitrous oxide (laughing gas), chloroform, and ether; (2) aerosol propellants (less commonly available now); and (3) volatile solvents such a glue, gasoline, and paint remover. The ready accessibility of glue and paint remover makes them particularly likely to be abused. The "high" produced by inhalants is of short duration, and chronic use carries a real risk of organic brain dysfunction.

Caffeine

Caffeinism is a good example of a substance dependency that is so widespread that it has seldom been classified as a disorder. However, the DSM specifically lists caffeine and tobacco abuse as disorders. Coffee, tea, most soft drinks (particularly cola drinks), and many common nonprescription drugs (such as aspirin compounds) provide a substantial dose of caffeine. Chocolate contains a related stimulant. At one time, certain Muslim sects that normally abstained from coffee had religious ceremonies that combined strong coffee and chanting to produce hallucinations and altered states of consciousness (Weil, 1972).

Many people have developed such a tolerance for caffeine that they are hardly aware of the common side effects, which include anxiety, irritability, gatrointestinal problems, and cardiac complications. When these side effects occur, they are commonly attributed to other causes, such as stress. In a double-blind experimental design, Veleber and Templer (1984) administered 150 mg, 300 mg, and 0 mg of caffeine to normal persons recruited by a newspaper ad. Caffeine was found to increase anxiety, as well as depression and hostility; the higher the dose, the greater the effect.

Nicotine

Nicotine, the principal active component of tobacco leaves, acts as a stimulant on persons who use it rarely. It raises the heart rate and increases the blood pressure by simultaneously inducing greater cardiac activity and constricting peripheral arteries. It reduces the appetite, especially for carbohydrates, such as sugar and simple starches, a fact that must be considered if gaining weight upon stopping smoking is to be avoided. Nicotine is also an effective pesticide (Bertinetti, 1980).

RESEARCH PROFILE

Smoking Intervention with Nursing Professionals, and Relapse

As the text notes, intervention efforts to help people stop smoking have not met with great success. However, a study by Scott et al. (1986) showed that (1) certain treatments can be effective and (2) any relapse quickly puts success in jeopardy. Scott and her colleagues put 19 nurses into a treatment group and 10 into a waiting-list control group. The latter group was told they would receive treatment later, but were studied along with the 19 going through treatment.

A novel, minimally intrusive treatment was used. Rather than asking the treated nurses to come to a clinic, a therapist visited them daily on their work unit to discuss problems and monitor progress. Those treated were provided a self-help manual that had them gradually cut down, or "fade," on the amount of nicotine, until a prescribed "quit day." Carbon dioxide (CO_2) levels in the blood, a direct reflection of the amount of smoking, were measured each day, and a graph of these measures was prominently posted on the wall of the nurse's work station. CO_2 levels were measured for two consecutive days after "quit day," three months later, and then at random unannounced times after that.

Twelve of the 16 subjects were abstinent for at least two days, and nine of those 12 were abstinent at three months, a rate as high or higher than many other studies that employed more extensive, intrusive, and/or expensive therapies. As with most such studies, there were further relapses, but approximately one third of the nurses continued to abstain.

Of particular interest is the fact that a single relapse led to a resumption of smoking 50 percent of the time, and 100 percent of those who relapsed twice eventually resumed smoking. Yet, symptoms of withdrawal were not mentioned as the primary cause of any of the relapses. These first relapses typically occurred at home (never at work where the treatment took place), during the evening, and usually in the presence of others where food, alcohol, and cigarettes were available. This suggests that habit (maintained by psychological factors) was crucial in promoting the initial relapses, but that the powerfully addicting factors (physiologic) then kicked in to generate a resumption of the smoking pattern.

The Case of Dr. S.

As a result of a severe flu attack at age 38, Dr. S. experienced an irregular heartbeat. His personal physician and colleague, Dr. F., told him that his habit of smoking cigars had caused it and advised him to stop smoking. When Dr. S. tried to do so, he became depressed and occasionally suffered an even worse pulse rate. After several attempts at stopping, he returned to smoking about 20 cigars a day and developed cancer of the jaw at age 67. Despite 33 operations and the removal of his entire jaw because of various cancerous and precancerous conditions, Dr. S. continued to smoke. At age 73 he developed angina pectoris (chest pains from heart disease), which was relieved whenever he stopped smoking. Yet although he continued to try to stop smoking, he could not. He died from cancer age age 83 after many years of severe suffering from operations, cancer, and heart disorder (Rodale, 1979).

Interestingly, Dr. S. did not experience any of the classic physical withdrawal symptoms when he stopped smoking. Nevertheless, his case is a good example of the psychological and physical habituating power of **nicotine,** especially considering who Dr. S. is: Sigmund Freud.

Approximately 20 percent of the U.S. population smokes with some regularity, and, as Sigmund Freud's case shows, nicotine is powerfully habituating. Statistically, two-pack-a-day smokers can expect to live about six years fewer than their nonsmoking peers, smokers in general are about 50 percent more likely than nonsmokers to require health care each year, and the smoke they disperse can be harmful to those around them. Historically, efforts to deter people from smoking, such as warnings from the Surgeon General's office, have had only limited effects, and those who do quit are extremely prone to relapse (Shiffman, 1984). In the seventeenth century, even Turkish sultan Murad IV's campaign of torturing and executing those addicted to tobacco was scarcely more effective, nor was a 1683 Chinese law that authorized beheading simply for possessing tobacco.

Etiology. Six major factors are usually considered to be crucial in initiating and maintaining tobacco addiction: (1) modeling and ease of access to tobacco, promoted by significant peers, authority figures, and media idols; (2) peer pressure, especially for early adolescents; (3) physiologic addiction; (4) habit and ritual; (5) the paradoxical tranquilizing effect of nicotine on the

Thanks in large part to widespread public smoking bans, many smokers have begun painful efforts to break their habits. (John Chiasson/Gamma-Liaison)

chronic smoker (pharmacologically, it is a stimulant); and (6) the fulfillment of personality needs (such as oral eroticism) (Schachter et al., 1977; Evans et al., 1981; Mills and Noyes, 1984; Bridgeman, 1988).

Treatment. Numerous researchers have examined ways to help individuals control their smoking (Hall et al., 1985; Sandler, 1985; Evans et al., 1981). Therapists have used scare tactics, such as showing films of people dying of lung cancer; applied shocks to clients when they smoke; and had clients smoke as fast as possible in a closed space to induce nausea. Behavioral rehearsal of positive nonsmoking habits, psychotherapy, group therapy, hypnosis, and a melange of other techniques have been tried.

Most of these efforts have had some limited success; none has shown complete success. In many cases, individuals are able to control their smoking significantly during the treatment phase, only to remit gradually afterward. The relapse rate is very high (Shiffman, 1984). Quitting all at once is the best strategy for most smokers, and gradual weaning from the chemical addiction to the nicotine itself, such as using nicotine gum, seems to help some heavy smokers (Hall et al., 1985). Continued success also requires that the significant persons around the smoker be supportive of a change to nonsmoking (Murray et al., 1984). Friends and family (particularly if they are also smokers) often give lip service to the smoker's pledge to quit, only to subvert—consciously or unconsciously—the person's efforts. As with many other substance abuse patterns, prevention is more efficient and effective than cure (Heath, 1986).

Evans and several colleagues (1981) reasoned that, because smoking frequently begins as a result of social influences, it might be possible to use still other social influences effectively to reduce or eliminate the behavior. Consequently, they devised a program that would train adolescents to recognize and cope with social pressures to smoke. This program employed cognitive inoculation, which strengthens an individual's existing attitudes by helping him or her anticipate and learn to deal with possible counterarguments.

The study involved female and male seventh graders in 13 schools in a large metropolitan area who were followed for three years. Evans et al. employed several experimental and control groups. Subjects in the experimental groups were exposed in varying degrees to films and posters with messages about either social pressuring that promoted smoking or the immediate consequences of smoking (such as analyses of nicotine and carbon monoxide blood levels, along with their attendant risks).

The results of the study supported the researchers' hypothesis that exposure to role models who successfully anticipate and deal with pressure to smoke has a significant influence on smoking behavior. Evans et al. found that by the end of the eighth and ninth grades, students in the experimental treatment groups smoked less frequently and intended to smoke less frequently than their counterparts in the control group.

The study by Evans et al., as well as that by Murray et al. (1984) and Mills and Noyes (1984), is important for at least two reasons. First, it reveals the extent to which the use of drugs, such as nicotine, appears to be under social control. Second, it illustrates the effectiveness of a social learning approach in modifying potentially health-threatening behaviors. Teaching adolescents to anticipate and deal effectively with pressure to smoke (or to use the other drugs discussed in this chapter) appeared quite successful compared with programs that merely emphasize the long-term negative consequences of smoking.

CHAPTER REVIEW

1. Our culture's general support of a high level of drug use facilitates a high level of abuse.

2. Substance abuse (defined in DSM as use for at least a month and life complications) becomes substance dependence if there is evidence of tolerance (needing more of the substance to get the same effect) or withdrawal (a specific set of symptoms upon reduction of dosage) and psychological dependence or pathological use.

3. In addition to the DSM categories (such as alcoholism and heroin abuse), both prescription and polydrug abuse patterns are common in our society.

4. Alcohol is a depressant, but because it acts first to suppress higher brain functions, it often results in a loss of inhibitions, which facilitates acting-out behavior. Some loss of inhibition is cognitively conditioned by the belief that one has consumed alcohol.

5. Like most other substance abuse patterns, alcoholism is a disorder with many possible causes. Genetic predisposition may be a factor in some cases, but social learning and psychological conflict variables (such as modeling, peer influences, cultural factors, avoidance of guilt, dependency, and depression) are usually the predominant causes. Thus, most alcoholics and abusers of other drugs require a multimodal treatment response, such as a program combining detoxification, AA, psychotherapy, Antabuse, and family therapy.

6. Although the abuse of barbiturates and diet-prescribed amphetamines has decreased somewhat in the past several years, abuse of

cocaine, the minor tranquilizers, marijuana, and phencyclidine has increased.

7. Tolerance to amphetamines builds rapidly, and increased usage can lead to psychotic-like behavior. Phencyclidine and LSD also easily produce psychotic-like behavior.

8. Cocaine, a stimulant, is a particularly favored drug of abuse in recent years. It is highly habituating, and in some ways is strongly addictive. The euphoria associated with cocaine use is probably a dopamine response.

9. Heroin appears especially suited to the abuser whose motivation is escape from conflict into passivity. Confrontation-style group therapy, methadone, and opiate antagonists are common treatment techniques.

10. Though legally available and commonly used, caffeine and tobacco produce strong patterns of physical and psychological dependence. As in all other substance abuse patterns, a strong decision to quit is an essential first step toward cure. Because societal attitudes play an especially important role in encouraging and supporting these habits, efforts at prevention are more efficient than those directed toward cure of a well-established pattern.

11. Although most people who use soft drugs (such as marijuana) do not necessarily go on to any significant use of hard drugs, those who do abuse hard drugs usually do so after a period of soft drug abuse.

TERMS TO REMEMBER

alcoholism
substance abuse
substance dependence
delerium tremens
Wernicke's syndrome
polydrug abuse

benzodiazepines
barbiturates
amphetamines
cocaine
marijuana
opiates

heroin
LSD (lysergic acid diethylamide)
hallucinogens
inhalants
caffeinism
nicotine

FOR MORE INFORMATION

Blane, H., and Leonard, K. (1987) *Psychological theories of drinking and alcoholism.* New York: Guilford. Probably the best available overview of theories not only as to why normal people drink, but also why some become addicted to alcohol

Gorski, T., and Miller, M. (1986) *Staying sober.* Independence, Mo: Independence Press. Avoids technical jargon, and offers solid, direct information on the abuser's other most difficult task, staying sober (the first is clearly deciding to quit, and doing it)

Julien, R. (1985) *A primer of drug action.* New York: W.H. Freeman. A readable and straightforward presentation of the physical effects of a wide range of drugs

Orford, J. (1985) *Excessive appetites: A psychological view of addiction.* New York: John Wiley. Does a fine job of relating commonly understood addiction patterns such as alcoholism and drug abuse to an addictive lifestyle orientation that can result in a dependency on people and things as well

Vaillant, G. (1983) *The natural history of alcoholism: Causes, patterns, and paths to recovery.* Cambridge, Mass.: Harvard University Press. The best available in-depth, longitudinal study of how alcoholism develops and persists in the lives of the individual cases that Vaillant has studied for many years

Washton, A. (1987) *Cocaine.* New York: Guilford. A highly readable exposition of all issues relating to a prominent addiction of modern times, cocaine

Weil, A. (1980) *The marriage of sun and moon.* Boston: Houghton Mifflin. Written in a less formal style, Weil's book provides an interesting philosophic and cross-cultural perspective on the issue of drug abuse

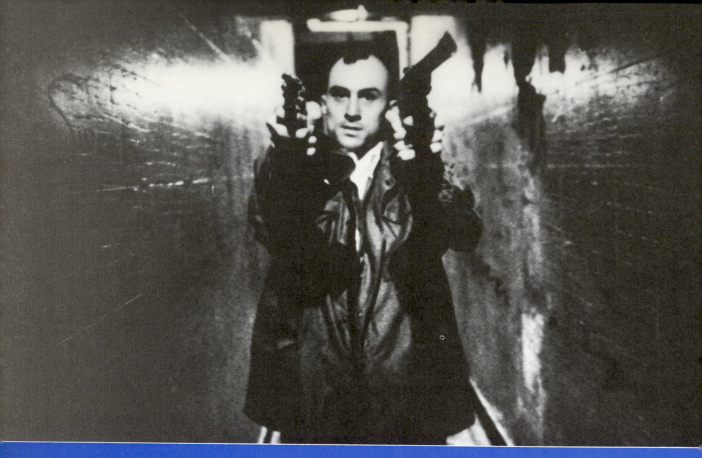

In *Taxi Driver*, Robert DeNiro plays an alienated loner who takes a night job as a New York City cabdriver. By the film's end, DeNiro becomes disgusted with society, shaves his head, arms himself with a small arsenal, and goes on a violent rampage through the city. (Museum of Modern Art/Film Stills Archive; © 1976 Columbia Pictures Industries Inc.)

THE PERSONALITY DISORDERS
Borderline Personality Disorder
Paranoid Personality Disorder
Schizotypal Personality Disorder
Schizoid Personality Disorder
Avoidant Personality Disorder
Passive-Aggressive Personality Disorder
Obsessive-Compulsive Personality Disorder
Narcissistic Personality Disorder
Histrionic Personality Disorder
Dependent Personality Disorder
Self-Defeating Personality Disorder
Antisocial Personality Disorder

THE CRIMINAL PERSONALITY VIOLENCE
The Explosive Disorder
Family Violence
Rape
Murder

DETERRING CRIME AND VIOLENCE THE IMPULSE DISORDERS
Pyromania
Kleptomania
Pathological Gambling
Trichotillomania
Overeating

12

Personality Disorders, Violence, and the Impulse Disorders

This chapter is about disorders that have a socially or interpersonally destructive component. They are long term, and are characterized by adequate reality contact. In most cases, individuals with these disorders do not label themselves as disordered, at least until they come under pressure from some external system such as marriage, family, job colleagues, or the criminal justice system (Levin, 1987). Quite a few of the individuals in these categories come in contact with the criminal justice system at some point in their lives, as we see in the case of Brad.

● The Case of Brad

Brad started off with two strikes against him. Born into poverty, he seldom saw his natural father, which was not surprising since his father spent quite a bit of time in the state prison and at other times kept busy with a variety of criminal and antisocial pursuits. Brad's mother tried to be a good parent, but was overwhelmed by the task, primarily because of her lack of financial resources and her sporadic alcoholic binges.

Brad had been difficult to control since infancy. However, it was unclear whether this resulted from a genetic or birth trauma, or simply reflected the poor parenting he had had from the start. He did poorly in school, mostly because he had difficulty keeping his attention focused for any length of time.

He started skipping school in the fifth grade and was chronically truant in high school. In his freshman year, he was arrested for viciously beating up a younger boy. He was apprehended in petty thefts numerous times in high school, accumulated a number of speeding and drunk driving offenses, and was suspected of molesting a young girl, though this latter charge was never proven.

Brad did graduate from high school, but more because of gift than gain. Shortly after he turned 19, he viciously assaulted a robbery victim who resisted. He was in prison for about a year and a half and committed virtually the same crime only a short time after his release. Despite many varied attempts at intervention from childhood on, Brad never changed in any significant way, and he spent most of his adult years in prison.

Brad's case highlights several of the disorders that could be described with the sociolegal label, "criminal personality." This chapter will examine the behavior of individuals, such as Brad, who are psychologically disturbed but who do not show a primary affective disorder, severe intrapsychic anxiety, or cognitive disorder. We will look at the personality disorders, the criminal personality and the related issue of violence, and the impulse disorders. Brad is a good example of one of the most common and socially destructive personality disorders, the antisocial personality disorder.

THE PERSONALITY DISORDERS

Personality disorders do not reach the psychotic proportions that the schizophrenic, paranoid, and affective disorders often do, nor do people with personality disorders perceive their behavior as disordered or unusual. They seldom become aware of their pattern unless forced to do so by others, such as a spouse or legal authorities (Clarke-Stewart, 1988). Yet whether it is theorized that such disorders occur because there are enduring genetically based personality "traits," or because the behavior has been so thoroughly reinforced that it becomes a consistent pattern, personality disorders are among the most frequently occurring patterns seen in clinical practice (Gardner, 1965; Millon, 1981).

Though not as bizarre as other disorders, personality disorders are severely maladaptive, because (1) the psychopathology is pervasive and thoroughly integrated in the personality, (2) the patterns are chronic, (3) parents with personality disorders tend to create significant psychopathology in their children, and (4) personality disorders are very difficult to treat (Doren, 1987; Danti et al., 1985).

We have already briefly described a few specific personality disorders in relation to other syndromes with which they are sometimes confused (such as the schizoid personality disorder with schizophrenia, and the paranoid personality disorder with the paranoid patterns). The following descriptions of

Ted Bundy, suspected of bludgeoning at least 30 college co-eds, was convicted for the murder of two. At his trial, when he attempted to assist his attorneys in his defense, his psychotic tendencies gradually began to exhibit themselves as he became violent at certain points in the proceedings.   (AP/Wide World Photos)

the personality disorders are listed in order of decreasing severity, similar to a classification system first proposed by Millon (1981), which has three basic groupings. At the first, the lowest level of personality integration, fall the borderline, paranoid, and schizotypal disorders. Profound difficulties with interpersonal relationships are common in these disorders, and characteristic behavior patterns include overt hostility and/or confusion. Next in order come the obsessive-compulsive, passive-aggressive, schizoid, and avoidant disorders. Persons with these personality traits are either ambivalent about in-

EXHIBIT

Personality Disorder Dimensions

The two behavioral dimensions shown below (active-passive; relating to others-distanced from others) are helpful in portraying some important ways in which the personality disorders differ from one another. Certain other disorders could also be placed on such scales; for example, a manic person appears at the extremes of the closely relating and activity dimensions, whereas a severely depressed person shows the opposite characteristics. These two dimensions, however, are most applicable to the personality disorders, because the initial label "disordered" usually comes as a result of behavioral and relationship characteristics rather than from self-report data. The horizontal dimension describes the predominant interpersonal relationship orientation; the vertical dimension, the general activity level initiated and maintained in the person's overall lifestyle. Thus, the dependent personality relates closely to others but is very passive, whereas the compulsive personality is generally quite active but at least moderately distanced from others.

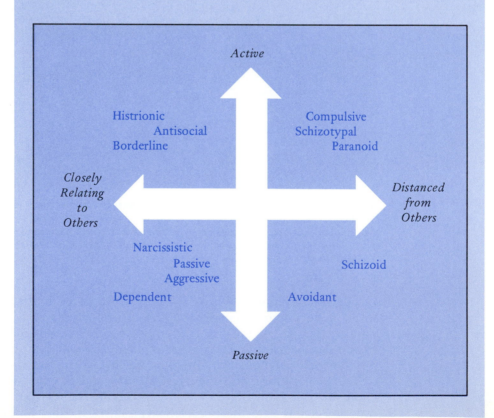

terpersonal relationships (obsessive-compulsives and passive-aggressives) or virtually isolated from external support. The last group, comprising the dependent, histrionic, narcissistic, and antisocial personalities, is characterized by relatively coherent, nonconflicted behavior patterns. Whether oriented toward or against other people, these individuals tend to function in comparatively effective ways, and, at least initially, function effectively interpersonally (Doren, 1987; Danti et al., 1985; Meyer, 1983; Millon, 1981). The graph in the accompanying exhibit locates each personality disorder on two important behavioral dimensions: (1) active-passive and (2) relating to others-distanced from others.

Borderline Personality Disorder

Borderline personalities are quite moody, emotionally unstable, and appear very liable to further personality deterioration. They are irritable, anxious, and occasionally spontaneously aggressive but have difficulty being alone. These interpersonally intense people may show identity problems similar to persons with the depersonalization disorder (see Chapter 6). This disorder was a confusing entity in the original DSM drafts, but now has been more clearly defined. At first glance, it may seem to overlap with the schizotypal personality disorder, as both imply an easy transition into a schizophrenic adjustment. However, individuals with the borderline personality disorder are neither as withdrawn socially nor nearly as bizarre in symptomatology as are schizophrenics. Though the DSM does not specifically mention it, this category seems to be a resurrection of an old term at one time much favored by clinicians, the emotionally unstable personality.

Persons with the borderline personality disorder do show obvious and significant emotional instability. There is some evidence that as these individuals improve they show more predictable behavior patterns, yet this is combined with increasingly evident narcissism. A diagnosis of borderline personality disorder requires at least five of the following: (1) unpredictable impulsivity in two areas such as sex, drug, or alcohol use; (2) physically self-damaging behaviors; (3) uncontrolled anger responses; (4) unstable interpersonal relationships; (5) unstable mood; (6) unstable identity; (7) persistent boredom experiences; and/or (8) avoidance of being alone.

This category is truly a variable syndrome, so it will therefore require equally variable treatment responses. It is also difficult to treat, and the success rate is not high.

Paranoid Personality Disorder

Paranoid personalities are suspicious, envious, rigid in emotions and attitudes, authoritarian, and hyperalert for intrusions into their psychological world. The paranoid personality disorder can be thought of as anchoring the

EXHIBIT

The Borderline Personality Disorder (BPD):
An Interesting but Problematic Diagnostic Category

As the text notes, the borderline personality disorder (BPD) is a relatively new diagnostic entity. Since its introduction to the mental health community, its use has rapidly increased. This is probably because the BPD is most relevant to (1) that large group of clients who manifest a wide range of emotional instability symptoms, and as a result don't easily fit other more specific diagnostic categories, and (2) BPD covers those clients who show some psychotic (though not primarily schizophrenic) symptoms, but not enough of them to warrant a psychotic diagnosis, and thus are hard to fit into other diagnostic categories.

Because of the popularity of the BPD diagnosis, however, it is being used with too many different types of clients. Thus, it loses a degree of its explanatory value by not being specific enough as a category.

The problems with the BPD diagnosis are compounded by increasing evidence that organic factors may play a part in some clients with this disorder. In a study published in *The Journal of Nervous and Mental Disease* (1987, *175(3)*), Gardner, Lucas, and Cowdry presented their research on the incidence of subtle neurologic disorders (brain or nervous system) in BPD clients. "Soft signs" include such behaviors as awkward foot tapping and hopping, difficulty in finger-thumb coordination, right-left confusion, difficulty in coordinating repetitive rapid movements, and mild problems in speech fluency. Soft signs *suggest*, but are not conclusive evidence of, neurologic disorder.

Gardner et al. (1987) gave thorough physical and psychological exams to matched BPD clients and normal controls. As hypothesized, a significantly greater number of soft signs were found in the BPD clients. However, it's also interesting that the majority of the controls showed at least one clear soft sign.

Gardner and his colleagues conclude that degrees of subtle, nonfocused neurologic dysfunction may be spread across the general population. This mild (in most cases nondebilitating, and in many cases not even noticeable in normal functioning) dysfunction could come from many sources: prenatal or birth trauma or infections, later high fevers, blows to the head, viral infections, and so on. As a group, BPD clients simply have more nonfocused neurological disorder, and it is significant enough to add to their psychological and physical dysfunction.

other end of the continuum of paranoid disorders from the most disturbed and fragmented pattern, paranoid schizophrenia (see Chapters 7 and 8). However, since there is neither thought disorder nor even a well-formed minor delusional system in the paranoid personality disorder, it is not listed under the DSM paranoid disorders and is not a psychotic condition. Modeling of parental or other significant others is more important in this disorder than in the psychotic paranoid conditions. Since paranoid personalities manifest hyperalertness toward the environment and have a chronic mistrust of most people, their information base is consistently distorted and their affect is constricted. Consequently, they find it difficult to adapt adequately to new situations or relationships, which is paradoxical because of their hyperalertness to their environment. So they may often be right in assuming that other people are against them. Yet the paranoia is usually a disabling overreaction to a low level of scrutiny by others.

Unless these individuals have almost absolute trust in another, they cannot develop intimacy and are continually seeking various ways to be self-sufficient. They avoid the emotional complexities of working out a meaningful relationship and tend to be litigious. For example, they may write negative letters to public figures, or bring lawsuits on minimal grounds. It is rare for them to come into therapy without significant coercion from others.

Schizotypal Personality Disorder

Schizotypal personalities show minor variations in their behavior and thinking similar to that manifested by schizophrenics. They are isolated interpersonally, somewhat suspicious, and illogical. Whereas the schizoid individual's behavior remains rather constant, the schizotypal person may, under stress, decompensate into actual schizophrenia. The essential difference between the schizotypal and schizoid personality disorders is that in addition to the disturbances in social functioning, the schizotypal personality disorder manifests peculiarities in the communication process. Schizotypal individuals are much more likely than the schizoid to show depression and anxiety, and because of the odd thinking patterns, they are more likely to have developed eccentric belief systems and become involved in fringe religious groups. The schizotypal personality is also more likely to be emotionally labile, overtly suspicious, and hostile of others than is the schizoid.

Schizoid Personality Disorder

Schizoid personalities are asocial, shy, introverted, and significantly defective in their ability to form social relationships, and are usually described as loners. The essential feature of this disorder is impairment in the ability to form adequate social relationships or, as author Joan Didion states in *The White Album*, they are "only marginally engaged in the dailiness of life" (p. 121). They have difficulty expressing hostility and have withdrawn from most social contacts. But, unlike that of agoraphobia (see Chapter 6), the behavior is ego-syntonic.

If, in addition to inadequate interpersonal skills, the person also shows peculiarities and difficulties in communication, the appropriate diagnosis is the schizotypal personality disorder. Schizotypals are more likely to have a family history of schizophrenia. Thus, that category predicts more consistently the eventual emergence of a schizophrenic disorder than does the schizoid personality disorder.

An avoidant personality may desire interpersonal relationships, but be too shy and inhibited to make the first move for fear of rejection.   (Mimi Forsyth/Monkmeyer Press Photo Service)

Schizoid personalities gravitate into jobs that require solitude, such as work as night watchmen. As they age or become vocationally dysfunctional, they are likely to move into a "skid row" situation. Even though they fantasize excessively and communicate in peculiar ways, they show no loss of contact with reality. Like the person with an avoidant personality disorder, soon to be discussed, the schizoid has inadequate interpersonal relations. Unlike one with an avoidant personality disorder, the schizoid does not care. Hence, therapy is quite difficult, as there is little motivation to change the essential feature.

Avoidant Personality Disorder

Avoidant personalities are shy and inhibited interpersonally, yet at the same time desire to have interpersonal relationships, which distinguishes them from persons with the schizotypal or schizoid personality disorders. They also do not show the degree of irritability and emotional instability seen in the borderline personality disorder.

A major feature of this chronic disorder is an unwillingness to tolerate risks in deepening interpersonal relationships. These persons are extremely sensitive to rejection and seem to need a guarantee ahead of time that a relationship will work out. Naturally, such guarantees are seldom available in healthy relationships. Thus, the friends they manage to make often show a degree of instability, or are quite passive.

In many ways, this disorder is similar to the anxiety disorders, since there is a degree of anxiety and distress, and low self-esteem is common. However, the behaviors that produce the distress are relatively ego-syntonic (that is, they are more acceptable to the avoidant personality than they are to a person with an anxiety disorder). The depression and anxiety of the avoidant disorder are related to the perceived rejection and criticism by others. This disorder is seen more often in women than men, and is relatively common. Any childhood disorder that focuses on shyness predisposes one to the avoidant personality disorder.

Passive-Aggressive Personality Disorder

Passive-aggressive personalities show a pattern commonly encountered in clinical practice, especially in marital problems. They live life as a double message, engaging others in dependency-oriented relationships and then expressing much resistance and hostility in the relationship. They are stubborn and inefficient, often procrastinate on deadlines, and resort to threats or pouting if confronted with their inconsistent behavior. The actual behavior expressed may be either passive or aggressive, but physical aggression seldom occurs.

Most parents have had the experience of a child pushing them to the limits of their control and then backing off. Like that child, the passive-aggressive becomes acutely sensitive to such limits and is consistently able to go that far but not farther. When this pattern becomes an integral part of a social and vocational lifestyle, a passive-aggressive personality disorder exists. Although these patterns are commonly modeled and learned in childhood, such a family usually reaches a state of mutual detente. The pattern then causes severe problems when it is transferred into any new intimate, consistent relationship, such as marriage.

The passive-aggressive personality disorder takes the standards and the belief systems of significant others and turns them around to immobilize the others effectively. The strategy (which is not thought to be a conscious behavior) is to present the "enemy" (often a person depended on) with a choice that forces one either to capitulate or to violate individual belief systems. That person is thus immobilized, yet has no adequate reason to justify retaliation. For example, one father used to demand strict adherence to a set of religious standards. One Sunday he asked his two sons to help him with work in the yard, a task they detested. They piously replied that they would like to but couldn't because "it was the Lord's day." They pointed out that they had been told in church that work on the Lord's day was wrong—a singular example of an effective passive-aggressive pattern, particularly since before this they had shown little interest in religion.

Obsessive-Compulsive Personality Disorder

Sometimes described as "workaholics without warmth," **obsessive-compulsive personalities** are overly controlled emotionally and find it hard to express warmth or caring. They are formal and perfectionistic, and they place inordinate value on work and productivity. This disorder is occasionally confused with the obsessive-compulsive disorder (which is an anxiety disorder; see Chapter 6), but there are significant differences between the two syndromes. First, the obsessive-compulsive personality seldom becomes obsessed about issues. Second, the term compulsive here refers to a lifestyle in which compulsive features are pervasive and chronic; it does not refer to a specific behavior. Third, the person with an obsessive-compulsive personality disorder is not upset, anxious, or distressed about his or her lifestyle, whereas anxiety is generic and often obvious at times in the functioning of the obsessive-compulsive disorder.

It is true that a degree of compulsivity is effective, particularly in our society. It becomes a problem when it overwhelms the rest of the personality. Paradoxically, obsessive-compulsives are often indecisive and poor planners of their time, a result of their narrow focus and concern with precision, even though the precision may be irrelevant. To diagnose an obsessive-compulsive personality disorder, the DSM requires consistent evidence of: (1) overemphasis on details to the exclusion of an overall perspective (they see the trees rather than the forest, and not even all of the trees); (2) constricted emotionality; (3) excessive devotion to vocation and productivity; (4) need for dominance in personal relationships; and (5) indecisiveness. One psychologist who had worked with a number of obsessive-compulsive personality disorder cases exclaimed, in a moment of frustration and sarcasm, "This is the type of person who can get a complete physical from a proctologist."

Narcissistic Personality Disorder

This category, which was new to DSM-III, and which clinicians continue to find to be a meaningful category, describes people who have an inflated sense of self-worth and care little for the welfare of others despite occasionally making a pretense of caring. They are asocial rather than antisocial. Such individuals may be a product of our modern social value systems. They manifest an unrealistic sense of self-importance, exhibitionistic attention seeking, inability to take criticism, interpersonal manipulation, and lack of empathy, with consequently substantial problems in interpersonal relationships. No doubt

narcissistic personality disorders have always existed, but it appears as if this pattern has become more common recently. It is not a surprising development when there are advertisements about "The Arrogance of Excellence," and self-help seminars urging people to live out the axiom "I'm Number One" (with little evidence that there is much room for a number two or number three). As the cultural historian Christopher Lasch (1978) so lucidly describes, a narcissistic personality disorder is a logical development from such societal values.

The pattern is usually evident in adolescence, and the disorder is chronic. As with the other personality disorders, narcissistic personalities only come to the attention of a clinician when coerced by circumstances, such as in a problem marriage. The prognosis for major change is moderate at best.

Histrionic Personality Disorder

Histrionic personalities have problematic interpersonal relationships that others perceive as superficial and shallow, as well as problematic marital and sexual adjustments. These persons are attention-seeking and overreactive, with the response being expressed more dramatically and intensely than is appropriate, hence the term histrionic. This category has traditionally been labeled the hysterical personality. However, hysteric wrongly suggests a disorder that parallels the causes and symptoms of what was previously labeled the hysterical neurosis.

Histrionic personalities may elicit new relationships with relative ease, as they appear to be empathic and socially able. However, they turn out to be emotionally insensitive and have little depth of insight into their own responsibilities in a relationship. They avoid blame for any difficulties in an interpersonal relationship, and in that sense, show a degree of the projection that is characteristic of the paranoid disorders. Even though they may be flirtatious and seductive sexually, there is little mature response or true sensuality. If one accepts the apparent sexual overture in the behavior, the histrionic individual may act as if insulted or even attacked.

There is controversy as to whether this disorder occurs with any frequency in males. This is not surprising, since the meaning of the Greek root term hystera is uterus. Ancient explanations for the disorder blamed an unfruitful womb, which became distraught and wandered about the body. Hippocrates thought marriage would cure hysteria by anchoring the womb. Even Freud suggested marriage as a cure. Since conflict over expressing sexual needs may be a factor, such medicine might even work at times. Sometimes, though, this medicine brings on "iatrogenic" problems that are worse than the "disease." However, it is clear that this disorder is found in males, but because the symptoms are a caricature of a traditional female stereotype, it is more common in women.

Dependent Personality Disorder

Dependent personalities have a great need to cling to stronger personalities who will make a wide range of decisions for them, and in certain cases they even change their beliefs to match those of a dominant personality, as in the shared paranoid disorder. Dependent personalities are naive and docile, and show little initiative. There is some suspiciousness of possible rejection, but not to the degree found in the avoidant personality disorder. In one way, dependent personality disorders can be seen as successful avoidant personality disorders. They have achieved a style that elicits the desired relationships, though at the cost of any consistent self-expression of their personality.

Since this is an exaggeration of the traditional feminine role, it is not surprising that it is more common in women. If the individual is not presently in a dependent relationship, anxiety and upset are common. Even in the middle of a dependent relationship, there is still residual anxiety over the possibility of being abandoned. To make a diagnosis of dependent personality disorder, the following should be noted with some consistency over a significant period of time: (1) they subordinate themselves to another to the point of ignoring their own essential needs; for example, they may tolerate physical abuse by a spouse; (2) they have low self-confidence and allow others to assume responsibility for decisions, so anxiety is experienced if they are left alone for any significant period of time. Not surprisingly, assertiveness training is a standard feature in the treatment of the dependent personality disorder.

Self-Defeating Personality Disorder

Self-defeating behaviors are integral to many forms of abnormal behavior, for example, alcoholism, phobias, and paranoid patterns. However, the specific category of **self-defeating personality disorder**, sometimes referred to as a masochistic personality, refers to individuals in whom such patterns are consistent and repetitive, especially in interpersonal relationships (Reich, 1987). Hence, self-defeating personality disorders are often "victims." However, the diagnosis is made only if there are self-defeating behaviors external to abuse or depression. This category is still controversial, and not accepted by many clinicians. The major critiques are (1) that it tends to shift the blame, by labeling the victim as abnormal, from the abuser (whether it is a form of physical or psychological abuse) to the victim, and (2) that it overlaps too highly with some of the other personality disorder categories, especially the borderline and dependent personalities (Reich, 1987).

Antisocial Personality Disorder

The **antisocial personality** is arguably the most important personality disorder, in terms of both its impact on society and complexity of psychological and legal issues. For this reason, we discuss it in far more detail than the other per-

For many juvenile delinquents, behavior is based on peer approval, with very little concern for approval by the adult, authoritarian world.   (Alon Reinniger/Leo de Wys, Inc.)

sonality disorders. Much of the material in this section reflects work by Meyer (1980, 1983) but is not repetitively referenced. Originally described in 1806 by Philippe Pinel and termed "manie sans delire" (mania without delusions), the essential characteristic of the antisocial personality disorder is the chronic manifestation of antisocial behavior in a person who is typically (1) unable to delay gratification, (2) amoral, and (3) impulsive. Other important characteristics are narcissism and an inability to deal effectively with authority. Distress usually occurs only as a result of immediate situational stress, and interpersonal relationships are shallow at best. Antisocial personalities display both an excessive need for environmental stimulation and a lack of response to standard social controls on behavior. The chronic nature of the pattern is reflected in a failure to profit from experience and is related to the inability to delay gratification. As in the introductory case of Brad, the pattern is already apparent in adolescence or even early childhood, and the disorder spans a broad performance spectrum, including school, work, and interpersonal behaviors.

The Case of the Hit Kids

Two teenagers in the Southwest, a 17-year-old boy and his 14-year-old sister, paid a 19-year-old friend $60 to shoot and kill their father when he came home from work one evening. The father and mother were divorced, and the father, who had sole care of the children, reportedly tried to be a good parent. The killer apparently missed with his first shot and had to chase the father all over the house. He discharged a hail of bullets that eventually killed the father. The son became distressed and left the house after the first shot; the daughter remained through it all.

The teenagers hid their father's body in a bedroom, cashed his last paycheck, took his credit cards, and went on a two-week spending spree. By the time they were apprehended, they had spent more than $3,000 on video games, televisions, and a variety of amusements. When apprehended by the police and asked why they had had their father killed, they replied, "He wouldn't let us do anything we wanted, like smoke pot."

The term antisocial personality represents the latest stage in an evolution through several terms. The DSM-I in 1952 discarded the traditional term psychopathic personality or psychopath (Cleckley, 1964). It was replaced by the term sociopathic personality, in an effort to emphasize the environmental factors presumably responsible for the disorder and to eliminate the negative connotations of the term psychopath. Nevertheless, both professionals and lay people continue to use the traditional term of **psychopath**. The DSM-II in 1968 discarded both terms and replaced them with the one still used in the DSM. The DSM specifies four criteria for a diagnosis of antisocial personality disorder: (1) evidence of the pattern before adulthood, (2) several indications of problematic work or academic performance, (3) manifestations of more than one type of antisocial behavior, and (4) impaired interpersonal relationships and violations of the rights of others.

Specific diagnostic considerations. Although evidence of antisocial behavior is usually seen before age 15, as in the case of Brad, the DSM discourages diagnosing anyone under age 18 as an antisocial personality. There are several reasons for this policy. Foremost is the ethical problem of applying a label that is liable to stigmatize a young person for life when his or her adjustment pattern is still not firmly set. For example, a young person might more appropriately be labeled a "subcultural socialized delinquent," that is, a person whose behaviors are generated almost totally by the need for peer or gang acceptance; these behaviors may change radically if peer contacts change.

As with Brad, antisocial personalities have definite problems adjusting to school, both socially and academically. Their learning deficiencies are often severe and may include functional illiteracy. Cleckley's (1964) early and influential assertion that psychopaths are often intellectually superior fits only the unique subsample he dealt with in his clinical practice. As a whole, antisocial personalities show lower-than-average scores on various measures of intelligence. Given their inability to adjust to school, this feature makes sense, especially if, as some researchers claim, genetic or brain dysfunction is involved (Zuckerman et al., 1980; Hare and Jutai, 1986).

Individuals who are impulsive, antisocial, and/or alcoholic and whose performance is only sporadically adequate will eventually sink to the bottom of any sociobehavioral group (Sanchez, 1986). It is, therefore, not surprising that antisocial personalites are predominantly from low socioeconomic levels, no matter what scale is employed. Their children have the double problem of trying to move out of a lower social class, while lacking either an adequate start or a model for appropriate behaviors and attitudes. There are no racial variables involved that cannot be explained more plausibly in terms of socio-economic level and/or societal response and restriction.

The DSM states that the antisocial personality is significantly more common in males. In males, signs are often obvious in early childhood, but in females they more commonly appear during puberty. These differences probably reflect societal roles and expectations, rather than inherent factors. In fact, along with feminism has come an increase in this disorder in females, accompanied by a lowered incidence of disorders centering on passivity. The accompanying case is a good example of psychopathy already evident in an early adolescent female.

Etiology.   As in many other areas of psychopathology, there are many theories about the cause of the antisocial personality disorder. Heredity, brain dysfunction, individual development experiences, and subcultural conformity have all been cited, and each is seen as the major factor by its proponents (Doren, 1987; Sanchez, 1986).

Physiological theories. In the nineteenth century, Lombroso advanced the theory that criminals possess distinctive physical features (such as low forehead). Although that theory now has been discredited among scientists, some modern research (Mednick and Christiansen, 1977) indirectly supports the idea that hereditary factors may underlie the antisocial personality by asserting that criminal behavior in general is hereditary. About 20 to 30 percent of most prison populations are antisocial personalities (Hare and Jutai, 1981). If a genetic difference does exist, it is unclear how it mediates behavior. Possibilities include low general intellectual ability, a specific learning deficit, brain dysfunction, or differences in the conditioning effects of standard disciplinary techniques. So far, data indicating a clear hereditary component are at best tentative, and no one has found a clear link to the mediating behaviors that actually produce the criminality.

Neurologically based theories of antisocial behavior have enjoyed some popularity, as they have with many other forms of psychopathology. Beginning with the phrenologists who associated bumps on various parts of the skull with certain behavioral predispositions, numerous efforts have been made to establish clear-cut brain–behavior relationships. Neurosurgeons, such as Wilder Penfield and his associates (Penfield and Rasmussen, 1950), have even produced maps of the brain's cortical surface by methodically stimulating minute areas with low-voltage electrical current and noting the specific behavioral responses.

It appears, however, that the key to understanding the neurologic underpinnings of psychopathic behavior lies within structures buried deep in the brain, far below the cortical surface stimulated by Penfield's electrodes. This region contains a group of structures collectively known as the limbic system, which mediates behaviors associated with emotions, motivation, and primitive survival. Collectively referred to by neurologists as the 4-F's (feeding, fighting, fleeing, and reproducing), these behaviors are controlled by a delicate, complex network of checks and balances in the intact brain. It has been found that removal of one such structure—the amygdala—is particularly likely to reduce aggressive human behavior. Yet opening a person's brain to pinpoint the source of a hypothetical dysfunction is still a risky affair, and it raises serious ethical issues. Less dangerous and invasive techniques have been devised to study the neuroanatomic correlates of psychopathy, including extensive monitoring of brain wave patterns using electroencephalograms (EEGs). To date, however, none has provided convincing data. Improvements in technique, such as the use of sophisticated computer scoring of specific aspects of EEGs, promise possible refinements.

Researchers already have found one possibly significant phenomenon: A greater proportion of aggressive antisocial personalities show abnormal temporal lobe slow-wave activity than do other subgroups of the criminal population. On the basis of this and similar research, Hare and Jutai (1981; 1986) have theorized that in at least some antisocial personalities, the essential dysfunction is in the temporal lobes and limbic system. Others have speculated that the dysfunction is in the frontal lobe. However, Hare and Jutai rather convincingly show there is not yet any good data to support such a hypothesis.

There has also been speculation that a chromosomal disorder may be involved in antisocial behavior (Jacobs et al., 1965). Most proponents lay the blame to an extra Y chromosone. The extra Y is correlated with a specific physical appearance called "Lincolnesque" (because Lincoln is thought to have had the XYY pattern). As yet, there is no evidence to support this. Even if there was, it would pertain to only a small proportion of aggressive individuals, as it is actually quite rare.

There is some evidence that aggressive antisocial personalities are disproportionately likely to be mesomorphic (muscular build) (Barrett, 1980). This theory is plausible, given that people who are slight in stature are less likely to be successful in using aggression to deal with the environment. Hence, such behaviors would tend to drop out of the repertoire of slightly built individuals, even with an initial influence of heredity or modeling. There is good evidence that less intelligent antisocial personalities are statistically more likely to be behaviorally impulsive and violent (Newman and Newman, 1987; Wilson and Herrnstein, 1985). Thus, in any one antisocial personality disorder, genetic variables, brain dysfunction, low intelligence, certain body builds, or a combination of these factors could contribute to the disorder (Doren, 1987).

Psychological theories. Two other areas of particular research interest that someday may be even more clearly linked with brain dysfunction correlates are the psychological variables of (1) stimulation-seeking behavior and (2) patterns of learning and parenting. Quay (1965) theorized that antisocial personalities are high in stimulation seeking, and are "unable to tolerate routine and boredom . . . impulsivity and lack of even minimal tolerance for sameness appear to be the primary and distinctive features" (p. 180). Subsequent research (Hare and Jutai, 1986; Zuckerman et al., 1980) supports this concept. These traits would fit with the lowered basal metabolism and level of physiologic arousal (i.e., more stimulation needed to generate the reinforcement of physiologic arousal) observed in many antisocial personalities (Quay, 1965; Zuckerman et al., 1980) and could also be tied to Hare's theory of temporal lobe and limbic system dysfunction.

Learning and psychopathy. Substantial evidence (Lykken, 1957; Doren, 1987) supports the existence of two discrete categories of antisocial personalities, reflecting different etiologies: *primary psychopathy*, in which the individual is extroverted, shows little anxiety or avoidance learning, and is especially resistant to social control; and *secondary psychopathy*, characterized by introversion, more anxiety, and greater potential for avoidance learning.

Lykken's innovative research suggests that these two subgroups also differ in the extent to which they can be conditioned by punishing stimuli. He divided criminal subjects into primary psychopaths, secondary psychopaths, and "normal" criminals and presented them with a "mental maze" containing a series of 20 decision-making points. At each point the subject had a choice of four levers, one of which was the correct choice and was denoted as such by a green light. If the green light flashed, the subject moved on to the next four levers. One of the other three levers at each point discharged a strong electric shock if pulled. Learning the sequence of correct levers was the overt task; avoidance of the punishment levers was the hidden task.

The three groups did not differ on the overt task, but the primary psychopaths were noticeably poorer than either the secondary psychopaths or the normal criminals at learning to avoid the punishing shock. The implication of these results is that primary psychopaths are less likely to be inhibited in behavior by standard punishments used to promote the development of normal social patterns. Schachter and Latane (1964) were able to replicate Lykken's findings. In addition, they found that the primary psychopaths made fewer errors when injected with adrenaline (a natural stimulant), while this adversely affected the performance of the other subjects. This offers another piece of support for Quay's stimulation-seeking hypothesis.

This line of research also produced another finding that may be significant: Primary psychopaths do respond like normal individuals to tangible reinforcers, such as money. They do not respond as well to negative reinforcers, such as electric shock or directions combined with social reprimand. Thus, if one presents punishment that is within their value system (such as loss of an immediate and tangible source of gratification), primary psychopaths will learn the response.

Parenting and psychopathy. Factors in early childhood development, particularly relationships with parents, also have been studied as possible causes of the antisocial personality disorder. Although these studies have found no clear evidence of a direct causal relationship between parenting and antisocial patterns, they have observed high rates of correlation between two styles of parenting and antisocial personalities (Doren, 1987; Sanchez, 1986).

One style is the cold and distant parent, whose influence leaves offspring unable to empathize with others or to understand the complexities of human relationships (Eisenberg and Miller, 1987). The other is the inconsistent parent whose unpredictability in administering rewards and punishments makes it impossible for the child to develop a clear identity or, more importantly, to respond to anything except concrete instructions. This last effect fits well with Lykken's research. Another frequent feature of inconsistent parenting is the double message (see Chapter 7), in which there is a significant discrepancy between verbalized rules and their actual enforcement.

In both patterns, the parents (or surrogates)—usually the father—often provide a clear and direct model for such behaviors as aggression, alcoholism, sexual promiscuity, and interpersonal manipulation. Both parenting styles produce individuals almost devoid of basic trust; the natural result is an inability to engage in committed interpersonal involvement (Eisenberg and Miller, 1987).

There are potential links among all these research findings. Other data (Meyer, 1980; Barrett, 1980) on the psychopath's slowness to develop conditioned responses in arousal systems, such as galvanic skin response (GSR), fit well with Quay's findings that the antisocial personality manifests a chronically high level of stimulation seeking because of inadequate central nervous system arousal; both of these results have a peripheral relation to brain dysfunction. All of these concepts can be tied to Lykken's and Schmauk's findings, and in any of these theories heredity could play a role.

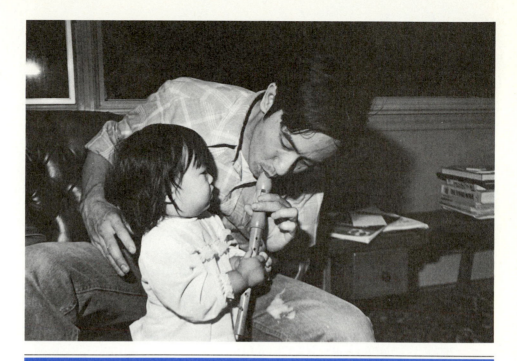

Although studies of parents' influence on early childhood development have proven inconclusive, there is a high correlation between cold or inconsistent parents and antisocial personality disorder. A loving, nurturing environment probably creates fewer psychopathic adults.   (Marilyn Pfaltz/Taurus Photos)

On the whole, the research suggests that heredity is important, though only as a predisposing factor and probably not in all cases. A genetic cause is a clear possibility in certain small subgroups of antisocial personalities. In most cases, however, emotional remoteness and inconsistent behavior in parents, combined with modeling and peer culture influences, appear to be the crucial variables. As Hare has consistently pointed out, one of the best predictors of adult psychopathy is having a parent who was psychopathic or alcoholic, or had the antisocial personality disorder.

Treatment.   Not surprisingly, antisocial personalities seldom present themselves to psychotherapists for study or treatment. When they do show up, they usually have been coerced, which compounds the problem.

In an ingenious effort to deal with this research sampling problem, Widom (1977) used newspaper ads to attract local antisocial personalities for treatment research. The ads were placed in an "underground" newspaper and read, "Wanted. Charming, aggressive, carefree people who are impulsively irresponsible but good at handling people and at looking after number one. Send name . . . etc." Of the 23 women and 45 men who responded, a number were selected for extensive interviewing, testing (which produced data in accord with the prior findings of Quay, Lykken, Hare, etc.) and possible therapy. In a similar vein, others have paid antisocial personalities to come to a treatment center to talk into a tape recorder, allegedly to obtain sociological background data on this population. Several clients liked this approach so well that they continued talking about themselves (thus, a form of psychotherapy) even after the pay stopped.

Yochelson and Samenow (1976) report success with a type of confrontation therapy. They tell their clients, usually incarcerated criminals, that they know all about their lies, their anger, and other specific antisocial behaviors. The objective is to increase the clients' "self disgust" and, indirectly, to impress or outdo them enough to get them to stay in therapy.

All of these maneuvers could be viewed as beating manipulators at their own game. No approach has been markedly successful.

Anthony Burgess' classic novel *A Clockwork Orange*, in which the protagonist is an excellent example of the antisocial personality, describes one extreme alternative mode of control—coercive conditioning of persons into new patterns of behavior. Conditioning people against their will may now be technologically feasible and could be effective; only public vigilance to preserve civil liberties prevents its use. The same is true of psychosurgery, which has yet to achieve prominence as a regulatory measure.

One important component in rehabilitating the psychopath, and possibly in the prevention of psychopathic tendencies from evolving into criminal acting-out, is providing an outlet for the stimulation-seeking component. Directing such a person into high-energy, high-risk activities such as mountain climbing, certain forms of racing, and into aggressive competitive sports can help. Sometimes a simple change of life circumstance can make a difference, as in the case of Don Johnson, star of television's "Miami Vice." Johnson had a problematic early childhood, showed a consistent pattern of delinquency while growing up in the Missouri Ozarks, had a long string of tumultuous and broken relationships with women, and was heavily into alcohol, drugs, and a fast-lane lifestyle before attaining fame in his role of Sonny Crockett on "Miami Vice" (*Newsweek*, 10/7/85, pp. 96–100). He apparently still enjoys any activity filled with "excitement," smokes incessantly, and is rather hyper in his behavior. For example, in a 1986 quote reported by the Associated Press, he said "It wasn't anything for me to knock off a case and a half of beer a day, a bottle of vodka, three or four good, healthy snifters of cognac, a couple of bottles of good wine and a couple of grams of coke. A day! And that's not to mention the eight or 10 odd joints." However, his fame and image now provide enough leeway and outlets for behaviors that in the average person might cause a drift into a clearly antisocial pattern.

THE CRIMINAL PERSONALITY

The **criminal personality** is a sociological term, not a DSM category. As we will see, it comprises a variety of different personalities who are involved in some way in criminal activity. Many different personality types function as criminals in our society; of these, the antisocial personality is only one specific psychological syndrome. Antisocial personalities account for no more than 30 percent of the overall prison population (Hare and Jutai, 1981).

However, the criminal who is also an antisocial personality is substantially different from the nonpsychopathic criminal. Hare and McPherson (1984) used a behavioral checklist that had already been established by prior research to be reliably effective in dividing prison inmates into psychopaths and nonpsychopaths. They then looked at a variety of other measures and found the following differences: (1) psychopaths are much more likely to engage in violent and aggressive behavior than are criminals in general, and (2) psychopaths are much more likely to use a weapon. Interestingly, the brighter the psychopath, the more likely he was to use a weapon.

Psychodiagnostician Edwin Megargee and several colleagues have developed an ongoing research program that has generated an excellent typology of the criminal personality. Using data primarily from the MMPI (see Chapter 3), they differentiated 10 criminal types in one prison population. On the basis of behavioral observations, social history data, and other psychological tests, they obtained validation for this classification and subsequently extended its use to other prison populations (Megargee and Bohn, 1977; Megargee and Corhout, 1977). Most importantly from the perspective of good research design, a researcher working independently of Megargee established the validity of the system in yet another prison (Edinger, 1979), and others have validated similar patterns (Doren, 1987; Wilson and Herrnstein, 1985).

The 10 types were first given alphabetical names (Able, Baker, etc.), but later (Megargee and Bohn, 1977) they were listed in order from the least to the most patholgical. The 10 criminal personality types are as follows.

1. *Items*, one of the larger subgroups in the prison population, show little or no emotional pathology. Items are generally outgoing, friendly, and nonaggressive and are likely to be incarcerated for victimless crimes, such as drug dealing. They come from the most stable and warm family backgrounds, make lasting and committed friendships, and show low recidivism rates. It would probably be feasible, and far less expensive, to place them on probation immediately.

2. *Easy* inmates suit their randomly assigned label well. They are brighter and have had more natural advantages than other criminal subgroups. However, although their backgrounds have been easier, they also take life easier—they are classic underachievers. They come from good

parental backgrounds, never appear particularly upset at being in prison, and have the lowest recidivism rate of all subgroups. Probation into academic-vocational training is advisable.

3. *Bakers*, a relatively small subgroup, are best conceptualized as neurotic delinquents, or as secondary psychopaths. Bakers are passive, socially isolated, alcoholic, anxious, and disruptive in a passive-aggressive fashion. A combination of an Alcoholics Anonymous program, supportive psychotherapy, and vocational counseling is the optimal treatment approach for these personalities.

4. *Ables* are often socialized delinquents. They are moderately sociopathic, self-assured, immature, and opportunistic. They are amoral rather than hostile or antisocial, and they function adequately when supervised. A controlled living situation in the community is probably the best solution for Ables.

5. *Georges* are similar to Ables except that they come from a more deviant family background and are also brighter. They are quiet but not passive loners—they "do their own time." Because their "career criminal" behavior is often economically motivated, any intervention must deal with that issue first.

6. Unlike the first five types, *Deltas* are a truly pathological group. They are "bright psychopaths"—sociable but amoral, impulsive, and easily provoked to violence. All the behavior characteristics and treatment issues applicable to the antisocial personality are relevant to Deltas.

7. *Jupiters* are a small subgroup who appear to be trying to make a more positive adjustment but are handicapped by a very deprived family background. The modeling is an enduring influence (Grusec et al., 1979). In contrast to Easys, Jupiters have motivation but few skills and low ability. A heavy emphasis on basic academic and vocational training and a supportive group experience, such as a halfway house, are necessary.

8. *Foxtrots* are not very intelligent, have poor educational and family backgrounds, and are antisocial and emotionally disturbed. They are abrasive and resent any demands or authority. Foxtrots need all the help they can get, but seldom respond to it. As a result, they have a high recidivism rate.

9. *Charlies* are particularly bitter, paranoid, and hostile antisocial loners. They all tend to be academically, intellectually, and socially deficient. This group has the highest probability of recidivism and of violent behavior, both in prison and in the community. In these terms, Charlies are the most disturbed criminals. Treatment usually involves the same techniques as for paranoid behavior.

10. *Hows* are similar to Jupiters in having the handicap of a deprived early environment, but they are more anxious than Jupiters and less inclined to

change themselves. They are unwilling loners; rather than withdrawing, they are rejected. This group needs virtually all types of interventions.

It is clear from Megargee and Bohn's classifications that there is no single criminal type. Their empirically derived and applicable system is likely to remain the standard for many years.

VIOLENCE

We have already discussed a number of personality patterns in which violence is a major factor. Later in this section we discuss another, the explosive disorder, along with three types of intrinsically violent events: family violence, rape, and murder.

Violence is high in U.S. society, and it continued to rise through 1985, even though nonviolent crimes started to decrease in the mid-1980s (Webster,

The availability of nondestructive outlets for aggression, such as contact sports, may curb violence within a society.   (450/Leo de Wys)

The Case of Jim

Although his father died when Jim was three, and the family was left with limited financial means, Jim generally had a happy childhood. One day, when he was 11, the doorbell rang while he was sitting in the living room playing a game. As Jim rose to open the door, his mother shouted at him not to open it. Typical of boys of that age, he accepted her words as a challenge and opened the door. His mother's boyfriend stepped in, and as his mother came out of the kitchen, the boyfriend took out a pistol and killed her. In the ensuing years, his brother and sister occasionally told him, usually when they had become angry at him, "You're the reason our mother is dead." Not surprisingly, Jim became increasingly withdrawn, and would occasionally show very angry outbursts.

Except in sports, where he excelled because he played with reckless abandon, Jim was shunned by his peers. They learned that he would take their taunts for quite awhile, but if he eventually responded it was with a dangerous rage. His academic performance deteriorated, and some of his teachers thought he was retarded. One quiet summer afternoon, when he was 18, he went to the middle of a downtown intersection and opened fire with a pistol, killing one person and injuring several others. After he ran out of bullets, he kept on pulling the trigger until he was subdued.

In prison, Jim spent much time in solitary confinement because of occasional outbursts of anger toward other inmates, though he was otherwise amiable and cooperative. For several months he received psychotherapy in the prison clinic, but made little progress. Then, during one session, the therapist used a gestalt therapy technique; Jim was to talk to an "empty chair" while imagining that his dead mother was sitting in it. After several false starts, Jim became more and more emotional. Finally he blurted out "I killed you," and for the first time since the day his mother had been shot, he wept. In subsequent sessions the therapist used similar techniques to help him get in touch with his real feelings and accept them. Jim later became involved in group therapy, showed marked improvement academically and socially. In fact, within one year he went from grade level six in the prison to graduating from high school and taking some college courses. He also took on several relatively complex and responsible jobs in the prison, and did them very well. After leaving the prison, he married and made a successful adjustment.

1985). The traditional debate among researchers is whether developed personality traits (possibly genetically based) cause violence, or whether violence is a response to social and situational cues such as frustration and modeling of aggression (Sanchez, 1986; Hare and Jutai, 1986; Olweus, 1979). Evidence of a higher rate of assaults in lower socioeconomic situations supports the second hypothesis, as does evidence that controlling access to guns lowers the rate of gun-related assaults. Alcohol is clearly a factor, since about 50 percent of violent crimes occur immediately after the perpetrator has drunk significantly. Even the level of caffeine intake has been related to a propensity for violence (Veleber and Templer, 1984).

Societal violence is also related to the level of violence in the family itself. Cummings et al. (1985) studied 90 two-year-old boys and girls by placing them two at a time in a home-like setting and having actors simulate a warm and friendly environment, then a heated argument, and eventually a friendly reconciliation. None of the anger was directed toward either child or toward their mothers, who were nearby but were engaged in other activities. Videotape analysis shows these children to be more distressed and to be more physically aggressive toward their playmates than children in a similar setting without the argument. These researchers repeated the same scenario a month later for 47 of the children, and the upset and aggression were even worse, with boys showing much more aggression and girls more distress. This directly supports the idea that continual family violence breeds violent and/or distressed children, and indirectly supports the theory that more realistic media portrayals of violence may breed distress and violence.

Another situational factor is the availability of nondestructive outlets for aggression. For example, despite Puerto Ricans' cultural emphasis on hospitality and personal dignity, their rate of murder and nonnegligent manslaughter is high, reflecting a lack of alternative expressive channels (effective catharsis experiences) (Tseng and Hsu, 1980).

On the other hand, Olweus (1979) and others (Beatty, 1987; Hare and Jutai, 1986) argue that while situational factors can spur aggressive behavior, innate factors in the individual are at least as important as situational variables in determining whether or not an individual becomes aggressive. Olweus (1979) reviewed 16 major studies on aggressive behavior and concluded that "the degree of consistency over time in aggressive behavior is much greater than has been maintained by proponents of a behavioral (situational) specificity position in the personality field" (p. 872). Olweus suggests that motivational systems (or personality traits) formed in early childhood are critical. These motive systems reflect physiologic temperament, exposure to violence, learning history, and modeling influences, and some of these factors may be related to genetic variables.

The Explosive Disorder

The accompanying case of Jim is an example of one of the few people who receives the DSM diagnostic label of **explosive disorder**. Many of these people end up in prisons. The syndrome is marked by an outburst of physical and/or verbal violence in a person who is not usually aggressive or hostile. The disorder is classified as either intermittent or isolated, according to the relative frequency of explosive outbursts.

The explosive disorder is sometimes referred to as an epileptoid personality, largely because it bears some resemblance to psychomotor epilepsy, in which orderly sequences of behavior are disrupted by episodic aggression and complete amnesia. However, although there is good evidence that central nervous system impairment underlies psychomotor epilepsy, there is little indication that it plays a role in the explosive disorder. The causes are primarily psychological, as in Jim's case, and cultural factors can increase the incidence. In the Malayan culture, for example, soldiers often became heroes by "running amok," inciting themselves into rages that resulted in outstanding combat performance; unfortunately, when they returned to their villages they often showed similar patterns (Tseng and Hsu, 1980).

Family Violence

There is a high level of family violence in our society (Mash and Terdal, 1988; Cummings et al., 1985). People are much more liable to be physically attacked, injured, or killed in their homes by a relative than they are in any other social context. Therefore, the most dangerous assignment that a police officer can be given is answering a family crisis call.

Two disturbingly frequent forms of family violence, child abuse and spouse abuse, are discussed in Chapter 16. One of every six couples has some kind of physical altercation each year, ranging from throwing things to using a knife or gun. The great majority of this violence takes the form of the husband abusing the wife. According to annual FBI statistics on spousal homicide, husbands and wives are victimized in almost equal numbers. However, wives are more likely to kill the husband in a desperate response to long-standing physical abuse. It is significant that about three-fourths of men who batter their wives were themselves battered as children, or observed their fathers beat their mothers (Sanchez, 1986; Webster, 1985).

Rape

An event on the night of March 18, 1983, demonstrated not only the horror of rape, but also the stigma and unusual burden of proof carried by the victims of that crime. On that night, a woman who went into Big Dan's bar in New Bedford, Massachusetts to buy a pack of cigarettes was gang raped for over two hours while the other patrons watched, or in some cases even cheered on the rapists. Though a public outcry eventually brought these rapists to justice, it's interesting how the onlookers seemed to assume that such behavior had a measure of acceptability.

Traditionally, the legal definition of **rape** has been the unlawful and unwanted penetration of a female's vagina by a male's penis, enforced by fear, physical control, or any other form of coercion. The traditional definition is too restrictive, since many rapists do not desire intercourse, but instead require the female to engage in some other sex practice, such as fellatio. There are documented cases of male victims of homosexual rape, and in a few extremely rare cases males have been physically coerced to have sex by females. However, in our discussion, rape will refer to physical coercion, overt or implied, by a male in a sexual encounter. Rape statutes do not require that the male have an orgasm, but the presence of semen is usually an important piece of evidence in prosecutions. Yet, it is estimated that in as many as a fourth of all rapes, the rapist has a potency problem that precludes ejaculation (Groth and Birnbaum, 1979).

Rape is as much a crime of violence as it is one of sexuality. The insult and assault to the victim go beyond the actual physical event of the rape itself (Heidensohn, 1986). Potentially demeaning physical examinations and nonsupportive questioning of the rape victim by police officials have abated somewhat in recent years, largely because of pressure from various women's groups and the increasing presence of female officers on police forces and in rape units. The defense attorney's too-often-used ploy of implying that the victim has always been "a loose woman" and in fact invited the rape is now restricted by Public Law 95-540, passed by Congress in October, 1978. This law limits the circumstances under which evidence of a rape victim's past sexual conduct is admissible in federal court; most states have now passed similar laws.

The incidence of rape is hard to determine, though the incidence of reported rape has continued to rise through the 1980s. Reported rapes account for five percent of all crimes of violence—about one in every 2,000 women per year. However, estimates are that only one of every 10 actual rape victims reports the assault to police. Only about one rapist in 20 is ever arrested; one in 30, prosecuted; and one in 50, convicted (Webster, 1985; Frazier and Borgida, 1985).

Most rapists are married, and although they may have regular sexual relations with their wives, their sexual performance during the rape is often impaired. More than half of reported rapes occur in the victim's home; in almost half the assailant is known to the victim. Like most other criminals, rapists are lower than average in intelligence (Abel et al., 1981; Webster, 1985).

Causes.   As with other violent behaviors, it is a mistake to assume that a single cause or personality pattern accounts for most rapes. Some theorists have claimed that elevation of male hormone levels or some other biochemical abnormality might incite rapists. So far, there is no convincing general evidence for this theory, although Rada et al. (1976) found somewhat higher levels of

EXHIBIT

Mistaken Views about Rape

Rape is an impulsive behavior Most rapes are planned, though in some cases no specific woman has been targeted. In many cases, the man develops a strong desire to rape someone, and then systematically seeks out a victim.

Men who rape are killers Certainly many men pose a real danger to the woman who is the victim. At the same time, probably not much more than one percent of victims are murdered, and less than half are physically injured.

Women are always safest in fighting back; or, Women are always safest in using passive techniques, e.g., guilt, to resist Most experts believe that immediately screaming as loud as one can, quickly hitting back and then running away is the best option, especially if one is in a situation where such escape is possible, or if people are around. But, no technique is the best for all situations. Inducing fear about sexual contact, e.g., saying one has a venereal disease, or cervical cancer, may be a good option in some instances.

Only attractive, sexy women are raped; or, Only virtuous women are raped Women of all ages (including infants and women in their eighties), physical appearances, and personal backgrounds have been victims of rape. Appearing vulnerable, and being in situations which suggest vulnerability and/or isolation, are more important predictors than level of physical attraction.

Rapists are oversexed and/or "sexual degenerates" A number of rapists actually have a relatively low sex drive and a sporadic sexual pattern. On the other hand, some are married and have otherwise good marriages. Many rapists appear to be motivated more by power or hostility than sexuality.

Rapists may avoid prosecution because of an intact hymen in a woman who was a virgin and allegedly penetrated, or because of a lack of semen Though either may be a useful piece of evidence, neither is required. Rapists often have a potency problem and some don't even ejaculate during the rape.

Rapes are commonly committed by strangers in dark or hidden places Actually, about half of the rape victims know their attacker, and many rapes occur on dates, a theme detailed in the novel and movie "Looking for Mr. Goodbar."

Exhibitionists and voyeurs will rape if given a chance A few voyeurs and exhibitionists do pose a danger to the victim, but most are passive and avoid any true interpersonal confrontation or interaction with the victim. Unfortunately, they don't wear signs to let us know which one is dangerous and which one is not.

White women are often raped by black men In the great majority of rapes, the victim and attacker are the same race.

Certain women enjoy being raped Simply untrue. Some women (and some men) enjoy sex play in which there is a veneer of being coerced or forced, but, in fact, both parties retain some control over what goes on.

plasma testosterone in the most violent rapists. Even in these cases, however, there is no proof that higher testosterone levels necessarily cause the behavior; they may merely be coincident with, or even result from, an incident of rape.

Cohen et al. (1969) developed a particularly useful classification for rapists that has since been widely adopted in the research literature. Their four categories are as follows.

1. *Displaced aggression type.* Sexual excitement in these rapists is absent or only slight. The primary motivation is to physically harm and degrade the victim. They may describe the act as uncontrollable, and the attack often follows an argument with a wife, girlfriend, or mother.

2. *Sex aggression diffusion type.* These people are often sadists, and the violence appears to be necessary for arousal. The rapists see the struggling of the victim as seductive. The rape is a pathological eroticization of aggressive behavior.

3. *Compensatory type.* Most rapists belong to this category, which involves less violence. These individuals use aggression only as a means of acquiring a sexual partner. They are usually in a high state of sexual and general physiologic arousal and are not otherwise antisocial. Although these rapists fantasize about winning the victim's heart with their sexual prowess, they have great feelings of sexual inadequacy and are likely to desist if the victim puts up much of a fight.

4. *Impulsive type.* These rapists appear to be purely opportunistic. The rape occurs unexpectedly, as an extension of predatory behavior after the commission of some other antisocial activity, such as a robbery, or under a gang mentality, such as is evident in the New Bedford case that opened this section. The victim just happens to be there. These individuals are narcissistic, and any harm to the victim is incidental but produces no real guilt.

Many theorists assume that for most rapists, violence and the nonconsent of the victim evoke sexual arousal. However, evidence of the existence of the displaced aggression type, in which the major feature is aggression with only mild arousal, has cast some doubt on that theory. Barbaree et al. (1979), using a mercury-filled tube that circled the penis to measure arousal, assessed rapists' and nonrapists' reactions to scenes of forced and nonforced sex. The sample of rapists showed the same level of arousal for both types of sex scenes, whereas the nonrapists were aroused only by the nonforced sex. This finding suggests that for certain rapists, forced sex simply fails to inhibit arousal, as it does in other people. Data collected by Abel et al. (1981), however, show that, unlike normal people, certain rapists require arousal by perceiving aggressiveness and selfishness in the victim.

EXHIBIT

Initial and Associated Deviation Patterns with Rape and Pedophilia

The bulk of the traditional clinical and research literature would lead one to believe that people who show a sexual deviation (paraphiliac) pattern consistently stay within that pattern. However, more in-depth and recent research by Abel and his colleagues found that at least 50 percent of the paraphiliac clients evaluated in their studies showed multiple diagnoses that overlapped a wide variety of paraphilias. In this vein, the following table shows the paraphiliac arousal pattern that developed initially for 411 of their clients who were then diagnosed either as rapists or child molesters as adults. These findings together suggest that those persons who are shown to have one pattern of paraphilia should be questioned extensively about other categories of deviant sexual arousal (Landis and Meyer, 1988).

Initial Deviant Behavior Patterns of Rapists and/or Child Molesters

First Paraphilia	Rapists (%)	Child Molesters (%)
Pedophilia	25.8	75.0
Rape	43.8	3.4
Exhibitionism	7.9	12.9
Transvestism	1.1	1.3
Fetishism	2.2	1.3
Voyeurism	9.0	3.0
Sadism and masochism	2.2	1.3
Obscene telephone calls	0	0.4
Frottage	5.6	1.3
Bestiality	1.1	0
Arousal to odors	1.1	0

Adapted from Abel, G., Rouleau, J., and Cunningham-Rathner, J. (1986) Sexually aggressive behavior. In: W. Curran, A. L. McGarry, and S. Shah (Eds.). *Forensic psychiatry and psychology*. Philadelphia: F. A. Davis Co.

Prevention.   Three features of our society make the prevention of rape by anyone but the potential victims both difficult and unlikely: (1) the mistaken but common sexist view, even among many police, legal, and judicial authorities, that women "ask for" or enjoy being raped; (2) the related low percentage of prosecutions and convictions of rapists, which poses little or no deterrent and in some cases may even encourage the behavior; and (3) the low incidence of treatment, successful or otherwise, of the few rapists who are convicted. Consequently—and unfairly—the burden of prevention falls on individual women.

Three major strategies are available to women to reduce their chances of being raped. All require some measure of distrust of males or passive or defensive behaviors that women have been trying to escape for many years.

1. Avoid contact with strangers. For example, women shouldn't open their doors to a person they do not know or cannot identify, and they shouldn't pick up hitchhikers.

2. If a woman is being harassed or followed, she should not handle the situation herself. Instead she should go to a friend or to the police.

3. Women should be prepared by learning karate or by carrying tear gas, a shrill police whistle, or a weapon. If a woman is threatened by a rape, remaining passive is only a moderately safe strategy, according to experts; strong, active resistance and flight are the best ways to avoid harm, especially if there are any other people in the vicinity. Some women have deterred a rape by claiming to have a venereal disease or cancer in the genital area. In general, if a woman can strongly resist, immediately escape, or persuade the rapist to see her as a person instead of as an object, she increases her chances of not being raped (Groth and Birnbaum, 1979).

Treatment of the Victim.   Rape victims, almost 80 percent of whom are single, divorced, or separated, show a variety of negative effects (Heidensohn, 1986). Virtually all suffer bruises or abrasions, and about five percent suffer severe injuries, such as fractures or concussions. Many suffer injury from being forced to perform fellatio or anal intercourse. Rape victims also suffer emotional trauma. Loss of self-esteem, anxiety, and depression are common reactions, though the recent use of well-trained rape squads who focus on helping the victim as much as on catching the perpetrator has helped. Work adjustment appears particularly negatively affected and sexual adjustment may be disrupted (LoPiccolo and Stock, 1986).

If a woman is raped, she should take the following steps.

1. As soon as she is alone, she should call the police or rape hot line, and also a trusted friend or relative to provide emotional support.

2. The victim should not take off her clothes, douche, or wash until the police have had a chance to gather corroborative evidence. Solid evidence can increase the chance of convicting the rapist, and thus increase conviction rates, which in turn may help deter future rapes (Frazier and Borgida, 1985).

3. If she lives alone, the victim should consider staying with a friend or relative for a few days.

4. The victim should not deny any of her feelings. If she continues to be anxious or upset, she should get professional help before symptoms crystallize or generalize.

RESEARCH PROFILE

Social Deviance and Alcohol Expectancy

The text in Chapter 11 describes research by Marlatt and his colleagues on the potency of an expectancy factor in alcohol-related behavior. A later study by George and Marlatt (1986) expanded this notion to the issue of social deviance.

Male subjects were recruited through campus posters and newspapers advertising "earn $5.00 for participation in an experiment on alcohol use and subjective judgment." The researchers used their standard research design: Some subjects expected to receive alcohol in a clear drink, only some of who actually did. Similarly, in a second group, all of whom expected to receive a nonalcoholic drink, some actually received alcohol. In addition, half of the subjects in each of these four subgroups were exposed to an anger provocation situation generated by a confederate of the experimenter; the other subjects were not so exposed. Subjects were then allowed to choose (both as to which slides and how long they watched) exposure to violent, erotic, violent-erotic, or neutral slides.

Unlike some earlier studies, anger provocation did not produce any especially significant effects in this study. However, consistent with prior studies, subjects who expected to receive alcohol reported higher levels of sexual arousal. This occurred regardless of whether or not they actually received alcohol.

Of probably greater significance was the new finding that subjects who expected to receive an alcoholic drink showed much greater interest in and reported more arousal toward the violent-erotic slides. Again, whether they had actually ingested alcohol was not important. The effect occurred only when they thought they had. This supports the hypothesis that an expectancy of having consumed alcohol becomes especially useful to the self-image when the would-be drinker acts on an opportunity to behave in socially deviant, undesirable, or unconventional ways. This effect derives from a message that is often communicated socially throughout our society. Thus, while alcohol may release some inhibitions physiologically, this additional psychological expectancy factor puts individuals and society at additional risk for destructive behaviors by people consuming alcohol, e.g., agression and rape.

Treatment of the Rapist. Very few rapists voluntarily seek treatment. And of that small percentage of rapists who are successfully prosecuted and are then somehow pushed into treatment, few cooperate wholeheartedly.

Castration and execution have been the traditionally preferred ways of dealing with rapists. They are effective deterrents for that individual rapist, but there is little evidence that these measures deter other rapists. Aversive techniques can be helpful in controlling the rape impulse, in much the same way that they are used to change a homosexual orientation to a heterosexual one (see Chapter 10). Drugs, such as medroxyprogesterone, have been used to lower the serum testosterone level in violent rapists, thereby reducing the likelihood of any sexual arousal at all (Walker, 1978; Walker and Meyer, 1981). The major difficulty in this treatment is getting the rapist to cooperate; also, the side effects of these drugs are substantial.

Murder

Murder is defined legally as nonjustifiable homicide. In the United States it is subclassified as first- or second-degree murder or first-degree manslaughter, depending on motivation and premeditation. The United States, with 18,692 reported murders in 1985, has the highest murder rate among North American and Western European countries (Bureau of Justice, 1985; Webster, 1985).

Most murders are committed by males under age 35. In 1975, four times as many males as females committed murder. Since then, the percentage of females has gradually increased (Heidensohn, 1986). A higher percentage of nonwhites than whites commit murder. About 40 percent of victims are strangers to the murderer, and in approximately 95 percent of all murders the killer and victim are of the same race. Sixty percent of murders involve guns, many of them cheap handguns known as "Saturday night specials." Interestingly, murders occur most frequently in December and least often in February (Webster, 1985).

Murder, like rape, is a behavior rather than an emotional disorder, and a wide variety of personality types are capable of committing it. Because murder, even more than rape, is frequently a crime of incidental impulse, the murderer is more commonly a reasonably normal individual. In fact, if authorities were to decide to release a group of prisoners by type of crime, first-degree murderers might be a good choice, for two reasons. First, because many are imprisoned for crimes of impulse rather than for planned, conscious behaviors, positive changes in their living conditions could radically reduce the probability that they will repeat their crime. Second, because they receive long sentences, they are likely to be older on the average than other criminal groups, and what psychopathy they do have may have dissipated. With increasing age, manifestations of psychopathy diminish, partly because in most people stimulation-seeking behavior lessens as they age (Zuckerman et al., 1980). By contrast, the potentially most dangerous inmates are those with a history of assault starting before age 18. They are statistically highly likely to be dangerous to others again (Bureau of Justice, 1985).

Causes. The data presented above confirm the theory that there is no common "killer personality." Although persons with a paranoid disorder are more likely to be dangerous to others than persons with an emotional disorder, there is a slight negative correlation between diagnosed mental disorder and murder. In fact, the per capita percentage of murders is higher in the general population that it is among former mental patients (Lunde, 1976).

As is noted in the Exhibit, murder rates tend to be highest on the weekend, and suicides at the beginning of the week (Klebba, 1981). One theory is that distress experienced on the weekend (which, if acted out in extreme form, would lead to murder), if unresolved, turns inward as the weekend ends, facilitating suicide. Lunde (1976) also finds that there is a higher rate of murder during a full moon. Most agree that this is simply a result of

EXHIBIT

Murder Rates versus Suicide Rates

Average Number of Homicides and Suicides, by Days of the Week

	Homicides	Suicides
Monday	48	78
Tuesday	43	75
Wednesday	43	72
Thursday	48	72
Friday	53	73
Saturday	74	72
Sunday	65	72

Adapted from data in Klebba (1981).

better visibility, because there is a similar correlation between murder and other weather conditions that promote visibility. So, contrary to the message of many frightening movies, if you want to take a walk in a dangerous neighborhood, you are advised to do it on a foggy, rainy night.

Prevention. Unlike schizophrenia or depression, murder is a discrete behavior, so the aim is prevention, not cure. Three strategies that would help are: (1) finding better methods of treating the antisocial and paranoid disorders; (2) providing more therapy for violence-prone families; and (3) curtailing the availability of cheap handguns, whose only apparent function is killing other humans. The great majority of guns used in murders are purchased for "self-defense," rather than for hunting or target shooting, so it is ironic that the victim is often the person who purchased the gun.

DETERRING CRIME AND VIOLENCE

An initial step in controlling societal violence is to reduce the amount of violence portrayed in the media, especially violence on television that is watched by children. In 1955 there were no violent, crime-oriented shows on television. By 1965, there were six hours of such shows per week, and by 1985 there were 27 hours of violent shows, nine hours of which appeared in the 8:00 p.m. time slot commonly viewed by children (Schwartz, 1985).

Society's eventual response to most of the patterns noted in this chapter is to imprison or even execute individuals displaying them. There has long been intense controversy in our society as to whether the death penalty is a deterrent to potential criminals. The use of the death penalty in legal codes may have been most widespread in eighteenth-century England, when criminal laws for 225 different offenses specified execution by hanging (Ignatieff, 1978).

Reviewing other studies, along with a sophisticated data analysis of his own, Bailley (1977) concluded that there is no clear evidence that the death penalty has a deterrent effect. But, at the same time, there is also no clear evidence that it is not a deterrent. Studies on the effect of the death penalty are limited by not knowing exactly how well-informed the public is about an execution or with what certainty executions occur as a result of committing a crime; any deterrence effect is dependent upon the perceptions of these events by the citizenry. The truth is, no one knows for certain whether the death penalty is a deterrent, and methodological problems make it unlikely that we ever shall. At the same time, there is much clearer data that deterrence is effective with lesser crimes (Montmarquette and Nerlove, 1985). Most experts feel that swiftness and certainty of punishment are more effective than severity of sentence. In the U.S. legal system, however, punishment is seldom either

The debate over whether imprisonment of convicts deters crime has raged for centuries. Even today, some argue that prisons create more criminals than they rehabiliate.   (Richard Hutchings/Photo Researchers, Inc.)

certain or swift. For example, if someone is mugged in Tokyo, there is close to a 50 percent chance of an arrest; the chance is about two percent in New York City.

There are some indexes that predict recidivism (a return to a prior pattern) for criminal behavior. The major predictor is a history of criminal offenses, especially if they occur before age 18 (Bureau of Justice, 1985). As noted elsewhere, "Behavior predicts behavior." Another variable that predicts recidivism is type of offense. Auto theft, burglary, larceny, forgery, and fraud all predict an eventual return to criminal behavior. So do being unmarried, having an unstable employment history, having had a very unstable or punitive early childhood, and having a history of drug use or alcohol abuse (Wilson and Herrnstein, 1985). Having been a mental patient is not necessarily predictive of criminal or violent behavior. Patients with arrest records prior to hospitalization have high crime rates after discharge. Patients without previous records have arrest and violent crime records equal to or lower than those of the general public (Lunde, 1976; Teplin, 1985).

Aside from making punishment more Swift, Sure, Severe, and Selective (focusing on the recidivism-prone individual), there are other possible ways to prevent violence and crime.

1. Reducing the level of child abuse and neglect should lower future levels of aggression (Finkelhor, 1985).

2. Putting more research and money into early socialization programs, such as Head Start and effective day care (Newman and Newman, 1987).

3. Reducing the amount of violence in the media should reduce both the number of models for aggression and the acceptance of aggression as a solution for conflicts or distress. Because research shows that this response tendency develops early, it is especially important to decrease the portrayal of violence in television programs for children (Schwartz, 1985).

4. Reducing aggressive militarism is important not only to lower respect for those who embrace violence as a way of life but also to reduce the chances of ultimate violence, a nuclear holocaust.

5. Reducing violence in such games as football and basketball that offer so many hero models to society might also help. These sports heros especially appeal to young males, the major perpetrators of most violent crimes (Mash and Terdal, 1988).

THE IMPULSE DISORDERS

The disorders discussed in this section (which, except for overeating, are DSM categories) may include violence, but their primary feature is impulsiveness, which may be evident in a variety of other behaviors. Two **impulse disor-**

ders that receive a fair amount of attention in the media are kleptomania and pyromania. Kleptomania, or compulsive stealing, is not uncommon; pyromania, or compulsive fire-setting, is rare. Other fairly widespread impulse disorders include pathological gambling and overeating.

Pyromania

It is estimated that as many as 80 percent of fires in businesses are caused by arson. However, these arsonists are more likely to be antisocial personalities hired for the purpose than true pyromaniacs. Some theorists have linked true **pyromania** to sexual pathology, and they assert that there is a specific sequence of fire-setting arousal and urination (Fenichel, 1945). In fact, however, there is little well-documented research on this disorder. What is known suggests that pyromania has its onset in childhood and is much more common in males than in females. Pyromaniacs are usually lonely, frustrated, and lacking in self-esteem. The fire-setting follows a buildup of tension and provides a sense of release or even pleasure. Pyromaniacs may show an inordinate interest in firefighting paraphernalia, and usually like to watch the results of their efforts, making detection easier than might be expected. The bizarre fantasy life that often accompanies pyromania is well portrayed in Barry Hannah's 1972 novel *Geronimo Rex*.

> And then I sat in my car in the garage for two hours one night thinking about *Dream of Pines* until I decided I wanted to see everything in it burn—the subdivisions and Pierre Hills, and especially those houses on the track like Ann's house, and Ann tangled up with her current lover in the back seat of a car parked in her front yard, Ann on fire like a building, with her ribs broiling in an x-ray view, and the guy she was with screeching as his crotch turned to embers and flames took his head. And you bet I wanted Harley Butte's house on fire: Harley lying in bed with his musical instruments having been made into molten brass by the fire before he wakes up, and then he wakes up to be scorched to death, howling, by the molten pool. I also wondered what my old man would do if he woke up with walls of fire in all corners of his room. I had a box of wooden matches with me and struck one by one in the car, studying each one from the initial ragged burst of yellow to the cool blue wavering blade at the last. I wanted Dream of Pines High School to burn too; to turn into the coal skeleton like the matches did.
>
> It's hard to tell whether my trumpet-playing profited by all this fire I was dreaming up (p. 57).

It is important to intervene as early as possible in pyromania. Because the behavior often reflects underlying family pathology, most cases warrant family therapy. Individual psychotherapy with the pyromaniac, especially when focused on changing self-verbalizations (the messages and self-instructions we all tend to subvocally repeat to ourselves) (Meichenbaum, 1977), is another potentially useful treatment. Multimodal programs also have successfully used two specific behavioral techniques. Overcorrection requires the client to make a new positive response in the area of conflict. An example would be public confession and restitution through working to repay the costs of the fire damage. Negative practice involves making the person perform the behavior until it becomes aversive. This might entail requiring the pyromaniac to strike a thousand or more matches one at a time within the confines of the therapy setting.

Kleptomania

Shoplifting (referred to in the retail trade as "inventory shrinkage") is a common crime in our society; statistics compiled by the U.S. Department of Commerce indicate that about one of every 12 shoppers is a shoplifter, and only one in 35 is apprehended. Many people shoplift for a thrill, to be "one of the gang," or to get something for nothing. A substantial number are kleptomaniacs have no real need or use for the stolen object; their solitary act is a response to an "irresistible impulse," followed by a sense of release. They

Shoplifting, a formal DSM category, resembles overeating in that behavior patterns are developed early in life and may involve compulsiveness.   (Robert Houser/Photo Researchers, Inc.)

are less likely than the "normal" shoplifter to be deterred by an increased probability of being punished (Montmarquette and Nerlove, 1985).

Early formulations about the causes of **kleptomania**, like those of pyromania, hypothesized sexual problems (Fenichel, 1945), but again, clear support for this claim has not been forthcoming. More recent formulations have focused on anxiety reduction, combined with a "training experience" in an adolescent peer group that engages in stealing. Kleptomaniacs frequently stole with friends during adolescence, and the reinforcement gained at that time established the later solitary behavior.

Khan and Martin (1977) saw a late-middle-aged male who was caught shoplifting and who showed recent evidence of cortical atrophy (degeneration of the front part of the brain). At first they thought the brain dysfunction had caused the behavior, but later they found that the kleptomania pattern had been established before the atrophy. This man's self-perceived loss of functioning because of the brain damage created anxiety and led him to increase his stealing behavior.

Kellam (1969) used aversive conditioning to cure a chronic kleptomaniac of shoplifting in department stores. Kellam filmed the client as he simulated his entire shoplifting sequence, then asked him to participate as vividly as he could in his imagination while the film was played back. A painful shock was adminsitered at critical points in the sequence. Clients who are highly motivated to change can use a variation of this technique by carrying a portable shock unit and self-administering a shock when the impulse to steal arises. If carrying such a unit is impossible for some reason, clients can be instructed to hold their breath until they experience discomfort, which acts as an aversive cue.

Pathological Gambling

Like kleptomania and pyromania, **pathological gambling** is a formal DSM category. About 60 percent of the overall population has participated in gambling of some form. Approximately five million Americans at some time in their lives show at least some characteristics of compulsive gambling, and conservative estimates are that there are over one million gamblers in the United States who meet the DSM criteria for pathological gambling (Goldstein et al., 1985). Compulsive gamblers, like antisocial personalities, are stimulation-seeking, and describe their life experience when not gambling as "boring." As with the stimulation-seeking component of the antisocial personality, some disorder or dysregulation of the brain may predispose one to pathological gambling (Goldstein et al., 1985). Most pathological gamblers work at jobs largely to make money to gamble. Others are more outwardly normal and may channel their gambling into more legitimate outlets, such as the commodities market, or playing lotteries.

Some researchers think that people get "hooked" on gambling because they are better at it than most and thus are more highly reinforced by success. To test this, Malkin and Syme (1985) took 16 male pathological gamblers and a matched group of 16 social or occasional gamblers, and gave them a chance to gamble for six different prize levels ($50 to $1,000) under seven different probabilities of winning (0.01 to 0.99) They found, somewhat surprisingly, that the pathological gamblers tended to bet more heavily when there was less probability of winning, and thus less effectively, whereas the occasional gamblers bet more under conditions in which there was a higher probability of winning. Different prize levels did not produce significant differences in amounts gambled.

It appears that several factors can predispose a person to pathological gambling. These include family values that emphasize material symbols rather than savings and financial planning, an absent parent before age 16, an extroverted and competitive personality, and a gambling model in the family. Tacit cultural acceptance of gambling also increases the number of abusers. For example, Chinese cultural values strongly disapprove of alcoholism, but approve of gambling as an acceptable channel for stimulation-seeking. As a result, the number of pathological gamblers is relatively high in Chinese cultures (Sanua, 1980). In the United States, Gamblers Anonymous, modeled on Alcoholics Anonymous, has been helpful for some. In most cases, the habit continues throughout life (Malkin and Syme, 1985).

Trichotillomania

The term **trichotillomania** was first introduced by Hallopeau in 1889 to designate a pattern of continuing irresistible urges to pull one's hair. It usually, though not always, focuses on the hair of the head, and often continues until all of the hair is pulled out. It generally starts in childhood in children who seem to use it as a distractor from a very chaotic family situation. It then continues in adulthood as a distractor from any stress or anxiety, just as overeating does for some other individuals. It is a difficult disorder to treat effectively, though some success has been had with aversive behavior control techniques.

Overeating

Americans seem to agree with the Duchess of Windsor's comment, "You can never be too rich or too thin." We have long been fascinated by weight, and its extreme manifestation termed **obesity**, and how to control it. In fact, overweight is a major public health problem in the United States (Epstein et al., 1985). A variety of possible physiologic causes can lead to obesity, including glandular disorder, developing an extensive level of adipose tissue (fat cells) through overeating in infancy, genetic predisposition, and, in some extremely rare cases, a tumor. In May, 1979, a team of surgeons at the University of California Medical Center successfully removed a benign ovarian tumor weighing more than 200 pounds. The woman, who had been gaining weight since her teens, had assumed she was simply getting fat.

Some overweight individuals engage in **bulimia**, a syndrome that involves gorging followed by purging. The essential feature of the pattern is binge eating, interspersed with periods of substantial depression. Because bulimaretics tend to be "extroverted perfectionists" (Casper et al., 1980), treatment often combines techniques to treat depression (Chapter 9) and compulsiveness (Chapter 5) with techniques aimed specifically at controlling overeating. Bulimia often alternates with periods of anorexia nervosa, a pattern of self-starvation (see Chapter 16 for a more detailed discussion of both bulimia and anorexia nervosa).

Although depression or compulsiveness may be involved, the great majority of overweight individuals are simply a result of the "too syndrome"; they eat too much and exercise too little, and the reasons given for not exercising enough are that they are too busy, sick, old, tired, or that exercise is too boring. For these people, the primary causes are psychological factors and loss of impulse control in the face of certain environmental cues (Van Strien, 1986).

Numerous techniques have been devised to control overweight. Some act to control the problem physically, while others combine behavior modification approaches in an overall program of weight loss.

Physical Control Techniques

1. *Intestinal bypass surgery.* A portion of the intestine or stomach is removed, so that food moves more quickly through the area and less is processed into energy. In one technique, the surgeon literally bypasses about 90 percent of the stomach by pulling it to one side and stitching it up. Basically, a two-quart container is transformed into a two-inch pouch. This procedure has all the dangers of major surgery and is reserved for very severe cases that have not responded to other techniques.

2. *Psychosurgery.* Lesions are produced in certain brain sites to reduce appetite. This technique also entails major surgery, and it has not been consistently effective.

3. *Stomach balloon.* Functionally a temporary gastric bypass, a balloon is guided down the throat to the stomach with a narrow, flexible tube, then is inflated to the size of a grapefruit. It minimizes overeating by making the client feel full. Unlike bypass surgery, it is relatively cheap, not especially dangerous, is reversible, and has few side effects or complications. It is effective for establishing an initial weight loss, but much of the weight returns unless behavioral lifestyle changes are firmly established.

4. *Metabolism drugs.* Drugs, such as the amphetamines, are used to raise metabolism and suppress appetite. Now that physicians are becoming more aware of the problematic side effects of these drugs and of their potential for dependency and abuse, they are less likely to prescribe them.

5. *Inhibitor drugs.* Research is progressing on drugs that will inhibit absorption of fat-producing carbohydrates or sugars during digestion. Phaseolamin reduces the absorption of starchy carbohydrates; substances being developed by various pharmaceutical companies can block the digestion of sugars. Theoretically, people could take these drugs, eat all they want at a meal, and gain little or no weight.

An Overall Program. Although a physical technique to curb weight gain can be useful in certain cases, a standard weight control program first developed by Richard Stuart (1967) in line with traditional behavioral principles has proved effective with virtually any client who will follow the plan. The difficulty lies in getting the client to persist in the program (Van Strien, 1986).

Rapid weight loss is ineffective in the long run. In fact, weight loss of more than a pound a week usually is nothing more than loss of water, which can quickly build up again. A weight loss program must entail a lifestyle change rather than a fad diet (Epstein et al., 1985), and the essential goals must be (1) move more, (2) eat less, and (3) markedly decrease the percent of fat in the diet.

1. Clients should eat only in designated places, such as at the dining table, since overweight people consistently associate eating with too many cues. For example, many people habitually get something to eat when they walk into a movie theater or sit down to watch television. After a while, sitting down in a theater or turning on a television actually brings on physiologically conditioned hunger responses. This negative use of the Premack principle (pairing, in time, a more commonly occurring behavior with a less frequent one raises the frequency of the latter) can be reversed by doing some form of exercise immediately upon performing the behavior, such as riding an exercise bike as soon as one turns on the television. Eventually this strategy develops the positive conditioned response of a desire to exercise rather than eat.

2. A related strategy is to do nothing else—such as watching television or reading—while eating.

3. Varying amounts of food should be left on the plate. Overweight individuals consistently leave less food on their plate than normal people do.

4. In general, the overweight are less aware of what, how much, and how they eat. At least initially, the overweight person should keep a diary of what is eaten. Forcing oneself to eat more slowly, taking smaller bites and chewing longer, increases awareness of these processes; and, as in biofeedback, increased awareness leads to changed behavior.

5. Eating a good breakfast is important. Many fat people skip breakfast, eat a light lunch, and then eat a lot in the late afternoon and at night, a time when calories are more likely to turn to fat than energy. Also, eating a number of smaller meals rather than one or two very big ones is advisable.

6. If any snacking is allowed, it should include only low-calorie foods, such as raw carrots or celery. Junk food should be kept from easy access.

7. Both eating and exercise behavior must be monitored. Exercise is critically important in achieving weight loss. Increasing exercise not only uses up calories, but it also acts to suppress appetite naturally. Extended exercise, such as walking, is usually more helpful than short bursts of strenuous exercise, mainly because it is more likely to become part of a person's lifestyle (Epstein et al., 1985).

As a last note, people who diet with amphetamines or powder formulas quickly rebound to their original weight (or more) once they go off the diet, probably because the metabolism rate has been changed. Also, staying on such diets for long periods of time can be physically harmful. Analogously, smokers often gain weight when they stop smoking. This is because smoking raises the metabolism rate. Thus, when one quits smoking, metabolism slows, so if exercise and eating levels remain the same, weight will be gained.

This chapter completes the sequence devoted to behavioral acting-out disorders, that is, sexual variations, drug use disorders, and the personality and impulse disorders and violence. The next chapter focuses on disorders in which brain dysfunction is a critical factor, that is, neuropsychology.

CHAPTER REVIEW

1. Although they do not show the evident anxiety, bizarreness, or severe loss of ability to function that characterizes many other disorder patterns, the personality disorders are chronic, common, and inflexible patterns of behavior that disrupt vocational and interpersonal functioning.

2. The antisocial personality disorder, which is related to the traditional concept of a psychopath, is marked by amorality, chronic breaking of society's rules, narcissism, and a high level of stimulation seeking. Like most of the personality disorders, any substantial cure is very difficult to achieve.

3. Megargee's empirically derived classification of criminal personalites reflects the diversity found in most prison populations.

4. The explosive disorder shows sporadic acting out of aggression, but not the associated brain dysfunction or disrupted memory during violent events that is typical in conditions like psychomotor epilepsy.

5. Rape is a pattern that typically includes a varying mixture of both sexual and aggressive motivation. Unlike normal people, the sexual arousal of rapists is not inhibited—and may even be promoted—by aggression-oriented sexual stimuli.

6. Persons who have been exposed to abuse or to modeling of aggression as children are more likely to show aggression as adults. The specific act of murder, however, is more often an immediate result of interpersonal conflict and passion than deliberate behavior.

7. The DSM impulse disorders, pathological gambling, kleptomania, and pyromania, represent responses to an "irresistible impulse," followed by a sense of release or even euphoria.

8. Overweight in most individuals is simply a result of eating too much and expending too little energy. Physical control techniques such as drugs or bypass surgery can help some severe cases. For people who are able to maintain a long-term program, behavioral techniques—such as eating in designated places and monitoring the specific eating patterns—are successful.

TERMS TO REMEMBER

personality disorders
borderline personality
paranoid personality
schizotypal personality
schizoid personality
avoidant personality
passive-aggressive personality
obsessive-compulsive personality
narcissistic personality
histrionic personality
dependent personality
self-defeating personality
antisocial personality

psychopath
criminal personality
violence
explosive disorder
rape
impulse disorders
pyromania
kleptomania
pathological gambling
trichotillomania
obesity
bulimia

FOR MORE INFORMATION

Doren, D. (1987) *Understanding and treating the psychopath*. New York: John Wiley. A fine overview of the issues related to the most important of the personality disorder patterns

Frazier, P., and Borgida, E. (1985) Rape trauma syndrome evidence in court. *American Psychologist* 40:984–993. An excellent article that discusses not only the issue of rape in general, but especially the problems of proving rape in the legal arena

Galski, T. (Ed.). (1986). *The handbook of pathological gambling*. Springfield, Ill.: Charles Thomas. Considers all aspects of an impulse disorder, pathological gambling, that appears to be on the rise in modern society

Goldstein, J. (1986) *Aggression and crimes of violence*. New York: Oxford University Press. A superb treatment of how aggression develops, and how general trends toward violence become manifest in specific violent criminal patterns

Heidensohn, F. (1986) *Women and crime*. New York: New York University Press. Dr. Heidensohn documents the increasing involvement of women in both violent and nonviolent crime, and she cites the various causes for this phenomenon

Layton, L., and Schapiro, B. (Eds.). (1986) *Narcissism and the text: Studies in the literature and the psychology of self*. New York: New York University Press. A collection of essays on the relation of literature to theories of the self, and how the self becomes distorted in such patterns as the personality disorders

Levin, D. (1987) *Pathologies of the modern self*. New York: New York University Press. A highly readable account of some of the personality disorders, e.g., the narcissistic and dependency patterns, that are facilitated by the factors peculiar to modern society

Megargee, E., and Bohn, M. (1979) *Classifying criminal offenders*. Beverly Hills, Calif.: Sage. A classic research study of the methodological and diagnostic problems encountered in the wide variety of persons inclined toward criminal behavior

Millon, T. (1981) *Disorders of personality*. New York: John Wiley and Sons. This definitive source book on the personality disorders also provides extensive coverage on the impulse disorders

Stearns, C., and Stearns, P. (1987) *Anger*. Chicago: University of Chicago Press. A sophisticated and provocative history of anger and its effects on the development of American society

V

Organic and Developmental Disorders

Despite his creator's efforts, Peter Boyle as the Monster in *Young Frankenstein* cannot conform to society's expectations of behavior. (Museum of Modern Art/Film Stills Archive; © 1974 20th Century-Fox Film Corporation)

13

Neuropsychological Deficits Associated with Central Nervous System Impairment

For centuries, scientists and physicians have been convinced that an analysis of brain functions holds the key to an understanding of much of human behavior. It has been only comparatively recently, however, that investigative research techniques have become sophisiticated enough to permit a detailed analysis of brain-behavior relationships. This chapter provides the reader with some basic background material fundamental to an understanding of how the brain and nervous system control and direct much of our behavior.

● The Case of Cecelia

Cecelia was 63 years old when she first had a stroke. She awoke early one morning unable either to speak or to move her right arm or leg. Her husband had gotten up earlier, and only discovered her condition when he came to see why she had not arisen at her accustomed time. Previously in fairly good health, she had noticed some tingling sensations up and down her right side during the previous few weeks, but had thought nothing of it.

At the hospital, a brain scan (CAT scan) showed an area of damage in the frontal lobe of the left hemisphere. An electroencephalogram (EEG) was also abnormal, noting irregular electrical discharges in the area of the left frontal lobe. Throughout all of this, Cecelia remained dimly conscious of what was going on around her, though she remembered little of it afterwards.

Following several days of observation, she was transferred to a treatment center specializing in rehabilitation of victims of stroke and accidents. She was evaluated by a team consisting of a physician and primary nurse, plus specialists in the areas of neuropsychology and occupational, speech, physical, and recreational therapies. At the time of admission, her level of alertness was markedly improved, and she was able to begin a program of rehabilitation right away. She made good progress, and was discharged one month later. At that time, she was able to move about with a walker, and could communicate her needs through a combination of gestures and brief statements. She was able to return home, largely because of a supportive family and an attentive husband, who was reluctant to admit her to a nursing home.

INTRODUCTION

Our discussions of abnormal behavior thus far have tended to focus on social and other environmental forces as sources of psychological problems. Collectively, these are referred to as *exogenous* variables, grouped together because they refer to forces that are outside, or *ex*ternal to, the individual. Discussions of exogenous variables are consistent with the idea that behavior patterns are influenced, if not directly controlled by, conditions in the person's environment.

However, it is equally important to consider another large class of variables known to have powerful effects on behavior. *Endogenous* variables exert their influence from *within* the individual. Constitutional factors, genetic influences, and inner psychological states such as feelings and thoughts are frequently cited as examples of endogenous variables. Constitutional factors involve biologically based mechanisms, of which the most important for this chapter is the brain.

The brain and a group of related structures compose what is termed the *central nervous system*, or *CNS*. It has been the object of intense research by scholars in such diverse fields as neuroanatomy, biochemistry, psychology, and even philosophy. Some of the basic structures of the CNS are depicted in the Exhibit on page 489. Psychologists are interested in how the CNS regulates a wide range of behavioral, emotional, and cognitive functions, which has led to the development of a speciality known as **neuropsychology**. Most neuropsychologists work in clinics or hospitals with patients who have some form of CNS damage. Strokes are one of the most common injuries seen, but neuropsychologists also work with patients having other CNS disorders such as epilepsy, multiple sclerosis, and Alzheimer's disease. Usually, the patient is first tested to determine what behaviors are impaired as a result of brain damage. Then, working with other specialists on a treatment team, the neuropsychologist develops a therapeutic program to help both the patient and family members compensate for the effects of the patient's disabilities.

To do this effectively requires knowledge drawn from several scientific disciplines other than psychology, including neuroanatomy, which deals with the structure and functions of the CNS; and neuropathology, the study of CNS disorders (Le Doux and Hirst, 1986). To this the neuropsychologist adds a background in specialized assessment and intervention techniques normally acquired as part of the training for a doctoral degree in psychology. Neuropsychology is a relatively new discipline, having evolved from painstaking research and clinical work over the past 100 years that has markedly altered the way in which the brain's role in behavior is perceived.

For centuries, people have been aware that the brain exerts a controlling influence on behavior, but many false starts and erroneous assumptions were made along the way before the true nature of this relationship began to emerge. A crude link was evidently established at least 7000 years ago, according to evidence from archaeological excavations. Scientists have unearthed ancient skulls with large holes cut in them, apparently to release evil spirits believed responsible for dangerous or erratic behavior. This crude ancestor of neurosurgery was actually not as farfetched as it sounds, for it is sometimes necessary to open a person's skull to relieve internal pressure in the event of a sudden buildup of fluids within the brain. The name for this procedure is **trepanning**, and it is most commonly performed on patients who have suffered serious head injuries.

Several thousand years later Hippocrates, the Greek physician, helped establish a connection between certain forms of atypical behavior and the diseased brain (see Chapter 1). He provided a rational alternative to the still-prevalent viewpoint that demonic possession was responsible for abnormal behavior.

It is a point worth making that there is quite a difference between discovering an association between abnormal behavior and brain disease and knowing how the brain regulates behavior in the normal individual. Most early theories about brain-behavior relationships were based on observations of the first type. Patients with many types of brain injuries were evaluated by neurologists and other medical specialists who attempted to correlate damage to specific areas (referred to as *lesions*) with predictable effects on behavior. One outcome of this approach was an emerging picture of the brain as an organ comprising many discrete parts, each of which controlled very specific functions (Bridgeman, 1988).

One interesting realization of this idea was the theory of *phrenology*, developed in Germany by Franz Gall in the early nineteenth century. Gall believed that the brain was the focal point of all mental life, and could be subdivided into regions controlling specific mental activities. Of particular note was his hypothesis that bumps on the skull signified underlying brain regions of exceptional inherited development. Phrenology captured the public's fancy, resulting in demonstrations and carnival-like road shows where people came to have the bumps on their head interpreted (Marx and Hillis, 1987).

The idea that the brain was associated with control of specific mental activities persisted long after interest in phrenology subsided. It eventually evolved into a widely accepted model of how the brain functions, known as *localizationist* theory. One early illustration of this theory likened the brain to a telephone switchboard with wires running to and from the various muscles and organs of the body. This analogy proved valid in certain respects, for it is true that nerve fibers carry messages to and from the brain to all regions of the body. However, the theory was less successful in explaining how mental and psychological processes are carried out. To suggest that thoughts, feelings, memories, and language skills each rely on brain structures physically independent of one another is to oversimplify things greatly (Kolb and Whishaw, 1985).

The physical structure of the brain in fact lends itself fairly well to theories that associate specific regions with particular functions. The outer layer of brain tissue is the **cerebral cortex**, and is divided into a right and left *cerebral hemisphere*, to be referred to as the *RCH* and *LCH*. The Exhibit depicts a side, or *lateral*, view of the LCH. The front, or *anterior*, part of the brain is to the left, while the rear (*posterior*) surface is on the right. The hemisphere is further subdivided into four regions, or *lobes*. These are named the **frontal, temporal, parietal,** and **occipital lobes**, and can all be seen in the Exhibit. Another important region, the *brainstem*, emerges from the lower portion of the brain, and continues through the pons and medulla to form the spinal cord. Just behind the brainstem is a structure known as the *cerebellum*. The distinctiveness of these structures has made it tempting to assign them specific functions. And indeed, early research tended to bear this theory out.

In 1846, a French neurologist named Paul Broca reported on a famous case that did much to advance the localizationist position. One of his patients abruptly lost the ability to speak shortly before he died, though he remained reasonably alert until the end. A postmortem examination revealed damage near the front LCH. Broca believed that the control of speech resided in this region, which was eventually named **Broca's area** in his honor.

It was not long before the effects of lesions in other parts of the brain were discovered to have relatively specific effects on cognition and behavior. The nineteenth century neurologist Carl Wernicke, discovered, for example, that patients lost the ability to comprehend speech when a region just behind Broca's area was damaged. Lesions in another region of the LCH were found to impair control of movement on the *opposite* side of the body, including that of the right hand. The LCH soon became associated with the control of a number of vital capabilities, eventually resulting in its designation as the *dominant* hemisphere.

EXHIBIT

Lateral View of Brain Showing the Following Structures:

Frontal Lobe	Parietal Lobe	Temporal Lobe
Occipital Lobe	Central Sulcus	Pre-central Gyrus
Post-central Gyrus	Sylvian Fissure	Cerebellum
	Medulla	Pons
		Brainstem

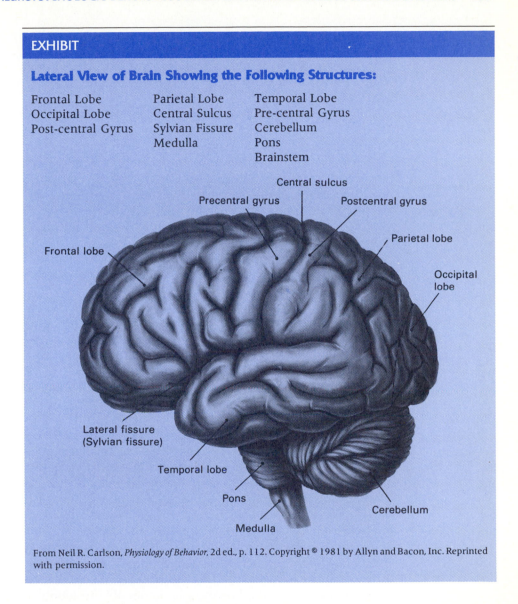

From Neil R. Carlson, *Physiology of Behavior*, 2d ed., p. 112. Copyright © 1981 by Allyn and Bacon, Inc. Reprinted with permission.

Despite an element of truth in this assertion, it is based on an erroneous assumption alluded to earlier. The problem lies in inferring the role of healthy brain tissue from observations of patients with *damaged* brain tissue. What is being localized is the symptom, rather than the function itself (Finger and Stein, 1982). In reality, a number of related brain centers are involved in the production of even such seemingly simple activities as drawing a line or repeating a word. A brain lesion in a specific area may interfere with performing some aspect of the task, without necessarily being responsible for the skill as a whole. Changes in behavior that occur following a brain lesion do not necessarily reveal what function that region served prior to injury; rather, they reveal the role of nonaffected brain tissue in the behavior of interest (Jackson, 1958).

An idea that ran somewhat counter to the localizationist theory of brain function attained support early in the twentieth century. Termed the theory of **equipotentiality**, it proposed that there is *not* in fact a simple one to one correspondence between brain structures and the behaviors they control. Proponents of equipotentiality believed that more than one region of the brain could control a given behavior. The theory was based on observations that nerve cell destruction in specific brain regions does not necessarily prohibit the subsequent reappearance of responses previously controlled by those cells. Related to equipotentiality theory was the Principle of Mass Action (Lashley, 1929), which stated that the amount of brain tissue damage by a lesion, rather than the location of the damage, essentially determined what the residual effects on behavior would be.

The theory of equipotentiality is particularly appealing because of its stress on the brain's adaptability. Numerous studies have documented the capacity of brain tissue either adjacent to or more remote from the site of a lesion to take over functions formerly associated with the damaged area (Smith and Sugar, 1975; Adamovich et al., 1984).

On the other hand, the equipotentiality theory has been criticized for several reasons, two of which seem especially important. First, there are limits to the flexibility of the CNS in adjusting to the effects of damage. The recovery of many patients with neurologic disease often stops far short of their preexisting capabilities, indicating that compensation by nonimpaired brain regions is only partially successful. Second, to a significant degree, brain regions do acquire functional assignments, which makes them less able to compensate for injury to other areas controlling different functions.

If neither the localizationist nor the equipotentiality theory provides an entirely satisfactory explanation of brain-behavior relationships, each has made important contributions to current knowledge in the area. What is needed is a theory that is able to merge the valid elements of both theories. There are in reality a number of recent advances in neural sciences that have helped resolve this dilemma. It would, however, be impossible to identify even a small proportion of the researchers who have made significant contributions. Instead, we have elected to discuss in some detail the work of one individual whose work has had a powerful influence on current models of how the brain functions. Alexander Luria was a Russian neuropsychologist whose many years of research and clinical work contributed significantly to current understanding of how the brain functions under normal conditions and, equally fascinating, how it is able to compensate for the effects of injury.

LURIA'S FUNCTIONAL ORGANIZATION OF THE BRAIN

Luria (1973) proposed a system of three interconnected functional units whose integration is essential for performing most behaviors. This represents a departure from strict localizationist theory, which assigned specific tasks to discrete brain regions. In contrast, Luria suggested that even behaviors that appear comparatively uncomplicated require the coordinated activity of multiple brain structures. Consequently, Luria placed a great deal more emphasis than the localizationists on how brain structures are *interconnected* with one another. On the other hand, Luria did not ascribe to the theory of equipotentiality, which argued against function localization. He proposed a model in which certain zones, or regions, of the CNS were responsible for particular functions. At the broadest level, there are three such regions. The first is the brainstem; second is the posterior portion of the cerebral hemispheres; and third is the area which encompasses the frontal lobes.

The first of these units, the brainstem, plays a key role in directing the individual's attention to incoming information. It also regulates the level of alertness and receptivity to stimulation. An especially important brainstem structure for controlling alertness is the *reticular activating system*, or **RAS**. Damage to the brainstem involving the RAS is frequently found in patients who experience prolonged unconsciousness, or *coma*. There is also some evidence linking a malfunction of the RAS to the syndrome of childhood hyperactivity. You may recall from an earlier chapter that the information processing deficits associated with schizophrenia have been found to stem in part from inadequate brainstem responses.

The second of Luria's three functional units includes a large portion of the cerebral cortex, encompassing the parietal, occipital, and temporal lobes (see Exhibit). This region is involved with the reception, analysis, and storage of information. It includes what Luria termed primary (sensory) and secondary (association) regions. The former are receptive centers for the various senses, including hearing, vision, and touch. Auditory impulses are transmitted to a portion of the temporal lobe; visual signals terminate in the occipital lobe; and tactile (touch) sensitivity is controlled by a region in the parietal lobe. In contrast, the secondary association areas lie adjacent to the sensory centers, and become highly interconnected with one another. Luria believed that these secondary regions integrate sensations from the various senses, thereby aiding the process of extracting meaning from incoming information. Connections between these and other brain structures that play an important role in memory provide a way of understanding how we are able to generate representations of sensory experiences and then store them for future reference. Exemplifying the concept of an association area is a structure called the **angular gyrus**, lying at the juncture of the parietal, occipital, and temporal lobes. More prominent on the left side than on the right, the angular gyrus undergoes additional, postnatal maturation as visual, auditory, tactile, and motor centers gradually become densely interconnected.

The primary and secondary association areas are frequently disrupted when brain injury occurs, due to the relatively large percentage of cortical tissue they occupy. Several characteristic impairment patterns associated with damage in these regions will be discussed in a later section of this chapter.

The third of Luria's basic neural components encompasses the frontal lobes, which are instrumental in planning and initiating behaviors, as well as more generally organizing sequences of responses that are carried out over a period of time. Luria attached a great deal of significance to frontal lobe structures, believing them to be essential to purposeful behavior.

According to Luria, virtually all behaviors depend on the coordinated integration of these three basic structural units. There are very few (if any) cognitive or behavioral capabilities that do not rely on integration for effective execution. For example, a moment's reflection will show how even so rudimentary a behavior as copying a line requires a high degree of integration within the brain, which might be broken down into a sequence of steps such as the following. First, becoming oriented and attentive to the figure activates the brainstem. The perception and analysis of the line to be copied could not occur without the visual areas. Executing the drawing calls on still another region, while the process of checking for accuracy and properly completing the task brings the frontal lobes into play.

The ideas that the CNS comprises a highly integrated structural system has greatly influenced many prominent theories of development and education (Filskov and Boll, 1986). As discussed by Gaddes (1981), these would include the holistic theories of cognitive development and education of Jean Piaget and Maria Montessori, and educational programs that stress the need for what is termed multisensory stimulation. According to this viewpoint, motor and sensory activity is essential for the development of higher-order cognitive skills. The significance of this for the present discussion lies in the fact that apparently, stimulation in one region of the CNS can impact on other areas as well, due to the high degree of integration among the various parts of the CNS. This is a highly significant discovery that was not predicted by any of the early theories of CNS organization already discussed.

COGNITIVE IMPAIRMENTS AND LOCALIZED CNS DAMAGE

Thus far, we have discussed some basic functional units of the intact CNS, using a model developed by Luria. Given this as a general background, we are now in a position to discuss the effects of localized brain damage on behavior. Let us consider the common types of cognitive impairments associated with damage to each of the four lobes in the cerebral hemispheres.

The four lobes of the brain are illustrated in the Exhibit. Notice how the surface of each lobe is convoluted, giving it a wrinkled appearance. The depressions, or crevices, in the cortical surface are known as *sulci*. The most prominent of these is the *central sulcus*, separating the frontal and parietal lobes. The **Sylvian fissure**, just above the temporal lobe, is like a sulcus except that it is much larger and deeper. It separates the temporal lobe from both the frontal and parietal lobes (Kolb and Whishaw, 1985).

Sections of the cortical surface bounded by two sulci are referred to as *gyri*. Two of these structures, the *precentral gyrus* and *postcentral gyrus*, appear in the Exhibit on either side of the central sulcus.

The Frontal Lobes

The frontal lobes occupy the largest proportion of cortical tissue and are among the last regions of the brain to mature (Filskov et al., 1981). Luria has accorded the frontal lobes considerable responsibility for the planning and organization of intentional behavior. It is not surprising, therefore, to find that many patients with frontal lobe lesions are unable to effectively regulate their behavior. There are, however, other types of impairments that may stem from frontal lobe damage, including a characteristic response pattern known as *perseveration*, problems with expressive language, and changes in emotional responsiveness (Kolb and Whishaw, 1985).

The regulation of purposeful activity is perhaps the most significant capability associated with the frontal lobes. The frontal lobes are highly interconnected with the rest of the brain and play a significant role in integrating incoming information from many regions. For example, the capacity to perceive and accurately copy a picture of something requires a high degree of integration between brain centers controlling visual perception and those involved in motor responses, such as hand movements. These regions are in fact located in very different parts of the brain. However, they are interconnected with each other and with the frontal lobes to achieve a high level of integration. Frontal lobe damage may impair this integration, resulting in poorly organized responses to such things as drawings that require a series of sequential steps. Typically, although patients with frontal lobe damage appear to understand the instructions for completing such a task, the end product is likely to lack organization and coherence. Walsh (1978) has identified several types of tests that seem particularly well suited to the assessment of frontal lobe damage. Among these are drawings, puzzles, and mazes, all of which require some degree of planning for accurate performance.

The ability to perform successfully tasks involving several steps requires more than just the ability to work according to a plan. It is also necessary to evaluate one's progress, make needed corrections, and determine when the work is finished. Some patients with frontal lobe damage find it difficult to terminate one response pattern and begin another, a symptom called

perseveration. An early study by Milner (1963), for example, found that frontal lobe damage impaired the ability to reclassify a group of pictures once they had been sorted on a particular dimension. A patient required to classify pictures of objects according to color, for example, would later find it difficult to shift and reclassify them according to shape or size.

There are other deficits associated with frontal lobe damage, as well. The neural structures needed for expressive speech are in the posterior frontal lobe of the LCH, as Broca first discovered. Damage in this area impedes fluent speech, symptomatic of a disorder known as *expressive aphasia* or *Broca's aphasia*. The speech of patients with this condition is painfully slow, labored, and at times unintelligible. It is what is referred to as *telegraphic speech*, where one or two key words—rather than full sentences—are used to convey the person's thoughts. Patients with Broca's aphasia come to rely on nonverbal gestures to get their ideas across.

There is yet another effect of frontal lobe damage, this time involving emotional responses. One of the earliest documented reports of this pattern involved a railroad worker named Phineas Gage, who was injured when an explosive charge ignited accidentally and drove a tamping iron through his skull. The iron pierced the frontal lobe region; there was little hope that he would survive. Remarkably, he lived for several more years and made a fairly good recovery, though he progressively became short-tempered, irritable, and impulsive. The effect of frontal lobe damage on emotions seems to take one of two distinct forms. In the first, the patient displays a syndrome marked by diminished anxiety, lack of concern for the future, and a pronounced loss of initiative. In the second form, patients become much more impulsive, facetious, and almost childlike in their behavior (Blumer and Benson, 1975).

The tranquilizing effect of frontal lobe damage on many patients is what prompted many neurosurgeons, before the advent of tranquilizing medications, to perform **lobotomies** on agitated patients in mental hospitals. In this operation, neural fibers normally connecting the frontal lobes with a group of subcortical structures collectively called the *diencephalon* are cut. Portions of the diencephalon regulate emotional expressiveness, and disconnecting this area from the frontal lobe had a calming effect that borders on apathy. Unfortunately, the operation was irreversible, and it rapidly fell into disfavor with the advent of psychotropic medications.

The Temporal Lobes

The temporal lobes are located behind and to the side of the frontal lobes. The Sylvian fissure, depicted in the Exhibit, forms the upper boundary of the temporal lobes. Two major types of deficits are commonly associated with temporal lobe lesions: disorders of memory, and a form of aphasia in which comprehension of speech is impaired. Perhaps the best known work on temporal lobe disorders was carried out by the neurosurgeon Wilder Penfield and the neuropsychologist Brenda Milner. One of Penfield's earliest discoveries was that mild electrical stimulation of certain portions of the temporal lobe evoked vividly detailed memories. Patients being operated on were brought out of anesthesia when electric current was applied, and typically reported that memories were replayed as if on a tape recorder. These and other investigations eventually led to the finding that damage in the left temporal lobe impairs memory for verbal information, whereas damage on the right side interferes with the ability to remember such nonverbal information as pictures and designs. In the unfortunate event of *bilateral* (affecting both right and left sides) damage, the patient is likely to show severe curtailment of almost all memory functions. Scoville and Milner (1957) published an interesting account of just such a patient. H.M., as he was known, had had sections of both temporal lobes removed to control severe epilepsy. Afterward, though he was of above-average intelligence, H.M. was unable to learn or remember virtually *any* new information. He constantly had to be reintroduced to people, places, and events. The tragedy of his situation may have been somewhat offset by the fact that he remembered little about what had happened to him or what he had done before the surgery (Milner et al., 1968).

Temporal lobe damage may also affect certain aspects of language. In particular, the posterior temporal lobe plays a crucial role in decoding speech. A lesion in this area may render the patient incapable of understanding what other people say. This disorder is frequently called either *fluent* or *Wernicke's aphasia*, in honor of the neurologist who first documented the condition. Patients with Wernicke's aphasia can speak so fluently that their pronunciation seems effortless. However, because they are unable to understand what is said to them, their speech is difficult to comprehend, since it is based on faulty comprehension. Because they are often unaware that their speech is confusing, patients with Wernick's aphasia sometimes become suspicious or angry when people appear perplexed by what they say (Gardner, 1976).

There are some interesting differences between the right and left temporal lobes in terms of what kind of auditory information they are most effective at processing. The most significant work in this area has been conducted by Doreen Kimura at the Montreal Neurological Institute. She developed a technique known as *dichotic listening*, which allows auditory stimulation to be delivered simultaneously but independently to the right and left ears. This is done using a two-channel tape recorder, and involves recording one signal on one channel and a different one on the other. The subject then listens to both tracks of the tape while wearing headphones that send one channel to the right ear and the other to the left. In a series of studies beginning in 1961, Kimura found consistent right ear superiority for word and number recognition (Kimura, 1961). When, for example, subjects hear two different sentences simultaneously, the one sent to the right ear has a greater probability of being accurately recalled. The implication of these results is that asymmetries in auditory recognition somehow reflect different

The Case of Tony

At age 23, Tony was in a serious automobile accident. The car in which he was riding was struck head-on, and although he was wearing a seat belt, Tony was thrown forward onto the dashboard and suffered a severe concussion. Unconscious only momentarily, he was apparently lucid by the time the ambulance arrived at the hospital. A CT scan performed at the time of admission indicated that some intracerebral bleeding had occurred, and that one of the bones of the skull had been fractured. Tony was hospitalized for several days, and was then discharged home to his parents. Within a week, however, the family was back at the institute for psychological consultation. Tony had become very forgetful, to the point of having to be prompted for even simple pieces of information he was presumed to know. He occasionally forgot the names of his brothers and sisters, and did not recognize his girl friend upon seeing her for the first time after the accident. His memory for certain events from the distant past seemed relatively intact, although a great deal of patience was needed to elicit accurate recall.

Tony was highly frustrated by this unexpected outcome. Before the accident, he had been a successful salesman who prided himself on having a good memory and being able to keep track of several hundred clients spread over a large geographic region. As events turned out, he was unable to resume work on even a limited basis for nearly a year after the accident.

At the rehabilitation institute, the neuropsychologist who worked with Tony began with some computer-based exercises to help him learn new strategies for remembering information. He learned to make use of visual images, key words, and prompts when learning new information, and also began to develop a written filing system that served as a source of information about his clients and sales work. With diligent practice, Tony made good progress in therapy, although his memory skills never approached their premorbid level, even after nearly a year of twice-weekly therapy and hours of practice. Tony instead learned to compensate for the effects of his impairment, and developed new strategies to help overcome the limitations imposed by his injury.

Tony eventually returned to sales work on a part-time basis. He made fewer sales calls, because each one took considerably more preparation than had previously been the case. Nevertheless, he made a good adjustment to his limitations in the aftermath of the accident, and was functioning well at a two-year follow-up visit.

functioning of the right and left temporal lobes, since many of the nerve fibers from each ear cross to the opposite side of the brain. Subsequent studies suggested that there is in fact just such an asymmetry, with the right ear/left hemisphere combination showing processing superiority for verbal material. However, this pattern is not something that is readily apparent, since the difference in processing efficiency appears to exist primarily when the two ears are stimulated simultaneously.

The Parietal Lobes

The parietal lobes are located behind the frontal and above the temporal lobes of each hemisphere. They are separated from the frontal lobe by the central sulcus, and from the temporal lobe by the Sylvian fissure (Kolb and Whishaw, 1985). The parietal lobe is the site of an important anatomical structure called the *angular gyrus* (Exhibit) that is found only in humans. This gyrus lies at the junction of the temporal, occipital, and parietal lobes, and serves to transmit information among other brain centers, such as those that regulate speech, motor, and visual functions. This structure is especially pronounced in the LCH, and is among the last cortical structures to mature.

Damage to the parietal lobe may thus interfere with the transmission of information between centers. But the parietal lobe is associated with important information processing capabilities of its own, as well, the most significant of which involves the ability to manipulate and conceptualize the spatial properties of objects. Being able to distinguish right from left, reading a map, and drawing pictures are all examples of activities that may be disrupted following damage to the parietal lobe. The RCH appears to play a relatively more dominant role in mediating these capabilities than the left, though damage in this region of either hemisphere can impair performance. (For a good example of the differing effects of right versus left parietal lobe damage, refer back to the human figure drawings discussed in Chapter 3.)

The parietal lobe also plays a role in processing various kinds of physical sensations. The *post-central gyrus* constitutes an area known as the **somesthetic cortex**, which processes sensations of pain, pressure, temperature, and feedback from muscles and joints. Frequently, parietal lobe damage will impair patients' awareness of both their surroundings and their own bodies. This symptom is called *neglect*, and involves a failure to adequately attend to either internal or external stimuli despite apparently intact sensation. Because nerve fibers carrying both visual and motor impulses cross from one side of the brain to the other, neglect is manifested on the side *opposite* the lesion. A patient with visual neglect may fail to attend to food on half of the tray, or shave only one side of his face. In severe cases, the patient may show *anosagnosia*, a form of neglect in which the side of the body opposite the lesion is utterly ignored, and treated as though it did not exist.

EXHIBIT

The Man Who Mistook His Wife For A Hat

Dr. P was an accomplished musician, active for many years in his community as both a singer and teacher. In his latter years, he developed a perplexing problem that puzzled his students, family, and physician: he became unable to recognize at sight people who were familiar to him. He had no trouble identifying people by the sounds of their voice, and was also able to name them if he could watch their movements.

At first, it was suspected that he had a visual problem, since he had diabetes, a disease known to affect eyesight. An examination proved negative, however, and it was at this point that he was referred to a neurologist. He was clearly highly intelligent, well-versed in a number of fields besides music. On most of the neurologic tests administered, he passed with flying colors, although the examination revealed somewhat abnormal reflex patterns on his left side. One reflex test required Dr. P. to remove his left shoe. When asked to replace it, however, he became confused and was unable to do so. He became confused as to the difference between his foot and his shoe.

Further testing revealed that he was unable to perceive whole images of objects. Instead, he attended to random details, which he was unable to piece together into wholes. He made many unusual errors of identification as a result of this impairment. When the neurologist paid a visit to Dr. P.'s house, he was startled to see the patient extend his hand in greeting to a grandfather clock. At other times, he literally mistook his wife for a hat, and was unable to identify her at sight. He was unable to identify well-known actors and actresses by sight, nor could he deduce the emotional states portrayed in their characters.

Utterly perplexed by many activities taken for granted by most people, Dr. P. appeared able to function only if he could incorporate music and movement into his world. He sang to himself continually, and in so doing was able to carry out many tasks that would otherwise have been impossible. His musical skills were exceptionally well retained, and aside from the unusual errors he made in

The Occipital Lobes

Adjoining and posterior to the parietal lobes lie the fourth major structural division of the cortex: the occipital lobes. The occipital lobes play a vital role in transforming visual sensations into meaningful images (Kolb and Whishaw, 1985). Patients who suffer occipital lobe damage are therefore likely to manifest impairments in some aspects of visual perception. A blind spot, or *scotoma*, is one symptom that may result from occipital lobe damage. Scotomas are often detected upon examination of the patient's field of vision, which normally describes a somewhat circular pattern from top to bottom and right to left. Blind spots consist of regions within the visual field where visual sensations are absent.

identifying people or objects, he was able to function remarkably well. He continued to teach and make music in this fashion until his death some years later due to a tumor in a region of his brain that processes visual information.

Dr. P.'s condition was described in great detail by the neurologist whom he had consulted. His inability to recognize things was determined to be a condition known in general terms as *agnosia*, a neurologically based disorder. More specifically, he suffered from *prosopagnosia*, a form of agnosia in which the person is unable to recognize faces of people, even those who are close family members. Prosopagnosia may even prevent people from identifying images of themselves, as in the case of one patient who was not sure that the face he saw in the mirror when he shaved every morning was really himself.

Prosopagnosia is of great interest to neuropsychologists for several reasons. First, it is not accompanied by impairments in vision per se; patients with the condition see quite well. This implies that the condition is due to an impairment in brain functioning not involving the eyes. Patients with this condition are unable to integrate features of complex visual images (like faces) into wholes for purposes of recognition. Like Dr. P., they are able to describe individual features of objects or people, but fail to organize their perceptions of things in a coherent fashion.

Studies of prosopagnosia have concluded that the condition is due to lesions in the right cerebral hemisphere. The finding in Dr. P.'s case of abnormal reflexes on the *left* side is consistent with this, since the right hemisphere controls the left side of the body, and vice versa. Studies to date suggest that accurate recognition of faces—even familiar ones—is a sophisticated task because faces themselves are such highly complex stimuli. Being able to differentiate people based on an analysis of their facial features alone is something that people tend to take for granted, but it is actually quite demanding in terms of the cognitive capabilities involved.

Sacks, O. (1985) *The man who mistook his wife for a hat.* New York: Summit Books.

Visual sensations eventually become transformed into identifiable images, a process that is carried out within the occipital lobes. The disruption of this capacity is known as **agnosia**, and involves a failure to visually recognize things, in the absence of a primary sensory deficit such as blindness.

Hemispheric Specialization

In addition to the specific functions associated with the four brain lobes, the right and left cerebral hemispheres appear to possess some specialized capabilities as well (Hertlage et al, 1987). The left hemisphere has the major

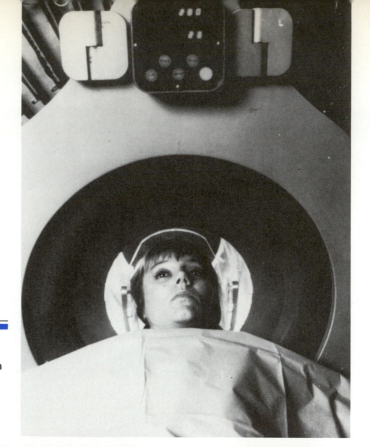

Positron Emission Tomography (PET) scans produce cross-sectional views of the brain's responses to stimuli by tracing the rate at which various brain regions use radioactive glucose that has been injected into the subject's bloodstream.   (top: Hank Morgan/Science Source, Photo Researchers, Inc.; bottom: NIH/Science Source, Photo Researchers, Inc.)

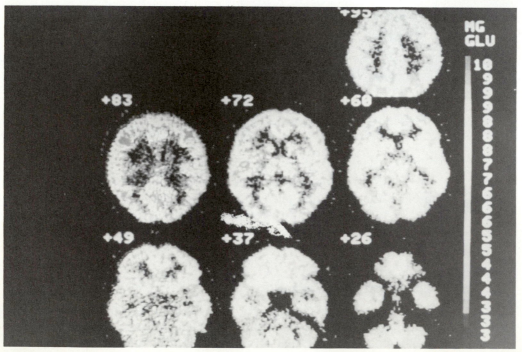

mediating role in speech and language, but the right cerebral hemisphere appears to have specialized functions of its own. There is, for example, considerable evidence that the right hemisphere plays a crucial role in the control of emotional expressions. A study by Sackheim et al. (1978) revealed some interesting patterns. In this study, pictures of human faces were split along the midline, and duplicates made of each half. Composite pictures were then assembled using two left-side and two right-side pieces. Subjects were shown the new composite photographs and had to evaluate the intensity of emotion expressed in each one. A consistent pattern emerged in which the left-side composite photographs were judged to be more highly emotionally expressive than were the right-side composite photos. The significance of this finding lies in the fact that the right hemisphere exercises predominant control over the left side of the body, including the face. The greater degree of emotional expression on the left side of the face was thus attributed to the mediating role of the right hemisphere.

DSM CLASSIFICATION OF CENTRAL NERVOUS SYSTEM IMPAIRMENT

Currently, there is considerable interest in the study and documentation of brain-behavior relationships. At a clinical level, this is reflected in increased emphasis on knowing some basic manifestations of brain damage. The DSM provides a general structure into which some of the symptoms of brain damage already discussed can be organized.

The DSM distinguishes between organic brain *syndromes* and organic mental *disorders*. The term "organic" has historically been used to denote CNS impairment, though it has in recent years fallen into disfavor because it lacks diagnostic specificity. **Organic brain syndromes** are patterns of psychological and behavioral symptoms that are independent of a particular causal factor. That is, they refer to symptoms that may arise from more than one condition. The abbreviation "OBS" is used in clinical settings to refer to Organic Brain Syndrome. Among the most common forms of OBS are *dementia, delirium*, and *amnesia*. There is in addition a personality syndrome associated with CNS impairment, called the organic personality syndrome.

The syndrome of dementia is marked by (1) impaired memory and (2) impairment in cognitive capabilities such as thought and reasoning. Delirium refers to disturbances of attention that are relatively short-lived. It involves a loss of orientation, although the patient remains conscious. Amnesia, or impaired memory, is most commonly manifested as the inability to recall the recent past. Many amnestic patients have relatively vivid memories dating back to childhood, but have great difficulty recalling, for example, what they have just eaten for dinner. Finally, patients with an organic personality

Alzheimer's, the most common form of senile disorder, recently played a role in a mercy killing. Roswell Gilbert, then 75, shot and killed his ailing wife, who suffered from Alzheimer's. He was found guilty of murder.   (AP/Wide World Photos)

syndrome manifest marked changes in personality or behavior. Impulsivity, heightened emotionality, apathy, or paranoid qualities may all be associated with this syndrome.

Dementia, delirium, amnesia, and the organic personality syndrome may accompany many forms of CNS impairment. Dementia, for example, may result from the effects of a stroke, from brain damage sustained in an auto accident, or as the result of a progressive neurologic disorder such as Alzheimer's disease. *Organic mental disorders*, on the other hand, refer to patterns of impairment associated with a specific dysfunction of the brain. The organic mental disorders are of two types. The first are those due to specific neurologic disorders frequently associated with advanced age. Primary degenerative dementia and multi-infarct dementia are the major disorders in the first group. Degenerative dementia is a progressive disease in which the patient's condition gradually worsens. Examples of degenerative dementias would include Alzheimer's disease and Pick's disease. In these conditions, there is an excessively rapid erosion in the network of nerve fibers that interconnect brain centers. As this process continues, the patient manifests a greater and greater degree of mental impairment.

Multi-infarct dementia is the other form of organic mental disorder. It reflects the fact that among older persons sudden disruptions of the brain's blood supply occur fairly commonly. These are referred to as *strokes* or *infarcts*. Many older hospitalized patients have been found to have multiple infarcts that have collectively impaired their mental processes; hence the term "multi-infarct dementia." Though not, strictly speaking, a degenerative condition, multi-infarct dementia is a disorder that often appears to worsen, as the collective effects of multiple infarcts gradually become evident.

There is also a group of organic mental disorders that are referred to as "substance induced." A variety of nonmedical substances contributing to this condition are listed in this category, and while it is not surprising to find alcohol and barbiturates among them, the presence of tobacco and caffeine may come as a surprise.

The organic mental disorders are encoded using both axes I and III of DSM. The particular disorder is listed on Axis I, while Axis III is used to denote the underlying biologic cause. A condition such as Alzheimer's disease would thus be listed on Axis I as "Primary Degenerative Dementia," and on Axis III as "Alzheimer's Disease." The remaining three axes are used as needed. Axis II, for instance, would be used only if the organic mental disorder was accompanied by a preexisting personality disorder. Axis IV would be used to denote psychosocial stressors that may be associated with the patient's condition. Axis V, used to specify the patient's highest level of function during the previous year, is useful in helping gauge just how debilitating the organic mental disorder is. Patients with progressive neurologic disease such as primary degenerative dementia show a more gradual path of declining capabilities than do patients with a history of strokes or auto accidents. This differing rate of change in psychological status will tend to be reflected on Axis V.

NEUROPSYCHOLOGICAL ASSESSMENT TECHNIQUES

Many test measures have been developed for assessing the effects of brain damage in both children and adults. A number of neuropsychological test batteries have been developed to provide comprehensive evaluations of the impact of CNS impairment on behavior. It has been well established that the administration of a comprehensive test battery provides more diagnostic validity than do measures of intellectual abilities or specific skills alone (Goldstein and Shelly, 1984). These collections of tests have come to be known as *neuropsychological test batteries*, and they are frequently used in medical settings along with other neurodiagnostic techniques to assess the nature and extent of CNS impairment. A number of test batteries have found widespread accep-

Computerized Tomography (CT Scan)

One of several neurodiagnostic techniques used to identify forms of brain damage, CT scans help determine the location and nature of CNS impairment.

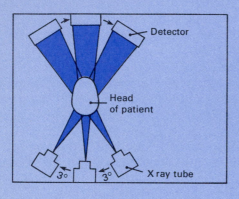
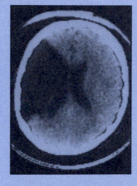
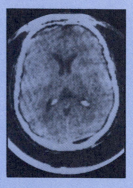

A. Schematic Explanation   B. Lesion in Left Hemisphere   C. Normal Brain

Source: Reprinted with permission from Carlson N.R. (1981) *Physiology of Behavior*, 2d ed. Boston: Allyn and Bacon. p. 149. (Scans courtesy of A. Kertesz.)

tance, although those developed by Benton (1975), Reitan and Davison (1974), and Smith (1981) are among the best known. Though initially conceived primarily as diagnostic tools to detect CNS impairment, neuropsychological test batteries have found other uses as well. Common applications include monitoring the effects of medications on cognition, providing pre- and postoperative data for neurosurgeons, and monitoring the recovery of cognitive skills in accident victims (Smith, 1981).

Neuropsychological testing is important for several reasons. Primary among these is that the measures assess capabilities mediated by the brain's cerebral cortex, which occupies a very large proportion of total brain mass. Routine neurologic investigations, by contrast, tend to focus on simpler response patterns that are not regulated by the cerebral cortex. A neurologic examination, for example, will evaluate reflex responses, basic coordination, and the status of nerves that carry sensory impressions to the brain. The combination of neurologic and neuropsychological evaluations ensures that the status of both lower (reflexive) and higher (cognitive) capabilities have been assessed.

Neuropsychological assessments are important for a second reason. Frequently, subtle alterations in behavior, cognition, or emotion provide the earliest clues to the presence of a neurologic disorder. Regardless of the specific cause, most forms of CNS impairment are accompanied by changes in orientation, memory, intellect, judgment, and affect (Sadock, 1975). Prompt detection of these changes and referral for a full neurologic work-up may aid in early identification and treatment of neurologic disease (Grant and Adams, 1986).

Because of the complexity of behavioral, cognitive, and emotional functions regulated by the CNS, a broad range of test measures is required to provide a thorough examination. Let us look in more detail at one such collection of tests, known as the Halstead-Reitan Neuropsychological Test Battery.

Halstead-Reitan Neuropsychological Test Battery

The **Halstead-Reitan Neuropsychological Test Battery** evolved from the work of psychologist Ward Halstead with adult brain-damaged subjects. In this form, it is known as the Halstead-Reitan Neuropsychological Test Battery. The battery was subsequently revised to accommodate two additional subject groups: the Halstead Neuropsychological Test Battery for Children is intended for children aged nine to 14; the Reitan-Indiana Neuropsychological Test Battery is for children aged five to eight (Reitan and Davison, 1974).

Four basic types of information are derived from the Reitan battery in establishing the presence and locus of CNS impairment. Normative data is used to compare a patient's performance against established criteria. **Pathognomonic signs**—unmistakable, invariant signs of brain damage—are derived from other measures. Tests comparing the right and left sides of the body (in effect, using the patient as his or her own control) constitute a third type of diagnostic information. Finally, pattern analysis is carried out as a means of linking certain configurations of test score groups to specific diagnostic categories.

In addition to a standardized test of intelligence, each battery comprises a number of individual tests with demonstrated sensitivity to brain damage. When accompanied by other measures of academic performance, the Halstead test batteries have been shown to have diagnostic utility in terms of characterizing the nature of a child's cognitive strengths and weaknesses and how these are likely to impact on specific academic skills (Rourke and Finlayson, 1978; Rourke and Strang, 1978).

The following measures are comprised in the test battery as used both with adults and older children (differences involve chiefly the number and complexity of various test items).

Categories test: This is a measure of concept recognition and abstract reasoning that has been shown to be sensitive to a wide range of impairments in brain functioning. The test consists of series of slides, each of which illustrates a specific principle or idea, based on feedback, which the subject must determine.

Tactual performance test: This test employs a form board with cutouts into which geometric forms can be placed. It is conducted with the subject blindfolded, relying only on tactile feedback. Three trials are conducted, one with each hand and one with both hands. Once the board has been put away and the blindfold removed, the subject is asked to draw a representation of the board and the figures in their respective places. This test measures tactile form discrimination and manual dexterity, as well as spatial memory capabilities.

Seashore rhythm test: Thirty pairs of brief rhythmic segments are played, and the subject is asked to decide whether the members of each pair are the same or different. Auditory discrimination and sustained attention are necessary for good performance on this test.

Speech sounds perception test: This is a test of sound discrimination in which the subject hears 60 nonsense words pronounced and then must select the word from four alternatives printed on the answer sheet. This is primarily a measure of auditory discrimination, but in addition requires visual discrimination and auditory-visual matching ability.

Finger tapping test: Manual dexterity is assessed for each hand by having the subject tap rapidly on a key attached to a counter for a series of 10-second trials. Ordinarily, the dominant hand is approximately 10 percent faster than the nondominant hand.

Aside from these basic measures, the test battery employs a number of measures assessing perceptual sensitivity in tactile, auditory, and visual modes. These measures are collectively referred to as the Reitan-Klove Sensory Perceptual Examination. Certain patterns of imperception constitute pathognomonic signs of brain damage, particularly when, despite adequate unilateral perception of stimulation, only one of two simultaneous stimuli is perceived.

Additional measures that may be employed in testing either children or adults, depending on the diagnostic issue, include the Reitan Aphasia Screening Test, a test of grip strength (employing a hand dynamometer), the Trial Making Test, and an assessment of lateral dominance.

Further modifications of the basic battery have been carried out to make the tests suitable for children aged five to eight. This version of the test is known as the Reitan-Indiana Neuropsychological Test Battery for Children. Several tests were devised especially for young children, most of which stress visual and motor skills.

Evaluation. Validation studies have been carried out with all three versions of the Halstead-Reitan batteries. Brain damaged and normal controls have been found to differ significantly on most of the measures included in the battery in studies of both older (Reed et al., 1965) and younger (Reitan, 1971) children. Moreover, extensive norms have been published for children in the older age group so that the impact of normal development on test performance can be gauged (Spreen and Gaddes, 1969).

Extensive validation studies of adults are likewise available for the Halstead-Reitan battery, and have been reviewed by Boll (1981). Moreover, there is some evidence suggesting the usefulness of the Halstead-Reitan battery in predicting functional behavioral adjustment (Heaton and Pendleton, 1981), although relatively few such studies have been conducted to date.

From a practical standpoint, the battery is quite lengthy and taxing for both patient and examiner alike. Particularly with children having attention disorders (a frequent concomitant of brain damage), or with adults with severely debilitating medical and/or neurologic conditions, administration of the entire battery can be quite time-consuming. Moreover, many of the individual tests are quite lengthy and difficult (the categories and tactual performance tests in particular). Attentional problems are more likely to interfere with tests of this nature than with measures that are shorter and more rapidly paced.

This limitation is a reflection of the larger issue concerning the origin of the test batteries: originally designed for use with adults, their format is most suitable to an older age group. Moreover, adaptation of tests for use with children has primarily involved simplifying adult measures, rather than developing an approach to assessment based on developmental theory.

On balance, the Reitan test batteries are widely used, comprehensive in scope, and, in the hands of a skilled examiner, can provide information that can help in planning remediation strategies.

COMMON SYMPTOMS OF CNS IMPAIRMENT

Amnestic Syndrome

The **amnestic syndrome** is the loss of memory that patients with traumatic head injuries commonly report (Squire, 1987). There are three aspects to the memory loss. First, memory for events up to the time of the trauma are impaired, a condition called *retrograde amnesia*. Typically, in anterograde amnesia memory for events from the distant past is the least impaired. Second, registration of information from the time of the accident onward is often impaired, a condition termed *anterograde amnesia*. This condition makes it difficult for patients to keep track of ongoing events, and people who otherwise seem quite well-oriented may forget much of what they have been told only moments earlier. As with anterograde amnesia, there is a gradient effect such that the memory problem tends to diminish with time. The third feature of the amnestic syndrome involves the inability to recall the moment of impact. Laboratory studies suggest that in most cases the physical shock of impact and the resultant brain trauma prevent memory traces for the event from being formed.

Seizures

The term **seizure** refers to a sudden electrical discharge from brain cells (Dodrill, 1981). A pattern of repeated seizures is called *epilepsy*, one of the most common neurologic disorders encountered. According to the Epilepsy Foundation of America (1975) up to two percent of the U.S. population suffers from some form of epilepsy. In over three quarters of all persons with epilepsy, the onset occurs before adolescence. Seizure disorders have been linked to psychological impairments that encompass intellectual, cognitive, and emotional domains. Temporal lobe seizures in particular have been linked to significant alterations in personality characteristics.

Among the most interesting correlates of seizure disorders is a collection of traits termed the "temporal lobe personality" (Valenstein and Heilman, 1979). Individuals with this disorder are described as experiencing intense emotional states, and tend to attribute unwarranted importance to trivial events. Slowed thought processes may be present, as may aggressive tendencies and a reduced sexual drive.

Seizures are normally treated with anticonvulsant medication, of which Dilantin is perhaps the most widely used. Although anticonvulsant medication is normally quite helpful in reducing seizure activity, an excessive dosage may have adverse effects on alertness and concentration. Careful monitoring of side effects is therefore essential when establishing the proper dose.

Dementia

Dementia is a general term used in the DSM to characterize the general effect of CNS impairment. The most common forms of dementia are associated with pathologic changes in the brain that accompany certain chronic degenerative neurologic disorders in the later stages of life (Joynt and Shoulson, 1979).

The two most common forms of degenerative dementia are *Alzheimer's disease* and *Pick's disease*. Alzheimer's disease involves a gradual, generalized deterioration of brain tissue. It affects a wide range of cognitive functions, including memory, visuomotor coordination, and abstract thought. Declining performance in these cognitive areas may be among the earliest signs of the disease. Attendant symptoms such as depression and distractibility make it easy to confuse Alzheimer's disease in the early stages with affective disorders. The disease runs its course in two to five years, resulting in death (Harding et al., 1985).

In *Pick's disease*, deterioration of brain tissue is confined largely to the frontal lobes. Erratic and impulsive episodes of behavior progress to more profound deterioration. As with Alzheimer's disease, death ordinarily results within two to five years.

Neither causes nor cures have as yet been identified for either of these forms of dementia, though fortunately the incidence rate is fairly low. Persons afflicted with either of these conditions have an emotionally wrenching effect on people around them, because in the advanced stages of the disease behavior is characterized by virtually total dependency.

Closed Head Injury

Head injury is a very common form of CNS impairment. Motor vehicle accidents, falls, and other traumatic events can produce brain injuries that result in significant alterations in behavior (Levin et al., 1987). The effects of head injury are typically assessed in two ways. First, during the period immediately following injury (acute phase), profound behavioral deficits are likely, including loss of consciousness or coma. Coma is believed to reflect injury to brainstem mechanisms that maintain alertness (Plum and Posner, 1980). As the brain gradually recovers from the initial shock, the generalized state of cognitive trauma resolves and is replaced by more stable and focal patterns of cognitive and behavioral deficits. Virtually all head trauma victims experience some aspect of the amnestic syndrome discussed earlier, possibly due to the fact that temporal lobe structures that play a significant mediating role in memory are particularly vulnerable to trauma and are easily damaged at the moment of impact (Levin et al., 1982).

TREATMENT OF BRAIN DAMAGE

The number of patients surviving CNS impairment of virtually all types has steadily increased in recent years (Brinkman, 1979). Regional trauma centers and other acute-care facilities have been successful in reducing mortality rates due to traumatic injury. However, programs designed to promote long-term recovery from such injuries have not been developed at an equally rapid pace.

Traumatic injuries involving CNS impairment create a number of problems for patients and their families (Williams and Long, 1987). The afflicted individual must cope with an increase in overall stress (despite reduced stress-coping capabilities), as well as with the negative impact of CNS damage on cognitive functions, which is typically related to a loss of occupational status (Long et al., 1984). Patients and family members are often faced with limited prospects when seeking services aimed at providing ongoing, long-term treatment. In many cases, transitional care provided at rehabilitation facilities is followed by discharge home at a time when the patient's medical condition may have stabilized but significant cognitive and emotional sequelae are very much in evidence.

Fortunately, this need has not gone entirely unheeded. There are at present a number of programs that have been designed specifically to work with persons with traumatic brain damage on a long-term basis. Such programs provide follow-up to services provided by acute-care and transitional rehabilitation facilities. At a general level, recovery processes can be assisted by programs that offer clients and their families the following services (Long et al., 1984): education regarding the nature and course of traumatic injury; stress management; activity planning and scheduling; cognitive retraining; and, when appropriate, vocational rehabilitation (Levin et al., 1987).

Specific rehabilitation techniques for use with brain-damaged patients fall into several classes. These include (1) psychotherapeutic techniques to promote management of stress and depression, (2) biofeedback techniques for tension control and motor retraining, (3) cognitive rehabilitation techniques designed to help the patient either reacquire lost skills or develop compensatory capabilities, and (4) the use of microcomputers to serve both prosthetic and retraining functions.

Psychotherapy

Recovery from the effects of brain damage is frequently accompanied by feelings of intense anxiety, depression, and, not infrequently, suicidal ideation. Somewhat paradoxically, the prospect of depression and suicide often increases as the patient's overall condition appears by objective standards to be improving. Several factors appear to be involved. First, recovery from coma and amnesia is replaced by a more conscious awareness of the extent of one's injuries and limitations. Second, the initial concern over whether or not the patient will survive is replaced with increasingly higher—and often unrealistic—expectations that a return to the premorbid level of functioning will in fact occur. Finally, the radical changes in one's environment and daily activities tend to cause a loss of positive reinforcement. The patient is cut off from accustomed social contacts and opportunities to perform activities and use skills that previously provided satisfaction and bolstered self-esteem. A sense of learned helplessness due to loss of control and predictability may set in, eventually evolving into a clinically significant depression (Rosenbaum and Palmon, 1984). For these and other reasons, psychotherapy should routinely be considered in working with the traumatically injured patient.

Therapeutic interventions for brain-injured patients may take any of several forms. Family counseling may be indicated because of the intense stress both patients and their families are likely to experience (Lezak, 1983). Behavioral modification techniques may be of help both in obtaining functional analyses of problems (Haynes, 1984) and in helping to manage residual difficulties such as chronic pain, impulsivity, lack of compliance with medical procedures, and other symptoms of posttrauma adjustment difficulties (Fordyce, 1976). Therapeutic interventions based on the analysis and alteration of the client's cognitions, or thought patterns, have proven helpful in treating depression (Beck et al., 1979b) and related disorders. In addition, the application of cognitive techniques, including cognitive restructuring (Kanfer, 1980) and thought stopping (Livingston and Johnson, 1979), have been discussed in the context of an integrated self-management program by Sawyer and Crimando (1984). Finally, cognitive rehearsal strategies to enhance task performance have been integrated into an approach termed Systematic Behavioral Response Rehearsal (SBAR) by Farley (1985). The major components of this include the following: (1) relaxation, (2) persistent practice, (3) self-instruction, (4) self-monitoring, (5) self-assessment, and (6) self-reinforcement.

Biofeedback and Relaxation Training

Stress, tension, and chronic pain associated with recovery from CNS impairment have been found to be responsive to treatment using various biofeedback and relaxation techniques (Schwartz, 1987). A review of representative studies reveals success in treating various types of headaches (Blanchard et al., 1982), particularly when "booster sessions" are employed (Andrasky et al., 1984); motor speech disorders (Driazan, 1984); joint pain (King et al., 1984; Furch and Gale, 1984); as well as with patients suffering strokes (Epstein et al., 1978).

Cognitive Retraining Procedures

A number of retraining programs have been developed to help remedy specific cognitive deficits associated with traumatic injury (Dryden and Golden, 1987). Perhaps the best known work in this area has been conducted by Diller and his associates at the Institute of Rehabilitation Medicine at New York University. A general review of these procedures reveals six basic areas to which rehabilitation efforts can be addressed: (1) assessment and management of medical problems; (2) impairments in sensory, motor, language, and/or cognitive areas; (3) management of skills needed for activities of daily living (ADL skills); (4) environmental structuring; (5) planning activity patterns; and (6) impacting on various aspects of the patient's social/vocational status (Diller and Gordon, 1981). Of these, the management of specific cognitive impairments—particularly in the area of memory and attention—has attracted considerable clinical and research interest in recent years (Levin et al., 1987). Techniques for assisting patients with residual memory deficits are described in detail by Wilson and Moffat (1984), who describe procedures employing visual imagery, verbal cueing, computer-based management assis-

RESEARCH PROFILE

Sex Differences in Impairment of Thinking Following Brain Damage

Sundet (1986) refers to literature suggesting that there are some differences in how men and women think and process information. One major concept in this regard is that women tend to use both hemispheres when processing information, while men are more likely to lean heavily on one, or the dominant, hemisphere. Sundet also carried out a study to provide indirect evidence relevant to this idea, by evaluating the effects of a unilateral (damage restricted to one side of the brain) brain lesion in men and women.

A group of 232 patients in the Oslo (Norway) City Hospital were tested with the Norwegian version of the Wechsler Adult Intelligence Test (WAIS; see Chapter 3); 83 ultimately met the criterion of clear unilateral brain damage (19 males and 15 females with a left-side brain lesion; 32 males and 17 females with a right-side brain lesion). These groups were generally comparable on such variables as age and amount of time between onset of disorder and time of evaluation.

The WAIS can be subdivided into tests that measure verbal-based skills and tests that are more of a measure of movement and coordination skills. Sundet found that unilateral brain lesions caused about equal impairment across both types of skills for women. But for men, unilateral lesions were more likely to severely disrupt one type of skill while leaving the other type relatively intact. Data from non-Western cultural groups is not available, but Sundet points out that this type of result appears consistent across Western cultures.

It is noteworthy that the overlap between men and women in cognitive performance is high, so sex differences actually account for only a small part of the total variance. At the same time, the results suggest there may be some differences, possibly culturally produced, as to how men and women process some types of information. Rehabilitation efforts need to take into account the different types of impairments in men and women that may result from similar brain traumas.

tance, and various other external aids such as timers, appointment schedulers, and prompting devices.

Attentional processes are a second area in which residual deficits are quite common following many forms of CNS impairment. Causes may range from damage to brainstem mechanisms controlling activation and arousal (Watson et al., 1974) to cortical damage resulting in failure to attend to visual areas on the side opposite the lesion (visual neglect) (Heilman, 1979). Remedial work with attentional deficits is described in a more recent review by Gummow et al., (1983). Tasks such as visual tracking and cueing attention to neglected areas, and tasks rewarding either visual or auditory vigilance have been devised as a means of helping patients cope with deficits of this type.

Additional remediation procedures have been developed for other aspects of cognition. Sivak et al. (1984), for example, describe a perceptual retraining program specifically designed to aid in driving skills. Programs such as these begin with a functional analysis of the patient's residual skills, then go on

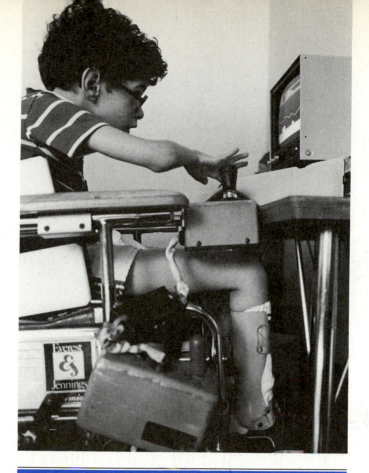

In the 1980s, record numbers of handicapped persons began using computers to communicate. Some use computers as an entertainment device; for others, computers are instrumental in their daily existence, sometimes even replacing damaged vocal chords or paralyzed limbs. (Joan Liftin/Archive Pictures)

to specify training activities designed both to provide remediation based on existing capabilities and compensation for irremediable deficits.

Computer-Assisted Rehabilitation

Recent developments in computer technology have carried over into rehabilitation efforts with brain-injured patients. Vanderheiden (1982) has provided a summary of potential applications for microcomputers with physically and mentally handicapped persons, including (1) the enhancement of visual and auditory stimulation, (2) control and manipulation of external devices, (3) recreational and developmental aids, (4) information management, and (5) cognitive/linguistic processing assistance.

There are a number of programs and systems designed to promote recovery of cognitive capabilities, such as those developed by Gianutsos at the New York University Rehabilitation Institute (Kurlychek and Glang, 1984) and by Bracy (1983).

In summary, a wide range of therapeutic techniques have been brought to bear on the problem of helping patients recover from the effects of CNS impairment. Psychotherapy, biofeedback, cognitive retraining, and computer-assisted rehabilitation are significant forces that can help in the treatment of brain-injured persons. To promote maximum recovery, it is vital that these procedures be deployed as rapidly as possible in the aftermath of brain damage (Levin et al., 1987). However, it should also be pointed out that the effectiveness of many of these techniques with brain-injured persons has yet to be conclusively proven. Even in such a traditional area as language therapy, questions remain as to its overall effectiveness (David et al., 1982). Particularly in the area of cognitive rehabilitation, definitive, methodologically sound studies are needed to demonstrate that the training itself, rather than secondary factors such as generalized stimulation, physiologic activation, or social interaction are responsible for changes in behavior (Gummow et al., 1983). These comments are made not so much to discredit therapeutic interventions as they are for the sake of keeping a proper perspective on the issue of rehabilitation effectiveness. It is one mistake to assume that even comprehensive therapeutic programs can routinely return patients to premorbid lifestyles, and another to assume that they are unsuccessful if they do not. Such techniques and procedures appear to aid naturally occurring processes of compensation and restitution, but are not of themselves sufficient to ensure complete recovery.

CHAPTER REVIEW

1. The brain has been linked to the control of behavior for centuries, but only recently have researchers begun to understand some of the complex relationships involved.

2. The four major structural regions of the brain are known as the frontal, temporal, parietal, and occipital lobes.

3. The Russian neurophysiologist Luria divided the brain into three functional areas: arousal, sensory-receptive, and regulatory/executive.

4. Damage to specific brain regions impairs certain behavioral and psychological functions. Frontal lobe damage impairs judgment and purposeful action; temporal lobe injury impairs memory functions; occipital lobe damage impairs visual processes; and parietal lobe damage impairs spatial abilities and bodily image.

5. The DSM system distinguishes between organic brain syndromes and organic mental disorders. The former are general patterns of impairment that may be associated with more than one type of brain damage. The latter refer to specific neurologic disorders.

6. Neuropsychological assessment procedures obtain information based on (a) normative data, (b) measures of lateralized functioning, (c) pathognomonic signs, and (4) functional profile analysis.

7. One of the best known neuropsychological assessment procedures, the Halstead-Reitan battery measures a broad range of cognitive and neurologic functions.

8. Among the more common syndromes associated with CNS impairment are amnesia, seizures, dementia, and closed head injury.

9. People who have suffered disabling brain damage can often be helped through rehabilitation and retraining procedures. Among the most promising of these are (a) psychotherapy, (b) biofeedback, (c) cognitive retraining, and (d) computer-assisted rehabilitation procedures.

TERMS TO REMEMBER

neuropsychology
trepanning
cerebral cortex
frontal lobe
temporal lobe
parietal lobe
occipital lobe
Broca's area
equipotentiality
RAS
angular gyrus

Sylvian fissure
perseveration
lobotomy
somesthetic cortex
agnosia
organic brain syndromes
Halstead-Reitan Test Battery
pathognomonic signs
amnestic syndrome
seizure
dementia

FOR MORE INFORMATION

Filskov, S., and Boll, T. (1986) *Handbook of clinical neuropsychology*. New York: Wiley. A good sourcebook for the topics, assessments, and treatments that are the focus of neuropsychology

Gardiner, H. (1974) *The shattered mind*. New York: Vintage. A sensitive clinician and astute observer of behavior provides a realistic appraisal of what patients with aphasic disorders experience on a day-to-day basis

Hanning, J. (Ed.). (1986) *Experimental techniques in human neuropsychology*. New York: Oxford. A valuable sourcebook that details the research methods neuropsychologists use to study human brain function and brain-behavior relationships

Lezak, M. (1983) *Neuropsychological assessment*, 2nd ed. New York: Oxford University Press. Lezak provides a comprehensive overview of the various tests and procedures available to neuropsychologists concerned with brain-behavior relationships

Reitan, R. M., and Wolfson, D. (1986) *Traumatic brain injury: Recovery and rehabilitation*. Tuscon, Ariz.: Neuropsychology Press. Ralph Reitan was an early pioneer in the field of neuropsychological assessment, and this is a thorough study, with helpful descriptive photos, of the effects on the brain of acute traumas incurred in automobile accidents and comparable events

Salmon, P., and Meyer, R. (1986) Neuropsychological assessment: 1-Adults; 2-Children. In: M. Kurke and R. Meyer (Eds.). *Psychology in product liability and personal injury law*. New York: Hemisphere Press. An overview of the various major neuropsychological assessment approaches for both adults and children

In *Charly,* Cliff Robertson plays a sensitive retarded man who competes against a mouse named Algernon in a variety of experiments designed to test intelligence. (Museum of Modern Art/Film Stills Archive; Cinerama)

14

Mental Retardation

Mental retardation is a disorder associated with the early years of development. It is a condition that tends to have widespread effects that, if severe, can profoundly impair adaptive functioning (Zigler and Hodapp, 1986). Fortunately, the majority of people diagnosed with mental retardation do not fall into this category. Instead, they are people who live fulfilling lives, frequently functioning in partially or fully independent living situations. This chapter provides an overview of the wide range of abilities and deficits associated with different levels of mental retardation, and concludes with a discussion of effective treatment and management procedures.

● The Case of Abe

Abe's father and mother were older than most parents when he was conceived. They had wanted children for years, but after two miscarriages Mrs. M. had given up hope of conceiving. She was surprised to find herself pregnant at age 44. Although her doctor warned Mrs. M. that, because of her age, there were risks to both child and mother, both she and her husband were determined to have the child.

Abe was born with a genetic defect known as Down syndrome, which results in mental retardation. Abe also possessed certain physical features characteristic of the disorder, including slanting eyes, low-set ears, and a large, protruding tongue. His parents loved him deeply, and were determined that he should have as normal an upbringing as possible. They politely but firmly resisted suggestions by well-intentioned friends and professionals that Abe be institutionalized.

Abe grew up free to roam about the countryside in which they lived. He did not learn to talk until he was about four, but well before that he showed an uncanny ability to communicate with stray animals that always seemed to follow him home. He was basically a loner; the few children who lived nearby in the neighborhood were frightened of his appearance and tended to avoid him. Although his father spent hours patiently trying to teach him how to play baseball and other games, Abe seemed too slow and uncoordinated to master any of them well. At age five, Abe was tested and formally diagnosed as having moderate mental retardation. Mr. and Mrs. M. found a day school program nearby for mentally retarded children, which Abe attended for about five hours each day. In later years, Abe continued to live at home with his parents, and worked in a sheltered workshop.

INTRODUCTION

Historically, individuals with limited mental capabilities were grouped together with other deviant members of society. The first correctional house in colonial Connecticut (established in 1722), for instance, housed retarded individuals along with common criminals. Current conceptions of mental retardation are more enlightened and humane, and stress the fact that it is a multifaceted disorder.

The prevailing concept of mental retardation has its roots in late nineteenth and early twentieth century investigations of mental abilities carried out by psychologists such as Galton and Binet. These researchers devised ways of quantifying mental abilities, and it was not long before tests based on these procedures were employed to classify people into ranges of intelligence. The term "mental retardation" was used to characterize individuals with below-average mental abilities (Marx and Hillix, 1987).

At first, it was presumed that such individuals would profit little from instruction, as a result of which many were simply institutionalized. In subsequent years, however, stereotypic views of the mentally retarded began to break down. In 1971 the United Nations General Assembly adopted a declaration on the rights of mentally retarded individuals.

Mental health and educational specialists define mental retardation in terms of deficits in both an individual's intellectual functioning and capacity to achieve a satisfactory level of social adjustment (Kail and Pellegrino, 1985). This viewpoint is reflected in the definition of mental retardation proposed by the American Association on Mental Deficiency (**AAMD**) (1977), which states:

Educators and administrators now find grouping retarded children with "normal" peers provides a rewarding environment for both groups.   (David Roberts/Photo Researchers, Inc.)

Mental retardation refers to significantly subaverage general intellectual function-ing existing concurrently with deficits in adaptive behavior, and manifested during the developmental period (p. 11).

The term "adaptive functioning" in the AAMD definition encompasses social adjustment as well as other manifestations of effective functioning. Despite diagnostic definitions that require evidence of both intellectual and social deficits, it is common to find intellectual impairment alone being used as the principle criterion in many clinics and schools (Huberty et al., and Ten Brink, 1980). The DSM classification system, however, retains the dual criteria, and its widespread influence has tended to promote the use of uniform diagnostic standards.

Mental retardation is a term used to characterize cognitive and social deficits; it does not imply a particular cause of these deficiencies. Genetic defects, neurologic damage, environmental trauma, and any other negative factors acting during early development can cause mental retardation. These factors can have other side effects as well, so that mental retardation is often found in individuals with diverse medical and physical problems.

ISSUES TO CONSIDER

Rights of Mentally Retarded Individuals

Below is the text of the United Nations Declaration on the Rights of Mentally Retarded Persons, adopted by the General Assembly in December 1971.

1. The mentally retarded person has, to the maximum degree of feasibility, the same rights as other human beings.

2. The mentally retarded person has a right to proper medical care and physical therapy, and to such education, training, rehabilitation, and guidance as will enable him to develop his ability and maximum potential.

3. The mentally retarded person has a right to economic security and to a decent standard of living. He has a right to perform production work or to engage in other meaningful occupation to the fullest possible extent of his capabilities.

4. Whenever possible, the mentally retarded person should live with his own family or with foster parents and participate in different forms of community life. The family with which he lives should receive assistance. If care in an institution becomes necessary, it should be provided in surroundings and other circumstances as close as possible to those of normal life.

5. The mentally retarded person has a right to a qualified guardian when this is required to protect his personal well-being and interests.

6. The mentally retarded person has a right to protection from exploitation, abuse and degrading treatment. If prosecuted for any offense, he shall have a right to due process of law with full recognition being given to his degree of mental responsibility.

7. Whenever mentally retarded persons are unable, because of the severity of their handicap, to exercise all their rights in a meaningful way, or it should become necessary to restrict or deny some or all of these rights, the procedure used for that restriction or denial of rights must contain proper legal safeguards against every form of abuse. This procedure must be based on an evaluation of the social capacity of the mentally retarded person by qualified experts and must be subject to periodic review and to the right of appeal to higher authorities.

Source: General Assembly Resolution No. 2856 (XXVI) of 20 Dec. 1971.

ASSESSMENT

Degrees of Retardation

Individuals with low intelligence quotients (IQs) do not form a homogeneous group, since IQs can range so widely even at a low level (Zigler and Hodapp, 1986). The AAMD and DSM classification systems currently recognize four

These drawings illustrate the differing abilities between normal and mentally retarded children. All were given the direction to draw a person, with no further prompts. (a) Self-portrait by Amelia, a normal four-year-old girl. (b) Drawing by Roy, a five-year-old boy with moderate developmental problems (delays in language, social and fine motor skills). (c) Drawing by Cindy, a four-year-old girl with left hemiparesis and left homonomous hemianopia.

The Case of Jean

Early in 1986, Jean apparently escaped the crunching poverty and danger of the Haitian streets when he was adopted by an American family. They had long wanted their own child and were delighted with this apparently bright, fun-loving 10-year-old with a handsome face and large brown eyes. Jean also was delighted. He suddenly had his own room, with his own stereo, television set, and the wide array of toys that economically comfortable Americans often provide their children. In Jean's words, "Me go to baseball. Me go to Disney. Every Sunday, I go in the church. I go in school. I go see basketball and football. Everyone place I see, I like. I go to Wendy's, I go to McDonald's." However, six months later, Jean's adoptive parents sedated him to keep down his upset, flew him back to Haiti, and simply un-adopted him by leaving him there.

At first glance, it would seem as if Jean was victimized by shallow, cruel parents who thought of him as a pet that could be returned to the pound if all did not work out. However, as reported by journalist Elenore Brecher in the March 29, 1987, edition of the Louisville *Courier-Journal*, all indications were that they had in reality given a tremendous effort to this venture, though they eventually concluded that keeping Jean would risk the survival of their marriage, as well as the happiness and even health of their soon-to-be delivered natural child.

Jean is not intellectually retarded, but he is socially retarded. While he had learned the skills needed to survive as an orphan in the worst of Haiti's slums, he was helpless in trying to adjust to middle-class America.

When frustrated or hindered he simply lashed out with violence or ran away from the situation. At school he tried to slash a girl with a razor blade, and bit a teacher, drawing blood. If his adoptive parents so much as touched each other, Jean would accuse them of bizarre sexual interests. As his father said, "My wife and I couldn't spend any time together because he was so belligerent. We were prisoners in our own home." He was very jealous toward their expected child. So much so, they felt they would have to keep Jean separated from the child. After consulting with a psychologist about Jean's problems, and the probable prognosis, they returned Jean to Haiti.

All indications are that Jean was at least average in natural intellectual power. He learned fast and well. But he had overlearned skills that were maladaptive to his new environment. Thus, just as some intellectually retarded individuals can show average levels of social skills, and thus make it on their own in the world, an absence of social skills even when accompanied by good intelligence can mean an inability to survive in that world.

levels of mental retardation, based on ranges of IQ scores (these values are based on the Stanford-Binet Intelligence Scale; the Wechsler Intelligence scales employ similar ranges): mild (IQ 52–67), moderate (36–51), severe (20–35), and profound (below 20). Mild retardation accounts for approximately 85 percent of all cases of mental retardation; 13 percent of all retarded persons are moderately retarded, while the remainder (two percent) fall within either the severe or profound range. Because mildly retarded individuals benefit significantly from educational and vocational training, they are also referred to as Educably Mentally Handicapped (**EMH**).

EXHIBIT

Expected Ability and Function Levels for Various Degrees of Mental Retardation

Level	Preschool Age (birth to 5 years)	School Age (6 to 21 years)	Adult (over 21 years)
Mild Retardation	Can develop social and language skills; less retardation in sensorimotor areas; seldom distinguished from normal until older	Can learn academic skills to approximately 6th grave level by late teens; cannot learn general high school subjects; needs special education, particularly at secondary-school levels	Capable of social and vocational adequacy with proper education and training; frequently needs guidance when under serious social or economic stress
Moderate Retardation	Can talk or learn to communicate; poor social awareness; fair motor development; may profit from self-help; can be managed with moderate supervision	Can learn functional academic skills to approximately 4th-grade level by late teens if given special education	Capable of self-maintenance in unskilled or semiskilled occupations; needs supervision and guidance when under mild social or economic stress.
Severe Retardation	Poor motor development; speech is minimal; generally unable to profit from training in self-help; little or no communication skills	Can talk or learn to communicate; can be trained in elemental health habits; cannot learn functional academic skills; profits from systematic habit training	Can contribute partially to self-support under complete supervision; can develop self-protection skills to a minimal useful level in controlled environment
Profound Retardation	Gross retardation; minimal capacity for functioning in sensorimotor areas; needs nursing care	Some motor development present; cannot profit from training in self-help; needs total care	Some motor and speech development; totally incapable of self-maintenance; needs complete care and supervision

Source: Adapted from Sattler, J.M. (1982) Assessment of children's intelligence and special abilities. Boston: Allyn and Bacon, Inc., p. 426.

As the degree of severity of mental retardation increases, the likelihood of associated physical and medical abnormalities also increases. Many mildly retarded people have no associated physical stigmata, and their limitations often do not become apparent until they encounter academic difficulties after starting school. In many cases, their condition reflects stunted intellectual development due to a deprived environment. Poverty, low social status, malnutrition, and a host of other factors may curtail the intellectual development of children who might otherwise have grown up with average or even above-average abilities. Such children are victims of **cultural-familial retardation**, a term that emphasizes environmental forces, not innate capabilities, as the cause of mental retardation.

Moderately retarded persons are capable of learning many basic communicative, educational, and vocational skills. Many are gainfully employed, and work productively in supervised settings. Job responsibilities need to be clearly specified, and behavioral techniques such as shaping are often employed in training programs.

Severely and profoundly retarded individuals require constant supervision and care. Most are also afflicted with physical or neurologic deficits, calling for a comprehensive program of institutionalized care (Tyson and Favell, 1987). Traditionally, people with severe or profound retardation were confined to custodial institutions, where they received little stimulation. More recently, behavioral techniques have been fruitfully applied in institutional settings to promote higher levels of functioning.

Distribution of IQ Scores

Many traits and physical characteristics are distributed throughout the general population in predictable proportions (Anastasi, 1987). A classroom survey, for example, would reveal that students vary systematically with respect to height and weight. The majority of those polled would be of average height or weight; a few would fall on either extreme. By counting the number of cases for each value of a variable (like height or weight), one arrives at a **frequency distribution** for that variable. Frequency distributions can be calculated for any variable, and IQ scores are no exception. It turns out that the frequency distribution of IQ scores approximates something called a normal, or "bell shaped," curve (see Exhibit).

The term "bell shaped" is an apt descriptor. Distributions that approximate normal curves are symmetrical, with a peak in the center and two tails tapering off to either side. Normal curves can be described mathematically in terms of two basic properties: the mean and the standard deviation. The mean is the average value of the distribution, while the standard deviation is a measure of how tightly the values all cluster around the mean. In a normal distribution, more than two thirds of all the values fall between the mean and one standard deviation above and below. About 13 percent of the scores fall between one

---

EXHIBIT

Range of IQ Scores

One criterion for diagnosing mental retardation is the individual's intelligence quotient, or IQ. According to guidelines established by the American Association on Mental Deficiency (AAMD), an IQ score below 70 is characteristic of persons diagnosed as mentally retarded. IQ scores are distributed within the general population according to a normal, or bell-shaped, curve, as shown here. This figure shows clearly that a relatively small percentage of people have either extremely low or extremely high IQ scores.

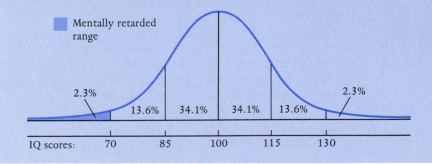

and two standard deviations from the mean, while only about 3 percent are found at a distance greater than two standard deviations above or below the mean.

In general, IQ tests have a mean of 100 and a standard deviation of about 15. Because IQ scores are normally distributed, this means that the majority of scores should fall within one standard deviation of the mean, or between 85 and 115. The percentage of IQ scores either greater or less than these values diminishes rapidly. About 14 percent of the population would have IQ scores between 70 and 85 and between 115 and 130. And only 2.3 percent would score less than 70 or more than 130.

By convention, mental retardation may be diagnosed in persons having IQ scores two standard deviations or more below the average. These would be individuals with IQ scores of 70 or less. Theoretically, about 2.3 percent of the population, or about five million people, would meet the intellectual criterion for mental retardation. In actuality, the number is higher, probably on the order of nearly seven million. The difference between the predicted (based on a theoretically normal distribution of IQ scores) and actual number of persons with mental retardation reflects the impact of many factors that tend to impair intellectual functioning.

Assessing Intellectual Skills

Because the diagnosis of mental retardation rests so heavily on the results of IQ tests, it is imperative that the test measures employed be both reliable and valid (see Chapter 3). Although a number of current tests meet both criteria, the two that have found the most widespread use in determining IQ are the Stanford-Binet Intelligence Scale and the revised Wechsler Intelligence Scale for Children (Anastasi, 1987). Precursors of the Stanford-Binet were explicitly designed to aid in school placement decisions for children of subaverage mental abilities. It won widespread acceptance for both its internal reliability and its consistency over time (Silverstein, 1982). More recently, diagnosticians have favored an analysis of IQ scores into component abilities, an approach better suited to the Wechsler scale.

Testing children with subaverage mental abilities requires sensitivity on the examiner's part as well as a valid and reliable test measure (Dean, 1987). For example, knowing whether probing for an answer will make a child feel upset or relieved is an important skill. Patience and understanding are other highly desirable traits needed to deal with the sometimes enigmatic behavior of retarded children. Sattler (1982) has pointed out, for example, that many of these children behave in ways that, though normally viewed as inappropriate, actually reflect efforts to cope with an intellectually challenging task. A child who attempts to leave the room, crawls under the table, or suddenly becomes beligerent may simply be reacting to unaccustomed demands imposed by the test questions. Some children act shy and inhibited when being tested, and know considerably more than is apparent from their responses. Effective examiners are able to discriminate between children with true mental limitations and those who perform poorly on tests for other reasons.

A child's behavior provides clues as to the reason for poor performance on IQ tests. Detailed analyses of the tests themselves provide additional clues as to the nature of the intellectual impairment. IQ tests such as the Wechsler scale sample a wide range of component skills. The Wechsler IQ scale for children, for example, includes among its subscales tests of vocabulary, abstract thinking, arithmetic, social judgment, short-term memory, and perceptual skills. Administration of the Wechsler IQ test results in a profile of test scores that comprise the IQ. The particular pattern formed by these measures tends to differ depending on the severity of mental retardation and the underlying etiological factors. Children with pervasive condition such as Down syndrome tend to score at uniformly low levels on most of the subscales. Cultural and/or environmental deprivation tends to impair performance on tests requiring good verbal and language skills. Mental retardation resulting from specific forms of brain damage can selectively impair memory or perceptual capabilities.

The task of a diagnostician assessing the intellectual capabilities of a retarded child goes beyond simply giving an IQ test. The child's behavior must be taken into account as a possible source of poor performance, and the examiner must be sensitive to a wide range of factors other than mental retardation that can impair performance. It is also important to analyze the IQ test for patterns of subtest scores that may help pinpoint the specific impact of etiological factors underlying mental retardation.

Assessing Functional Behavior

The diagnosis of mental retardation requires not only intellectual assessment, but analysis of more functional behaviors, such as social skills, as well. There are several standardized instruments for assessing social skills. Two of the most widely used are the **Vineland Social Maturity Scale** and the **Adaptive Behavior Scale**.

The Vineland Social Maturity Scale is commonly used to assess day-to-day skills not evaluated by IQ tests. Parents or other adults directly involved with the child rate their behavior on six dimensions: self-help, self-direction, communication, socialization, locomotion, and occupational orientation. These skills are all developmentally based, meaning that the child's age determines what skills in each category should be developed. The test provides age norms for each of the six functional areas. In conjunction with the results of an IQ test, the Vineland profile of adaptive behavior provides a thorough assessment of mental and adaptive capabilities that is well suited to the task of diagnosing mental retardation.

The AAMD has also developed a protocol for assessing adaptive behavior. Known as the Adaptive Behavior Scale (ABS), this questionnaire is also filled out by the child's parents or other significant adults. The ABS evaluates the following four general functional areas: functional independence, physical capabilities, communication skills, and social maturity. As with the Vineland, items on the ABS are related to developmental stages. In the Exhibit containing a sample of the ABS, notice how the behaviors in each of the four areas are linked to different degrees of retardation, depending on the chronological age of the child. For example, a child of three who communicates in two- or three-word sentences, names simple objects, and understands simple directions would be considered to be mildly retarded, since these are all skills generally characteristic of children about a year younger. These skill levels would be associated with moderate retardation in a six-year-old, severe retardation in a nine-year-old, and profound retardation in persons 12 and older.

Early Detection

There is some controversy about the age at which mental retardation can reliably be detected. Early studies by the psychologist Nancy Bayly and others revealed low correlations between IQ scores for very young children (age two to three) and for the same children when retested at age 10. Other studies,

---

EXHIBIT

Sample from the Adaptive Behavior Scale

Highest Level of Adaptive Behavior Functioning in a Six-Year-Old Moderately Retarded Child

Independent functioning. Feeds self with spoon with considerable spilling or messiness; drinks unassisted; can pull off clothing and put on same; tries to help with bath or hand washing but still needs considerable help; indicates toilet accident and may indicate toilet need.

Physical. May climb up and down stairs but not alternating feet; may run and jump; may balance briefly on one foot; can pass ball to others; transfers objects; may do simple form-board puzzles without aid.

Communication. May speak in two- or three-word sentences; names simple common objects; understands simple directions; knows people by name.

Social. May interact with others in simple play activities, usually with only one or two others unless guided into group activity; has preference for some persons over others.

Age and Level Indicated by Behavior

3 years	Mild
6 years	Moderate
9 years	Severe
12 + years	Profound

Source: Adapted from Grossman, H.J. (Ed.). (1983) *Classification in mental retardation.* Washington, D.C.: American Association on Mental Deficiency, pp. 204–205.

---

such as that by Werner et al. (1968) suggest that children who perform poorly on IQ tests when very young are likely to score in a comparable range when retested several years later.

Early detection of mental retardation and other debilitating conditions is of course desirable for a number of reasons. Early detection and prompt intervention can rectify conditions that may cause retardation. For example, the metabolic disorder phenylketonuria (**PKU**), described later, results in serious mental deterioration if undetected. Prompt diagnosis and dietary regulation can arrest the progression of the disorder. Even when it is not possible to prevent mental retardation, early detection and rapid deployment of learning resources geared to the child's developmental level can maximize benefits from critical early experience and minimize the loss of self-esteem that frequently accompanies negative self-evaluations of intellectual or social skills.

Prenatal genetic counseling has become increasingly popular in recent years. Such consultations are routinely recommended to parents who are known or potential carriers of genetic aberrations. For example, the incidence of Tay-Sachs disease, which results in mental retardation and premature death, is abnormally high in certain Jewish sects. It is a recessive trait, meaning that both parents must contribute the necessary gene in order for the disorder to occur. Couples wishing to have children can be screened for the presence of the recessive trait associated with Tay-Sachs disease (and other genetically based disorders) and advised about the risks of pregnancy.

During pregnancy, it is also possible to detect certain genetic abnormalities with a technique called **amniocentesis**. Using a long hollow needle inserted through the mother's uterine wall, the physician draws a sample of fluid from the amniotic sac, which envelops the fetus. This fluid contains some fetal cells, each genetically identical to the fertilized egg (or zygote) that was formed at the time of conception. The chromosomal structure of these cells is then analyzed for the presence of genetic defects such as Tay-Sachs disease or Down syndrome.

Through the procedure of amnioscentesis, physicians can detect some genetic abnormalities in unborn fetuses. (SIU/Photo Researchers, Inc.)

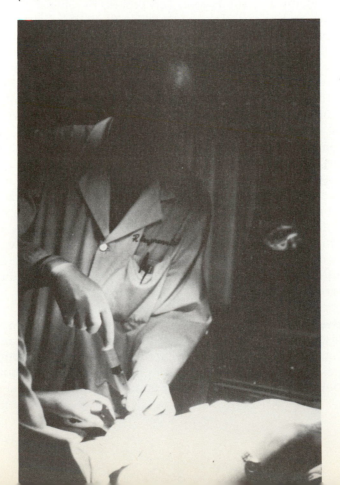

ETIOLOGY

According to available estimates (Karp et al., 1978), mental retardation has been positively linked with other 200 distinct causes, with many other factors suspected of causing the condition. For the purposes of this discussion, attention is focused on two types of causative factors: those reflecting a genetic basis and those stemming from brain damage.

Genetic Factors

To gain an appreciation for the way in which genetic factors can contribute to mental retardation, it is necessary to introduce some basic principles of genetic development (Bridgeman, 1988).

Upon conception, a zygote, or fertilized egg, is formed. The zygote has 23 pairs of chromosomes, one member of each pair being contributed by the mother and one by the father. Arranged on each chromosome are millions of genes, which are the carriers of inherited traits. Within a few hours after conception has occurred, the zygote splits into two cells identical to each other and identical to the zygote. This process of replication and cell division, called **mitosis**, is the mechanism by which the billions of cells in the body are formed, each containing the same genetic information as the original zygote.

As this process of cell division continues during pregnancy, certain cells subdivide in quite another way. In a process known as **meiosis**, the cells divide, but the chromosomes do not replicate themselves as they do in mitosis. Instead, the 23 pairs of chromosomes separate, one member of each pair going to each of two new cells. Cells formed by meiosis are known as sex cells, or gametes, each of which has only 23 chromosomes instead of the 46 found in all somatic cells. In females, gametes are referred to as ova, or eggs. Of the thousands of ova formed prenatally, only a very few will ever be fertilized after the woman reaches menarche, or childbearing age. The male, in contrast, continues to produce gametes, called sperm cells, well into advanced age.

At conception, an ovum and a sperm—each with its 23 chromosomes—unite to form a zygote. Each parent contributes half of the new cell's total of 46 chromosomes. During subsequent mitosis, each new cell contains a genetic code derived equally from each parent. This genetic code, much like a blueprint, is called the individual's **genotype**. A corresponding **phenotype**, or observed characteristic, may or may not be manifested.

Recessive Trait Disorders.
Inherited traits that occur infrequently (like Tay-Sachs disease) are generally controlled by recessive genes. Many metabolically based forms of mental retardation are linked to recessive genes.

Recessive traits are manifested only if both parents contribute the necessary gene. Dominant traits, on the other hand, require the critical gene from only

EXHIBIT

Mitosis

Mitosis, the process by which a somatic cell replicates itself

Source: From Carlson, N.R. (1981) *Physiology of behavior,* 2nd ed. p. 317. Boston: Allyn and Bacon, Inc. Reprinted with permission.

one parent. It is possible for an individual to carry a recessive gene for a particular characteristic without actually manifesting it. Recessive traits vary in frequency of occurrence, and those associated with mental abnormalities tend to be quite rare. Of these, the most common are a group of metabolic disorders including phenylketonuria (PKU), galactosemia, and amaurotic family idiocy. Less frequent is a recessive gene that causes the infant to be born with an abnormally small head (microcephaly) and, inevitably, to be mentally retarded.

PKU and galactosemia result from a lack of enzymes necessary for various metabolic processes. PKU occurs when the amino acid phenylalanine is not metabolized by an enzyme ordinarily produced in the liver. This results in toxic levels of phenylalanine which, if not controlled, eventually cause generalized deterioration of the brain and nervous system. PKU occurs frequently enough that hospitals do blood tests on all newborn infants to screen for elevated phenylalanine levels. In galactosemia, another metabolic disorder linked to a recessive trait, metabolism of a carbohydrate contained in milk fails to take place. Like PKU, galactosemia results in a highly toxic condition with widespread, generalized effects.

In both PKU and galactosemia, dietary treatments have proven successful in arresting the course of the disorder and preventing mental retardation. Children with PKU, for example, are placed on diets that restrict their phenylalanine intake for the first six or seven years of life. Although physical growth is somewhat retarded by this regimen, it prevents the occurrence of retardation. Similarly, children with galactosemia exclude milk from their diets. The resultant restricted intake of calcium can negatively effect bone development, but the risk of mental retardation is lowered substantially.

Chromosomal abnormalities. Normal somatic cells contain 46 chromosomes. Variations in this number lead to serious deformities during prenatal development and account for a high percentage of spontaneous abortions (Robinson and Robinson, 1970). **Down syndrome**, also known as mongolism, is the most common of these disorders, accounting for about 10 percent of all cases of moderate to severe mental retardation. About 90 percent of cases of Down syndrome are due to a condition called **trisomy 21**, in which the 21st pair of chromosomes is accompanied by a third chromosome. This results in a total of 47, rather than 46, chromosomes. The liklihood of trisomy 21 increases with the age of the mother. Although women over age 35 account for a relatively small proportion of total births, they produce a disproportionate number of children with Down syndrome due to trisomy 21.

The genetic abnormalities associated with trisomy 21 and several other similar conditions are most common in women who conceive comparatively late in life. One of the reasons for this is that there is a heightened risk that the ova of older women have been exposed to potentially hazardous agents such as radiation, toxic chemicals, or other environmental pollutants whose effects are only now beginning to be documented.

Down syndrome, the common name for trisomy 21, affects many facets of development. Many children born with the disorder eventually succumb to heart failure, and they show higher rates of other systemic disorders as well. Physical features characteristic of the condition include a small head, low-set ears, protuberant tongue, and slanted eyes, which led the disorder to be referred to as mongolism.

Heightened concern about the impact of toxic environmental agents on many aspects of life has led to more careful study of Down syndrome and other disorders originating before birth. Recent surveys have reported that the overall percentage of babies born with Down syndrome has remained constant from year to year. However, Uchida et al. (1968) reported a drop in the mean age of mothers giving birth to children with Down syndrome between 1960 and 1967. This trend supports the contention that hazardous environmental agents may contribute to earlier degeneration of female ova. Thus, given higher birth rates among younger women, the possibility exists that Down syndrome could become more prevalent. Environmental toxins

Nutrition plays a key role in physical and psychological development. This severely malnourished child has a greater chance of suffering from disorders than a child who grows up with a stable, balanced diet. (AP/Wide World Photos)

may be playing an increasingly prominent role in the etiology of mental retardation and other chronic, disabling conditions.

Brain Damage

The large proportion of children with severe neurologic conditions associated with mental retardation attests to the vulnerability of the developing brain (Kolb and Whishaw, 1985). Considerable research has been done to determine the effects of brain injury during the pre- and perinatal period on later behavior. One outcome of this research has been the identification of critical periods of brain development during which certain nutritional needs must be met. The first of these occurs at between 10 and 20 weeks of gestation, when brain cells undergo rapid multiplication. During this period the mother's nutritional status has a direct bearing on the development of the fetal nervous system. Severe nutritional deprivation can impair the maturation of developing structures that eventually are comprised in the brain and nervous system.

A second critical period occurs during the first year of life, when nutritional factors are again important determinants of neurologic development. The child must receive adequate supplies of fats known as lipids. Lipids are essential to the process of **myelination** (see Exhibit). Myelin is a lipid-based substance that forms a protective covering around nerve cell fibers. Myelin functions much like the insulation on a wire that transmits electric current, ensuring that the minute electric currents passing from nerve to nerve are not diminished in strength.

Another important phase of neurologic growth also takes place in the first year. As nerve cells mature, tiny tendrils known as dendrites grow from the nerve axon (see Exhibit) and become interconnected with the axons of nearby nerve cells. Dendrites look like tiny branches, and the comparatively large nerve axon resembles the trunk of a tree. Because of this, the process of dendrite growth has been termed **dendritic arborization**, the latter word the Latin equivalent of "tree."

The production of brain cells, myelination, and dendritic arborization are all critical aspects of brain development, which take place at a very rapid pace both prenatally and during the first year of life. All are dependent on adequate nutrition. Studies of malnourished children have shown that the effects of inadequate nutrition can be devastating. For example, Pollit and Thomson (1977) reviewed a series of studies demonstrating conclusively that malnourished infants are markedly less sensitive to stimulation than normal infants. Cravioto et al. (1966) identified three adverse effects of prolonged malnutrition on early development: (1) a loss of available learning time; (2) interference with mental development during critical periods for learning; and (3) apathy and other indications of low motivational states. Children with these symptoms, according to Cravioto et al., have a high probability of being diagnosed as mentally retarded.

Other factors may have deleterious effects on the neophyte brain as well. Complications during the birth process that deprive the newborn of an

EXHIBIT

Nerve Cell Processes

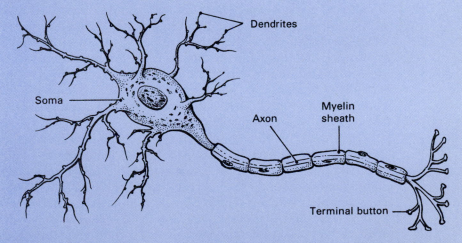

Figure A. Dendritic Arborization. In a process known as dendritic arborization, tiny tendrils, much like miniature tree roots, form on the stem, or axon, of nerve cells and become densely interconnected. Dendritic arborization appears to affect the efficiency with which electrical impulses are transmitted through the nervous system.

Source: From Carlson, N.R. (1981) *Physiology of behavior,* 2d ed., p. 20. Boston: Allyn and Bacon, Inc. Reprinted with permission.

Dendrites

Soma

Axon

Myelin sheath

Terminal button

Figure B. The Principal Structures or Regions of a Multipolar Neuron. In another important process, myelination, nerve axons are encased in a sheath composed of substances known as lipids. Acting like an insulator on a piece of wire, myelin aids in the efficient transmission of nerve impulses from one fiber to another.

Source: Carlson, 1981, p. 21. Reprinted with permission.

adequate oxygen supply can have very harmful effects. The effects of oxygen deprivation, or **anoxia**, are widespread, and may effect such diverse areas as motor coordination, mental development, memory skills, and activity level. Severe oxygen deprivation at birth is likely to result in permanent, irreversible brain damage and severely disabling mental retardation.

The number of potentially disabling conditions associated with brain maturation underscores the vulnerability of the developing infant. The impact of conditions such as malnutrition and anoxia is often widespread and chronic, leaving the child permanently disabled.

Other Factors

Mental retardation, as we have seen, is not caused by a single factor (Zigler, 1986). Most psychologists view the intellectual and social deficits characteristic of mental retardation to be the result of adverse genetic or environmental factors, frequently a combination of both. Children of all intellectual levels benefit from the experience of an enriched environment, which can compensate to varying degrees for innate biological limitations. Conversely, an impoverished environment can have a significant, adverse effect on children of any potential intellectual level. A report by Bradley and Caldwell (1976) revealed a significant correlation between ratings of the quality of childrens' home environment during infancy and their IQ scores at age four and a half. Bradley and Caldwell found that two factors were important for subsequent intellectual development: (1) ample opportunities for stimulating interactions with the mother or primary caretaker, and (2) adequate provision of play materials and varied experiences on a day-to-day basis. Correlational findings such as these, however, are open to more than one interpretation, only one of which is that enriched experiences have a positive influence on IQ scores. It is also possible that mothers who provide enriching stimulation do so because they have children who respond enthusiastically. It might also be argued, in support of a genetically based explanation of enrichment effects, that highly competent and intelligent mothers naturally provide this sort of stimulation to offspring who are equally endowed.

To choose among these plausible explanations would require studies demonstrating that children initially raised in deprived environments show marked improvements in IQ scores when transferred to more hospitable surroundings. In fact one such survey by Clarke and Clarke (1976) has reported considerable evidence—some of it quite dramatic—that such gains are possible. Clarke and Clarke's survey suggested at least two conclusions with respect to mental retardation. First, raising a child in a stimulating, emotionally secure environment can to some degree offset inherited limitations on intellectual development. Second, studies revealing large gains in IQ scores of children initially diagnosed as mentally retarded indicate that some forms of retardation are environmentally, rather than biologically, based. In fact, the

RESEARCH PROFILE

Nutrition and Precursors of Intelligence

It has long been recognized that malnourishment has adverse effects on physical growth and development. Only recently, however, have the effects of malnutrition on psychological development begun to be understood. In a significant series of studies, Lester (1975) tested groups of normal and malnourished infants in Guatemala to determine the effects of deprivation on sensitivity to the environment. Lester studied a specific reaction known as an orienting response (OR), which normally occurs when one is exposed to novel stimulation. This "what is it?" response basically serves as an alerting mechanism. The OR is believed to be an important component in learning, since it appears that, for learning to occur, attention must be directed toward the source of the necessary information. One of the characteristic reactions of OR is brief deceleration of the heart rate. Repeated stimulation results in a gradual extinction of this response as the subject becomes accustomed, or habituates, to the stimulus.

Lester studied the heart rate responses of normal and malnourished infants, using two loud tones as stimuli. Nearly 60 percent of the children in the normal group showed an OR to the first presentation of the sounds. Repeated presentation of either tone resulted in habituation. If the other tone was then presented, the OR recurred in nearly 30 percent of the children. In marked contrast, no more than 10 percent of the infants in the malnourished group gave any signs of an OR when the tones were sounded. As a group, these children tended to be lethargic and unresponsive.

Lester's data indicated that the children's physiologic mechanisms associated with attention and alertness were at best minimally responsive. This finding suggests that the infants were relatively insensitive to what was going on around them. In the long run, such a lack of sensitivity predisposes children to develop subaverage mental abilities, often within the range of mental retardation.

term "cultural-familial retardation," mentioned earlier, accurately portrays the status of many children who, though classified as mentally retarded, manifest no biologic deficiencies. Typically, these are children whose IQ scores fall in the mildly retarded range and who often manifest dramatic signs of improvement when provided with enriching, stimulating educational programs. Even within this group, however, biologic as well as environmental factors can play contributory roles in determing the child's level of functioning.

In practice, it is seldom necessary to determine unequivocally the cause of poor intellectual and social adaptation. The key factor in working with retarded children is their capacity to learn. This capacity exists at all levels of mental retardation to at least some degree, even in individuals requiring constant supervision and custodial care.

The Case of Mark

Mark was the last of four children, born 10 years after his next oldest sibling. Of the four, he was the slowest to develop. His mother kept track of developmental milestones for the other children, and found that Mark was somewhat delayed in learning to walk and talk. A shy child, he nonetheless liked being around people and in fact, even as a three-year-old, became quite anxious if left to himself. No specific physical abnormalities were evident, but Mark's parents were convinced that he was somehow abnormal.

Psychological testing when Mark was four confirmed their suspicions of slow development. His IQ score fell within the range of mild mental retardation, and an assessment of adaptive behavior skills indicated that he was functioning about one year behind his age level. Because the problem had been detected early, Mark's parents were able to arrange a comprehensive treatment program for Mark by the time he entered the public school system.

Mark was placed in a small class for children with mild mental handicaps. Aides worked with the regular teacher to provide each of the children with individual tutoring and attention. One of the specific areas where Mark was noticeably slow involved language skills, and this was given special attention.

During Mark's first year in the program, he received intensive training in learning to associate pictures of objects with their names. One activity he especially liked involved looking through magazines with his teacher, taking turns pointing out pictures of objects, which he would then try to identify. The teacher would give him one or two clues about the name, but if he failed to identify it with these hints, she would make the first sound of the word and wait for him to supply the rest.

As simple as this game-like activity sounds, it helped Mark in three ways. First, identifying objects in pictures helped sharpen visual discrimination skills. Naming and labeling the objects promoted more active use of language skills. Third, the social context of the activity added to Mark's feelings of acceptance and competence. He derived great comfort from the relationship formed with his teacher and the aide, and as a result became much more confident in other social situations.

There is no magical ending to Mark's story; his IQ did not abruptly increase by 30 or 40 points. But he did make steady progress in the program, and by the end of the first year was able to participate in some classwork with nonimpaired children—a concept known as "mainstreaming." The contact proved very helpful to Mark, especially in terms of social development. He continued on in this fashion for several years, and eventually entered a vocational program in food preparation and cooking—a move that surprised everyone. He eventually obtained work in the food service department of a large company that had a policy of hiring persons with mental handicaps who had demonstrated practical skills.

TREATMENT

In general, early detection of mental retardation results in the greatest chances for substantial improvement in intellectual and adaptive functioning (Schaefer, 1988; Erickson, 1978). Children with mental retardation who begin attending school have been shown to profit from some general training procedures oriented toward problem-solving skills. The Israeli psychologist Feuerstein (1979) found that many children with borderline or mild mental retardation approach academic situations in a passive manner, and as a result fail to develop effective problem-solving skills. Feuerstein identified three primary factors underlying this passivity, and proposed remedial strategies to promote more active responses. The first factor involves a characteristically nonanalytic approach to problems in which the child responds impulsively without considering all the relevant information. Getting the child to slow down, consider all the aspects of the problem, and generate a thoughtful solution is a helpful remedial strategy. A second limitation of retarded children is that their view of the world tends to be fragmentary and disconnected, partly because they form so few associations between their experiences. Words such as "like," "similar," or "different" are noticeably absent from their vocabularies. Helping them to see how things are alike and how they differ is one way of helping overcome this limitation (Apbib et al., 1987). Third, many of these children have to be trained to recognize a problem; they are not initially aware, for instance, that a statement posing a question requires a series of logical steps before the question can be answered. Helping a child to first detect and then comprehend the issues posed by, for instance, a request to define and illustrate the meaning of a word is one way of creating a greater sensitivity to problem-solving strategies.

There are other intervention strategies that also have proven effective for children with mental retardation. In terms of basic cognitive and perceptual skills development, Crawford and Siegal (1982) have reported success in training retarded children to improve their visual discrimination skills. They use a combination of immediate feedback and attention-directing cues to promote discrimination efficiency. For example, training children to identify differences between pictures of two animals would involve prompting the child to look at each picture in turn, compare the specific features of each, and point out the differences.

The use of cueing, prompting, and other techniques for directing the attention of children towards the task at hand have been widely employed. Many institutional programs have trained staff members in these techniques, which provide the child with a structured approach to problem-solving but still leave room for personal discovery (Page et al., 1982). The accompanying case report illustrates the effectiveness of cognitive stimulation programs in promoting an active approach to school work for a young child with mild retardation.

Language training represents another important area of cognitive skills training for children with mental retardation. Grieve (1982) found that many

Programs such as the Special Olympics give mentally retarded and handicapped children a much needed feeling of accomplishment.   (Abraham Menashe/Photo Researchers, Inc.)

mentally retarded children are significantly lacking in the language skills needed for basic problem-solving and arithmetic skills. Stimulating the use of language to describe the child's environment and day-to-day experiences has been advocated (Friedman et al., 1987). Intervention beginning as early as infancy has been proposed to help develop these types of skills (Sharav and Shlomo, 1986). Lombardino et al. (1982) found that the communicative responsiveness of children with Down syndrome could be enhanced through active modeling of speech patterns and questions by the mother.

A variety of socially oriented interventions also have been employed with mentally retarded children. Modeling is an effective technique for teaching many skills (Bandura, 1977), and there are indications that retarded children profit from exposure to competent models as much as nonretarded children (Sarinski, 1982).

Incorporating mentally handicapped children into play activities is a worthwhile therapeutic activity. According to Field et al. (1982), mentally retarded children tend to seek out such contact spontaneously, and make extensive efforts to interact with nonhandicapped peers. An inevitable benefit of this type of social integration is enhanced self-esteem, which is known to correlate positively with cognitive performance (Wolf and Wenzl, 1982).

Psychological counseling has proven helpful for victims of certain genetic abnormalities like PKU and galactosemia. The prognosis for these children is relatively good for achieving at least average levels of functioning, but only if they adhere to strict dietary regulations. Psychotherapy with both the afflicted child and other family members can prove invaluable in helping to deal with the frustrations caused by the restrictions.

Intervention strategies need to be sensitive to a child's level of retardation. As the severity of mental retardation increases, psychological interventions tend to become more behaviorally oriented. With highly impaired institutionalized individuals, it is often necessary to devise programs to manage behavior that may be injurious to the patient and staff (Barrett, 1986b). Successful reports of interventions based on combined reward and punishment contingencies have been reported (Lockwood and Bourland, 1982; Durand, 1982). Behaviorally based training in self-care and personal hygiene has also proven successful, even for severely retarded individuals (Smith and Wong, 1981).

Mental retardation is a multifaceted problem that encompasses a wide range of physical, psychological, and social factors (Zigler and Hodapp, 1986). As a result, the multimodal approach to intervention stressed throughout this book is generally quite appropriate. But beyond the varied needs of children with mental retardation lie other issues to be addressed. According to Eggert (1982), a truly comprehensive approach to intervention for mental retardation must take into account (1) the handicap itself and how it affects the child's development; (2) problems encountered by the family in coping with the impairment; (3) prevailing stereotypic social attitudes toward mental retardation; and (4) the capacity of the community to respond to the needs of mentally retarded persons.

CHAPTER REVIEW

1. Historically, mental retardation was associated with many forms of deviance, including criminal behavior, sexual aberrations, and physical abnormalities. Mentally retarded persons were often treated as common criminals.

2. Mentally retarded persons differ widely in their degree of intellectual and functional impairments. Currently, four levels of mental retardation are recognized: mild, moderate, severe, and profound.

3. AAMD guidelines diagnose mental retardation on the basis of (1) subaverage intellectual performance; and (2) impaired adaptive functioning.

4. Early detection of mental retardation is possible via an analysis of genetic material withdrawn from the amniotic sac. Through amniocentesis, the fetus' chromosomal structure can be analyzed for genetic characteristics associated with known forms of mental retardation.

5. A variety of factors have been identified that can cause mental retardation, including genetic abnormalities, brain damage, and the effects of an impoverished early upbringing.

6. Genetic abnormalities known to cause mental retardation include both recessive trait disorders (such as PKU) and chromosomal abnormalities (Down syndrome).

7. Brain damage sustained early in life can cause mental retardation. The widespread deficits associated with mental retardation are frequently caused by factors with widespread effects, such as oxygen deprivation at birth or chronic malnutrition during the following months.

8. Treatment of mental retardation requires that goals be set within the framework of the client's strengths and limitations. The vast majority of mentally retarded persons have at least reasonable aptitudes for learning.

9. For individuals whose performance is in the "borderline" range of functioning, cognitive training may prove helpful. This approach helps people become more active and involved in their surroundings.

TERMS TO REMEMBER

AAMD
EMH
cultural-familial retardation
frequency distribution
Vineland Social Maturity Scale
Adaptive Behavior Scale
PKU
amniocentesis
mitosis

meiosis
genotype
phenotype
Down syndrome
trisomy 21
myelination
dendritic arborization
anoxia

FOR MORE INFORMATION

Barrett, R. (1986) *Severe behavior disorders in the mentally retarded*. New York: Plenum. An indepth analysis of the behavior disorders that often accompany mental retardation, along with ways to treat and cope with them

Dean, R. (1987) *Introduction to assessing human intelligence*. Springfield, Ill.: Charles Thomas. Unique in its focus on the assessment of intelligence across the life span, this text stresses the evaluation of cognitive functioning and learning problems, with specific reference to mental retardation

Feldman, D. (1987) *Nature's gambit: Child prodigies and the development of human potential.* Offering an interesting perspective on mental retardation by way of contrast to the opposite end of the intelligence continuum, this is a scientifically sound and clear description of what it's like for someone who grows up as an intellectual prodigy

Tyson, M., and Favell, J. (1987) *Mental retardation—children.* In: V. Van Hasselt, P. Strain, and M. Hersen (Eds.). *Handbook of developmental and physical disabilities.* Elmsford, N.Y.: Pergamon Press provides a comprehensive overview of the basic cognitive and behavioral impairments associated with the early manifestations of mental retardation

Nicholas Cage and Holly Hunter unexpectedly find themselves in charge of bringing up unfinished furniture heir Nathan Arizona, Jr. (played by T.J. Kuhn) in the film *Raising Arizona.* (IMP/GEH Stills Collection; © 1987 20th Century-Fox Film Corporation)

CHAPTER

15

Psychological Disorders of Childhood

It may come as something of a surprise to learn that children, like adults, are vulnerable to psychological distress. A wide range of mental disorders has been associated with early development, ranging from fairly common problems like bed wetting (enuresis) to more rare, but more disabling conditions like infantile autism (Roberts, 1986). This chapter discusses a representative group of psychological disorders unique to childhood. A number of the disorders already discussed in this book, including conditions such as depression, stress, and certain psychological disorders (such as the gender identity disorder of childhood), may all have their roots in early experience.

● The Case of Charlie

Because of persistent academic problems, Charlie, age seven, was seen by a psychologist. His test scores from kindergarten revealed him to be a child of at least average mental abilities. When tested two years later, however, his scores had dropped: an IQ test indicated his performance to be within the borderline mentally retarded range—a significant overall decline. In effect, his development appeared to have been arrested at the level of a five year old.

Further assessment revealed that Charlie had not learned much during his first two years of school. He was highly distractible and difficult to manage unless given constant, individualized attention. However, the large class size precluded this. Thinking that he might be "hyperactive," the family physician prescribed Ritalin for Charlie. Ritalin is a stimulant medication that paradoxically calms down some hyperactive children. Charlie, however, was so sedated that he slept much of the day, and the medication was discontinued. To keep him from falling even further behind, Charlie's parents tried to work with him on assignments each evening, but soon gave up in frustration.

The psychologist developed a multimodal intervention program consisting of home tutoring, part-time placement in a "resource room" at school, and carefully monitored medication. By hiring a tutor who specialized in helping children who were slow learners, Charlie's parents experienced less frustration and found enjoyable things to do with him unrelated to school work. The school system in which Charlie was enrolled had a comprehensive program for learning-impaired children. It was discovered that Charlie's low performance on the IQ test was due in part to excessive distractibility. In reality, he was a child of average overall abilities with specific areas of learning impairment, particularly reading. This knowledge enabled the school to develop an educational plan for Charlie that made use of both a regular classroom and a specialized "resource room." Not only did Charlie receive added instruction, but he was given far more individualized attention than had been the case previously. Finally, Charlie was once again started on Ritalin, only this time the dosage was carefully monitored. The initial trial had over-sedated him, so half the original dosage was administered. The effects on his behavior were monitored for two weeks via classroom observation, until it became evident that Charlie was staying alert and aware of his surroundings without being distracted by them.

Gradually, Charlie's school performance improved. His attention became more focused, and the tutoring he received in the resource room improved his reading skills. These improvements in turn led to heightened feelings of self-esteem, and Charlie began to show greater interest in school. When tested at the end of the school year, Charlie was found to be making good progress, and he finished the year ranked in the middle third of his class.

INTRODUCTION

The case of Charlie illustrates several important points concerning assessment and intervention issues with children. First, many psychological problems are not detected until children enter school. Charlie's history revealed a consistent pattern of nearly constant activity. Highly reactive as an infant, he would start crying at the slightest disturbance. Raised by parents who did not consider his sensitivity to be a problem, Charlie's problems did not really become evident until he started school. Second, childhood disorders tend to stem from multiple causes; it is rare to find a condition that can be clearly traced to a single etiological factor (Wender, 1987). In Charlie's case, both biological and social factors appeared to contribute to his distractibility. The combination of Ritalin with individualized academic tutoring proved an effective means of addressing both factors. Third, it is often difficult to precisely diagnose psychological disorders in childhood, and it was only recently that the DSM classification system was expanded to include a section on childhood disorders. Until recently, Charlie's problems might have elicited such diagnostic labels as "hyperactive"; "minimally brain damaged"; "learning disabled"; and even "mentally retarded." With the advent of the DSM system, however, conditions such as Charlie's can be defined more precisely. According to current terminology, his condition would be diagnosed as Attention-deficit Hyperactivity disorder about which more will be said later.

The psychological problems of children have begun to occupy the attention of clinicians only comparatively recently. Much more attention was initially devoted to disordered behavior in adults. Until recently, children were perceived as miniature, imperfect versions of adults with few uniquely defining characteristics. As a result, there were few systematic efforts to learn about the nature of children's problems. (One of the few disorders diagnosed in the mid-nineteenth century, for example, was masturbatory insanity, which many people attributed to juvenile sexual experimentation.)

Beginning with the early twentieth century, however, interest in children burgeoned. In 1896 Lightner Witmer established the first treatment clinic in America for children. Sigmund Freud's theories concerning the childhood origins of adult neurosis stimulated interest in the impact of early experiences on development. Later, Arnold Gesell and other developmental psychologists began collecting precise data on the ages at which many capabilities—such as walking and speaking—developed. As a result of these theories and empirical investigations, childhood came to be perceived as a unique and vital phase of the life span that has major implications for later development (Pope et al., 1987)

A complete discussion of childhood psychological disorders is beyond the scope of this chapter; entire books, such as those by Knopf (1979), Quay and Werry (1979), and Weiner (1982) have been written on the subject. Our intent, rather, is to provide a representative overview of the area by discussing several of the most clinically significant disorders of childhood. Most of these conditions have been incorporated into the DSM classification system.

The disorders discussed in this chapter are arranged according to the average age at onset. Generally speaking, disorders occurring early in life are linked to hereditary and/or biological factors, whereas those developing later are almost invariably linked to social and environmental forces. Infantile autism, the first disorder discussed, is a good example of a biologically based condition present from birth. Anxiety reactions, in contrast, generally develop in response to unpleasant experiences in the child's social environment. Fears of abandonment, separation, and negative responses to strangers are all related to social experiences.

It is easier to understand the nature of childhood psychological disorders if one first has some appreciation for the characteristics of normal development (Gelfamel et al., 1987). This chapter begins, therefore, with a consideration of some basic processes related to the psychological and physical development of children.

DEVELOPMENTAL PROCESSES

There is no single psychological theory that can encompass the broad scope of childhood development (Achenbach, 1982). Infancy and childhood are periods of rapid change in such diverse areas of development as language, social skills, thinking processes, sexuality, and physical maturation (Pellegrini, 1986). Explaining how each of these capabilities matures requires highly specialized knowledge. There are, for example, psychologists whose work focuses exclusively on language development, and others who primarily study thought processes. It can be difficult to gain an overview of how the different facets of development result in a coordinated pattern of growth. The exhibit on page 549 illustrates some important milestones in specific areas of development, each of which has been studied by a different investigator. The Exhibit depicts the stages of psychosexual, psychosocial, cognitive, and moral development as proposed by Freud, Erikson, Piaget, and Kohlberg, respectively. Each of these individuals has formulated a **stage theory** to account for certain developmental events (Clarke-Stewart et al., 1988).

Stage theories ascribe a logical sequence to development, such that each new level attained represents a higher degree of maturity and a greater capacity for complex forms of behavior. The transition from one stage to the next does not occur abruptly, so there are seldom sudden, abrupt changes in a child's behavior. Instead, children acquire the characteristics of a given stage of development in a gradual, almost imperceptible way. The age at which a child achieves a given stage of maturity can vary considerably from one child to the next. Regardless of the actual age of onset, however, stage theories assume that all children pass through each stage in the same order. Failure to mature at a given level may delay or preclude maturation at the next.

Freud's model of **psychosexual development** (see Chapter 2) proposed a series of developmental stages differing according to how sexual energies are discharged (Masling, 1982). Implicit in his developmental scheme is the idea that sexual energies are gradually channeled away from self-centered pleasure seeking toward graftification based on interpersonal contact. This is one way the sexual behavior of mature adults differs from that of young children. The process of moving from one stage of psychosexual development to the next is a lengthy one fraught with potential problems. Freud believed that many forms of adult psychopathology could be traced to arrested development during earlier stages of psychosexual maturation.

EXHIBIT				
Phases of Early Development				
Age Span	Psychosexual Development (Sigmund Freud)	Psychosocial Development (Erik Erikson)	Cognitive Development (Jean Piaget)	Moral Development (Lawrence Kohlberg)
Infancy (Birth–2)	Deriving pleasure passively, by taking things in (oral stage)	Establishing trust in one other person (trust versus mistrust)	Maturity of motor skills, manipulation of objects (sensori-motor stage)	Simple reactions to pleasure, pain; behavior oriented toward meeting personal needs (preconventional)
Preschool (2–5)	Experiencing pleasure via eliminative functions (anal stage) Early experience of genital pleasure (phallic stage)	Achieving limited personal autonomy (autonomy versus shame) Learning to take the initiative in relating to others (initiative versus guilt)	Acquisition of language, appreciation of symbols (pre-operational stage)	Behavior that leads to approval by others; behavior that conforms to existing laws and regulations (conventional)
School Age (6–13)	Submersion of genital pleasure to other, socially sanctioned activities (latency stage)	Becoming productive, industrious, and cooperative (industry versus inferiority)	Capacity for abstract thought (concrete operations stage)	
Adolescence (13 +)	Achievement of mutually pleasurable genital sexuality (heterosexual genital stage)	Achieving a sense of personal integrity distinct, but not divorced from, others (identity versus diffusion)	Development of sophisticated reasoning ability, capacity for hypothetical thought (formal operations stage)	Awareness of common good and of universal principles (postconventional)

Erik Erikson's theory of **psychosocial maturation** analyzes in detail the course of social development (Erikson, 1963). He proposed a series of stages in social development that extends across the entire lifespan. According to Erikson, interactions with other people, from infancy onward, strongly influence one's personal identity. Social development proceeds by stages from extreme dependence on others during infancy to stages of greater maturity in which people contribute as much to relationships as they receive in return. Failure to make this transition can inhibit the ability to form satisfying personal relationships and result in feelings of aimlessness and alienation.

Piaget's model of **cognitive development** focuses on the maturation of mental abilities. Each of four stages of cognitive growth brings with it added capabilities for abstract, rational thought (Piaget, 1976). Because such skills are highly valued both in school and in occupational settings, most children are pushed to develop reasoning and analytical skills. The developmental progression in cognitive development begins in infancy when infants explore their world by touching and manipulating objects. They next develop language capabilities, which allows them to talk about objectives, people, and events (Franklin and Barten, 1988). The capacity to think about and solve problems first develops during the early school years, and is carried to highly sophisticated levels in adolescence.

As is true of other stage theorists, Piaget assumed that a child deprived of necessary stimulation during one level of development would be handicapped in attaining the next (Sugarman, 1987). For example, an infant deprived of opportunities to practice sensory and motor skills would be likely to show deficient cognitive skills as a school-age child. In extreme cases of deprivation, drastic curtailment of cognitive development may occur, resulting in mental retardation.

Lawrence Kohlberg developed a stage theory of **moral development,** which traces the formation of moral and ethical values (Kohlberg, 1963). His research suggested that moral integrity evolves from the painful and pleasurable sensations associated with punishments and rewards. Initially, children behave in socially appropriate ways to gain approval and avoid being punished. Later, they learn to base their actions on more abstract moral principles such as the "Golden Rule," or certain humanistic and religious ideals (Colby et al., 1987).

Moral development may be arrested or curtailed at any stage of development, which may then have adverse effects on social adjustment. Both juvenile delinquency and antisocial behavior have been linked to deficits in moral development.

Sexual, social, cognitive, and moral development encompass but a small number of dimensions on which maturation takes place. Something as specific as emotional expressiveness has been the object of considerable developmental research, resulting in a growing body of research literature suggesting that as children mature, they undergo significant changes in the way they express their feelings.

Physical development is also important, and has been the subject of considerable research (Osofsky, 1987). One of the most important researchers in this area was Arnold Gesell. He was among the first to demonstrate that many aspects of development operate according to approximate timetables, which, if excessively tampered with, can lead to maladjustment (Gesell and Thompson, 1929). Thus, according to Gesell, parents who push their children too rapidly risk upsetting internal forces governing maturation. There are many reports of poorly adjusted individuals pushed to high achievement levels in school before they were ready to handle the associated pressures

EXHIBIT

The Early Development of Various Human Emotions

Month	Pleasure-Happiness	Fear-Wariness	Anger-Rage	Phases of Emotional Development
0	Nondirected smile	Startle/pain	Upset due to; covering the face, physical restraint, extreme discomfort	No responsive emotions
1	Turning toward	Reflexive attention		Turning toward
2				
3	Pleasure		Rage (frustration)	Positive mood
4	Delight, laughter	Wariness		
5				
6				Active participation
7	Joy	Anger		
8				
9		Fear of strangers		Attachment
10				
11				
12	Elation	Anxiety, immediate fear	Angry mood, petulance	Practicing
18	Positive valuation of self-affection	Shame	Defiance	Emergence of self
24			Intentional hurting	
36	Pride, love		Guilt	Play and fantasy

The age specified is neither the first appearance of the affect in question nor its peak occurrence; it is the age when the literature indicates that the reaction is common. *Adapted from* Sroufe, L.A. (1979) *Socioemotional development.* In: J. Osofsky (Ed.). *Handbook of infant development.* New York: Wiley.

(Bettelheim, 1967). Gesell argued persuasively that education and training must be properly matched to the child's developmental level. Aimed too high, the effect would be to frustrate the child and engender anxiety. Pegged too low, and boredom or apathy would result.

Gesell is perhaps best known for having established comprehensive developmental norms covering a wide range of behavioral capabilities. This information proved invaluable both as a source of data on normal developmental

Most children learn to walk according to an approximate timetable; parents who push their children to achieve before they are ready may cause maladjustment problems that last into adulthood.   (Charles Harbutt/Archive Pictures)

trends and as a standard against which to assess children whose maturation was either exceptionally slow or fast. As a result of Gesell's work, it was learned, for example, that children learn to walk at an average age of just over one year, and begin speaking shortly thereafter.

Gesell's norms provided psychologists with a statistical criterion of abnormality that was previously lacking. It became possible, for example, to test infants only a few months old for indications of abnormally slow development that might indicate the presence of mental retardation or other disorders associated with early development. Of course, there are many behaviors for which precise developmental norms are not available. For example, it is impossible to state at precisely what age a child should form his or her first friendship, or say with certainty how old children should be before leaving the house unaccompanied. Nonetheless, an appreciation for the basic developmental norms first documented by Gesell underlies all current models of both normal and abnormal development (Clarke-Stewart et al., 1988).

Each of the developmental psychologists discussed thus far has focused on specific aspects of maturation. All share a conviction that, at each stage of development, adequate stimulation is necessary for continuing development. These stages have been termed **critical periods** (Caldwell, 1962), and are important because they strongly influence the course of subsequent growth. Millon (1981) later applied the concept of critical periods to an analysis of personality development. He has proposed that the child's central nervous system is sensitive to different classes of stimuli as maturation progresses. Infants, for example, are highly responsive to being touched, fed, and kept warm. Collectively, these stimuli engender feelings of pleasure and security. Later on, opportunities to explore one's environment and manipulate objects are sought, contributing to a child's curiosity and independence. Security and independence, outgrowths of these early experiences, provide a basis for self-esteem, feelings of self-worth, and other manifestations of a healthy personality.

THE ASSESSMENT OF ABNORMAL BEHAVIOR

The psychological disorders in childhood are classified separately from adult mental disorders in the DSM system, for several reasons. First, the rapid pace of development during the first years of life creates unique psychological vulnerabilities (Osofsky, 1987). Second, there are certain disorders, primarily biologically based, whose onset occurs only during childhood. Third, the manifestations of mental disorders found in both children and adults do not always take the same form. For example, adults with depression are invariably sad and mournful. Depressed children, on the other hand, seldom show such pervasive dysphoria. Instead, their emotional state is determined far more by external (environmental) than internal (cognitive) factors. As a result, their depression may take the form of excessive activity, which wards off feelings of unhappiness.

Although it is well established that children and adults may have distinctive sets of psychological problems, there is less agreement about the precise nature of mental disorders in children (Glow et al., 1982). There are several reasons for this. First, until the advent of classification systems like the DSM, few specific diagnostic criteria existed for any disorders. Second, even with more specific criteria, levels of agreement among teachers, parents, psychologists, and physicians about a child's specific problems may nonetheless be low. Part of the difficulty has to do with the relationships each person has with the child and how attuned each is to problem areas. Parents, for example, are often quite astute at identifying problematic behavior (Thompson and Bernal, 1982), but frequently give inaccurate descriptions of their childrens' early development (Hetherington and Martin, 1979). Finally, children themselves do not necessarily agree with the way in which their parents (and presumably other adults) evaluate their behavior (Herjavic and Reich, 1982). One of the most important services provided by clinical psychologists in assessing children lies in integrating the varied perceptions of the problem into a unified diagnostic impression (Anastasi, 1987).

Steps have been taken in recent years to help reduce the amount of confusion in assessing childhood psychological disorders. Gesell's research on patterns of normal development has provided statistical criteria for assessing abnormality. A second area of refinement is reflected in the proliferation of empirical rating scales and observational measures that attempt to describe problem behaviors in precise terms. The individual items on rating scales are often evaluated using a statistical procedure called factor analysis to determine whether or not they cluster into related groupings. For example, Hewitt and Jenkins (1946) factor-analyzed data derived from ratings of disturbed children. They found that the ratings tended to categorize children as being antisocial ("unsocialized aggressive"), sociable ("socialized delinquent"), or isolated ("overinhibited") (Quay and Werry, 1979). Other factor analytic studies have been used to classify children as sensitive, hyperactive, aggressive, and fearful (Miller, 1967; Achenbach and Edelbrock, 1978).

The development of the DSM system has led to further refinement of procedures for assessing mental disorders in childhood. The DSM recognizes numerous types of mental disorders uniquely associated with the period of development beginning with infancy and extending through adolescence.

Of course, other mental disorders may be diagnosed in childhood as well. For example, the affective disorders, schizophrenia, substance use disorders, and virtually all other conditions normally associated with adulthood may occur in children as well. These disorders have all been discussed in previous chapters. Intellectual disorders, the first of the DSM disorders of childhood, are associated with mental retardation, the topic of Chapter 14.

EXHIBIT

DSM Childhood Disorders

Representative Disorders Usually First Evident in Infancy, Childhood, or Adolescence

1. Overt behavioral: (a) attention deficit-hyperactivity disorder, (b) conduct disorder

2. Emotional: (a) anxiety disorders of childhood or adolescence, (b) gender identity disorder

3. Physical: (a) eating disorders, (b) tic disorders, (c) elimination disorders

4. Developmental: (a) pervasive developmental disorders, (b) specific developmental disorders, (c) mental retardation

EXHIBIT

Representative Childhood Disorders: Traditional and DSM Designations

Clinical Name	DSM Designation	
	General Category	Specific Title
Infantile autism	Developmental disorders	Pervasive developmental disorder (Axis II): Autistic disorder
Childhood schizophrenia	Developmental disorders (Schizophrenic disorders)*	Pervasive developmental disorder not otherwise specified (Axis II):
Asthma	Psychological factors affecting physical condition (Axis I)*	
Enuresis and encopresis	Physical disorders	Other disorders with physical manifestations (Axis I): Functional enuresis, functional encopresis
Hyperactivity	Overt behavioral disorders	Attention deficit—hyperactivity disorder (Axis I):
Anxiety reaction	Emotional disorders	Anxiety disorders of childhood or adolescence (Axis I)
Conduct disorder	Overt behavioral disorders	Conduct disorder

*Designations not limited to childhood.

REPRESENTATIVE DISORDERS

The following disorders are discussed within the framework of the DSM system. Included are disorders with (1) overt behavioral, (2) emotional, (3) physical, and (4) developmental characteristics.

These disorders are discussed in chronological order, beginning with conditions first evident in infancy. Infantile autism and Pervasive Developmental Disorder Not Otherwise Specified (PDDNOS to use DSM terminology) are the first disorders considered. The former is present at birth, while the latter develops within the first two years. The DSM system classifies both as pervasive developmental disorders, to convey the widespread degree of impairment evident in children afflicted with either condition. In both conditions, there is gross impairment in social skills as well as other evidence of highly disturbed behavior.

Next in order are three conditions usually found in children of preschool or later age: asthma, enuresis, and encopresis. The final three conditions discussed—hyperactivity, anxiety reactions, and conduct disorders—are most commonly associated with school-age children. Though sometimes evident earlier in life, they most often become the object of concern *after* children have made the transition from home to school.

Infantile Autism (DSM 'Autistic Disorder')

Infantile autism is a disorder first described by Leo Kanner in 1943. It is characterized by pervasive impairment in communication skills and by markedly poor social adjustment (Cohen and Donnellan, 1987). Infantile autism is classified in the DSM system as a pervasive developmental disorder because of the global impairments associated with it.

This autistic child exhibits typical tendencies to avoid social situations and to respond strangely to stimuli (in this case, an overhead light). (David M. Grossman/Photo Researchers, Inc.)

As initially described in a group of 11 children studied by Kanner, autism consisted of four features: (1) an inability to relate to other people that was present from birth; (2) failure to develop communicative language skills; (3) marked distress in response to even minute changes in the environment; and (4) a combination of subaverage intelligence and highly developed, but narrowly defined, capabilities. The latter are referred to as **islets of performance,** and constitute one way that autism can be discriminated from mental retardation. (The mental abilities of mentally retarded persons are uniformly low.) Islets of performance have been found in areas as varied as arithmetic skills, feats of memory, and artistic skills (see Exhibit).

Islets of performance are not the only feature that distinguish autism from mental retardation. Rutter (Rutter and Schopler, 1978) found that children with autism showed greater variability on IQ tests, were more prone to epileptic seizures, and had poorer language skills. Rutter also found autism more likely than mental retardation to be concentrated in children of upper middle-class families, although the validity of this assertion has since been questioned.

The DSM has retained many of Kanner's original symptoms in its definition of autism. It employs the following diagnostic criteria.

1. Onset before 30 months of age
2. Pervasive lack of responsiveness to other people
3. Grossly deficient language development
4. Peculiar speech patterns, such as echolalia (repeating words in a parrotlike fashion)
5. Bizarre responses to stimuli (such as reacting violently to a whisper)
6. Absence of delusions, hallucinations, or loose associations (any of which would suggest a psychotic disorder, such as schizophrenia)

Other symptoms of autism found in some, but not all, children with the disorder include **choreiform movements** and **self-stimulation.** Choreiform movements are rapid, whirling motions that sometimes resemble free-form dancing. Self-stimulation may take any of several forms, from rapid flapping of the hands to potentially harmful behaviors such as hand banging, pinching, and even biting oneself.

Etiology. Kanner originally believed that autism was caused by parents who were emotionally cold and aloof (Eisenberg and Kanner, 1956). The parents in his original sample of autistic children were indeed highly intelligent, but rigid and compulsive. He coined the phrase **refrigerator parent** to describe these individuals, and stimulated considerable research interest in the social origins of autism (Rimland, 1964). Recent studies, however, show that the incidence of psychological problems among parents of autistic children is no

EXHIBIT

Islets of Performance: Extraordinary Artistic Ability of a Young Child with Early Infantile Autism

This drawing gives a clear indication of the degree to which some autistic children possess remarkable skills in specific areas (islets of performance).

Source: From Selfe, L. (1977) *Nadia: A case of extraordinary drawing ability in an autistic child.* London: Academic Press, Inc. Reprinted with permission.

greater than average (Quay and Werry, 1979). Many parents have developed problems as a result of having an autistic child, so great are the attendant stresses in many cases. Psychiatrist John Ksar (1968) wrote a compelling account of the ordeals he was subjected to while seeking treatment for his own autistic child. His efforts to secure help were initially met with blame, suspicion, and even hostility. Fortunately, current treatment programs for autism are sensitive to the needs of parents, and generally incorporate them into the overall intervention plan.

Recent evidence that autism is biologically based and present from birth has done much to improve attitudes toward the parents of autistic children (Bridgeman, 1988). Pre- or perinatal abnormalities—as yet not clearly specified—are presumed to lie at the root of autism (Knobloch and Pasamanick, 1975; Ornitz and Ritvo, 1976). It has been found, for example, that children with autism do not establish solid bonds with their mothers. This process, referred to as **attachment** (Clancy and McBride, 1975) is manifested in normal children through behaviors such as making eye contact, clinging, smiling, and vocalizing. Autistic children, in contrast, tend to be unresponsive and physically rigid.

Impaired attachment constitutes the first evidence of poor social relationships in autism. As autistic children grow older, their capacity to relate to others is further impaired by failure to develop communicative language skills. Most authorities on autism now agree that language impairment constitutes the most disabling aspect of the disorder, and that the problem may be neurologically based. For example, Blackstock (1978) presented evidence that autistic children show indications of right cerebral hemisphere dominance, in contrast to the left dominant pattern of normal children. Speech and language skills are associated with the left hemisphere, whereas the right hemisphere processes essentially nonverbal information such as music and visuospatial data. The fact that autistic children have poor language skills but frequently show splinter skills in nonverbal areas provides support for a view of the disorder as being neurologically based (Schoplen and Mesibou, 1987).

Language development in autistic children is a reliable predictor of eventual adjustment. Knopf (1979) has found that the sophistication of language usage by age five is highly predictive of the degree of overall impairment in adolescence and early adulthood. Language deficits have far-reaching consequences. Not only do they predict poor adjustment in adulthood, but they also interfere with the registration and interpretation of experiences early in life.

Impaired language is one symptom of a broader pattern of cognitive deficits that adversely affect experiences associated with early development (DeMyer, 1976; Ornitz and Ritvo, 1976). Inborn, biologically based conditions like autism disturb early development in two principle ways. First, they impair the registration and interpretation of incoming information that is normally used to develop mental representations of one's environment. As a result, autistic children may develop a view of the world that is fragmentary, or which differs substantially from that of normal children. Second, inborn conditions like autism markedly impair social adaptation, beginning with the attachment to the mother and extending to other relationships. Thus, autistic children are handicapped from the beginning both perceptually and socially as a result of underlying neurologic dysfunctions.

Autism is one of the most disabling and difficult to treat of the childhood disorders (Cohen and Donnellan, 1987). While most autistic children possess isolated skills and show some improvement with treatment, few achieve really satisfactory levels of adjustment. As a result, most eventually require the structure and protection of hospital or institutional settings. Weiner (1982) reports that about 50 percent of autistic children are institutionalized by adolescence. Children with the poorest prognosis are those with chronic, longstanding symptoms and highly impaired language skills. The degree to which neurologic abnormalities, birth complications, physical abnormalities, and maternal stress are reported also have a bearing on prognosis (Harper and Williams, 1975).

Intervention. Pervasive developmental disorders like autism require comprehensive intervention to achieve even minimal results. Most programs are tailored to the specific needs of individual children and employ highly intensive, structured, and stimulating activities. This is especially true of the two most common intervention models for autism and related disorders: behavior therapy and milieu therapy.

Behavior therapy. Behavior therapists begin with a comprehensive assessment of an autistic child's functional skills, then design a program based on principles of operant conditioning to encourage behavior that is desirable and eliminate that which is maladaptive (Cohen and Donnellan, 1987). The focus of many programs is on the development of useful social and communication skills. Ferster (1961) was among the first psychologists to systematically employ behavioral techniques in the treatment of autism. He made extensive use of **shaping,** which involves breaking down complex behaviors into small components, each of which can individually be practiced and mastered. Shaping has been applied to areas such as social skills training (Hingtgen et al., 1965) and language development (Lovaas, 1977).

Sometimes it is necessary to use aversive conditioning with autistic children to eliminate self-injurious behavior such as chronic head-banging or self-mutilation. Lovaas and others have described procedures for administering mild electric shock in response to self-mutilating behavior, a procedure that has drawn some criticism.

Behavioral techniques have in general proven successful in modifying the behavior of autistic children, although it takes a long time and painstaking repetition to achieve even modest goals. Rutter (1968) has noted that improvements in language skills of autistic children are frequently at a very mechanical level, and seldom generalize to situations where language must

ISSUE TO CONSIDER

Treatment for Noah

Coping with the reality of raising a severely handicapped child can be difficult for parents. In "A Child Called Noah" (*Life,* October 23, 1970) and in two subsequent books, Joshua Greenfeld recounted the agonies and pleasures of raising a child whose numerous diagnoses included autism, brain damage, mental retardation, and "severe emotional disturbance." Because Noah's condition was not apparent at birth, his parents only gradually became aware that he was different from other children.

Noah's attractive physical appearance belied the profound limitations in his behavioral and language skills. Until he was a few months old, there was no indication that anything was wrong. At nine months, he failed to roll or sit the way most children do, but the pediatric examination was otherwise normal. A few months later, when signs of developmental delays became apparent, Noah's parents took their son through numerous consultations, examinations, and diagnostic procedures. Diagnostic labels were changed so frequently that they inevitably lost any meaning.

Despite the contradictory diagnoses, certain symptoms were obvious. The most important was Noah's inability to communicate with others predictably or effectively. At times he was hypersensitive to voices and other sounds but at other times he appeared insensitive or indifferent to them. Intelligible speech was almost nonexistent. As a result, Noah appeared to live in a world of his own.

Noah's parents eventually found some assistance through a behaviorally oriented language training program directed by Dr. O. Ivar Lovaas, a psychologist at UCLA. The training, however, produced limited results. Noah gradually acquired a few reliably conditioned response patterns: by the time he was five, he had been successfully toilet trained. He also manifested rudimentary imitative speech when reinforced for verbal responses.

In later years, Noah's condition showed minimal improvement. In *A Place for Noah* (1978), Greenfeld says he has few illusions left about the possibility of a miraculous cure; instead he tries to focus on small gains, such as people and programs showing a genuine concern for Noah. Ultimately, Noah will probably require long-term institutional care, despite the efforts of his parents to seek a cure for his condition.

Noah's situation reveals some of the limitations of traditional medical and psychological intervention. Noah apparently suffers from a variety of conditions, including brain damage, mental retardation, and severe developmental disabilities. These diagnostic terms merely describe Noah's symptoms, and treatment programs are limited in their capacity to improve his overall condition.

be applied in more complex, flexible ways (such as in social interactions). Some researchers have reported greater success with nonverbal communications systems such as sign language (Bonvillian et al., 1981), but, in general, most behaviorally based programs are considered successful if they are able to help autistic children achieve very rudimentary communication skills.

Milieu therapy. Milieu therapy provides the autistic child with a carefully controlled environment that is highly supportive and nurturant. As a rule, autistic children respond well to highly structured, caring settings (Schopler, 1974). Using milieu therapy to treat autism can be traced to Bruno Bettelheim (1967), who founded the Orthogenic School in Chicago to treat severely debilitating disorders of childhood. Bettelheim works with children who would be classified in the DSM system as having pervasive developmental disorders, and would thus include autism. He attributes severe psychopathology in childhood to traumatic early experiences, such as abuse or gross mistreatment of a child by the parents. His position with regard to autism is therefore similar to Kanner's original contention that parent-child interactions lay the groundwork for the disorder.

The therapeutic milieu provided by Bettelheim is highly structured in many ways, but is also quite permissive. He believes that removing the child from the home in itself is a significant step in therapy. Separation of parent and child gives both parties a chance to benefit from therapeutic interventions.

The child is treated with practically infinite patience and understanding. This approach is designed to help seriously disturbed children overcome their fears of personal involvement and gradually learn to develop a sense of trust in other people. Such children often act out in bizarre or unpredictable ways. Milieu therapists tolerate such behavior, provided it does not risk injury to the child or others. It is interpreted as the child's way of working through the trauma still associated with negative early experiences, and is believed to constitute a form of catharsis.

Although Bettelheim and others have made impressive claims for the effectiveness of milieu therapy, there has been little actual research to document these assertions. There are indications (Quay and Werry, 1979) that children with autism and other pervasive developmental disorders do best in highly organized treatment programs. Both the behaviorally oriented and milieu approaches discussed here meet this criteria.

The most important prognostic factor regarding autism appears to be the severity of the condition when it is first detected. Severely afflicted children are unlikely to show significant improvement in even the best treatment program. Support for this assertion comes from a follow-up study by Kanner (1971) on the 11 children he had diagnosed as autistic 30 years earlier. Of these eleven, all of whom had been diagnosed with autism early in life, only one was living with any degree of independence. Similarly, a long-term reevaluation of 120 autistic children by DeMyer et al. (1973) revealed that more than two thirds required long-term supervision or institutionalization.

Pervasive Developmental Disorder Not Otherwise Specified (PDDNOS)

PDDNOS is the name used in the DSM system to describe children previously referred to as having childhood schizophrenia. Recently, a distinction has

EXHIBIT

Characteristics of Childhood Schizophrenia and Infantile Autism

Clinical Aspects	Childhood Schizophrenia	Early Infantile Autism
Onset	Gradual, between age two to 11, after period of normal development.	Gradually apparent, but may have been present from birth.
Social and interpersonal	Decreased interest in external world; withdrawal; loss of contact; impaired relations with others.	Failure to show anticipatory postural movements; insistence on sameness; seems to be off in own world, even when around others.
Intellectual and cognitive	Thought disturbance; perceptual problems; distorted time and space orientation; below-average IQ.	High spatial ability; good memory; low IQ but seems to have intellectual potential.
Language	Disturbances in speech; mutism, or speech is not used for communication; bizarre associations.	Disturbances in speech; mutism, or speech is not used for communication; very literal; delayed echolalia; pronoun reversal; *I* and *yes* absent until age six.
Affect	Defect in emotional responsiveness and rapport; decreased, distorted, and/or inappropriate affect.	Inaccessible and emotionally unresponsive to people.
Motor	Bizarre body movements; repetitive and stereotyped motions; motor awkwardness; distortion in mobility.	Head banging and body rocking; remarkable agility and dexterity; preoccupation with mechanical objects; spinning, repetitive movements.
Physical and developmental patterns	Unevenness of somatic growth; disturbances of normal rhythmic patterns; abnormal EEG.	Peculiar eating habits and food preferences; normal EEG.
Family	High incidence of mental illness.	High intelligence and educational and occupational levels; low divorce rate and incidence of mental illness.

Source: Adapted from Rimland, B. (1964) *Infantile autism.* New York: Appleton-Century-Crofts, pp. 67–76, and Knopf, I.J. (1979) *Childhood psychopathology: A developmental approach.* Englewood Cliffs, N.J.: Prentice-Hall, p. 246, with permission of Bernard Rimland and Prentice-Hall.

been made between the adult and childhood forms of schizophrenia. Before 1933, Bleuler's original diagnostic criteria for a schizophrenic-like condition called *dementia praecox* were uncritically applied to children. Subsequently, the term *dementia praecoxissima* (*very* early insanity) came into vogue, but the diagnostic criteria did not really distinguish between childhood and adult variants. In 1933, however, Potter proposed that **childhood schizophrenia** be considered a distinct diagnostic entity to be applied only to prepubertal children. Based on his observations of seriously disturbed children, Potter proposed the following diagnostic criteria (Goldfarb, 1970, pp. 769–770):

1. Generalized retraction of interest in the environment
2. Unrealistic thinking, feeling, and acting
3. Disturbances of thought, manifested in incoherent speech
4. Defect in emotional rapport
5. Distorted emotional expressiveness
6. Bizarre behavior patterns

Most of these characteristics are implicit in the newer DSM diagnostic criteria for PDDNOS. Both terms designate a severe form of psychopathology in which interpersonal relationships are profoundly impaired and the child's overall behavior is unusual and at times bizarre. The disorder is presumed, moreover, to emerge following a period of relatively uneventful development. However, the fact that DSM does not use the term "schizophrenia" to describe this disorder is significant. It is meant to clearly disassociate PDDNOS from schizophrenia as diagnosed in an adolescent or adult. This distinction is made even clearer by the exclusion of symptoms that are considered the hallmark of schizophrenia in adults: delusions, hallucinations, or loose associations.

There is some question as to the need for a DSM category of PDDNOS (Achenbach, 1982). Although there are some seriously disturbed children who meet the basic criteria, their behavior is often difficult to differentiate from that of children with autism. The age of onset is the principle factor that differentiates the two disorders, but it is sometimes difficult to determine in an individual case the precise age of onset. Use of the term "childhood schizophrenia" may have contributed to the impression that the behavior of these children is fundamentally different from that of children with autism. In practical terms, however, children with either condition behave in largely similar ways, and have comparable needs for comprehensive care and therapy. Many programs do not attempt to differentiate the two conditions, preferring instead to focus on definable aspects of the child's behavior. This is especially true of behaviorally oriented programs, which focus to a greater degree on modifying observable behavior than on making diagnostic distinctions.

Asthma

Although not discussed as a childhood disorder in the DSM system, asthma is an important and interesting condition. It involves an interplay between biological and psychological factors, and could therefore be associated with the condition "Psychological Factors Affecting Physical Condition" (see Chapter 5). Asthma is an episodic respiratory dysfunction marked by constriction of the small bronchial passages in the lungs. The resultant symptoms include labored breathing, wheezing, and tightening of the chest. Asthma attacks are often quite painful and frightening, and a severe attack may completely incapacitate an individual for several hours unless prompt treatment is instituted.

Asthmatic attacks may be triggered by a variety of factors, including allergens, respiratory infections, and psychological stressors (Rees, 1964). Physiologically, asthma results from overreaction of the parasympathetic nervous system, a division of the autonomic nervous system. Asthma can be treated effectively with sympathomimetic medications such as epinephrine.

Etiology.   Although asthma is clearly due to physical causes, it is widely viewed as a psychophysiological disorder, meaning that both psychological and physical factors may have important contributory roles in the course of the disorder. The contribution of psychological factors to asthma is generally explained in one of two ways. The earliest viewpoint, consistent with psychodynamic theory, was that asthma reflects unresolved intrapsychic conflicts. Physiological explanations of asthma, on the other hand, favor the stress diathesis model (see Chapter 5), which predicts that stress causes physical breakdowns in the weakest, most vulnerable physical organs.

Sternbach (1966) proposed an explanation of asthma and related disorders that is consistent with the stress diathesis model. He postulated that three conditions were needed to trigger an asthma attack: (1) a vulnerable organ system that reacts in a characteristic fashion to a variety of stressors, a condition known as **response stereotypy;** (2) exposure to stressful situations; and (3) the breakdown of mechanisms that normally regulate responses to stressors. These mechanisms range from changes in body chemistry to large-scale behavioral responses, such as taking a vacation to "get away from it all."

Psychodynamic explanations of asthma emphasize the significance of unresolved conflicts in predisposing an individual to asthma attacks. Such theories assume that direct expression of the conflict is too threatening to the individual, who instead acts it out in an indirect or symbolic manner. Alexander et al. (1968) proposed that asthma symbolizes fear and anger over separation from the mother, and is a stifled "cry for help." Undoubtedly, the symptoms of a severe asthma attack—ashen face, labored breathing, convulsive chest—are guaranteed to keep the child's caretaker close to the child. From a behavioral perspective, this would suggest that secondary gain factors are operating, and that the asthma attack is reinforced by having a highly significant need (for mother's attention) met.

Available research data has tended to provide more support for psychophysiological than psychodynamic explanations of asthma. There are relatively few generalizations that can accurately be made about asthmatic children. Purcell (1963) has noted that asthmatic children may differ on any of the following variables: (1) the child's, or, with very young children, the parents', perception of events related to the onset of asthma attacks; (2) the nature of the child's responses to separation from significant figures; (3) biological characteristics; and (4) the degree of psychopathology manifested by either parents or child. One consistent finding that has emerged is that asthmatic children can be reliably classified according to whether or not they obtain rapid relief from an attack by being removed from the home situation and hospitalized.

Treatment. A multimodal approach to treatment is generally appropriate in treating asthma, particularly when stress factors have been identified that have a contributory role. Psychological intervention is important when behavioral, cognitive, and interpersonal factors are believed to exacerbate the asthma (Creer, 1982).

Some asthmatic children undergo rapid remission of their symptoms when separated from their families and hospitalized (Purcell and Weiss, 1970). Although this would appear to implicate family conflict as a cause of asthma attacks, it is not conclusive proof, because the hospitalized child is also removed from the source of irritating allergens. However, family conflict can contribute significantly to asthma, a fact that was demonstrated by Purcell et al., (1972). They studied a group of asthmatic children who showed virtually complete remission when their families temporarily left home—despite ongoing exposure to allergens. Such children, it appears, are members of family systems that generate sufficient stress to either trigger or intensify physiological reactions like asthma. In these situations, family therapy can help reduce overall stress levels by promoting more supportive and effective interactions among members (Weiss and Wieder, 1982).

Individual therapy can also be effective. Behavioral techniques in particular appear to be quite helpful in treating asthmatic children. For example, Moore (1965) reported successful application of SDT procedures in aiding breathing patterns of asthmatic children. More recently, Alexander (1980) discussed the use of behavior therapy in reducing the anticipatory fears experienced by many victims of asthma.

Enuresis

Enuresis, or accidental urinary incontinence after bladder control has been established, occurs frequently in young children. In its most common form, bedwetting (technically **nocturnal enuresis**), it affects up to 20 percent of all children up to the age of seven (Quay and Werry, 1979). Normally, children achieve bladder control by the age of two or three, and most enuretic children have demonstrated bladder control during some period of early development.

Etiology. Psychodynamic, developmental, and behavioral explanations of enuresis have all been advanced. From a psychodynamic perspective, urinary incontinence is seen as an expression of anger or hostility towards parents (Masling, 1982). The occurrence of enuresis once the child has achieved bladder control is viewed as a form of regression, the return to a more primitive mode of functioning in response to stress or conflict. The birth of a sibling, for example, often triggers regression in young children accustomed to being the center of attention. The onset of bedwetting at such times constitutes the child's means of expressing anger at having been abandoned, and usually succeeds in restoring parental attention. Psychotherapy is frequently recommended to help the child work through the trauma that triggered the regressive behavior, but there is currently little available outcome research attesting to its helpfulness (Lovibond and Coote, 1969).

Viewed from the perspective of developmental theory, enuresis is seen as the result of inappropriately timed bladder training. MacKeith (1968) has proposed that the critical period for bladder training is between ages one and a half to four and a half. Before this time, the child's bladder musculature is too immature to benefit from training. Premature efforts to teach bladder control frequently cause disappointment in parents and anxiety in the child. Conversely, training at too advanced an age may be difficult because the enuretic habit has become well established.

Behaviorally oriented clinicians such as Mowrer and Mowrer (1938) and Azrin et al. (1974) view enuresis as a failure to acquire normal eliminative habits. Like developmental psychologists, behaviorists stress the need for muscular maturity before training can be instituted. However, they are less likely to think in terms of critical periods for acquiring the necessary habits, arguing that appropriate reinforcers can be found for children of practically any age.

The behavioral perspective has gained widespread popularity for two reasons (Hersen and Van Hasselt 1987). First, there has been little evidence to support the psychodynamic assertion that enuresis is caused by emotional conflicts. Early studies supporting this hypothesis were based on samples of children referred to clinics with other problems, many of whom just happened to be enuretic as well. Since then, epidemiological studies such as Rutter et al.'s (1973) have shown that enuretic children who are not seen by physicians tend to show overall lower levels of psychopathology than those who are referred for medical treatment. The lack of a clear-cut relationship between emotional conflict and bedwetting makes the straightforward behavioral method of treating the symptom seem highly appropriate.

The success of behavioral treatment for enuresis accounts for this method's popularity. Behavioral interventions, when properly implemented, have been shown to be highly effective in treating the disorder in comparatively short periods of time.

Enuresis is seldom reported in adolescence, even if its occurrence in early childhood goes untreated. However, the importance of early intervention cannot be overemphasized, since chronic enuresis may have a negative effect on a child's social development. When enuresis persists, the fear of ridicule will discourage the child from participating in social activities such as camping or overnight visits with friends.

Treatment. Medical treatment of enuresis commonly employs the drug imipramine, which is also used to treat mild anxiety. Most children show a reduction in bedwetting with daily 50-milligram doses of imipramine, which can generally be tapered off after about two months of use. Relapse rates, however, tend to be high once the medication is discontinued (Knopf, 1979). A further disadvantage of medication is that it is a passive form of treatment, which teaches the child little self-control.

Psychologically based treatment of enuresis has employed primarily classical or operant conditioning techniques.

The first effective application of classical conditioning to treating enuresis is attributed to Mowrer and Mowrer (1938). They pioneered what came to be known as the **bell and pad** approach. This procedure makes use of a sheet filled with absorbent material sandwiched between two layers of fabric coated with aluminum (the pad). An electrode attached to each aluminum layer is connected via a circuit to a bell. When the sleeping child urinates, the middle layer of the pad becomes wet, completing a circuit between the outer layers. This causes the bell to ring, awakening the child before the bed is completely soaked.

In practice, this system has proven quite effective in curtailing enuresis, and the device is perennially advertised in catalogs and department stores. However, the procedure does not always achieve quick results, and relapse rates are high once the bell and pad are removed (Doleys, 1977).

The problem with a classical conditioning approach seems to lie in some procedural flaws in the conditioning procedure. In classical conditioning terminology, the bell is the unconditioned stimulus (US) that awakens the child, the unconditioned response (UR). The conditioned stimulus (CS) should be bladder pressure sufficient to awaken the child, the conditioned response (CR). For conditioning to occur, the sound of the bell should be paired with bladder pressure signifying a need to urinate. In practice, however, bladder pressure actually precedes the sound of the bell, since by the time the bell rings the bladder may be nearly empty. The strength of the conditioning procedure is diminished because the CS and US do not occur together. The child is just as likely to be conditioned to awaken *after* wetting the bed as before wetting the bed.

The lack of control over the CS (bladder pressure) constitutes a significant flaw in the conditioning procedure, enough to interfere with the formation of a strong conditioned response.

Operant conditioning techniques have also been employed to treat enuresis. One such approach has been termed "dry bed" training (Azrin et al., 1974). Dry bed training is related to a successful program designed to teach initial toileting skills (Azrin and Foxx, 1974). The program provides concentrated practice in going to the bathroom during a period of a few days. During this time, the child's fluid intake is kept high, creating frequent urges to urinate. Through practice, the child learns to associate bladder pressure with going to the bathroom, and also gets to practice the muscular contractions needed to keep from voiding at other times. Trips to the bathroom are rewarded liberally with praise. Failure to get to the bathroom on time is associated with moderately aversive consequences, such as having to wash clothes or bedsheets that have been wet. Azrin et al. have reported encouraging results with this approach, as have other researchers (Griffiths et al., 1982). Griffiths et al. note that the success of this program depends on considerable time and attention, particularly when the program is initiated. All in all, however, operant modification of bedwetting has proven a highly effective form of intervention.

Encopresis

Encopresis is fecal soiling in children who have previously learned bowel control, and who have no diagnosed neuromuscular disorders (Schaefer, 1979). In contrast to enuresis, encopresis usually occurs during the day. Encopresis is considered to be a more serious problem than enuresis, and is often associated with significant psychological problems. Psychoanalysts have associated encopresis with conflicts arising during the anal stage of personality development, when issues of autonomy are at stake. Irregular bowel control is seen as being related to adult personality patterns involving hostility and indirect expression of anger. Encopresis itself is often seen as a means of expressing anger toward a parent the child cannot confront directly. Sometimes, the disorder reflects more deeply seated and pathological disturbances, and in extreme cases playing with or smearing feces may occur.

Even if not accompanied by indications of serious psychopathology, encopresis should be treated promptly because of the social stigma attached to failure in regulating bowel activity. Despite the likelihood of scorn and ridicule from peers, encopretic children often maintain the behavior because it elicits concerned attention from parents. Encopretic children frequently manifest other signs of infantile behavior related to conflicting patterns of dependency and hostility. Encopresis is also reported in many children diagnosed as psychotic and in those with markedly subaverage mental abilities.

The disorder has been successfully treated with operant conditioning procedures employing rewards for appropriate toileting behaviors (Knopf, 1979), and other techniques such as overcorrection training (Butler, 1977). Overcorrection involves extensive training in behavior patterns incompatible with encopresis (Craighead et al., 1981). For example, a child may extensively practice the behavior of going to the bathroom and sitting on the toilet so that when the real need to eliminate arises the appropriate behaviors will be automatic. Approaching the problem from quite another standpoint, family therapy has been successful in treating encopresis, particularly when the behavior constitutes a form of hostility stemming from interpersonal conflicts between family members (Andolfi, 1978; Schaefer, 1988).

Hyperactivity (DSM: Attention-deficit Hyperactivity Disorder)

Children are confronted with the need to effectively regulate their behavior and focus their attention as they enter the school years. This capacity is in part under voluntary control; in fact, the term "self-control" is often used in discussing problems related to paying attention. The control of attention and behavior also depends in part on maturation of a brain structure that controls the organism's overall level of alertness. Located in the brainstem (which connects the cortex with the spinal cord), this structure is referred to as the **reticular activating system (RAS).** As the RAS matures, the child's ability to regulate behavior and control attention improves correspondingly. There is a certain sense of purposefulness in the average eight-year-old child that is not apparent in a preschooler.

Some children, however, fail to acquire the inhibitory controls that are normally apparent in most children by the time they start school (Wender, 1987). It is estimated that at least five percent of school-age children have problems in this area (U.S. Department of Health, Education, and Welfare, 1971). Such children are distractible, inattentive, and restless, and they often are extremely active. These behaviors are usually first detected during the early school years, though in many cases they have been present for some time without being viewed as problematic. Greater expectations for disciplined behavior in the typical classroom quickly reveal children with problems in this area (Ross and Ross, 1976). Excessive activity is one of the most common complaints made about young children, and parents as well as teachers are likely to label such behavior as "hyperactivity" when it becomes problematic (Lambert, 1987).

Etiology. Hyperactivity has been the target of considerable research and debate (Rie and Rie, 1980). Strauss and Lehtinen (1947) first described the **hyperactivity syndrome** as a pattern of excessive activity and distractibility resulting from mildly impaired brain functioning. This term later came to be used interchangeably with the term **minimal brain damage.** Claims of an association between poorly controlled behavior and brain damage have persisted to the present, even though only a small percentage of restless, overly active children have diagnosable brain damage. The long-standing association between activity level and brain integrity is due in part to the known association between certain neurologic disorders and excess activity (Schulman et al., 1965). For example, an epidemic of cerebral meningitis (an inflammation of the tissue covering the brain) during World War I left many children with residual symptoms of excessive activity and restlessness.

Brain damage can affect activity level in other ways as well. It is known, for instance, that the higher (cerebral) brain centers normally exert an inhibitory effect on lower centers. Thus, under normal circumstances, the cerebral cortex serves to inhibit the expression of more primitive forms of behavior, of which excessive activity is one. In the event of damage to the cerebral cortex, however, the inhibitory effect is diminished, giving rise to behaviors normally unexpressed. Neurologic damage affecting the cerebral cortex may therefore have the effect of reducing inhibitory control over lower centers and releasing behavior patterns that may include excessive activity (Bridgeman, 1988).

RESEARCH PROFILE

The Effects of Early Hyperactivity in Adulthood

It is well known that children who show hyperactivity in childhood often show behavior problems at the same time. It is generally assumed that this can lead to adjustment problems in adulthood, though it was only in the mid-1980s that data became available to clarify the issue.

Lambert et al. (1987) studied 117 boys born between 1960 and 1965, 50 of whom had been clearly identified as hyperactive when they were children, and 58 control subjects who were comparable in other respects.

Upon follow-up, several significant differences were found between these two groups. Specifically, 19 percent of the hyperactive boys, as opposed to 3 percent of the controls, had had trouble with law enforcement agencies; 14 percent had been suspended from school more than once, compared with only 2 percent of the controls, and there were many more cases of later school failure and emotional and interpersonal difficulties among the hyperactive boys.

However, outcomes were not uniform within the group of hyperactive boys. By the time of early adulthood, 20 percent of the boys were actually free of problems and no longer considered hyperactive by family, teachers, or physicians; 37 percent were no longer treated for hyperactivity but continued to show a variety of other problems; and 43 percent were till being treated for hyperactivity and continued to show evidence of learning, behavior, or emotional problems.

It's worthy of note that virtually all of the hyperactive boys had received a variety of treatment interventions. Of course, there is no way of knowing if the outcome might have been worse without these interventions, yet it is also obvious that the interventions were not markedly successful, and that hyperactivity in childhood predicts a rather high possibility of problems later in life.

Some children who are excessively active have been found to actually show signs of central nervous system *under*arousal. This is due to abnormally low activation of the RAS, which normally prevents activity level from being either too high or too low. An underactive RAS fails to inhibit certain behaviors, one of which is the pattern of heightened activity associated with hyperactivity.

Studies by Satterfield and Dawson (1971) have shown that a substantial percentage—perhaps one third—of children described as hyperactive show low levels of brain arousal states as measured using electroencephalograms (EEGs) and galvanic skin response (GSR). Other researchers have found that many hyperactive children manifest low reactivity of the sympathetic nervous system, which, in conjunction with the RAS, plays a role in arousal level (Rosenthal and Allen, 1978). This characteristic pattern has also been found in many psychopathic individuals, which may help explain the link between hyperactivity in early childhood and later tendencies toward delinquency. Many factors other than brain damage may be associated with hyperactivity

EXHIBIT

Disorders and Conditions Associated with Hyperactivity

Metabolic and endocrine disorders—hyperthyroidism

Toxic conditions—lead poisoning

Allergy—particularly food allergies

Sensory disorders—deafness, blindness

Temperament—normal variant of psychological functioning

Maturational lag—immaturity of central nervous system

Central nervous system impairment—acute encephalitis, chronic brain syndrome

Learned reaction—response to environmental social stressors

Psychoneurosis—phobia

Personality disorder—pathological personality traits, juvenile delinquency

Psychosis—severe behavioral disturbance such as schizophrenia

Source: Ross, D.M., and Ross, S.A. (1976) *Hyperactivity: Research, theory, and action.* New York: John Wiley and Sons, p. 7.

as well. Ross and Ross (1976) have cataloged many potential contributing factors, some of which are shown in the accompanying Exhibit.

In addition to being aware of the many factors that may underlie hyperactive behavior, diagnosticians also need to be sensitive to the differing manifestations of hyperactivity. For example, children who are both highly active and aggressive comprise a distinctive diagnostic grouping (O'Leary and Steen, 1982). Some childrens' heightened activity is associated with anxiety and fearfulness—the excessive activity provides a means of ridding oneself of excessive tension (Lambert, 1987).

Given that hyperactivity may stem from any of several causes, and that its manifestations may differ from one child to the next, it's not surprising that it is not a distinct diagnostic category in the DSM system. Instead, it is diagnosed only as a symptom that may or may not accompany a diagnosis of attention deficit disorder (Kirby and Grimley, 1986).

Treatment. Specific treatment for excessive activity may involve chemotherapeutic, behavioral, or cognitive interventions. Surprisingly, stimulant medications like dextroamphetamine and Ritalin are the most frequently used medications. Their effect has been explained by Wender (1971, 1987), whose research has shown that stimulants act to arouse the RAS so that it exerts its normal inhibitory control over behavior. According to Wender's theory, stimulants correct the hyperactive child's condition of chronic CNS underarousal. There is also evidence that Ritalin may enhance selective attention as well, and thereby serve as an effective means of controlling distractibility (Flintoff et al., 1982). Wender and other researchers emphasize, however, that not all hyperactive children are sedated by Ritalin and other stimulants. For some, the effect is to further heighten activity and distractibility. The implication of this finding is that Ritalin should be administered in small dosages initially and its effects carefully monitored.

Even when Ritalin is effective in diminishing hyperactive behavior, problems in other areas may remain. For example, hyperactive children who are low school achievers do not automatically improve in their school work when excessive activity is brought under control. A study by Rie et al. (1976) found, for example, that although hyperactive children treated with Ritalin showed an overall drop in activity level, their school performance did not improve significantly. In conjunction with cognitive and behavioral techniques, however, Ritalin can be an effective part of an intervention program.

The most effective psychological intervention techniques for treating hyperactivity are behaviorally and cognitively based (Hersen and Van Hasselt, 1987). In particular, operant conditioning procedures have been found highly successful in regulating excessive activity and increasing attention span (O'Leary and O'Leary, 1972; Ayllon et al., 1975). Ayllon et al.'s study offered direct evidence that a token reinforcement system could provide an effective alternative to medication. The children in this study were evaluated under three different conditions: during a trial medication period using Ritalin, following the medication trial, and during the time a token economy program was in effect. Withdrawal of medication led to an expected increase in activity levels. But subsequent implementation of the token economy system controlled activity levels to a degree comparable to that achieved by the Ritalin. Moreover, the academic performance of the children improved significantly under the token economy program, whereas medication brought about no such improvement. The authors concluded that contingency management can control activity levels and at the same time promote academic performance as well.

Cognitive techniques have also proven effective in helping manage hyperactivity and promoting self-control (Dryden and Golden, 1987). Many hyperactive children in fact lack the capacity to regulate their own behavior and direct their attention at will. Instead, they are diverted by one irrelevant source of stimulation after another. Such children have been described as having an external **locus of control,** meaning that environmental forces dictate their behavior (Linn and Hodge, 1982). Cognitive behavior modification therapy offers a means of helping such children internalize effective control mechanisms. Extensively developed by Meichenbaum (1977), cognitive procedures are used to teach children the use of "self-talk," or covert vocalizations, to help direct their own behavior. The child is taught to practice using statements and sometimes images that are brought into play while a task is being performed. For example, while working in a classroom filled with potential distractions, a child might learn to say such things as "Focus!" or "Stay on task!" to avoid having his or her attention diverted.

Imagery is sometimes used in this regard as well. An overly active child, for example, might be taught to use visual imagery to slow down. The image of being a large hippopotamus wallowing in a mud bath can be employed with many children in a way that is both enjoyable and effective.

The effects of cognitive therapy are visible in more than one way. Effective behavior control, of course, is the principal desired outcome, and cognitive techniques have proven highly successful in this regard. Also significant, however, is the finding that cognitive strategies promote feelings of mastery and competence—children take a great deal of personal satisfaction in being able to effectively monitor and control their behavior (Kendall and Branswell, 1982).

Anxiety Disorders

Children and adults alike are vulnerable to the distressful feelings and tensions that accompany anxiety (Shaw et al.,1987). Freud, among the first to formulate a general theory of anxiety, viewed it as a signal alerting the individual to a state of potential danger. Separation from one's mother, abandonment, sudden exposure to an unfamiliar environment, and the trauma associated with birth are all events capable of generating significant levels of anxiety (Masling, 1982). More recent formulations of anxiety ascribe to the concept of a warning system, but broaden the scope of events considered to be anxiety-arousing (Goodwin, 1986). Recent research on anxiety has also provided more detailed information about both the cognitive and physical manifestations of anxiety (Marks, 1987). There is ample evidence that vulnerability to anxiety results from the interplay between one's biological makeup and the thought patterns activated in the face of potentially threatening events (Shaw et al., 1987).

Psychological disorders in which anxiety is a major component are very prevalent in childhood (Emmelkamp, 1982). Despite the idyllic images often associated with childhood, it is a period full of stressful and bewildering events. Although most children cope effectively with anxiety-arousing events, a great many do not. Such children generally seem tense, irritable, and preoccupied. Frequently socially inhibited, they tend to ruminate about disasters and catastrophes that seldom come to pass. Other symptoms commonly found in children who are anxious include fear, tension, sadness, and depression (Quay and Werry, 1979). These children are seldom obnoxious, even when in states of acute distress. Instead, they tend to become quiet and withdrawn, as a result of which their disturbance may easily be overlooked.

Common to virtually all **anxiety disorders** in the DSM system is a change in the child's environment that is perceived as somehow threatening. The three categories of anxiety disorders in the DSM system—separation anxiety disorder, avoidant disorder, and overanxious disorder—are all associated with social or environmental conditions that the child is unable to effectively cope with.

In separation anxiety, children become inordinately distressed when separated from a parent or other significant adult figure. Separation anxiety is often a two-way street; parents can convey as much anxiety as their children, and intensify the child's reaction. Children who refuse to go to school or engage in other activities that place them out of touch with their parents are generally considered to manifest separation anxiety. Note that the disorder, separation anxiety, is different from a normal pattern of distress also known as separation anxiety but associated with social development early in life. This type of normal anxiety is discussed later in this section.

Children with an avoidant disorder are apprehensive about contact with other people (Jones et al., 1986). Preferring situations where they can remain in control, they tend to shy away from contact with people other than family members and perhaps a few close friends. The avoidant disorder tends to be

Anxiety is not a purely adult condition. Drug and sex abuse, complicated family relationships, peer pressure, and the rough environment of cities contribute to childhood anxiety and stress. (Hiroji Kubota/Magnum)

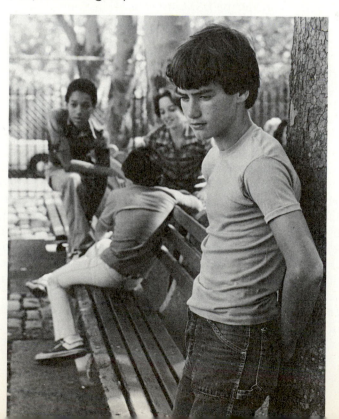

associated with painful experiences of rejection or mistreatment causing a child initially sociable by nature to become cautious and mistrustful.

The overanxious disorder is characteristic of children who show a generalized pattern of tension and anxiety. Such children tend to overreact to situations they perceive as threatening but which do not in fact pose a realistic danger.

The particular fears experienced by children vary somewhat depending on their age and maturity level. Infancy, for example, is a time when most children experience what is termed "stranger anxiety" and "separation anxiety." Stranger anxiety describes the infant's distress at being exposed to unfamiliar people. Infants quickly develop schemas, or representations, of family members and other people they're constantly exposed to, and anxiety results when they are confronted by a face that does not fit with any currently existing schema (Clarke-Stewart et al., 1988).

Stranger anxiety usually first occurs between six and eight months of age, by which time most children's cognitive development has progressed to the point where they have formed detailed schemas. Within a few months, however, stranger anxiety diminishes, largely as a function of increasingly sophisticated cognitive development and the incorporation of many new schemas. Children adapt more quickly to new people and situations, as a result of which less anxiety is evident (Osofsky, 1987).

Between 12 and 18 months of age, separation anxiety makes its appearance. Not the same as the DSM disorder of the same name, separation anxiety is a normal phase of development. Separation anxiety is marked by acute distress when children are separated from their parents or caretaker. Children continue to protest for some time after the separation occurs, indicating that they have a clear memory of the parent who is absent. As with stranger anxiety, separation anxiety is really a manifestation of maturing cognitive skills: perceptual discrimination capabilities based on visual schematas are a prerequisite to stranger anxiety, while the capacity to remember someone when they're absent is necessary for separation anxiety to occur (Shaw et al., 1987).

Older children experience anxiety due to other causes (Jersild and Holmes, 1935). Anthony (1970) proposed a developmental model of children's anxiety reaction patterns. He noted, for example, that preschoolers tend to fear animals and imaginary creatures conjured up in stories and in their own fantasies. Elementary school children, in contrast, are fearful of personal injury, school failure, ridicule, the prospect of death, and physical illness.

School refusal is also a common manifestation of anxiety in school-age children (Kahn et al., 1980). Most common in children just beginning school, school refusal can remain a problem for years unless treated effectively (Achenbach and Edelbrock, 1981). As already mentioned, school refusal is generally a sign of separation anxiety, more than a real dread of going to school (Kelly, 1973). Parents of such children often feel ambivalent about school attendance, a fact not lost on the child. Sometimes, parents create anxiety by heightening the risk of the child leaving. A parent who says "If you don't behave more respectfully toward me, you'll come home from school some day and find me gone!" can be virtually assured that the child in question will develop a strong fear of leaving home.

Virtually all techniques for treating school refusal involve both the child and the parent (Schaefer, 1988). Parents are taught to provide the child with a sense of stability and security in the home environment. They are also encouraged to deal with their own fears and misgivings so that they do not communicate double messages to the child. Children being treated for school refusal are generally worked into the school setting as quickly and firmly as possible, often over their initial objections. If they view home as a secure base from which to venture forth, their anxieties will generally diminish rapidly.

In many instances, anxiety during childhood is transient, and dissipates with specific treatment (Goodwin, 1986). Even intense fears of specific objects or events tend to diminish with time. A study by Miller et al. (1972) found that reducing fear through systematic desensitization or traditional psychotherapy resulted in only marginally greater improvement in children with phobias than no treatment at all. A follow-up study months later found only seven percent of the subjects still phobic.

From a developmental standpoint, the dissipation of childhood anxieties reflects the maturation of cognitive skills allowing the child to better cope with threatening events. For example, Elkind (1976) suggested the increasing capacity of preschool children to think about things sometimes gets out of hand and leads to unregulated—and frightening—fantasies. Young children frequently frighten themselves by thinking about Darth Vader, or the "bogey-man." Later on, they learn to distinguish between reality and fantasy, and show diminished anxiety about the products of their imagination.

Not all children handle anxiety so adaptively. Indeed, anxiety-based disturbances account for a significant number of referrals to child treatment centers. Generally, intervention appears warranted when a child shows intense and prolonged anxiety that is out of proportion to the feared situation.

Children with disabling anxiety can be helped in several ways. **Play therapy** (Axline, 1969) is an effective medium for children to work through their anxieties. In play therapy, the child is encouraged to act out conflicts using such play materials as dolls and other figures. Manipulating these objects allows the child to re-enact anxiety-provoking situations in a symbolic manner. Any anxiety that surfaces in the play session can be addressed and dealt with by the therapist. The accompanying Case Study provides an example of how play therapy was effectively used in the treatment of an anxious child.

Behavioral techniques also have proven effective in treating anxiety disorders. Successful effects have been obtained with modeling, desensitization, operant conditioning, and cognitive structuring (Emmelkamp, 1982). An especially effective procedure involves having children watch adult role models demonstrate active coping behaviors (Cartledge and Milburn, 1986). This is a

The Case of Sally

Sally had been in a serious automobile accident when she was four. The car in which she was riding was hit by an oncoming vehicle that swerved across the median. Sally's mother, who was driving, managed to swerve to the side of the road, but could not avoid a collision. Sally was not seriously hurt, and her mother sustained only minor injuries. However, Sally became intensely anxious after the accident, and developed an aversion to riding in cars. She began to have nightmares, and started wetting her bed. Despite her parents' efforts to calm her, Sally's anxiety seemed to grow more intense as time passed. Her parents eventually took her to see a child psychologist.

In an early session with Sally, the psychologist introduced some play materials consisting of a house, dolls to represent family members, and a car. Initially, Sally ignored the car completely and contented herself with "playing house" and dressing up the figurines. Significantly, she kept all the dolls in close contact with each other and in the immediate vicinity of the doll house. Subtly encouraged by the therapist, she began to play with the car but would never take it far from the house. During one session, while moving the car across the table, she stood up abruptly, took a large box of building blocks, and dramatically emptied it over the car and the dolls. "All gone," she announced, and indeed all the figures were buried out of sight underneath the blocks. This marked the beginning of a breakthrough for Sally. It marked her first open acknowledgment of the trauma associated with the accident. She replayed this scenario many times, eventually coming to realize that she could recover the dolls and resume playing with them. In symbolic form, this helped her to realize that the accident had done no permanent harm either to herself or to her mother, and that she needn't continue to be fearful of an event now long past. Gradually, Sally's play behavior became more creative and imaginative as she gradually worked through the anxieties associated with the accident. Within six months treatment was terminated and she was no longer enuretic or fearful of riding in cars.

procedure often used intuitively by parents and teachers to help children master new situations. In vivo desensitization, another effective procedure, puts the child into direct but controlled contact with the anxiety-provoking situation. Training can then be carried out teach the child responses incompatible with the anxiety that was previously aroused.

Conduct Disorders

Conduct disorders are an important part of the DSM classification system, for they encompass virtually all diagnostic categories in which acting-out behavior is the primary symptom. Conduct disorders and a related condition known as oppositional disorder are important for two reasons. First, they constitute the majority of referrals to many mental health centers providing children's services. Prevalence estimates for conduct disorders as high as 25 percent of the general population have been cited (Robins, 1981). Second, the behavior patterns characteristic of the acting-out disorders are highly predictive of adult conduct. This means that children diagnosed as having a conduct disorder or its precursor, the oppositional disorder, are at risk for adult forms of psychopathology in which acting out or antisocial behavior is the cardinal feature.

The behaviors associated with conduct disorders are highly visible and offensive (Quay, 1987). Quay and Werry (1979) identified fighting, temper tantrums, disobedience, and destructiveness as common correlates of conduct

Temper tantrums may indicate existence of a deeper conduct disorder, and could lead to adult forms of antisocial behavior. (Ed Lettau/Photo Researchers, Inc.)

disorders. Such behavior is more common in boys than in girls, in part as a result of society's differential encouragement of aggressiveness in the two sexes.

The DSM system describes conduct disorders as involving repetitive patterns of conduct that violate either the rights of others or societal norms. There is a lengthy list of behavior patterns that meet these criteria, including rape, mugging, assault, theft, truancy, lying, vandalism, and fire setting. Whereas the behavior of many children on occasion appears antisocial in nature, the diagnosis of conduct disorders requires evidence of a chronic, habitual pattern of violating the rights of others or society.

There are three subtypes of conduct disorder in the DSM system: (1) group type; (2) solitary aggressive type, and (3) undifferentiated type. Conduct disorder with aggressive behavior is characterized by persistent violation of the rights of others. Confrontations with victims, physical assault, and violent behavior are all associated with the "solitary aggressive" subtype.

The term "group type" is used to identify children who have established clear peer-group relationships. Children who have patterns of socialized delinquency generally show strong peer group affiliation. Relationships with adults and those outside their particular clique are often treated with suspicion and hostility.

The terms "conduct disorder" and "juvenile delinquency" are frequently used interchangeably. But while they are generally used to refer to similar types of behavior, "delinquency" is a legal term while "conduct disorder" has its roots in psychiatric terminology. Technically, delinquency is reserved for people who have been apprehended within the legal system and formally convicted of wrongdoing. Not surprisingly, many children with conduct disorders go on to establish patterns of delinquent behavior. A child is judged to have a conduct disorder solely on the basis of his or her behavior, not as a result of having been convicted within the legal system.

Etiology. Conduct disorders develop in response to both genetic and environmental forces that promote behavior that routinely violates social expectations. Bijou and Redd (1975) have described conduct disorders in terms of "behavior excesses" associated with a lack of impulse control. Hewitt and Jenkins (1946), in their discussion of conduct disorders, distinguished between unsocialized aggressive individuals and those who were socialized. Children in the former group had generally been deprived of the secure, trusting relationships with adults that normally provide the basis for social adjustment. As a result, they developed independently of people, and learned to rely chiefly on themselves (Quay, 1987). Socialized delinquents were described by Hewitt and Jenkins in much the same terms as the "group type" in DSM: social delinquency involves a pattern of strong peer-group attachment in which outsiders are treated with suspicion and often hostility. These factors all point out ways in which social (that is, environmental) factors can result in conduct disorder

ISSUE TO CONSIDER

Children Who Kill Parents

Psychodynamic theorists long ago documented the frequency of aggressive fantasies in children (Gedo, 1986; Lewis, 1981). Many of these fantasies involve murdering others, and more specifically, focus on the murder of a parent. The frequency of such fantasies has commonly been contrasted to the rarity of actual murders by children.

Within the psychodynamic tradition, facilitating the expression of such fantasies via play and/or talking about them has been seen as effective in reducing any compulsion to act them out in reality. Of course, lack of physical strength, lack of access to lethal means, and immature cognitive abilities relevant to long-term planning also serve to reduce any such acting-out.

However, parricide (the killing of a parent) does occur, and in his book *The Kids Next Door: Sons and daughters who kill their parents* (New York: Wm. Morrow), Greggory Morris (1987) vividly describes such children and their families. It's somewhat comforting to find that, except for accidents (usually related to too-easy access to lethal means), most children who kill parents do so in response to chronic physical or sexual abuse. While not making any murder a rational or reasonable response, this makes it more understandable. Another significant group of parricides occurs with severely disturbed children. In this group, especially when the child is schizophrenic, those few who do kill do so quite unpredictably, and even when parents are seemingly loving and concerned.

Children and early adolescents who kill present particular problems for the legal system. Recently, a seven-year-old shot and killed a playmate. After talking to him, the police formally arrested him for murder, citing the fact that he first consistently denied everything, then talked about it in a fashion that indicated rational planning and an awareness of what he had done. The prosecuting attorney's office later dropped the charges.

Mozart was writing great works of music at age five, so it is conceivable that a seven-year-old child could rationally plan a murder and be reasonably aware of the implications of death. The present legal system, however, is not really equipped to deal with the subtle aspects of children's thought processes. From the standpoint of the law, there is little real difference between an adult murderer and one seven years of age. And even if one were to clarify the differences in a meaningful way, there is nothing to ensure that the court's response would necessarily be therapeutic. It is interesting to note that children, as a rule, are generally perceived as being more "treatable" than adults. But such distinctions are blurred in the legal system, which judges criminal behavior more by its impact on society, and less by the characteristics of the individual accused of the crime.

patterns. But both genetic and physical factors have been implicated in the development of antisocial tendencies (Doren, 1987).

The contribution of genetic factors in particular was underscored in a study by Cadoret and Cain (1980). These researchers showed that children of antisocial parents, when reared by adoptive parents, are more likely to develop conduct disorders than are other adopted children. In terms of specific physical factors that promote delinquency, it has been suggested (Anolik, 1983) that these individuals typically do not show high levels of alertness and awareness on a day-to-day basis. Adult criminals recover more slowly from environmental stimuli than do noncriminals, in part due to a biologically generated need for more than the average level of stimulation (Doren, 1987).

Family relationship patterns have a significant role in the precursors of delinquent behavior. For example, parents who use physical punishment to control aggression may eventually succeed in suppressing overt manifestations of violence, but nonetheless end up modeling for the child the very behaviors they are trying to eliminate. Children are of course exposed to other sources of aggressive role models, particularly through television. Constant exposure to television shows that depict violence has been linked to acting-out tendencies. For example, Eron (1980) found that a clear preference for violent TV shows in young children was highly predictive of aggressive behavior 10 years later. Parental attitudes and child-rearing techniques also have been demonstrated to have a role in fostering acting-out behavior. Schafer (1961) has identified two key dimensions of parenting styles that are predictive of delinquent behavior and other forms of childhood psychopathology. The first dimension is control (ranging from permissive to restrictive), while the second involves emotional tone (warmth to hostility). Generally, parents whose behavior lies at the extremes of these dimensions are the ones most likely to have children with antisocial tendencies. Although conduct disorders often have their origins in behavior patterns beginning at home, referrals for treatment generally reach significant proportions only after children have reached school age. Wahler (1976) noted that parents of younger children are often more concerned about behavioral deficits, age-inappropriate behavior, and sex-role behavior patterns than they are about hostile or aggressive tendencies.

Intervention.   Socially-based programs are among the most common for dealing with delinquency and conduct disorders. Most of these are based on the idea that social and economic factors push many children into delinquent patterns. Job programs and funding to improve academic skills have both been tried as means of alleviating conditions that give rise to delinquency.

School-based programs have reported some success in modifying antisocial behavior. Grammar and middle-school programs that employ psychological consultations and exposure to effective role models in classroom settings have proven especially helpful in treating children with conduct disorders (Greenwood and Zuring, 1985).

Behaviorally oriented programs have proven successful as well (Hersen and Van Hasselt, 1987). A case in point is the CASE project (Center et al., 1982) at the National Training School for Boys. CASE stands for "Contingencies Applicable to Special Education"; it is a program designed to modify both social and academic skills based on principles of operant conditioning.

The well-known Achievement Place program for delinquent youths has claimed considerable success in the application of token economies and group-oriented treatment (Solnick et al., 1981). One of the principal therapeutic effects derived from programs such as Achievement Place concerns the fact that participants reside at the center, having been removed from the delinquent subculture that promoted many of their behavior problems in the first place.

Not surprisingly, family and parental therapy is highly advocated by many clinicians (Brantley and Sutker, 1984). Many programs that focus on parents promote the development of effective child-management techniques, most of which are based on behavioral procedures. Disciplinary techniques are stressed, particularly those that provide an alternative to physical punishment (which has untoward effects from the standpoint of modeling and imitation). Time-out procedures are frequently recommended as a means of applying somewhat unpleasant contingencies without physically traumatizing the child.

Overall, effective management of problems related to conduct disorders involves gaining control over the child's physical and social environment (Schaefer, 1988). Children with patterns of socialized delinquency need to develop substitutes for peer-group patterns that promote internal allegiances but advocate antisocial behavior in other contexts. Those with unsocialized patterns of aggressiveness can probably best be helped by intervention programs that attempt to inculcate socialization skills and clearly associate antisocial behavior with negative contingencies. As a rule, programs that use behavioral techniques are the most effective in attaining these goals. For these to succeed, it is necessary to gain as much control as possible over the child's day-to-day environment.

This completes an overview of some common childhood psychological disorders. We have examined a series of conditions associated with different stages of development, beginning with autism, a neurologic disorder present at birth, and ending with conduct disorders, whose origins in childhood and adolescence owe much to the child's environment. The next chapter will continue this developmental perspective, considering in turn disorders of adolescence, adulthood, and aging.

CHAPTER REVIEW

1. The DSM classification system for disorders of childhood and early development is distinct from that for adults. This reflects increasing recognition that children have unique capabilities, problems, and needs.

2. Development during infancy and early childhood proceeds rapidly and on many fronts simultaneously. The pace and diversity of early development carries with it both opportunities for greater maturation and risks of maladjustment.

3. As children develop, the impact of social and environmental forces becomes increasingly prominent. As far as psychopathology is concerned, disorders evident at birth or shortly thereafter are almost exclusively due to innate, or biologically based, conditions.

4. Children with pervasive developmental disorders, such as infantile autism, manifest widespread impairments in social and interpersonal adjustment. Although therapy, especially behaviorally oriented therapy, has proven helpful in promoting better adjustment, the overall recovery rates for these disorders are low.

5. Asthma, a psychophysiological disorder, afflicts both children and adults. Evidence is accumulating suggesting that asthma in many children is a response to familial stress and tension; in many cases, removing the child from the stressful situation causes the symptoms to disappear quickly.

6. Toilet training can be a major focus of conflict for children. Both bedwetting (enuresis) and soiling (encopresis) are commonly reported in early childhood, after the age at which children have achieved bowel and bladder control. Of the two disorders, encopresis is generally considered to be more serious.

7. Children diagnosed as hyperactive show excessive poorly organized behavior patterns. Some are helped by the paradoxical strategy of administering stimulant medication; it appears to stimulate brain centers that normally inhibit excessive activity.

8. Anxiety disorders and conduct disorders reflect extremes of a behavioral dimension extending from introverted to extroverted.

9. Children with conduct disorders are more visible, and consequently are referred for treatment more frequently, than are children whose anxiety is often accompanied by passivity and withdrawal.

TERMS TO REMEMBER

stage theory
psychosexual development
psychosocial maturation
cognitive development
moral development
critical periods
islets of performance
choreiform movements

self-stimulation
refrigerator parent
attachment
shaping
PDDNOS
response stereotypy
nocturnal enuresis
encopresis

bell and pad
reticular activating system (RAS)
hyperactivity syndrome
minimal brain damage
locus of control
anxiety disorders
play therapy
conduct disorders

FOR MORE INFORMATION

Adams, P.L. (1973) *Obsessive children: A sociopsychiatric study.* New York: Bruner/Mazel. A collection of case studies by a child psychoanalyst that portrays deeply disturbed children in a graphic, yet humane and compassionate, manner

Pellegrini, A. (1986) *Applied child study.* Hillsdale, N.J.: Lawrence Erlbaum. Written for all professionals and students who interact closely with children, this is an overview of developmental theory and its applications in the areas of language, cognition, social competence, and play

Pope, A., McHale, S., and Craighead, W. (1987) *Self-esteem enhancement with children and adolescents.* Elmsford, N.Y.: Pergamon. Describes techniques for assessing and improving a most important variable in childrens' functioning: self-esteem

Reeve, R., and Kauffman, J. (1987) Learning disabilities. In: V. Van Hasselt, P. Strain, and M. Hersen (Eds.). *Handbook of developmental and physical disabilities.* Elmsford, N.Y.: Pergamon. A good reference for information on one of the major causes of adjustment problems and psychological disorders in children: Learning disabilities

Schaefer, C.E., and Millman, H.L. (1981) *How to help children with common problems.* New York: Van Nostrand Reinhold. A practical, useful text that provides detailed descriptions of common childhood disorders and various treatment strategies

Schaeffer, C., and O'Common, K. (1983) *Handbook of play therapy,* and Schaeffer, C., and Reid, S. *Game play: Therapeutic use of childhood games,* both published by John Wiley. These companion volumes not only give an excellent overview of historical and modern developments in play therapy, but also discuss the use of games in assessing children and aiding them in developing more effective communication skills

Growing up is hard to do, as the young characters in the 1985 film *Stand By Me* discover. (IMP/GEH Stills Collection; © 1985 Columbia Pictures Industries Inc.)

16

Psychological Disorders of Adolescence Through Old Age

Most people understand that many of the childhood disorders discussed in Chapter 15 are at least in part a response to the challenges of growing up. But these challenges don't cease at the end of childhood. This chapter focuses on disorder patterns in adolescence, adulthood, and old age that are significantly related to the developmental challenges of those periods.

● The Case of Patsy

Patsy, a bright and attractive young woman, was the apple of her parents' eyes throughout childhood. Patsy was a model child, both at school and at home, in contrast to her older brother Larry, who was rebellious and had experimented with drugs. However, as Patsy moved into adolescence, she began to withdraw from some of her friends and become much more secretive around home. She seemed uninterested in relationships with boys, but she began to show some anxiety about her physical appearance. Though she had never been overweight, she began to diet occasionally, skipped family meals whenever she was allowed to, and expressed a strong fear of becoming too fat.

Her parents had always seemed to have a perfect marriage. But when Patsy was an adolescent, her parents became very upset with each other over two issues. The first was her mother's desire to return to school, get a graduate degree, and then go to work full-time. The second was whether or not to place Patsy's maternal grandmother in a nursing home. At this point, Patsy's dieting became so intense that whenever she ate at all, she would cause herself to vomit. Her weight dropped rapidly from 120 to 85 pounds, and she resisted any attempts to talk about the problem. She was hospitalized and was diagnosed as having anorexia nervosa, but resisted any treatment attempts, even efforts to feed her intravenously. The strife that her parents had experienced disappeared as their concern for Patsy increased. Also, Patsy's maternal grandmother suffered a severe stroke, and now obviously had to be hospitalized. As the family problems lessened, Patsy began to respond to treatment and continued her improvement at home following discharge. However, she showed residual symptoms, which included obsessive-compulsive patterns (see Chapter 5), difficulties in expressing feelings, and physical problems, including irregular menstrual periods and intestinal disorders.

Adolescence is a phase of life when a number of psychological disorders may first be encountered (Mash and Terdal, 1988). The rebelliousness and drug involvement shown by Patsy's older brother, Larry, is one form that resultant disorders may take. Some children act out their confusion or distress in more extreme ways (juvenile delinquency, extreme drug abuse, and so on). Others are equally distressed, but show it in more passive forms, such as Patsy's pattern of anorexia nervosa, or possibly in school problems. These developmental disorders of adolescence are the focus of the first part of this chapter.

Just as the challenges of adolescence may predispose one to psychological disorders, so may those tasks and difficulties associated with adulthood and old age. For example, the stresses that Patsy's parents experienced are the type that often generate marital discord. In more extreme cases, spouse or child abuse may occur.

In a similar vein, advancing age brings about physical changes and alterations in life roles (for example, retirement or loss of a spouse) that predispose many older persons to disorders such as depression and hypochondriasis. The developmental disorders of adulthood and old age are examined later in this chapter.

By developmental disorders, we mean disorders that stem from the difficulties and tasks of various life-span developmental tasks. Some disorders, such as suicide, may appear at virtually any age, yet show unique characteristics when associated with developmental challenges. These issues will provide the focus for this chapter.

EXHIBIT

Four Most Common Emotional Disorders*—By Age and Sex

	Rank	18-24 yr	25-44 yr	45-54 yr	65 + yr	Total
MALES	1	Alcohol abuse/ dependence	Alcohol abuse/ dependence	Alcohol abuse/ dependence	Severe cognitive impairment	Alcohol abuse/ dependence
	2	Drug abuse/ dependence	Phobia	Phobia	Phobia	Phobia
	3	Phobia	Drug abuse/ dependence	Dysthymia	Alcohol abuse/ dependence	Drug abuse/ dependence
	4	Antisocial personality	Antisocial personality	Major depressive episode—not based on grief reaction	Dysthymia	Dysthymia
FEMALES	1	Phobia	Phobia	Phobia	Phobia	Phobia
	2	Drug abuse/ dependence	Major depressive episode not based on grief reaction	Dysthymia	Severe cognitive impairment	Major depressive episode—not based on grief reaction
	3	Major depressive episode—not based on grief reaction	Dysthymia	Major depressive episode—not based on grief reaction	Dysthymia	Dysthymia
	4	Alcohol abuse/ dependence	Obsessive-compulsive disorder	Obsessive-compulsive disorder	Major depressive episode—not based on grief reaction	Obsessive-compulsive disorder

*Based on six month prevalence rates, from St. Louis, Baltimore, and New Haven, and adapted from Myers, J. et al., *Archives of General Psychiatry*, 1984, 41, 959–970

DEVELOPMENTAL DISORDERS OF ADOLESCENCE

Only in the past hundred years has adolescence been considered a distinct, significant phase of the life span (Santrock, 1987). In the late nineteenth century, the American psychologist G. Stanley Hall first characterized this period as simply a transition from childhood to adulthood. Freud considered adolescence significant chiefly because it marks the onset of genital sexual matura-

Adolescence may be marred by a number of psychological disorders associated with an individual's struggle to "fit in." However, adolescents are often capable of forging strong interpersonal bonds, perhaps falling in love for the first time.   (Globe Photos)

tion. In contrast, Erik Erikson, more concerned with social behavior, treated adolescence as a period of crisis during which a sense of personal identity is formed. Erikson coined the term **identity crisis** to characterize this phase of development. Modern developmental theorists describe adolescence as a time when the individual's views of self and society change radically (Newman and Newman, 1987). This last view embraces the earlier concepts: While young people are trying to evolve their own sense of *personal* identity, they are also using their physical capacity and drive to pursue *interpersonal* experiences, all the while coping with such challenges as (1) increasing academic demands; (2) beginning to choose a vocational direction; (3) deciding on values related to sexuality, gender roles, marriage, and so on; (4) learning to accept rapid body changes and a new body image; and (5) developing independence.

Sorting out these complex issues requires considerable emotional and cognitive sophistication. According to the developmental psychologist Jean Piaget, adolescence is a period of significant maturation in cognitive capabilities (Santrock, 1987). These skills allow the individual to reflect upon the self and others more objectively than a child can. The clear benefit is that the adolescent can imagine and plan things without having to act them out concretely. On the other hand, the capacity for abstract thought brings with it tendencies toward rumination and introspectiveness. Most adolescents spend considerable time imagining how they appear to others, often magnifying their personal faults and becoming acutely self-conscious in the process. This struggle for a sense of identity and equilibrium, and eventual maturity, is inevitable and natural.

Maturity requires change, which brings with it the potential for deviance. Viewed in this light, many of the problems of adolescence may be seen as extensions of normal developmental trends. For example, many teenagers experiment with drugs, and some get to the point of abusing them. Often this begins with a simple urge to experience a change in one's state of consciousness.

In learning to assume conventional adult roles, teenagers encounter many of the problems of older persons. They can become depressed, even suicidal; they experience anxiety and tension; they have problems with their sexuality; they may abuse drugs, alcohol, and other substances. However, although they are susceptible to many problems of adulthood, teenagers are often treated like children, with no significant responsibilities and attendant rewards.

Personal Identity

The majority of adolescents appear well adjusted and healthy, despite the upheaval and conflict attributed to this period. Indeed, several studies suggest that most adolescents share their parents' value systems, remain close to them throughout this stage, and experience a smooth transition into adulthood (Santrock, 1987). This is significant because effective support systems increase the ability to deal with stress during any phase of life. On the other hand, there is ample evidence (Coles and Stokes, 1985) that disturbed communication patterns among parents and teenagers have serious consequences for later developments.

Temporary or prolonged failure to achieve personal adjustment and an integrated and coherent sense of self occurs frequently enough to warrant a DSM diagnostic category called the **identity disorder**. Uncertainty and distress usually focus on several issues such as career choice, friendship patterns, sexual orientation, or moral values. A formal diagnosis requires evidence of severe subjective distress over such issues for at least three months, along with evidence of impairment of social or academic functioning. Identity disorder is especially likely to be reported in late adolescence, when it is important for teenagers to psychologically separate from their immediate family in order to establish a distinct identity (Mash and Terdal, 1988).

EXHIBIT

Potential Severe Disorder Reactions in Response to Developmental Challenges during Adulthood

Adjustment Disorders
(see Chapter 5)

Adjustment disorders are patterns in which an otherwise healthy person shows emotional disruption in response to significant personal traumas (such as divorce or the death of a child) or environmental changes (such as hurricanes). Disturbing memories and even nightmares mark these disorders.

Anxiety Disorders
(see Chapter 6)

Anxiety disorders are composed of the anxiety states and the phobic disorders. Anxiety states reflect more diffuse concerns, almost a fear of life and/or the world in general; phobic disorders are more specific (such as a fear of public speaking or of snakes).

Depression and Suicide
(see Chapter 9)

Depression is a common response to losses of all types (such as loss of a job or the death of a parent or friend). If it becomes chronic, it severely disrupts general functioning. If accompanied by a sense of hopelessness, the person may consider suicide, although suicide ideation may also occur as a result of a rational evaluation of a situation (such as a diagnosis of a painful and/or costly and clearly terminal disease).

Dissociative and Withdrawal Disorders
(see Chapters 6 and 7)

Dissociative and withdrawal disorders are marked by a lessening of the ability to keep the self organized and effective in the face of the ordinary and extraordinary challenges of life. Dissociative disorders, disruptions of an ongoing sense of self, may be the self's coping reaction to unexpected trauma (such as loss of a mate); withdrawal is a more chronic pattern that in severe forms may be manifested as schizophrenic symptomatology.

Drug and Alcohol Disorders
(see Chapter 11)

Drug and alcohol disorders occur for a variety of reasons, including pressure from peer behavior standards or increasing addiction. Such patterns can also be a means of avoiding the ambivalence and risk inherent in many of the developmental challenges that occur from adolescence through old age.

Paranoid Disorders
(see Chapter 8)

Paranoid persons have a chronic mistrust of others and often feel persecuted or at least misunderstood. In severe cases, they may develop delusions (inaccurate belief systems) of jealousy or of being persecuted; these beliefs may be accompanied by grandiose delusions of being very special or important.

Paraphilias and Sexual Dysfunctions
(see Chapter 10)

The sexual dysfunctions and paraphilias receive much attention in adulthood. The paraphilias (such as fetishism) reflect deviant and maladaptive modes of sexual arousal and release; sexual dysfunctions (such as premature ejaculation) are patterns in which the inability to function adequately sexually causes intrapersonal anxiety and/or interpersonal difficulties.

Personality and Impulse Disorders
(see Chapter 12)

Personality disorders are chronic and primarily learned behavior patterns (such as histrionic or passive-aggressive patterns) that become especially maladaptive when a person encounters the intimacy and consistent interpersonal challenges of adulthood. The impulse disorder patterns (such as pyromania and explosive disorder) are common in both adolescence and adulthood, and again reflect inadequate coping with both impulses and interpersonal stresses.

Psychophysiological and Stress Disorders
(see Chapter 5)

Psychophysiological and stress disorders are physical disorders (such as headaches or high blood pressure) in which a psychological component (such as a type A behavior pattern or pent-up anger) plays a major part in producing the physical disturbance. Any change in a person's world may generate stress, which can accumulate to produce a later physical or psychological disorder.

Suicide

Adolescence and early adulthood are periods of high risk for suicide, higher than at any other time except old age. During 1979, 4,245 males and 1,001 females, aged 15 to 24, committed suicide in the United States. Differences in method used are broken down as follows:

	Males	Females
Handguns, and other firearms	2,705	511
Hanging, strangulation, suffocation	713	93
Drugs and other substances	225	232
Gases/vapors	275	62
Miscellaneous	327	103
Total	4,245	1,001

From 1968 to 1978, the suicide rate for males aged 15 to 19 increased from 5.0 to 7.9 per 100,000 (for males of all ages it increased from 7.8 to 12.6; for females of all ages, up to 3.0 from 2.2 [U.S. Dept. of Health and Human Services, 1984]). Suicide attempts by children under age 12 are rare. Suicide is discussed in Chapter 9, but mentioned again here because of its unique characteristics in adolescence.

Most studies of adolescents who attempt suicide report that the event is preceded by periods of deterioration in coping abilities (Petti and Larson, 1987). To learn more about contributory factors, Jacobs (1971) interviewed 50 adolescents within 48 hours of their suicide attempts. He concluded that suicide attempts generally represent the culmination of a process in which adolescents view themselves as becoming progressively isolated from meaningful social relationships. When compared with a matched group of control subjects, more adolescents who attempted suicide had both a long-standing history of psychological problems and a significant increase in such problems after the onset of adolescence. They experienced a progressive breakdown of coping skills, and in the days and weeks preceding the attempt withdrew from meaningful social relationships into a state of hopelessness. Nearly three-fifths gave obvious warning signals, including rebellion, delinquent acts, withdrawal, and running away, before their attempt. If such acting-out behavior occurs in an adolescent with an inhibited or introverted personality, it is especially predictive of suicide attempts. As regards early signs, children who experienced respiratory distress for more than one hour during delivery or whose mother suffered a chronic disease during the pregnancy had a higher risk for suicide during their teen years.

Drug Abuse

Drug (or substance) abuse is a particularly significant problem among even "normal" adolescents, such as Patsy's brother, who was described in the case that introduced this chapter. Peele (1984) notes that in the last half of the 1970s and the beginning of the 1980s, approximately 40 percent of high school seniors (50 percent of male seniors) said they drank at least five drinks in a single setting at least once in the two weeks prior to when they were surveyed. He also notes that the trend in teen drinking is toward binge drinking rather than mild, regular drinking. At the same time, a 1984 survey of 17,000 high school seniors by Johnson, Bachman, and O'Malley (Fischman, 1985) of the Institute for Social Research at the University of Michigan showed a decline in the use of other drugs (except cocaine, which has risen somewhat) from the late 1970s through 1984.

Huba et al. (1979) note that the popular concept of a single, general drug culture among adolescents is a myth and that, as a general rule, beginning adolescent drug abusers do not belong to highly atypical or deviant groups. Such personality factors as extroversion, need for autonomy, and rebelliousness predispose certain adolescents to reject traditional social role models, leaving them more vulnerable to influence from peers and to deviant preference patterns.

Drugs can have an important role in peer socializing. Shared experiences have a powerful appeal because they draw people together and give them a sense of belonging, an appeal particularly strong during adolescence. From this perspective, drug use by a group is unlikely to involve "hard" drugs, which have an intrinsically isolating effect. However, even the use of marijuana presents a paradox. The sharing implied in passing a joint around is diminished by the intensely subjective and personal experiences that follow, even though adolescents assume that others share their experiences and perceptions. It is this highly social nature of many early experiences with drugs that sets adolescents apart from veteran adult users (Zucker, 1986; Murray et al., 1984).

Some adolescents turn to drugs for other reasons. Many become disillusioned with society and are unwilling to work within the confines of normal social institutions (Santrock, 1987). For these individuals, drugs appear to offer a means of obliterating the cares and concerns of day-to-day life. Unfortunately, the psychological and physiological complications that may result can be devastating.

Adolescents, like adults, react to drugs and other experiences in a variety of ways, in part depending upon their expectancies (Brown, 1985a). Some experiment and stop at that point; others become addicted to and controlled by progressively more powerful agents. Although most adolescents who use alcohol or marijuana do not progress to more potent drugs, progressive substance use is more frequent among adolescents who begin by using comparatively nonlethal drugs. Few progress to hard drugs without first using alcohol or

Anorexics exhibit an intense concern, usually unfounded, regarding weight gain. At the time this photo was taken, this girl was combatting her anorexia through treatment. (Susan Rosenberg/Photo Researchers, Inc.)

tobacco and then marijuana, according to thorough study of 2,036 students by Mills and Noyes (1984). They also found that the drug involvement was correlated with earlier age of first usage, amount of alcohol use, cigarettes, and marijuana, and the amount of spending money available. Thus, the social sanction of certain drugs may itself be a contributing factor to later experimentation with and use of potentially more harmful ones.

Anorexia Nervosa

Anorexia nervosa, described in this chapter's opening case, is an initially nonorganic disorder characterized by a voluntary refusal to eat, which results in a 25 percent or greater loss of body weight. It was described by the eleventh century Persian physician, Avicenna, and first named by the physician William Gull in 1874. Anorexia occurs most frequently in adolescent and young adult females (Abraham and Jones, 1985). In extreme cases, the weight loss may be life-threatening, and may require coercive treatment, including tube and in-travenous feeding, as well as medication. Though still comparatively rare, the disorder has recently received increasing national publicity. Approximately one in every 250 females between the ages of 12 and 18 develops this dis-order, and follow-up studies now estimate mortality rates at between 5 and 10 percent. Young women are especially at risk for anorexia nervosa if they: (1) are Caucasian, (2) are upper-middle class, (3) show obsessive-compulsive traits (see Chapter 6), (4) avoid family meals, and (5) are preoccupied with trying on clothes and posing before a mirror (Agras, 1987; Bruch, 1986).

One clue about why the disorder is more common in females comes from some rather clever research by Fallon and Rozin (1985). They showed a set of nine figure drawings (arranged from somewhat underweight to somewhat overweight) to 248 male and 227 female undergraduates and asked them to indicate their current body figure, their ideal figure, the figure they felt would be most attractive to the opposite sex, and the opposite sex figure to which they would be most attracted. For men, the current, ideal, and most attractive male figures were almost identical. But for women, their perception of their own current figure was significantly heavier than the most attractive figure, which in turn was heavier than the ideal female figure. Both sexes err in estimating what the opposite sex would find attractive, but in opposite directions. Men think women like a figure in men of a heavier stature than the women reported they really do like, and women think that men like women to be thinner than the men actually reported they like. So, overall, Fallon and Rozin find that men's perceptions tend to keep them satisfied with their figures, while women's perceptions place pressure on them to lose weight. Thus, the greater incidence of dieting, anorexia, and bulimia among women is not surprising.

DSM points out that the term *anorexia* (literally, "loss of appetite") is somewhat inappropriate, for loss of appetite does not ordinarily occur until rather late in the course of the illness. Rather, the essential features of anorexia nervosa are an intense concern about becoming overweight and a persistent, unwarranted feeling of being fat. This is combined with a refusal to maintain appropriate body weight for one's age and height, with a weight loss of at least 25 percent. For individuals under 18 years of age, a projected and extrapolated weight at 18 may be used as the criterion.

This apparently voluntary self-starvation is seen primarily in middle and upper socioeconomic classes of women. It typically occurs first during puberty as a young woman becomes more conscious of her self-image. Sexuality may be channeled into the eating area, as these women usually avoid sexual acting-out. After the "sin" of eating, they may resort to self-induced vomiting and laxatives to "cleanse" the body of food (Bruch, 1986; 1973). Some anorectics also show episodes of bulimia (binge-eating), and, in general, they are more disturbed than anorectics who do not show bulimia.

The parents of the anorectic are typically very controlling, though caring, individuals. It could be argued that such controlling behaviors are a result of having an anorectic child, rather than being a contributing factor. However, all indications are that these family patterns were in place before the anorexia nervosa developed (Agras, 1987; Bruch, 1986). As a result, the anorectic appears to use the disorder to regain some control in the family, that is, as a statement of independence in one of the few areas that she can control.

Treatment. The fact that anorectics are frequently resistant to treatment may be seen as another aspect of their estrangement from their environment. However, significant weight loss and other associated signs, including menstrual cessation, generally result in medical consultation followed by hospitalization. At this point, treatment generally focuses on inducing weight gain, with or without the patient's cooperation. Later it becomes important to deal with the conditions that induced the weight loss, so that the person will not revert to old patterns upon discharge from the hospital. For this reason, psychological intervention is often closely integrated with medical treatment. Several programs have been developed and implemented with reportedly high levels of success. Currently, behavior modification programs and family intervention—either singly or in combination—appear to be the treatments of choice, although there is recent evidence that cognitively based therapy can be effective as well for both anorectics and bulimorectics (Garner, 1986).

Bulimia

The converse pattern from anorexia nervosa is **bulimia**, a chronic pattern of binge eating. The word itself comes from the Greek words for ox and hunger; bulimia is also known as the gorge-purge syndrome. It is a contributor to obesity, as well as a problem in its own right (Polivy and Herman, 1985). The essential features, according to DSM, are recurrent binge eating combined with depression and remorse following the binges, with awareness that the pattern is disordered and cannot be stopped. Bulimia is associated with eating in an inconspicuous manner using high-calorie foods, and with attempts to control weight by dieting or vomiting. Some bulimics even become abusers of ipecac, a drug that induces vomiting.

Striegel-Moore and her associates (1986) find that the following factors predispose to a bulimic pattern: (1) either an obsessive-compulsive or addictive personality pattern, (2) acceptance of a traditional female role, (3) middle- to upper-class social status, (4) attendance at a college or university away from home, (5) early physical maturation, (6) a lower metabolic rate, (7) higher stress, (8) tendencies toward depression, (9) a history of dieting attempts, (10) family valuing of appearance and thinness, and (11) a high belief in the ability to use one's will to control self and the world.

While anorectics are typically shy, but passively controlling and stubborn, bulimorectics (even those who are also anorectic) are more likely to be extroverted perfectionists who attempt to control their peers in direct ways.

Some bulimorectics are obese, though many are of normal weight. On the other hand, anorectics are usually almost cadaverously thin (Bruch, 1986). Both disorder groups come from families in which food is a focus, a means of socializing or obtaining recognition (Agras, 1987). Anorectics will often cook exotic meals for others, although they may eat only a small portion themselves. Bulimorectics do not usually like to cook because they are afraid they will eat all the food before the guests show up.

Treatment.   The bulimoretic can respond to many of the same therapy techniques noted for the anorectic. In addition, an adolescent group therapy experience is also helpful. This provides a sense of control, as well as a source of feedback. The adolescent group can be useful for anorectics as well, but only after they have made substantial improvements through other techniques. The bulimorectic also may need counseling for simple control of eating behaviors, similar to counseling used with the more standard problem of obesity and persistent eating disorders.

Juvenile Delinquency and Social Aspects of Abnormality

Juvenile delinquency encompasses recurring instances of truancy, drug use, and sexual precocity, as well as more explicitly unlawful behavior. The term itself actually refers to a particular legal status rather than to a clinically defined disorder. Most of what would be legally termed juvenile delinquency is included in the DSM under the term **conduct disorders**. The conduct disorders are subdivided into two categories: the group type and the solitary aggressive type. Juvenile delinquency is the product of the individual juvenile's behavior and decisions, but it also reflects a social environment typically characterized by family fragmentation, differential affluence and mobility, and a materialistic ethic that allows the end to justify the means (Geismar and Wood, 1986). Use of the term conduct disorders does, however, avoid the legal implications of the term "delinquent."

Most studies suggest a dramatic increase in the past couple of decades in the aggressive conduct disorders (Sechrest, 1986; Marohn, 1982). A 1981 analysis of juvenile crime by the U.S. Department of Justice indicates that at least 27 percent of all serious crimes, including criminal homicide, forcible rape, robbery, aggravated assault, and arson, are committed by individuals under 18 years old, an age group that makes up only 10 percent of the population. Males between the ages of five and 20 represent 35 percent of those arrested for violent crimes. Research indicates that most juvenile delinquents are repeat offenders (recidivists), and while it is generally agreed that males exhibit more delinquent behavior (of a more aggressive type) than females, the frequency, variety, and severity of delinquent acts among females is increasing (Montmarquette and Nerlove, 1985; Achenbach and Edelbrock, 1984).

EVOLUTION OF AGGRESSIVE DELINQUENCY

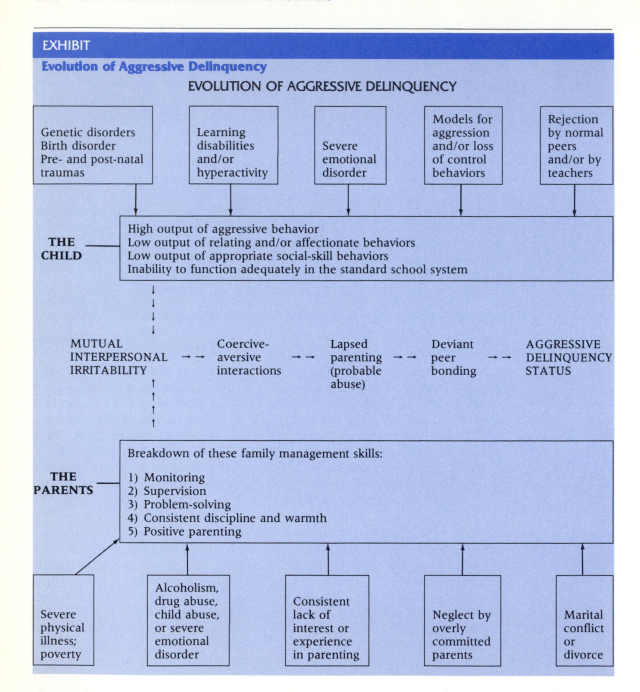

There is clear evidence that delinquency occurs at virtually all levels of society, although there is general agreement that there is a higher percentage of juvenile offenders among the lower socioeconomic classes (Santrock, 1987). Currently there is an increase in reported delinquency both among more youthful juveniles and among those of higher socioeconomic status (Mash and Terdal, 1988).

Cross-cultural evidence indicates that juvenile delinquency and conduct disorders also exist in most other countries (Sechrest, 1986). In this country, there is a higher incidence of delinquency among ethnic minorities than in the overall population. This finding reflects the economic and political status of these groups within the larger culture. Studies in England, Mexico, and China all found youths engaging in antisocial behavior (Rohner et al. 1980; Yang, 1981).

This increase in reported incidents of delinquency may be due to any of several factors. Better record-keeping procedures, an increase in detection, decrease of parental supervisory responsibility, weak societal deterrence methods, as well as a real increase in incidence rates may all be relevant (Montmarquette and Nerlove, 1985). Undoubtedly, one influential factor is the population increase in the mid-1960s of adolescents. Other factors, however, such as the increased incidence of juvenile offenses attributed to females, strongly suggest that social transgressions within this age group are actually rising, and are being ascribed to an increasingly broad cross-section of youths (Heidensohn, 1986; Sechrest, 1986).

Causes. Many delinquent acts involve aggressive or destructive behaviors, the types of behaviors most liable to evoke immediate social retribution. Attempts to explain this have typically focused on three major sources: (1) instinctive aggression, (2) frustration with consequent aggression, and (3) learned aggression via modeling and imitation. An aggressive act may stem from any of these factors, either singly or in combination. An example of how two of these factors may combine in a single instance occurs when a young child from a family of low socioeconomic status regularly watches a broad sample of daily television shows. First, the presentation of desirable but unattainable possessions or goals may generate frustration; second, exposure to aggressive role models influences later behavior.

Genetic studies indicate that instinctive temperament factors are important in generating aggression (also see Chapter 12). Editha Nottelmann, a researcher at the National Institute of Mental Health, reported on a relation between hormone levels and delinquent behavior at the May, 1985, meeting of the American Association for the Advancement of Science. She found that boys with lower testosterone and higher androstenendione levels and girls with lower dehydroepiandrosterone sulphate levels showed higher rates of delinquent behavior.

The second cause noted, based on the **frustration-aggression hypothesis**, asserts that frustration is a potent determinant of aggression. Life in a poverty-stricken environment entails continual frustration as people of limited means and resources struggle to meet basic needs. This accounts in part for the high rates of delinquency associated with youngsters from low socio-economic backgrounds. Frustration may also derive from other areas. Children who are intellectually inferior, emotionally disturbed, learning disabled, hyperactive, or otherwise handicapped in the pursuit of competence in school and social challenges are also likely to express their frustration and seek a sense of identity in delinquent pursuits (Geismar and Wood, 1986). Yet those who join gangs may actually be quite conformist in this quest for identity, hence the DSM term of group conduct disorder.

Social learning theorists emphasize modeling and imitation in the genesis of delinquent behavior, and point out that parental behavior is a crucial source of learning for children. Accordingly, delinquent behavior is usually associated with home environments in which violence and aggression are presented, observed, and perhaps condoned (Geismar and Wood, 1986).

Social Environment and Delinquency. Of course, not all delinquent behavior can be accounted for in this fashion. Although family interactions apparently affect the likelihood of delinquency, modeling and imitation appear to be only one mechanism by which these behaviors are learned. For example, Knopf (1979) discussed three types of interaction patterns associated with delinquent behavior. The first pattern involves a permissive home atmosphere in which the child has numerous early opportunities to establish independent behavior. The second pattern is one in which extremely strict (and perhaps punitive) parents generate resentment, hostility, and aggression. The third pattern likely to breed delinquent behavior is one in which parental control is erratic, so that the child develops without consistent behavioral guidelines.

Along with impaired family relationships, various disorders and school-age social interaction patterns appear to be predictive of delinquency (Sechrest, 1986). In particular, children who later manifest chronic patterns of antisocial behavior often display hyperactivity or behavior problems early in school. Many such children fail to develop any real sensitivity to others' needs, so the traditional self-absorption of adolescence develops further into true narcissism (Levin, 1987).

Treatment. According to Empey (1978), efforts to treat juvenile delinquency evolved from Retribution, through Restraint or confinement, to Rehabilitation (the "three Rs"). In reviewing past and current efforts to deal effectively with delinquency, Empey and others have stressed the complexity of the issues involved. The treatment of delinquency defies easy solutions.

Varying degrees of success have been reported with behavioral methods (Achenbach and Edelbrock, 1984). The degree of external control exercised

EXHIBIT

Factors in Juvenile Delinquency

Sociocultural

Poverty

Breakdown of family unit

Loss of religion as socializing influence

Breakdown of discipline in schools

Media portrayals of violence

Teenage unemployment

Familial

History of family criminality

Low socioeconomic-education level

Broken home

Domineering mother/inadequate father

Absence of or rejection by father or mother

Abusive and/or alcoholic parent

Personal

Birth-trauma, brain dysfunction

Retardation

Hyperactivity and/or dyslexia

Chronic illness as a child

Significant emotional instability

School avoidance and/or failure

High-stimulation seeking

Alcohol or drug abuse

Negative peer influence

Major stress or loss

over the juvenile's environment significantly affects the outcome. In a typical intervention program, constructive, prosocial behavior is rewarded, perhaps through the use of a token economy system. Undesirable or inappropriate behaviors are either ignored or penalized. Nevertheless, the extent of change successfully incorporated into behavioral patterns is limited.

If the problem is not yet too severe, increasing the parent's skills as behavior managers, combined with social and academic skills training for the child, can be effective. This often needs to be combined with general family therapy sessions that act to channel the more specific gains from the other approaches. If this is not effective, placement outside the home is often necessary. Unfortunately, such placement is often in an institution in which the child models more delinquent behaviors and treatment is minimally effective (Geismar and Wood, 1986).

However, one such comprehensive residential treatment approach, modeled on Achievement Place, has shown promise (Phillips et al., 1973). In Achievement Place, and other similar programs, a peer culture is substituted for the family social structure, and a token economy is used to reward appropriate behavior. Residents eventually advance to a merit system in which they learn to maintain appropriate behavioral patterns without tangible reinforcers. An overall assessment of this program by Hoefler and Bornstein (1975) notes that residents frequently make dramatic changes while enrolled in the program; however, extending or maintaining these positive changes in the outside world is difficult. Change is easier to effect in a highly organized, controlled environment. Many individuals, particularly delinquents discharged from treatment settings, often revert to previous behavioral patterns after returning to their customary environments.

THE COLLEGE STUDENT

For young people in our society who choose to attend college, the experience is a major transition point into adulthood. Some of the identity crisis issues discussed in this section continue as challenges throughout the college years, and many of the tasks of adulthood are gradually encountered here. However, it is clear that issues of *performance* often become particularly acute during the college years. This can especially become a problem in two areas: public presentations and taking tests.

Public Performance Anxiety

In Chapter 5, we discussed the social phobia, an extreme form of **public performance anxiety** (Liebowitz, et al., 1985b), and the reader is referred to that section for a more thorough discussion of causes and types of professional intervention that are appropriate. But, the milder form, public performance anxiety, often first clearly encountered in college, is not at all uncommon. As with the severe forms, this anxiety often reflects a combination of self-esteem problems and a lack of skills specific to the public performance situation

(Emmelkamp et al., 1985). In fact, the first edition of the *Book of Lists* cites being asked "to say a few words" as the most commonly feared event in our society. Even in this milder form, the fear of presenting in public can be a devastating hindrance to careers in such areas as teaching, law, and business. The following suggestions have been successfully used by many clients to reduce such fear.

1. Most importantly, remind yourself consistently that (a) it is both normal, and yet controllable, to have some fear about public speaking, and (b) audiences seldom become aware of the anxiety in even the most nervous of speakers. When they do, they are usually sympathetic and empathetic rather than hostile, realizing that "there but for the grace of God go I."

2. Run through your presentation in your imagination—seeing yourself as vividly as you can, and doing it as a very good speaker would. Don't allow images of nonsuccess; stop and start over envisioning yourself do it well, all the way through.

3. Alternate Step 2 with actual physical practice—out loud with all the motions. Ideally, videotape yourself (unless this creates too much anxiety for you) and critique yourself.

4. Remember when you give your speech to try to (a) vary the pace, volume, pitch, and gestures; (b) use "natural" gestures, not stiff or exaggerated ones; (c) use relatively simple sentence structures, and occasionally use words that easily elicit images in your audience (for example, "spinetingling").

5. Have four or five basic points, under one unifying theme, that you want to get across. Memorize these, as well as your opening and closing lines, and if you feel the need, write them on a small card in bold print, so you feel as if you have some "safety valves" in the event you have forgotten something.

6. If you are giving a speech in a strange place, visit it the day before, or maybe a half-hour before your talk, just to get a little more comfortable with the place. Run through Step 2 again, using the actual images of this room.

7. Try to release any nervous energy ahead of time, maybe by thinking of a favorite joke or story or doing some stretching exercises (or maybe giving a "primal scream," see Chapter 4).

8. Just before you start, take several deep breaths, inhaling slowly and exhaling fully, while reminding yourself of the ideas in Step 1.

9. As you get into your speech, pick a few people in various parts of the room who appear to be friendly and attentive, and make eye contact with them throughout the speech.

10. If you make a mistake, be prepared (through separate practice of this technique using Steps 2 and 3 above) to rescue yourself, maybe with a little chuckle or laugh at yourself, e.g., "Sorry about that, I always make mistakes as the full moon approaches." If you want a model for such behavior, try Johnny Carson. Much of his success over the years rests on the clever rescue of poor jokes and casual preparation.

Test Anxiety

Test anxiety is not unusual, and some anxiety about tests is functional. It helps us to prepare, and then to give our best effort. However, test anxiety, like many other psychological disruptions, is a good coping strategy that has become exaggerated or distorted. **Test anxiety** usually occurs when the person has become overconcerned about doing well, has poor study habits, has low self-esteem, or has had an academic failure experience that was embarrassing or otherwise upsetting (Spielberger et al., 1976).

In its severe forms, it may require professional intervention, possibly using such techniques as systematic desensitization of relaxation training. Some college counseling centers or student health services even offer specific training programs to combat test anxiety. However, a great many students suffer at least a mild form of test anxiety, and there are several things one can do on one's own to help the situation.

1. Closely examine the attitudes that have been communicated to you by your parents, both by their words and deeds. Remind yourself that you should expect yourself only to make a good *effort*, not necessarily attain one of the top scores.

2. Make sure that you have kept up with the material throughout the course. Avoid "cramming," a process that increases test anxiety.

3. Try to learn to relax, both as the anxiety builds up and at the time of the test. Learning a simple relaxation pattern is advised; for example, proceeding from the head to the toes, alternately flexing and then relaxing each set of muscles, followed by three or four very slow deep breaths.

4. Familiarity with the content and format of the anticipated test helps reduce test anxiety. Develop a model of the test that you expect in a class, and then take it under even more stringent time limits than you will have in class. You can even give yourself some overall practice by playing several verbal or written production games under short time limits.

5. Learn how to pace your efforts. During any practice tests, state your pace out loud, i.e., how long you expect to spend doing what.

6. Learn the habit of quickly skipping the most difficult questions. First do all those questions you can at least reasonably handle, and then go back later to the difficult ones. That way you won't waste time getting "stuck"

on a difficult question, and you will have more confidence and less test anxiety when you come back to it.

7. Prior to any scheduled test, make sure you get a good night's sleep and a good breakfast, and then leave for the test under as comfortable and relaxed circumstances as possible.

8. Immediately, but in an easy-going fashion, go over any returned tests. Try to understand how you made any errors in preparation or test-taking strategy so that you feel better prepared the next time.

College Student Suicide

The increased emphasis on performance typical of the college years results in a number of suicides caused by performance failure (Shneidman, 1985). Not surprisingly, the majority of these suicides are very similar in cause, treatment, and prevention to suicides in general (see Chapter 9) and to suicide in adolescence (as discussed earlier in this chapter) (Petti and Larson, 1987).

However, Seiden's (1966) pioneering study of college student suicides found (1) a higher proportion of actual as opposed to attempted suicides among females, though males still showed a higher absolute number of suicides, (2) college students who committed suicide more often were language or literature majors, and (3) they more often were older and/or foreign students. Also overrepresented were graduate students who had done very well academically as undergraduates, but were now doing poorly, and undergraduates who had excelled in high school and were now doing less well, even though they were getting adequate grades. Interestingly enough, the incidence of student suicides peaked in October and February. One could theorize that it was not the anticipatory anxiety and upset about tests that led to suicide, but rather the initial negative grade reports plus some time to ruminate about them. This suggests that inappropriate expectancies were a critical cause. As Seiden (1966) puts it,

> The demands that they imposed upon themselves were so exacting, that they were destined to suffer frustration and disappointment no matter how well they fared. . . . Whereas they had previously been crackerjack students in high school or junior college, excelling without much difficulty, (any) drop in grade points . . . threatened their feelings of self-esteem (p. 391).

As you may recall, such a loss of self-esteem can also lead to paranoid disorders, but when turned inwardly may lead to suicide. Clues as to whether or not someone may be genuinely suicidal, and actions to take at such times, are discussed in Chapter 9.

As a person moves out of adolescence and the college years, a variety of challenges and tasks come to the foreground of one's world: the developmental challenges of adulthood.

The Case of Irene

Irene is a 32-year old accountant who has been married for nine years. She referred herself to a private psychologist just after breaking off an affair with a younger colleague in the accounting firm in which she is a partner. Several sessions revealed that she was dissatisfied with her life in general and that she might want to consider a new career. There was no evidence of classic depression or anxiety or of other standard psychopathology.

Irene grew up as the oldest of three children in a warm and caring upper-middle-class family. She was an excellent student, starred in volleyball in high school, and participated in Junior Achievement programs. She went on to college, enjoyed it, and did well. After earning a degree in accounting, she started working for a reputable firm. She married a man she met in her senior year in college, and three years later they had a child. To friends, she had always appeared to be happy in the marriage, yet she now says it has "always been all right, never great."

The outstanding characteristics of Irene's case are her lack of previous mental disorder or even of adjustment problems, her possession of the elements that most people would say are necessary for "the good life," and a pervasive sense of dissatisfaction despite these apparent advantages.

DEVELOPMENTAL DISORDERS OF ADULTHOOD

Childhood, adolescence, and old age have received much attention as specific periods of adjustment, but it was not until the review of the experimental literature by Pressey et al. (1939) that the field of adult psychology emerged. LaVoie (1980) has noted the diversity of opinion about the specific ages that define adulthood. Most experts, however, agree that the early twenties to the mid-sixties is a reasonable span (Clarke-Stewart et al., 1988). Most of the pathological patterns discussed in previous chapters (such as alcoholism, schizophrenia, and depression) also can be viewed as problems of adulthood, and these are noted in the accompanying exhibit. That material, of course, will not be repeated here. However, several specific disorders, such as Irene's, are primarily conditioned and elicited by attempts to cope with the tasks associated with adulthood.

General Changes during Adulthood

A variety of psychological and physical changes occur in adulthood (Zarit and Zarit, 1987; Cohler and Boxer, 1984). Overall intellectual ability slowly declines during this period, although specific aspects such as crystallized intelligence (accumulated information content) may increase even into the sixties. Intellectual abilities involving visual-motor skills and the processing of new information tend to decline the most in later adulthood. Botwinick (1981) discovered, however, that individuals who are high in intellectual ability drop less than those of lesser ability. Furthermore, a sudden drop in verbal intellectual ability (that is, a terminal drop) often predicts an earlier death.

Several associated physical changes commonly occur. The percentage of sleep with rapid eye movement (REM) decreases, and there is more slow-wave brain activity. Hearing acuity decreases, and in general people begin to hear primarily in the right ear.

Presbyopia, or farsightedness, increases as the lenses of the eyes thicken. Simple physical reaction times are not markedly slowed, but there are decreases in complex-choice reaction times. Good nutrition, adequate exercise, and a sense of meaningful existence all help to slow the aging process (LaVoie, 1980; Zarit and Zarit, 1987).

Personality Changes

Levinson (1978; 1986) describes a theory of aging based on a series of life stages that is similar in many respects to that of Erik Erikson. Both suggest that certain tasks must be completed at each stage before a person can progress to the next. For example, the tasks of the period termed "entering the adult world" are (1) to keep one's options open, yet (2) to begin to develop a stable life structure. The basic incompatibility of these two tasks is a partial cause of the allegedly inherent crisis people face at about age 30. For example, Irene's attempt to hold on to the positive stability in her life while reaching out for new options in her personal and vocational world illustrates how this conflict can emerge. In many cases, actual changes (such as divorce or a change in vocational emphasis) represent direct attempts to resolve these conflict patterns (Guerin et al., 1986).

One of the most controversial of Levinson's formulations is that of the **midlife transition**. He sees this as a time of dramatic reevaluation, a time to search for new meanings. In essence, this concept reflects the earlier thinking of Carl Jung, who saw the task of *individuation* (creating a personal sense of self and meaning) as emerging most forcefully in the second half of life. It is a time when many evaluate for the first time their achievements and direction in terms of the fact that they actually will die. Sustained psychotherapy with Irene revealed that these concerns underscored her verbalized worries about her job and marriage.

Many literary works have starkly portrayed these concerns and crises. Willy Loman in Arthur Miller's play *Death of a Salesman* is one example. Levinson asserts that Eugene O'Neill wrote *The Iceman Cometh* in the aftermath of his own debilitating midlife crisis. In that play, O'Neill depicts a tavern in which all the customers are middle-aged men who continue to verbalize their youthful illusions even though they have lost all sense of meaning about their futures. The Iceman is symbolic of death, inevitably moving in when hope leaves.

Yet both O'Neill and Jung appear to have been spurred to their finest creativity by their own midlife crises, as have Freud, anthropologist Margaret Mead, artists Goya and Gauguin, and architect Frank Lloyd Wright. Others, such as Sinclair Lewis and Dylan Thomas, failed to deal adequately with their midlife crises and ceased to be productive. William Shakespeare, whose *Timon of Athens* and *King Lear* portray abrupt character transformations in middle-aged men that lead to their ruin, is said to have retired from marital sex before age 45 and from writing plays and poetry at 46.

Most would agree that Levinson has identified a crisis that affects most individuals at some point during the midlife period (Newman and Newman, 1987). However, an incidental problem to publicizing the inevitability of certain stages is that people who have not experienced them begin to feel abnormal. Also, some may facilitate the occurrence of such a crisis by strongly expecting that one will happen. As Neugarten (1979) points out, the concept of sequential stages simply does not fit every experience, and Levinson's hypotheses, like most other endeavors in this area, are based on limited data, gathered by retrospective self-reports, and using mostly male subjects.

Whether or not one accepts the sequences described by Levinson (1978; 1986), Vaillant (1977), or others, it is clear that most people undergo general personality changes in their adult years (Cohler and Boxer, 1984). Shaie and Geiwitz (1982) describe a series of transitions in cognitive behaviors, aimed first at gaining greater responsibility and control of the environment and finally at a resimplification of life demands, with a focus on immediate life concerns and the inevitability of death.

Most people keep three to four good friends throughout the life cycle, although these are commonly replaced over time, and one of the predictors of positive psychological health is access to and use of a confidant. Other common predictors of positive adjustment as people age are (1) a satisfying marriage, (2) competence in a meaningful occupation, (3) a positive feeling about one's own childhood experience, (4) access to and support from liked siblings, and (5) positive achievements of one's children (LaVoie, 1980). A satisfying marriage appears to be more important to older males than to females.

Of course, the prediction of satisfactory psychological adjustment presupposes that people are not forced to alter their lifestyles in a radical fashion (Goldston, 1986). Changes in one or more of these areas are likely to occur, especially in advanced age, and may have a significant impact on the continuity of behavior patterns. For example, an abrupt change in economic security may occur upon forced retirement; a friend or loved one may suddenly die, leaving a social void; physical illness may intrude on an otherwise satisfactory retirement.

Marriage and Family

Two major related structures affecting the happiness and psychological stability of adults are marriage and the family. About 95 percent of persons in the United States will marry during their lifetime, and although these relationships often provide satisfaction and happiness, marital and family disharmony are still major problems (Cohler and Boxer, 1984).

The Family as a System. Economic, social, and psychological pressures can significantly alter patterns of family life. For example, the cost of raising a child to age 17 between 1961 and 1978 was conservatively estimated at more than $40,000, not including the mother's probable loss of income when not

---

EXHIBIT

Representative Behavioral Contract Used in Family Therapy

Behavior agreed upon	in exchange for the	Reinforcement agreed upon
Ken, age 18, will take out the garbage each night within 10 minutes after supper, will receive no school grades lower than a C, and will avoid raising his voice against Dad in any discussion.		Ken is allowed to keep a TV in his room and to use the family car two times a week without extensive questioning as to where he goes.
Sue, age 16, agrees to go out on a single date with Howard no more than once a week, to be in by midnight, and to show no evidence of drinking.		Sue is allowed to play the flute (even poorly) one hour a day four times a week without being hassled by anyone, and will receive a $5 bonus to her allowance each week.
Dad will not drink at home before 8:00 P.M., will accompany Mom to dinner at the Green Derby (her favorite restaurant) or a movie twice a week, and will do both in a good humor.		Dad is free to play golf and bowl up to four different times during the week.
Mom will not smoke at home, will accompany Dad to one sports event a week, and will do so in a good humor.		Mom is free to play bridge up to four different times during the week.

employed during that time. Couples are having fewer children, are waiting longer before raising families, and are more likely to share childrearing with others. These changes reflect efforts to adapt to significant cultural changes. Also, the long-term viability of the highly revered, somewhat mythical nuclear family is now questioned more than ever (Levinson, 1986; Weiss and Wieder, 1982). When there is a problem, it is logical to focus treatment on the entire family as the "client."

Family Therapy. Practitioners of **family therapy** view psychopathology as symptomatic of impaired communications between two or more family members, rather than as a condition affecting a single person (Guerin et al., 1986). There is a tendency for families to engage in "scapegoating," in which a single family member takes the blame for being "sick" and in need of treatment. Some families are reluctant to share collective responsibility for the impaired behavior of one individual.

Family therapy is most appropriate when (1) the family is using a family member as a scapegoat or safety valve for family distress; (2) a psychologically

ABNORMALITY ACROSS CULTURES

The Expectant Father Across Cultures

In modern society, fathers are encouraged to participate in the birth experience, even up to going into the delivery room. However, even where fathers, through social expectations, are kept out of the birth process, they often end up participating vicariously. L. Bogron in a 1986 paper in the *International Journal of Family Psychiatry* on "The Couvade Syndrome" (p.123–136) notes that it was not uncommon for soldiers away on duty during World War II to experience abdominal pain during their wives' pregnancy.

However, in most Western nations, males are not encouraged to express physical or psychological distress about their partner's pregnancy. Rather, they are expected to provide support and encouragement for the expectant mother, despite sharing the anticipatory anxiety of (1) a major lifestyle change (especially if it is a first child), (2) a further subdivision of time and attention both to and from existent family members, and (3) increased economic and psychological demands.

Certain other cultures have different attitudes toward gender identity and allow a more direct sharing of the physiologic experiences associated with pregnancy and birthing (Bogron, 1986). Probably the most dramatic example of this is *couvade*, most commonly seen in some of the primitive tribes of the coastal regions of Belize (Tseng and Hsu, 1980), though similar patterns have been increasingly noted in Westernized cultures, including the United States. In couvade, the father actually goes to bed and imitates the activities of childbirth while the woman is having the baby. The father also occasionally shows some of the symptoms of late pregnancy, such as swelling of the limbs, breasts, or abdomen.

Many adult couples find a sense of satisfaction and harmony in marriage, despite divorce statistics to the contrary.   (Randy Matusow/Archive Pictures)

disturbed family member is aided by changes in family structure to support the positive individual changes that he or she needs to make; or (3) the changing roles of a family member (such as a son or wife seeking more independence) are creating family disruption (Walrond-Skinner, 1976; Weiss and Wieder, 1982). Family therapy is not considered appropriate when family members are extremely anxious and unable to express emotional feelings verbally. Likewise, families that are conflict-habituated or are already rapidly deteriorating offer little likelihood of a successful therapeutic outcome (Guerin et al., 1986).

Marital satisfaction.   Marriage can be a source of fulfillment and satisfaction to many, and being married is a strong positive predictor for recovery from most psychological (and physical) disorders. Thus, it is a concern that since 1890 the proportion of couples obtaining a divorce has approximately doubled every 30 years. Demographics now predict that nearly half of all couples married in the 1980s will eventually divorce (Weitzman, 1985).

Of course, not all marital disharmony ends in divorce. Some couples even seem to relish living in a conflict-laden marriage. The contact provided by

EXHIBIT

Predicting Marital Happiness

As noted in the text, variables such as similar interests and personality type can be used to predict marital stability and happiness. A more detailed theory developed by psychologist Robert Sternberg of Yale University was presented to the 1985 annual meeting in Los Angeles of the American Psychological Association.

Sternberg points out that love has three components, represented by the three sides of a triangle: (1) an emotional component—primarily those feelings of intimacy and bondedness experienced in close relationships, (2) a motivational component—the drives that lead to physical attraction and sexual involvement, and (3) a cognitive component—in the short run it determines the decision whether or not one loves another, and in the long run whether or not to maintain that love.

Sternberg uses a triangle to stand for each person in a couple, with the length of each side designating the strength of that person's three components, with the overall size or area of the triangle designating the degree of over- or underinvolvement in the relationship. This gives a more graphic representation to a couple of their relative type and level of involvement in a relationship, and helps them see areas that need changing if the marriage is to work.

In a relationship termed "liking," only the emotional component is truly available, and seldom leads to marriage. But six other combinations of these factors are found in marriages, and predict varying levels of interaction and satisfaction.

1. Infatuation—high motivational arousal, little emotional or cognitive commitment. People are impulsive, and often blind to various issues in the partner, e.g., falling in love with a married person. The relationships are often destructive.

the conflict appears to be preferable to the risks of ending the relationship (Weiss and Wieder, 1982). The estimates of significantly unhappy couples that continue in marriages vary from 15 to 30 percent. Even normally happy couples have an average of one nonproductive fight a week. But distressed couples fight on almost every day that they have a reasonable amount of contact.

Generally, the older a person is at the time of marriage, the less marital disharmony he or she experiences. Also, the higher one's socioeconomic class, the greater the marital satisfaction. This reflects the importance of financial problems in generating marital disharmony. Nevertheless, data on

2. Empty love—high cognitive commitment, little motivational or emotional involvement. Found in arranged marriages or in long-term stagnant relationships. Any apparent closeness is unstable unless some motivational or emotional components do develop.

3. Romantic love—strong motivational and emotional components, little cognitive commitment. Strong physical and emotional bonds develop here, but this type of love usually produces turbulent, intense relationships that are unstable unless a cognitive component also develops.

4. Compassionate love—significant cognitive and emotional components, with little motivational arousal. Marriages of this sort resemble long-term committed friendships, and at most there is only sporadic passion and sexuality.

5. Fatuous love—high on motivational and cognitive components, but low on emotional arousal. It is termed fatuous because the commitment is physical without the stabilizing factor of emotional investment, which takes longer to develop. The whirlwind or Hollywood-style romance and marriage is an example of this often ultimately destructive pattern.

6. Consummate love—all three components are present. The best of all marriages.

Sternberg and others note that divorces often occur because (1) people choose partners on the basis of what is important to them at the time, not what will be in the long run; and (2) some of the qualities that were initially attractive, for example, "he's the strong, silent type," later become aversive ("he never talks to me"). The qualities that increased in importance over time are sharing values, willingness to change in response to one another, willingness to tolerate each other's flaws, and a reasonable match in religious beliefs; while those qualities that turned out to be less important than most people thought they would be are willingness to listen attentively, how interesting each partner seemed to the other, and how each responds to the other's parents and family.

upper-middle-class couples also show a steady decline in marital satisfaction throughout the first 10 years of marriage.

Companionship activity is a most efficient predictor of marital happiness. Marital happiness is positively influenced by social status, inversely related to the number of children, and is also related to birth order rank. For example, a first-born husband and later-born wife have a statistically higher chance of happiness than do a couple who both were only children, for an only child is not likely to have had the experience of sharing. It is also important to note that statistically there are *many* exceptions to these findings (Guerin et al., 1986).

Arguments between couples are normal, but may be symptomatic of deeper communication problems or unrealistic expectations. (Ann Chwatsky/Leo de Wys)

Marital therapy. **Marital therapy,** as currently practiced, looks on the couple as the client because most unhappy marriages are characterized by communication problems, maladaptive behaviors elicited by the couple, and unrealistic expectations (Weiss and Wieder, 1982). There is a change from the focus of individual therapy on intrapsychic anxiety and conflict to the interpersonal interactions of the couple. Experienced marital therapists usually combine several theoretical approaches, including gestalt therapy, transactional analysis, and behavior and communication theories (see Chapter 4). The paradoxical techniques and systems analysis techniques of people like Bowen, Satir, or Haley (see Chapter 4) are especially useful here (Seltzer, 1986; Guerin et al., 1986). The first goal of the marital therapist is to make the disordered interactions clear to the couple, then to help in developing more satisfying ones. One common technique employs some form of the **"fair fight" rules** that reflect the early insights of Bach and Wyden (1969). The couple contracts to observe these rules to change a destructive fight into a productive exchange.

Most couples also need to develop more effective communication skills. Eisler et al. (1973) have emphasized the inability of distressed couples to express either positive or negative feelings. Eisler et al. first make videotapes so that the partners can see when they have communicated one message

EXHIBIT

Two New Approaches to Common Marital Problems

There is wide variety in the conflicts that distress marriages. However, it is generally agreed that in order to save a distressed marriage, changes almost always have to be made in two processes: communication and everyday behavioral responses.

M. Scarf, in her book *Intimate Partners* (1987) (New York: Random House), describes two techniques that couples can employ to deal with these processes. The first, "Talking and Listening," aimed at bettering communication, has the couple select one hour each week during which each partner has one half of the hour to talk out loud about his or her self only. The other partner is to listen attentively, but is allowed no verbal response whatsoever. Most importantly, the person talking is not allowed to say anything about the spouse or the relationship, only about himself or herself as a separate person, his joys, hurts, likes, dislikes, feelings about life, and so on.

Equally important is that when the task is finished, no discussion of it is ever to take place, that is, neither can respond to the other. This prevents the occurrence of what Scarf terms the "projective identification system," in which "for example, a wife perceives her own feelings of inferiority and inadequacy as being her husband's thoughts and feelings about "her"—she needs to sustain the projection by experiencing her own self-accusations as coming from him—and "she must (albeit she does so quite unconsciously) provoke him to treat her like an incompetent dodo, thus enabling her to fight the bad feelings as they exist and become manifest in him instead of experiencing them as painful feelings that exist within" (pp. 191–192). Thus, the restriction of follow-up discussion paradoxically clarifies communication.

The second technique, "Odd day, even day," a more behavioral task, assigns the odd weekdays to one spouse, the even weekdays to the other (Sundays are kept free to "practice their pathology"). Then, on a particular spouse's day, that spouse is allowed to make one "intimacy request" and the partner must meet it on that day, assuming it is under the spouse's behavioral control to do it. So, requests such as "I want you to be committed forever," "I want you to make love to me 50 times," "I want you to adore me" are out. Even requests like "I want you to be tender and loving" are not helpful. They need to be put in more behavioral terms, like "I'd like a nice gentle, loving massage for the next half hour," "Help me think through a problem I had at the office."

Both of the above tasks, from different perspectives, work to break the control struggles and negative behavioral habits that are at the center of most distressed marriages, and indeed, of most long-term relationships of any type.

verbally while sending an opposite one nonverbally. Such monitoring and correction can be effective in changing disturbed communication, particularly when therapy includes attention to the underlying feelings.

Behaviorists have underscored the value of using explicit contracts between the partners to replace the confusing, unarticulated expectancies and demands that are characteristic of distressed couples (Weiss and Wieder, 1982). This systematic negotiation of agreements attempts to translate requests for intangibles, such as changes in attitude, into requests for changes in specific behavior. As in an earlier example with family therapy, this contract is often in written form. The means of endorsing the contract may be only the general commitment to change that is assumed to exist (a good-faith contract), or it may be specific consequences (a quid pro quo contract). In a quid pro quo contract, the husband might agree to perform specific housework tasks, while the wife might agree to accompany him (or not to accompany him) to a football game. If either partner fails to do his or her part, the other has no obligation. Both Levy (1979) and Jacobsen (1978), in separate studies, found both good faith and quid pro quo contracting approaches to be effective.

Divorce

Despite evidence that effective treatments are available for sexual dysfunctions, distorted communications, and other marital problems, many couples seek a divorce. The upward spiral of the divorce rate has stopped in recent years, though it is still estimated that nearly 50 percent of new marriages will end in divorce. From a cross-cultural perspective, anthropologist Helen Fisher (1987) surveyed the archives of the United Nations' demographic yearbooks to trace patterns of divorce in 58 countries, including the United States, Russia, Egypt, Samoa, France, New Zealand, and Costa Rica. She found three striking similarities among all cultures: (1) women tended to divorce (or were divorced) in the midst of their reproductive years (between 25 and 29), (2) after being married for an average of four years, and (3) bearing a single child. One could interpret this data in diverse ways, in large part depending on who instigated the divorce, and that data was not available. In any case, although most people find that a divorce produces some positive consequences, significant distress is also a frequent result (Weitzman, 1985).

Economic status is an initial consideration, because two households will have to be supported. If there are children, several specific stresses result, including the difficulties of being a single parent (95 percent of whom are female) and the disorganization in family routine (Weitzman, 1985). With or without children, role adjustment and interpersonal problems are inevitable, and loneliness and consequent depression are common. Remarriage may help allay loneliness, but it has also been found that stepfamilies experience more psychological stress than do original nuclear families. Indeed, the noted authority on childrearing, Dr. Benjamin Spock, who originally was rather moderate in his comments on the problems of dealing with a stepchild, later spoke of stepparenting as a "naturally accursed" relationship after he himself experienced life as a stepparent (Associated Press Dispatch, Aug. 12, 1985).

Spouse Abuse

There's no place like home, for either happiness or violence. As a marriage breaks down, the potential for violence soars. It may be directed toward the child (see the following discussion of child abuse), or toward the spouse (Browne and Finkelhor, 1986).

There has been increasing attention to **spouse abuse** in recent decades (Meyer et al., 1988). The type of violence in spouse abuse ranges from verbal abuse to physical assault. Also, rape is being increasingly recognized within the marriage as a form of spouse abuse. Estimates of couples who experience physical violence at some time in a marriage range from 30 to 60 percent. And it is clear that the amount of reported violence is far less that the amount of actual violence (Jouriles and O'Leary, 1985), a point vividly made by the noted mystery-fiction writer Ed McBain in his 1961 short story "J" reprinted in *The Ethnic Detectives* by Pronzini and Greenberg (1985).

> *"She wouldn't press charges," Hawes said knowingly.*
> *"Charges, hell. There wasn't any beating, according to her. She's got blood running out of her nose, and a shiner the size of a half-dollar . . .—but the minute I get there, everything's calm and peaceful". . .*
> *"She said, 'Oh, we were just having a friendly little family argument.'. . . So I asked her how she happened to have a bloody nose and a mouse under her eye and—catch this, Cotton—she said she got them ironing." (p. 310).*

In most cases the wife is the victim, though there are a few reports where the husband was abused (Sonkin et al., 1985). Family therapy can be helpful on occasion here, though often by the time the abuse pattern has been made public, the bonding between the two parties has been so violated that reconciliation is highly improbable. It's worth noting that a great many spouse abusers were themselves abused as a child by one or both of their parents.

Child Abuse

While the abuse of children throughout history has been well documented (Belsky, 1980) and has been generally abhorred, for a long time few efforts to prevent it were actually made. It is ironic that the first formal legal intervention in a child-abuse case, that of Mary Ellen in New York in 1875, had to be prosecuted through animal protection laws and was primarily a result of the efforts of the Society for the Prevention of Cruelty to Animals (Cross, 1984). In the past 25 years, however, **child abuse** has become a national issue, and all 50 states, partly spurred by the federal Child Abuse Prevention and Treatment Act, have established legislation for the identification of and

EXHIBIT

Cross-Cultural Considerations In Child Abuse

Cross-cultural research has not only examined patterns of child abuse in various cultures but has also attempted to relate abuse patterns to childrearing practices and views of child development. As a result, such research may indicate possible causes for abuse in Western societies as well.

Child abuse is a problem in a wide variety of cultures, with both the age and temperament of the abused child and the presence of parental stressors influencing abuse in the same way it does in the U.S. culture. There are reported differences, however. Sex ratios of abused children differ by culture, with a relatively even ratio in the U.S., a slightly higher rate for males in Japan, two males to one female in Greece, and one male to three females in Malaysia (Walker, 1987; Cross, 1984).

The relationship of abuse to infanticide has also been explored. Infanticide appears to be much less frequent in pastoral or agricultural societies than in hunting, gathering, or fishing societies. Two groups that practice infanticide are the Kung San in the Kalahari, who bury defective infants alive, and the Netsilik Eskimos, who use female infanticide to maintain the male-female ratio at 3:2. Yet neither of these groups practice other types of child abuse, and parents are devoted to their children. Thus, infanticide appears to be of evolutionary significance in such groups (Prescott, 1979; Walker, 1987).

Cultures with extended families tend to show little child abuse. Collective childrearing appears to buffer possible maladaptive interactions. Among the Zulu tribes of Africa, a breakdown in the extended family is accompanied by increasing child abuse, which had formerly been virtually nonexistent.

In a lengthy analysis of the relationship of various cultural practices and child abuse, based on a summary of 20,000 significant correlations among 400 cultures, Prescott (1979) reported a strong relationship between physical and corporal punishment of children and the following factors, among others: inferior status of women, high incidence of mother-child households, low physical affection of infants, and sporadic meeting of infants' needs. Prescott sees abuse as a result of low levels of physical affection leading to somatosensory deprivation, with the infant's lack of pleasure during a formative period preventing the proper balance between pain and pleasure systems in the brain. Whether or not this physiological explanation has any long-term validity, the cross-cultural material Prescott presented points to the contributions of differing childrearing practices.

intervention with abusive families. As a result, the number of identified cases has grown enormously, from 7,000 to 8,000 annually in 1967 and 1968 to over 700,000 in 1978, and most experts believe the number is still increasing.

Because of the private nature of abuse and the reluctance of both perpetrators and victims to reveal it, reported cases of child abuse are generally believed to represent only a portion of actual cases. Estimates do vary, but the 1980 National Incidence Study of Child Abuse and Neglect *conservatively* estimated that 652,000 children under 18 are abused or neglected yearly, a rate of 10.5 children per 1,000. Deaths from abuse reportedly number from 700 to 2000 per year. Generally, such acts of violence decrease with increasing age of the children (National Center on Child Abuse and Neglect, 1981).

Much of the discussion of the incidence and etiology of child abuse in this section refers to both physical abuse and sexual abuse. Issues that are very specific to sexual abuse, however, will be noted, and the reader is also referred to the discussions of pedophilia and incest in Chapter 10.

Etiology.   There are several major causes of child abuse. In rare cases, one of these causes may be primary, but in most cases, several of the following causes are usually contributing (Belsky, 1980; Cross, 1984; Browne and Finkelhor, 1986).

1. *Incompetence.* Far too many parents come to this crucial task with little preparation or support (for example, poverty markedly increases the potential for child abuse). When the task overwhelms them, they don't have extra support or financial resources, and may react with harsh punishments in an attempt to regain control.

2. *Frustration.* In a similar vein, the demands of childrearing are too much for an immature personality, who lashes out in retaliation at the cause for these demands. Remorse may follow, though the damage is done.

3. *Disturbance.* Psychological and physical disturbances that are not generated by the child (for example, schizophrenia, drug and alcohol abuse, mental retardation, or a disrupted marriage) generate problems that in turn facilitate child abuse.

4. *Modeling.* The child who has been abused, or who has witnessed a pattern of spouse abuse, is much more likely to become an abuser than the average child.

5. *Characteristics of the child.* Children who have characteristics that make frustration or disappointment more likely (for example, hyperactivity, physical or psychological handicaps) are more likely to be abused. The amount of parental bonding and the vulnerability of the child are also relevant. Thus, stepchildren and younger children are more often the victims.

6. *Cultural attitudes.* Child abuse is more likely in a culture or subgroup to the degree that competition, rather than cooperation, is emphasized or that physical punishment is accepted as a common childrearing technique.

Sexual abuse.   The various theories that are used to explain physical child abuse are also often relevant to cases of sexual child abuse. Psychodynamic features include the interaction of such parental factors as marital discord, personality disorder, loss of an important relationship or fear of disintegration of the family, and emotional deprivation. Finkelhor (1985) related sexual abuse to extreme masculine socialization practices and views, which include

EXHIBIT

Predisposing Variables in Child Abuse

Many factors contribute to the ultimate emergence of an episode of physical and/or sexual child abuse (Belsky, 1980; Cross, 1984; Finkelhor, 1985). These factors are found within three contributing systems: (1) sociocultural, (2) familial, and (3) individual. To the degree these factors are present, the probability of an occurrence of child abuse is heightened.

1. Sociocultural

   a. lack of affirmation and support of the family unit
   b. lack of emphasis on parent training skills as a prerequisite to parenting
   c. acceptance of and high media visibility of violence
   d. acceptance of corporal punishment as a central childrearing technique
   e. emphasis on competitiveness rather than cooperation
   f. unequal status for women
   g. low economic support for schools and day care facilities

2. Familial

   a. low socioeconomic and educational level
   b. little availability of friends and extended family for support
   c. single-parent or merged-parent family structure
   d. marital instability
   e. family violence as common
   f. low rate of family contact and information exchange
   g. significant periods of mother absence
   h. high acceptance of family nudity
   i. low affirmation of family member privacy
   j. "vulnerable" children, i.e., to the degree they are young, sick, disturbed, retarded, or emotionally isolated

3. Individual (the parent)

   a. history of abuse as a child
   b. low emotional stability and/or self-esteem
   c. low ability to tolerate frustration and inhibit anger
   d. high impulsivity
   e. lack of parenting skills
   f. high emotional and interpersonal isolation
   g. problems in handling dependency needs of self or others
   h. low ability to express physical affection
   i. unrealistic expectancies for child's performance
   j. acceptance of corporal punishment as a primary childrearing technique
   k. presence of drug or alcohol abuse

the equating of sexuality and affection, the importance of heterosexual success to self-identity, a focus on sexual acts rather than relationships, and the acceptance of younger and smaller sexual partners.

The seriousness of disorder in the child resulting from sexual abuse appears to depend on several factors (Browne and Finkelhor, 1986). More serious problems are likely if (1) the offender is in a close relationship to the child, such as the father, (2) the sexual activity includes genital contact, and especially if this includes penetration, (3) the child is older at the time of abuse, (4) the abuse is frequent and/or of long duration, (5) the child has strong negative feelings about the abuse and/or is somehow aware of its wrongness, and (6) much upset and/or distress occurs around the event, for example, court testimony.

Differential diagnosis. Unless someone admits abuse, diagnosis may be problematic. Physical trauma alone is rarely a sufficient basis, although certain patterns of injury may strongly suggest nonaccidental or repeated physical abuse (Cross, 1984). A device for remembering the major *physical* signs of abuse is the "4 Bs": unexplained or unusual *b*ruises, *b*urns, *b*ald spots, or *b*leeding. Bruises around the head or face, and easily protected areas such as the abdomen; multiple bruises, especially if spread over the body; or bruises in the shape of an object, such as a hand, are especially indicative. Likewise, burns of all types should cause concern, especially cigarette burns, burns with a specific shape, such as an iron, and burns that suggest that the hand has been immersed in liquid or that liquid has been poured on the body. Concern should be even greater if the child provides an explanation that does not fit the injury.

Behavioral signs of physical abuse (as well as the often accompanying emotional abuse) include inappropriate crying or fearfulness; cruelty by the child to animals or smaller children; extremes of behavior, such as marked aggressiveness or passivity; self-destructive behavior or accident proneness; problems with school tasks and peers; shrinking from physical contact; wearing clothes that seem more designed to cover the body than to keep one warm. These signs are especially important if the symptoms are a change in behavior pattern for that child. In addition, delinquency, drugs abuse, anorexia nervosa, and excessive fearfulness and avoidance of parents may reflect an abuse situation in older children and adolescents.

There are also problems in diagnosing sexual abuse. The behavioral signs of physical abuse, noted above, are often found in cases of sexual abuse as well. In addition, behaviors found in victims of sexual abuse include extreme secrecy, excessive bathing, indications of low self-worth, provocative or promiscuous sexual patterns, appearing more worldly than friends, and suddenly possessing money or items that could have been used to bribe the child to keep quiet. Specific physical signs of sexual abuse are pain, rashes, itching or sores in the genital or anal areas, frequent urinary infections, and frequent vomiting or enuresis (Finkelhor, 1985; Cross, 1984). Unfortunately, as many as 75 percent of sexual abuse victims don't show easily detectable signs of trauma to the vagina. Recently, detection has been improved by painting the vaginal tissue with toluidine blue dye, which highlights the damage.

Intervention.   Treatment of specific parental psychopathologies, such as drug or alcohol abuse or the disturbed marriage, may help in the specific case, as will training in more effective parenting. But the greatest changes will come with efforts at prevention (for example, parent training *before* becoming parents, the reduction of the percentage of very young and/or single parents without enough skills or resources) or cultural change (for example, efforts to reduce the acceptance of the common use of physical discipline) (Belsky, 1980; Cross, 1984; Browne and Finkelhor, 1986).

DEVELOPMENTAL PROBLEMS OF ADVANCED AGE

Adulthood is a period commonly associated with vocational and career development and, in many cases, the assumption of family responsibilities. This period gradually gives way to developmental changes associated with advancing age, which often brings with them fundamental alterations in lifestyle, interests, and adjustment patterns. This is especially true for women, who, on the average, can be expected to outlive their husbands. As a rule, successful adjustment earlier in life is a good predictor of how a person of either sex will adjust to advancing age (Clarke-Stewart et al., 1988).

In coping with stressful life events and in dealing with the prospect of mortality, older persons necessarily experience and express a full range of emotional reactions, including anxiety, guilt, grief, anger, hopelessness, and perhaps also laughter and serenity. However, there is a common tendency in our society to react to emotional expression in older persons with caution and concern. Frequently, marked changes in behavior or emotional control are viewed as signs of incipient progressive dementia or senility. However, older people experience transient difficulties just like everyone else, and, in fact, may adjust better to them (Himmelfarb and Murrell, 1984; Murrell, 1986). Thus, it is important to distinguish these from disorders that actually portend a more serious decline. Most of the latter are associated with the declining integrity of the central nervous system (see Chapter 13).

Like younger people, aged individuals can suffer from a wide variety of psychological afflictions. However, there are more impediments to successfully treating older persons. First is the tendency to view many problems in advanced age as indications of irreversible, progressive disease processes. For example, occasional memory lapses, though common among people of all ages, are evaluated far more critically in older persons because memory problems have traditionally been the hallmark of senility. While it is true that cognitive limitations afflict some older persons, these may simply reflect a lack of early training or education, rather than irreversible disease (Levinson, 1986). Second, older persons may resist either evaluation or treatment, because they fear substantial changes in their daily routines. Third, physicians, psychologists, and other health-care providers may resist treating older persons because they lack knowledge, experience, or empathy with that age group. Finally, families of older persons may resist treatment for them because of the prospect of added financial strain or, in some cases, ambivalence toward the benefits of treatment.

A loving, active relationship between older people can be a source of comfort in the face of advancing uncertainties and infirmities. (Nancy Kaye/Leo de Wys, Inc.)

Myths and Facts about Aging and Mental Health

Many people, especially adolescents and young adults, hold a variety of misconceptions about the effects of aging. The following chart describes a number of these misconceptions as they specifically relate to mental health. An excellent source of information in this regard is Erdman Palmore's (1987) *The Facts on Aging Quiz: A handbook* (New York: Springer), and a number of the following statements are adapted from this source.

1. The incidence of schizophrenia and manic disorders increases with age

2. Most nursing-home patients suffer from mental disorders

3. The incidence of "neurotic" disorders, e.g., the anxiety disorders, increases with age

4. Disturbance of thought processes (confusion, memory problems), often referred to as dementia, inevitably occur as a person ages

5. Conversations with demented persons tend to increase their level of confusion

1. False; the rates for both decrease

2. True; most research indicates that mental disorder (including both organic and functional mental disorders) is a major cause for confinement in nursing homes

3. False; the rates stay approximately the same

4. False; only about 15 percent of persons over age 65 exhibit dementia

5. False; such conversations are not only pleasurable to such persons, but are of help in slowing the progress of the dementia

Depression

Depression is by far the most common functional disorder in the elderly. As discussed in Chapter 9, depression is a condition characterized by a generalized slowing of activity patterns, commonly accompanied by "blue" moods or dysphoria.

One of the more thorough research studies on aging persons was conducted by Stan Murrell and his colleagues (Murrell et al., 1983; Himmelfarb and Murrell, 1984; Murrell, 1986). They carried out a study of 3,000 Kentuckians 55 and older, using a sample designed to be quite similar to the U.S. population in that age range. They employed in-depth interviews (for most subjects at five different times at six-month intervals) and administered a wide variety of questionnaires and psychological tests.

6. Rates of disruption and divorce increase with age

6. False; they decrease

7. Major depression is more common among older persons than among younger persons

7. False; although older persons incur more loss-generated depressions (e.g., retirement, deaths of friends), they show lower rates of chronic depression

8. Suicide rates are higher for older persons

8. True and false; they become higher for males, and lower for females

9. Poor nutrition may cause mental disorder in older people

9. True; a number of older persons eat nutritionally unbalanced meals, which in turn causes confusion and depression

10. Psychotherapy is seldom effective with older persons

10. False; studies indicate that psychotherapy is effective across all age ranges

11. Older people use more mental health services than do younger persons

11. False; and probably unfortunately so; older people use mental health services at a rate of little more than half as much as younger persons

Murrell and his colleagues did find a fairly high level of depression (13.7 percent of the male sample and 18.2 percent of females were above a cutoff point used to indicate depression in older persons) and anxiety (17.1 percent of males and 21.5 percent of females). The most important finding was the very strong relationship of depression (and to a slightly lesser extent of anxiety) to self-reported physical health problems. Unfortunately, there was a low readiness, approximately three percent, to seek or use mental health interventions to deal with this anxiety and depression. Interestingly enough, while self-reported kidney and bladder disease, heart or lung problems, hardening of the arteries, and stroke were especially likely to generate depression and anxiety, high blood pressure, cancer, diabetes, or stomach ulcers were not. There were some clear, positive findings as well. For one thing, these older persons, often thought of as frail by the young, seem to take most crises and problems with more ease than younger persons, almost as if they had been inoculated against such stresses by time. Also, they were found to be much more active and coping than had been expected, and without particularly significant financial problems in most cases.

Hypochondriasis

Physical infirmities are an inevitable consequence of aging, but individuals differ in their adaptations to physical afflictions. As discussed in Chapter 6, the DSM includes **hypochondriasis** (a person believing he or she is disordered, in spite of advice or evidence to the contrary) among the somatoform disorders. Although hypochondriacal complaints are most prevalent among 30- to 50-year-old persons, they are also fairly common among aged people. The factors associated with hypochondriasis are an atmosphere of illness, strong dependency relationships, channeling of psychological conflict, and reinforcement. For some older persons, hypochondriacal symptoms may serve as a passive means of expressing feelings too threatening to convey directly. Less obvious, perhaps, but often significant is the extent to which symptoms can provide a means of symbolically identifying with a deceased loved one. Such tendencies become more pronounced with age because an increasing number of factors threaten the older person's well being. Thus, people who have established patterns of extreme self-scrutiny in early life are likely to intensify these behaviors in later years (Newman and Newman, 1987).

In some cases, individuals *believed* to be hypochondriacal have entirely legitimate concerns. Older individuals are more likely than younger ones to experience multiple side effects from medical treatments, often because the person is being treated for several afflictions simultaneously (sometimes by different specialists). Although conscientious physicians attempt to obtain knowledge of elderly patients' medication inventories, it is not uncommon for patients to be taking several medications that, when taken concurrently, may produce uncomfortable or even dangerous side effects. Subsequent complaints may go unheeded, especially if the person has a history of chronic physical complaints. Thus, the problem of distinguishing real from imagined physical complaints is particularly difficult in the elderly.

Sexual Dysfunction

Sexual problems are being reported among older persons with increasing frequency (Allgeier and Allgeier, 1988). One reason is that with society's heightened awareness of the aspects of sexuality in all phases of the life cycle, older people are becoming more open to discussing formerly taboo subjects such as sex. As Butler and Lewis have pointed out, "It is frequently assumed that (1) older people do not have sexual desires; (2) they could not make love even if they wanted to; (3) they are too fragile physically and it might hurt them; (4) they are physically unattractive and therefore sexually undesirable; and (5) anyway, the whole notion is decidedly shameful and perverse" (1977, p. 112).

In fact, neither men nor women necessarily lose their capacity for sexual activity except as the result of specific physical diseases. Although women lose at menopause their ability to bear children, many actually report an increase in sexual desire in later years. Most men do not totally lose sexual potency, and sperm are constantly regenerated. Both sexes retain the capacity for sexual intercourse indefinitely. Differences in sexual arousal patterns between young and elderly individuals appear to be limited to a few factors. Sexually active individuals generally report diminished frequency of intercourse; men generally report that penile erections take more time to achieve and may be sustained for comparatively shorter periods; and women tend to report a lessening of vaginal lubrication (LoPiccolo and Stock, 1986). With patience, perspective, and more persistence in stimulation, these factors can be compensated for, however, and in no way appear to diminish the capacity for sexual pleasure between the partners who are aware and adaptable.

Treatment of Disorders

Because older persons are likely to encounter a series of stressful events within a comparatively short time, psychological services should be readily available to them (Goldston, 1986). The client's age does not appreciably affect the outcome of treatment of functional disorders. For example, standard techniques used to treat depression—tricyclic antidepressants, monoamine oxidase inhibitors, neuroleptics, electroconvulsive therapy, and psychotherapy—have been employed successfully with both younger and older persons (Jamison, 1979). However, pharmacological treatment of older persons requires careful management for two reasons. First, appropriate dosage levels differ with age; generally, the lower metabolic efficiency of an older person's system dictates lower dosage levels. Second, the fact that older persons are likely to be taking other medications increases the likelihood of adverse side effects. Therefore, chemotherapy for functional disorders in older persons requires careful history taking beforehand, close supervision during treatment, and follow-up evaluations.

Dementia

When a significant, *global* decline in mental abilities is noted, the term **dementia** is often used to describe the condition (Bridgeman, 1988). Dementia refers to a significant loss of mental abilities resulting from any of a wide variety of conditions involving central nervous system impairment. The reader is referred to Chapter 13 for a discussion of general neuropsychological issues, as these are at least as relevant to older persons as they are to anyone else.

The Case of Sylvia

Sylvia, age 75, was referred for psychological evaluation as part of an effort to determine the basis for what seemed to be rather peculiar behavior. Recently, on one of her frequent shopping trips, she had inexplicably become lost on the way home. Somewhat frightened, she drove about aimlessly, and while on an unfamiliar road disregarded a stop sign. Apprehended by a police officer, she appeared flustered and confused. Upon further questioning, she continued to display confusion and disorientation. The officer ascertained Sylvia's address by calling in her license plate number, then led her home. She was cited for the traffic violation and had her license revoked pending a medical consultation.

Upon initial examination, Sylvia proved coherent and well oriented, and subsequent psychological testing corroborated this finding. History data gathered on her at this time indicated that Sylvia had led a normal, happy, and productive life, with no prior evidence of any psychological dysfunction. It was concluded that she had probably suffered a temporary disruption of blood supply to the brain as a result of a mild stroke. This type of challenge to psychological functioning from increasing physical problems is not uncommon for people as they age. Although signs of residual impairment appeared slight, a thorough review of Sylvia's medical records revealed at least two previous incidents of reported brief memory lapses and confused states, one of which was accompanied by slight weakening on the left side of the body. Sylvia also had a history of chronic hypertension. By themselves none of these occurrences appeared to produce significant impairment, but evidence suggested that her overall condition had deteriorated somewhat during the past two years.

Later judged unable to drive safely, Sylvia was thus deprived of mobility and independence. Fortunately, the compassionate judge took note of her situation and arranged for follow-up intervention through a social worker. The social worker made contact with another woman who, though younger than Sylvia and able to drive, did not have a car. The two developed a strong companionship and ultimately decided to merge households. Sylvia continues to have her ups and downs, and while it is very probable that she has had some minor strokes during the past six months, she has had no debilitating strokes during that time. Her hypertension has been more effectively controlled by medication, and probably by stress reduction through being able to share her responsibilities with someone.

Despite increased potential for dementia, old age need not be a time of inactivity or hopelessness; many independent elderly people attribute their longevity and ongoing happiness to activities that promote a feeling of self worth. (Rocky Weldon/Leo de Wys)

According to the DSM, dementia is an organic brain syndrome involving the loss of intellectual capabilities resulting in a significant disruption of day-to-day functioning. Thus defined, dementia is not associated with a particular phase of the life cycle, for intellectual abilities can be disrupted by a wide range of factors at almost any stage of development. However, because dementia refers to a loss of *acquired* intelligence, it is typically not diagnosed before early adulthood, and then usually in conjunction with central nervous system impairments. Symptoms of dementia are commonly reported among the elderly, and differential diagnoses of dementia are often more difficult to make for elderly people. Traditionally, dementia was associated with the latter part of the life span and was often used synonymously with the term **senility**. However, the terms are not identical. Senility implies an irreversible decline of abilites; dementia does not.

It should also be noted that such a loss may also be relatively minor, as well as occasionally reversible. This is well portrayed in the story of the elderly couple sitting watching television one night. The woman said she felt like a sundae and asked if her husband would mind going to get her one.

"I'd be glad to," he said.

"Well, get a pencil and write it down," she said.

"No need, I got it," he said.

"Well, I want vanilla ice cream with chocolate syrup—you'd better write it down or you'll forget."

"No, I can remember. Vanilla ice cream, chocolate syrup and. . ."

EXHIBIT

Individual Variations in Test Performance among Elderly Persons

Most psychological tests of cognitive and intellectual abilities are scored according to age-related norms, reflecting the manner in which performance varies as a function of age (Anastasi, 1987). However true it may be that age affects one's psychological status, it is erroneous to assume that age alone is highly predictive of test performance. Work by Marilyn Alpert, Edith Kaplan, and others points up the need to consider individual variations in patterns of test performance, irrespective of the subject's age—especially when the purpose of an assessment is to test for evidence of central nervous system (CNS) impairment.

Alpert and Kaplan (1980) employed a brief test battery that has been administered to over 2,000 people participating in a study on normal aging processes. For one part of this battery, subjects draw several designs from memory, after viewing each for 10 seconds. Tests like this, which assess memory performance, are very important components of clinical evaluations.

The first design (Figure A) consists of two crossed lines with two pairs of boxes facing each other. Ordinarily, this item is evaluated in terms of overall accuracy according to a scoring system. Alpert and Kaplan went further, evaluating the *qualitative* features of their subjects' drawings. This evaluation is important because although such test items typically have only one "best" solution, errors can be made in many ways.

The researchers felt that an analysis of error variations might help in distinguishing between drawings reflecting normal aging processes and those suggestive of some underlying CNS disturbance. They were thus especially interested in how their subjects handled the task in comparison with how most subjects do it: typically, a subject draws two crossed lines, then adds the boxes. As can be seen in Figure B, the percentages of both men and women who drew the design in this manner remained quite high through age 74, even for subjects whose scores were relatively low. Beyond that age, however, striking variations were evident in how subjects went about drawing the design. Of the subjects who received relatively high scores, about half of the males and nearly 100 percent of the females maintained the strategy preferred by younger subjects. However, low-scoring subjects of both sexes appeared to divert significantly from the preferred strategy; less than 25 percent of the women, and almost none of the men, employed it.

Figure C shows examples of error patterns by subjects with relatively high and relatively low scores. Subjects with relatively high scores erred chiefly in their placements of the boxes; all three correctly crossed two lines of approximately equal length at about 90 degrees. Low-scoring subjects, on the other hand, tended to produce designs varying considerably from the standard, failing to cross, or in some cases even draw, connecting lines. It appeared as if they failed to retain an overall concept of what the design looked like and instead became preoccupied with segmented details.

Alpert and Kaplan attributed considerable significance to these findings. When they were combined with results of other tests, a pattern emerged suggesting central nervous system impairment in patients whose drawings were comparably degraded. Performance quality was comparable to patients with damage in the frontal region of the nondominant hemisphere.

There are several important implications of Alpert and Kaplan's work. First, it emphasizes the extent to which individual differences in performance are as characteristic of the elderly as of any other group. Second, it suggests ways in which test performance indicative of normal aging processes can be differentiated from that which may reflect underlying CNS pathology. Finally, it points up the importance of evaluating qualitative, as well as quantitative, features of test performance when conducting an assessment. A consideration of these factors makes it easy to see why psychological assessment demands considerable powers of observation and involves considerably more than the mechanical administration and scoring of tests.

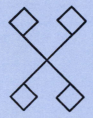

Figure A. The first stimulus figure on the visual reproduction subtest of the Wechsler Memory Scale.

Figure B. Drawing strategies of male and female aging subjects.

Figure C. Sample errors of aging individuals on the visual reproduction subtest of the Wechsler Memory Scale.

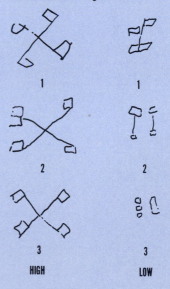

Figure A reproduced by permission from the Wechsler Memory Scale-Form 1. Copyright 1948 by the Psychological Corporation. All rights reserved. Figures B and C reprinted from Alpert and Kaplan (1980) by permission of authors and publisher.

EXHIBIT

Cross-Cultural Research In Geropsychiatry

A number of countries have in recent years undertaken research to learn more about the process of aging and the psychological needs of elderly persons. In a number of both Western and non-Western nations, the elderly are beginning to be an increasing percentage of the overall population, resulting in greater needs for both physical and mental health-care facilities (Clarke-Stewart et al., 1988).

One of the most prominent research surveys conducted on this topic was the United States–United Kingdom Cross-National Project, begun in 1965. As described by Gurland and Zubin (1982), one facet of this project has been to examine the epidemiology of various physical, mental, and psychological disorders among the elderly. The study pointed out both similarities and differences in terms of how the psychological status of elderly individuals was perceived in the two participating nations.

Among the most interesting findings of the study involved the diagnosis of dementia, a neurologically based condition affecting intellect, memory, and other cognitive capabilities. Project researchers in the United States found that their criteria and those employed by psychiatric medical staff in London hospitals were in good agreement regarding the relatively low number of patients in each country diagnosed as having dementia. In contrast, standard diagnostic procedures employed in New York City hospitals selected for the study consistently overdiagnosed dementia. In particular, it was found that patients with depression, a functional disorder, were consistently regarded as having dementia. A serious implication of this finding was that patients so diagnosed were unlikely to receive appropriate intervention of either a chemotherapeutic or psychotherapeutic nature.

The authors of this study point out that the diagnosis of dementia depends on a thorough assessment of multiple factors affecting both the patient's background and current behavior patterns. Evidence currently suggests that a combination of heritability factors in conjunction with significant psychosocial stressors frequently may lead to dementia or related conditions. There are clear indications that one of the most important factors determining the degree of functional impairment in such conditions as dementia involves the social network of which the individual is a part. A study cited by the authors of this article noted that social network ties consistently emerged as among the most prominent indices of survival and adaptation in a list

"Whipped cream and a cherry on top. Got all that?"

The husband assured her, and a half-hour later he returned and handed her a sack. She pulled out a ham sandwich.

"I told you to write it down," she said. "I wanted mustard on it."

For a diagnosis of dementia, the DSM requires three psychological deficits: a significant lessening of intellectual abilities; memory deficits; and at least some evidence of impaired higher-order cognitive functions, such as speech and language, judgmental abilities, or abstract thinking. Damage to the brain that included socioenconomic status, smoking and alcohol consumption, patterns of physical activity, and general health practices. It would therefore appear that adequate assessment of a patient suspected of having dementia would have to take into account social, as well as neurologic, factors.

The issue of diagnosing dementia is an interesting one from a cross-cultural perspective. Currently, there are four principle sources of data in making the diagnosis: impaired adaptation, psychological test performance, general medical status, and neurologic integrity. It appears on the basis of the Cross-National project data that all of these factors are not given sufficient weight, at least in certain diagnostic settings. The employment of one measure least equivocal and unaffected by psychosocial factors—neurologic integrity—is the very measure most likely to be overlooked in diagnostic screening programs, due to the expense and time involved. As a result, persons with psychosocial indicators correlated with (but not specifically indicative of) dementia currently run a risk of having the condition diagnosed when in fact alternative diagnoses (such as affective disorder) may be equally feasible.

In helping determine the prevalence of disorders such as dementia in cross-cultural contexts, it would be clearly advantageous to employ multiple criteria such as the four mentioned here. Many complex questions are raised by this diagnostic issue: Are patterns of adaptation required for adequate functioning constant across different cultures? Is dementia more likely to be diagnosed in cultural settings where an overall higher level of adaptation is the norm? Are there specific factors (such as nutritional status, disease prevalence, and the like) that affect the manifestations of changes in brain structure associated with dementia?

Research projects like the United States–United Kingdom National Project are likely to provide answers to such questions. They will help improve our understanding of the psychological and physical processes involved in aging, and will begin to clarify the extent to which environmental and cultural forces may be brought to bear on minimizing the impact of biologically based conditions such as dementia.

Source: Gurland, B.J., and Zubin, J. (1982) The United States–United Kingdom Cross-National Project: Issues in cross-cultural psychogeriatric research. In: L.L. Adler (Ed.). *Cross cultural research at issue.* New York: Academic Press.

and nervous system almost always results in deficiencies in at least one of these areas (Reitan and Wolfson, 1986). The effects are not necessarily permanent, although the extent of structural damage at the time of detection has a bearing on eventual outcome. There are at least three conditions commonly associated with dementia in elderly persons: degenerative diseases of the nervous system, vascular disease (disruption of blood supply to the brain), and substance-induced states.

The most common degenerative conditions, Alzheimer's disease and Pick's disease, are typically first diagnosed in middle to late middle age and are often referred to collectively as the presenile dementias. Estimates of the prevalence of Alzheimer's disease range from 1.5 to 3 million, with 20 percent of persons over 80 suffering from it. Current practice is to minimize the distinction between onset ages and instead to focus on degenerative conditions of both early and later onset, which are not distinctly different processes. Whatever the age of onset, these degenerative conditions can be fatal within five or six years of onset and are accompanied by progressive, irreversible dementia.

Dementia associated with vascular disease may or may not prove irreversible, largely depending upon the severity of the disorder. In addition to more serious and debilitating vascular disorders, such as strokes, elderly people (and others with a propensity to develop vascular disease) are susceptible to slight disruptions of brain blood supply that may be accompanied by transient symptoms of dementia. Psychological tests cannot always assess these states with any precision, and by the time the patient is tested the symptoms have often dissipated. There are reported cases in which individuals, their judgmental capabilities apparently diminished by a mild vascular disruption, have made impulsive decisions, such as selling the family home below market value, only to be tested and found unimpaired.

In the accompanying case report, Sylvia's condition clearly fits the description of an organic mental disorder termed **multi-infarct dementia** in the DSM. Multi-infarct dementia is a condition in which there are periodic neurologic and psychological manifestations of impaired brain blood flow. Frequently this impairment results when blood vessels supplying particular regions of the brain either become blocked or rupture. In Sylvia's case, a combination of chronic hypertension and weakening blood vessel walls caused ruptures, or infarcts, resulting in transient cognitive disruption (Reitan and Wolfson, 1986).

Dementia associated with substance ingestion commonly occurs as a case of alcohol abuse, but may also occur as a side effect of medication taken to control other problems (Persad, 1986). Elderly people whose medical treatment is not adequately coordinated may be taking a variety of medications to control any of several problems, and unexpected side effects may include symptoms of dementia.

Treatment.   It is often assumed that the presence of central nervous system impairment rules out therapeutic intervention for dementia. In the future, partial or total brain transplants may be feasible. However, at present there is some promising data available suggesting that certain cognitive skills may be amenable to remediation. Zarit et al. (1982), for example, reported some limited success in memory training of older patients with dementia. They discovered, however, that it is often difficult to generalize the effects of training to everyday situations. Piracetam and pentoxifylline have been found to be useful in lessening the effects of multi-infarct dementia. Drugs such as tetrahydroaminoacrine (THA), a drug discovered in 1909 but only recently applied to persons with Alzheimer's disease, is effective in reversing the accompanying memory problems but does not interrupt the course of the disease itself.

In our own experience, working effectively with elderly persons in rehabilitation settings depends on the following: (1) setting clear and reasonable goals; (2) working to restore acquired skills rather than teaching new ones (this process may involve training in the use of alternative strategies to help compensate for acquired limitations); and (3) gradually incorporating staff and, most desirably, family members into the treatment program.

Terminal Drop

Terminal drop is a sudden decline in cognitive functions that is predictive of impending death. An early study by Kleemeier (1961) noted an association between rapidly declining performance on IQ tests and imminent death. Subsequent investigations have tended to support these early findings, although the relationship is far from perfect. Several explanations of these findings are possible (Newman and Newman, 1987). It may be that for many elderly individuals death is preceded by a generalized period of decline affecting many areas, including cognitive skills. Or a decline in cognitive test performance may reflect comparatively discrete deterioration of central nervous system structures on which test performance is highly dependent. It is also known that some aging individuals "disengage" themselves from their environment. The apathy and disinterest they display in any interpersonal situations includes test sessions, where rapport between subject and examiner and motivation to perform are vital. In any case, the establishment of a predictive relationship between death and cognitive skills is clearly important.

While many older people are besieged by disorders, most survive them to lead an enjoyable old age. Rather than showing the apathy noted in the phenomenon of terminal drop, most show the healthier attitude so vividly described by the poet Dylan Thomas:

> *Do not go gentle into that good night*
> *Old age should burn and rave at close of day.*
> *Rage, rage against the dying of the light.*

CHAPTER REVIEW

1. Adolescence has traditionally been viewed as a period of heightened conflict, when the potential for psychological maladjustment is high. An important aspect of cognitive development during adolescence is heightened self-awareness and, frequently, self-consciousness.

2. Developing a sense of personal identity has been seen by many as one of the chief developmental tasks of adolescence. This development involves achieving a sense of personal worth and integrity that is independent of one's social network.

3. Adolescence and early adulthood are high-risk periods for suicide, particularly among males. The typical pattern of adolescent suicide is a gradual reduction of coping abilities until the individual reaches a point of extreme hopelessness.

4. Drug and substance abuse are both commonly thought of as significant adolescent problems. Nonetheless, cultural values that promote the use of chemical agents for a wide range of purposes contribute to a climate of relative permissiveness regarding drug use.

5. Anorexia nervosa is a condition in which an individual voluntarily refuses food, leading to extreme weight loss. Bulimia is a chronic pattern of binge eating, referred to as the gorge-purge syndrome. More common in females than in males, both have been viewed as extreme reactions to fears of becoming obese.

6. Juvenile delinquency describes a legal status and is probably the most common pattern of deviance in adolescence. As with substance abuse, delinquency may stem in part from relatively permissive social attitudes toward violence and aggression. In both cases, adolescents are exposed to adult role models, both directly and via various media, that exert powerful modeling influences.

7. Several issues and problems, in particular performance anxiety, test anxiety, and certain suicide patterns, often affect college students.

8. Researchers have only recently given adulthood and advanced age attention as distinct developmental periods.

9. Most physical powers slowly decline throughout adulthood. Although some facets of intelligence remain stable or even increase slightly, those depending on visual-motor abilities and the ability to process new information tend to decrease.

10. The concept of a midlife transition remains largely unvalidated by specific research findings. For many adults, however, a change of lifestyle and attitude is as radical as those that occur during adolescence.

11. General predictors of positive psychological health in the latter part of adulthood are (a) access to a friend who can function as a confidant, (b) access to liked siblings, (c) a satisfying marriage, (d) competency in a meaningful occupation, (e) a happy childhood, and (f) positive achievements by one's children.

12. Although marriages can be positive relationships, close to half of all first marriages are predicted to end in divorce. Marital therapy attempts to clarify the distorted communications and to eliminate nonproductive patterns in the relationship.

13. The experience of older persons may include a relatively large number of stresses within a short period of time. These can severely tax the coping skills of older persons.

14. Attitudes toward the treatment of psychological problems appear to differ for older and younger persons. Problems in advanced age are often viewed as inevitable and irreversible; as a result, there is less motivation to pursue vigorous treatment with older persons.

15. A common myth about older persons is that their sex drive diminishes radically. Older persons may even be thought of as strange or abnormal when they show an interest in sex. There is ample evidence that the sex drive can remain active and compelling throughout life.

16. Mental abilities are often assumed to diminish in advanced age. There appears to be some slowing of certain mental processes in many older persons, but this slowdown does not appear to significantly affect overall levels of intellectual function. For example, people whose mental abilities were above average in their youth tend to retain these capabilities throughout life.

TERMS TO REMEMBER

adolescence
identity crisis
identity disorder
anorexia nervosa
bulimia
juvenile delinquency
conduct disorders
frustration-aggression hypothesis
public performance anxiety
test anxiety
midlife transition
family therapy

passive-aggressive personality
narcissistic personality
histrionic personality
marital therapy
"fair fight" rules
spouse abuse
child abuse
hypochondriasis
dementia
senility
multi-infarct dementia
terminal drop

FOR MORE INFORMATION

Brownell, K., and Foreyt, J. (Eds.). (1986) *Handbook of eating disorders*. New York: Basic Books. A thorough overview of all the eating disorders, with a focus on anorexia nervosa and bulimia

Butler, R.M. (1975) *Why Survive? Being old in America*. New York: Harper and Row. This Pulitzer-Prize–winning book brings many of the issues confronted by older persons into sharp, and sometimes painful, focus

Erikson, E. (1968) *Identity youth and crisis*. New York: W.W. Norton. Erikson's classic text about the transition from childhood into adulthood includes extensive discussion of his well-known term "identity crisis."

Geismar, L., and Wood, K. (1986) *Family and delinquency*. New York: Human Sciences Press. This book thoroughly examines delinquency, and relates it to family issues

Giovacchini, P. (1986) *Developmental disorders: The transitional space in mental breakdown and creative integration*. Northvale, N.J.: Jason Aronson. Giovacchini discusses how the process of change and development as we grow from birth to old age can result in either mental disorder or positive growth

Keniston, K. (1965) *The uncommitted: Alienated youth in American society*. New York: Dell. Probes deeply into the disenchantment and alienation that affect many adolescents and young adults

Van Hasselt, V., and Hersen, M. (1987) *Handbook of adolescent psychology*. Elmsford, N.Y.: Pergamon. Provides a good overview of the problems that are encountered in adolescence

Viorst, J. (1986) *Necessary losses*. With wit, wisdom, and compassion, she analyzes the stages of our lives, including the painful loss of closeness to our mothers, the complexities of marriage, and even the varieties of dying

Yogman, M., and Brazelton, T. (1987) *In support of families*. Cambridge, Mass.: Harvard University Press. In addition to a good overview of problems faced by most families, this book examines the implications of the family for public policy

Legal and Ethical Issues

You couldn't even prove the White House staff sane beyond a reasonable doubt.
Edwin Meese
Attorney General and counselor to Ronald Reagan

Al Pacino plays a feisty trial attorney who fights flaws in the criminal justice system in . . . *And Justice for All.* (Museum of Modern Art/Film Stills Archive; © 1979 Columbia Pictures Industries Inc.)

MENTAL HEALTH LAW
  Criminal versus Civil Cases
CRIMINAL LAW ISSUES
  Criminal Responsibility
  Competency to Stand Trial
  The Insanity Defense
  Competency to Be Executed
CIVIL LAW ISSUES
  Competency to Make a Will
  Guardianship
  Civil Commitment
  The Prediction of Dangerousness
PATIENTS' RIGHTS
  The Right to Treatment and the Right to
    Refuse It

The Right to Privacy as It Relates to
  Homosexuality
The Right to a Humane Environment
OTHER LEGAL AND ETHICAL ISSUES
  Confidentiality and Privileged
    Communication
  Reporting Child Abuse
  Defining the Client
  Malpractice and the Mental Health
    Professional
  The Detection of Deception
**VALUES, DILEMMAS, AND
ABNORMAL BEHAVIOR**

17

Legal and Ethical Issues

Many of the disorders and cases that have been described throughout this book have a related legal or ethical component, in addition to the psychological issues. Even though many of these legal and ethical issues have been with us for a long time, they are still controversial. As we see in the case of Z.L., a central reason for the controversial nature of these issues is that they often require a decision about balancing the rights or the good of the individual against the rights or good of a group of others, for example, the victims or potential victims, or even against the good of society as a whole.

● The Case of Z.L.

Z.L. has been admitted to mental hospitals twice over the past 10 years, once on a voluntary basis and once on an involuntary basis. She has a deep distrust of people, which reaches paranoid proportions when she is under a high level of stress. Although she has apparently never harmed herself or others, she is viewed as having potential for hostile, aggressive acting-out behavior under extreme conditions.

Over the course of several weeks her therapist at a local mental health center recently noted a rapid deterioration in her functioning, as evidenced by faster and more hurried speech, a lack of clarity in the logical relationships in her thoughts, a sharp increase in paranoid thinking, and extreme emotional variability. At this time, Z.L. refuses to enter a mental hospital voluntarily because of concerns about the loss of personal freedom and control over her life and about the various treatments to which she may be subjected. Although these concerns are based in reality, her current paranoid state precludes Z.L.'s being able to examine the pertinent issues in a realistic, adaptive manner. Taking these issues under consideration as well as the possible risks to both Z.L. and others, should Z.L.'s therapist try to have her involuntarily committed to the hospital? If she were committed, would it be in violation of her constitutional rights? Would such rights be violated if she were forced to take certain treatments such as medication or electroconvulsive treatment (ECT)? If she were not committed and then harmed another person, would she likely be found not guilty by reason of insanity? Or could her therapist be held responsible for the harm Z.L. inflicted, if any?

EXHIBIT

The Various Duties of the Forensic Psychologist or Psychiatrist as Fact-Finder in the Legal Arena

Criminal defendant	_____	Competent to stand trial?
Criminal defendant	_____	Criminally responsible, or "insane"?
Criminal defendant	_____	Competent to be executed?
Witness to event	_____	Competent enough in perception and information processing
Child witness	_____	Mature enough to testify?
Criminal victim	_____	Credible, or psychotic fantasy?
Criminal victim	_____	Degree of psychological damage
Offender	_____	Dangerous to release?
Juvenile offender	_____	Emotionally and cognitively mature enough to stand trial as an adult? Dangerous to be released?
Parole candidate	_____	Rehabilitated? Dangerous to release?
Mental patient	_____	Dangerous to community? To self?
Parent	_____	Responsible enough to have custody of child?
Testator	_____	Competent to make a valid will?
Contracting party	_____	Competent to make binding contract?

Adapted from Curran, W., and Pollack, S. (1986) Mental health and justice. In: W. Curran, A.L. McGarry, and S. Shah (Eds.). *Forensic psychiatry and psychology.* Philadelphia: F.A. Davis.

Once a patient with a mental disorder is involuntarily confined to a hospital, some of his constitutional rights are suspended in order to protect himself and society.   (Michael O'Brien/Archive Pictures)

These and other legal and ethical issues are the topic of this chapter. Many of the related legal issues are faced every day by psychologically normal individuals. However, as with Z.L., the issues are more often underscored by the presence of abnormal emotion or behavior, as can be seen from the following review of some of the disorders we have seen in past chapters and the legal issues each highlights.

The first issue in this chapter, competence (to stand trial or to handle one's life affairs), is relevant to many of the disorders we have covered in this book, such as schizophrenia or severe depression. However, since competence so often involves the question of intellectual ability, the issue is almost always raised with persons encountering the legal system who have mental retardation or central nervous system impairment.

The next topics, criminal responsibility and insanity and competency to be executed, naturally involve those psychotic disorders in which there is a potential loss of reality contact, that is, schizophrenia, the paranoid disorders, and the bipolar disorder and severe depression. But the insanity defense has also been raised where there is a posttraumatic stress disorder, a severe obsessive-compulsive neurosis, alcoholism, psychopathy, and even some of the impulse patterns such as pathological gambling, kleptomania, and pyromania. However, other than with the presence of the psychotic disorders, courts have not given much credence to such claims, though the presence of any of these disorders is sometimes effective as a mitigating factor in requesting a lesser sentence.

At this point we move from discussing primarily criminal cases to civil cases (see the upcoming discussion on the differences between these two areas). The first topic in the civil area is also an issue of competency, the competency to make a will. The next topic, civil commitment, is concerned with confining someone who is "a danger to self or others." The "danger to self" component naturally involves suicide potential, as well as those people who cannot take care of themselves because of a psychotic disorder, retardation, central nervous system impairment, or aging. The concept of dangerousness to others commonly involves a paranoid component, as well as some of the sexual disorders and the personality and impulse disorders.

Individuals with any of the above disorders who are confined to a hospital or prison can be the focus of a right to treatment or even a right to refuse treatment. Both institutionalized and noninstitutionalized clients are concerned with the confidentiality of the material they disclose. The issue of defining the client becomes particularly relevant when a mental health professional is dealing with a person referred by the courts or other government agencies or when a parent brings a child for treatment.

Many of the diagnoses in this book could be related to a decision as to whether or not the victim is truly injured or is malingering in a personal injury case (Grote et al., 1986) and issues such as assessing chronic pain, level of intellectual ability, and degree of brain damage, are obviously important. In all of these issues, detecting the level of truth in a client's report becomes a critical problem.

MENTAL HEALTH LAW

Both criminal and civil law in this country are rooted in the concept that an individual's behavior is a matter of choice and that for the most part people freely choose their actions. However, society and the legal profession generally agree that the mentally abnormal are less free when making choices than are normal individuals (Beatty, 1987; Bartol, 1983). Because of insufficient contact with reality, people with mental disorders are not held legally responsible for criminal acts. Furthermore, when a person with a mental disorder is placed in a hospital involuntarily in order to protect the individual or to protect society, some of that person's constitutional rights are suspended. How are these legal issues, raised by problems of mental health, decided?

In order to administer justice there must be special legal rules for disordered people, and these special rules make up the branch of law known as mental health law. The field of **forensic psychology**, or forensic psychiatry, concerns itself with those issues or cases in which there is both a significant psychological and legal component.

Mental health law encompasses a wide variety of statutes, both federal and state, concerned with degree of free choice and degree of responsibility. These can be broken down into overall areas such as issues of competence, criminal responsibility, civil commitment, mental patients' rights, and so forth, as we will do in this chapter. Mental health law is changing at a rapid pace. In fact, approximately three fourths of the states have revised their mental health laws in the past decade (Smith and Meyer, 1987). These changes indicate considerable controversy over legal and ethical issues.

Criminal versus Civil Cases

Criminal law deals with violations against the laws of a society, (murder, burglary, and so on). **Civil laws** are designed to resolve nonviolently and fairly disputes between persons or parties (a child custody hearing), or to decide how far the state or government can go in exerting its interests against private parties or individuals (committing someone to a mental institution because they are dangerous to others). For example, personal injury cases, as well as suits involving damages for breaking confidentiality or violating rights, are also in the domain of civil law, that is, where one citizen or group is requesting a form of satisfaction from another. The **standard of proof** is the degree of evidence required to come to a legal decision, and it depends upon the type of case (Landis and Meyer, 1988). The standard of proof in most civil law is "a preponderance of the evidence," in other words, whoever produces more than 50 percent of the evidence should win. In criminal law, some arm of the government, acting for all citizens, takes action against an alleged lawbreaker, and society has decided that the standard of proof should be more stringent in such cases. Thus, the government must prove its case "beyond a reasonable doubt." It is not exactly clear if that standard can be tied to any specific percentage in either the minds of jurors or judges (Kagehiro and Stanton, 1985). Judges, including the Supreme Court, consistently refuse to define the standard more specifically. Somewhere in between these two standards of proof is a third one, that of "clear and convincing evidence," the standard of proof required in a civil case to commit a person to a mental institution for confinement and treatment. The **burden of proof** defines who has the primary responsibility to prove a specific point in a case. For example, the phrase in criminal law "innocent until proven guilty" is a way of saying the prosecutor, rather than the defendant, has the burden of proof.

Sometimes the lines between civil and criminal law become blurred, as is evident in the 1986 Supreme Court case of *Allen* v. *Illinois*. Even though Allen was never criminally convicted of a crime, he was incarcerated under the Illinois Sexually Dangerous Persons Act (sex psychopath law). He claimed a violation of his right to avoid self-incrimination because the court had ordered him to submit to two psychiatric examinations and these exams were the basis for determining him to be a sexually dangerous person. The Court, with Justice Rehnquist writing the majority opinion, noted that the right to avoid self-incrimination does not apply to civil cases. He ruled, based on the facts that the person would be released when no longer dangerous and that the purpose of the law here was to provide treatment rather than punishment, that this was, in fact, a civil case. However, the Illinois sex psychopath law requires proof of a criminal sexual assault, provides a jury trial with many of the rights of a criminal trial, establishes a "beyond a reasonable doubt" standard of proof (the standard used in criminal trials), and permits the person to be incarcerated in a maximum-security prison.

The various minority opinions of those judges who dissented from the majority opinion (the case was decided 5-4) emphasized the great loss of liberty, the stigma, and the criminal trial–like aspects of the process. The dissent noted that the state might now be able to create "an entire corps of 'dangerous person' statutes to shadow its criminal code." By claiming commission of criminal offenses, findings of mental disorders and predictions of "criminal propensities," and a goal of "treatment" (rehabilitation), the state could confine people in maximum-security institutions (prisons) for indeterminate periods as *civil* offenders.

CRIMINAL LAW ISSUES

Criminal Responsibility

In order for a person to be found guilty of an alleged crime there must be proof of criminal responsibility. A person can be held criminally responsible only if it can be shown that the accused had criminal intent, or **mens rea**, a state of mind *during* the commission or omission of an act designated as criminal. It is this legal concept of "mens rea" (translated as "guilty mind") that is brought into question when a person thought to be mentally disturbed is accused of a crime. The legal question that must be answered is, "What was the defendant's state of mind at the time of the alleged crime?" If it can be shown that the defendant was "insane" at the time of the crime, the defendant will not be held criminally responsible for the act. However, the first question to be answered is whether or not the defendant is competent to stand trial. Both questions about state of mind must be answered, and judges and lawyers typically call on psychologists and psychiatrists for assistance with such issues. We shall first look at the issues of competence to stand trial and then at the issue of criminal responsibility and the insanity defense. Then we will look at the issue of competency in civil laws, such as competency to make a will.

Legal Aspects and Definitions of Violent Crime in the United States

I. Murder—A killing which is "calculated, in cold blood" or with "malice aforethought" (or a guilty mind).

    A. First degree—includes:
        (1) an intent to effect death with "malice aforethought"
        (2) deliberate act
        (3) premeditated act

    B. Second degree—includes:

        (1) an intent to effect death, "malice aforethought"
        (2) without deliberation or premeditation. In essence, most states define second degree murder as any murder which is not a first-degree murder

II. Felony Murder Doctrine—If in the act of committing a felony the death of one of the victims is brought about, this is murder and it is not necessary to demonstrate intent, deliberation, or premeditation.

III. Manslaughter—Homicide that lacks malice aforethought:

    A. Voluntary (nonnegligent)—Intentional killing without "malice aforethought"; often described as homicide "in hot blood" and often takes place due to provocation.

    B. Involuntary (negligent)—Unintentional killing without "malice aforethought," for example, vehicular homicides.

IV. Assault—Involves offering to give bodily harm to a person or placing him or her in fear of such harm. Assault is an attempted, but uncompleted, battery.

V. Battery (aggravated assault)—"An offensive, uncontested to, unprivileged and unjustified offensive bodily contact." Battery includes mens rea, where the contact was intentional or resulted from wanton misconduct and in which bodily harm takes place.

VI. Statutory Rape—Sexual relations with a victim under the age of consent.

VII. Forcible Rape—Forcible and unlawful sexual relations with a person against her or his will. Rape is defined in the traditional common law as "carnal knowledge of a female forcibly and against her will."

Competency to Stand Trial

The first question that must be answered in a criminal case is whether or not the defendant is competent to stand trial; the legal question here becomes "What is the defendant's state of mind at the time of the trial?" Thus, a competency evaluation is necessary and must be conducted before criminal responsibility can be determined through a trial. In most states, the requirements for **competency to stand trial** are that defendants (1) must be able to understand the nature of the proceedings against them and (2) must be able to assist counsel in their own defense before and during the trial. Interview techniques and psychological tests are usually employed by psychologists, at the request of the attorneys in the case or the court itself, to evaluate competency (Grisso, 1986).

Defendants found incompetent to stand trial are routinely denied bail and are held in jail to await a change in their mental condition so that they will become competent to stand trial. They are cut off from family, friends, and other social supports, which in turn may further disrupt their emotional condition, delaying further their competence to stand trial. Until recently, incompetence to stand trial meant confinement in a mental institution for years, perhaps even a lifetime. In 1972, however, the U.S. Supreme Court

The question of competency to stand trial became an issue in the case of John W. Hinckley, Jr., who attempted to assassinate President Reagan in 1981. (AP/Wide World Photos)

ruled that the length of pretrial confinement must be limited to the reasonable period of time necessary to determine whether the defendant is likely to become competent to stand trial in the foreseeable future (*Jackson* v. *Indiana*, 1972). If unlikely to become competent, the defendant must be released or the state must institute civil commitment proceedings.

Defense attorneys are accused (sometimes accurately) of raising the competency issue (as well as the insanity defense) whenever the prosecution has a strong case against their client. Prosecutors who have weak cases may raise the competency issue in order to delay the trial in the hope that defense witnesses may die or leave the area, or that in some other way they may be able to strengthen their case. For example, in 1987 the Supreme Court held in *Buchanan* v. *Kentucky* that a psychological examination used in the competency trial could later be used in the criminal trial.

One further issue concerning competency demands attention. Even some psychotic people may at times be lucid enough to meet the competency requirements, especially when charged with lesser offenses. With the advent of antipsychotic drugs, this issue became even more complex. If the drugs do allow a return of lucidity, is it fair for the defendant to stand trial when under the influence of such drugs? Recall that such drugs often make people groggy and passive, not the best of states under which to stand trial. Furthermore, the person's genuinely abnormal behavior probably substantiates an insanity plea in the jurors' minds, and antipsychotic drugs may well eliminate such behavior. In any case, if the person is judged competent to stand trial, the issue of insanity may be raised.

The Insanity Defense

Insanity is the legal term that refers to a condition that excuses persons from criminal responsibility for the alleged act, thereby protecting them from the penalties imposed on those who are found guilty of wrongdoing. Though an insanity defense may be raised in any criminal trial, it is more often raised in "capital" or potential death-penalty cases (see the Exhibit, "Pro and Con Death Penalty Arguments"). However, contrary to what many believe, insanity pleas are rare compared with the total number of criminal cases tried (Caplan, 1984). In the first place, in order to plead insanity the defendant, in effect, admits to having committed the crime. If he or she is then found not to be insane, prison confinement or, in some cases, the death penalty will very probably be ordered. Even if found not guilty by reason of insanity, the defendant may be civilly committed for "treatment," a confinement that might last longer than a prison term. For these reasons, defense attorneys rarely use the insanity defense. Nonetheless, there must be standards or tests by which insanity can be determined, and there are four important historical developments or court rulings that bear on this issue.

The Case of John Hinckley, Jr.

On March 30, 1981, shortly after 2:30 P.M., John Hinckley attempted to assassinate President Ronald Reagan as the president came out of the Washington Hilton hotel. He was able to fire all six Devastator (exploding) bullets from his .22 caliber revolver before he was subdued. Four men, including President Reagan, were hit, but all survived. Subsequent testimony in Mr. Hinckley's seven-week trial indicated that he carried out the attack to impress and therefore capture the love of movie star Jodie Foster, who was then a student at Yale University.

Mr. Hinckley was born in Oklahoma in 1955, and experienced an apparently normal childhood and adolescence. After graduation from high school in 1973, he started college work at Texas Tech in Lubbock. But he quickly had problems. He started to daydream of success in areas of such as music or politics, and in 1976 he went to Hollywood hoping to sell his music there. He failed completely, and spent a lot of his time daydreaming and watching movies. His favorite was "Taxi Driver," which he saw 15 times. Taxi Driver focused on an assassination plan related to an unrequited love, and co-starred Jodie Foster. He moved back to Lubbock in 1977, and his functioning began to decline even more (Caplan, 1984). He became involved with the American Nazi movement, bought his first firearm, and began to publish the "American Front Newsletter," which virtually no one subscribed to. Yet he fabricated membership lists from 37 states and appointed himself national director.

By 1980, he had begun experiencing panic attacks, had gained 60 pounds, had purchased other guns, and began attempting to reach Jodie Foster by phone at Yale. He did talk to her on September 20, 1980, but her obviously noncommittal response resulted in this entry in his diary: "My mind was at the breaking point. A relationship I had dreamed about went absolutely nowhere. My disillusionment with everything was complete" (Caplan, 1984, p. 38). Though he began seeing psychiatrist John Hooper in October of 1980, and continued into February of 1981, he did not really disclose any of his more bizarre thoughts. He also took numerous plane flights, apparently stalking both Presidents Carter and Reagan. On March 29, 1981, he arrived by bus in Washington, coming from Los Angeles. After writing a final love letter to Miss Foster, he went to the Washington Hilton on March 30 to begin his fateful vigil.

Since there was little disagreement on the facts of the case, the seven-week trial focused on Mr. Hinckley's psychological condition, with overall costs probably exceeding $2,000,000. Interestingly, the defense had originally offered to plea bargain a guilty plea if the sentences would have been allowed to run concurrently rather than consecutively, thus allowing Mr. Hinckley to be up for parole in 15 years. Under various political pressures, the prosecution declined. During the trial, mental health experts differed sharply on whether or not he was insane at the time of the crime, but after almost three days of deliberation, the jury found him not guilty by reason of insanity on all 13 counts. He was automatically committed to St. Elizabeth's Hospital in Washington, D.C., to stay there until he is judged to no longer be dangerous as a result of his mental illness.

In the weeks following his trial, 26 different bills were submitted to modify the federal insanity statute. Two major changes ultimately resulted. First, the volitional (will or emotion) component was removed, leaving the cognitive component (deficit in understanding as a result of mental disorder) as the only insanity plea available in a federal (not state) court. Second, the burden of proof, that is, whose responsibility it is to prove sanity, shifted from the prosecution to the defense. Numerous states have since followed this example of the federal courts.

Legal definitions of insanity. The first important ruling was handed down in 1834 by an Ohio court. The so-called "irresistible impulse" standard held that a person should be acquitted if he or she could not "resist" committing the criminal act. The problem, obviously, is that juries must distinguish between resistible and irresistible impulses. Pathological gamblers, kleptomaniacs, pyromaniacs, psychopaths, alcoholics, and obsessive-compulsives could logically employ this defense, but juries have seldom been convinced by such arguments (Caplan, 1984).

The second important decision is the M'Naghten rule, which was handed down in 1843 by a British court. The defendant, Daniel M'Naghten, claimed that the "voice of God" had instructed him to kill Sir Robert Peel, the English prime minister. In his attempt to do so, M'Naghten had mistakenly killed Peel's secretary. M'Naghten was found not guilty under a vaguely worded insanity defense. Because of the political nature of the crime, The English House of Lords was enraged about M'Naghten's acquittal (a reaction not unlike that of the U.S. Congress and the general population when John Hinckley was acquitted by reason of insanity of attempting to assassinate Ronald Reagan.) Indeed, Queen Victoria, who had her political differences with her Prime Minister, but who was also upset with the M'Naghten verdict, made both points simultaneously in a comment to the effect that anyone attempting to assassinate this particular prime minister should be presumed to be sane. In any case, a convocation of top judges was brought together to come up with an acceptable definition of insanity, and they determined that:

> *. . . to establish a defense of insanity, it must be clearly proved that, at the time of the committing of the act, the party accused was laboring under such a defect of reason, from disease of the mind, as not to know the nature and quality of the act he was doing; or if he did know it, that he did not know he was doing what was wrong (Caplan, 1984).*

This "right-wrong" concept has been criticized by numerous experts for singling out cognition (i.e., not *knowing* the nature of the act or not *knowing* it was wrong) when, in the opinion of these experts, cognitive activity cannot be separated from emotion or any other mental activity (Shapiro, 1986; Caplan, 1984). Nonetheless, many states in the U.S. do apply this as the sole test, and most other states use it as one standard in determining insanity.

Probably in response to the restrictiveness of M'Naghten, the third rule was made in 1954 in the case of *Durham* v. *United States*. The Durham rule states that "an accused is not criminally responsible if his unlawful act was the product of a mental disease or mental defect." However, the term mental illness is so vague and broad that it can include the mental condition of most offenders, affording great (some would say too much) liberty to the examiner. Also, it is very difficult to view an offense as a "product" of an alleged condition. As a result, the Durham rule has been discarded even by those states that originally adopted it.

More recently, the American Law Institute (ALI) formulated and adopted its own guidelines for the insanity defense in its Model Penal Code of 1962:

1. *A person is not responsible for criminal conduct if at the time of such conduct as a result of mental disease or defect he lacks substantial capacity either to appreciate the criminality (wrongfulness) of his conduct or to conform his conduct to the requirements of law.*

2. *As used in the article, the terms "mental disease or defect" do not include an abnormality manifested only by repeated criminal or otherwise antisocial conduct (Section 4.01).*

The ALI test was seen by most experts as a significant improvement because the phrases "substantial capacity," "appreciate the criminality of conduct," and "conform conduct to the law" allow the jurors themselves, as opposed to the expert witnesses, to decide whether or not the defendant should be held responsible for misconduct, and because it excludes psychopaths from the insanity defense (Doren, 1987). However, others believe that the ALI rule does not vary significantly from M'Naghten and that each rule now available lacks concise definitions of terms that can be clearly related to observable behavior (Bartol, 1983).

The public outcry over the acquittal by reason of insanity of John Hinckley eventually led to the passage by Congress in 1984 of the Insanity Defense Reform Act (Shapiro, 1986) (see the accompanying Case of John Hinckley). Under the ALI rule, there was essentially a two-part test: the inability to appreciate the criminality (or wrongfulness) (and it could matter in the jury's decision which is emphasized or understood of one's behavior), and the inability to conform one's behavior to the requirements of law. Under the new congressional standard (which is the law in federal trials, and commonly serves as a model for future changes in state laws that govern state trials), the "inability to conform one's behavior" component has been dropped, bringing us back very close to the "knowing right from wrong" M'Naghten test. Other important features of the 1984 act are (1) expert witnesses may present evidence and opinions only on the evidence, and are not allowed to render an opinion on the "ultimate issue" of whether or not the defendant is insane; (2) unlike prior standards, there is a provision for *automatic* civil commitment if the person is acquitted of legal guilt by reason of insanity; (3) the defense now has the burden of proving insanity, whereas the prosecution traditionally has had the burden of proving the person was not insane; and (4) the standard of proof required for establishing insanity has been raised from a "preponderance of evidence" to "clear and convincing evidence" (Shapiro, 1986).

In some states, a defendant may be found to be "guilty but mentally ill." If found guilty but mentally ill, the person usually receives a set sentence. He or she then receives treatment until deemed as not needing treatment, whereupon they go to prison to serve the remainder of the sentence. Finally, a few states have recently adopted a bifurcated rule whereby a defendant is tried in two phases. In the first phase, the defendant is simply presumed to be sane, and guilt or innocence is determined. If found guilty, the defendant then has the option of pleading insanity, and the second phase of the trial determines whether or not the plea is valid. Thus, the bifurcated rule allows defendants to be found guilty but also insane (Smith and Meyer, 1987).

Evaluation of the insanity defense. Both practical and moral problems are raised by the insanity defense. It was mentioned earlier that distinguishing between resistible and irresistible impulses poses a difficult problem for a jury. But this is no more or less difficult than determining the sanity or insanity of a defendant or of determining whether or not a defendant did, in fact, lack "substantial capacity" to appreciate or conform to the law. In addition to being highly subjective, these judgments must, in the case of the insanity defense, be made about crimes that may have occurred months or years before the trial. Professionals have almost as much difficulty with retrospective diagnoses as do juries (Bersoff, 1986), and the experts are on occasion diametrically opposed in their opinions. However, improvement in the professional's contribution has come about because of (1) better training and credentials, (for example, the emphasis on using psychologists and psychiatrists who are board certified in the forensic area), and (2) the use of better validated scales for assessing insanity (Rogers, 1986).

A further criticism of the insanity defense comes from the radical psychiatrist Thomas Szasz (1960; 1986), who contends that mental illness is a myth

---

Post Reagan Assassination Attempt Insanity Defense Changes

Here are the states that made insanity defense reforms after John Hinckley's assassination attempt on President Reagan:

Alaska: Added guilty-but-mentally-ill option.

Arizona: Changed burden, standard of proof, commitment rules.

Arkansas: Changed release, commitment procedures.

California: Changed test of insanity.

Colorado: Changed insanity test, burden of proof, release rules.

Connecticut: Changed test, proof burden, commitment rules.

Delaware: Added guilty-but-mentally-ill option.

Florida: Changed release, commitment procedures.

Georgia: Added guilty-but-mentally-ill; changed release rules.

Hawaii: Changed burden of proof, release, commitment rules.

Idaho: Changed insanity test, release, commitment rules.

Illinois: Changed burden, standard of proof, release rules.

Indiana: Changed insanity test, release, commitment rules.

Iowa: Changed burden, standard of proof, release rules.

Kentucky: Added guilty-but-mentally-ill option.

Maryland: Changed burden, standard of proof, trial, release rules.

Minnesota: Changed burden of proof, release, commitment rules.

Missouri: Changed release and commitment procedures.

Montana: Changed insanity test pre-Hinckley.

---

since all behavior is purposeful and deliberate. Given this premise, people who commit hostile or dangerous acts do so because they mean to do so, and Szasz proposes that labeling such a person as insane denies any true meaning or value to his or her behavior. Along with a few others, such as Hardisty (1973), Szasz further believes that psychology and psychiatry use the term "mental illness," at least in part, to maintain power in influencing legal determinations of mental states. Szasz also asserts that being acquitted by reason of insanity has more dire consequences than being convicted of a crime. Persons convicted of crimes are usually incarcerated for specific periods of time, after which their freedom is restored. People who have successfully pleaded an insanity defense are often given indeterminate civil commitments, though in most states such commitment is not automatic but requires a separate commitment process. Their eventual freedom from a mental hospital thus depends

Nebraska: Changed burden, standard of proof.

New Hampshire: Changed release, commitment procedures.

New Mexico: Created guilty-but-mentally-ill option.

New York: Changed burden, standard of proof, release rules.

North Carolina: Changed release and commitment procedures.

North Dakota: Changed test, burden, standard of proof, trial, release, commitment rules.

Oklahoma: Changed trial, release, commitment rules.

Oregon: Changed insanity test.

Pennsylvania: Added guilty-but-mentally-ill option.

South Carolina: Added guilty-but-mentally-ill option.

South Dakota: Changed burden of proof, release, commitment procedures; created guilty-but-mentally-ill option.

Tennessee: Changed release and commitment procedures.

Texas: Changed insanity test, release, commitment procedures.

Utah: Changed burden, standard of proof, release, commitment procedures; created guilty-but-mentally-ill option.

Vermont: Changed burden, standard of proof.

Washington: Changed release and commitment procedures.

Wyoming: Changed burden and standard of proof.

Source: USA Today, April 16, 1987. Reprinted with permission.

on a staff decision that they are no longer dangerous. Such a decision could be a long time in coming. However, in actual practice, most are released before the sentence for the alleged crimes would have run its course.

Competency to Be Executed

In a death penalty case, even though the person may have been found competent to stand trial, and then in the subsequent trial found to be both sane and guilty of the offense, he or she may even later be found so confused or disturbed as to be "incompetent to be executed." There is a long history of not executing the incompetent. Reasons for this include that (1) they cannot participate effectively in any last minute appeals, (2) it is inhumane and cruel, (3) it provides no deterrence to others, (4) it does not have retributive value,

EXHIBIT

Pro and Con Death Penalty Arguments

As noted in the text, the insanity defense probably receives the most visibility in capital, or death penalty, cases. This is probably because the public often perceives the insanity defense as helping a vicious criminal to escape his or her just deserts. The following are some of the typical pro and con arguments relevant to the death penalty.

Arguments against capital punishment include:

- Executing someone is an irreversible step; thus, the rare execution of an innocent person cannot be undone.

- Even though there may be good reasons to support an execution, the state functions as a killer, and, in turn, society can become dehumanized.

- The death penalty has not been proven to deter others from similar crimes.

- Because of long delays and appeals, the processing of cases involving the death penalty is more costly than life imprisonment, and a mandated death penalty sentence may raise difficulties in finding juries willing to find defendants guilty.

- The enactment of capital punishment has always been discriminatory. In the U.S., the majority of those executed have been black.

Arguments in favor of the death penalty include:

- Employing the death penalty where appropriate discourages private revenge and vigilantism.

- The death penalty is sanctioned in the Bible as well as by historical tradition as a culturally approved manner of dealing with heinous offenders.

- It is an effective deterrent in preventing cold-blooded murder.

- It could easily be made more economical than the permanent, lifelong warehousing of the most dangerous criminals.

- It clearly deters the person who is executed from doing any more damage to individuals or society.

- As regards retribution, it is reasonable to say that those who kill innocent persons in cold blood deserve similar punishment.

and (5) it prevents the condemned from making a final religious peace. In the 1986 case of *Ford* v. *Wainwright*, the Supreme Court held that the cruel and unusual punishment provision of the Eighth Amendment prohibits the state from executing a prisoner who is incompetent. The Court split on the various issues in the case, but, in effect, this was a 5–4 decision, with Justice Marshall writing the opinion. A practical problem may be that because competency can change from time to time, the competency of a prisoner may be raised repeatedly, right up to the moment of execution. As one forensic psychologist put it, not altogether in jest, this would at least help provide steady employment for forensic psychologists.

CIVIL LAW ISSUES

Competency to Make a Will

Another competency decision, in this case made in a civil trial, is whether the deceased person was competent to have made a valid will, referred to in the law as "testamentary capacity." **Competency to make a will** may be voided either because of the inability to know enough about the issues or to form the intention to dispose of property, or the existence of "insane delusions" (it's a bit of a challenge to define a sane delusion). As a result, senility and psychosis are common reasons why persons may not have been competent when they made out their wills. Yet neither eccentricities, mistaken beliefs, old age, nor odd or unreasonable provisions in the will establish incompetence (Grisso, 1986).

Psychologists are occasionally called upon either to challenge or support the validity of a will by making a "psychological autopsy." A **psychological autopsy** is simply an examination and interpretation of all available, relevant information about the person's mental condition at time the will was made. This could include health and work records; letters, diaries, and business papers; and interviews with people who knew the individual. The difficulty is, of course, in making a decision about someone whom the psychologist very possibly never met, and for whom usually only sketchy information exists as to his or her mental condition when the will was made.

Psychologists also have been used to support the validity of a will at the time it is written. The psychologist simply examines the person at the time, and the attorney files the report of that evaluation with the will. If the psychologist comes to a negative finding, the attorney usually then goes shopping for another psychologist. The validity of a will can also be strengthened by having the person videotaped while making it and stating its provisions, and this approach, combined with a positive psychological evaluation at that time, significantly reduces any possibility of a later effective challenge.

Guardianship

Another competency issue in civil law, the competency to handle one's own financial and personal affairs, is termed **guardianship**. The guardianship system exists to protect the incompetent from personal and financial harm, but it also protects society and the family of the incompetent. Guardianship systems have existed since ancient times. In early Rome, for example, there were extensive laws for the protection of the property of the incompetent.

The legal criteria defining this type of incompetency have traditionally been quite vague, using such phrases as "unable to manage his own affairs." More recent statutes have attempted to be somewhat more specific, for example, "lacks sufficient understanding or capacity to make, communicate or implement responsible decisions concerning his personal property." The usual bases for such incompetency are dementia (from old age or physical trauma), the severe mental disorders such as schizophrenia or paranoia or major depression, or chronic alcohol or drug addiction.

There are not many strong research studies on the operation of the incompetency system. But the evidence that exists suggests that too often the system is haphazard, uncertain, and not necessarily for the benefit of the ward. For example, despite the incompetent person's right to attend the competency hearing and to be represented by attorneys, studies in Los Angeles and New York found that wards were seldom present and seldom adequately represented by attorneys. In Los Angeles, for example, in 84 percent of the cases the only people present at the hearing were the judge, the petitioner (the person trying to have the potential ward declared incompetent), and the petitioner's attorney (Smith and Meyer, 1987).

Civil Commitment

When persons of questionable mental health, such as Z.L., are deprived of freedom by the state and compelled to accept treatment, it is called **civil commitment**. The state may exercise civil commitment either to protect such people from themselves—the "parens patriae," or parental, power of the state,—or to protect society from such people—the police power of the state. In order to assert this power, each state must have its own statutes that articulate the standards and procedures to be followed both prior to and during commitment. Most such laws require (1) proof of the existence of mental illness and (2) some indication that the person is dangerous to self or others. The complex issue of dangerousness will be discussed in more detail shortly.

In general, there are two types of commitment procedures: formal and emergency. Formal or judicial commitment is by order of a court. Formal does not mean, however, that the procedure is the usual **adversary process**, that is, two sides, one of who may be a prosecuting attorney for the state, each have an attorney arguing their position as strongly as possible before a judge. Commitment is usually initiated by a relative, friend, employer, or any other responsible person. Although such persons may testify, a judge often makes a decision based solely on the testimony or written reports from psychological, medical, or psychiatric experts. Rarely is a jury trial requested, although it is available if requested; and in some cases, neither the "experts" nor the affected person are present. If the judge allows commitment, the person is confined (with periodic review) in a mental institution until the mental disorder is alleviated to the satisfaction of the court, usually upon advice of the treating therapist. Although the average length of stay is usually only a couple of weeks up to a few months, anyone facing involuntary civil commitment is potentially "susceptible to lifelong deprivation of rights and liberties in most states" (Bartol, 1983, p. 94).

An informal emergency commitment does not initially involve a court. The police can take any person acting bizarrely to a state hospital. A responsible citizen can ask the police to pick up someone he or she believes to be dangerous by swearing out a mental health warrant. In most states, two professionals may then sign a temporary, informal commitment order that will allow the affected person to be confined for a period of time, usually ranging from one to three days. Incarceration for longer periods requires a formal commitment.

Recent trends in civil commitment.   Voluntary commitments outnumber involuntary commitments, though the reverse was true before 1970. However, it is impossible to know how many people "voluntarily" enter mental hospitals under threat of civil commitment from family members, mental health professionals, or police officers. Though estimates vary, many suspect that this percentage may be as much as 50 percent (Szasz, 1986; Grisso, 1986). Nonetheless, mental health professionals and the courts are increasingly reluctant to commit involuntarily persons of questionable mental health.

Recent trends include requirements that an individual threatened with civil commitment be given the right to written notice of the hearing and the right and opportunity to counsel, requirements that there be "clear and convincing" evidence, and similar safeguards. In contrast, the 1987 Supreme Court case of *U.S.* v. *Salerno* upheld the concept of "preventive detention" which becomes a kind of civil commitment for those who are charged with a crime but are not mentally ill. Finally, there is a trend toward viewing dangerousness as being related more to situational variables than to an unchanging personality trait (Smith and Meyer, 1987). For instance, a person may be deemed dangerous if allowed total independence to live where and how he or she chooses, but not dangerous if living in a halfway house or other sheltered quarters and taking prescribed antipsychotic drugs under medical supervision. Since commitment laws require that the "least restrictive alternative" to freedom be provided when treating the mentally disturbed, institutionalization may not be necessary in all cases.

The Prediction of Dangerousness

Dangerousness, as it applies to involuntary civil commitment, is ambiguous and problematic. Specifying the criterion as "imminent dangerousness" is an improvement. However, there are still problems. Does dangerousness include emotional harm, cognitive harm, and economic harm, as well as physical harm? What about harm to property? How severe or frequent must harm be to justify police intervention? Although some suggest limiting dangerousness to acts intended to do physical harm to self or others, the courts have not concurred and positions on this matter vary from state to state.

Even if an acceptable definition of dangerousness were found, only a part of the problem would be solved, since the accurate **prediction of dangerousness** is then required. Mental health professionals have not proven they have any consistent ability to predict dangerous or violent behavior (Monahan, 1981; Stone, 1975). Conversely, neither can an absence of potential for violent behavior be clearly determined. There is a strong tendency to overpredict dangerousness since a professional who fails to protect a community by *not* detecting a person who eventually engages in violent behavior pays a heavy price, not only from a negative stigma because of high media visibility, but also because of the potential expense of legal proceedings, and in some cases, a high malpractice settlement. Given a choice between being safe and being criticized or held responsible for the possible repercussions of releasing a possibly dangerous person, most profesionals choose the safe route.

The Tarasoff case.   The difficulty of accurately predicting dangerousness and the legal issues involved were illustrated in a 1976 California case, generally referred to as the "Tarasoff case" (Mills et al., 1987). The treating psychologist at the U.C.-Berkeley mental health clinic determined that one of his patients, Mr. Poddar, was dangerous and probably meant it when he said he intended to kill a woman, Ms. Tarasoff, who was avoiding his romantic approaches. The clinic called the campus police, told them about the situation, and requested they pick up Mr. Poddar to have him taken to a hospital for a civil commitment evaluation. The police went to Mr. Poddar's house, talked to him, decided there was no problem, and left. Poddar later did kill Ms. Tarasoff. He was tried and on the basis of diminished mental capacity was found guilty of involuntary manslaughter rather than first- or second-degree murder. Interestingly enough, Poddar later returned to his native India and reportedly is living contentedly as a normal married family man.

The California court held that the Tarasoff estate could sue the clinic on the basis that it failed to take reasonable action to protect her, such as warning Tarasoff about Poddar's intention to kill her. In fact, the suit was directed at a whole range of University of California functionaries, from the clinic personnel and campus police up to the Board of Regents. Ironically, throughout the legal process, the campus police were the only group never found to be liable. The obligation described by the court is to take "reasonable steps" to protect the intended victim: the court seemed to emphasize a "duty to warn" the intended victim of the danger, only one of many ways a "duty to protect" could be carried out. A major concern is the implication in the Tarasoff decision and some subsequent decisions that therapists are liable if they "should have known" of the danger. This opens the door to a jury deciding that even though there was never any actual threat, the therapist should have been able to assess the danger anyway. This would raise a difficult task, accurately predicting a person's dangerousness, to a virtually impossible one.

The Tarasoff court seemed to be saying to mental health professionals something to the effect, "You have always been delighted and desirous of the 'expert' role in such situations; we're simply saying you have to be liable for it." Mental health professionals have responded with an emphasis on the difficulties of making such predictions (Mills et al., 1987). Of course, since this was a decision of the California Supreme Court, it has no compelling legal effect in any other state. But it has been influential. Other states have followed with various statutes of this sort. In 1986, the Kentucky legislature mandated that when a client threatened harm to a specific person, for example, "I hate my ex-wife, and I'm going to kill her," the mental health professional has to (1) warn the victim, (2) notify the police in the victim's area, (3) notify the police in the client's area, and (4) take out a civil commitment warrant to have the client detained or picked up for evaluation. If the threat is nonspecific, "I feel so upset, I want to just go out and shoot until this gun is empty," the professional is still obligated to take the last two steps (Smith and Meyer, 1987).

Related Issues.   Even though many courts are responding to this issue, a number of related issues remain unsettled. Does the therapist's obligation extend to a threat to property, rather than just to persons? Most might agree that it does in certain situations (as in an intent to destroy as many of the great art works in the world as the person can), but most believe it would not be worth voiding confidentiality if the client has said he or she might break a neighbor's window in anger. The difficulty is where to set the limits. A related issue that is now debated by therapists is whether they have the duty to warn prospective sexual contacts if their client has AIDS. Neither the courts or therapists have indicated any clear trend on what to do here.

The difficulty in predicting dangerousness should not be surprising. Events such as suicide or homicide are rare, and the rarer an event, the more difficult it is to predict (Maltsberger, 1986; Levin, 1987). What results in actuality are many false positives. False positives here mean that people who are labeled dangerous do not engage in dangerous behavior after having been predicted to do so. For example, if a clinician predicts that 10 people will commit dangerous acts and six of them follow the prediction, then there is a 60 percent rate of true positives and a 40 percent rate of false positives. If civil commitment were the outcome of this prediction, then for every six actually dangerous individuals committed to a mental institution, there would be four committed who were not dangerous. We said earlier that it is safer for clinicians to overpredict dangerousness and, in fact, most studies indicate that overprediction does occur, not at a rate of just 40 percent but at a rate of 60 to 70 percent (Monahan, 1981; Szasz, 1986). In criminal law, it is usually said to be better for 10 guilty persons to go free than for one innocent person to suffer. In civil commitment then, the question is how many harmless people (false positives) are we willing to sacrifice to protect ourselves from one violent person?

Note that the studies indicating this high level of overprediction cannot exactly replicate life as it is. It is not desirable or ethical to carry out the exact experiment, which would necessitate predicting the dangerousness of a large number of people threatened with commitment, letting them go, and then keeping track of them to see if the predictions were accurate or not. Obviously, the danger to society makes a study of this nature highly unethical. Thus we are left with imperfect ways of determining how valid clinicians' predictions of dangerousness at commitment hearings actually are.

Also, none of the studies which have caused such pessimism about predicting dangerousness have examined the issue of emergency commitment, that is, a short commitment, without a legal hearing, of 24 to 48 hours. Most studied people who were in mental hospitals for varying lengths of time and who were then released. However, these same studies have been used in arguments against emergency commitment, and there are those who take exception to this practice. Monahan (1978; 1981) has posited that it is probably far easier and surer to predict dangerousness in an emergency situation since (1) the individual may be threatening violence and appear out of control, (2) the threatened victims may be on hand, (3) the intended weapon is likely to be immediately available, and (4) a dangerous outburst may appear imminent. Also, the person may also have been violent in the past, a good predictor of present or future violence. It would seem that a prediction of violence under such circumstances would be much more accurate. Needless to say, the same constraints stated previously prevent an exact testing of the validity of such predictions. It seems we must be satisfied with logical and prudent judgments made by fallible mental health professionals. Though imperfect, they provide the best information available (Mills et al., 1987; Monahan, 1981).

PATIENTS' RIGHTS

We have stated previously that civil commitment occurs when persons of questionable mental health are deprived of freedom by the state and compelled to accept treatment. Until recent decades, however, "treatment" was never asserted as a constitutional right of mental patients, nor were certain other basic human rights guaranteed them.

The Right to Treatment and the Right to Refuse It

The right of mental patients to treatment and their right to refuse treatment have been prominent issues in the past decade.

The law has traditionally recognized a strong individual interest in controlling what is done to our bodies (*Griswold* v. *Connecticut* (1985); *Roe* v. *Wade* (1975); *Zablock* v. *Redhail* (1978); *Stantosky* v. *Kramer* (1982)). This interest has constitutional protection and is central to a constitutional right to privacy, as recognized by the Supreme Court. It is also the primary reason for requiring that informed consent be obtained before potentially dangerous medical treatments, such as ECT and psychosurgery (Valenstein, 1986).

If the individual right to make decisions concerning treatment is important in physical therapies, it may be equally important where the treatment involves changing mental activity. This treatment may have physical consequences (from certain psychotropic drugs, psychosurgery, or from electroconvulsive therapy), mental consequences (changing the thought patterns or ability to have certain thoughts) and social consequences (for example, loss of job or friends because of the stigma associated with some forms of treatment). Thus a patient might wish to refuse treatment to avoid either changes in personality, which successful treatment might cause, physical side effects, or social consequences of treatment. Naturally, a patient can't make reasonable treatment decisions without being offered treatments that could be effective, and then, without coercion, being allowed to decide whether or not to accept those treatments.

The **right to treatment** and the **right to refuse treatment** are most commonly considered in connection with institutionalized, involuntary mental patients. But treatment issues may also arise regarding other institutionalized persons, such as prisoners and mental patients who cannot fully make decisions for themselves. Also, the mentally retarded and disabled, children, and other legally incompetent individuals are not permitted by the law to make some of these decisions for themselves. Even purely voluntary mental patients may raise some right-to-treatment issues, such as refusing prescribed medications.

Deinstitutionalization.   Central to any right to treatment has been the notion of providing the **least restrictive alternative** of the forms of treatment. For example, a patient should not be placed on a locked ward if an open ward with grounds privileges would be sufficient. Combining this with the attendant iatrogenic problems (the committed patient's passivity and loss of initiative, breakdown of friendship networks, and so on) of treating people in institutions and the higher costs of institutional care, it's not surprising that there has been a trend toward deinstitutionalization. This trend was first spurred by the 1957 case of *Donaldson* v. *O'Connor*, wherein Donaldson had been committed to a Florida state mental hospital for 14 years as mentally ill and dangerous on the complaint of his son that his father had been saying his food had been poisoned. Donaldson, a Christian Scientist by religion, had refused ECT and medication, but the hospital had refused to give him the occupational

In the 1970s and 1980s, many cities were hit with a new population problem: homelessness. Many "bag people" are former mental hospital patients, for whom deinstitutionalization meant literally hitting the streets. (AP/Wide World Photos)

therapy he requested. The court held he could not be institutionalized without treatment or without continuing proof of present dangerousness.

Deinstitutionalization is a policy of preference for placing persons at home, or if necessary in small day-care or night-care facilities in the home community. Deinstitutionalization has been applied to the mentally disordered and mentally retarded, and now, in some cases, to incarcerated criminals as well. Indeed, Governor DiPrete of Rhode Island announced plans in late 1986 to totally deinstitutionalize care for the retarded in that state, and to place those persons in the community.

Deinstitutionalization has the positive aspects of avoiding the above problems. But, there have been some negative results. For many individuals, home care is not available or not adequate. Those who cannot reintegrate into the community often become homeless wanderers—the Skid Row derelicts and "bag ladies," who are very often mentally disturbed. Homelessness can be especially difficult for women. There are traditional services and even some social acceptance for the wandering derelict male. There are much less of these for females. Also, the number of homeless mentally disturbed older people is increasing, and this is a population in which women outnumber men.

As a result of deinstitutionalization, mentally disturbed people are more likely to come into conflict with some law. Society then deals with these people through the criminal justice system rather than the mental health system. This change has been called the criminalization of the mentally disturbed. Society needs to confront more effectively the negative effects of what is, for the most part, a positive policy, i.e., deinstitution alization.

Current and future issues in deinstitutionalization and treatment rights.

Most legal issues regarding deinstitutionalization and the rights to treatment and to refuse treatment are of relatively recent origin. However, the actual extent to which these rights are going to be validated and supported by legal decisions is unclear. As a result, involuntarily hospitalized mental patients so far do not have any greater sense of freedom in decision-making when ordered to take chemotherapy (Smith and Meyer, 1987; Valenstein, 1986). The debate over these rights is likely to continue. As even more effective therapies are developed, especially to the degree they can be effective whether or not the patient cooperates in the treatment, the debate will intensify. The existence of clearly effective therapies, on one hand, may make the right to receive treatment more important for some people. On the other hand, the increased efficacy of treatment may cause more people to refuse treatment to prevent a form of governmental "mind control."

Courts have not yet clarified whether the right to refuse treatment refers to any treatment or a particular kind of treatment. The complexity of this issue may best be understood by posing several questions. If a patient is acutely suicidal and refuses electroconvulsive therapy (ECT) and the drugs prescribed in lieu of the ECT, what should the hospital do? Should it provide around-the-clock surveillance of the patient? If that kind of attention were provided the suicidal patient, would the care of other patients suffer? What about their rights? Realistically, what is the state's ability to provide appropriate security and care if all patients can refuse certain forms of treatment? Or should the judgment of a mental health professional override a refusal of treatment by a patient? As these questions demonstrate, the right to refuse treatment is an especially complex issue.

The Right to Privacy as It Relates to Homosexuality

Many arguments designed to buttress a right to refuse treatment (as well as supporting the expectations for confidentiality and privilege, which will be discussed shortly) come from the generally accepted constitutionally based **right to privacy**. An important development in this area, as well as for our society's perspective on homosexuality, came in the 1986 Supreme Court decision of *Bowers* v. *Hardwick*. In this case, decided 5–4, with the majority opinion written by Justice White, the Court upheld a Georgia statute making consensual sodomy ("sexual act involving the sex organs of one person and the mouth or anus of another") a felony. The major basis for the decision was that the right to privacy does not include homosexual activity (as evidenced by the fact that most states had sodomy laws when the Bill of Rights and Fourteenth Amendment were adopted), and, therefore, there is no constitutional protection for that activity. Interestingly enough, the Court ruled that the issue of heterosexual sodomy, which is also prohibited by the Georgia law, was not yet before the Court.

In a final paragraph that at first received little attention, but which may well be significant in the long run, the Court said that "majority sentiments about the morality of homosexuality" could be the rational, constitutional basis for the prohibition against sodomy. Presumably the Court was referring here to a political majority, since the Georgia statute had been passed and not repealed.

A strong dissenting opinion held that the right of privacy included private, consensual sexual conduct in the home. Quoting an early Supreme Court Justice, Oliver Wendell Holmes Jr., the dissenters found it "revolting to have no better reason for a rule of law than that . . . it was laid down in the time of Henry IV."

Ironically, there are few arrests for private, consensual sodomy even in the 24 states (and Washington, D.C.) that have such laws. However, the indirect impact is significant, since it allows for a return to criminalization of victimless crimes, a reduction in the scope of the constitutional right of privacy, and the promotion of antihomosexual attitudes and laws. This approach would seem to allow approval of the criminalization of a broad range of nondangerous, victimless crimes.

The Right to a Humane Environment

Some have argued that patients (and to a lesser degree prisoners) have a right to a humane environment. The strongest case for a right to a humane environment came in 1972, in the case of *Wyatt* v. *Stickney*, when a federal court ordered the state of Alabama to upgrade conditions in its hospitals for the retarded and the mentally disabled. It's not surprising that conditions were chaotic and antitherapeutic in these Alabama hospitals, since, for example,

RESEARCH PROFILE

Privacy and a Humane Environment

The text discusses the 1972 landmark case of *Wyatt* v. *Stickney*, a decision that influenced many subsequent cases. However, as we note in the text, many of the reforms were never fully carried out. Also, research by O'Reilly and Sales (1987) suggests that some of the reforms and the assumptions on which they were based were not entirely appropriate.

These researchers studied two long-term wards (with 35 and 28 patients, respectively) at a public long-term facility for the mentally ill in Arizona, a facility that met virtually all of the standards mandated by the Wyatt case and subsequent decisions. With the exception of a few patients who were too disturbed to respond effectively, each patient was thoroughly evaluated with structured interviews and rating scales. Some interesting results emerged.

Consistent with all of the legal decisions, privacy was found to be highly important to the great majority of patients. One assumption of the Wyatt-type court decisions was that privacy is primarily visual, and this is generated by visual screens of various sorts. However, these researchers found that freedom from noise and physical intrusions, which are not really dealt with in these decisions, were equally important components of privacy, and were not being met in this hospital, which actually exceeded the Wyatt standards.

One interesting and important question remains unanswered. It's reasonable to assert that some standards have to be upgraded simply on humane grounds, whether or not they actually cause some positive change in the patients. But the Wyatt type decisions seem to assume that upgrading hospital conditions would lead to psychological improvement, quicker discharge, and fewer relapses, in patients.

So far there is no clear evidence that it does. It's true that privacy does positively affect the interactions between therapist and patient, and improves the patient's mood and self-esteem. Yet O'Reilly and Sales also point to several experts who argue that making many overall improvements in the hospital environment can even have a negative effect—to the degree that the hospital becomes a "country club," many patients will be content to become institutionalized rather than return to their prior impoverished circumstances. Most experts disagree with such an idea, but as yet it has not been fully evaluated by solid empirical research.

at that time less than fifty cents per day per patient was spent on food. The court ordered increased staffing by better personnel, better physical conditions, and more freedoms and privileges. The court affirmed a right to treatment within a humane environment, and attempted to specify certain minimum requirements that would fulfill this, such as rights to (1) privacy and dignity, (2) an opportunity for voluntary religious worship, (3) a satisfying and nutritionally adequate diet, (4) screens to provide privacy in toilets and sleeping rooms for more than one patient, (5) an opportunity for visitation with the opposite sex, and so on. Unfortunately, the state was slow to implement these orders, citing lack of funds, which resulted in the appointment by the

Modern mental hospitals make an effort to provide disturbed people with a humane environment. Treatment often includes rehabilitation programs, such as art therapy. (M.E. Warren/Photo Researchers, Inc.)

court of an overseer to monitor progress in this regard. In 1987, supervision of the situation was turned back to the state of Alabama, as much progress had been made (Bales, 1987).

There have been other state and federal court decisions that have lent some support to the notion of a right to a humane environment, but, as yet, the Supreme Court has not clearly affirmed such a right as constitutionally based, and until it does, lower court decisions have to be considered as somewhat tentative.

OTHER LEGAL AND ETHICAL ISSUES

We have thus far looked mostly at legal trends in which the mental health professional is brought into a court as a consultant on cases that at least potentially involve a criminal offense. However, there are a variety of other dilemmas and issues related to the legal system that face mental health professionals today, such as confidentiality in the professional relationship, claims of malpractice, and so on.

Confidentiality and Privileged Communication

Confidentiality is a commitment by a professional person such as a lawyer, psychologist, or physician not to reveal information obtained from or provided by the client. At least three reasons have been identified for the importance of confidentiality in therapy. First, without a guarantee of confidentiality, patients may not be completely open or may be reluctant to enter into therapy at all. In many forms of therapy, patients are expected to reveal the most intimate and private aspects of their lives. Patients believing that such communications might be repeated to others would be understandably reluctant to talk freely. Second, a most important ingredient in the therapeutic relationship is trust (Meyer et al., 1988). Without the confidence that therapists will not reveal their secrets, some patients may not develop a trusting relationship. Finally, confidentiality promotes the privacy of individuals by allowing them to control extremely personal information about themselves.

It is important to distinguish confidentiality from privileged communication. Confidentiality refers to broad ethical and legal obligations to protect the secrets of a client's life from disclosure to others. **Privileged communication** refers specifically to the legal protection of the communications in evaluations and therapy from disclosure in court. According to law, communications between husband and wife, physician and patient, pastor and penitent, attorney and client, and more recently, mental health professional and client, is privileged communication and cannot be used in court.

Protecting the confidentiality of patients has been an ethical obligation of the helping professions for centuries. Several features are common to these ethical guidelines. First, each offers a broad statement of the obligation of confidentiality. Second, they all stipulate that the client or patient can allow the release of confidential information. This right implies an important principle: confidentiality protects clients or patients, and the decision to release information is theirs, not the therapist's. A third common feature is the recognition of exceptions to confidentiality.

Most people agree that society's interests are best served if communications between certain people are kept private, particularly in regard to the legal system. However, within these privileged relationships there are exceptions. Although the limits provided by these exceptions may vary some from state to state, generally, the privileged communication for the mental health professional–client relationship is eliminated for any of the following reasons.

1. If a therapist has reason to believe a child (whether a client or not) has been either physically, emotionally, or sexually abused, the therapist is required to report it within a specific time frame, such as 24 or 36 hours.

2. If a client has been accused of a crime and has requested a sanity determination, the therapist may give the results of such determination to the proper authorities and, perhaps, to the court.

3. If a client has been the victim of a crime, his or her therapist's records can in certain instances be subpoenaed during the trial.

4. If a client initiated therapy in the hope of evading the law for having committed a crime or for planning to do so, there is no entitlement to privilege.

5. If a client accuses a therapist of malpractice, the therapist can disclose whatever information about the therapy is necessary for a defense.

6. If a therapist believes a client is dangerous to himself or others and that disclosure of such information is necessary to protect the client or others, the therapist cannot remain silent.

The treatment of children also presents problems of confidentiality. Ordinarily parents have the right to have information concerning their children until the children reach the age of majority, 18 in most states, although this right has been modified in some states. Yet, a release of information from therapy may often be harmful, depending upon the age of the child. A five-year-old child presents different problems from an adolescent who will be very concerned about his or her independence from parental scrutiny. When parents bring a child for treatment, the mental health professional may establish a contract with the parents in which the parents agree that they will not receive, or be able to demand, information about the therapy. When therapy is undertaken without the consent of parents, however, and the parents discover the therapy and demand information concerning it, the therapist may have to disclose the information. The parents can persist in a demand for the information and may be able to obtain a court order for it.

The increasing use of insurance, health maintenance organizations (HMOs), government-funded programs, and other third-party payments for therapy threatens confidentiality in several ways. Most payers require some information concerning the basis of, reasons for, and extent of therapy. This information may be shared with other institutions and insurance companies. In some instances it may also be available to an employer who is paying for the insurance. In addition, third-party payers, such as HMOs, are increasingly establishing auditing and review systems that require the release of information to review committees. This means even more individuals will have access to private information. Hospitalization is particularly likely to be reviewed extensively. In yet another instance, if the therapist is accused of fraud for wrongful billing, the criminal investigation may result in the subpoena of patients' records to establish proof of fraud. Since the release of such information is often necessary to obtain payment for services, mental health professionals will have continuing conflicts between obtaining payment and protecting confidentiality.

Reporting Child Abuse

Child abuse reporting statutes are relatively new, yet now exist in all 50 states. The tendency has been to expand the groups of persons who are required to report child abuse. The early statutes required physicians to report, but it is now common to require reports from all medical and mental health professionals, social service workers, teachers, and law enforcement officers. Other states require "anyone" or "any person" suspecting or knowing of child abuse to report it. Reporting any "mild suspicion," however, easily leads to overreporting.

Although states vary in the definition of abuse, it generally includes two (or commonly all) of the following: (1) physical injury, (2) sexual molestation, (3) emotional injury, and (4) neglect, though neglect, a more passive violation, may be kept as a separate statistic. There is ordinarily a requirement that the injury be "serious" or a "serious threat to welfare." However, these terms are generally left undefined or are so broadly defined that the resultant uncertainty produces substantial confusion about what is meant by child abuse and neglect.

There are positive aspects to a broad definition of child abuse. Emotional injuries are real and should be recognized by the law (Grote et al., 1986). Yet, the National Study of Child Abuse found that nearly 60 percent of suspected child abuse cases reported to child protection agencies could not be substantiated (U.S. Center on Child Abuse and Neglect, 1981). The problem of overreporting is significant: The National Study estimated, on the basis of 1979–1980 statistics, that 1.1 million child abuse and neglect reports are filed with child protective service agencies each year, and more than 600,000 of these probably cannot be substantiated, even using the broad definitions often employed by the protective service agencies. More recent estimates of the number of reports of child abuse are as high as 1.7 million per year (Smith and Meyer, 1987).

Paradoxically, the confusion concerning the definition of child abuse and neglect may also contribute to significant failure to report. The National Study found that 68 percent of the children who were specifically identified by the Study as being within the scope of abuse and neglect (using a definition probably somewhat narrower than many statutes) were *not* reported to the child protection agency or otherwise known to the child protection agency.

One controversial problem, especially noted in the area of child sexual abuse, follows from the commonly held belief that "children never lie about being sexually abused." But the fact is that a few children do lie about this, some report fantasies of sexual abuse that did not occur, and sometimes children report being sexually abused as a result of suggestion, coaching, or coercion from others (Underwager et al., 1986). In the majority of cases where there is no apparent reason why there would be a distortion of the truth, children who report having been sexually abused should be assumed to be telling the truth.

Professionals who interview the child have to be careful not to introduce a bias one way or another about what they expect the child to say. Some use anatomically correct dolls when interviewing very young alleged victims. However, as yet there are no good data on nonabused child responses to such interviews. Using such dolls could introduce a bias. Since alleged victims may be very intimidated about testifying in open court, some courts have allowed these children to testify from another room by television or videotape. The problem here is that the constitutional right of the alleged perpetrator of the abuse to confront effectively the testimony of the accuser may then be violated (Smith and Meyer, 1987; Underwager et al., 1986).

Actual abuse that is not dealt with will result in serious harm to the child. At the same time, false reports, even if made in good faith, can disrupt families, invade privacy, and make personal and professional relationships more difficult.

Defining the Client

When an adult pays a clinician for help with a problem that does not involve the judicial system, that adult is clearly the client. When parents pay a clinician to help their child with a problem that affects only the family, the issue of who is the client becomes a little clouded. As noted earlier, the clinician will advise the parents that what occurs between the clinician and the child will generally be kept confidential. On the other hand, a clinician may be hired by an adult person's family to help the family obtain the civil commitment of that person. Or a clinician may be engaged to evaluate someone for competency to stand trial or to determine if someone accused of a crime was mentally ill at the time of the alleged crime. In these instances the clinician is potentially serving more than one client. Thus he or she must define the client clearly to all concerned, or function unethically and run the risk of a malpractice suit (Bersoff, 1986).

Malpractice and the Mental Health Professional

A malpractice suit is a civil rather than criminal case. **Malpractice** suits can arise in any area in which a client feels the professional has failed the client, whether the failure is a result of incompetence, deliberate wrongdoing, or unintentional injury. Claims of malpractice against mental health professionals have risen steadily in the last decade (Smith and Meyer, 1987). Yet, mental health professionals still have much lower rates of malpractice than do health-care professionals, such as physicians, who deal primarily with physical problems. There are several reasons for this. For one, the "standard of practice" (the methods that are generally accepted in the profession) for mental health professionals is not as clearly or precisely defined as it is in many areas of physical medicine. The standard practice for treatment of appendicitis is generally agreed upon; the standard practice for treatment of schizophrenia is not. In fact, most areas of mental health therapy give therapists considerable latitude in determining what constitutes reasonable care.

Second, not only is it often difficult to determine whether a breach of reasonable care has *occurred* in mental health, but it is often equally difficult to determine whether a breach has *caused an injury* to the patient. A client claiming that faulty mental health therapy caused an injury may have a difficult time demonstrating that therapy was actually the cause. Indeed, since patients often are suffering from some form of mental illness before seeking the assistance of a therapist, any psychological injury received during or after therapy may appear to be nothing more than part of the preexisting mental illness.

Third, the nature of most injuries apt to result from mental health malpractice makes winning a lawsuit difficult. Emotional injuries are very real and may be very painful, but are generally not as obvious or gruesome as physical injuries (Levin, 1987). A mangled limb or scarred body presents dramatic evidence of injury; a mangled psyche or ego is much less evident.

While these are the primary reasons for fewer malpractice suits against mental health professionals, there are others, such as the type of close relationship that mental health professionals have with their clients. A person may see a surgeon only briefly before and after surgery and thus is not likely to develop the type of close personal relationship that often makes a psychotherapy client hesitant about filing suit. Also, clients who have been injured in psychotherapy may be reluctant to file a legal claim because doing so would destroy their claim to privileged communication and potentially allow their conflicts in emotional and personal relationships to become public.

As a result, the more similar a treatment is to physical medicine treatments, and the shorter and more impersonal it is, the more likely a malpractice suit may occur. For example, chemotherapy, psychosurgery, and electroconvulsive therapy (ECT) are more likely to generate a malpractice claim than is psychotherapy (Valenstein, 1986).

The most common and most successful claims against mental health professionals result from alleged sexual contact between professional and client. Nanette Gartrell (1987) notes that the problem is not rare. She directed a survey of 5,574 psychiatrists randomly selected from the files of the American Medical Association. Of the 1,442 psychiatrists who returned a confidential questionnaire, 7 percent of male and 3 percent of female psychiatrists, for an overall rate of 6 percent, acknowledged having sex with their patients. About two thirds of the affairs began shortly after the clients stopped regular treatment sessions. But this is still a clear ethical violation. It was surprising and upsetting to mental health professionals in general that many of these psychiatrists thought a sexual relationship might even be good for their client, and only 40 percent of those professionals who acknowledged having sex with

An Example of a Professional Code of Ethics

A professional code of ethics acts to stipulate and govern the relevant behaviors of its members. For example, the following is the preamble to the code of ethics of the American Psychological Association (APA), along with a list of the areas that the total document speaks to. The full code goes into considerable detail about what is expected in each area. Members of the APA who are found (by a committee of the APA) to be in violation of any of these ethical principles may be expelled from the organization. State licensing boards then often take action against a psychologist who has been dropped from the APA membership because of an ethical violation.

The preamble to the APA Code of Ethical Principles of Psychologists states:

Psychologists respect the dignity and worth of the individual and strive for the preservation and protection of fundamental human rights. They are committed to increasing knowledge of human behavior and of people's understanding of themselves and others and to the utilization of such knowledge for the promotion of human welfare. While pursuing these objectives, they make every effort to promote the welfare of those who seek their services and of the research participants that may be the object of study. They use their skills only for purposes consistent with these values and do not knowingly permit their misuse by others. While demanding for themselves freedom of inquiry and communication, psychologists accept the responsibility this freedom requires: Competence, objectivity in the application of skills, and concern for the best interests of clients, colleagues, students, research participants, and society. In pursuit of these ideals, psychologists subscribe to principles in the following areas:

1. Responsibility
2. Competence
3. Moral and legal standards
4. Public statements
5. Confidentiality
6. Welfare of the consumer
7. Professional relationships
8. Assessment techniques
9. Research with human participants
10. Care and use of animals

Acceptance of membership in the American Psychological Association commits the member to adherence to these principles [American Psychological Association, 1981, p. 633].

The APA Committee on Scientific and Professional Ethics and Conduct responds to all inquiries and complaints about possible ethical violations by APA members.

their clients had sought therapy or consultation with a colleague because of this behavior. These violations are not confined to psychiatrists, and the problem is such that insurance underwriters for most psychologists will not cover damages from claims of this sort (Smith and Meyer, 1987).

Professional mental health organizations.   While the courts decide malpractice suits and also enforce any violations of criminal law, ethical violations have traditionally been dealt with first by professional organizations, such as the American Psychological Association, American Psychiatric Association, American Nurses Association, and National Association of Social Workers. These organizations all have sets of ethical principles that members must adhere to. In most states, a pledge to follow these guidelines is written into the professional licensing law. In such states anyone practicing that profession has to follow the principles, even if they don't happen to belong to one of these professional organizations. Contrary to popular belief, not all persons licensed in a profession by a state have to belong to the relevant professional organization. In most instances, however, a client may lodge a complaint with these organizations or with the parallel state organization, such as the state psychological association. These organizations only have the authority to void the professional's membership in that organization; but they often refer matters to state licensing boards, for a possible loss of license. In some cases, there is a referral to the criminal justice system. For example, some cases of sexual contact between professional and client have been construed by the courts as involving assault, battery, or fraud.

Voluntary mental health organizations.   In addition to professional organizations, there are a variety of voluntary mental health organizations that any interested citizen may join. In many instances, major changes in the practice of mental health were brought about by voluntary organizations rather than by professionals. Prominent among the many voluntary mental health groups are the National Association for Mental Health and the National Association for Retarded Children. They have been particularly effective in developing resources for improving conditions in institutions and for promoting court cases in the area of patients' rights and confidentiality. Similar efforts at the local level by these groups, as well as groups with interest in a specific disorder, such as the Schizophrenia Association, offer emotional and financial support to individuals and families affected by mental disorder. As noted throughout this book, certain voluntary organizations, such as Alcoholics Anonymous, take on an important direct role in treatment. Interestingly enough, such organizations, or other less commonly recognized treatment agents such as ministers or counselors, are seldom the target of a malpractice suit. This is probably because they are not seen as liable by clients and their attorneys even though they become liable any time they take on a treatment role, whether they are paid for such services or not.

The Detection of Deception

The ability to detect deception is critical to all the legal issues we have presented in this chapter, as well as in the diagnosis of the disorders discussed throughout this book, especially with factitious disorder and chronic pain and malingering. Furthermore, these three syndromes are often central to determining the validity of a claim in a personal injury suit, such as a claim for damages following an auto accident.

Malingering. **Malingering** is a DSM category, and is defined as the voluntary presentation of physical or psychological symptoms. Malingering is recognizable by the circumstances of the situation, rather than from the person's individual psychology, as is true of a factitious disorder. Malingering is likely to occur in job screening, military and criminal justice situations, or wherever a psychological or physical disability has a payoff, such as money from a successful suit or avoidance of combat. It occurs more commonly in the early to middle adult years, is more common in males than in females, and often follows an actual injury or illness. Problematic employment history, lower socioeconomic status, or an associated antisocial personality disorder are also common predictors of malingering (Landis and Meyer, 1988).

Techniques in deception detection. The detection of faked symptoms is always difficult. Recently, psychologists have shown an interest in adding physiological methods, such as the polygraph, into such examinations. The **polygraph** is a device that simultaneously gives several physiological measures, usually blood pressure, pulse, respiration, and/or galvanic skin response (a measure of electrical conductivity across the skin—related to the degree of moisture on the skin). Such measures provide an index of psychophysiological arousal of the client, which polygraphers assume (and this is an inaccurate assumption in some cases) is a direct indication of whether or not the client is telling the truth. Unfortunately, most states are passing laws that allow the title of "polygrapher" and "lie detection examiner" only for individuals who have specific, but actually very limited and often inadequate, training.

The Office of Technology Assessment, which provides data on important technological matters to the U.S. Congress, reviewed all of the available research on the polygraph (U.S. Congress-OTA, 1983). This review concluded that the polygraph may be useful in isolated cases when the information in question is very narrow and specific. But it found the technique far less useful if (1) the examiner is "fishing for information, (2) the subject is not convinced of the polygraph's efficacy, or (3) the examiner is not well qualified, a finding corroborated by other reviews (Alpher and Blanton, 1985; Lykken, 1980; Landis and Meyer, 1988).

Other physiologically based methods of detecting deception produce even less satisfactory results. These methods include analysis of micro-tremors in the voice, monitoring of respiration by using a radar-like device, and the study of the dilation of the small blood vessels (capillaries) in the eye. As yet, none of these techniques has shown any validity in well-controlled, independent studies (Landis and Meyer, 1988).

Psychologists usually employ interview techniques, observations of behavior, and psychological tests (see Chapter 3) to assess deception. Systematized interview observations or techniques that change the mind set or expectancy of the person taking the test help assess the truthfulness of response. Several consistent behavioral cues have been noted in dishonest individuals. For example, on the average, such individuals nod and gesture more than the honest interviewees do, and they have less frequent foot and leg movements. They also talk less, speak more slowly, and at the same time have more speech errors and smile more often. In addition, the dishonest interviewees tend to take positions that are physically farther from the interviewer. High voice pitch and many hand movements, relative to the individual's standard performance, are also indicative of deception (Ekman, 1985).

There is no real support for the idea that people who are deceiving will necessarily avoid eye contact. There is some evidence that females will look longer into the eyes of male examiners while lying, but perhaps not into a female examiner's eyes. These same cross-sex results hold for males as well, but not as markedly (Burns and Kintz, 1976).

With reference to the mind set in which the test is taken, Macciocchi and Meyer (1981) told certain people that the test that they were going to take had built-in scales to detect deception. These subjects provided more honest response patterns than those who were given only general encouragement to be honest in their responses. Of even more importance, one group of subjects was told that if there was any hint in the psychological tests that they might have been deceptive, they would be given a standard lie detection examination (physiological condition). They were then even more honest and self-disclosing in their response patterns, when compared with the threat of detection only by psychological test scales. In both the physiological condition and the psychological test condition, the subjects were more honest than when there was no threat of further assessment if it was thought they were lying.

Even when the most effective means of lie detection are employed, discerning malingering is difficult. This is just one more reason why the assessment and treatment of all of the mental disorders discussed throughout this book will continue to be a complex and challenging task.

VALUES, DILEMMAS, AND ABNORMAL BEHAVIOR

Laws and ethical principles reflect the values and generally accepted assumptions of a society. When these values or assumptions change, political dilemmas arise around these changes. The laws then change, though sometimes slowly. As noted at the outset of this chapter, one of the most basic societal dilemmas is how to balance the rights or the good of the individual against

EXHIBIT

Developing Positive Mental Health

This book has necessarily emphasized abnormal behavior, the negative end of the mental health continuum. However, there are individuals who have developed above-average mental functioning. Certain researchers, such as Abraham Maslow and Carl Rogers, have emphasized positive mental health, as opposed to psychopathology. The principles through which many experts agree individuals can reach positive mental health have been well articulated by Dr. Oakley Ray, a clinical psychologist at the Nashville Veterans Administration Medical Center, and author of *The Good Life* (1983). The following principles are in part adapted from his book.

1. The anticipation of a situation is often more distressing or important to us than is the actual situation itself.

2. Our interpretation of our experiences is often more important than the actual experiences.

3. Facing the sources of our fears until we feel they are mastered, even if we are anxious and upset while doing so, is the only way to overcome them.

4. Some factors in each of us are strongly influenced by genetic factors, and, as such, it is probably more effective to develop ways to cope with these factors than to try to directly change them.

5. Ambiguity or uncertainty about life situations is anxiety-producing and aversive.

6. Most of us will go to great lengths to impose structure or meaning even where there is none. The belief that we are in control of a situation decreases

the good of society as a whole. This dilemma will probably be with us for a long time. This is healthy, because the ability to openly discuss and move politically one way or another on this dimension is one mark of a free society.

In closing, we note other value-based dilemmas that are likely to continue into the foreseeable future. Attitudes will change not only as the assumptions of our society change, but also as research provides new information relevant to the following dilemmas.

1. How much freedom should a severely mentally disordered person have to decide what kind of treatment he or she should receive? In a related vein, what degree of input should children have in the treatment they receive?

2. To what degree should a mentally disordered person be held liable for the consequences of his or her behavior? This goes to the issues of (a) how much free choice anyone has, and (b) how much of that ability to make a free choice is hindered by a specific form of abnormal behavior?

3. Should treatment ever be imposed on a criminal despite his or her wishes to the contrary? For example, the available literature on brainwashing

aversiveness or anxiety, even if that belief is false, and even if we have never actually done anything to change the situation.

7. When we expect to fail in a situation, we are very likely to avoid the situation, or take inadequate steps to cope with it. The predicted failure is thus more likely to occur; this in turn decreases self-esteem, increases depression, and makes future failure more likely.

8. Doing what we can to prevent psychological (and physical) disorder is less costly and distressing, both emotionally and financially, than the efforts it takes to cure disorder.

9. Purposefully accumulating positive experiences, and then preserving these positive experiences in memory and in symbols (photos, for example), lead to a positive self-image and protect our "self" from the effects of negative experiences.

10. Developing positive mental health is attained by working directly and purposefully toward the components of good mental health, which are: a clear and accurate picture of our world (good reality testing); flexibility in the face of change and stress; a positive personal identity that includes a sense of self-worth and some unique competencies; mutually satisfying interpersonal relationships, friendships, and loves; the capacity to relax and enjoy life; and the ability to give of ourselves to others and become involved with something outside and beyond ourselves.

11. We should acknowledge our failures and defeats, work to change them and to repair any damage, but always be ready to forgive ourselves and start again.

says that this is possible now, and will be even more probable in the future, but at present our society usually says no.

4. Following up on the last two points, when mentally disordered persons commit crimes, should they be dealt with in the mental health system or the criminal justice system?

5. What degree of responsibility, legally and ethically, should mental health professionals bear toward the clients (or patients) in their care?

6. What level of accuracy should be expected of mental health professionals in predicting whether their clients are dangerous to themselves or to others?

7. How much control should society exert over a suicidal individual who is not psychotic and who is apparently able to rationally process information?

8. Is psychological pain and injury as real as physical pain and injury? For example, in a practical application, should personal injury victims be compensated in an equal fashion for psychological and physical injuries?

9. Should society spend as much money, for example, through equal levels of coverage in insurance policies and government programs, for psychological disorder as it does for physical disorder? Should public monies be spent to promote psychological well-being or personal growth, or just to cure disorders?

10. Given that there are finite resources to spend on mental health, how much should be spent on prevention rather than cure? Throughout this book we have pointed to methods of prevention. We have also noted that in the long run, dollar for dollar, more change comes from prevention than cure. This would suggest the emphasis should be placed on prevention. But if this is the chosen direction, it means a lower standard of care for those presently being treated, and possibly even an abandonment of effort toward some of the mentally disordered, such as the elderly derelicts and bag ladies discussed earlier in this chapter.

Research will provide information relevant to these and similar issues. But they are primarily issues of social policy or choice rather than issues of fact. They will continue to be areas of discussion and decision for many years.

CHAPTER REVIEW

1. Psychologically normal individuals often face legal and ethical issues, and the presence of abnormal behavior highlights these issues.

2. Criminal law is concerned with violations against the rules of society. Civil law is designed to fairly and nonviolently resolve disputes between individual parties, and sometimes between the state and an individual. The standard of proof in criminal law is "beyond a reasonable doubt," and in civil law it is typically a "preponderance of the evidence." In a few situations, a compromise standard, "clear and convincing evidence," is used. The burden of proof defines who has the primary responsibility to prove a specific point.

3. To establish criminal responsibility usually requires establishing "mens rea," or a guilty mind. The first step, though, is to establish if the accused is competent to stand trial, using the criteria of whether or not they understand the charges and can assist the attorney. If that is established, the accused could plead insanity, (an absence of mens rea). The trend is back to a variation of the M'Naghten rule, a cognitive test of whether the accused understands the criminality of the act.

4. Even after being found guilty of a capital crime, a person may subsequently be found incompetent to be executed.

5. Two important competency issues in civil law are the competency to make a will and the competency to handle one's personal and financial affairs (guardianship).

6. Persons who are found to be (a) mentally ill and (b) dangerous to self or others can be civilly committed to a hospital for treatment. Mental health professionals, ever since the Tarasoff case of 1976, have been held to stricter liability for predicting the dangerousness of their clients, even though accurate predictions in this regard are very difficult to make.

7. There has been an increasing emphasis on defining whether a client has a right to treatment, and then of whether he or she has a right to refuse certain treatments, both of which have been related to a right to privacy. In a related vein, persons who have been civilly committed should receive the least restrictive alternative form of treatment, and in a humane environment.

8. Confidentiality is a commitment by a professional person not to reveal information obtained from or provided by the client. Privileged communication refers specifically to the legal protection of the communications obtained in evaluation and in therapy from disclosure in court. There are various specific conditions, for example, reporting child abuse, that void privileged communication.

9. Claims of malpractice against mental health professionals have risen steadily in the past decade. Primary reasons for such malpractice claims are sexual contact with a client, violations of confidentiality, and treatments that have an invasive or intrusive component, such as ECT or medication.

10. A critical task in many cases with a legal component is the detection of deception, as malingering is often an issue. A common technique in lie detection exams is the use of the polygraph.

TERMS TO REMEMBER

forensic psychology	competency to make a will	least restrictive alternative
criminal law	psychological autopsy	deinstitutionalization
civil law	guardianship	right to privacy
standard of proof	civil commitment	confidentiality
burden of proof	adversary process	privileged communication
mens rea	prediction of dangerousness	malpractice
competency to stand trial	right to treatment	malingering
insanity	right to refuse treatment	polygraph

FOR MORE INFORMATION

Grisso, T. (1986) *Evaluating competencies*. New York: Plenum. The best overall presentation of the actual techniques for deciding competency in a wide range of legal issues, including criminal responsibility, child custody, and the traditional competencies, i.e., to stand trial, make a will, or manage one's affairs

Monahan, J. (1981) *Predicting violent behavior*. Beverly Hills, Calif.: Sage. Still the definitive book on both the psychological research and legal issues relevant to this important topic.

Neely, M., and McMurty, R. (1986) *The insanity file: The Case of Mary Todd Lincoln*. Carbondale, Ill. Southern Illinois University Press. Though the term insanity was used at the time of the trial of Mary Todd Lincoln, the wife of President Abraham Lincoln, the focus of the book is actually on her competency to manage her own affairs. This is an interesting presentation, with much supporting historical material, as well as information on issues such as the treatments used in those times.

Smith, S., and Meyer, R. (1987) *Laws, behavior, and mental health: Policy and practice*. New York: New York University Press. Provides an overview of all the issues on the interface of the disciplines of law and psychology, including criminal responsibility; competency; informed consent; right to treatment and to refuse treatment; courtroom and jury process; human experimentation; and legal issues related to specific disorders such as psychopathy, the sexual disorders, and the impulse disorders

Szasz, T. (1986) *Insanity: The idea and its consequences*. New York: Wiley. Offers a history of the insanity defense as well as the arguments by a radical psychiatrist for dropping the insanity defense

Valenstein, E. (1986) *Great and desperate cures*. New York: Basic Books. A renowned neuropsychologist discusses intrusive and coercive treatments, particularly focusing on psychosurgery, ECT, some of the chemotherapies, and their legal and social implications

Glossary

AAMD: The abbreviation for the American Association for Mental Deficiency, a group that promotes and protects the rights of persons with mental retardation.

Abnormal: A comprehensive term, meaning "away from the normal," that includes other psychological descriptors such as "bizarre," "disordered," "different," "diseased," and "deviant."

Abnormal psychology: A sub-area of psychology having to do with the study, assessment, treatment, and prevention of abnormal behavior.

Acetaldehyde: A colorless, water-soluble liquid used primarily in the synthesis of organic compounds.

Achievement motivation: A term used by David McClelland to characterize an individual's level of aspiration. The TAT has proven to be an effective measure of achievement motivation.

Acrophobia: Fear of heights.

Acute: Sudden.

Actualization: The process of achieving one's maximum potential.

Adaptive Behavior Scale (ABS): A rating scale developed by the American Association for Mental Deficiency used to evaluate adaptive behavior as part of the process of assessing mental retardation.

Addiction: Dependence on an agent, such as a drug, because of physiological or biochemical changes induced by that agent. Addiction is often manifested by either withdrawal symptoms upon stopping use of the drug or the need for increasing amounts to achieve the same effect.

Adjustment disorder: Emotional disability occurring in response to an identifiable stressful event, such as divorce or loss of a job.

Adolescence: The phase of development marking the transition from childhood to adulthood, including genital sexual maturation.

Adversary process: Legal process in which both sides in a dispute are expected to present as strong a case as possible for their position before an impartial judge.

Affect: A general term referring to mental processes associated with moods, feelings, emotions, and temperament; the subjective experience of emotion.

Affective disorders: A condition in which the main symptoms are disturbances in mood. The four major categories of this disorder are major depression, dysthymic disorders, bipolar disorders, and cyclothymic disorders.

Agnosia: A neurologic disorder in which there is a failure to recognize common objects, despite intact sensory capabilities. In visual agnosia, a patient is unable to recognize objects or their pictures by sight.

Agoraphobia: A phobic fear of being alone and without recourse to help from others.

Alcoholism: Excessive consumption of alcohol resulting in physical or psychological dependency and impairment of perceptual and cognitive functioning.

Alienation: A sense of apartness from others, often combined with a lack of integration in the self or with a sense that one is behaving in conformity to social rules and the demands of others rather than in response to one's true psychological needs.

Alzheimer's disease: A form of dementia involving the gradual generalized deterioration of brain tissue and accompanied by depression and distractibility, usually ending in death within five years.

Ambivalence: Simultaneous existence of seemingly contradictory emotions or attitudes, e.g., love and hate.

Amnesia: A temporary loss of the ability to recall personal information.

Amnestic syndrome: A form of memory impairment in which the patient is unable to recall information, usually from the immediate past.

Amniocentesis: A test used during pregnancy to detect genetic abnormalities.

Amphetamines: A group of stimulant drugs commonly used to treat hyperactive children and as a prescribed dieting aid.

Analogue measures: A behavioral term referring to the collection of data under conditions that are similar, or analogous, to real world settings. Examples of analogue measures include role playing and laboratory-based observation of a client's behavior.

Angular gyrus: A neural structure at the juncture of parietal, temporal, and occipital lobes that integrates information from all three regions.

Anhedonia: Loss of ability to gain pleasure from life.

Anorexia nervosa: A disorder characterized by a voluntary refusal to eat, resulting in a 20 percent or greater loss of body weight.

Anoxia: A deficiency of oxygen.

Antiandrogens: Drugs, such as medroxyprogesterone acetate and cyproterone acetate, used to treat male pedophiles, exhibitionists, and rapists by reducing testosterone levels so that sexual arousal is minimal or absent.

Anticipatory anxiety: A state of high tension in advance of an event or situation that an individual perceives as potentially threatening.

Antipsychotic medication: Powerful drugs that help control the florid symptoms of psychotic disorders.

Antisocial personality: A disorder characterized by amoral and impulsive behavior, narcissism, and an inability to learn from experience.

Anxiety: A state of psychological distress fundamental to many mental disorders.

Anxiety Disorders: A group of psychological disorders characterized by excessive tension and worry, which may be linked to a specific situation (phobias) or which may involve generalized distress (anxiety states).

Anxiety states: A subgroup of the Anxiety Disorders. They differ from the other subgroup, the phobic disorders, in that the concern of an individual with an anxiety state is directed toward less specific concerns.

Arteriosclerosis: Hardening or thickening of the arteries.

Asphyxia: A combination of anoxia and increased carbon dioxide tension in the blood.

Assertiveness training: A set of techniques, including role playing, designed to help the client more effectively express and satisfy needs that have been inappropriately expressed.

Assessment: A process of gathering information about clients and their problems for the purpose of planning effective psychological intervention.

Association: A term used by behaviorists to refer to the connections established between events occurring at the same time. Pavlov demonstrated the principle of association by presenting an unconditioned and conditioned stimulus simultaneously.

Associative learning: Learning that occurs as a result of the development of stimulus and response elements.

Ataxia: A lack of muscle coordination, usually in the arms and legs.

Atrophy: Disintegration and wasting resulting from interference of necessary sustenance due to disease, disuse, and/or injury.

Attachment: Attachment refers to the process through which the young of all species form a strong bond with their caretaker at or shortly after birth.

Attribution: The process of placing responsibility for a change or causal path.

Autism: A developmental disorder characterized by a pervasive lack of responsiveness to other people, gross deficiency in language development, echolalia, and bizarre responses to the environment.

Autogenic training: A form of self-hypnosis accomplished through deep breathing and meditative activity.

Aversion therapy: A behavior therapy in which actual or imagined performance of an undesirable behavior is simultaneously paired with a negative event (such as self-generated imagery that elicits disgust, electric shock, or a nausea-inducing drug).

Aversive: Characterizes any stimulus that suppresses or stops a particular behavior. A component of pain is often, though not always, one aspect of the aversive stimulus.

Avoidant personality: A disorder in which a person shows a heightened sensitivity to social rejection, a lack of personal initiative, and an absence of self-assertive behaviors.

Barbiturates: Sedatives, used to induce sleep, that quickly produce dependency.

Baseline: Level of response prior to intervention.

BASIC ID: The term used by Lazarus to characterize seven basic areas of functioning: Behavioral, Affective, Sensation, Imagery, Cognition, Interpersonal, and Drugs (i.e., physiological/pharmacological).

Behavioral contracting: An agreement between therapist and client specifying the behaviors expected of the client and the rewards for performing them.

Behavioral observation: A naturalistic or structured observation technique used to learn how a person's accustomed surroundings affect behavior. Specific behaviors are targeted for observation.

Behavioral therapies: Specific techniques such as systematic desensitization therapy (SDT), implosion therapy, aversion therapy, overcorrection, and negative practice.

Behaviorism: A theory that emphasizes the influence of outside forces on a person's observable behavior.

Benzodiazepines: A group of minor tranquilizers, including Valium, that cause muscle relaxation and reduce anxiety.

Bestiality: Sexual intercourse with animals.

Beta blockers: A class of medications originally used to control cardiac angina that have been found helpful in the treatment of anxiety associated with performance situations (e.g., public speaking, musical performances, etc.).

Biased sample: A sample in an experimental design that produces distorted data because of erroneous selection of the sample.

Biofeedback: Any method that enables clients to monitor and obtain continuous information about a physiological process. A client can learn to manipulate these processes with the aid of visual or audio cues from a machine.

Bipolar Disorder: One of the affective disorders characterized by a pattern of mood swings alternating between intense depression and elation.

Birth trauma: Stress attendant on the birth process, which Freud believed to be the precursor of anxiety.

Bizarre: Suggests behavior that differs extremely from norms of the society and also connotes disintegration of behavioral patterns and inadequate coping patterns.

Body systems: In general, a group of related organs or structures that function interdependently in the performance of certain bodily functions. For example, the circulatory system governs the circulation of body fluids and includes the lymphatic and cardiovascular systems.

Borderline personality: A disorder characterized by moodiness, emotional instability, irritability, proneness to boredom, and difficulty in being alone.

Brainstem: Lower brain regions that regulate activation and arousal, among other functions.

Broca's area: A region in the posterior frontal lobe that controls the motor activity necessary for spoken language. Damage to Broca's area inhibits the ability to speak.

Bulimia: Binge eating interspersed with self-induced vomiting.

Burden of proof: The definition of who has the primary responsibility to prove a point, usually referring to a legal case.

Caffeinism: A substance dependency with various side effects, such as anxiety or irritability and gastrointestinal and cardiac complications.

Capgras's syndrome: A condition closely allied to the paranoid disorders involving the delusion that the important people in one's life are impostors.

Castration: The surgical removal of the testicles or ovaries. On a symbolic level, castration refers to interpersonal behaviors in which one person damages another's self-esteem and sense of self-worth.

Catatonic schizophrenia: A form of schizophrenia characterized by extreme stupor or agitation as well as uncontrollable motor and verbal behavior.

Catecholamine theory: The theory that depression reflects an alteration in the level of chemicals that facilitate nerve transmission in the brain, possibly due to a deficiency in the neurotransmitter norepinephrine.

Catharsis: One of the effects of therapy, in which the client experiences a great sense of emotional and psychological relief. Catharsis frequently accompanies the achievement of insight into one's own personal conflicts.

Causation: One factor or variable directly generates an effect.

Central nervous system: The brain and spinal cord.

Central nervous system disorders: Disorders affecting brain functions, divided into two groups: *diffuse* *disorders,* such as Korsakoff's syndrome, syphilis, and multiple sclerosis; and *focal neurologic disorders,* such as vascular disease, brain tumors, and epilepsy.

Cerebral cortex: The largest tissue mass of the brain, associated with the localization of sensory, cognitive, and intellectual functions.

Chemotherapy: The use of chemical agents to treat disorders, more commonly referred to as drug therapy.

Child abuse: Physical, sexual, or emotional abuse of a child; may also refer to neglect, a more passive form of abuse.

Childhood psychopathology: The study of childhood psychological disorders, including the development of effective intervention strategies.

Childhood Schizophrenia: A severe disorder acquired in early childhood involving severely impaired communication and general adaptive capabilities.

Chlorpromazine: A drug (trade name Thorazine) commonly used to treat schizophrenia.

Chromosomal anomalies: Abnormalities resulting from the presence of more (or less) than 46 chromosomes in an individual's genetic cells.

Chronic: Development over a long period, as opposed to acute, or abrupt, development.

Civil commitment: Legal status defining an individual as a (1) mentally ill, and (2) dangerous to self or others, leading to confinement.

Civil laws: Laws designed to fairly and nonviolently settle disputes between persons or parties.

Civilian disaster syndrome: Traumatic reaction to a disaster such as a plane crash, characterized by periods of shock and denial and followed by a reality phase and a recovery period.

Classical conditioning: A learning process in which a neutral stimulus, repetitively paired with reinforcement, eventually elicits a conditioned response.

Client-centered therapy: A term used by Carl Rogers to describe psychotherapy designed to promote self-expression and personal growth. Client-centered therapy emphasizes the need for people to determine their own course of action, rather than to follow the dictates of parents, teachers, or therapists.

Cocaine: A stimulant derived from coca leaves, originally used medically as a local anesthetic, that provides a sense of euphoria.

Cognitive: A term referring to modes of knowing, such as reasoning, judging, and imagining. Cognitive functions are usually associated with intellectual functions, in contrast to those of affect, or the will.

Cognitive behaviorism: A behavioral model that emphasizes the role of thought, or cognitive, processes in regulating behavior.

Cognitive behavior modification: A form of therapy combining cognitive and behavioral techniques to change beliefs, thoughts, and self-verbalizations.

Cognitive conditioning: The development of a thinking pattern through repetitive pairing of thoughts of the acquired behavior with thoughts that either reinforce or suppress it by aversive means.

Cognitive development: Refers to the development of thinking and reasoning skills as studied by Piaget and others.

Cognitive mediators: Mental events that intervene between stimuli and responses.

Cognitive therapy: A form of therapy that emphasizes changing beliefs, thoughts, and feelings.

Collective unconscious: A component of the unconscious, which, according to Jung, is the repository of timeless cultural themes and symbols possessed by every human being.

Combat stress: Mental problems caused by prolonged exposure to the fatigue, uncertainty, and danger of combat.

Common channel: The factor through which generic and mediating factors in a disorder become manifest, e.g., an attention and information processing deficit in schizophrenia.

Community psychology: An approach to psychological intervention that seeks to eliminate environmental conditions leading to mental illness.

Competency to make a will: Legal status of being able to understand the issues and have the ability to form a sane, though not always obviously rational, intent to dispose of one's property.

Competency to stand trial: Legal status, usually defined as (1) understanding the proceedings and (2) being able to adequately assist one's attorney.

Compulsion: A behavior that appears to have been performed without any conscious decision, often reflecting long-term character traits and, in some individuals, behavior that is performed against their own will and desires.

Concordance: Amount of similarity in events or characteristics, e.g., in a study of twins.

Concussion: A disruption of consciousness; often associated with memory problems, disorientation, and some amnesia.

Conditioned response: In classical conditioning, a response that becomes associated with a specific stimulus through learning.

Conditioned stimulus: In classical conditioning, a stimulus that acquires the capacity to elicit a response on the basis of training.

Conduct Disorders: A class of behavior disorders in which the underlying characteristic is a disregard for social conventions and standards of behavior.

Confidentiality: Ethically based commitment by a professional not to reveal information obtained from or provided by the client.

Conflict-generated behaviors: Behaviors that a person implements in conflict situations as a means of coping with the conflict. These may be retained in the person's overall functioning even after the conflict has been resolved.

Continuous sleep therapy: A therapeutic regimen of prolonged enforced sleep.

Controlled experiment: An experiment in which the experimenter can exert the desired level of control over the variables that will be manipulated.

Conversion Disorder: A DSM disorder, one of the somatoform disorders, characterized by dramatic, incapacitating symptoms that usually have symbolic meaning.

Convulsive therapy: Therapies in which the induction of a convulsion, by drug or electric shock, is a central feature.

Coronary prone: A condition of particular susceptibility to a heart attack, often reflecting personality factors (the type A person) as well as genetic and environmental factors.

Correlation: The existence of an observed relationship between variables, as distinct from causation, in which one variable directly affects or generates the other variable.

Criminal law: Branch of law concerned with an individual's violation against laws of society, and the consequent required societal response.

Criminal personality: An overall term to cover the wide variety of personality types who can become involved in criminal behavior.

Critical periods: Stages in development when the maturing organism is especially sensitive to certain classes of stimulation. Critical periods offer an opportunity for especially rapid development in specific areas.

Cross-cultural research: Research that observes behavior patterns in various cultures to determine the common social practices or environmental conditions related to behavior.

Cross-sectional method: Research in which the performance of people of different ages is compared.

Crystallized intelligence: R. B. Cattell's term for intellectual skills based on previously acquired knowledge.

Cultural-familial retardation: A pattern of social and economic deprivation frequently associated with borderline levels of intellectual and adaptive functioning.

Cyclothymic disorder: A combination of manic and depressive components at a chronic but nonpsychotic level.

Defense mechanisms: Response patterns employed to avoid what would otherwise be overwhelming levels of anxiety.

Deinstitutionalization: A policy of placing institutionalized persons at home or in a community facility.

Delerium: Acute brain disorder marked by confusion and disorientation, often accompanied by visual or auditory hallucinations.

Delerium tremens: Referred to as "DTs," occurs in about five percent of people withdrawing from alcohol. Delerium, sometimes accompanied by distress and pain.

Delusion: An inaccurate belief that cannot be changed by rational argument or a demonstration of relevant facts.

Dementia: A significant loss of mental abilities that results from a variety of conditions and involves impairment of the central nervous system.

Dendritic Arborization: A process that takes place during early neurological development, in which nerve fiber axons develop densely branching tendrils, or dendrites, that interconnect with dendrites of other nerve fibers.

Dependent personality: Naive, passive, and docile (though occasionally suspicious) individuals who subjugate their needs to others in order to attain and maintain relationships.

Dependent variable: The results in an experiment that occur as the result of manipulations of the independent variables.

Depersonalization: A disruption or alteration in one's self-image and identity resulting in temporary or permanent loss of contact with reality. Mild experiences of depersonalization, without significant impairment in other areas of life, are fairly common in young adults as they go through a period of relatively rapid identity change and development.

Depressant: A drug that acts to reduce cognitive and physiological behavior and reactions and usually also reduces anxiety and tension. Common depressants are alcohol, tranquilizers, barbiturates, and narcotics.

Depression: In moderate manifestations, a condition characterized by negative feelings about the self, pessimism about the future, a general sense of inadequacy, and a slowed activity rate. More extreme forms involve withdrawal into the self, possible development of a sense of hopelessness, and perhaps delusions of guilt and inadequacy.

Determinants: Features of Rorschach responses such as color, form, shading, and texture. An analysis of determinants aids in the interpretation of a subject's emotional and motivational status.

Deviant: Characterizes behavior that differs markedly from some accepted standard of conduct defined within the group as normal. Deviant behavior often carries a negative connotation.

Diathesis: An inherent predisposition.

Different: Like deviant, characterizes behavior that departs significantly from the accepted norm, but does not necessarily have a negative connotation.

Differential diagnosis: The process of distinguishing between disorders—either physically or mentally based—that may share some characteristics.

Direct experience learning: Lessons learned from one's own life experiences rather than from external sources such as books or the verbalized experience of others.

Direct suggestion: Straightforward recommendations made to clients under hypnosis suggesting new ways of thinking and acting.

Disease model: A theory of abnormal behavior in which persons with psychological problems are viewed as recipients of specific disorders, in much the same way that medical patients are afflicted with diseases.

Disordered: Characterizes a lack of integration in behaviors and a reduction in the ability to cope in various dimensions of life.

Disorganized (hebephrenic): A form of schizophrenia marked by disrupted or incoherent speech and markedly inappropriate affect, e.g., silly giggling.

Dissociative disorder: A disorder in which certain functions of the personality are separated from the self, often accompanied by lack of awareness between these separated aspects of the self.

Dopamine: One of a number of neurotransmitter chemicals in the brain.

Double-blind method: An experimental design in which both the on-site experimenters and the subjects are unaware of how the independent variable has been manipulated.

Down syndrome: Also known as "mongolism"; a genetically-based disorder associated with mental retardation and characteristic physical features including slanted eyes, low-set ears, and protuberant tongue.

Dream interpretation: A technique frequently employed by Freud to help him understand the often hidden nature of his client's unconscious psychological conflicts.

DSM system: A widely used assessment system for mental disorders developed by the American Psychiatric Association.

DSM-III: A recent edition of the *Diagnostic and Statistical Manual of Mental Disorders,* published by the American Psychiatric Association.

Dyslexia: Impaired reading ability; if impairment is total, it is termed alexia.

Dyspareunia: Pain accompanying intercourse.

Dysthymic disorder: Depression, at a chronic but nonpsychotic level.

Ego: Freud's term for a personality structure which controls much of day-to-day behavior, and which serves as a "buffer zone" between the id and the superego.

Ego-alien: Characterizes behaviors and emotions that the person views as inconsistent with his or her decision or values; that is, the person does not consider them part of the essential self.

Ego-dystonic homosexuality: Referring to a homosexual who wishes to change sexual preference because of internal conflicts, e.g., not because of a desire to have children.

Ego ideal: A component of the superego; represents highly desirable traits and characteristics toward which the individual strives.

Ego loss: The psychological (and often physical) loss of a person or object one is attached to.

Ego states: Clearly separated patterns of behavior, often accompanied by separate moods and affects.

Ego-syntonic: Characterizes behaviors and emotions that the person considers consistent with the decisions, ideals, and values of the self.

Electra complex: Freud's term for the incestuous attraction of young girls to their fathers during the phallic stage of psychosexual development. It is analagous to the Oedipal conflict experienced by young male children.

Electroconvulsive therapy: The use of electric shock to induce convulsions, used in the treatment of severe depression and other disorders.

Electroencephalography (EEG):   The monitoring of electrical activity of the brain with a machine by means of electrodes taped to the skull.

Electrosleep therapy: A therapeutic program involving prolonged sleep, induced by passing mild electric current through the brain.

EMH: Educably Mentally Handicapped. This term is used to characterize persons with mild mental retardation who are likely to profit from educational and training programs.

Empathy: The capacity to see things from another person's point of view.

Empiricism: A philosophic viewpoint that maintains that sensory experiences provide the basis for all knowledge.

"Empty-nest" syndrome: The complex of feelings and emotions experienced by parents when their children no longer need any direct care from them and leave the home.

Encopresis: Failure to control one's bowels, which results in fecal soiling beyond the age at which toilet training has been successfully taught.

Endogenous: Originating from internal causes or situations.

Endorphins: Brain-produced chemicals that act to suppress pain, and may induce euphoria.

Enlightenment: A goal of many Eastern meditative techniques, enlightenment is a state of full personal awareness that can only be achieved following years of practice and spiritual discipline.

Enuresis: In its most common form, bedwetting. In general, the term refers to urinary incontinence, whether occurring during the day or night.

Epilepsy: A disruption of consciousness during which convulsions (seizures) may occur. *Petit mal* epilepsy is marked by momentary loss of consciousness, usually accompanied by eye-blinking. *Grand mal* epilepsy involves generalized convulsions that cause the individual to fall to the ground and thrash about uncontrollably. *Psychomotor* epilepsy is marked by a number of periods of relatively normal behavior, occasionally marked by violent acts the individual does not remember.

Equipotentiality: A term used by Lashley in reference to the capability of different regions of the cerebral cortex to mediate the same behavioral or cognitive function.

Erectile dysfunction: An inability to achieve or maintain an erection; commonly referred to as impotence.

Ergot: A poison derived from a fungus; causes convulsions and abnormal behavior.

Essential hypertension: A general term for high blood pressure, the cause of which is not specified.

Etiology: The underlying cause of a mental disorder.

Exhibitionism: The exposure of the genitals to a stranger to obtain sexual arousal.

Existential therapy: A therapy that emphasizes increased consciousness and articulation of personal choices, and responsibility for the consequences of choices made.

Exogenous: Originating from external causes or situations.

Explosive disorder: A disorder marked by an outburst of physical or verbal violence in a person who is not usually aggressive or hostile.

Extinction: Causing a response to lessen or cease by not reinforcing it.

Factitious disorder: The faking of a disorder or disability, to achieve a unique psychological gratification, such as enjoyment of the nurturance accompanying hospitalization.

False negative: An inaccurate prediction or diagnosis that there is no disorder.

False positive: An inaccurate prediction or diagnosis that there is disorder.

Family therapy: A form of therapy that views psychopathology as impairment in communication among family members, rather than as a condition affecting a single person, and focuses on the entire family as the client.

Fear: The emotional response generated by an actual external threat.

Fetishism: A condition in which nonliving objects are used as the exclusive or consistently preferred method of stimulating sexual arousal.

Fixation: In psychodynamic theory, fixation means that the child's maturation is arrested at a specific stage of psychosexual development.

Flight of ideas: A rapid progression from one thought to another.

Fluid intelligence: R. B. Cattell's term for intellectual skills manifested in rapid decision-making processes and other manifestations of flexible thinking.

Forensic psychology: Sub-area of psychology concerned with matters having a significant component from both the fields of law and psychology.

Frequency distribution: A statistical term describing the relationship between different values of a variable and the frequency with which they occur. Two important characteristics of frequency distributions are the mean, or average value, and the standard deviation, a measure of how widely values in the distribution vary.

Frontal lobe: The foremost region of the brain, believed to play a role in the regulation and planning of behavioral responses.

Frotteurism: Obtaining sexual gratification by touching and rubbing against a stranger.

Frustration-aggression hypothesis: A concept that conditions that generate frustration subsequently lead to aggression.

Fugue: A period of amnesia marked by leaving home and often accompanied by wandering and a change of identity and occupation.

Future Shock: Alvin Toffler's term for a sense of insecurity and dread resulting from feelings of being unable to cope with the swift changes that occur in modern living.

Gender disorder: Contradiction between sexual anatomy and a deeply felt conviction one should be the other sex.

General Adaptation Syndrome (GAS): A reaction pattern to stress first identified by Hans Selye, the GAS involves high levels of physiological and physical activitation designed to cope with perceived stress.

Generalization: The ability to apply skills and new behaviors learned in one situation or environment to other situations.

Generalized anxiety disorder: A chronic version of the panic disorder, characterized by a general physiological stress syndrome.

Generic: Characterizes a nonspecific cause of an action or disorder.

Genotype: The genetic code contained in the 46 chromosomes of an individual's cells.

Grandiose: Reflecting an exaggerated belief in one's abilities and powers. If the exaggeration is significant, it may be termed a delusion.

Graves disease: A hyperthyroid condition in which a high level of apprehension and anxiety commonly results in paranoid and confused thoughts and hallucinations.

Guardianship: Legal status defining one as in need of assistance in handling one's personal or financial affairs.

Gynemimesis: High identification with the opposite sex, cross-dress, may take hormones, but stop short of transsexual surgery. Usually a disorder of males.

Habituation: The process of becoming dependent on anything, such as a drug, through consistent use. Habituation is usually accompanied by a strong need to return to the use of that agent.

Hallucinations: Sensory experiences in the absence of appropriate stimuli, e.g., hearing something that is not there.

Hallucinogens: A substance that induces hallucinations.

Halstead-Reitan Test Battery: One of the most widely used neuropsychological test batteries in current use.

Hemodialysis therapy: The use of an artificial kidney machine to purify the blood of any toxic elements, sometimes used in the treatment of schizophrenia.

Heterosexuality: A sexual preference for, or activity with, someone of the opposite sex.

Hierarchy: Used in systematic desensitization, hierarchies are groups of stimulus images arranged in order according to the degree of anxiety which each evokes.

Hippocampal formations: A number of small areas of the brain that lie below the cortical formations and are critical to the integration of behavior, especially memory functions.

Histamine: A substance commonly found in the body where tissues are damaged. If given intravenously, histamines cause skin flushing, lowered blood pressure, secretion of gastric acid, and headache. Antihistamines, often used in the treatment of allergies, act to reduce these effects.

Histrionic personality: A disorder characterized by attention seeking, the need for a high level of emotional responsiveness from others, and extremely reactive behaviors.

Homeostasis: The balance maintained in a psychologically healthy system as members consistently adjust to each other to maintain predictable patterns.

Homosexuality: A sexual preference for, or activity with, someone of the same sex.

Humanistic therapy: Therapy based on treating the whole person rather than on impersonal analysis. Examples are client-centered therapy, existential therapy, reality therapy, and Gestalt therapy.

Hyperactivity: A pattern of excessive activity and distractibility in children.

Hyperactivity syndrome: A pattern of excessively active behavior originally believed to reflect underlying brain damage. A variety of physical and psychological factors have since been identified that may give rise to hyperactive behavior.

Hypertension: Higher than normal blood pressure for one's age.

Hypnosis: A state marked by heightened suggestibility toward another person, the hypnotist; usually accompanied by a sleeplike state and "trance" behaviors. Amnesia for events during hypnosis may or may not occur.

Hypochondriasis: A DSM somatoform disorder characterized by the strong conviction that one is seriously ill, in the absence of clear documenting evidence.

Hypothesis: An idea to be tested experimentally.

Hysteria: A traditional term, not incorporated in DSM-III, that refers primarily to neurotic patterns in which there is high suggestibility, dramatic behaviors, emotional instability, and manipulative interpersonal behaviors. It also refers to conversion hysteria, in which physical symptoms such as blindness or paralysis symbolically or directly reflect a psychological conflict.

Iatrogenic: Refers to disorder that is the result of treatment for another disorder.

Id: The most primitive part of one's personality. According to Freud's theory of psychosexual development, the id is a repository of primitive drives and impulses whose expression is normally controlled by both the ego and superego.

Identity crisis: Acute upset related to an identity disorder: an attempt to define the parameters of the self.

Identity disorder: An impairment of social or occupational functioning caused by anxieties related to educational, interpersonal, and vocational decisions.

Imipramine: A medication commonly used to treat anxiety disorders that has also been used successfully in the treatment of childhood nocturnal enuresis.

Implosion therapy: A behavioral therapy based on the technique of flooding, in which the therapist tries to maximize anxiety to help the client overcome fear of a particular stimulus.

Impulse disorders: Acting-out disorders such as kleptomania, pyromania, pathological gambling, and overeating.

Incest: Socially prohibited sexual interaction between close family members.

Independent variable: The variable in an experiment that is systematically manipulated by the experimenter.

Information processing: The ability to take pieces of information and process them accurately and optimally.

Informed consent: A legal term denoting the provision of complete information about a technique, including possible negative and positive outcomes of participation, prior to a client's participation in the technique or experiment.

Inhalants: A group of drugs, including anesthetics such as nitrous oxide, aerosol propellants, and volatile solvents, some of whose chronic abuse can cause organic brain dysfunction.

Inhibition: A hesitancy to behave in a certain manner due to a mental blockage.

Insanity: Legal status or condition excusing a person from responsibility for an alleged criminal act.

Institutionalization: A process of adapting to a specific environment whose demands may differ markedly from those of a normal environment.

Intellectualization: The tendency to talk or think about a problem while avoiding its emotional impact and not doing anything to cope with the problem.

Interpersonal: Refers to anxieties or conflicts generated between two or more persons.

Intrapersonal: Refers to anxieties or conflicts generated within the self, such as conflicting belief systems.

In vitro: Describes experiments conducted under laboratory, rather than real world, conditions.

In vivo: Describes experiments conducted under actual conditions.

Juvenile delinquency: Types of deviant behaviors among adolescents that elicit an official control response from a societal agency.

Kleptomania: Compulsive stealing by a person who has no obvious need or use for the object stolen.

Korsakoff's amnestic syndrome: A form of amnesia associated chiefly with chronic alcoholism, in which patients appear unable to retain new knowledge, although both their conscious awareness and recall of past events are often intact.

Labile: Refers to variability in responsiveness.

Learned helplessness (LH): A theory of depression development that is marked by helpless behavior and thoughts, sometimes caused by inconsistent parenting.

Learning-avoidance theory: A theory that the symptoms of obsessions and compulsions are methods evolved for controlling anxiety.

Least restrictive alternative: Legal concept, asserting that persons forced to receive treatment should receive the least restrictive form that is available and effective.

Level of significance: The degree of probability that the results of a specific experiment could have been obtained by chance.

Libido: Freud's term for biological energy that is channeled into one's activities according to the dictates of the pleasure principle.

Lithium: A chemical element used to treat mania.

Litigious: A high inclination to undertake legal actions against others, often over minor issues.

Lobotomy: A neurosurgical procedure in which the frontal lobe is disconnected from the rest of the brain. Lobotomies were performed on violent and aggressive patients because of their tranquilizing effects; they created an irreversible state of apathy.

Longitudinal studies: Research designed to test the same group periodically so that development can be traced over a designated period.

Lysergic acid diethylamide (LSD): A psychotomimetic drug that causes hallucinations and delusions of varying intensity.

Maintenance variables: Factors such as social isolation, scapegoating, and learned helplessness, that act to solidify and maintain a person's status as a schizophrenic.

Major depression: A severe, often psychotic, form of depression.

Maladaptive behavior: Abnormal behavior.

Malingering: The faking of a disorder or disability in order to avoid responsibility, duty, or the expectancies of others.

Malpractice: Legal concept that a professional is responsible as a result of incompetent, malicious, or negligent behavior.

Mania: Behavior characterized by hyperactive motor and cognitive behaviors, as well as excitement and impulsiveness.

Marijuana: A plant whose active component, tetrahydrocannabinol (THC), induces sleepiness and mild euphoria.

Marital therapy: A form of therapy that deals with the distressed couple as the client.

Masochism: The intentional acceptance of activities that generate pain or humiliation to produce sexual excitement.

Mediating variables: Perceptual, attentional, and information-processing deficits in schizophrenics.

Medical (organic) model: The concept that mental disturbance results from physical disease and should therefore be treated with physical methods.

Megavitamin therapy: The administration of large doses of specific vitamins, especially the B vitamins, in the treatment of mental disorders.

Meiosis: The division of cells without reduplication of chromosomes to form gametes, each of which has 23 chromosomes.

Meningitis: Inflammation of the tissue surrounding the brain and spinal cord.

Mens rea: A criminal state of mind; "guilty mind."

Mental disorder: A specific pattern of abnormal behavior.

Mental retardation: Slowness in mental development, classified by markedly subaverage IQ scores.

Metabolism: The breakdown of a substance directly into carbon dioxide and water by oxidation, with the remainder absorbed directly into the intestinal tract instead of being processed through the more complex digestive system.

Midlife crisis: Upset or maladaptive behavior associated with a midlife transition.

Midlife transition: A period of reevaluation of life goals and roles, often occurring in middle age.

Migraine headache: A severe form of vascular headache that is frequently incapacitating. Treatment employing thermal feedback and other techniques to decrease brain blood vessel dilation is generally called for.

Milieu therapy: A form of institutional therapy emphasizing a concerned and supportive staff, pleasant surroundings, meaningful and purposeful activities, and a deemphasis on restrictions.

Model: A systematic set of related facts and hypotheses used to generate further experiments designed to verify or disprove the ideas that flow from the model.

Modeling: A specific form of observational learning in which a person is shown the behavior intended to replace previous problematic behavior.

Mood: A consistent or pervasive emotion that influences our view of the world.

Moral development: As used by Kohlberg, the stage-wise process of achieving a mature capacity to make ethical and moral judgments.

Motor behavior: Actions involving at least large muscle groups, such as movements of the arms and legs, or overall body movements.

Multi-infarct dementia: Dementia caused by a series of strokes in the brain.

Multiaxial classification: A procedure employed in DSM for rating mental disorders on several axes or dimensions.

Multimodal approach: A theory of therapeutic intervention that holds that a variety of therapeutic techniques is necessary for the optimal treatment or case management of almost all disorders.

Multimodal therapy: The flexible and practical use of diverse therapeutic techniques in the treatment of mental disorders.

Multiple personality: A disorder in which one person has two or more dissociated personalities, each a complete identity with a consistent set of behavioral and social patterns.

Multiple sclerosis: A degenerative disease resulting from multiple lesions in the white matter of the brain and characterized by impaired mobility, coordination, and vision.

Munchausen syndrome: A believable presentation of fictitious physical symptomatology to elicit and sustain multiple hospitalizations.

Myelination: The process by which nerve cell fibers are coated with a fatty sheath that improves electrical conductivity along the nerves.

Myths: Traditional beliefs that evolve in a particular society to reflect the society's expectations. Myths may determine normal behaviors in that society.

Narcissism: An exaggerated concern with the self, usually marked by defensive behaviors designed to protect the self and a lack of sensitivity to the needs of others, although the individual may verbalize sensitivity to and concern for others.

Narcissistic personality: A disorder in which interpersonal difficulties are caused by an inflated sense of self-worth, exhibitionistic behavior to obtain admiration, and indifference to the welfare of others.

Naturalistic observation: The observation of behavior in its natural setting.

Neobehaviorism: A refinement of simple associative learning that includes mental, or cognitive, processes.

Neologism: New word; a sign of schizophrenia.

Neurology: The study of the brain and nervous system.

Neuron: An individual nerve cell.

Neuropsychologist: A psychologist—usually a clinical psychologist by training—who specializes in the relationships between brain function and dysfunction in various behavioral patterns.

Neuropsychology: The scientific study of brain-behavior relationships.

Neurosis: A general term for comparatively mild mental disorders, reflecting maladaptive behavior patterns that are typically amenable to therapeutic intervention.

Neurotic: A traditional term used in earlier DSMs to describe disorders supposedly produced by anxiety. The DSM-III replaced the term with other descriptors, such as the anxiety, factitious, somatoform, and dissociative disorders.

Neurotransmitter: A hormone-like chemical that communicates signals between nerve cells.

Nicotine: A drug contained in tobacco that can produce psychological or physical dependency.

Obesity: Significant overweight.

Objective self-awareness: The capacity, highly valued among humanistic psychotherapists, to have a clear understanding of one's needs and motivations.

Objective-subjective stress theories: Theories along a range of dimensions, diverging on the notion of whether the stressor resides primarily in the external agent (objective) or in the individual's perception of the external stressor (subjective).

Obsession: A persistent and often irrational idea or set of ideas.

Obsessive-compulsive disorder: A disorder in which there is excessive concern with detail, organization, punctuality, and routine, often accompanied by embarrassment about such behaviors and extreme measures to hide them from the scrutiny of others.

Obsessive-compulsive personality: A disorder characterized by emotional control and distance, conformity, excessive concern with details, interpersonal dominance, and high orientation toward efficiency and productivity, with a significant lack of interpersonal warmth and emotional responsivity.

Occipital lobes: The posterior portion of the brain, known primarily as the site of the primary visual cortex.

Oedipal conflict: Freud's name for the incestuous desires of male children in the phallic stage of psychosexual development to sexually possess their mothers. The term is drawn from the Greek myth in which the tragic figure Oedipus unknowingly killed his father and married his mother.

Operant conditioning: An associative learning process through which desired responses are immediately followed by rewards, or reinforcements.

Operational definition: The description of a phenomenon in terms that can be measured.

Opiates: A group of painkilling narcotic drugs, including morphine and heroin, that induce euphoria, usually followed by lethargy and sleepiness.

Organic Brain Syndrome: A generic term used to describe the presence of diffuse cerebral impairment.

Organic mental disorders: Organic brain syndromes that can be attributed to a specific transient or permanent dysfunction of the brain.

Overt behavior: External and measurable behaviors.

Panic disorder: An anxiety state marked by episodic anxiety reactions and accompanied by a sustained high level of psychological tension.

Paradigm: A pattern or model that defines concepts and procedures.

Parameter: A defining criterion.

Paranoid: Describes behavior dominated by a defensive and distancing attitude toward others, often accompanied or generated by delusions.

Paranoid personality: A chronic, nonpsychotic disorder wherein the person is suspicious, hyperalert, litigious, and has difficulty allowing others to see any vulnerability.

Paranoid personality disorder: A nonpsychotic pattern marked by suspiciousness, hyperalertness, and an inability to become psychologically vulnerable to others.

Paranoid psuedocommunity: The group of individuals who share the paranoid's distorted beliefs and thus act to maintain those beliefs.

Paranoid schizophrenia: A form of schizophrenia in which the client shows persecutory or grandiose beliefs, sometimes accompanied by hallucinations and fragmented associations. Paranoid schizophrenics show less impaired judgment and are usually more intelligent than other schizophrenics.

Paraphilias: The sexual disorders, including fetishism, transvestism, zoophilia, pedophilia, exhibitionism, and voyeurism.

Parasympathetic nervous system: A division of the autonomic nervous system that is generally activated under conditions of high stress.

Parietal lobe: A region of the brain which processes information pertaining to visuospatial configurations.

Parkinson's disease: A chronic nervous disorder characterized by muscular weakness, muscular tremors, bodily rigidity, and a peculiar style of walking.

Participant observer: A role ascribed by Sullivan to therapists who retain the capacity to evaluate clients while interacting with them.

Passive-aggressive personality: A personality pattern in which hostility is expressed indirectly.

Pathognomonic signs: Neurologic diagnostic signs that imply a very specific form of brain damage.

Pathological gambling: An impulse disorder characterized by irresistible impulses to gamble.

Patient role: The passive and non-decision–making role assumed by or imposed on a patient in an institution in which the person allows others to take responsibility for even minor decisions.

Pederasty: The sexual initiation of young boys by older men.

Pedophilia: A preference for sexual experiences with sexually immature persons, sometimes involving force or coercion.

Performance anxiety: Anxiety about performance that in turn disrupts the performance; often cited as an explanation for sexual dysfunction.

Perseveration: A response pattern characteristic of many patients with frontal lobe lesions, in which a single response is continuously repeated in a rigid, inflexible manner.

Personality disorders: Maladaptive patterns of behavior that are chronic, thoroughly integrated in the personality, and difficult to treat, partly because affected people do not perceive themselves as disordered.

Personality inventories: Instruments used to infer underlying general personality traits and often based on response patterns to large numbers of specific questions.

Personality pattern theory: The theory, now generally discredited, that stress disorders are a direct representation of a person's psychic conflicts.

Phenotype: An observed characteristic that expresses an underlying hereditary characteristic.

Phenylketonuria (PKU): A condition in which lack of an enzyme causes toxic levels of phenylalanine that, if not controlled, eventually cause deterioration of the central nervous system.

Phobia: An irrational but strong, persistent, and usually disabling fear triggered by a specific stimulus or set of stimuli, such as a phobic fear of heights (acrophobia).

Phobic disorders: A subgrouping of the anxiety disorders with the concern of the individual being directed at more specific targets than is true in the anxiety states, the other subgroup.

Phrenology: The practice, now largely discredited, of linking personality traits to bumps on the skull that were believed to reflect underlying areas of brain development.

Pick's disease: A form of presenile dementia that begins with episodes of erratic, impulsive behavior and results in profound deterioration and death, usually within five years.

PKU: PKU, or phenylketonuria, is a genetically based metabolic disorder which, if untreated, results in mental retardation.

Placebo effect: A response to a placebo—an inert or neutral agent—as though it had potency or therapeutic effect.

Pleasure principle: Freud's description of a motivating force that causes people to seek out pleasurable experiences and sensations.

Polydrug abuse: The use of several prescription or nonprescription drugs that cause physical or psychological dependency.

Polygraph: A machine, also known as a lie detector, that measures the reactions of body systems such as heart rate, blood pressure, and respiration. Systems chosen for measurement depend on the individual polygrapher's theories and mandates of state law.

Posthypnotic suggestions: Suggestions made to clients under hypnosis intended to affect their behavior once they emerge from the hypnotic state.

Posttraumatic stress disorder: An anxiety disorder with disabling psychological reactions subsequent to a severe trauma or catastrophe.

Premenstrual Syndrome: A specific disorder, often marked by depression, related to premenstrual changes.

Premorbid: Referring to the level of functioning prior to the onset of disorder.

Premack principle: The principle that states that a high-probability behavior will reinforce and increase the occurrence of a low probability behavior with which it is paired.

Premature ejaculation: The inability of a male to exericse voluntary control over the ejaculatory reflex, so that he reaches orgasm too quickly.

Preparedness: A concept that people are inherently predisposed toward developing certain types of phobias, e.g., of snakes or heights.

Presenile dementia: A state of mental deterioration due to neurologic disease, with onset between middle age and advanced age.

Prevalence: Frequency of disorder within a specific population.

Primitive conflict: Conflicts and anxieties originally generated during the earliest stages of life that continue to have some relationship to the issues of that period, such as fear of abandonment or the loss of basic support systems.

Privileged communication: Legal protection from disclosure of communications within a professional relationship.

Prognosis: Predicted outcome.

Projection: A defense mechanism in which a person denies some impulse and attributes it to others.

Projective tests: Tests that confront the subject with a comparatively ambiguous stimulus, responses to which are organized according to the client's particular needs and motivations.

Psychic determinism: A belief, prevalent in Freud's time, that mental forces outside conscious awareness controlled behavior.

Psychoanalytic therapy: The form of therapy based on the work of Freud in which the therapist studies the client's unconscious by analyzing transference reactions and interpreting dreams.

Psychodynamic therapies: Forms of therapy influenced by Freudian theory but emphasizing the interpersonal context and principles of social psychology.

Psychogenic pain disorder: A DSM disorder, one of the somatoform disorders, in which the patient is troubled by significant levels of physical pain that have no apparent medical basis.

Psychological autopsy: An after-the-fact, e.g., after a person is dead, examination of an individual's psychological status.

Psychopath: *See* Antisocial personality.

Psychophysiological: Characterizes the interaction of psychological and physiological factors in the genesis of a disorder. Psychological factors usually play a larger causal role, although the physiological disorder is often the manifested symptom.

Psychosexual arousal dysfunction: In females, either an inability to maintain the swelling and lubrication responses of sexual excitement necessary to complete intercourse, or an inability to achieve orgasm. In males, either an inability to retain erection necessary to attain or provide sexual gratification, or an inability to achieve orgasm.

Psychosexual development: Freud's description of the process through which one achieves adult sexual maturation.

Psychosis: A mental disorder sufficiently severe to result in personality disorganization and a loss of contact with reality.

Psychosomatic: *See* Psychophysiological.

Psychosomatic disorder: A term formerly used to describe disorders in which psychological factors contributed significantly to physical problems. The DSM system uses the term "Psychological Factors Affecting Physical Conditioning" in referring to comparable conditions.

Psychosurgery: A surgical procedure aimed at changing or controlling emotions and behavior through the destruction of brain tissue.

Psychotherapy: The interaction between a psychologist or psychiatrist and a client, aimed at helping the client modify feelings, attitudes, or behavior.

Public performance anxiety: A specific type of performance anxiety; usually generated by a requirement to make a public presentation.

Pyromania: Compulsive setting of fires.

Rape: The use or threat of violence by a male to force a female into a sexual encounter.

RAS: RAS stands for Reticular Activating System, a region of the brainstem that controls one's level of alertness.

Rational-emotive therapy (RET): A form of therapy developed by Albert Ellis that seeks to identify and eliminate irrational cognitive beliefs believed to interfere with effective functioning.

Reality testing: The ability to obtain a clear and accurate picture of the world by effectively observing and interacting with the world.

Recessive trait disorders: Inherited disorders, including many metabolically based forms of mental retardation, that appear only if each parent contributes a recessive gene carrying the trait for the disorder.

Reciprocal inhibition: A behavioral technique utilized in systematic desensitization that involves training a relaxation response to anxiety-arousing cues.

Refrigerator parent: An early term used to describe parents of autistic children, who were erroneously believed to be cold and unemotional.

Regression: Reversion to an earlier and less adaptive level of psychological functioning.

Regression hypnotherapy: A form of hypnosis in which the client is made to regress to earlier developmental periods and recreate early experiences.

Reinforcer: The consequence of a response that makes it more likely that that response will occur again.

Reliability: A statistical concept that refers to the consistency of a test measure.

Repression: A defense mechanism that attempts to totally block out awareness of a disturbing memory or a disrupting impulse.

Resistance: A term used by Freud in reference to psychological impediments to psychoanalytic therapy. Resistances reflect the action of defense mechanisms, which bar from consciousness impulses, drives, and traumatic memories that reside in the id.

Response stereotypy: The characteristic response pattern of a vulnerable organ system to stress.

Right to privacy: Legal concept, usually asserting that the Constitution establishes a right to be free from unwarranted intrusions on personal privacy.

Right to refuse treatment: Legal concept, usually asserting that involuntarily confined persons may refuse some or all treatment without negative consequences.

Right to treatment: Legal concept, usually asserting that involuntarily confined persons have a legal right to adequate treatment while confined.

Role playing: Simulating real-world social interactions through practice and rehearsal.

Rorschach inkblot test: A frequently used projective technique in which a clinician associates a person's responses to 10 symmetric inkblots with aspects of personality such as dominant traits, underlying motives, and areas of conflict.

Sadism: The real or simulated infliction of pain or humiliation to produce sexual excitement.

Schizoaffective: A disorder marked by clear features of both schizophrenia and affective disorder, usually depression.

Schizoid personality: A chronic pattern of asocial, inhibited, and isolating behaviors.

Schizophrenia: A subcategory of psychosis characterized by significant and consistent thought disorder.

Schizophrenogenic: Generally describes destructive behaviors exhibited by parents in their interactions with their children that may facilitate the development of schizophrenia in the children.

Schizophrenogenic parents: Parents who, according to the double-bind theory of schizophrenia, foster disturbances in children by constantly placing them in no-win, "damned if you do, damned if you don't" situations.

Schizotypal personality: A chronic disorder with symptoms that appear to be less severe but similar to those of schizophrenia. Under stress, they may decompensate into schizophrenia.

Secondary gain: The reward or gain that a person experiences in the process of being disordered. Secondary gains often act to maintain the disorder.

Self-actualization: A term used by humanistic psychologists to refer to an underlying human motive toward high levels of personal fulfillment and accomplishment.

Self-defeating personality: A personality disorder marked by a pattern wherein the person often becomes a victim and/or fails. Masochism is often present. A controversial category, as some assert it shifts blame from the aggressor to the victim.

Self-esteem: Feelings and beliefs about one's personal worth.

Senility: Dementia attributed to aging.

Sensate focus: A therapy for sexual dysfunction that orients clients to focus on the process of experiencing and giving pleasure rather than trying to perform sexually or "spectatoring" while sexually involved.

Sexual dysfunction: Sexual problems such as psychosexual arousal dysfunction, inhibited sexual desire, premature ejaculation, vaginismus, and dyspareunia.

Sexual identity: One's psychological view of oneself as male or female.

Shame-humiliation theory: A theory of paranoid behavior based on the idea that paranoid behavior is generated by the self to avoid experiences of humiliation or shame.

Shaming: A parenting style that depends primarily on the inducement of embarrassment and guilt and the suppression of assertiveness.

Shaping: A term used by behavioralists to describe the process of teaching complex behavior patterns by breaking them down into simple components, each of which is systematically reinforced.

Shared paranoid disorder (folie a deux): A disorder marked by the sharing of a delusional system, in which one person passively incorporates the psychosis of another into his or her own belief system.

Siblings: Offspring of the same parent or parents.

Simple phobia: A phobia focused on very specific objects or situations.

Single subject experiment: An experimental design, using only one subject, in which conditions are systematically varied in order to assess the consequent effects.

Social learning theory: An extension of learning theory that focuses on the mechanisms by which social behavioral patterns are learned.

Social phobia: Persistent anxiety about the possible scrutiny of one's behavior by others.

Somatic: Pertaining to the body.

Somatization Disorder: A DSM disorder, one of the somatoform disorders, referring to a pattern of chronic, multiple complaints beginning before age 30.

Somatoform: Refers to disorders with physical symptoms but reflecting a primary psychological conflict and disorder.

Somatogenic: Disorder in the physical body (soma) is the psychological disorder.

Somesthetic cortex: A region of the cerebral cortex that mediates sensations of temperature, pressure, pain, and feedback from joints and muscles.

Somnambulism: Sleepwalking, a nondistressing, learned behavior that does not appear to have any psychologically generated, dissociative component.

Spontaneous remission: Recovery in the absence of any known therapeutic intervention.

Spouse abuse: Physical or emotional abuse of a spouse.

Stage Theory: An approach to studying human development which postulates that maturation takes place through a series of identifiable stages.

Standard of proof: Degree of evidence required to come to a legal decision.

Stanford-Binet Intelligence Scale: A widely used measure of general intelligence in children. The Stanford-Binet has evolved to its present form from a screening test developed in the late 19th century by Alfred Binet.

Statistical rarity: An uncommon occurrence, defined as such by data or statistics, rather than by reasoning or inference.

Stimulant: A drug, such as amphetamines, that produces increased cognitive and physiological behavior, accompanied by feelings of increased alertness and energy.

Stimulation-avoidant: A personality trait of withdrawing from or avoiding stimulation, often seen in schizophrenia.

Stimulus void: A reduction in the stimuli to which a person is usually oriented and responsive, often as a result of the loss of an important object or person in one's world.

Stress: A general term referring to stimuli that elicit physiological responses characterized by high levels of activation, alertness, and tension.

Stroke: Rupture or blockage of a brain blood vessel.

Stupor: An unresponsive state, with total or partial unconsciousness.

Subjective discomfort: An individual's own judgment as to whether or not he or she is content with feelings or functioning.

Substance abuse: A level of alcohol or drug abuse characterized by either psychological dependence or a pathological pattern of use.

Substance dependence: A level of alcohol or drug abuse requiring fulfillment of the criteria for substance abuse and the additional factor of either tolerance or withdrawal.

Suicide: Taking one's own life.

Superego: The third and last major component of personality development, according to Freud's theory of psychosexual development. The superego is analogous to one's conscience, promoting morally correct and responsible behavior.

Sylvian fissure: A large cleft in the cerebral cortex that separates the frontal and temporal lobes.

Symptom: A manifestation or sign of disorder.

Symptom substitution: The appearance of new signs of psychological distress following successful treatment for other symptoms.

Syndrome: A cluster or pattern of symptoms found in a particular disorder.

Syphilis: An infectious venereal disease whose initial symptoms are sores or chancres at the infection site. If left untreated, syphilis can result in paretic psychosis and death.

Systematic desensitization: The use of relaxation exercises in therapy to alleviate anxiety associated with a feared object or event.

Systems Theory: A perspective on abnormal behavior which focuses on interactions between group and family members as the source of abnormal behavior.

Systolic/diastolic pressure: Pressure exerted by the heart when pumping blood (systolic) and when at rest (diastolic).

Tardive dyskinesia: A disorder involving impairments in motor and memory skills that results from chronic treatment with antipsychotic medications.

Taxonomy: The accurate observation and classification of phenomena.

Temporal lobe: One of the four major subdivisions of the cerebral cortex, the temporal lobes mediate memory skills and auditory comprehension capabilities.

Terminal drop: An abrupt decline in cognitive functions that may be predictive of impending death.

Test anxiety: A specific form of performance anxiety; anxiety in anticipation of, or during, the process of being tested.

Thematic Apperception Test (TAT): A projective test developed by Henry Murray to assess the preoccupations and themes concerning clients' social environments.

Thought disorder: A problem in thinking that is not related to retardation but is seen in various manifestations such as unique or bizarre logic, skipped premises in analytic thinking, and unusual associations of words.

Token economy: A program in an institution that rewards clients for positive behaviors with tokens that can be exchanged for privileges or goods, such as cigarettes.

Tranquilizers: A class of commonly prescribed medications used to alleviate symptoms of anxiety and agitation.

Transactional analysis: A form of therapy that analyzes various manipulative interpersonal behaviors as a way of helping people conceptualize disturbed interpersonal relationships.

Transference: The process by which a patient's outside relationships strongly influence the nature of his or her relationship with the therapist. In transference, people ascribe to new acquintances characteristics of people who have significantly shaped their development.

Transmethylation hypothesis: A theory that a change in the molecular structure of norepinephrine might produce a hallucinogen in the brain that could cause schizophrenia.

Transsexualism: A condition characterized by an individual's strong and persistent identification with the opposite sex, manifested by a desire for a change of sexual apparatus through hormone therapy and surgery and by cross-dressing that is not done for sexual excitement.

Transvestism: The seeking of sexual arousal by wearing clothes of the opposite sex.

Tremor: Repetitious and spastic muscle movements.

Trepanning: A primitive surgical technique practiced by primitive man in which an opening was cut in the skull of a deranged individual to release the evil spirits believed responsible for aberrant behavior.

Trichotillomania: A disorder marked by persistent pulling of one's own hair, often resulting in baldness and secondary infection.

Trisomy 21: The genetic condition associated with Down syndrome, so named because of an extra (third) chromosome attached to the 21st pair.

Type A/B personality: Contrasting behavior patterns linked to differential vulnerability to cardiac problems. Type A individuals, those most vulnerable, are hard driving, competitive, and aggressive.

Unconditional positive regard: A term from humanistic psychology referring to the capacity to accept people as they present themselves, without passing judgment.

Unconditioned response: In classical conditioning, a response automatically elicited by a specific stimulus without prior training. Salivation in response to the sight of food is an example of an unconditioned response.

Unconditioned stimulus: In classical conditioning, a stimulus that automatically elicits a specific response without prior training. Touching a hot stove is an unconditioned stimulus that automatically causes one's hand to be withdrawn.

Vaginismus: Intense involuntary spasms of the vaginal musculature that make intercourse extremely painful or impossible.

Validity: The extent to which a test instrument accurately measures what it is intended to measure.

Vineland Social Maturity Scale: A scale of adaptive behavior used in the assessment of mental retardation.

Voyeurism: The repetitive seeking out of situations in which to observe the sex organs or sexual activity of others as a means of stimulating arousal and orgasm.

Wechsler scales: Intelligence tests widely used in current clinical practice.

Wernicke's syndrome: Neurologic disorder marked by confusion, ataxia, and ophthalmoplegia; indicates a thiamine deficiency.

Word salad: Confused and jumbled combination of words and phrases; a symptom of schizophrenia.

Zoophilia: A rare condition in which animals are used as the exclusive or preferred method of sexual stimulation.

References

Abad, V., and Boyce, E. (1979) Issues in the psychiatric evaluation of Puerto Ricans: A socio-cultural perspective. *Journal of Operational Psychology 10,* 28–29.

Abel, G., Becker, J., Blanchard, E., and Flanagan, B. (1981) The behavioral assessment of rapists. In J. Hays, T. Roberts, and K. Solway (Eds.), *Violence and the violent individual.* New York: SP Books.

Abraham, K. (1916) (1960) The first pregenital stage of the libido. In *Selected papers on psychoanalysis.* New York: Basic Books.

Abraham, S., and Jones, D. (1985) *Eating disorders.* New York: Oxford.

Abrams, D., and Wilson, T. (1979) Effects of alcohol on social anxiety in women: Cognitive versus physiological processes. *Journal of Abnormal Psychology, 88,* 161–173.

Abramson, L., Seligman, M., and Teasdale, J. (1978) Learned helplessness in humans: Critique and reformulation. *Journal of Abnormal Psychology, 87,* 49–74.

Abroms, G., Taintor, Z., and Lhamon, W. (1966) Percept assimilation and paranoid severity. *Archives of General Psychiatry, 14,* 491–496.

Achenbach, T.M. (1982) *Developmental psychopathology* (2nd ed.). New York: John Wiley and Sons.

Achenbach, T.M., and Edelbrock, C.S. (1978) The classification of child psychopathology: A review and analysis of empirical efforts. *Psychological Bulletin, 85,* 1275–1301.

——— . (1981) Behavioral problems and competencies reported by parents of normal and disturbed children aged 4 through 16. *Monographs of the Society for Research in Child Development, 46,* Serial 188.

——— . (1984) Psychopathology of childhood. In M. Rosenweig and L. Proter (Eds.), *Annual Review of Psychology* (Vol. 35). Palo Alto, Calif: Annual Reviews.

Achterberg, J., and Lawlis, G.F. (1980) *Bridges of the bodymind.* Champaign, Ill.: Institute for Personality and Ability Testing.

Adamovich, B., Henderson, J., and Auerbach, S. (1984) *Cognitive rehabilitation of closed head injured patients.* San Diego: College-Hill Press.

Adams, H.E., Freuerstein, M., and Fowler, J.L. (1980) Migraine headache: Review of parameters, etiology, and intervention. *Psychological Bulletin, 87,* 217–237.

Adams, J. (1978) *Psychoanalysis of drug dependence.* New York: Grune & Stratton.

Adams, P.L. (1973) *Obsessive children: A sociopsychiatric study.* New York: Bruner/Mazel.

Adams, P. (1985) The obsessive child: A theory update. *American Journal of Psychotherapy, 39,* 301–313.

Agras, W. (1987) *Eating disorders.* New York: Pergamon.

Agras, W.S., Barlow, D.H., Chapin, H.N., Abel, G.G., and Leitenberg, H. (1974) Behavior modification of anorexia nervosa. *Archives of General Psychiatry, 31,* 279–306.

Ahyi, R. (1979) Victoire sur les mort. Réflexions sur la clinique de deuil à propos de hoxosudide. (Victory over death. Reflections on therapy for mourning through "hoxusudide.") *Psychopathologie africaine, 15,* 141–157.

Akers, W.S., Kazdin, A.E., and Wilson, G.T. (1979) *Behavior therapy.* San Francisco: W.H. Freeman.

Albee, G. (1980) A competency model must reflect the defect model. In L. Bond and J. Rosen (Eds.), *Primary prevention of psychopathology* (Vol. 4). Hanover, N.H.: University Press of New England.

———. (1982) Preventing psychopathology and promoting human potential, *American Psychologist, 37,* 1043–1050.

Albin, R. (1979) Adult rites of passage. *APA Moniter, 10(1),* 5.

Alexander, A.B. (1980) The treatment of psychosomatic disorders: Bronchial asthma in children. In B.B. Lahey and A.E. Kazdin (Eds.), *Advances in child clinical psychology* (Vol. 3). New York: Plenum Press.

Alexander F., French, T., and Polleck, G.H. (1968) *Psychosomatic specificity* (Vol. 1). Chicago: University of Chicago Press.

Allen v. *Illinois,* U.S., S. Ct., 54 U.S. Law Week (USLW) 4966-4971 (1986)

Allgeier, A., and Allgeier, E. (1988) *Sexual interactions.* Lexington, Mass: D.C. Heath.

Alpert, M.S., and Kaplan, E. (1980) Organic implications of neuropsychological deficits in the elderly. In L.W. Poon, J.L. Fozard, L.S. Cermak, D. Arenberg, and L.W. Thompson (Eds.), *New directions in memory and aging.* Hillsdale, N.J.: Erlbaum Associates.

Alpher, V., and Blanton, R. (1985) The accuracy of lie detection. *Law and Psychology Review, 9,* 67–75.

American Association on Mental Deficiency. (1977) *Manual on terminology and classification in mental retardation.* Washington, D.C.: American Association on Mental Deficiency.

American Psychiatric Association. (1968) *Diagnostic and statistical manual of mental disorders* (2nd ed.). Washington, D.C.: American Psychiatric Association.

———. (1980) *Diagnostic and statistical manual of mental disorders* (3rd ed.). Washington, D.C.: American Psychiatric Association.

American Psychological Association (1981) *Code of Ethical Principles.* Washington, D.C.: American Psychological Association.

Anastasi, A. (1986) Evolving concepts of test validation. In M. Rosenweig and L. Porter (Eds.), *Annual Review of Psychology* (Vol. 37). Palo Alto, Calif: Annual Reviews.

———. (1987) *Psychological testing,* (6th ed.). New York: Macmillan.

Andolfi, M. (1978) A structural approach to a family with an encopretic child. *Journal of Marriage and Family Counseling, 4,* 25–29.

Andrasky, F., Blanchard, E.B., Neff, D.F., and Rodichok, L.D. (1984) Biofeedback and relaxation training for the chronic headache: A controlled comparison of booster treatments and regular contacts for long-term maintenance. *Journal of Consulting and Clinical Psychology, 52(4),* 609–615.

Anolik, S.A. (1983) Family influences upon delinquency: Biosocial and psychosocial perspectives. *Adolescence, 18(71),* 489–498.

Anthony, E.J. (1970) The behavior disorders of childhood. In P.H. Mussen (Ed.). *Carmichael's manual of child psychology* (3rd ed.). New York: John Wiley and Sons.

Apfelbaum, B. (1977) The myth of the surrogate. *Journal of Sex Research, 13,* 238–249.

Appelbaum, P., and Gutheil, T. (1980) Drug refusal: A study of psychiatric inpatients. *American Journal of Psychiatry, 137,* 340–348.

Arbib, M., Conklin, J., and Hill, J. (1987) *From schema theory to language.* New York: Oxford University Press.

Ard, B. (1977) Sex in lasting marriage: A longitudinal study. *Journal of Sex Research, 13,* 274–285.

Arieti, S., and Bemporad, J. (1978) *Severe and mild depression.* New York: Basic Books.

Asarnow, J.R., Lewis, J.M., Doane, J.A., Goldstein, M.J., and Rodnick, E.H. (1982) Family interaction and the course of adolescent psychopathology: An analysis of adolescent and parental effects. *Journal of Abnormal Child Psychology, 10(3),* 427–444.

Ashman, A. (1982) Cognitive processes and perceived language performance of retarded persons. *Journal of Mental Deficiency Research, 26(3),* 131–141.

Axline, V.M. (1969) *Play therapy* (Rev. ed.). New York: Ballantine Books.

Ayllon, T. and Azrin, N. (1968) *The token economy: A motivational system for therapy and rehabilitation.* New York: Appleton-Century-Crofts.

Ayllon, T., Layman, D., and Kandel, H.J. (1975) A behavioral-educational alternative to drug control of hyperactive children. *Journal of Applied Behavior Analysis, 8,* 137–146.

Azrin, N.H., and Fox, R.M. (1974) *Toilet training in less than a day.* New York: Simon and Schuster.

Azrin, N.H., Sneed, T.J., and Fox, R.M. (1974) Dry-bed training: Rapid elimination of childhood enuresis. *Behavior Research Therapy, 12,* 147–156.

Bach, G., and Wyden, P. (1969) *The intimate enemy.* New York: William Morrow.

Bacon, M. (1974) Dependency, the conflict hypothesis and frequency of drunkenness. *Quarterly Journal for the Study of Alcoholism, 35,* 863–876.

Bagarozzi, D., Jurich, A., and Jackson, R. (Eds.) (1982) *Marital and family therapy: New perspectives in theory, research, and practice.* New York: Human Sciences Press.

Bandura, A. (1977) *Social learning theory.* Englewood Cliffs, N.J.: Prentice-Hall.

Barnett, R., Biener, L., and Baruch, G. (1987) *Gender and stress.* New York: The Free Press.

Barrett, R. (1986) *Severe behavioral disorders in the mentally retarded.* New York: Plenum Press.

Bateson, G. (1972) *Steps to an ecology of mind.* New York: Ballantine Books.

Bailley, W. (1977) Imprisonment v. the death penalty as a deterrent to murder. *Law and Human Behavior, 1,* 239–260.

Bakan, D. (1971) Twelve to sixteen: Early adolescence. *Daedalus,* 979–995.

Bakwin, H., and Bakwin, R.M. (1972) *Behavior disorders in children.* Philadelphia: W.B. Saunders.

Baldessarini, R. (1977) *Chemotherapy in psychiatry.* Cambridge, Mass.: Harvard University Press.

Bales, J. (1987) Alabama case settled, still debated. *APA Monitor, 1,* 22.

Ball, J.C., Ross, A., and Simpson, A. (1964) Incidence and estimated prevalence of recorded delinquency in a metropolitan area. *American Sociological Review, 29,* 90–93.

Balloun, K., and Holmes, D. (1979) Effects of repeated examinations on the ability to detect guilt with a polygraphic examination: A laboratory experiment with a real crime. *Journal of Applied Psychology, 64,* 316–322.

Ban, T., Lehmann, H., and Deutsch, M. (1977) Negative findings with megavitamins in schizophrenic patients: Preliminary report. *Communications in Psychiatry, 1,* 119–122.

Bandura, A. (1969) *Principles of behavior modification.* New York: Holt, Rinehart and Winston.

———— . (1977) *Social learning theory.* Englewood Cliffs, N.J.: Prentice-Hall.

———— . (1981) In search of pure unidirectional determinants. *Behavior Therapy, 12,* 30–40.

Bandura, A., Taylor, C., Williams, S., Mefford, I., and Barchas, J. (1985) Catecholamine secretion as a function of perceived coping self-efficacy. *Journal of Consulting and Clinical Psychology, 53,* 406–414.

Barbaree, H., Marshall, W., and Lanthier, R. (1979) Deviant sexual arousal in rapists. *Behavior Research and Therapy, 17,* 215–222.

Barker, P. (1986) *Basic family therapy* (2nd ed.). New York: Oxford University Press.

Barlow, D., Abel, G., and Blanchard, E. (1979) Gender identity change in transsexuals. *Archives of General Psychiatry, 36,* 1001–1007.

Barnes, G., and Prosen, H. (1985) Parental death and depression. *Journal of Abnormal Psychology, 94,* 64–69.

Baron, R.A. (1977) *Human aggression.* New York: Plenum Press.

Barrett, C. (1981) Personal communication.

———— . (1980) Personality (character) disorders. In R. Woody (Ed.), *The encyclopedia of clinical assessment.* San Francisco: Jossey-Bass.

———— . (1986) Use of disulfiram in the psychological treatment of alcoholism. *Bulletin of the Society of Psychologists in the Addictive Behaviors, 4(4),* 197–205.

Barrett, R. (1986) *Severe behavioral disorders in the mentally retarded.* New York: Plenum Press.

Bartlett, P., and Low, S. (1980) Nervios in rural Costa Rica. *Medical Anthropology, 4,* 523–559.

Bartol, C.R. (1983) *Psychology and American law.* Belmont, Calif.: Wadsworth.

Bausell, R. (1986) *Experimental methods.* New York: Harper & Row.

Beatty, J. (1987) *Biological basis of behavior.* Chicago: Dorsey.

Beck, A. (1967) *Depression.* New York: Harper & Row.

———— . (1976) *Cognitive therapy and the emotional disorders.* New York: International Universities Press.

Beck, A., Kovacs, M., and Weissmann, A. (1979) Assessment of suicidal ideation: The scale for suicidal ideation. *Journal of Consulting and Clinical Psychology, 47,* 343–352.

Beck, A.T., Rush, A.J., Shaw, B.F., and Emery, G. (1979) *Cognitive therapy of depression.* New York: Guilford.

Beck, S.J., Beck, A.G., Levitt, E.E., and Molish H.B. (1961) *Rorschach's test: Processes* (Vol. 1) (3rd ed.). New York: Grune & Stratton.

Becker, J. (1987) Personal communication.

Becker, V., Skinner, L., Abel, G., and Treacy, E. (1982) Incidence and types of sexual dysfunctions in rape and incest victims. *Journal of Sex and Marital Therapy, 8,* 65–74.

Bedrosian, R., and Beck, A. (1979) A principle of cognitive therapy. In M. Mahoney (Ed.), *Psychotherapy process: Current issues and future directions.* New York: Plenum Press.

Bedrosian, R.C., and Beck, A.T. (1980) Principles of cognitive therapy. In M.J. Mahoney (Ed.), *Psychotherapy process.* New York: Plenum Press.

Begleiter, H., Porjesz, B., and Chou, C. (1981) Auditory brain stem potentials in chronic alcoholics. *Science, 201,* 1064–1066.

Behavior Today (1986) Landmark depression study: Psychotherapy as effective as drug therapy. *Behavior Today, 11 (26–27),* 1–3.

Belanky, G. (1987) *Contemporary studies in combat psychiatry.* Westport, Ct.,: Greenwood Press.

Belkin, G. (Ed.) (1980) *Contemporary psychotherapies.* Boston: Houghton Mifflin.

Bellack, A., Hersen, M., and Kazdin, A. (Eds.) (1982) *International handbook of behavior modification and therapy.* New York: Plenum Press.

Bellak, L. (1975) *The Thematic Apperception Test, the Children's Apperception Test, and the Senior Apperception Test in clinical use* (3rd ed.). New York: Grune & Stratton.

Belsky, J. (1980) Child maltreatment: An ecological integration. *American Psychologist, 35,* 320–335.

Bemporad, J. (1977) My most unusual sexual case. *Medical aspects of human sexuality, July,* 40.

Bennett, A. (1947) Mad doctors. *Journal of Nervous and Mental Disease, 106,* 118.

Benson, D.F., and Blumer, D. (1975) *Psychiatric aspects of neurologic disease.* New York: Grune & Stratton.

Benton, A.L. (1975) Psychological tests for brain damage. In A.M. Freedman, H.I. Kaplan, and B.J. Sadock (Eds.), *Comprehensive textbook of psychiatry,* (Vol. 1) (2nd ed.). Baltimore: Williams and Wilkins.

Berenbaum, H., Oltmanns, T., and Gottesman, I. (1985) Formal thought disorder in schizophrenics and their twins. *Journal of Abnormal Psychology, 94,* 3–16.

Berger, P. (1978) Medical treatment of mental illness. *Science, 200,* 974–981.

Berger, S.M. (1962) Conditioning through vicarious instigation. *Psychology Review, 69,* 450–466.

Bergin, A. (1971) The evaluation of psychotherapeutic outcomes. In A. Bergin and S. Garfield (Eds.), *Handbook of psychotherapy and behavior change: An empirical analysis.* New York: John Wiley and Sons.

Berkowitz, L., and Le Page, A. (1967) Weapons as aggression-eliciting stimuli. *Journal of Personality and Social Psychology, 3,* 202–207.

Berne, E. (1964) *Games people play.* New York: Grove.

Bernheim, K.F., and Lewine, R.J. (1979) *Schizophrenia: Symptoms, causes, treatments.* New York: W.W. Norton.

Bersoff, D. (1986) Psychologists and the judicial system: Broader perspectives. *Law and Human Behavior, 10,* 151–166.

Bertinetti, J. (1980) Substance abuse. In R. Woody (Ed.), *The encyclopedia of clinical assessment.* San Francisco: Jossey-Bass.

Bettelheim, B. (1967) *The empty fortress.* New York: Free Press.

Bieber, I., Dain, H., Dince, P., Drellich, M., Grand, H., Gundlach, R., Kremer, M., Rifkin, A., Wiber, C., and Bieber,T. (1962) *Homosexuality: A psychoanalytical study.* New York: Random House.

Bijou, S., and Redd, W. (1975) Behavioral therapy for children. In D. Freedman and J. Dyrud (Eds.), *American handbook of psychiatry.* New York: Basic Books.

Billings, A., and Moos, R. (1985) Psychosocial processes of remission in unipolar depression. *Journal of Consulting and Clinical Psychology, 53,* 314–325.

Birren, J.E. (1964) *The psychology of aging.* Englewood Cliffs, N.J.: Prentice-Hall.

Blachly, P. (1977) Attitudes, data, and technological promise of ECT. *Psychiatric Opinion, 14,* 9–12.

Black, J. (1968) Further considerations of psychosomatic factors in allergy. *Psychosomatic Medicine, 30,* 202–208.

Black, J., Jennings, P., Harvey, E., and Payson, E. (1964) Interaction between allergic potential and psychopathology in childhood. *Psychosomatic Medicine, 26,* 307–320.

Blackstock, E.G. (1978) Cerebral asymmetry and the development of early infantile autism. *Journal of Autism and Childhood Schizophrenia, 8,* 339–353.

Blackwell, B. (1977) Benzodiazepenes: Drug abuse and data abuse. *Psychiatric Opinion, 16,* 10, 37.

Blair, J., and Justice, R. (1979) *The broken taboo.* New York: Human Sciences Press.

Blanchard, E., Theobald, D., Williamson, D, Silver, B., and Brown, D. (1978) Temperature feedback in the treatment of migraine headaches. *Archives of General Psychiatry, 35,* 581–588.

Blanchard, E.B., Andrasik, F., Neff, D.F., Arena, J.G., Ahles, T.A., Jurish, S.E., Pallmeyer, T.P., Saunders, N.L., Teders, S.J., Barron, K.D., and Rodichok, L.D. (1982) Biofeedback and relaxation training with three kinds of headache: Treatment effects and their prediction. *Journal of Consulting and Clinical Psychology, 50,* 562–575.

Blanchard, R., Steiner, B., and Clemmensen, L. (1985) Gender dysphoria, gender reorientation, and the clinical management of transsexualism. *Journal of Consulting and Clinical Psychology, 53,* 295–304.

Blane, H., and Leonard, K. (1987) *Psychological Theories of Drinking and Alcoholism.* New York: Guilford.

Blatt, S., Quinlan, D., Chevron, E., McDonald, C., and Zuroff, D. (1982) Dependency and self-criticism: Psychological dimensions of depression. *Journal of Consulting and Clinical Psychology, 50,* 113–114.

Bleuler, E. (1930) Primary and secondary symptoms in schizophrenia. *Zeitschrift für Generalische Neurologische Psychiatrie, 124,* 607.

Bliss, E., and Zwanziger, J. (1966) Brain amines and emotional stress. *Journal of Psychiatric Research, 4,* 189–198.

Bliss, E., and Jeppsen, E. (1985) Prevalence of multiple personality among inpatients and outpatients. *American Journal of Psychiatry, 142,* 250–251.

Bloch, S., and Crouch, E. (1987) *Therapeutic factors in group psychotherapy.* New York: Oxford University Press.

Blumer, D., and Benson, D.F. (Eds.) (1975) Personality changes with frontal and temporal lobe lesions. In *Psychiatric aspects of neurological disease.* New York: Grune & Stratton.

Bogerts, B., Meertz, E., and Schonfeldt-Bausch, R. (1985) Basal ganglia and limbic system pathology in schizophrenia. *Archives of General Psychiatry, 42,* 784–791.

Boll, T.J. (1981) The Halstead-Reitan neuropsychology battery. In S.B. Filskov and T.J. Boll (Eds.), *Handbook of clinical neuropsychology.* New York: Wiley-Interscience, pp. 418–452.

Bonnard, A. (1961) Truancy and pilfering associated with bereavement. In S. Lorand and H.I. Schneer (Eds.), *Adolescents: Psychoanalytic approach to problems and therapy.* New York: Hoeber.

Bonvillian, J.D., Nelson, K.E., and Rhyne, J.M. (1981) Sign language and autism. *Journal of Autism and Childhood Schizophrenia, 11,* 125–137.

Bornstein, P., and Bornstein, M. (1986) *Marital therapy.* Elmsford, N.Y.: Pergamon Press.

Boswell, J. (1980) *Christianity, social tolerance, and homosexuality.* Chicago: University of Chicago Press.

Botwinick, J. (1981) Neuropsychology of aging. In B. Filskov and T. Boll (Eds.), *Handbook of clinical neuropsychology.* New York: John Wiley and Sons.

Boulanger, G., and Kadushin, C. (Eds.) (1986) *The Vietnam veteran defined.* Hillsdale, N.J.: Lawrence Erlbaum.

Bourne, P. (1970) Military psychiatry and the Vietnam experience. *American Journal of Psychiatry, 127,* 481–488.

Bowers v. *Hardwick,* U.S. S. Ct., 54 (USLW) 4919 (1986).

Bowlby, J. (1980) *Attachment and loss* (Vol. 3). New York: Basic Books.

Bozarth, M., and Wise, R. (1985) Toxicity associated with long term intravenous heroin and cocaine self-administration in the rat. *Journal of the American Medical Association, 284,* 81–83.

Bracy, O.L. (1983) Computer based cognitive rehabilitation. *Cognitive Rehabilitation, 1(1),* 7–8.

Bradley, R.H., and Caldwell, B.M. (1976) Early home environment and changes in mental test performance in children from 6 to 36 months. *Developmental Psychology, 12,* 93–97.

Braff, D., and Saccuzzo, D. (1985) The time cause of information processing deficits in schizophrenia. *The American Journal of Psychiatry, 142,* 170–174.

Braginsky, D., and Braginsky, B. (1976) The myth of schizophrenia. In P. Magaro (Ed.), *The construction of madness.* New York: Pergamon Press.

Brandsma, J. (1979) *Outpatient treatment of alcoholism.* Baltimore: University Park Press.

Breier, A., Charney, D., and Henninger, G. (1984) Major depression in patients with agoraphobia and panic disorder. *Archives of General Psychiatry, 41,* 1129–1135.

Brenner, D. (1982) *The effective psychotherapist.* New York: Pergamon Press.

Brenner, M. (1973) *Mental illness and the economy.* Cambridge, Mass.: Harvard University Press.

Breslar, D. (1979) *Free yourself from pain.* New York: Wallaby.

Briddell, D., Rimen, D., Caddy, G., Krawitz, G., Sholis, D., and Wenderlin, R. (1978) Effects of alcohol and cognitive set on sexual arousal to deviant stimuli. *Journal of Abnormal Psychology, 87,* 418–443.

Bridgeman, B. (1988) *Biology of behavior.* New York: Wiley.

Brinkman, S.D. (1979) Rehabilitation of the neurologically impaired patient: The contribution of the neuropsychologist. *Clinical Neuropsychology, 1,* 39–44.

Brody, L. (1985) Gender differences in emotional development. *Journal of Personality, 53,* 102–149.

Brody, D., Saccuzzo, D., and Braff, D. (1980) Information processing for masked and unmasked stimuli in schizophrenia and old age. *Journal of Abnormal Psychology, 89,* 617–622.

Bronfenbrenner, U. (1977) Toward an experimental ecology of human development. *American Psychologist, 32,* 513–531.

———. (1979) *The ecology of human development.* Cambridge, Mass.: Harvard University Press.

Brown, G., and Harris, T. (1979) *Social origins of depression.* Riverside, N.J.: Free Press.

Brown, S. (1985) Expectancies versus background in the prediction of college drinking patterns. *Journal of Consulting and Clinical Psychology, 53,* 123–130.

Brown S. (1985) *Treating the alcoholic.* New York: John Wiley and Sons.

Browne, A., and Finkelhor, D. (1986) Impact of child sexual abuse. *Psychological Bulletin.* New York: The Free Press.

Bruch, H. (1973) *Eating disorders.* New York: Basic Books.

Bruch, H. (1986) Anorexia nervosa: The therapeutic task. In K. Brownell and J. Foreyt (Eds.) *Handbook of Eating Disorders.* New York: Basic Books.

Bryer, K. (1979) The Amish way of death. *American Psychologist, 34,* 255–261.

Buchanan vs. *Kentucky,* 107 S.Ct. 989, 55 L.W. 5026 (1987).

Bullough, V. (1976) *Sexual variance in society and history.* New York: John Wiley and Sons.

———. (1978) *Homosexuality, past and present.* New York: Garland.

Bureau of Justice (1985) *Capital Punishment 1984.* Washington, D.C.: Bureau of Justice.

Burns, J., and Kintz, B. (1976) Eye contact while lying during an interview. *Bulletin of the Psychonomic Society, 7,* 87–89.

Busse, E.W. (1954) The treatment of hypochondriasis. *Tristate Medical Journal, 2,* 7–12.

Bustamante, J., and Ford, C. (1977) Ganser's syndrome. *Psychiatric Opinion, 14,* 39–41.

Butcher, J.N. (1987) *Computerized psychological assessment.* New York: Basic Books.

Butler, J.F. (1977) Treatment of encopresis by overcorrection. *Psychological Reports, 40,* 639–646.

Butler, R.N., and Lewis, M.I. (1977) *Aging and mental health.* St. Louis, Mo.: Mosby.

Butters, N. (1979) Amnestic disorders. In K.M. Heilman and E. Valenstein (Eds.), *Clinical neuropsychology.* New York: Oxford University Press.

Cadoret, R., O'Gorman, T., Troughton, E., and Heywood, E. (1985) Alcoholism and antisocial personality: Interrelationships, genetic, and environmental variables. *Archives of General Psychiatry, 42,* 161–167.

Cadoret, R., Troughton, E., and O'Gorman, T. (1987) Genetic and environmental factors in alcohol abuse and antisocial personality. *Journal of Studies on Alcohol, 48,* 1–8.

Caldwell, B.M. (1962) The usefulness of the critical period hypothesis in the study of filiative behavior. *Merrill-Palmer Quarterly of Behavior and Development, 8,* 229–242.

Calhoun, K., and Atkeson, B. (1987) *Treatment of victims of sexual assault.* New York: Pergamon Press.

Campbell, D.T., and Stanley, J.C. (1963) *Experimental and quasi-experimental designs for research.* Chicago: Rand McNally.

Campbell, D., Sanderson, R., and Laverty, S. (1964) Characteristics of a conditioned response in human subjects during extinction trials following a single traumatic conditioning trial. *Journal of Abnormal and Social Psychology, 68,* 627–639.

Cann, D., and Donderi, D. (1986) Jungian personality typology and the recall of everyday and archetypal dreams. *Journal of Personality and Social Psychology, 50,* 1021–1030.

Caplan, G. (1964) *Principles of preventive psychiatry.* New York: Basic Books.

Caplan, L. (1984) *The insanity defense.* Boston: David R. Godin.

Carlson, N.R. (1980) *Physiology of behavior* (2nd ed.). Boston: Allyn and Bacon.

Carman, J., and Wyatt, R. (1979) Calcium: Pacesetting the periodic psychoses. *American Journal of Psychiatry, 136,* 1033–1039.

Carpenter, E. (1985) Conditioning, *Psychology Today, 5,* 11–12.

Carrington, P. (1984) Modern forms of meditation. In R.L. Woolfolk and P.M. Lehrer (Eds.), *Principles and practice of stress management.* New York: Guilford.

Cartledge, G., and Milburn, J. (1986) *Teaching social skills to children.* New York: Pergamon Press.

Casper, R., Eickert, E., Halmi, K., Goldberg, S., and Davis, V. (1980) Bulimia. *Archives of General Psychiatry, 37,* 1030–1035.

Cattell, R.B. (1987) *Psychotherapy by structured learning theory.* New York: Springer.

Caudill, B., and Marlatt, A. (1975) Modeling influences in social drinking: An experimental analogue. *Journal of Consulting and Clinical Psychology, 43,* 405–415.

Cautela, J. (1972) Covert conditioning. In M.A. Jacobs and L.B. Sachs (Eds.). *The psychology of private events: Perspectives on covert response systems.* New York: Academic Press.

———— . (1967) Covert sensitization. *Psychological Record, 20,* 458–468.

Cautela, J., and Kearney, A. (1986) *The covert conditioning handbook.* New York: Springer.

Cawley, R. (1974) Psychotherapy and the obsessional states. In H. Beech (Ed.), *Obsessional states.* London: Metheun.

Centerwall, B., and Criqui, M. (1978) Prevention of the Wernicke-Korsakoff syndrome. *New England Journal of Medicine, 299,* 285–289.

Cerek, D.T., Hendrikson, W., and Holmes, D.J. (1961) Delinquency addiction in parents. *Archives of General Psychiatry, 282,* 357–262.

Chambless, D., Foa, E., Graves, G., and Goldstein, A. (1979) Flooding with Brevital in the treatment of agoraphobia: Countereffective. *Behavior Research and Therapy, 17,* 243–251.

Chambless, D., Caputo, G., Bright, P., and Gallagher, R. (1984) Assessment of fear in agoraphobics. *Journal of Consulting and Clinical Psychology, 52,* 1090–1097.

Chambless, D., Sultan, F., Stern, T., O'Neill, C., Garrison, S., and Jackson, A. (1984) Effect of pubococcygeal exercise on coital orgasm in women. *Journal of Consulting and Clinical Psychology, 52,* 114–118.

Chambless, D. (1985) The relationship of severity of agoraphobia to associated psychopathology. *Behaviour Research and Therapy, 23,* 305–310.

Cheek, D. (1965) Emotional factors in persistent pain states. *American Journal of Clinical Hypnosis, 8,* 100–110.

Cheek, D., and LeCron, L. (1968) *Clinical hypnotherapy.* New York: Grune & Stratton.

Cheek, R., and Miller, M. (1981) The use of behavior modification techniques in developing socially appropriate behaviors in substance abusers. In J. Lowinson and P. Ruiz (Eds.), *Substance abuse: Clinical problems and perspectives.* Baltimore: Williams & Wilkins.

Cheng, L., and Hummel, L. (1978) The Munchausen syndrome as a psychiatric condition. *British Journal of Psychiatry, 133,* 20–21.

Chethik, M. (1986) Levels of borderline functioning in children: Etiological and treatment considerations. *American Journal of Orthopsychiatry, 56,* 109–119.

Chevron, E., Quinlan, P., and Blatt, S. (1978) Sex roles and gender differences in the experience of depression. *Journal of Abnormal Psychology, 87,* 680–683.

Chowka, P. (1979) Pushers in white. *East-West Journal, 9,* 30–37.

Christiansen, H. (1964) *Handbook of marriage and the family.* Chicago: Rand McNally.

Chusid, J.G. (1976) *Correlative neuroanatomy and functional neurology* (16th ed.). Los Altos, Calif.: Lange.

Ciminero, A., Calhoun, K., and Adams, H. (1986) *Handbook of behavioral assessment.* New York: John Wiley and Sons.

Clancy, H., and McBride, G. (1975) The isolation syndrome in childhood. *Developmental Medicine and Child Neurology, 17,* 198–219.

Clare, A. (1985) Invited review: Hormones, behavior, and the menstrual cycle. *Journal of Psychosomatic Research, 29,* 225–233.

Clarke, A.M., and Clarke, A.D.B. (Eds.) (1976) *Early experience: Myth and evidence.* New York: Free Press.

Clarke, R.V.G., and Cornish, D.B. (1978) The effectiveness of residential treatment for delinquents. In L.A. Hersov, M. Berger, and D. Shaffer (Eds.), *Aggression and antisocial behavior in childhood and adolescence.* Oxford: Pergamon Press.

Clark-Stewart, A., Friedman, S., and Perlmutter, M. (1988) *Lifespan development.* New York: Wiley.

Cleckley, H. (1964) *The mask of sanity* (4th ed.). St. Louis, Mo.: Mosby.

Cochran, S. (1984) Preventing medical noncompliance in the outpatient treatment of bipolar affective disorders. *Journal of Consulting and Clinical Psychology, 52,* 873–878.

Cohen, A.K. (1955) *Delinquent boys: The culture of the gang.* Glencoe, Ill.: Free Press.

Cohen, D.J., and Donnellan, A.M. (1987) *Handbook of autism and pervasive developmental disorders.* New York: Wiley.

Cohen, M., Seghorn, T., and Calmas, W. (1969) Sociometric study of sex offenders. *Journal of Abnormal Psychology, 74,* 249–255.

Cohen, R., and Smith, F. (1976) Socially reinforced obsessing: Etiology of a disorder in a Christian Scientist. *Journal of Consulting and Clinical Psychology, 44,* 142–144.

Cohler, B., and Boxer, A. (1984) Personal adjustments, wellbeing, and life events. In C. Malatesta and C. Izard (Eds.), *Emotion in adult development.* Beverly Hills: Sage.

Colby, A., Kohlberg, L., et al. (1987) *The measurement of moral judgment.* New York: Cambridge University Press.

Colby, K.M. (1976) Clinical implications of a stimulation model of paranoid processes. *Archives of General Psychiatry, 33,* 854–857.

——— . (1977) Appraisal of four psychological theories of paranoid phenomenon. *Journal of Abnormal Psychology, 86,* 54–59.

Colby, K.M., and Enea, H. (1967) Heuristic methods for computer understanding of natural language in context-restricted on-line dialogues. *Mathematical Biosciences, 1,* 1–25.

Coles, R., and Stokes, G. (1985) *Sex and the American teenager.* New York: Harper & Row.

Cone, J., and Foster, S. (1982) Direct observation in clinical psychology. In P. Kendall and J. Butcher (Eds.), *Handbook of research methods in clinical psychology.* New York: John Wiley and Sons.

Cone, J.D., and Hawkins, R.P. (Eds.) (1977) *Behavioral assessment: New directions in clinical psychology.* New York: Bruner/Mazel.

Confer, W., and Ables, B. (1982) *Multiple personality.* New York: Human Sciences Press.

Conger, J. (1964) The effects of alcohol on conflict behavior in the albino rat. *Quarterly Journal of Studies on Alcohol, 12,* 1–29.

Conger, J.J., and Miller, W.C. (1966) *Personality, social class, and delinquency.* New York: John Wiley and Sons.

Constantino, G., Malgody, R., and Rogler, L. (1986) Cuentotherapy: A culturally sensitive modality for Puerto Rican children. *Journal of Consulting and Clinical Psychology, 54,* 639–645.

Corbett, L. (1976) Perceptual dyscontrol: A possible organizing principle for schizophrenia research. *Schizophrenia Bulletin, 2,* 249–265.

Corcoran, K., and Fischer, J. (1987) *Measures for clinical practice.* New York: The Free Press.

Cornelius, J., Soloff, P., and Reynolds, C. (1984) Paranoia, homicidal behavior, and seizures associated with phenylpropanolamine. *American Journal of Psychiatry, 141,* 120–121.

Corsini, R. (Ed.) (1981) *Handbook of innovative psychotherapies.* New York: John Wiley and Sons.

Cox, D., and Daitzman, R. (1980) *Exhibitionism.* New York: Garland.

Cox, D., Freundlich, A., and Meyer, R. (1975) Differential effectiveness of EMG feedback, verbal relaxation instructions and medication placebo with tension headaches. *Journal of Clinical and Consulting Psychology, 43,* 892–898.

Coyne, J. (1976) Depression and the response of others. *Journal of Abnormal Psychology, 85,* 185–193.

Craighead, W.E., Kazdin, A.E., and Mahoney, M.J. (1981) *Behavior modification: Principles, issues, and applications* (2nd ed.). Boston: Houghton Mifflin.

Crain, W.C. (1980) Theories of development: Concepts and applications. Englewood Cliffs, N.J.: Prentice-Hall.

Cravioto, J., DeLicardie, E.R., and Birch, H.G. (1966) Nutrition, growth, and neuro-integrative development: An experimental and ecologic study. *Pediatrics, 38,* 319.

Crawford, K.A., and Siegal, P.S. (1982) Improving the visual discrimination of mentally retarded children: A training strategy. *American Journal of Mental Deficiency, 87(3),* 294–301.

Creer, T.L. (1982) Asthma. *Journal of Consulting and Clinical Psychology, 50(6),* 912–921.

Crits-Cristoph, P., and Singer, J. (1981) Imagery in cognitive-behavior therapy: Research and application. *Clinical Psychology Review, 1,* 19–32.

Cross, C. (1984) *Child abuse and neglect.* Washington, D.C.: National Education Association.

Crow, T.J., Johnstone, E.C., Longden, A.J., and Owen, F. (1978) Dopaminergic mechanisms in schizophrenia: The antipsychotic effect and the disease process. *Life Sciences, 23,* 563–568.

Cummings, E.M., Ianotti, R., Zahn-Waxler, C. (1985) Influence of conflict between adults on the emotions and aggression of young children. *Developmental Psychology, 21,* 136–143.

Curran, J., Monti, P., and Corriveau, D. (1982) Treatment of schizophrenia. In A. Bellack, M. Hersen, and A. Kazdin (Eds.), *International handbook of behavior modification and therapy.* New York: Plenum Press.

Currie, P., and Ramsdale, D. (1984) Paranoid psychosis induced by tocainide. *British Medical Journal, 288,* 606–607.

Dahlkoetter, J., Callahan, E., and Linton, J. (1979) Obesity and the unbalanced energy equation: Exercise versus eating habit change. *Journal of Consulting and Clinical Psychology, 47,* 898–905.

Dahlstrom, W.G., Lachar, D., and Dahlstrom, C.E. (1986) *MMPI patterns of American minorities.* Minneapolis: University of Minnesota Press.

Danish, S., and D'Angelli, A. (1980) Promoting competence and enhancing development through life development intervention. In L. Bond and J. Rosen (Eds.), *Primary prevention of psychopathology* (Vol. 4). Hanover, N.H.: University Press of New England, 1980.

Danti, J., Adams, C., and Morrison, T. (1985) Children of mothers with borderline personality disorder. *Psychotherapy, 22,* 28–35.

David, R., Enderby, P., and Bainton, D. (1982) Treatment of acquired aphasia: Speech therapists and volunteers compared. *Journal of Neurology, Neurosurgery, and Psychiatry, 45,* 957–961.

Davidson, W.S., and Seidman, E. (1974) Studies of behavior modification and juvenile delinquency: A review, methodological critique, and social perspective. *Psychological Bulletin, 81,* 998–1011.

Davis, B., Pfefferbaum, A., Krutzik, S., and Davis, K. (1981) Lithium's effect on parathyroid hormone. *American Journal of Psychiatry, 138,* 489–492.

———. (1978) Dopamine theory of schizophrenia: A two-factor theory. In L.C. Wynn, R.L. Cromwell, and S. Matthyse (Eds.), *The nature of schizophrenia: New approaches to research and treatment.* New York: John Wiley and Sons.

Davis, J. (1976) Recent developments in the treatment of schizophrenia. *Psychiatric Annals, 6,* 33–50.

Davison, G. (1976) Homosexuality: The ethical challenge. *Journal of Consulting and Clinical Psychology, 44,* 157–162.

———. (1978) Not can but ought: The treatment of homosexuality. *Journal of Consulting and Clinical Psychology, 46,* 170–172.

Dean, R. (1987) *Introduction to assessing human intelligence.* Springfield, Ill.: Charles Thomas.

Deitch, D., and Zweben, J. (1981) Synanon: A pioneering response in drug abuse treatment and a signal for caution. In J. Lowinson and P. Ruiz (Eds.), *Substance abuse: Clinical problems and perspectives.* Baltimore: Williams & Wilkins.

Delaney, B. (1981) Is Uncle Sen insane? Pride, humor, and clique formation in a northern Thai home for the elderly. *International Journal of Aging and Human Development, 13,* 137–150.

Dell, L., Ruzicka, M., and Palisi, A. (1981) Personality and other factors associated with gambling addiction. *International Journal of the Addictions, 16,* 149–156.

DeMause, L. (1974) *The history of childhood.* New York: Psychohistory Press.

DeMyer, M. (1976) The nature of the neuropsychological disability in autistic children. In E. Schopler and R. Reichler (Eds.), *Psychopathology and child development: Research and treatment.* New York: Plenum Press.

DeMyer, M., Barton, S., DeMyer, W., Norton, J., Allen, J., and Steele, R. (1973) Prognosis in autism: A follow-up study. *Journal of Autism and Schizophrenia, 3,* 199–246.

Depue, R. (1979) *The psychobiology of depressive disorders.* New York: Academic Press.

Depue, R., Slater, J., Wolfstetter-Kausch, H., Klein, D., Goplerud, E., and Farr, D. (1981) A behavioral paradigm for identifying persons at risk for bipolar depressive disorder: A conceptual framework and five validation studies. *Journal of Abnormal Psychology, 90,* 381–438.

Derner, G.F., Aborn, M., and Canter, A.H. (1952) The reliability of the Wechsler-Bellevue subtests and scales. *Journal of Consulting Psychology, 16,* 272–277.

Deutsch, T.A. (1969) The physiological basis of memory. *American Review of Psychology, 20,* 85–104.

Diller, L., and Gordon, W.A. (1981) Rehabilitation and clinical neuropsychology. In S.B. Filskov and T.J. Boll (Eds.), *Handbook of clinical neuropsychology.* New York: Wiley-Interscience, pp. 702–733.

Dizmang, L.H., Watson, J., May, P.A., and Bopp, J. (1974) Adolescent suicide at an Indian Reservation. *American Journal of Orthopsychiatry, 44,* 43–49.

Dodrill, C.B. (1981) Neuropsychology of epilepsy. In S.B. Filskov and T.J. Boll (Eds.), *Handbook of clinical neuropsychology.* New York: Wiley-Interscience, pp. 366–395.

Doerfler, L., and Chaplin, W. (1985) Type III error in research on interpersonal models of depression. *Journal of Abnormal Psychology, 94,* 227–230.

Doleys, D. (1977) Behavioral treatment for nocturnal enuresis in children: A review of the literature. *Psychological Bulletin, 84,* 30–43.

Donovan, J. (1986) An etiologic model of alcoholism. *Archives of General Psychiatry, 143,* 1–11.

Doren, D. (1987) *Understanding and treating the psychopath.* New York: John Wiley and Sons.

Dorus, E., Pandey, G., Shaughnessy, R., Gavira, M., Eriksen, S., and Davis, J. (1979) Lithium transport across red cell membrane. *Science, 205,* 932–934.

Draguns, J. (1980) Psychological disorders of clinical severity. In H. Triandis and J. Draguns (Eds.), *Handbook of cross-cultural psychology: Psychopathology.* Boston: Allyn and Bacon.

Draizan, A. (1984) Clinical EMG feedback in monitoring speech defects. *Archives of Physical Medicine and Rehabilitation, 65,* 481–484.

Drew, C.J., and Hardman, M.L. (1977) *Mental retardation: Social and educational perspectives.* St. Louis, Mo.: Mosby.

Dryden, W., and Golden, W.L. (1987) *Cognitive-behavioral approaches to psychotherapy.* New York: Hemisphere.

Dupont, R. (Ed.) (1981) *Phobias: A comprehensive survey of modern treatments.* New York: Bruner/Mazel.

Durand, V.M. (1982) A behavioral/pharmacological intervention for the treatment of severe self-injurious behavior. *Journal of Autism and Developmental Disorders, 12(3),* 243–251.

Durham v. *United States,* 214 F. 2d 962, 874–875 (D.C. Cir. 1954).

Durkheim, E. (1951) *Suicide.* New York: Free Press.

Eaton, W. (1986) *The sociology of mental disorders.* New York: Praeger.

Edinger, J. (1979) Cross-validation of the Megargee MMPI typology for prisoners. *Journal of Consulting and Clinical Psychology, 47,* 234–242.

Eggert, D. (1982) Family environmental and developmental variables in mental retardation: A multidimensional approach. *Exceptional Child, 29(2),* 87–99.

Ehrlich, P., and McGeehan, M. (1985) Cocaine recovery support groups and the language of recovery. *Journal of Psychoactive Drugs, 17,* 11–17.

Eisdorfer, C., and Friedel, R. (Eds.) (1977) *Cognitive and emotional disturbance in the elderly.* Chicago: Year Book Medical.

Eisenberg, L. (1956) The autistic child in adolescence. *American Journal of Psychiatry, 112,* 607–612.

Eisenberg, L., and Kanner, L. (1956) Childhood schizophrenia. *American Journal of Orthopsychiatry, 26,* 556–564.

Eisenberg, N., and Miller, P. (1987) The relation of empathy to prosocial and related behaviors. *Psychological Bulletin, 101,* 91–119.

Eisler, R., Hersen, M., and Agras, W. (1973) Videotape: A method for the controlled observation of nonverbal interpersonal behavior. *Behavior Therapy, 4,* 420–425.

Ekman, P. (1985) *Telling lies.* New York: Norton.

Elkind, D. (1976) Cognitive development and psychopathology: Observations on egocentrism and ego defense. In E. Schopler and R. Reichler (Eds.), *Psychopathology and child development: Research and treatment.* New York: Plenum Press.

———. (1967) Middle-class delinquency. *Mental Hygiene, 51,* 80–84.

Ellis, A. (1970) *The essence of rational psychoanalysis: A comprehensive approach to treatment.* New York: Institute for Rational Living.

———. (1973) *Humanistic psychotherapy: The rational-emotive approach.* New York: McGraw-Hill.

———. (1979) A note on the treatment of agoraphobics with cognitive modification versus prolonged exposure "in vivo." *Behavior Research and Therapy, 17,* 162–164.

Ellis, A., and Grieger, R.M. (1986) *Handbook of rational-emotive therapy,* (Vol. 2). New York: Springer.

Ellis, P.L. (1982) Empathy: A factor in antisocial behavior. *Journal of Abnormal Child Psychology, 10(1),* 123–134.

Emmelkamp, P. (1982) Anxiety and fear. In A. Bellack, M. Hersen, and A. Kazdin (Eds.), *International handbook of behavior modification and therapy.* New York: Plenum Press.

Emmelkamp, P., Mersch, P., Vissia, E., and Van Der Helm, M. (1985) Social phobia: A comparative evaluation of cognitive and behavioral interventions. *Behaviour Research and Therapy, 23,* 365–370.

Empey, L. (1978) *American delinquency.* Homewood, Ill.: Dorsey Press.

Endicott, J., Nee, J., Andreasen, P., Clayton, P., Keller, M., and Coryell, W. (1985) Bipolar II—Combine or keep separate. *Journal of Affective Disorders, 8,* 17–28.

Endler, N., and Edwards, J. (1987) Vulnerability and stress. In C. Last and M. Hersen (Eds.) *Handbook of anxiety disorders.* Elmsford, N.Y.: Pergamon Press.

Enna, S., Malick, J., and Richelson, E. (Eds.) (1981) *Antidepressants.* New York: Raven.

Epilepsy Foundation of America (1975) *Basic statistics on the epilepsies.* Philadelphia: F.A. Davis.

Epstein, L., Wing, R., Koeske, R., and Voloski, A. (1985) A comparison of life-style exercise, aerobic exercise, and calisthenics in weight loss in obese children. *Behavior Therapy, 16,* 345–356.

Epstein, L.H., Malone, P.R., and Cunningham, J. (1978) Feedback influenced changes in stroke patients. *Behavior Modification, 2,* 387–402.

Erdelyi, M. (1985) *Psychoanalysis: Freud's cognitive psychology.* New York: Freeman.

Erikson, E. (1963) *Childhood and society* (2nd ed.). New York: W.W. Norton.

———. (1968) *Identity youth and crises.* New York: W.W. Norton.

———. (1978) *Adulthood.* New York: W.W. Norton.

Eron, L.D. (1980) Prescription for reduction of aggression. *American Psychologist, 35,* 244–252.

Eron, L. (1982) Parent-child interaction, television violence, and aggression in children. *American Psychologist, 37,* 197–211.

Essman, W., and Valzelli, L. (Eds.) (1981) *Current developments in psychopharmacology* (Vol. 6).New York: SP Books.

Evans, R.I., Rozelle, R.M., Maxwell, S.E., Raines, B.E., Dill, C.A., Guthrie, T.J., Henderson, A.J., and Hill, P. (1981) Social modeling films to deter smoking in adolescents: Results of a three-year field investigation. *Journal of Applied Psychology, 66,* 399–414.

Evans, R., and Koelsch, W. (1985) Psychoanalysis arrives in America. *American Psychologist, 40,* 942–948.

Everly, G., and Rosenfeld, R. (1981) *The nature and treatment of the stress response.* New York: Plenum Press.

Ewing, J., Rouse, B., and Aderhold, R. (1979) Studies of the mechanism of oriental hypersensitivity to alcohol. In M. Galanter (Ed.), *Biomedical issues and clinical effects of alcoholism.* New York: Grune & Stratton.

Exner, J.E. (1974) *The Rorschach: A comprehensive system* (Vol. 1). New York: Wiley-Interscience.

Exner, J. (1978) *The Rorschach: A comprehensive system: Current research and advanced interpretation* (Vol. 2). New York: John Wiley and Sons.

Eysenck, H.J., and Rachmans, S. (1965) *The causes and cures of neurosis.* London: Routledge and Kegan Paul.

Fabry, J. (1980) Depression. In R. Woody (Ed.), *Encyclopedia of mental assessment.* San Francisco: Jossey-Bass.

Fairfield, R. (1972) *Communes, Japan.* San Francisco: Alternatives Foundation.

Fallon, A., and Rozin, P. (1985) Sex differences in perceptions of desirable body shape. *Journal of Abnormal Psychology, 94,* 102–105.

Farberow, N. (1975) *Suicide in different cultures.* Baltimore: University Park Press.

Farley, R.C. (1984) The effects of a self-instructional self-management training package on the generalization and maintenance of selected interview skills: A pilot study. *Journal of Applied Rehabilitation Counseling, 15(2),* 50–53.

Fawcett, J., Scheftner, W., Clark, D., Hedeker, D. et al. (1987) Clinical predictors of suicide in patients with major affective disorders. *American Journal of Psychiatry, 144,* 35–40.

Feldman, M., and MacCulloch, M. (1965) The application of anticipatory avoidance learning to the treatment of homosexuality. *Behavior Research and Therapy, 2,* 165–183.

Fenichel, O. (1945) *The psychoanalytic theory of neuroses.* New York: W.W. Norton.

Fenz, W.D. (1975) Strategies for coping with stress. In I.G. Sarason and C.D. Spielberger (Eds.). *Stress and anxiety* (Vol. 2). New York: Hemisphere (Wiley).

Ferster, C. (1961) Positive reinforcement and behavioral deficits of autistic children. *Child Development, 32,* 437–456.

———. (1965) Classification of behavior pathology. In L. Krasner and L. Ullman (Eds.), *Research in behavior modification.* New York: Holt, Rinehart and Winston.

———. (1979) A functional analysis of depression. *American Psychologist, 34,* 174–181.

Ferster, C., and Culbertson, S. (1982) *Behavior principles* (3rd ed.). Englewood CLiffs, N.J.: Prentice-Hall.

Feuerstein, R. (1979) *The dynamic assessment of retarded performers.* Baltimore: University Park Press.

Field, T.M., Roseman, S., De Stefano, L.J., and Knewler, J. (1982) The play of handicapped preschool children with handicapped and nonhandicapped peers in integrated and non-integrated situations. *Topics in Early Childhood Special Education, 2(3),* 28–38.

Figley, C. (Ed.) (1978) Psychosocial adjustment among Vietnam veterans: An overview of the research. In *Stress disorders among Vietnam veterans.* New York: Bruner/Mazel.

———. (1981) Working on a theory of what it takes to survive. *APA Monitor, 12(3),* 9.

Filskov, S., and Boll, T. (1986) *Handbook of clinical neuropsychology.* New York: John Wiley and Sons.

Filskov, S.B., Grimm, B.H., and Lewis, J.A. (1981) Brain-behavior relationships. In S.B. Filskov and T.J. Boll (Eds.), *Handbook of clinical neuropsychology.* New York: Wiley-Interscience, pp. 39–73.

Fine, E., and Steel, R. (1979) Brain damage in early alcohol dependency. In M. Galanter (Ed.), *Biomedical issues and clinical effects of alcoholism.* New York: Grune & Stratton.

Finger, S., and Stein, D.G. (1982) *Brain damage and recovery.* New York: Academic Press.

Fink, M. (1979) *Convulsive therapy: Theory and practice.* New York: Raven.

Finkelhor, D. (1979) *Sexually victimized children.* New York: Free Press.

———. (1985) *Child sexual abuse.* New York: Free Press.

Fischman, J. (1985) Drug abuse. *Psychology Today, 19(4),* 22.

Fisher, C., Schiani, R., Edwards, A., Davis, D., Reitman, M., and Fine, J. (1979) Evaluation of nocturnal penile tumescence in the differential diagnoses of sexual impotence. *Archives of General Psychiatry, 36,* 431–437.

Fisher, H. (1987) Personal communication.

Fisher, K. (1982) TV and the mentally ill. *APA Monitor, August,* 12–13.

Fisher, L., and Wilson, T. (1985) A study of the psychology of agoraphobia. *Behavior Research and Therapy, 23,* 97–108.

Flanagan, T.J., Hindlang, M.J., and Gottfredson, M.R. (Eds.) (1980) *Sourcebook of criminal justice statistics, 1979.* Washington, D.C.: Government Printing Office.

Flaxman, J. (1976) Quitting smoking. In W. Craighead, A. Kazdin, and M. Mahoney (Eds.),*Behavior modification.* Boston: Houghton Mifflin.

Flintoff, M.M., Barron, R.W., Swanson, J.M., Ledlow, A., and Kinsbourne, M. (1982) Methylphenidate increases selectivity of visual scanning in children referred for hyperactivity. *Journal of Abnormal Child Psychology, 10(2),* 145–161.

Foa, E., and Kozak, M. (1986) Emotional processing of fear: Exposure to corrective information. *Psychological Bulletin, 99,* 20–35.

Ford v. *Wainwright,* U.S., S. Ct., 54 (USLW) 4799 (1986).

Ford, C., and Beach, F. (1951) *Patterns of sexual behavior.* New York: Harper & Row.

Fordyce, W. (1976) *Behavioral methods for chronic pain and illness.* St. Louis: C.V. Mosby.

Forey, J., Scott, L., Mitchell, R., and Gotto, A. (1979) Plasma lipid changes in the normal population following behavioral treatment. *Journal of Consulting and Clinical Psychology, 47,* 440–452.

Forgione, A. (1976) Instrumentation and techniques. The use of mannequins in the behavioral assessment of child molesters: Two case reports. *Behavior Therapy, 7,* 678–685.

Foy, D., Sipprelle, R., Rueger, D., and Carroll, E. (1984) Etiology of posttraumatic stress disorder in Vietnam veterans: Analysis of premilitary, military, and combat exposure influences. *Journal of Consulting and Clinical Psychology, 52,* 79–87.

Framo, J. (1979) Family theory and therapy. *American Psychologist, 34,* 988–992.

Frankl, V. (1975) Paradoxical intention and deflection. *Psychotherapy: Theory, research, and practice, 12,* 226–237.

Franklin, M.B., and Barten, S.S. (1988) *Child language.* New York: Oxford University Press.

Frazier, P., and Borgida, E. (1985) Rape trauma syndrome evidence in court. *American Psychologist, 40,* 984–993.

Frederick, C.J. (1978) Current trends in suicidal behavior in the United States. *American Journal of Psychotherapy, 32,* 172–200.

Freud, S. (1953) Three essays on the theory of sexuality. In J. Strachey (Ed.), *Standard edition of the complete works of Sigmund Freud* (Vol. 7). London: Hogarth Press. (Originally published, 1930.)

———. (1960) *A general introduction to psychoanalysis.* New York: Washington Square Press.

———. (1965) *A general introduction of psychoanalysis.* New York: Washington Square Press.

Friedberg, J. (1975) Let's stop blasting the brain. *Psychology Today, 35,* 18–26.

———. (1976) *Shock treatment is not good for your brain.* San Francisco: Glide.

———. (1977) ECT as neurologic injury. *Psychiatric Opinion, 14,* 16–19.

Friedman, M., and Rosenman, R. (1959) Association of specific overt behavior patterns with blood and cardiovascular findings. *Journal of the American Medical Association, 169,* 1289–1296.

Friedman, M., and Rosenman, R. (1974) *Type A behavior and your heart.* New York: Knopf.

Friedman, M.J., Schneiderman, C.K., West, A.U., and Capson, J.A. (1986) Measurement of combat life stress among Vietnam combat veterans. *American Journal of Psychiatry, 193(4),* 537–539.

Friedman, S.L., Scholnick, E.K., and Cocking, R.R. (1987) *Blueprints for thinking.* New York: Cambridge University Press.

Frith, C. (1984) Schizophrenia,memory, and anticholinergic drugs. *Journal of Abnormal Psychology, 93,* 339–341.

Frumkin, K., Nathan, R., Prout, M., and Cohen, M. (1978) Nonpharmacologic control of essential hypertension in man: A critical review of the experiments literature.*Psychosomatic Medicine, 40,* 294–320.

Fulkerson, S. (1965) Some implications of the new cognitive theory for projective tests. *Journal of Consulting Psychology, 29,* 191–197.

Fuller, G. (1978) Current status of biofeedback in clinical practice. *American psychologist, 33,* 39–48.

Furch, D.P., and Gale, E.N. (1984) Biofeedback and relaxation therapy for chronic temporomandibular joint pain: Predicting successful outcomes. *Journal of Consulting and Clinical Psychology, 52(6),* 928–935.

Fuse, T. (1980) Suicide and culture in Japan: A study of Seppuku as an institutionalized form of suicide. *Social Psychiatry, 15,* 57–63.

Gabe, J., and Williams. P. (Eds.) *Tranquilizers: Social, psychological, and clinical perspectives.* London: Tavistock.

Gaddes, W.H. (1981) An examination of the validity of neuropsychological knowledge in educational diagnosis and remediation. In G.W. Hynd and J.E. Obrzut (Eds.), *Neuropsychological assessment and the school-age child.* New York: Grune & Stratton, pp. 27–84.

Gaffney, R., Lurie, S., and Berlin, F. (1984) Is there familial transmission of pedophilia? *The Journal of Nervous and Mental Disease, 172,* 546–548.

Gallagher, D.E., Thompson, L.W., and Peterson, J.A. (1982) Psychosocial factors affecting adaptation to bereavement in the elderly. *International Journal of Aging and Human Development, 14(2)*, 79–95.

Ganzer, V.J., and Sarason, I.G. (1973) Variables associated with recidivism among juvenile delinquents. *Journal of Consulting and Clinical Psychology, 40*, 1–5.

Gardner, D., Lucas, P., and Cowdry, R. (1987) Soft sign neurological abnormalities in borderline personality and normal control subjects. *The Journal of Nervous and Mental Disease, 175*, 177–180.

Gardner, E. (1965) The role of the classification system in outpatient psychiatry. In M. Katz, J. Cole, and W. Barton (Eds.), *The role and methodology in psychiatry and psychopathology.* Washington, D.C.: U.S. Public Health Service.

Gardner, H. (1976) *The shattered mind.* New York: Vintage Books.

Garfield, S. (1974) *Clinical psychology: The study of personality and behavior.* Chicago: Aldine.

———. (1981) A 40-year appraisal. *American Psychologist, 36*, 174–183.

Garmezy, N. (1978) New approaches to a developmental overview of schizophrenia. Paper presented at the annual meeting of the American Psychological Association, Toronto.

Garner, D. (1986) Cognitive therapy for anorexia nervosa. In K. Brownell and J. Foreyt (Eds.), *Handbook of eating disorders.* New York: Basic Books.

Garner, D.M., and Bemis, K.M. (1982) A cognitive-behavioral approach to anorexia nervosa. *Cognitive Therapy and Research, 6(2)*, 123–150.

Gartrell, N. (1987) Personal communication.

Gatchel, R.J., and Mears, F. (1982) *Personality theory, assessment, and research.* New York: St. Martin's Press.

Geismar, L., and Wood, K. (1986) *Family and delinquency.* New York: Human Sciences Press.

Gelfand, D.M., Jenson, W.R., and Drew, C.J. (1987) *Understanding child behavior disorders* (2nd ed.). New York: Holt, Rinehart, and Winston.

George, W., and Marlatt, G.A. (1986) The effects of alcohol and anger on interest in violence, erotica, and deviance. *Journal of Abnormal Psychology, 95*, 150–158.

Gerner, R.H. (1979) Depression in the elderly. In O.J. Kaplan (Ed.), *Psychotherapy of aging.* New York: Academic Press.

Gesell, A. (1954) The ontogenesis of infant behavior. In L. Carmichael (Ed.), *Manual of child psychology* (2nd ed.). New York: John Wiley and Sons.

Gesell, A., and Thompson, H. (1929) Learning and growth in identical infant twins: An experimental study by the method of co-twin control. *Genetic Psychology Monograph, 6*, 1–124.

Gibson, D. (1978) *Down's syndrome: The psychology of mongolism.* London: Cambridge University Press.

Gilbert, D. (1979) Paradoxical tranquilizing emotion-reducing effects of nicotine. *Psychological Bulletin, 86*, 645–661.

Gillis, J., and Blevins, K. (1978) Sources of judgmental impairment in paranoid and nonparanoid schizophrenics. *Journal of Abnormal Psychology, 87*, 587–596.

Gilmour, D.R., and Walkey, F.H. (1981) Identifying violent offenders using a video measure of interpersonal distance. *Journal of Consulting and Clinical Psychology, 49*, 287–291.

Girdano, D.A., and Everly, G.S. (1986) *Controlling stress and tension* (2nd ed.). Englewood Cliffs, N.J.: Prentice-Hall.

Gladstein, G., and Associates (1987) *Empathy and counseling: Explorations in theory and research.* New York: Springer-Verlag.

Glasser, W., and Zunin, L. (1973) Reality therapy. In R. Corsini (Ed.), *Current psychotherapies,* Itasca, Ill.: Peacock.

Glatt, M. (1974) *A guide to addiction and its treatment.* New York: John Wiley and Sons.

Glow, R.A., Glow, P.H., and Rump, E.E. (1982) The stability of child behavior disorders: A one year test–retest study of Adelaide versions of the Connors teacher and parent rating scales. *Journal of Abnormal Child Psychology, 10(1)*, 33–60.

Glueck, S., and Glueck, E.T. (1950) *Unraveling juvenile delinquency.* New York: Commonwealth Fund.

———. (1970) *Toward a typology of juvenile offenders.* New York: Grune & Stratton.

Goldfarb, W. (1970) Childhood psychosis. In D. Mussen (Ed.), *Carmichael's manual of child psychology* (3rd ed.). New York: John Wiley and Sons.

Goldman, H., Gomer, F., and Templer, D. (1972) Long-term effects of electroconvulsive therapy upon memory and perceptual-motor performance. *Journal of Clinical Psychology, 28*, 32–34.

Goldstein, A., Lopez, M., and Greenleaf, D. (1979) Nontransferability of therapeutic gains. In A. Goldstein and F. Kanfer (Eds.), *Maximizing treatment gains.* New York: Academic Press.

Goldstein, A., and Myers, C. (1985) Relationship-enhancement methods. In F. Kanfer and A. Goldstein (Eds.), *Helping people change.* Elmsford, New York: Pergamon Press.

Goldstein, G., and Shelly, C. (1984) Discriminative validity of various intelligence and neuropsychological tests. *Journal of Consulting and Clinical Psychology, 52(3)*, 383–389.

Goldstein, L., Manowitz, P., Nora, R., Swartzburg, M., and Carlton, P. (1985) Differential EEG activation and pathological gambling. *Biological Psychiatry, 20*, 1232–1234.

Goldstein, M., Hand, I., and Hahlweg, K. (Eds.) (1986) *Treatment of schizophrenia,* New York: Springer-Verlag.

Goldstein, M., and Strachan, A. (1987) The family and schizophrenia. In T. Jacob (Ed.), *Family interactions and psychopathology.* New York: Plenum Press.

Goldston, S. (1986) Primary prevention: Historical perspectives and a blueprint for action. *American Psychologist, 41,* 453–460.

Gomes-Schwartz, B. (1978) Effective ingredients in psychotherapy: Prediction of outcome from process variables. *Journal of Consulting and Clinical Psychology, 46,* 1023–1035.

Gonzales, L., Lewinsohn, P., and Clarke, G. (1985) Longitudinal follow-up of unipolar depressives. *Journal of Consulting and Clinical Psychology, 53,* 461–469.

Goodwin, D.W. (1986) *Anxiety.* New York: Ballantine.

Goodwin, D., Schulsinger, F., Hermansen, L., Quze, S., and Winokur, G. (1973) Alcohol problems in adoptees raised apart from alcoholic biologic parents. *Archives of General Psychiatry, 128,* 289–343.

Gorski, T., and Miller, M. (1986) *Staying sober.* Independence, Mo.: Independence Press.

Gotlib, I., and Colby, C. (1987) *Treatment of depression.* New York: Pergamon Press.

Gottesman, I., and Shields, J. (1972) *Schizophrenia and genetics: A twin study vantage point.* New York: Academic Press.

Gottlieb, B.H. (1975) The contribution of natural support systems to primary prevention among four social subgroups of adolescent males. *Adolescence, 10,* 207–220.

Graham, J.R. (1987) *The MMPI* (2nd ed.) New York: Oxford University Press.

———. (1978) The Minnesota Multiphasic Personality inventory (MMPI). In B.B. Wolman (Ed.), *Clinical diagnosis of mental disorders.* New York: Plenum Publishing.

Graham, T., Kaplan, B., Covenoni-Huntley, J., James, S., Becker, C., Hames, C., and Heyden, S. (1978) Frequency of church attendance and blood pressure elevation. *Journal of Behavioral Medicine, 1,* 37–43.

Grant, I., and Adams, K. (1986) *Neuropsychological assessment of neuropsychiatric disorders.* New York: Oxford University Press.

Graves, R. (1955) *Collected poems.* Garden City, N.J.: Doubleday.

———. (1980) *A.E. Housman: The scholar poet.* New York: Scribners.

Graves, T. (1970) The personal adjustment of Navajo Indian migrants to Denver, Colorado. *American Anthropologist, 72,* 35–54.

Gray, H., and Hutchinson, H.C. (1964) The psychopathic personality: A survey of Canadian psychiatrists' opinion. *Canadian Psychiatric Association Journal, 9,* 450–461.

Gray, S. (1975) The insanity defense: Historical developments and contemporary relevance. In R. Allen, E.

Ferster, and J. Rubin (Eds.), *Readings in law and psychiatry.* Baltimore: Johns Hopkins University Press.

Greaves, G. (1980) Multiple personality 165 years after Mary Reynolds. *Journal of Nervous and Mental Disorders, 186,* 557–596.

Green, R. (1985) Gender identity in childhood and later sexual orientation. *The American Journal of Psychiatry, 142,* 339–341.

Greenberger, E., Steinberg, L.D., and Vaux, A. (1981) Adolescents who work: Health and behavioral consequences of job stress. *Developmental Psychology, 17,* 691–703.

Gregory, R.J. (1987) *Adult intellectual assessment.* Boston: Allyn and Bacon.

Grieve, R. (1982) Mentally retarded children's abilities in the process of comparison. *American Journal of Mental Deficiency, 87(2),* 180–185.

Griffiths, P., Neldrum, C., and McWilliam, R. (1982) Drybed training in the treatment of nocturnal enuresis in childhood: A research report. *Journal of Child Psychology and Psychiatry, 23(4),* 485–495.

Grisso, T. (1986) *Evaluating competencies.* New York: Plenum Press.

Griswold v. *Connecticut,* 381 U.S. 479 (1985).

Grob, C. (1983) *Mental illness and American society, 1875–1940.* Princeton, N.J.: Princeton University Press.

Grob, C. (1985) Single case study: Female exhibitionism. *The Journal of Nervous and Mental Disease, 173,* 253–256.

Grof, S. Personal communication, 1986.

Grote, C., Kaler, D., and Meyer, R. (1986) Personal injury. In M. Kurke and R. Meyer (Eds.), *Psychology in product liability and personal injury litigation.* New York: Hemisphere.

Groth, A., and Birnbaum, J. (1979) *Men who rape.* New York: Plenum Press.

Gruenewald, D. (1978) Analogues of multiple personality in psychosis. *International Journal of Clinical and Experimental Hypnosis, 26,* 1–8.

Gruenewald, D. (1984) On the nature of multiple personality: Comparison with hypnosis. *The International Journal of Clinical and Experimental Hypnosis, 32,* 170–190.

Grusec, J., Kucynski, L., Rushton, J., and Simutis, Z. (1979) Learning resistance to temptation through observation. *Developmental Psychology, 15,* 233–240.

Guerin, P., Fay, L., Bruden, S., and Kautto, J. (1986) *The evaluation and treatment of marital conflict.* New York: Basic Books.

Gummow, L., Miller, P., and Dustman, R.E. (1983) Attention and brain injury: A case for cognitive rehabilitation of attentional deficits. *Clinical Psychology Review, 3,* 255–274.

Gur, R., Gur, R., Skolnick, B., Caroff, S., Obrist, W., Resnick, S., and Reivich, M. Brain function in psychiatric disorders. *Archives of General Psychiatry, 42,* 329–334.

Gur, R. (1978) Left hemisphere dysfunction and left hemisphere overactivation in schizophrenia. *Journal of Abnormal Psychology, 87,* 226–238.

Guthrie, G., and Tanco, P. (1980) Alienation. In H. Triandis and J. Draguns (Eds.), *Handbook of cross-cultural psychology: Psychopathology.* Boston: Allyn and Bacon.

Guttman, H. (1973) A contraindication for family therapy: The prepsychotic or postpsychotic young adult and his parents. *Archives of General Psychiatry, 29,* 352–355.

Guy, J.D. (1987) *The personal life of the therapist.* New York: Wiley.

Haier, R., Murphy, D., and Buchsbaum, M. (1979) Paranoia and platelet MAO in normals and non-schizophrenic psychiatric groups. *American Journal of Psychiatry, 136,* 308–310.

Haley, J. (1959) *Strategies of psychotherapy.* New York: Grune & Stratton.

———. (1973) *Uncommon therapy: The psychiatric technique of Milton H. Erickson.* New York: W.W. Norton.

Hall, J. (1962) A histological investigation of the auditory pathways in neonatal asphyxia. *Acta Oto-Laryngologica, 54,* 369–375.

Hall, S., Tunstall, C., Rugg, D., Reese, T., and Benowitz, N. (1985) Nicotine gum and behavioral treatment in smoking cessation. *Journal of Consulting and Clinical Psychology, 53,* 256–258.

Hamilton, S., and Bornstein, P. (1979) Broad-spectrum behavioral approach to smoking cessation. *Journal of Consulting and Clinical Psychology, 47,* 598–600.

Hankoff, L., and Einsidler, B. (Eds.) (1979) The dialectics of suicide. In *Suicide.* Littleton, Mass.: PSG Publishing.

Harding G., Wright, C., and Orwin, A. (1985) Primary presenile dementia: The use of visual evoked potential as a diagnostic indicator. *British Journal of Psychiatry, 147,* 532–539.

Hardisty, J.H. (1973) Mental illness: A legal fiction. *Washington Law Review, 48,* 735–762.

Hare, R.D. (1970) *Psychopathy: Theory and research.* New York: John Wiley and Sons.

Hare, R., and McPherson, L. (1984) Violent and aggressive behavior by criminal psychopaths. *International Journal of Law and Psychiatry, 7,* 35–50.

Hare, R., and Jutai, J. (1986) Psychopathy, stimulation-seeking, and stress. In J. Strelau, F. Farley, and A. Gale (Eds.), *The biological bases of personality and behavior* (Vol. 2). New York: Hemisphere.

———. (1981) Psychopathy and violence. In J. Hays, T. Roberts, and K. Solway (Eds.), *Violence and the violent individual.* New York: SP Books.

Harlow, H.F., Gluck, J.P., and Suomi, S.J. (1972) Generalization of behavioral data between nonhu-

man and human animals. *American Psychologist, 27,* 709–716.

Harman, R. (1982) Personal communication.

Harpe, S. (1979) *Headaches.* Chicago: Budlong.

Harper, J., and Williams, S. (1975) Age and type of onset as critical variables in early infantile autism. *Journal of Autism and Childhood Schizophrenia, 5,* 25–36.

Harre, R. (1987) *The social construction of emotions.* New York: Basil Blackwell.

Hartlage, L. et al. (1987) *Neuropsychological assessment.* New York: Springer.

Hartmann, E., Milofsky, E., Vaillant, G., Oldfield, M., Falke, R., and Ducey, C. (1984) Vulnerability to schizophrenia. *Archives of General Psychiatry, 41,* 1050–1056.

Hasek, J. (1930) *The good soldier Schweik.* New York: Ungar.

Hatch, J., Fisher, J., and Rugh, J. (1986) *Biofeedback,* New York: Plenum Press.

Hatfield, L., Petrilli, A., and Tourney, G. (1975) Hormonal relationships in homosexual men. *American Journal of Psychiatry, 132,* 228–290.

Hathaway, S.R., and McKinley, J.C. (1943) *Minnesota multiphasic personality inventory: Manual.* New York: Psychological Corporation.

Havighurst, R.J., Bowman, P.H., Liddle, G.P., Matthews, C.V., and Pierce, J.V. (1962) *Growing up in River City.* New York: John Wiley and Sons.

Hayashida, Y., Mitani, Y., Hosomi, H., Amemiya, M., et al. (1986) Auditory brain stem responses in relation to the clinical symptoms of schizophrenia. *Biological Psychiatry, 21,* 177–188.

Haynes, S.N. (1984) Behavioral assessment of adults. In G. Goldstein and M. Herson (Eds.), *Handbook of psychological assessment.* New York: Pergamon Press, pp. 369–401.

Hays, J., Roberts, T., and Solway, K. (Eds.) (1981) *Violence and the violent individual.* New York: SP Books.

Hays, P. (1976) Etiological factors in manic-depressive psychoses. *Archives of General Psychiatry, 33,* 1187–1188.

Heath, R. (1960) A biochemical hypothesis on the etiology of schizophrenia. In D. Jackson (Ed.), *The etiology of schizophrenia.* New York: Basic Books.

Heath, D. (1986) Drinking and drunkeness in a transcultural perspective. *Transcultural Psychiatric Research, 23,* 7–42.

Heaton, R., and Pendleton, M.G. (1981) Use of neuropsychological tests to predict adult patients' everyday functioning. *Journal of Consulting and Clinical Psychology, 49,* 807–821.

Heidensohn, F. (1986) *Women and crime.* New York: New York University Press.

Heilbrun, A. (1978) Projective and repressive styles of processing aversive information. *Journal of Consulting and Clinical Psychology, 46,* 156–164.

————— . (1979) Psychopathy and violent crime. *Journal of Consulting and Clinical Psychology, 47,* 509–516.

Heilbrun, A., Blum, N., and Goldreyer, N. (1985) Defensive projection: An investigation of its role in paranoid conditions. *Journal of Nervous and Mental Disease, 173,* 17–25.

Heilman, K., and Valenstein, E. (Eds.) (1979) *Clinical neuropsychology.* New York: Oxford University Press.

Heilman, K.M. (1979) Neglect and related disorders. In K.M. Heilman and E. Valenstein (Eds.), *Clinical neuropsychology.* New York: Oxford University Press, pp. 268–307.

Heller, J. (1966) *Something happened.* New York: Knopf.

Helman, C. (1981) "Tonic," "fuel," and "food": Social and symbolic aspects of the long-term use of psychotropic drugs. *Social Science and Medicine, 15B,* 521–533.

Hendrix, E., and Meyer, R. (1976) Toward more comprehensive and durable client changes: A case report. *Psychotherapy: Theory, Research, and Practice, 13,* 263–266.

Hendrix, E., Thompson, L., and Rau, B. (1978) Behavioral treatment of an "hysterically" clenched fist. *Journal of Behavior Therapy and Experimental Psychiatry, 9,* 273–276.

Herjavic, B., and Reich, W. (1982) Development of a structured psychiatric interview for children: Agreement between child and parent on individual symptoms. *Journal of Abnormal Child Psychology, 10(3),* 307–324.

Herman, S., Barlow, D., and Argras, W. (1974) An experimental analysis of classical conditioning as a method of increasing heterosexual arousal in homosexuals. *Behavior Therapy, 5,* 335–347.

Hersen, M. (1981) Complex problems require complex solutions: *Behavior Therapy, 12,* 15–29.

Hersen, M., and Breuning, S. (1986) *Pharmacological and behavioral treatment.* New York: John Wiley and Sons.

Hersen, M., and Van Hasselt, V.B. (1987) *Behavior therapy with children and adolescents.* New York: Wiley.

Hersen, M. et al. (1984) Effects of social skill training, amitriptyline, and psychotherapy in unipolar depressed women. *Behavior Therapy, 15,* 21–40.

Hesbacher, P. (1976) Psychotropic drug prescription in family practice. *Comprehensive Psychiatry, 17,* 607–615.

Hetherington, E., and Martin, B. (1979) Family interaction in H.C. Quay and J.S. Werry (Eds.), *Psychopathological disorders of childhood* (2nd ed.). New York: John Wiley and Sons.

Hewitt, L.E., and Jenkins, R.L. (1946) *Fundamental patterns of maladjustment: The dynamics of their origin.* Springfield, Ill.: State of Illinois.

Higginbotham, H.N. (1976) A conceptual model for the delivery of services in non-Western settings. *Topics in Cultural Learning, 4,* 44–52.

Higgins, J. (1979) *Day of Judgment.* New York: Holt, Rinehart and Winston.

Hill, S., and Mikhael, M. (1979) Computerized transaxial topographic and neuropsychological evaluations in chronic alcoholics and heroin abusers. *American Journal of Psychiatry, 136,* 598–602.

Himmelfarb, S., and Murrell, S. (1984) The prevalence and correlates of anxiety symptoms in older adults. *The Journal of Psychology, 116,* 159–167.

Hingtgen, J., Sanders, B., and DeMyer, M. (1965) Shaping cooperative responses in early childhood schizophrenia. In L. Ullman and L. Krasner (Eds.), *Case studies in behavior modification.* New York: Holt, Rinehart and Winston.

Hippius, H. (1972) The current status of treatment for depression. In P. Kielholz (Ed.), *Depressive illness.* Baltimore: Williams & Wilkins.

Hoefler, S.A., and Bornstein, P.H. (1975) Achievement place: An evaluative review. *Criminal Justice and Behavior, 2,* 146–168.

Hoffmann, A. (1979) How LSD originated. *Journal of Psychedelic Drugs, 11,* 53–60.

Hokanson, J., DeGood, D., Forrest, M., and Brittain, T. (1971) Availability of avoidance behaviors for modulating vascular-stress responses. *Journal of Personality and Social Psychology, 19,* 60–68.

Holinger, P. (1979) Violent deaths among the young: Recent trends in suicide, homicide, and accidents. *American Journal of Psychiatry, 136,* 1144–1147.

Hollender, M., Brown, G., and Roback, H. (1977) Genital exhibitionism in women. *American Journal of Psychiatry, 134,* 436–438.

Hollingshead, A., and Redlich, R. (1958) *Social class and mental illness: A community study.* New York: John Wiley and Sons.

Hollon, S., and Beck, A. (1978) Psychotherapy and drug therapy: Comparison and combinations. In S. Garfield and A. Bergin (Eds.), *Handbook of psychotherapy and behavior change.* New York: John Wiley and Sons.

Holmes, T., and Rahe, R. (1967) The social readjustment rating scale. *Journal of Psychosomatic Medicine, 11,* 213–218.

Holroyd, K.A., and Andraski, F. (1982) Do the effects of cognitive therapy endure? A two-year follow-up of tension headache sufferers treated with cognitive therapy or biofeedback. *Cognitive Therapy and Research, 6,* 325–333.

Holtzman, W.H. (1968) The Holtzman inkblot technique. In A.I. Rabin (Ed.), *Introduction to modern projective techniques.* New York: Springer.

Holzman, A., and Turk, D. (1986) *Pain management.* Elmsford, N.Y.: Pergamon.

Homme, L. (1965) Perspectives in psychology: Control of coverants, the operants, the operants of the mind. *Psychological Record, 15,* 501–511.

Honzik, M.P., MacFarlane, J.W., and Allen, L. (1948) The stability of mental test performance between two and eighteen years. *Journal of Experimental Education, 17,* 309–324.

Horn, J.L., and Cattell, R.B. (1967) Age difference in fluid and crystallized intelligence. *Acta Psycholojica, 26,* 107–129.

Householder, J., Hatcher, R., Burns, W., and Chasnoff, I. (1982) Infants born to narcotic-addicted mothers. *Psychological Bulletin, 92,* 453–468.

Huba, G., Wingard, J., and Bentler, P. (1979) Beginning adolescent drug use and peer and adult interaction patterns. *Journal of Consulting and Clinical Psychology, 47,* 265–276.

Huberty, T.J., Koller, J.R., and Ten Brink, T.D. (1980) Adaptive behavior in the definition of mental retardation. *Exceptional Children, 46(4),* 256–261.

Hugdahl, K., and Ohman, A. (1977) Effects of instruction on acquisition and extinction of electrodermal response to fear-relevant stimuli. *Journal of Experimental Psychology: Human Learning and Memory, 3,* 608–618.

Hunt, N. (1967) *The world of Nigel Hunt: The diary of a mongoloid youth.* Beaconsfield: Darwen Finleyson.

Hurst, M., Jenkins, C., and Rose, D. (1978) The assessment of life change stress: A comparative and methodological inquiry. *Journal of Psychosomatic Medicine, 40,* 126–141.

Ignatieff, M. (1978) *A just measure of pain.* New York: Pantheon.

Imperato-McGinley, J., Peterson, R., Antier, T., and Sturla, E. (1979) Androgens and the evolution of male-gender identity among male pseudohermaphrodites with 500 reductase deficiency. *New England Journal of Medicine, 300,* 1233–1237.

Jackson, J.H. (1958) *Selected writings of John Hughlings Jackson, Volume II.* London: Staples Press.

Jackson v. *Indiana*, 406 U.S. 715 (1972).

Jacob, T. (1987) *Family interaction and psychopathology.* New York: Plenum Press.

Jacob, T. (1986) Alcoholism and family interaction. Nebraska Symposium on Motivation: Alcohol and Addictive Behavior. Lincoln, Neb.

Jacobs, A. (1971) *Adolescent suicide.* New York: Wiley-Interscience.

Jacobs, A., Brunton M., and Melville, M. (1965) Aggressive behavior, mental subnormality, and the XYY male, *Nature, 208,* 1351–1352.

Jacobs, L. (1977) The impotent king: Secondary impotence refractory to brief sex therapy. *American Journal of Psychotherapy, 31,* 97–103.

Jacobsen, N. (1978) Specific and nonspecific factors in the effectiveness of a behavioral approach to the treatment of marital discord. *Journal of Consulting and Clinical Psychology, 46,* 442–452.

Jacobson, E. (1970) *Modern treatment of tense patients.* Springfield, Ill.: Charles Thomas.

Jamison, K.R. (1979) Manic-depressive illness in the elderly. In O.J. Kaplan (Ed.), *Psychopathology of aging.* New York: Academic Press.

Janis, I. (1950) Psychologic effects of electric convulsive treatments. Part 1: Post-treatment amnesia. *Journal of Nervous and Mental Disease, 129,* 359–382.

Jarvik, M. (1967) The psychopharmacological revolution. *Psychology Today, 1,* 51–59.

Jayne, C. (1984) Effect of pubococcygeal exercise on female sexuality: Comment on Chambless et al. *Journal of Consulting and Clinical Psychology, 52,* 269–270.

Jeffrey, R., and Wing, R. (1979) Frequency of therapist contact in the treatment of obesity. *Behavior Therapy, 10,* 186–192.

Jellinek, E. (1960) *The disease concept of alcoholism.* New Haven: Hillhouse Press.

Jenkins, R.L., and Hewitt, L. (1944) Types of personality structure encountered in child guidance clinics. *American Journal of Orthopsychiatry, 14,* 84–94.

Jersild, A.T., and Holmes, F.B. (1935) *Children's fears,* (Child Development Monograph 20). New York: Bureau of Publications, Teachers College, Columbia University.

Jeste, D., Potkin, S., Sinha, S., Feder, S., and Wyatt, R. (1979) Tardive dyskenesia-reversible and persistent. *Archives of General Psychiatry, 36,* 585–590.

Johnson, B., and Anger, W. (1982) Behavioral toxicology. In W. Rom (Ed.), *Environmental and occupational medicine.* Boston: Little, Brown.

Jones, M. (1971) Personality antecedents and correlates of drinking patterns in women. *Journal of Consulting and Clinical Psychology, 36,* 61–70.

Jones, W., Cheek, J., and Briggs, S. (1986) *Shyness.* New York: Plenum Press.

Jouriles, E., and O'Leary, K. (1985) Interspousal reliability of reports of marital violence. *Journal of Consulting and Clinical Psychology, 53,* 419–421.

Joynt, R.J., and Shoulson, I. (1979) Dementia. In K. Heilman and E. Valenstein (Eds.),*Clinical Neuropsychology.* New York: Oxford University Press.

Julien, R. (1985) *A primer of drug action.* New York: W.H. Freeman.

Justice, R., and Justice, B. (1981) Treatment of child-abusing families. In J. Hays, T. Roberts, and K. Solway (Eds.), *Violence and the violent individual.* New York: SP Books.

Kagehiro, D., and Stanton, W. (1985) Legal vs. quantified definitions of standards of proof. *Law and Human Behavior, 9,* 159–178.

Kahn, J.H., Nursten, J.P., and Caroll, C.M. (1980) *Unwillingly to school: School phobia or school refusal?* (3rd ed.). New York: Pergamon Press.

Kahn, R., McNair, D., Lipman, R., Covi, L. et al. (1986) Imipramine and chlordiazepoxide in depressive and anxiety disorders. II. *Archives of General Psychiatry, 43,* 79–85.

Kail, R., and Pellegrino, J. (1985) *Human intelligence.* New York: W.H. Freeman.

Kallman, F. (1946) The genetic theory of schizophrenia: An analysis of 691 schizophrenic twin index families. *American Journal of Psychiatry, 103,* 309–322.

———. (1952) Comparative twin study in the genetic aspects of male homosexuality. *Journal of Nervous and Mental Disease, 115,* 283–298.

Kandel, D., and Faust, R. (1975) Sequence and stages in patterns of adolescent drug use. *Archives of General Psychiatry, 32,* 923–932.

Kanfer, F.H. (1977) Self-regulation and self-control. In H. Zeier (Ed.), *The psychology of the twentieth century* (Vol. 4). Zurich: Kindler Verlag.

Kanfer, F.H. (1980) Self-management methods. In F. Kanfer and A. Goldstein (Eds.), *Helping people change: A textbook of methods.* New York: Pergamon Press, pp. 334–389.

Kanfer, F.H., and Phillips, J.S. (1970) *Learning foundations of behavior therapy.* New York: John Wiley and Sons.

Kanner, L. (1971) Follow-up study of eleven autistic children originally reported in 1943. *Journal of Autism and Childhood Schizophrenia, 1,* 14–19.

Kaplan, B. (Ed.) (1964) *The inner world of mental illness.* New York: Harper & Row.

Karon, B. (1976) The psychoanalysis of schizophrenia. In P. Magaro (Ed.), *The construction of madness.* New York: Pergamon Press.

———. (1981) The Thematic Apperception Test (TAT). In A. Rabin (Ed.), *Assessment with projective techniques.* New York: Springer.

Karon, B., and VanDenBos, G. (1972) Psychotherapeutic technique and the economically prone patient. *Psychotherapy: Theory, research, and practice, 9,* 111–119.

Karp, E., Morgenstern, M., and Michal-Smith, H. (1978) Diagnosing mental deficiency. In B. Wolman (Ed.), *Clinical assessment of mental disorders.* New York: Plenum Publishing.

Karson, C., and Bigelow, L. (1986) The paranoid quotient. *Acta Psychiatrica Scandinavica, 73,* 39–41.

Kasl, S., and Cooper, C. (1987) *Stress and health.* New York: Guilford.

Kaslow, F., and Sussman, M. (1982) *Cults and the family.* New York: Haworth.

Keefe, F., and Gil, K. (1987) Chronic pain. In V. Hasselt, P. Strain, and M. Hersen (Eds.) *Handbook of developmental and physical disabilities.* Elmsford, N.Y.: Plenum Press.

Kellam, A. (1969) Shoplifting treated by aversion to a film. *Behavior Research and Therapy, 7,* 125–127.

Kelly, E. (1973) School phobia: A review of theory and treatment. *Psychology in the schools, 10,* 33–42.

Kelly, G. (1955) *The psychology of personal constructs* (Vol. 2). New York: W.W. Norton.

———. (1977) Personal construct theory and the psychotherapeutic interview. *Cognitive Therapy and Research, 1,* 355–362.

Kelly, J.J. (1970) The quest for valid preventive interventions. In C.D. Spielberger (Ed.), *Current topics in clinical and community psychology* (Vol. 2). New York: Academic Press.

Kelly, W. (Ed.) (1985) *Post-traumatic stress disorder and the war veteran patient.* New York: Bruner/Mazel.

Kembler, K. (1980) The nosologic validity of paranoia (simple delusional disorder). *Archives of General Psychiatry, 37,* 695–706.

Kendall, P.C., and Branswell, L. (1982) Cognitive-behavioral self-control therapy for children: A components analysis. *Journal of Consulting and Clinical Psychology, 50(5),* 672–689.

Kendler, H. (1987) *A history of psychology.* Chicago: Dorsey.

Kendler, K., Heath, A., Martin, N., and Eaves, L. (1986) Symptoms of anxiety and depression in a volunteer twin population. *Archives of General Psychiatry, 43,* 213–221.

Keniston, K. (1965) *The uncommitted: Alienated youth in American society.* New York: Dell.

Kerlinger, F. (1985) *Foundations of behavioral research.* New York: Holt, Rinehart and Winston.

Kessler, J. (1966) *Psychopathology of childhood.* Englewood Cliffs, N.J.: Prentice-Hall.

Kestenbaum, C. (1979) Children at risk for manic-depressive illness: Possible predictors. *American Journal of Psychiatry, 136,* 1206–1208.

Kety, S. (1975) Biochemistry of the major psychoses. In A. Freedman, H. Kaplan, and B. Sadock (Eds.), *Comprehensive textbook of psychiatry* (Vol. 2). Baltimore: Williams and Wilkins.

———. (1976) Genetic aspects of schizophrenia. *Psychiatric Annals, 6,* 6–15.

Kety, S., Rosenthal, D., Wender, P., Schulsinger, F., and Jacobsen, B. (1978) The biologic and adoptive families of individuals who became schizophrenic. In L. Wynne, R., Gramwell, and S. Matthyse (Eds.), *The nature of schizophrenia.* New York: John Wiley and Sons.

Khan, K., and Martin, I. (1977) Kleptomania as a presenting feature of cortical atrophy. *Acta Psychiatrica Scandinavia, 56,* 168–172.

Kiell, N. (1976) *Varieties of sexual experience.* New York: International Universities Press.

Kilminster, S., and Jones, D. (1986) Perceived control and the cold pressor test. *Stress Medicine, 2,* 73–77.

Kimura, D. (1961) Some effects of temporal lobe damage on auditory perception. *Canadian Journal of Psychology, 15,* 156–165.

King, A.C., Ahles, J.A., Martin, J.E., and White, R. (1984) EMG biofeedback-controlled exercise in chronic athletic knee pain. *Archives of Physical Medicine and Rehabilitation, 65(6),* 341–343.

King, M.G. (1987) *Stress: Theory and practice.* Orlando, Flor.: Harcourt-Brace.

Kinsey, A., Pomeroy, W., and Martin, C. (1948) *Sexual behavior in the human male.* Philadelphia: W.B. Saunders.

Kinsey, A., Pomeroy, W., Martin, C., and Gebhard, P. (1953) *Sexual behavior in the human female.* Philadelphia: W.B. Saunders.

Kipper, D., and Ginot, E. (1979) Accuracy of evaluating videotape feedback and defense mechanisms. *Journal of Consulting and Clinical Psychology, 47,* 493–499.

Kirby, E., and Grimley, L. (1986) *Understanding and treating attention deficit disorder.* New York: Pergamon Press.

Klebba, A. (1981) Comparison of trends for suicide and homicide in the United States, 1900–1976. In J. Hays, T. Roberts, and K. Solway (Eds.), *Violence and the violent individual.* New York: Spectrum Publications.

Klee, S., and Meyer, R. (1981) Alleviation of performance deficits of depression through thermal biofeedback training. *Journal of Clinical Psychology, 37,* 515–518.

Kleemeier, R.W. (1961) Intellectual change in the senium, or death and the IQ. Presidential address to the American Psychological Association.

Klein, D., Depue, R., and Slater, J. (1985) Cyclothymia in the adolescent offspring of parents with bipolar affective disorder. *Journal of Abnormal Psychology, 94,* 115–127.

Kleinmuntz, B. (1967) *Personality measurement.* Homewood, Ill.: Dorsey Press.

Kluft, R. (1987) An update on the multiple personality disorder. *Hospital and Community Psychiatry, 38,* 363–373.

Knight, R., and Sims-Knight, J. (1979) Integration of linguistic ideas in schizophrenia. *Journal of Abnormal Psychology, 88,* 191–202.

Knobloch, H., and Pasamanick, B. (1975) Some etiological and prognostic factors in early infantile autism. *Pediatrics, 55,* 182–191.

Knopf, I.J. (1979) *Childhood psychopathology.* Englewood Cliffs, N.J.: Prentice-Hall.

Kobasa, S. (1979) Stressful life events, personality, health: An inquiry into hardiness. *Journal of Personality and Social Psychology, 37,* 1–11.

Kohlberg, L. (1978) The cognitive developmental approach to behavior disorders: A study of the development of moral reasoning in delinquents. In G. Serban (Ed.), *Cognitive defects in the development of mental illness.* New York: Bruner/Mazel.

————. (1963) The development of children's orientations toward a moral order, 1: Sequence in the development of moral thought. *Vital Humana, 6,* 11–33.

Kohut, H. (1977) *The restoration of the self.* New York: International University Press.

Kolata, G. (1979) Mental disorders: A new approach to treatment? *Science, 203,* 36–38.

————. (1979) New drugs and the brain. *Science, 205,* 774–777.

Kolb, B., and Whishaw, I.Q. (1985) *Fundamentals of human neuropsychology* (2nd. ed.). New York: W.H. Freeman.

Kolb, L.S. (1963) Therapy of homosexuality. In J. Masserman (Ed.), *Current psychiatric therapies.* New York: Grune & Stratton.

Koluchová, J. (1976) A report on the further development of twins after severe and prolonged deprivation. In A.M. Clarke and A.D.B. Clark (Eds.), *Early experience: Myth and evidence.* New York: Free Press, Chapter 5, pp. 56–66.

Korchin, S.J. (1976) *Modern clinical psychology: Principles of intervention in the clinic and community.* New York: Basic Books.

Kosovich, D. (1978) Sexuality through the centuries. *Psychiatric Opinion, 15,* 15–17.

Kozak, M., Foa, E., and McCarthy, P. (1987) Obsessive-compulsive disorder. In C. Last and M. Hersen (Eds.), *Handbook of Anxiety Disorders.* Elmsford, N.Y.: Plenum Press.

Kraepelin, E. (1896) *Lehrbuch der psychiatrie* (5th ed.). Leipzig: Barth.

Krantz, D. (1977) The Santa Fe experience. In S.B. Sarason (Ed.), *Work, aging, and social change.* New York: Free Press.

Krasner, L. (1962) The therapist as a social reinforcement machine. In H.H. Strupp and L. Luborsky (Eds.), *Research in psychotherapy.* Washington, D.C.: American Psychological Association.

Krassner, H., Brownell, K., and Stunkard, A. (1979) Cleaning the plate: Food left over by overweight and normal persons. *Behavior Research and Therapy, 17,* 155–156.

Kubler-Ross, E. (1969) *On death and dying.* New York: Macmillan.

Kudrow, L. (1978) Managing migraine headache. *Psychosomatics, 19,* 685–693.

Kurlychek, R.T., and Glang, A.E. (1984) The use of microcomputers in the cognitive rehabilitation of brain-injured persons. In M.D. Schwartz (Ed.), *Using computers in clinical practice.* New York: Haworth Press, pp. 245–256.

Kysar, J.E. (1968) The two camps in child psychiatry: A report from a psychiatrist father of an autistic and retarded child. *American Journal of Psychiatry, 125,* 103–109.

Lacy, W., and Hendricks, J. (1980) Developmental models of adult life: Myth or reality. *International Journal of Aging and Human Development, II,* 89–110.

Laing, R.D. (1979) *The facts of life.* New York: Ballantine Books.

Lambert, N., Hartsough, C., Sassone, D., and Sandoval, J. (1987) Persistence of hyperactivity symptoms from childhood to adolescence and associated outcomes. *American Journal of Orthopsychiatry, 57,* 22–32.

Lambourn, J., and Gill, D. (1978) A controlled comparison of simulated and real ECT. *British Journal of Psychiatry, 133,* 514–519.

Landis, E., and Meyer, R. (1988) *Detecting deception.* Chicago, Dorsey.

Landman, J., and Dawes, R. (1982) Psychotherapy outcome: Smith and Glass's conclusions stand up under scrutiny. *American Psychologist, 37,* 504–516.

Lang, A., Goechner, D., Adesso, V., and Marlatt, A. (1979) Effects of alcohol on aggression in male social drinkers. *Personality and Social Psychology Bulletin, 5,* 169–172.

Lansky, D., and Wilson, G. (1977) Alcohol, expectations, and sexual arousal in males: An information processing analysis. *Journal of Experimental Psychology: General, 106,* 3–40.

Larson, J., Johnson, J., and Easterbrooks, M. (1979) Sensation seeking and antisocial behavior: Some laboratory evidence. *Personality and Social Psychology Bulletin, 5,* 169–172.

LaRusso, L. (1978) Sensitivity of paranoid patients to nonverbal cues. *Journal of Abnormal Psychology, 87,* 463–471.

Lasch, C.(1978) *The culture of narcissism.* New York: W.W. Norton.

Lashley, K.S. (1929) *Brain mechanisms and intelligence.* Chicago: University of Chicago Press.

LaVoie, J. (1980) Adult development. In R. Woody (Ed.), *The encyclopedia of clinical assessment.* San Francisco: Jossey-Bass.

Lazar, B., and Harrow, M. (1985) Paranoid and nonparanoid schizophrenia. *Journal of Clinical Psychology, 141,* 145–151.

Lazarus, A. (1971) *Behavior therapy and beyond.* New York: McGraw-Hill.

———. (1981) *The practice of multimodal therapy.* New York: McGraw-Hill.

———. (1985) *Casebook of multimodal therapy.* New York: Guilford.

———. (1987) *In the mind's eye.* New York: Guilford.

LeDoux, J.E., and Hirst, W. (1986) *Mind and brain.* New York: Cambridge University Press.

Lehrer, P.M., Woolfolk, R.L., Rooney, A.J., McCann, B., and Carrington, P. (1983) Progressive relaxation and meditation. A study of psychophysiological and therapeutic differences between two techniques. *Behavior Research and Therapy, 21,* 651–662.

Leighton, A. (1982) *Caring for mentally ill people: Psychological and social barriers in historical context.* London: Cambridge University Press.

Leitenberg, H. (1965) Is time out from positive reinforcement an aversive event? *Psychological Bulletin, 64,* 428–441.

Lenneberg, E.H., and Long, B.S. (1974) Language development. In *Psychology and the handicapped child.* Washington, D.C.: Government Printing Office (DHEW Publication OE 73-05000).

Leo, V. (1985) The ups and downs of creativity, *Time, 124(15),* 76.

Lester, B.M. (1975) Cardiac habituation of the orienting response to an auditory signal in infants of varying nutritional status. *Developmental Psychology, 11,* 432–442.

Lester, D., Beck, A., and Mitchell, B. (1979) Extrapolation from attempted suicides to completed suicides: A test. *Journal of Abnormal Psychology, 88,* 78–80.

Levin, D. (Ed.) (1987) *Pathologies of the modern self.* New York: New York University Press.

Levin, H.S., Benton, A.L., and Grossman, R.G. (1982) *Neurobehavioral consequences of closed head injury.* New York: Oxford University Press.

Levin, H.S., Grafman, J., and Eisenberg, H.M. (1987) *Neurobehavioral recovery from head injury.* New York: Oxford University Press.

Levine, E.M., and Kozak, C. (1979) Drug and alcohol use, delinquency, and vandalism among upper middle class pre- and post-adolescents. *Journal of Youth and Adolescence, 8,* 92–101.

Levine, S. (1979) Barriers to the attainment of ejaculatory control. *Medical Attempts of Human Sexuality, 13,* 32–56.

Levinson, D. (1978) *The seasons of a man's life.* New York: Knopf.

Levinson, D. (1986) A conception of adult development. *American Psychologist, 41,* 3–13.

Levy, D. (1979) Two styles of marital therapy. Unpublished paper, University of Louisville.

Lewandowski, K., and Graham, J.R. (1972) Empirical correlates of frequency occurring two-point MMPI code types: A replicated study. *Journal of Consulting and Clinical Psychology, 39,* 467–472.

Lewine, R. (1981) Sex differences in schizophrenia: Timing or subtypes. *Psychological Bulletin, 90,* 432–444.

Lewis, D.O., and Balla, D.A. (1976) *Delinquency and psychopathology.* New York: Grune & Stratton.

Lewis, D., and Winokur, G. (1983) The familial classification of primary unipolar depression: Biological validation of distinct subtypes. *Comprehensive Psychiatry, 24,* 295–301.

Lewis, H. (1981) *Freud and modern psychology.* New York: Plenum Press.

Lewis, H. (1985) Depression vs. paranoia: Why are there sex differences in mental illness. *Journal of Personality, 53,* 151–178.

Lewis, M., and Griffin, P. (1981) An explanation for the season of birth effect in schizophrenia and certain other diseases. *Psychological Bulletin, 89,* 589–596.

Lewis, R., Gerber, L., Stein, S., Stephen, R., Grosser, B., Velick, S., and Undenfriend, S. On B_H-Leu⁵— Endorphin and schizophrenia. *Archives of General Psychiatry, 36,* 237–239.

Lewinsohn, R., and Hoberman, H. (1982) In A. Bellack, M. Hersen, and A. Kazdin (Eds.), *International handbook of behavior modification and therapy.* New York: Plenum Press.

Lewy, A., Nurnberger, J., Wehr, T., Pack, D., Becker, L., Powell, R., and Newsome, D. (1985) Supersensitivity to light: Possible trait markers for manic-depressive illness. *The American Journal of Psychiatry, 146,* 725–727.

Lezak, M. (1983) *Neuropsychological assessment* (2nd ed.). New York: Oxford University Press.

Lieblum, S., and Pernin, L. (Eds.), *Principles and practice of sex therapy.* New York: Guilford.

Liebman, R., Minuchin, S., and Baker, L. (1974) An integrated treatment program for anorexia nervosa. *American Journal of Psychiatry, 131(4),* 432–436.

Liebowitz, M., Gorman, J. Fryer, A., Levitt, M., Dillion, D., Levy, G., Appleby, H., Anderson, S., Palij, M., Davies, S., and Klein, D. (1985a) Lactate provocation of panic attacks. *Archives of General Psychiatry, 42,* 709–714.

Liebowitz, M., Gorman, J., Fryer, A., and Klein, D. (1985b) Social phobia: Review of a neglected anxiety disorder. *Archives of General Psychiatry, 42,* 729–735.

Lincoff, G., and Mitchell, D. (1977) *Toxic and hallucinogenic mushroom poisoning.* New York: Van Nostrand Reinhold.

Linn, R.J., and Hodge, G.K. (1982) Locus of control in childhood hyperactivity. *Journal of Consulting and Clinical Psychology, 50(4),* 592–593.

Lipowski, Z. (1975) Psychophysiological cardiovascular disorders. In A. Freedman, H. Kaplan, and B. Sadock (Eds.), *Comprehensive textbook of psychiatry* (Vol 2). Baltimore: Williams & Wilkins.

Lipton, M. (1979) Lithium: Developments in basic and clinical research. *American Journal of Psychiatry, 136,* 1059–1061.

Livingston, R.H., and Johnson, P.C. (1979) Covert conditioning and self-management in rehabilitation counseling. *Rehabilitation Counseling Bulletin, 22,* 330–337.

Lobel, B. (1984) *Depression,* Rockville, Md.: Department of Health and Human Services (DHHS publication # (ADM)) 84-1318.

Lobitz, W., and Post, R. (1979) Parameters of self-reinforcement and depression. *Journal of Abnormal Psychology, 88,* 33–41.

Lockwood, K., and Bourland, G. (1982) Reduction of self-injurious behaviors by reinforcement and toy use. *Mental Retardation, 20(4),* 169–173.

Lombardino, L.J., Klein, M.P., and Saine, T.J. (1982) Maternal interrogatives during discourse with language learning normal and Down's syndrome children: A preliminary clinical taxonomy. *Education and Training of the Mentally Retarded, 17(3),* 222–226.

Long, B. (1986) The prevention of mental-emotional difficulties. *American Psychologist, 41,* 825–829.

Long, C.J., Gouvier, W.D., and Cole, J.C. (1984) A model of recovery for the total rehabilitation of individuals with head trauma. *Journal of Rehabilitation, 70,* 39–45.

Looney, J.D., and Gunderson, E. (1978) Transient situational disturbances: Course and outcome. *American Journal of Psychiatry, 135,* 660–663.

LoPiccolo, J. (1985) Advances in the diagnosis and treatment of sexual dysfunction. Convention Workshop. Kentucky Psychological Association, Louisville.

LoPiccolo, J., and Stock, W. (1986) Treatment of sexual dysfunction. *Journal of Consulting and Clinical Psychology, 54,* 158–167.

Loraine, J., Ismael, A., Adamopoulos, R., and Dove, G. (1970) Endocrine function in male and female homosexuals. *British Medical Journal, 4,* 406.

Lorenz, K. (1966) *On aggression.* New York: Harcourt, Brace.

Lorr, M., Klet, C., and McNair, D. (1963) *Syndromes of psychosis.* New York: Pergamon Press.

Lovass, O.I. (1977) The autistic child. *Language development through behavior modification.* New York: Irvington.

Lovibond, S., and Caddy, G. (1970) Discriminated aversive control in the modification of alcoholics' drinking behavior. *Behavior Therapy, 1,* 437–444.

Lovibond, S., and Coote, M. (1969) Enuresis. In M.C. Costello (Ed.), *Symptoms of psychopathology.* New York: John Wiley and Sons.

Lowinson, J. (1981) Methadone maintenance in perspective. In J. Lowinson and P. Ruiz (Eds.), *Substance abuse: Clinical problems and perspectives.* Baltimore: Williams & Wilkins.

Lowinson, J., and Ruiz, R. (Eds.) (1981) *Substance abuse: Clinical problems and perspectives.* Baltimore: Williams & Wilkins.

Luisada, P. (1981) Phencyclidine. In J. Lowinson and P. Ruiz (Eds.), *Substance abuse: Clinical problems and perspectives.* Baltimore: Williams & Wilkins.

Lunde, D. (1976) *Murder and madness.* San Francisco: San Francisco Book Co.

Luria, A.R. (1973) *The working brain.* New York: Basic Books.

Luria, Z., Friedman, S., and Rose, M. (1986) *Human Sexuality.* New York: John Wiley and Sons.

Lutzker, J., and Martin, J. (1981) *Behavior change.* Monterey, Calif.: Brooks/Cole.

Lykken, D.T. (1979) *A tremor in the blood.* New York: McGraw-Hill.

Lykken, D. (1980) *A tremor in the blood.* New York: McGraw-Hill.

————. (1957) A study of anxiety in the sociopathic personality. *Journal of Abnormal and Social Psychology, 55,* 6–10.

Lyons, J., Rosen, A., and Dysken, M. (1985) Behavioral effects of tricyclic drugs in depressed inpatients. *Journal of Consulting and Clinical Psychology, 53,* 17–24.

Maas, H., Kuypers, J. (1974) *From thirty to seventy.* San Francisco: Jossey-Bass.

MacDonald, M., Lidsky, T., and Kern, J. (1979) Drug instigated effects. In A. Goldstein and F. Kanfer (Eds.). *Maximizing treatment gains.* New York: Academic Press, 429–444.

MacKeith, R. (1968) A pregnant factor in the organs and primary nocturnal anxiety in the third year of life. *Developmental Medicine and Child Neurology, 10,* 465–470.

Macciocchi, S., and Meyer, R. (1981) Unpublished paper.

Mack, J.C. (1969) Behavior ratings of recidivist and non-recidivist delinquent males. *Psychological Reports, 25,* 260.

Madsen, W. (1964) *Mexican-Americans of south Texas.* New York: Holt, Rinehart and Winston.

Magero, P. (1980) *Cognition in schizophrenia and paranoia.* Hillsdale, N.J.: Erlbaum Associates.

Mahoney, M.J. (1974) *Cognition and behavior modification.* Cambridge, Mass.: Ballinger.

Maisto, S., Sobell, L., and Sobell, M. (1979) Comparison of alcoholics' self-report of drinking behavior with reports of collateral informants. *Journal of Consulting and Clinical Psychology, 47,* 106–112.

Malamuth, N., and Spinner, B. (1980) A longitudinal content analysis of sexual violence in the best-selling erotic magazines. *Journal of Sex Research, 16,* 226–237.

Malkin, D., and Syme, G. (1985) Wagering preferences of problem gamblers. *Journal of Abnormal Psychology, 94,* 86–91.

Maltsberger, J. (1986) *Suicide risk.* New York: New York University Press.

Marengo, J., and Harrow, M. (1985) Thought disorder. *The Journal of Nervous and Mental Disease, 173,* 35–43.

Marks, I. (1978) Behavior psychotherapy of adult neuroses. In S. Garfield and A. Bergin (Eds.), *Handbook of psychotherapy and behavior change.* New York: John Wiley and Sons.

Marks, I. (1987) *Fears, phobias, and rituals.* New York: Oxford University Press.

Marks, V. (1979) *The search for the manchurian candidate.* New York: Bantam.

Marmor, J. (Ed.) (1980) Preface to *Homosexual behavior.* New York: Basic Books.

Marohn, R. (1982) Adolescent violence: Causes and treatment. *Journal of the American Academy of Child Psychiatry, 21,* 354–360.

Marsella, A. (1980) Depressive experience and disorder across cultures. In H. Triandis and J. Draguns (Eds.), *Handbook of cross-cultural psychology: Psychopathology.* Boston: Allyn and Bacon.

Marshall, W., Parker, L., and Hayes, B. (1982) Treating public speaking problems. *Behavior Modification, 6,* 147–710.

Marx, M., and Hillix, W. (1987) *Systems and theories in psychology* (4th ed.) New York: McGraw-Hill.

Mash, E., and Terdal, L. (1988) *Behavioral assessment of childhood disorders* (2nd ed.). New York: Guilford.

Masling, J. (Ed.) (1982) *Empirical studies of psychoanalytic theories.* Hillsdale, N.J.: Erlbaum Associates.

Maslow, A.H. (1968) *Toward a psychology of being.* New York: Van Nostrand Rinehold Company.

Maslow, A.H. (1954) *Motivation and personality.* New York: Hayes and Low.

Mason, A., Nerviano, V., and DeBurger, R. (1977) Patterns of antipsychotic drug use in four southeastern state hospitals. *Diseases of the Nervous System, 38,* 541–545.

Masters, W. (May 7, 1973) *International Herald Tribune* (Paris), 6.

Masters, W., and Johnson, V. (1970) *Human sexual inadequacy.* Boston: Little, Brown.

————. (1979) *Homosexuality in perspective.* Boston: Little, Brown.

Masters, W., Johnson, V., and Kolodny, R. (1982) *Human Sexuality.* Boston: Little, Brown.

Matarazzo, J.D. (1972) *Wechster's measurement and appraisal of adult intelligence* (5th ed.). Baltimore: Williams & Wilkins.

————. (1979) Intellectual functioning in chronic alcoholism. *Journal of Continuing Education in Psychiatry, June,* 13–24.

Matarazzo, J. (1986) Computerized clinical psychological test interpretations: Unvalidated plus all mean and no sigma. *American Psychologist, 41,* 14–42.

Matarese, S.M., and Salmon, P.G. The concept of deviance in utopian societies. *Midwest Quarterly,* in press.

Mathew, R., Claghorn, J., and Largen, J. (1979) Craving for alcohol in sober alcoholics. *American Journal of Psychiatry, 136,* 603–606.

Mathews, A. (1977) Recent developments in the treatment of agoraphobia. *Behavioral Analysis and Modification, 2,* 64–75.

———— . (1978) Fear-reduction research and clinical phobias. *Psychological Bulletin, 85,* 390–404.

Matthews, K., and Saal, F. (1978) Relationship of type A coronary-prone behavior pattern to achievement, power, and affiliation motives. *Psychosomatic Medicine, 40,* 630–636.

Matthyse, S. (1978) Current status of biochemistry in schizophrenia. Paper presented at the annual meeting of the American Psychological Association, Toronto.

Mattsson, A., Seese, L.R., and Hawkins, J.W. (1969) Suicidal behavior as child psychiatric emergency. *Archives of General Psychiatry, 20,* 100–105.

Mavissakalian, M., Turner, S., and Michelson,L. (Eds.) (1985) *Obsessive-compulsive disorder.* New York: Plenum Press.

Mawrer, R., Cadoret, R.J., and Cain, C. (1980) Cluster analysis of childhood temperament data on adoptees. *American Journal of Orthopsychiatry, 50(3),* 522–534.

May, R. (1977) *The meaning of anxiety.* New York: W.W. Norton.

May, W., Barlow, D., and Hay, L. (1981) Treatment of stereotypic cross-gender motor behavior using covert modeling in a boy with gender identity confusion. *Journal of Consulting and Clinical Psychology, 49,* 388–394.

McCabe, M. (1977) ECT in the treatment of mania: A controlled study. *American Journal of Psychiatry, 134,* 688–690.

McCarty, S.M., Siegler, I.C., and Logue, P.E. (1982) Cross-sectional and longitudinal patterns of three Wechsler memory scale subtests. *Journal of Gerontology, 37(2),* 169–175.

McClelland, D. (1979) Inhibited power motivation and high blood pressure in men. *Journal of Abnormal Psychology, 88,* 182–190.

McConaghy, N. (1982) Sexual deviations. In A. Bellack, M. Hersen, and A. Kazden (Eds.), *International handbook of behavior modification and therapy.* New York: Plenum Press.

McGuigan, F. (1970) Covert oral behavior during the silent performance of language tasks. *Psychophysiological Bulletin, 74,* 309–326.

McGuire, W.L. (1974) Communication persuasion models for drug education: Experimental findings. In M. Goodstadt (Ed.), *Research on methods and programs of drug education.* Toronto: Addiction Research Foundation.

McIntosh, J.L., and Santos, J.F. (1980) Suicide among native Americans: A compilation of findings. *Omega, 11(4),* 303–316.

McNeal, E., and Cimbolic, P. (1986) Antidepressants and biochemical theories of depression. *Psychological Bulletin, 99,* 361–374.

Mednick S., and Christiansen, K. (1977) *Biological basis of criminal behavior.* New York: Halstead.

Megargee, E. (1981) Methodological problems in the prediction of violence. In J. Hays,T. Roberts, and K. Solway (Eds.), *Violence and the violent individual.* New York: SP Books.

Megargee, E., and Bohn, M. (1977) Empirically determined characteristics of the ten types. *Criminal Justice and Behavior, 4,* 149–210.

———— . (1979) *Classifying criminal offenders.* Beverly Hills, Calif.: Sage.

Megargee, E., and Corhout, B. (1977) A new classification system for criminal offenders: Revision and refinement of the classification rules. *Criminal Justice and Behavior, 4,* 125–148.

Mehrabian, A., and Weinstein, L. (1985) Temperament characteristics of suicide attempters. *Journal of Consulting and Clinical Psychology, 53,* 544–546.

Meichenbaum, D. (1977) *Cognitive behavior modification.* New York: Plenum Press.

Meichenbaum, D. (1985) Cognitive behavior modification. In F. Kanfer and A. Goldstein (Eds.), *Helping people change.* Elmsford, New York: Pergamon Press.

Meier, C.A. (1986) *Soul and body: Essays on the theories of C.G. Jung.* San Francisco: Lapis Press.

Meiselman, K. (1978) *Incest.* San Francisco: Jossey-Bass.

Meissner, W. (1978) *The paranoid process.* New York: Jason Aronson.

Meister, R. (1980) *Hypochondria.* New York: Taplinger.

Mellinger, G., Balter, M., Manheimer, I., and Perry, H. (1978) Psychic distress, life crisis, and use of psychotherapeutic medications. *Archives of General Psychiatry, 35,* 1045–1054.

Menninger, K. (1938) *Man against himself.* New York: Harcourt, Brace.

———— . (1958) *Theory of psychoanalytic technique.* New York: Harper Torchbooks.

Menolascino, F.J. (1977) *Challenges in mental retardation: Progressive ideology and services.* New York: Human Sciences Press.

Mercer, J.R. (1973) *Labeling the mentally retarded.* Berkeley: University of California Press.

Merriam, K. (1976) The experience of schizophrenia. In P. Magero (Ed.), *The construction of madness.* New York: Pergamon Press.

Meyer, R. (1972) The acute mental effects of marijuana. In *Biochemical and pharmacological aspects of dependence and reports on marijuana research.* Haarlem, The Netherlands: De Ernen F. Bohn N.V.

———— . (1973) Delay therapy: Two case reports. *Behavior Therapy, 4,* 709–711.

———— . (1975) A behavioral treatment approach to

sleepwalking associated with test anxiety. *Journal of Behavioral Therapy and Experimental Psychiatry, 6,* 202–220.

———— . (1977) Legal and social ambivalence regarding homosexuality. *Journal of Homosexuality, 2,* 281–287.

———— . (1980) *The antisocial personality.* In R. Woody (Ed.), *The encyclopedia of mental assessment.* San Francisco: Jossey-Bass.

———— . (1981) Chronisch hoher blutdruck, essentieller hochdruck, und hemmung von aggression. *Sonderdruck aus aggression und frustration als psychologisches problem* (Vol. 1). Darmstadt: Wissenschaftliche Buchgesellschaft.

———— . (1983) *The clinician's handbook: The psychopathology of adulthood and late adolescence.* Boston: Allyn and Bacon.

Meyer, R., Barrett, C., and Hays, J. (1983) *Forensic psychology.* New York: Plenum Press.

Meyer, R., and Freeman, W. (1977) A social episode model of human sexual behavior. *Journal of Homosexuality, 2,* 123–131.

Meyer, R., and Karon, B. (1967) The schizophrenogenic mother concept and the TAT. *Psychiatry, 30,* 173–179.

Meyer, R., Landis, E., and Hays, J. (1988) *Law for the psychotherapist.* Chicago: Dorsey.

Meyer, R., and Osborne, Y. (1987) *Case studies in abnormal behavior.* Boston: Allyn and Bacon.

Meyer, R., and Smith, S. (1977) A crisis in group therapy. *American Psychologist, 32,* 638–643.

Meyer, R., and Tilker, H. (1976) The clinical use of direct hypnotic suggestion. In E. Dengrove (Ed.), *Hypnosis and behavior therapy.* Springfield, Ill.: Charles Thomas.

Meyer, T.P. (1962) The effects of sexually arousing and violent films on aggressive behavior. *Journal of Sex Research, 8,* 324–331.

Mezzich, J., and Berganza, C. (Eds.) (1984) *Culture and psychopathology.* New York: Columbia University Press.

Miall, W. (1961) The epidemiology of essential hypertension. In J. Cort, V. Fend, Z. Hejl, and J. Jirka (Eds.), *Psychopathology of essential hypertension.* Prague: State Medical Publishing House.

Miklowitz, D., Strachan, A., Goldstein, M., and Doane, J. et al. (1986) Expressed emotion and communication deviance in the families of schizophrenics. *Journal of Abnormal Psychology, 95,* 60–66.

Mikulich, D. (1979) Health psychology practice with asthmatics. *Professional Psychology, 10,* 580–588.

Milby, V. (1981) *Addictive behavior and its treatment.* New York: Springer.

Miller, I., and Normann, W. (1979) Learned helplessness in humans: A review and attribution-theory model. *Psychological Bulletin, 86,* 93–118.

Miller, J.G. (1978) *Living systems.* New York: McGraw-Hill.

Miller, L.C. (1967) Louisville behavior check list for males 6–12 years of age. *Psychological Reports, 21,* 885–896.

Miller, L.C., Barrett, C.L., Hampe, E., and Noble, H. (1972) Comparison of reciprocal inhibition, psychotherapy, and waiting list control for phobic children. *Journal of Abnormal Psychology, 79,* 269–275.

Miller, M.L., Chiles, J.A., and Barnes, V.E. (1982) Suicide attempters within a delinquent population. *Journal of Consulting and Clinical Psychology, 50(4),* 491–498.

Miller, S., Saccuzzo, D., and Braff, D. (1979) Family structure and depression in female college students: Effects of parental conflict, decision-making power, and inconsistency of love. *Journal of Abnormal Psychology, 88,* 398–406.

Miller, W. (1978) Lower class cultures as a generating milieu of gang delinquency. *Journal of Social Issues, 15,* 5–19.

Millon, T. (1981) *Disorders of personality, DSM-III: Axis II.* New York: John Wiley and Sons.

Mills, C., and Noyes, H. (1985) Patterns and correlates of initial and subsequent drug use among adolescents. *Journal of Consulting and Clinical Psychology, 52,* 231–243.

Mills, M., Sullivan, G., and Eth, S. (1987) Protecting third parties: A decade after Tarasoff. *American Journal of Psychiatry, 144,* 68–74.

Milner, B. (1963) Effects of different brain lesions on card sorting. *Archives of Neurology, 9,* 90–100.

Milner, B., Corkin, S., and Teuber, H.L. (1968) Further analysis of the hippocamipal amnesia syndrome: Fourteen year follow-up study of H.M. *Neuropsychologia, 6,* 215–234.

Mineka, S., and Cook, M. (1986) Immunization against the observational conditioning of snake fear in rhesus monkeys. *Journal of Abnormal Psychology, 95,* 307–318.

Mineka, S., Davidson, M., Cook, M., and Keir, R. (1984) Observational conditioning of snake fear in rhesus monkeys, *Journal of Abnormal Psychology, 93,* 355–372.

Minuchin, S. (1974) *Families and family therapy.* Cambridge, Mass.: Harvard University Press.

———— . (1977) Research report in J. Segal, *Psychosomatic diabetic children and their families.* Rockville, Md.: National Institute of Mental Health (DHEW Publication ADM, 77-477).

Mirsky, A., and Duncan, C. (1986) Etiology and expression of schizophrenia. In M. Rosenzweig and L. Porter (Eds.), *Annual Review of Psychology* (Vol. 37). Palo Alto, Calif.: Annual Reviews.

Mischel, W. (1968) *Personality and assessment.* New York: John Wiley and Sons.

Mischel, W. (1986) *Introduction to personality: A new look* (4th ed.). New York: Holt, Rinehart and Winston.

Mitchell-Heggs, N., Kelly, D., and Richardson, A. (1976) Stereotactic limbic leucotomy: A follow-up at sixteenth month. *British Journal of Psychiatry, 128,* 226–240.

Modestin, J., and Hodel, J. (1977) How blind is a double-blind trial really? Concerning the validity of controlled investigations. *International Pharmacopsychiatry, 12,* 129–136.

Monahan, J. (1978) The prediction of violent criminal behavior: A methodological critique and prospectus. In A. Blurastein (Ed.), *Deference and incapacitation: Estimating the effects of criminal sanctions on crime rates.* Washington, D.C.: National Academy of Sciences.

Monahan, J. (1981) *Predicting violent behavior.* Beverly Hills, Calif.: Sage.

Money, J., and Lamacz, M. (1984) Gynemimesis and gynemetophilia: Individual and cross cultural manifestations of a gender-coping strategy hitherto unnamed. *Comprehensive Psychiatry, 25,* 392–403.

Money, J., and Weideking, C. (1980) Gender identity/role normal differentiation and its transpositions. In B. Wolman (Ed.), *Handbook of human sexuality.* Englewood Cliffs, N.J.: Prentice-Hall.

Monohan, J. (1981) *Predicting violent behavior.* Beverly Hills: Sage.

Montmarquette, C., and Nerlove, M. (1985) Deterrence and delinquency: An analysis of individual data. *Journal of Quantitative Criminology, 1,* 37–58.

Montmarquette, C., and Nerlove, M. (1985) Deterrence and delinquency. *Journal of Quantitative Criminology, 1,* 37–58.

Moore, N. (1965) Behavior therapy in bronchial asthma: A controlled study. *Journal of Psychosomatic Research, 9,* 257–276.

Morey, L., Skinner, H., and Blashfield, R. (1984) A typology of alcohol abusers: Correlates and implications. *Journal of Abnormal Psychology, 93,* 408–417.

Morgan, C.D., and Murray, H.A. (1935) A method for investigating fantasies: The Thematic Apperception Test. *Archives of Neurology and Psychiatry, 34,* 289–306.

Morgan, J. (1981) Amphetamines. In J. Lowinson and P. Ruiz (Eds.), *Substance abuse: Clinical problems and perspectives.* Baltimore: Williams & Wilkins.

Mowrer, O., and Mowrer, W. (1983) Enuresis: A method for its study and treatment. *American Journal of Orthopsychiatry, 8,* 436–447.

Munich, R. (1977) Depersonalization in a female adolescent. *International Journal of Psychoanalytic Psychotherapy, 6,* 187–197.

Murphy, J., Sobol, A., Neff, R., Olivier, D., and Leighton, A. (1985) Stability of presence: Depression and anxiety disorders. *Archives of General Psychiatry, 41,* 990–1000.

Murphy, L., and Frank, C. (1979) Prevention: The clinical psychologist. In M. Rosenweig and L. Porter (Eds.), *Annual Review of Psychology.* Palo Alto, Calif.: Annual Reviews.

Murray, D., Luepker, R., Johnson, C., and Mittelmark, M. (1984) The prevention of cigarette smoking in children. *Journal of Applied Social Psychology, 14,* 274–288.

Murrell, S. (1986) Personal communication.

Murrell, S., Himmelfarb, S., and Wright, K. (1983) Prevalence of depression and its correlates in older adults. *American Journal of Epidemiology, 117,* 173–185.

Mussen, P., Honzik, M., and Eichorn, D. (1982) Early adult antecedents of life satisfaction at 70. *Journal of Gerontology, 37(3),* 316–322.

Myers, J., Weissman, M., Tischler, G., Holzer, C., Leof, P., Orvaschel, H., Anthony, J., Boyd, J., Burke, J., Kramer, M., and Stoltzman, R. (1984) Six-month prevalence of psychiatric disorders in three communities. *Archives of General Psychiatry, 41,* 959–970.

Nagler, S. (1985) Overall design and methodology of the Israeli high risk study. *Schizophrenia Bulletin, 11,* 38–47.

Nathan, P., and Marlatt, A. (1978) *Experimental and behavioral approaches to alcoholism.* New York: Plenum Press.

Nathan, P., Titler, N., Lowenstein, L., Solomon, P., and Rossi, A. (1979) Behavioral analysis of chronic alcoholism. *Archives of General Psychiatry, 36,* 419–430.

National Center on Child Abuse and Neglect. (1981) *Child Sexual Abuse* (DDHS Pub. No (DHDS) 81-30166) Wash. D.C.: U.S. Government Printing Office.

National Commission on Marijuana and Drug Abuse. (1973) *Drug use in America: Problems in perspective.* Washington, D.C.: Government Printing Office.

National Institute of Mental Health Staff. (1977) *Lithium in the treatment of mood disorders.* Rockville, Md.: National Institute of Mental Health.

Naylor, G., and Martin, B. (1985) A double-blind outpatient trial of indalpine vs. mianserin. *The British Journal of Psychiatry, 147,* 306–309.

Nelson, R.O., and Hayes, S.C. (Eds.) (1986) *Conceptual foundations of behavioral assessment.* New York: Guilford Press.

Nemiah, J. (1975) Obsessive compulsive neurosis. In A. Freedman, H. Kaplan, and B. Sadock (Eds.), *Comprehensive textbook of psychiatry* (Vol. 2). Baltimore: Williams & Wilkins.

Nerviano, V. (1976) Common personality patterns among alcoholic males: A multivariate study. *Journal of Consulting and Clinical Psychology, 44,* 104–110.

Neugarten, B. (1979) Time, age, and the life cycle. *American Journal of Psychiatry, 136,* 887–894.

Neugarten, B., Crotty, W., and Tobin, S. (1964) *Personality in middle and late life.* New York: Atherton Press.

Neuringer, C. (1979) Relationship between life and

death among individuals of varying levels of suicidality. *Journal of Clinical and Consulting Psychology, 47*, 407–408.

Newman, B., and Newman, P. (1987) *Development through life*. Chicago: Dorsey.

Nikolouski, O., and Fernandez, J. (1978) Capgras Syndrome as an aftermath of chickenpox encephalitis. *Psychiatric Opinion,15*, 39–43.

Norcross, J.C. (1986) *Handbook of eclectic psychotherapy*. New York: Bruner/Mazel.

Norton, G., Harrison, B., Hauch, J., and Rhodes, L. (1985) Characteristics of people with infrequent panic attacks. *Journal of Abnormal Psychology, 94*, 216–221.

Noyes, R., Clancy, V., Crowe, R., Hoench, P., and Slyman, D. (1978) The familiar prevalence of anxiety neurosis. *Archives of General Psychiatry, 35*, 1058–1059.

O'Brien, C., and Greenstein, R. (1981) Treatment approaches: Opiate antagonists. In J. Lowinson and P. Ruiz (Eds.), *Substance abuse: Clinical problems and perspectives*. Baltimore: Williams & Wilkins.

O'Donnell, J. (1985) *The origins of behaviorism*. New York: New York University Press.

Olbrisch, M. (1977) Psychotherapeutic interventions in physical health. *American Psychologist, 32*, 761–777.

O'Leary, K., and O'Leary, S. (1972) *Classroom management: The successful use of behavior modification*. New York: Pergamon Press.

O'Leary, S.G., and Steen, P.L. (1982) Subcategorizing hyperactivity: The Stony Brook Scale. *Journal of Consulting and Clinical Psychology, 50(3)*, 426–432.

Olson, D. (1970) Marital and family therapy: Integrative review and critique. *Journal of marriage and Family, 32*, 501–538.

Oltmanns, T. (1978) Selective attention in schizophrenia and manic psychoses: The effect of distraction on information processing. *Journal of Abnormal Psychology, 87*, 212–225.

Oltmanns, T., and Maher, B. (1988) *Delusional beliefs*. New York: Wiley.

Olweus, P. (1979) Stability of aggressive reaction patterns in males: A review. *Psychological Bulletin, 86*, 852–875.

O'Reilly, J., and Sales, B. (1987) Privacy for the institutionalized mentally ill: Are court-ordered standards effective? *Law and Human Behavior, 11*, 41–53.

Orford, J. (1976) A study of the personalities of excessive drinkers and their wives, using the approaches of Leary and Eysenck. *Journal of Consulting and Clinical Psychology, 44*, 534–545.

Orford, J. (1985) *Excessive appetites: A psychological view of addiction*. New York: John Wiley and Sons.

Ornitz, E., and Ritvo, E. (1976) The syndrome of autism.: A critical review. *American Journal of Psychiatry, 44*, 534–545.

Orton, S.T. (1928) Specific reading disability-strephosymbolia. *Journal of the American Medical Association, 90*, 1095–1099.

Osgood, C., Luria, Z., Jeans, R., and Smith, A. (1976) The three faces of Evelyn: A case report. *Journal of Abnormal Psychology, 85*, 247–286.

Osmond, H., and Smythies, J. (1962) Schizophrenia: A new approach. *Journal of Mental Science, 98*, 309–315.

Osofsky, J. (1987) *Handbook of infant development*. New York: Wiley.

Ounsted, C., and Lynch, M. (1976) Family pathology as seen in England. In R.E. Helfer and C.H. Kempe (Eds.), *Child abuse and neglect*. Cambridge, Mass.: Ballinger.

Overmeir, J., and Seligman, M. (1967) Effects of inescapable shock upon subsequent escape and avoidance responding. *Journal of Comparative and Physiological Psychology, 63*, 28–33.

Page, T.J., Iwata, B.A., and Reid, D.H. (1982) Pyramidal training: A large scale application with institutional staff. *Journal of Applied Behavioral Analysis, 15(3)*, 335–351.

Pahnke, W. (1963) Drugs and mysticism. Unpublished doctoral dissertation. Harvard University.

Pallis, C., and Bamji, A. (1979) McIlroy was here. Or was he? *British Medical Journal, 6169*, 973–975.

Pane, W. (1977) Organ weights in rats with activity stress ulcer. *Bulletin of the Psychonomic Society, 9*, 11–13.

Pankratz, L. (1981) A review of the Munchausen syndrome. *Clinical Psychology Review, 1*, 65–78.

Parker, G. (1979) Parental characteristics in relation to depressive disorders. *British Journal of Psychiatry, 134*, 138–147.

Parsons, O., and Prigatano, G. (1978) Methodological considerations in clinical neuropsychological research. *Journal of Clinical and Consulting Psychology, 46*, 608–619.

Patterson, G.R. (1971) Behavior intervention procedures in the classroom and the home. In A.E. Bergin and S.L. Garfield (Eds.), *Handbook of psychotherapy and behavior change: An empirical analysis*. New York: John Wiley and Sons.

Patterson, R. (1975) *Maintaining effective token economies*. Springfield, Ill.: Charles Thomas.

Pauly, I. (1968) The current status of the change of sex operation. *Journal of Nervous and Mental Disease, 147*, 460–471.

Pearce, K., Schauer, A., Garfield, N., Olde, C., and Patterson, T. (1985) A study of post traumatic stress disorder in Vietnam veterans. *Journal of Clinical Psychology, 41*, 9–41.

Peele, S. (1985) The cultural context of psychological approaches to alcoholism. *American Psychologist, 39*, 1337–1351.

Peele, T. (1977) *The neuroanatomic basis for clinical neurology* (3rd ed.). New York: McGraw-Hill.

Pellegrini, A. (1986) *Applied child study*. Hillsdale, N.J.: Lawrence Erlbaum.

Penfield, W., and Rasmussen, T. (1950) *The cerebral cortex of man: A study of the localization of functions*. New York: Macmillan.

Penk, D. (1978) The dilemma of law and psychiatric equity. *Corrective and Social Psychiatry and Journal of Behavioral Technology, 24*, 77–85.

Penk, W., Robinowitz, R., Roberts, W., Patterson, E., Dolan, M., and Atkins, H. (1981) Adjustment differences among male substance abusers varying in degree of combat experience in Vietnam. *Journal of Consulting and Clinical Psychology, 49*, 426–437.

Perls, F., Hefferline, R., and Goodman, P. (1958) *Gestalt therapy*. New York: Julian.

Perry, R.W., and Lindell, M.K. (1987) *Handbook of disaster response planning*. New York: Hemisphere Press.

Persad, E. (1986) *Use of drugs in psychiatry*. Lewiston, N.Y.: Hogrefe International.

Peselow, E., Baxter, N., Fieve, R., and Barouche, F. (1987) The dexmethasone suppression test as a monitor of clinical recovery. *American Journal of Psychiatry, 144*, 30–35.

Petti, T., and Larson, C. (1987) Depression and suicide. In V. Van Hasselt and M. Hersen (Eds.), *Handbook of adolescent psychology*. New York: Pergamon Press.

Phillips, D. (1974) The influence of suggestion on suicide. *American Sociological Review, 39*, 340–354.

Phillips, D. (1986) The effects of mass media violence on suicide and homicide. *Newsletter of the American Academy of Psychiatry and the Law, 11*, 29–31.

Phillips, E.L. (1968) Achievement place: Token reinforcement procedures in a home-style rehabilitation setting for pre-delinquent boys. *Journal of Applied Behavior Analysis, 1*, 213–223.

Phillips, E.L., Phillips, E.A., Fixson, D.L., and Wolf, M. (1973) Achievement place: Behavior shaping works for delinquents. *Psychology Today, 7*, 75–79.

Piaget, J. (1976) The stages of the intellectual development of the child. In N.S. Endler, L.R. Boulter, and H. Osser (Eds.), *Contemporary issues in developmental psychology* (2nd ed.). New York: Holt, Rinehart and Winston.

Piercy, F.P., Sprenkle, D.H., et al. (1986) *Family therapy sourcebook*. New York: Guilford Press.

Pitts, F., Schuller, A., Rich, C., and Pittas, A. (1979) Suicide among U.S. women physicians, 1967–1972. *American Journal of Psychiatry, 136*, 694–696.

Place, E., and Gilmore, G. (1980) Perceptual organization in schizophrenia. *Journal of Abnormal Psychology, 89*, 409–418.

Plum, F., and Posner, J. (1980) *The diagnosis of stupor and coma*. Philadelphia: F.A. Davis.

Polivy, J., and Herman, C. (1985) Dieting and binging. *American Psychologist, 40*, 193–201.

Pollack, J. (1979) Obsessive-compulsive personality: A review. *Psychological Bulletin, 86*, 225–241.

Pollio, H. (1982) *Behavior and existence: An introduction to empirical humanistic psychology*. Monterey, Calif.: Brooks/Cole.

Pollit, E., and Thomson, C. (1977) Protein calorie malnutrition and behavior: A view from psychology. In R.J. Wurtman and J.J. Wurtman (Eds.), *Nutrition and the brain*. New York: Raven.

Pope, A., McHale, S., and Craighead, E. (1987) *Self-esteem enhancement with children and adolescents*. Elmsford, N.Y.: Pergamon Press.

Potkin, S., Cannon, H., Murphy, P., and Wyatt, J. (1978) Are paranoid schizophrenics biologically different from other schizophrenics? *New England Journal of Medicine, 299*, 61–65.

Powers, E., and Witmer, J. (1951)*An experiment in the prevention of delinquency: The Cambridge-Somerville Youth Study*. New York: Columbia University Press.

President's Commission on Law Enforcement and Administration of Justice. (1967) *Juvenile delinquency and youth crime*. Washington, D.C.: Government Printing Office.

President's Commission on Obscenity and Pornography. (1970) *The report of the commission on obscenity and pornography*. New York: Bantam Books.

Pressey, S., Janney, J., and Kuhlen, R. (1939) *Life: A psychological survey*. New York: Harper & Row.

Price, K., Tryon, W., and Raps, C. (1978) Learned helplessness and depression in a clinical population: A test of two behavioral hypotheses. *Journal of Abnormal Psychology, 87*, 113–121.

Prien, R., Kupfer, D., Mansky, P., et al. (1984) Drug therapy in the prevention of reoccurrences in unipolar and bipolar affective disorders. *Archives of General Psychiatry, 41*, 1097.

Prince, R. (1980) Variations in psychotherapeutic procedures. In H. Triandis and J. Draguns (Eds.), *Handbook of cross-cultural psychology: Psychopathology*. Boston: Allyn and Bacon.

Pritchard, C. (1979) Stable predictors of recidivism. *Criminology, 17*, 15–21.

Pritchard, W. (1986) Cognitive event-related potential correlates of schizophrenia. *Psychological Bulletin, 100*, 43–66.

Prochaska, J. (1979) *Systems of psychotherapy*. Homewood, Ill.: Dorsey Press.

Proskauer, S., and Rolland, R.S. (1975) Youth who use drugs. In R.E. Grinder (Ed.), *Studies in adolescence*. New York: Macmillan.

Purcell, K. (1963) Distinctions between subgroups of asthmatic children: Children's perceptions of events associated with asthma. *Pediatrics, 31*, 486–494.

Purcell, K., and Weiss, J. (1970) Asthma. In C. Costello

(Ed.), *Symptoms of psychopathology*. New York: John Wiley and Sons.

Purcell, K., Weiss, J., and Hahn, W. (1972) Certain psychosomatic disorders. In B. Wolman (Ed.), *Manual of child psychopathology*. New York: McGraw-Hill.

Putnam, R. (1984) The psychophysiologic investigation of multiple personality disorder: A review. *Psychiatric Clinics of North America, 7*, 31–39.

Quay, H.C. (1965) Psychopathic personality as pathological stimulation-seeking. *American Journal of Psychiatry, 122*, 180–183.

————. (1979) Classification. In H.C. Quay and J.S. Werry (Eds.), *Psychopathological disorders of childhood* (2nd ed.). New York: John Wiley and Sons.

Quay, H.C. (1987) *Handbook of juvenile delinquency*. New York: Wiley.

Quick, J.C., Bhagat, R.S., and Dalton, J.E. (1987) *Work Stress*. Westport, Ct.: Praeger.

Rabin, A. (1986) *Projective techniques for adolescents and children*. New York: Springer.

Rabin, I.A. (1981) *Assessment with projective techniques: A concise introduction*. New York: Springer.

Rabkin, J. (1979) Criminal behavior of discharged mental patients: A critical appraisal of the research. *Psychological Bulletin, 86*, 1–27.

Rachman, S. (1980) *Obsessions and compulsions*. Englewood Cliffs, N.J.: Prentice-Hall.

Rada, R., Laws, D., and Kellner, R. (1976) Plasma testosterone levels in the rapist. *Psychosomatic Medicine, 38*, 257–268.

Rado, S. (1928) The problem of melancholia. *International Journal of Psychoanalysis, 9*, 420–438.

Rahe, R., Hervign, L., and Rosenman, R. (1978) Heritability of type A behavior. *Psychosomatic Medicine, 40*, 478–486.

Raisanen, M., Virkkunen, M., Huttunen, M., Furman, B., and Karkkainen, J. (1984) Increased urinary excretion of bufotenin by violent offenders with paranoid symptoms and family violence. *Lancet, 2*, 700–701.

Rajneesh, B. (1975) *The book of secrets* (Vol. 2). New York: Harper & Row

Rakic, Z., and Ignjatonic, M. (1983) Paranoid phenomena and sexual impotence in males. *Psihijatrija Danos, 15*, 27–33.

Rankin, H. (1982) Control rather than abstinence as a goal in the treatment of excessive gambling. *Behaviour Research and Therapy, 20*, 185–187.

Raphael, B. (1986) *When disaster strikes*. New York: Basic Books.

Raymond, J. (1976) *The transsexual empire*. Boston: Beacon Press.

Redd, W., Porterfield, A., and Anderson, B. (1979) *Behavior modification*. New York: Random House.

Reed, H.B.C., Reitan, R.M., and Klove, H. (1965) Influence of cerebral lesions on psychological test performance of older children. *Journal of Consulting Psychology, 29*, 247–251.

Rees, L. (1964) The importance of psychological allergic and infective factors in childhood asthma. *Journal of Psychosomatic Medicine, 7*, 253–262.

Reese, W. (1979) A model for human psychopathology. *American Journal of Psychiatry, 136*, 1168.

Regan, D. (1987) *Visual evoked potentials in physiology, sensory physiology and medicine*. New York: John Wiley and Sons.

Reich, J. (1987) Prevalence of DSM-III-R self-defeating (masochistic) personality disorder in normal and outpatient populations. *The Journal of Nervous and Mental Disease, 175*, 52–54.

Reich, W. (1980) The case of General Grigorenko: A psychiatric examination of a Soviet dissident. *Psychiatry, 43*, 303–323.

Reilly, S., and Muzzekari, L. (1979) Responses of normal and disturbed adults and children to mixed messages. *Journal of Abnormal Psychology, 88*, 203–208.

Reisman, D., and Benney, M. (1956) The sociology of the interview. *Midwest Sociologist, 18*, 3–15.

Reitan, R.M. (1971) Sensorimotor functions in brain-damaged and normal children of early school age. *Perceptual and Motor Skills, 33*, 655–664.

Reitan, R.W., and Davison, L. (1974) *Clinical neuropsychology: Current status and applications*. Washington, D.C.: V.H. Winston and Sons.

Reitan, R., and Wolfson, D. (1986) *Traumatic brain injury* (Vol. I). Tucson, Ariz.: Neuropsychology Press.

Rekers, G. (1977) A typical gender development and psychosocial adjustment. *Journal of Applied Behavior Analysis, 10*, 559–571.

Reppen, J. (Ed.) (1985) *Beyond Freud: A study of modern psychoanalytic theories*. Hillsdale, N.J.: The Analytic Press.

Resnick, P., Calhoun, K., Atkeson, B., and Ellis, E. (1981) Social adjustment in victims of sexual assault. *Journal of Consulting and Clinical Psychology, 49*, 705–712.

Reynolds, D. (1980) *The quiet therapies*. Honolulu: University of Hawaii Press.

Richards, W.S., and Thorpe, G.L. (1978) Behavioral approaches to the problems of later life. In M. Storandt, I.C. Siegler, and M.F. Elias (Eds.), *The clinical psychology of aging*. New York: Plenum Press.

Riddick, C., and Meyer, R. (1973) The efficiency of automated relaxation training with response contingent feedback. *Behavior Therapy, 4*, 331–337.

Rie, H.E., and Rie, E.D. (Eds.) (1980) *Handbook of minimal brain dysfunction: A critical view*. New York: Wiley-Interscience.

Rie, H., Rie, E.D., Stewart, S., and Ambuel, T. (1976) Effects of methylphenidate on underachieving children. *Journal of Clinical and Consulting Psychology, 44,* 250–260.

Rimland, B. (1964) *Infantile autism.* New York: Appleton-Century-Crofts.

Rimm, D., and Masters, J. (1979) *Behavior therapy.* New York: Academic Press.

Rioch, M.J., Elkes, C., Flint, A.A., Udansky, B.S., Newman, R.G., and Silber, E. (1973) National Institute of Mental Health pilot study in training mental health counselors. *American Journal of Orthopsychiatry, 23,* 678–689.

Roberts, M. (1986) *Pediatric psychology.* New York: Pergamon.

Roberts,T., Mock, L., and Johnstone, E. (1981) Psychological aspects of the etiology of violence. In J. Hays, T. Roberts, and K. Solway (Eds.), *Violence and the violent individual.* New York: Spectrum Publications.

Robins, L., and Helzer, J. (1986) Diagnosis and clinical assessment: The current state of psychiatric diagnosis. In M. Rosenzweig and L. Porter (Eds.), *Annual Review of Psychology* (Vol. 37). Palo Alto, Calif.: Annual Reviews.

Robinson, D. (1981) *An intellectual history of psychology.* New York: Macmillan.

Robinson, H.B., and Robinson, N. (1970) Mental retardation. In P.H. Mussen (Ed.),*Carmichael's manual of child psychology* (3rd ed.). New York: John Wiley and Sons.

Rockwell, D.A. (1978) Social and familial correlates of antisocial disorders. In W.H. Reid (Ed.), *The psychopath.* New York: Bruner/Mazel.

Rodale, J. (1979) *If you must smoke.* Emmaus, Penn.: Rodale Books.

Roe v. *Wade,* 410 U.S. 113 (1975).

Rogers, C. (1951) *Client-centered therapy.* Boston: Houghton Mifflin.

—————. (1959) A theory of therapy, personality, and interpersonal relationships, as developed in the client-centered framework. In S. Koch (Ed.), *Psychology: A study of a science* (Vol. 3). New York: McGraw-Hill.

—————. (1961) *On becoming a person.* Boston: Houghton Mifflin.

—————. (1980) *A way of being.* Boston: Houghton Mifflin.

Rogers, R. (1986) The R-CRAS and criminal responsibility evaluations: An update. *Bulletin of the American Academy of Forensic Psychology, 7,* 6–7.

Rohner, E., Rohner, R., and Roll, S. (1980) Perceived parental acceptance–rejection and child's reported behavioral dispositions—a comparative and intercultural study of Mexican and American children. *Journal of Cross-Cultural Psychology, 11,* 213–223.

Rohwer, W.D., Jr., Ammon, P.R., and Cramer, P. (1974) *Understanding intellectual development.* Hinsdale, Ill.: Dryden Press.

Rosen, A. (1979) Case report: Symptomatic mania and phencyclidine abuse. *American Journal of Psychiatry, 136,* 118–119.

Rosen, A., Rekers, G., and Bentler, P. (1978) Ethical issues in the treatment of children. *Journal of Social Issues, 34,* 60–72.

Rosen, J. (1953) *Direct Analysis.* New York: Grune & Stratton.

Rosenbaum, M., and Palmon, N. (1984) Helplessness and resourcefulness in coping with epilepsy. *Journal of Consulting and Clinical Psychology, 52(2),* 244–253.

Rosenberg, S., and Farrell, M. (1976) Identity and crisis in middle-aged men. *International Journal of Aging and Human Development, 7,* 153–170.

Rosenhan, D. (1973) On being sane in insane places. *Science, 179,* 365–369.

Rosenthal, R.H., and Allen, T.W. (1978) An examination of attention, arousal, and learning dysfunctions of hyperkinetic children. *Psychological Bulletin, 85,* 689–715.

Rosenthal, T., and Bandura, A. (1978) Psychological modeling: Theory and practice. In S. Garfield and A. Bergin (Eds.), *Handbook of psychotherapy and behavior change.* New York: John Wiley and Sons.

Rosenzweig, S. (1986) *Freud and experimental psychology.* St. Louis, Mo.: Rana House.

Ross, A.O. (1981) *Child behavior therapy.* New York: John Wiley and Sons.

Ross, D.M., and Ross, S.A. (1976) *Hyperactivity: Research, theory, and action.* New York: John Wiley and Sons.

Rourke, B.P., and Finlayson, M.A.J. (1978) Neuropsychological significance of variations in patterns of academic performance: Verbal and visual-spatial abilities. *Journal of Abnormal Child Psychology, 6,* 121–133.

Rourke, B.P., and Strang, J.D. (1978) Neuropsychological significance of variations in patterns of academic performance: Motor psychomotor, and tactile-perceptual abilities. *Journal of Pediatric Psychology, 3,* 62–66.

Rourke, B., Fisk, J., and Strang, J. (1986) *Neuropsychological assessment of children.* New York: Guilford.

Rouse v. *Cameron,* 373 F.2d 451 (D.C. Cir. 1966).

Rowan, J. (1983) The Reality Game: *A guide to humanistic counseling and therapy.* London: Routledge & Kegan Paul.

Rubens, R., and Lapidus, L. (1978) Schizophrenic patterns of arousal and stimulus barrier functioning. *Journal of Abnormal Psychology, 87,* 207–216.

Rubin, L. (1976) *Worlds of pain: Life in the working class family.* New York: Basic Books.

—————. (1980) The empty nest: Beginning or ending? In L. Bond and J. Rosen (Eds.), *Primary prevention of psychopathology* (Vol. 4). Hanover, N.H.: University Press of New England.

Rubinstein, E. (1981) Effects of television on violent behavior. In J. Hays, T. Roberts, and K. Solway (Eds.), *Violence and the violent individual*. New York: SP Books.

Rutter, M. (1983) Cognitive deficits in the pathogenesis of autism. *Journal of Child Psychology and Psychiatry*, 24(4), 513–532.

Rutter, M. (1987) Temperament, personality and personality disorder. *British Journal of Psychiatry, 150*, 443–458.

Rutter, M., and Schopler, E. (Eds.) (1978) *Autism: A reappraisal of concepts and treatment*. New York: Plenum Press.

Rutter, M., Yule, W., and Graham, P. (1973) Enuresis and behavioral deviance: Some epidemiological considerations. In I. Kolvin, R. MacKeith, and S. Meadow (Eds.), *Bladder control in enuresis*. London: Wm. Heinemann.

Saccuzzo, D. (1977) Bridges between schizophrenia and gerontology: Generalized or specific deficits? *Psychological Bulletin, 84*, 595.

Sackheim, H.A., Gur, R.C., and Saucy, M. (1978) Emotions are expressed more intensely on the left side of the face. *Science, 202*, 434–436.

Sadock, B.A. (1975) Organic brain syndromes: Introduction. In A.M. Freedman, H.I. Kaplan, and B.J. Sadock (Eds.), *Comprehensive textbook of psychiatry*. (Vol. 1), (2nd ed.). Baltimore: Williams & Wilkins, pp. 757–768, 1060–1064.

Saghir, M., and Robins, E. (1979) Homosexuality, Part 1: Sexual behavior of the female homosexual. *Archives of General Psychiatry, 36*, 192–201.

Salzinger, S., Antrobus, J., and Glick, J. (Eds.) (1980) The ecosystem of the "sick" kid. In *The ecosystem of the "sick" child*. New York: Academic Press.

Sanchez, J. (1986) Social crises and psychopathy. In W. Reid, D. Dorr, J. Walker, and J. Bonner (Eds.), *Unmasking the psychopath*. New York: W.W. Norton.

Sandler, J. (1985) Aversion methods. In F. Kanfer and A. Goldstein (Eds.), *Helping people change*. Elmsford, N.Y.: Pergamon Press.

Santosky v. *Kramer*, 455 U.S. 745 (1982).

Santrock, J. (1987) *Adolescence*. Dubuque, Iowa: Wm. C. Brown.

Sanua, V. (1980) Familial and sociocultural antecedents of psychopathology. In H. Triandis and J. Draguns (Eds.), *Handbook of cross-cultural psychology: Psychopathology*. Boston: Allyn and Bacon.

Sarbin, T., and Mancuso, V. (1980) *Schizophrenia: Medical diagnosis or moral verdict?* Elmsford, N.Y.: Pergamon Press.

Sarinski, K. (1982) Effects of etiology and cognitive ability on observational learning of retarded children. *International Journal of Rehabilitation Research, 5(1)*, 75–78.

Satir, V. (1967) *Conjoint family therapy* (Rev. ed.). Palo Alto, Calif.: Science and Behavior Books.

Satterfield, J.H., and Dawson, M.E. (1971) Electrodermal correlates of hyperactivity in children. *Psychophysiology, 8*, 191–197.

Sattler, J. (1982) *Assessment of children's intelligence and special abilities* (2nd ed.). Boston: Allyn and Bacon.

Sawyer, H.W., and Crimando, W. (1984) Self-management strategies in rehabilitation. *Journal of Rehabilitation, 50(1)*, 27–30.

Scarpitti, F.R. (1965) Delinquent and nondelinquent perception of self, values, and opportunity. *Mental Hygiene, 49*, 399–404.

Schachter, S. (1971) Eat, eat. *Psychology Today, 7*, 44–47, 78–79.

Schachter, S., and Latane, B. (1964) Crime, cognition, and the autonomic nervous system. Nebraska Symposium Motivation. Lincoln, Neb.

Schachter, S., Silverstein, B., Kozlowski, L., Perlick, D., Herman, C., and Liebling, B. (1977) Studies of the interaction of psychological and pharmacological determinants of smoking. *Journal of Experimental Psychology: General, 106*, 3–40.

Schaefer, C.E. (1979) *Childhood encopresis and enuresis*. New York: Van Nostrand Reinhold.

Schaefer, C.E., and Millman, H.L. (1981) *How to help children with common problems*. New York: Van Nostrand Reinhold.

Schaefer, C. (1988) *Innovative interventions in child and adolescent therapy*. New York: Wiley.

Schafer, E.S. (1961) Conveying conceptual models for maternal behaviour and for child behaviour. In J.C. Glidewell (Ed.), *Parental attitude and child behaviour*. Springfield, Ill.: Charles Thomas.

Schaie, K.W., and Schaie, J. (1977) Clinical assessment and aging. In J.E. Birren and K.W. Schaie (Eds.), *Handbook of the psychology of aging*. New York: Van Nostrand Reinhold.

Schaie, K., and Geiwitz, J. (1982) *Adult development and aging*. Boston: Little, Brown.

Schmauk, F.J. (1970) Punishment, arousal, and avoidance learning in sociopaths. *Journal of Abnormal and Social Psychology, 76*, 325–335.

Schneidman, E. (1979a) An overview: Personality, motivation, and behavior theories. In L. Hankoff and B. Einsidler (Eds.), *Suicide*. Littleton, Mass.: PSG Publishing.

———. (1979b) Suicidal logic. In W. Sahakiam (Ed.), *Psychopathology Today*. Itasca, Ill.: Peacock.

Schneidman, E., and Farberow, N. (Eds.) (1957) *Clues to suicide*. New York: McGraw-Hill.

Schopler, E. (1974) Changes of direction with psychotic children. In M.A. Davids (Ed.), *Child personality and psychopathology: Current topics* (Vol. 1). New York: John Wiley and Sons.

Schopler, E., and Mesibov, G.B. (1987) *Neurobiological issues in autism.* New York: Plenum.

Schover, L., Friedman, J., Weiler, S., Heiman, J., and LoPiccolo, J. (1982) Multiaxial problem-oriented system for sexual dysfunctions. *Archives of General Psychiatry, 39,* 614–619.

Schreiber, F. (1974) *Sybil.* New York: Warner.

Schreibman, L.A., and Koegel, R.L. (1979) A guideline for planning behavior modification programs for autistic children. In S.M. Turner, V.S. Calhoun, and H.E. Adams (Eds.), *Handbook of behavior therapy.* New York: John Wiley and Sons.

Schuckit, M., and Morrissey, E. (1979) Drug abuse among alcoholic women. *American-Journal of Psychiatry, 136,* 607–611.

Schulman, J., Kaspar, J., and Thrane, F. (1965) *Brain damage and behavior: A clinical experimental study.* Springfield, Ill.: Charles Thomas.

Schulsinger, F., Parnas, J., Petersen, E., Schulsinger, H., Teasdale, T., Mednick, S., Muller, L., and Silverton, L. (1984) Cerebral ventricular size in the offspring of schizophrenic mothers. *Archives of General Psychiatry, 41,* 602–606.

Schulz, D. (1981) *A history of modern psychology.* New York: Academic Press.

———. (1982) *The changing family: Its function and future.* Englewood Cliffs, N.J.: Prentice-Hall.

Schulz, R. (1982) Emotionality and aging: A theoretical and empirical analysis. *Journal of Gerontology, 37(1),* 42–51.

Schwartz, M. (1987) *Biofeedback.* New York: Guilford.

Schwartz, S. (1985) Symposium on violence in the media. Annual Convention of American Psychological Association. Los Angeles.

Scott, R., Prue, D., Denier, C., and King, A. (1986) Worksite smoking intervention with nursing professionals. *Journal of Consulting and Clinical Psychology, 54,* 809–813.

Scoville, W., and Milner, B. (1957) Loss of recent memory after bilateral hippocampal lesions. *Journal of Neurology, Neurosurgery, and Psychiatry, 20,* 11–21.

Sechrest, L. (1986) Sociological perspectives on youth violence. In S. Apter and A. Goldstein (Eds.), *Youth violence,* Elmsford, N.Y.: Pergamon Press.

Sechzer, J., Faro, M., and Windle, W. (1973) Studies of monkeys asphyxiated at birth: Implications for minimal cerebral dysfunction. *Seminars in Psychiatry, 5,* 19–34.

Segal, J., and Yahraes, H. (1979) *A child's journey.* New York: McGraw-Hill.

Seiden, R. (1966) Campus tragedy: A study of student suicide. *Journal of Abnormal and Social Psychology, 71,* 389–399.

Seif, M., and Atkins, A. (1979) Some defensive and cognitive aspects of phobias. *Journal of Abnormal Psychology, 88,* 42–51.

Seixas, F. (1981) Alcohol. In J. Lowinson and P. Ruiz (Eds.), *Substance abuse: Clinical problems and perspectives.* Baltimore: Williams & Wilkins.

Seligman, M. (1975) *Helplessness: On depression, development, and death.* San Francisco: W.H. Freeman.

Selling, L. (1940) *Men against madness.* New York: Greenberg.

Seltzer, L. (1986) *Paradoxical strategies in psychotherapy.* New York: John Wiley and Sons.

Selye, H. (1956) *The stress of life.* New York: McGraw-Hill.

Shah, S. (1981) Dangerousness: Conceptual, prediction, and public policy issues. In J. Hays, T. Roberts, and K. Solway (Eds.), *Violence and the violent individual.* New York: SP Books.

Shakow, D. (1977) Segmental set. *American Psychologist, 32,* 129–139.

Shapiro, D. (1984) *Psychological evaluation and expert testimony.* New York: Van Nostrand Rheinhold.

Shapiro, D. (1986) The Insanity Defense Reform Act of 1984. *Bulletin of the American Academy of Forensic Psychology, 7,* 1–6.

Shapiro, D., and Giber, D. (1978) Meditation and psychotherapeutic effects. *Archives of General Psychiatry, 35,* 294–302.

Shapiro, S. (1981) *Contemporary theories of schizophrenia: Review and synthesis.* New York: McGraw-Hill.

Sharav, T., and Shlomo, L. (1986) Stimulation of infants with Down syndrome: Long-term effects. *Mental Retardation, 24,* 81–86.

Shaw, B. (1977) Comparison of cognitive therapy and behavior therapy in the treatment of depression. *Journal of Consulting and Clinical Psychology, 45,* 543–551.

Shaw, B.F., Cashman, F.E., Segal, Z., and Mallis, T.M. (1987) *Anxiety disorders.* New York: Plenum Press.

Sheehy, G. (1976) *Passages.* New York: Dutton.

Shemberg, K., and Levanthal, D. (1984) Conceptualization and treatment of paranoid schizophrenia. *Psychotherapy, 21,* 370–376.

Shiffman, S. (1984) Cognitive antecedents and sequelae of smoking relapse crises. *Journal of Applied Social Psychology, 14,* 296–309.

Shneidman, E. (1985) *Definition of suicide.* New York: John Wiley and Sons.

Silber, S. (1987) Personal communication.

Silney, A. (1980) Sexuality and aging. In B. Wolman (Ed.), *Handbook of human sexuality.* Englewood Cliffs, N.J.: Prentice-Hall.

Silverman, L. (1976) Psychoanalytic theory: The reports of my death are greatly exaggerated. *American Psychologist, 31,* 621–637.

Silverstein, A.B. (1982) Note on the constancy of the IQ. *American Journal of Mental Deficiency, 87(2),* 227–228.

Silverton, L., Finello, K., Mednick, S., and Schulsinger, F. (1985) Low birth weight and ventricular enlargement in a high-risk sample. *Journal of Abnormal Psychology, 94,* 405–409.

Simon, E. (1981) Recent developments in the biology of opiates: Possible relevance to addiction. In J. Lowinson and P. Ruiz (Eds.), *Substance abuse: Clinical problems and perspectives.* Baltimore: WIlliams & Wilkins.

Simon, S. (1987) Personal communication.

Simon, W., and Gagnon, J. (Eds.) (1970) Psychosexual development. In *The sexual scene.* Chicago: Aldine.

Siomopoulos, V., and Goldsmith, J. (1976) Sadism revisited. *American Journal of Psychotherapy, 30,* 631–640.

Sivak, M., Hill, C.S., Henson, D.L., Barclay, P.B., Sliber, S.M., and Olson, P.L. (1984) Improved driving performance following perceptual training in persons with brain damage. *Archives of Physical Medicine and Rehabilitation, 65,* 163–167.

Sizemore, C., and Pittillo, E. (1977) *"I'm Eve."* Garden City, N.J.: Doubleday.

Sklar, L., and Anisman, H. (1979) Stress and coping influence tumor growth. *Science, 205,* 513–515.

Skolnick, A. (1966) Motivational imagery and behavior over twenty years. *Journal of Consulting Psychology, 30,* 463–478.

Slavney, P., Breitner, J., and Rabins, P. (1977) Variability of mood and hysterical traits in women. *Journal of Psychiatric Research, 12,* 155–160.

Smith, A. (1962) Ambiguities in concepts and studies of "brain damage" and "organicity." *Journal of Nervous and Mental Disease, 135,* 311–326.

———. (1975) Neuropsychological testing in neurological disorders. In W.J. Friedlander (Ed.), *Advances in neurology* (Vol. 7). New York: Raven.

——— . (1981) Principles underlying human brain functions in neuropsychological sequelae of different neuropathological processes. In S.B. Filskov and T.J. Boll (Eds.), *Handbook of clinical neuropsychology.* New York: John Wiley and Sons.

Smith, A., and Sugar, O. (1975) Development of above normal language and intelligence 11 years after left hemispherectomy. *Neurology, 25,* 813–818.

Smith, M., and Glass, G. (1977) Meta-analysis of psychotherapy outcome studies. *American Psychologist, 32,* 995–1008.

Smith, M., Glass, G., and Miller, T. (1980) *The benefits of psychotherapy.* Baltimore: Johns Hopkins University Press.

Smith, P.S., and Wong, H. (———) Changes in bladder function during toilet training of mentally handicapped children. *Behavior Research of Severe Developmental Disabilities, 2(2),* 137–155.

Smith, R. (1976) Voyeurism: A review of the literature. *Archives of Sexual Behavior, 5,* 585–609.

Smith, S., and Meyer, R. (1980) Workings between the legal system and the therapist. In D. Cox and R. Daitzman (Eds.), *Exhibitionism.* New York: Garland.

Smith, S., and Meyer, R. (1987) *Law, behavior, and mental health: Policy and practice.* New York: New York University Press.

Snyder, S. (1976) Dopamine and schizophrenia. *Psychiatric Annals, 6,* 23–31.

Snyder, S., and Karacan, I. (1981) Effects of chronic alcoholism on nocturnal penile tumescence. *Psychosomatic Medicine, 43,* 423–430.

Sobell, M., Sobell, L., Ersner-Hershfield, S., and Nirenberg, T. (1982) Alcohol and drug problems. In A. Bellack, M. Hersen, and A. Kazdin (Eds.), *International handbook of behavior modification and therapy.* New York: Plenum Press.

Socarides, C. (1976) Psychodynamics and sexual object choice, 2: A reply to Friedman. *Contemporary Psychoanalysis, 12,* 370–378.

Solnick, J., et al. (1981) The relationship between parent-youth interaction and delinquency in group homes. *Journal of Abnormal Child Psychology, 9(1),* 107–119.

Solomon, K. (1982) Social antecedents of learned helplessness in the health care setting. *The Gerontologist, 22(3),* 282–287.

Solovay, M., Shenton, M., and Holzman, P. (1987) Comparative studies of thought disorders: 1. Mania: 2. Schizoaffective disorder. *Archives of General Psychiatry, 44,* 13–30.

Sommers, A. (1985) "Negative symptoms": Conceptual and methodological problems. *Schizophrenia Bulletin, 11,* 364–379.

Sotile, W., and Kilman, P. (1977) Treatment of Psychogenic female sexual dysfunctions. *Psychological Bulletin, 84,* 619–633.

Spanos, N., Weekes, J., and Bertrand, L. (1985) Multiple personality: A social psychological perspective. *Journal of Abnormal Psychology, 94,* 362–376.

Spiegel, H., and Spiegel, D. (1978) *Trance and Treatment,* New York: Basic Books.

Spielberger, C.D. (1972) *Anxiety: Current trends in theory and research.* New York: Academic Press.

Spielberger, C., Anton, W., and Bedell, J. (1976) The nature and treatment of test anxiety. In M. Zukerman and C. Spielberger (Eds.), *Emotions and anxiety.* New York: John Wiley and Sons.

Spielberger, C., Sarason, I., and Milgram, M. (1981) *Stress and anxiety* (Vol. 8). Washington: Hemisphere.

Spiess, W., Geer, J., and O'Donohue, W. (1984) Premature ejaculation: Investigation of factors in ejaculatory latency. *Journal of Abnormal Psychology, 93,* 242–245.

Spitzer, R., Forman, J., and Nee, J. (1979) DSM-III field trials: Initial interrater diagnostic reliability. *American Journal of Psychiatry, 136,* 815–817.

Spitzer, R., Cohen, J., Fliess, J., and Endicott, J. (1967) Quantification of agreement in psychiatric diagnosis: A new approach: *Archives of General Psychiatry, 17,* 83–87.

Spotts, J., and Shontz, F. (1984) Drug-induced ego states. I. Cocaine: Phenomenology and implications. *The International Journal of the Addictions, 19,* 119–151.

Spreen, O., and Gaddes, W.H. (1969) Developmental norms for 15 neuropsychological tests ages 6 to 15. *Cortex, 5,* 171–191.

Springer, S.P., and Deutsch, G. (1981) *Left brain, right brain.* San Francisco: W.H. Freeman.

Squire, L.R. (1987) *Memory and brain.* New York: Oxford University Press.

Squire, L., and Chase, P. (1975) Memory functions six to nine months after electroconvulsive therapy. *Archives of General Psychiatry, 32,* 1557–1564.

Squire, L., Slater, P., and Miller, P. (1981) Retrograde amnesia and bilateral ECT. *Archives of General Psychiatry, 38,* 89–95.

Stampfl, T.G., and Levis, D.J. (1967) Essentials of implosive therapy: A learning-theory-based psychodynamic behavioral therapy. *Journal of Abnormal Psychology, 72,* 496–503.

Starkey, M. (1961) *The devil in Massachusetts.* Garden City, N.J.: Doubleday.

Stasiek, C., and Zetin, M. (1985) Organic manic disorders. *Psychosomatics, 26,* 394–399.

Stein, R. (1971) *Disturbed youth and ethnic family patterns.* Albany: State University of New York Press.

Steinberg, F. (1979) The delineation of an MMPI symptom pattern unique to lithium responses. *American Journal of Psychiatry, 136,* 567–569.

Steinbrueck, S., Maxwell, S., and Howard, G. (1983) A meta-analysis of psychotherapy and drug therapy in the treatment of unipolar depression with adults. *Journal of Consulting and Clinical Psychology, 51,* 856–863.

Stemback, R.A. (1966) *Principles of psychophysiology.* New York: Academic Press.

Stephenson, P. (1979) Hutterite belief in evil eye: Beyond paranoia and toward a general theory of invidia. *Culture, Medicine, and Psychiatry, 3,* 247–265.

Stern, G.S., McCants, T.R., and Pettine, P.W. (1982) Stress and illness: Controllable and uncontrollable life events' relative contributions. *Personality and Social Psychological Bulletin, 8,* 140–145.

Sternbach, R.A. (1966) *Principles of psychophysiology.* New York: Academic Press.

Sternberg, R.L. (1985) *Beyond IQ.* New York: Cambridge University Press.

Steronko, R., and Woods, D. (1978) Impairment in early stages of visual information processing in nonpsychotic schizotypic individuals. *Journal of Abnormal Psychology, 87,* 481–490.

Stone, A. (1975) *Mental health and law: A system in tran-* sition. Washington, D.C.: U.S. Government Printing Office.

Storandt, M., Siegler, I.C., and Elias, N.F. (Eds.) (1978) *The clinical psychology of aging.* New York: Plenum Press.

Strachey, J. (Ed.) (1957) *Standard edition of the complete works of Sigmund Freud.* London: Hogarth Press.

Strassberg, D., Roback, H., Cunningham, J., McKee, E., and Larson, P. (1979) Psychopathology in self-identified female-to-male transsexuals, homosexuals, and heterosexuals. *Archives of Sexual Behavior, 8,* 491–496.

Strauss, A.S., and Lehtinen, L.E. (1947) *Psychopathology and education of the brain-injured child.* New York: Grune & Stratton.

Strauss, J. (1985) Negative symptom: Future developments of the concept. *Schizophrenia Bulletin, 11,* 457–460.

Strauss, J., Boker, W., and Brenner, H. (1986) *Psychosocial treatment of schizophrenia,* Lewiston, N.Y.: Hogrefe.

Striegal-Moore, R., Silberstien, L., and Rodin, J. (1986) Toward an understanding of risk factors for bulimia. *American Psychologist, 43,* 246–263.

Strub, R.L., and Black, F.W. (1980) *The Mental Status Examination in neurology.* Philadelphia: F.A. Davis.

Strupp, H. (1978) Psychotherapy research and practice: An overview. In S. Garfield and A. Bergin (Eds.), *Handbook of psychotherapy and behavior change.* New York: John Wiley and Sons.

Strupp, H., and Hadley, S. (1979) Specific vs. nonspecific factors in psychotherapy. *Archives of General Psychiatry, 36,* 1125–1136.

Stuart, L., and Abt, L. (1981) *Children of separation and divorce.* New York: Van Nostrand Reinhold.

Stuart, R. (1967) Behavior control over eating. *Behavior Research and Therapy, 5,* 357–365.

Stunkard, A. (1972) New therapies for the eating disorders. *Archives of General Psychiatry, 26,* 391–398.

Sturgis, E., and Adams, H. (1978) The right to treatment: Issues in the treatment of homosexuality. *Journal of Consulting and Clinical Psychology, 46,* 165–169.

Sue, S., and Zane, N. (1987) The role of culture and cultural techniques in psychotherapy. *American Psychologist, 42*(1), 37–45.

Sugarman, S. (1987) *Piaget's construction of the child's reality.* New York: Cambridge University Press.

Sugihara, Y., and Plath, D. (1969) *Sensei and his people.* Berkeley: University of California Press.

Sullivan, H.S. (1954) *The psychiatric interview.* New York: W.W. Norton.

Sullivan, W. (1982) New study backs thesis on witches. *New York Times, August,* 29, 30.

Sundet, K. (1986) Sex differences in cognitive impairment following unilateral brain damage. *Journal of Clinical and Experimental Neuropsychology, 8,* 51–61.

Sussman, G. (1974) Psychopathia sexualis. *National Lampoon, June.*

Swanson, D., Bonhert, P., and Smith, J. (1970) *The paranoid.* Boston: Little, Brown.

Swanson, L., and Biaggio, M. (1985) Therapeutic perspectives on father-daughter incest. *The American Journal of Psychiatry, 142,* 667–674.

Swartz, M., Hughes, D., Blazer, D., and George, L. (1987) Somatization disorders in the community. *The Journal of Nervous and Mental Disease, 175,* 26–33.

Sweeney, P., Anderson, K., and Bailey, S. (1986) Attributional style in depression: A meta-analytic review. *Journal of Personality and Social Psychology, 50,* 974–999.

Szabo, S. (1980) Stress and ulcers. *Stress, 1,* 25–36.

Szasz, T. (1960) The myth of mental illness. *American Psychologist, 15,* 113–118.

Szasz, T.S. (1961) *The myth of mental illness.* New York: Harper & Row.

———. (1974) The myth of mental illness: Three addenda. *Journal of Humanistic Psychology, 14,* 11–19.

———. (1978) *Psychiatric slavery.* New York: Free Press.

Szasz, T. (1987) *Insanity: The idea and its consequences.* New York: John Wiley and Sons.

Talland, G. (1965) *Deranged memory.* New York: Academic Press.

Tarasoff v. *Regents of the University of California,* 42 Cal. 3d 425, 551 P. 2d 334,131 Cal. Rpts. 14 (1976).

Taylor, W., and Martin, M. (1944) Multiple personality. *Journal of Abnormal Social Psychology, 39,* 281–300.

Telch, M., Agras, W., Taylor, C., Roth, W., and Gallen, C. (1985) Combined pharmacological and behavioral treatment for agoraphobia, *Behaviour Research and Therapy, 23,* 325–336.

Tennov, D. (1977) *Psychotherapy: The hazardous cure.* Garden City, N.J.: Doubleday, Anchor Books.

Teplin, L. (1985) The criminality of the mentally ill: A dangerous misconception. *The American Journal of Psychiatry, 142,* 593–599.

Teri, L. (1982) The use of the Beck depression inventory with adolescents. *Journal of Abnormal Child Psychology, 10(2),* 277–284.

Teyber, E. (1988) *Process and relationship in psychotherapy.* Chicago, Ill: Dorsey Press.

Thase, M., Reynolds, C., Glanz, L., Jennings, J., et al. (1987) Nocturnal penile tumescence in depressed men. *American Journal of Psychiatry, 144,* 89–92.

Thigpen, C., and Cleckley, H. (1984) On the incidence of multiple personality: A brief communication. *The International Journal of Clinical and Experimental Hypnosis, 32,* 63–66.

Thomas, A., and Chess, S. (1977) *Temperament and development.* New York: Bruner/Mazel.

Thompson, J., Jarvie, G., Lahey, B., and Cureton, K. (1982) Exercise and obesity: Etiology, physiology, and intervention. *Psychological Bulletin, 91,* 55–59.

Thompson, R.J., and Bernal, M.E. (1982) Factors associated with parent labeling of children referred for conduct problems. *Journal of Abnormal Child Psychology, 10,* 191–202.

Tiger, L. (1979) *Optimism: the biology of hope.* New York: Simon and Schuster.

Tollison, C., and Adams, H. (1979) *Sexual disorders.* New York: Gardner.

Tomporowski, P., and Ellis, N. (1986) Effects of exercise on cognitive processes: A review. *Psychological Bulletin, 99,* 336–346.

Toolan, J.M. (1971) Depression in adolescents. In J.H. Howells (Ed.), *Modern perspectives in adolescent psychiatry.* New York: Bruner/Mazel.

Torrey, E. (1979) *Schizophrenia and civilization.* New York: Jason Aronson.

Torrey, E., and Peterson, M. (1976) The viral hypothesis of schizophrenia. *Schizophrenia Bulletin, 2,* 136–146.

Towbin, A. (1978) Cerebral dysfunctions related to perinatal organic damage: Clinical-neuropathic correlations. *Journal of Abnormal Psychology, 87,* 617–635.

Triandis, H., and Draguns, J. (Eds.) (1980) *Handbook of cross-cultural psychology: Psychopathology.* Boston: Allyn and Bacon, 1980.

Tripp, C. (1976) *The homosexual matrix.* New York: New American Library.

Trotter, S. (1976) Federal Commission OKs psychosurgery. *APA Monitor, 7,* 4–5.

Tsai, M., Feldman-Summer, S., and Edgar, M. (1979) Childhood molestation: Variables related to differential impacts on psychosexual functioning in adult women. *Journal of Abnormal Psychology, 88,* 407–417.

Tseng, W., and Hsu, J. (1980) Minor psychological disturbances of everyday life. In H. Triandis and J. Draguns (Eds.), *Handbook of cross-cultural psychology: Psychopathology.* Boston: Allyn and Bacon.

Tsuang, M., Farasone, S., and Fleming, J. (1985) Familial transmission of major affective disorders: Is there evidence supporting the distinction between unipolar and bipolar disorders? *British Journal of Psychiatry, 146,* 268–271.

Tuchman, B. (1978) *A distant mirror.* New York: Knopf.

Turk, D.C., Meichenbaum, D., and Genest, M. (1983) *Pain and behavioral medicine: A cognitive-behavioral perspective.* New York: Guilford.

Turkat, I. (1985) Formulation of paranoid personality disorder. In I. Turkat (Ed.), *Behavioral case formulation.* New York: Plenum Press.

Turkington, C. (1982) Depression seen induced by decline in NE levels. *APA Monitor, 13(11),* 6.

Turkington, C. (1985) First mental hospital in colonies

restored at Williamsburg. *American Psychological Association Monitor, 16(5),* 38.

Turner, S., Beidel, D., and Nathan, S. (1985) Biological factors in obsessive-compulsive disorders. *Psychological Bulletin, 97,* 430–450.

Turner, S.M., and Hersen, M. (1984) *Adult psychopathology.* New York: Wiley-Interscience.

Tursky, B. (1979) Biofeedback research methodology: Need for an effective change. In R. Gatchel and K. Price (Eds.), *Clinical application of biofeedback: Appraisal and status.* Elmsford, N.Y.: Pergamon Press.

Tymoczko, T. (1979) The four-color problem and its philosophical significance. *Journal of Philosophy, 76,* 3–16.

Tyson, M., and Favell, J. (1987) Mental retardation—children. In V. Van Hasselt, P. Strain, and M. Hersen (Eds.), *Handbook of Developmental and Physical Disabilities.* Elmsford, N.Y.: Pergamon Press.

U.S. v. *Salerno,* 107 S.Ct. 2095, 55 L.W. 4663 (1987).

U.S. Center on Child Abuse and Neglect, National Study of the Incidence and Severity of Child Abuse and Neglect (DHHS 1981).

U.S. Congress, Office of Technology Assessment (1983) *Scientific validity of polygraph testing* (OTA-TM-H-15). Washington, D.C.: U.S. Government Printing Office.

U.S. Department of Health, Education, and Welfare. (1971) *Report of the conference on the use of stimulant drugs in the treatment of behaviorally disturbed young school children.* Washington, D.C.: U.S. Government Printing Office.

U.S. Department of Health and Human Services (1984) *Adolescence and depression* (DHHS Publication No. (ADM) 84-1337). Rockville, Md.: National Institute of Mental Health.

Uchida, I.A., Holunga, R., and Lawler, C. (1968) Maternal radiation and chromosomal aberrations. *Lancet, 2,* 1045–1049.

Ullman, L., and Krasner, L. (Eds.) (1965) *Case studies in behavior modification.* New York: Holt, Rinehart and Winston.

———. (1975) *A psychological approach to abnormal behavior.* Englewood Cliffs, N.J.: Prentice-Hall.

Underwager, R., Wakefield, H., Legrand, R., Bartz, C., et al. (1986) The role of the psychologist in the assessment of cases of alleged sexual abuse of children. Annual Meeting. American Psychological Association: Washington, D.C.

Ursin, H., Baade, E., and Levine, S. (1978) *Psychobiology of stress.* New York: Academic Press.

Vaillant, G. (1977) *Adaptation to life.* Boston: Little, Brown.

Vaillant, G. (1983) *The natural history of alcoholism: Causes, patterns, and paths to recovery.* Cambridge, Mass.: Harvard University Press.

Valenstein, E. (1986) *Great and desperate cures.* New York: Basic Books.

Valenstein, E. (1986) *Great and desperate cures: The rise and decline of psychosurgery and other radical treatments for mental illness.* New York: Basic Books.

Valenstein, E., and Heilman, K.M. (1979) Emotional disorders resulting from lesions of the central nervous system. In K.M. Heilman and E. Valenstein (Eds.), *Clinical neuropsychology.* New York: Oxford University Press.

Van Dyke, C. (1981) Cocaine. In J. Lowinson and P. Ruiz (Eds.), *Substance abuse: Clinical problems and perspectives.* Baltimore: Williams & Wilkins.

Van Strien, T. (1986) *Eating behaviour, personality traits, and body mass.* Lewiston, N.Y.: Hogrefe.

Vanderheiden, G. (1982) Computers can play a dual role for disabled individuals. *Byte, 7(9),* 136–ff.

Vaz, E.W. (1967) *Middle-class juvenile delinquency.* New York: Harper & Row.

Vega-Lahr, N., and Field, T. (1986) Type A behavior in preschool children. *Child Development, 57,* 1331–1348.

Veleber, D. and Templer, D. (1984) Effects of caffeine on anxiety and depression. *Journal of Abnormal Psychology, 93,* 120–122.

Verba, H., Barnard, G., and Holzer, C. (1979) The intelligence of rapists: New data. *Archives of Sexual Behavior, 8,* 375–378.

Verghese, A., Large, P., and Chiu, E. (1978) Relationship between body build and mental illness. *British Journal of Psychiatry, 132,* 12–15.

Vestre, N. (1984) Irrational beliefs and self-reported depressed mood. *Journal of Abnormal Psychology, 93,* 239–241.

Virkunen, M. (1976) Victim-precipitated pedophilia offenses. *British Journal of Criminology, 15,* 175–179.

Wadden, T., and Anderton, C. (1982) The clinical use of hypnosis. *Psychological Bulletin, 91,* 215–243.

Wahler, R.G. (1976) Deviant child behavior within the family: Developmental speculations and behavior change strategies. In H. Leitenberg (Ed.), *Handbook of behavior modification and behavior therapy.* Englewood Cliffs, N.J.: Prentice-Hall.

Walker, L. (Eds.) (1987) *Handbook on sexual abuse of children.* New York: Springer.

Walker, P. (1978) The role of antiandrogens in the treatment of sex offenders. In B. Qualls, J. Wincze, and D. Barlow (Eds.), *The prevention of sexual disorders.* New York: Plenum Press.

Walker, P., and Meyer, W. (1981) Medroxyprogesterone acetate treatment for paraphiliac sex offenders. In J. Hays, T. Roberts, and K. Solway (Eds.), *Violence and the violent individual.* New York: SP Books.

Wallace, D.H., and Wehner, G. (1971) Pornography and attitude change. *Journal of Sex Research, 7,* 116–125.

Wallerstein, J.S., and Kelly, J.B. (1980) The effects of parental divorce: The adolescent experience. In S.I.

Harrison and J.T. McDermott (Eds.), *New directions in childhood psychopathology* (Vol. 1). New York: International Universities Press.

Walmsley, S.A., and Allington, R.L. (1982) Reading abilities of elderly persons in relation to the difficulty of essential documents. *The Gerontologist, 22,* 36–38.

Walrond-Skinner, S. (1976) *Family therapy: The treatment of natural systems.* London: Routledge & Kegan Paul.

Walsh, L.W. (1978) *Neuropsychology.* New York: Churchill Livingstone.

Warren, L. and Tomlinson-Keasey, C. (1987) The context of suicide. *American Journal of Orthopsychiatry, 57,* 41–48.

Warrington, E.K. (1969) Constructional apraxia. In M.P.J. Vinken and G.W. Bruyn (Eds.), *Handbook of clinical neurology* (Vol. 4). Amsterdam: North Holland Publishing Co., 1969.

Washton, A. (1987) *Cocaine.* New York: Guilford.

Watson, C., and Buramen, C. (1979) The frequencies of conversion reaction symptoms. *Journal of Abnormal Psychology, 88,* 209–211.

Watson, R.T., Heilman, K.M., Miller, B.D., and King, F.A. (1974) Neglect after mesencephalic reticular formation lesions. *Neurology, 24,* 294–298.

Watt, N., Grubb, T., and Erlenmeyer-Kimling, L. (1982) Social, emotional, and intellectual behavior at school among children at high risk for schizophrenia. *Journal of Consulting and Clinical Psychology, 50,* 171–181.

Watts, A. (1957) *The way of Zen.* New York: Pantheon.

Watzlawick, P., Beavin, J., and Jackson, D. (1974) *Pragmatics of human communication.* New York: W.W. Norton.

Waxler, N. (1984) Culture and mental illness. In J. Mezzich and C. Berganza (Eds.), *Culture and psychopathology.* New York: Columbia University Press.

Webster, W. (1985) *FBI Crime Statistics Report—7/27/85.* Washington, D.C.

Weil, A. (1972) *The natural mind.* Boston: Houghton Mifflin.

Weiner, I.B. (1982) *Child and adolescent psychopathology.* New York: John Wiley and Sons.

Weiner, M. (1979) Haloperidol, hyperthyroidism, and sudden death. *American Journal of Psychiatry, 136,* 717–718.

Weiner, M. (1986) *Cognitive-experiential therapy.* New York: Bruner/Mazel.

Weisenberg, T., and McBride, L. (1964) *Aphasia: A clinical and psychological study* (2nd ed.). New York: Hafner.

Weiss, R., and Wieder, G. (1982) Marital and family distress. In A. Bellack, M. Hersen, and A. Kazdin (Eds.), *International handbook of behavior modification and therapy.* New York: Plenum Press.

Weitzman, L. (1985) *The divorce revolution.* New York: The Free Press.

Welch, M., and Kartub, P. (1978) Socio-cultural correlates of incidence of impotence: A cross-cultural study. *Journal of Sex Research, 14,* 218–230.

Wells, D., and Leventhal, D. (1984) Perceptual grouping in schizophrenia: Replication of Place and Gilmore. *Journal of Abnormal Psychology, 93,* 231–234.

Wender, P. (1971) *Minimal brain dysfunction in children.* New York: Wiley-Interscience.

Wender, P.H. (1987) *The hyperactive child, adolescent, and adult.* New York: Oxford University Press.

Werner, E.E., Honzik, M.P., and Smith, A.S. (1968) Prediction of intelligence and achievement at ten years from twenty months pediatric and psychologic examinations. *Child Development, 39,* 1063–1075.

White, L. (1979) Erotica and aggression: The influence of sexual arousal, positive affect, and negative affect on aggressive behavior. *Journal of Personality and Social Psychology, 37,* 591–601.

Wickramsekera, I. (1976) Aversive behavior rehearsal for sexual exhibitionism. In I. Wickramsekera (Ed.), *Biofeedback, behavior therapy and hypnosis.* Chicago: Nelson-Hall.

Widom, C.S. (1977) A method for studying noninstitutionalized psychopaths. *Journal of Consulting and Clinical Psychology, 45,* 674–683.

Wierzbicki, M. (1987) Similarity of monozygotic and dizygotic child twins in level and lability of subclinically depressed mood. *American Journal of Orthopsychiatry, 57,* 33–40.

Wijesinghe, B. (1977) A case of frigidity treated by short-term hypnotherapy. *International Journal of Clinical and Experimental Hypnosis, 25,* 63–67.

Wikler, A. (1970) Some implications of conditioning theory for problems of drug abuse. In P. Blachly (Ed.), *Drug abuse: Data and debate.* Springfield, Ill.: Charles Thomas.

Williams, J.M., and Long, C.J. *The rehabilitation of cognitive disabilities.* New York: Plenum Press.

Wilsnack, S., and Wilsnack, R. (1986) Antecedents and consequences of drinking and drinking problems in women: Patterns from a U.S. National Survey. Nebraska Symposium on Motivation: Alcohol and Addictive Behavior. Lincoln, Neb.

Wilson, A., Blanchard, R., and Davidson, W. (1984) Disulfiram implantation: A dose response trial. *Journal of Clinical Psychiatry, 45,* 242–247.

Wilson, B.A., and Moffat, N. (1984) *Clinical management of memory problems.* Rockville, Maryland: Aspen Systems Corporation.

Wilson, G., and Gosselin, C. (1981) *Sexual variations: Fetishism, sadomasochism, and transvestism.* New York: Simon and Schuster.

Wilson, J., and Herrnstein, R. (1985) *Crime and human nature.* New York: Simon and Schuster.

Wilson, W. (1978) Can pornography contribute to the

prevention of sexual problems? In C. Qualls, J. Wincze, and D. Barlow (Eds.), *The prevention of sexual disorders.* New York: Plenum Press.

Winer, D. (1978) Anger and dissociation: A case study of multiple personality. *Journal of Abnormal Psychology, 87,* 368–372.

Winokur, G. (1979) Unipolar depression. *Archives of General Psychiatry, 36,* 47–52.

Winslow, R.V. (Ed.) (1973) *Juvenile delinquency in a free society* (2nd ed.). Belmont, Calif.: Ackerson.

Wittchen, H., and Semler, G. (1986) Diagnostic reliability of anxiety disorders. In I. Hand and H. Wittchen (Eds.), *Panic and phobias.* New York: Springer-Verlag.

Wolf, T.M., and Wenzel, P.A. (1982) Assessment of relationship among measures of social competence and cognition in educable mentally retarded-emotionally disturbed students. *Psychological Reports, 50(3),* 695–700.

Wolfgang, M. (1978) Violence in the family. In I. Kutash, S. Kutash, and L. Schlesinger (Eds.), *Violence.* San Francisco: Jossey-Bass.

Wolin, S., Bennett, L., and Noonan, D. (1979) Family rituals and the recurrence of alcoholism over generations. *American Journal of Psychiatry, 136,* 589–593.

Wolman, B.B. (Ed.) (1978) *Clinical diagnosis of mental disorders: A handbook.* New York: Plenum Press.

Wolpe, J. (1958) *Psychotherapy by reciprocal inhibition.* Stanford: Stanford University Press.

———. (1981) Behavior therapy versus psychoanalysis: Therapeutic and social implications. *American Psychologist, 36,* 252–283.

———. (1987) Carbon dioxide inhalation treatments of neurotic anxiety. *The Journal of Nervous and Mental Disease, 175,* 129–133.

Woolfolk, R., and Richardson, F. (1978) *Stress, sanity and survival.* New York: Sovereign Books.

Woolfolk, R.L., and Lehrer, P.M. (1984) Clinical applications. In R.L. Woolfolk and P.N. Lehrer (Eds.), *Principles and practice of stress management.* New York: Guilford.

World Health Organization. (1979) *Schizophrenia: An international follow-up study.* New York: Wiley-Interscience.

Wright, E. (1939) Medieval attitudes toward mental illness. *Bulletin of the History of Medicine, 7,* 353–356.

Wurmser, L. (1981) Psychodynamics of substance abuse. In J. Lowinson and P. Ruiz (Eds.), *Substance abuse: Clinical problems and perspectives.* Baltimore: Williams & Wilkins.

Wurtman, R., Growden, J., and Barbeau, A. (1979) *Choline and lecithin in neurologic and psychiatric diseases.* New York: Raven.

Wyatt v. *Stickney,* 325 F. Supp. 781 (M.D. Ala. 1971).

Wyatt, R., and Togrow, J. (1977) A comparison of equivalent clinical potencies of neuroleptics as used to treat schizophrenia and affective disorders. *Journal of Psychiatric Research, 13,* 91–98.

Wynne, L., Cromwell, R., and Matthyse, P. (Eds.) (1978) *The nature of schizophrenia.* New York: John Wiley and Sons.

Yalom, I., and Lieberman, M. (1971) A study of encounter group casualties. *Archives of General Psychiatry, 25,* 16–30.

Yang, K. (1981) Problem behavior in Chinese adolescents in Taiwan. *Journal of Cross-Cultural Psychology, 12,* 213–231.

Yochelson, S., and Samenow, S. (1976) *The criminal mind.* New York: Jason Aronson.

Young, L. McKinney, W., and Lewis, J. (1973) Induction of adrenal catecholamine synthesizing enzymes following mother-infant separation. *Nature New Biology, 246,* 94–96.

Zablock v. *Redhail,* 434 U.S. 374 (1978).

Zarit, J., and Zarit, S. (1987) The physiology and psychology of normal aging. In L. Carstensen and B. Edelstein (Eds.), *Handbook of Clinical Gerontology.* Elmsford, N.Y.: Pergamon Press.

Zarit, S.H., Zarit, J.M., and Reever, K.E. (1982) Memory training for severe memory loss: Effects on senile dementia patients and their families. *The Gerontologist, 22,* 373–377.

Zeichner, A., and Pihl, R. (1979) Effects of alcohol and behavior contingencies on human aggression. *Journal of Abnormal Psychology, 88,* 153–160.

Zeiss, A., Rosen, G., and Zeiss, R. (1977) Orgasm during intercourse: A treatment strategy for women. *Journal of Consulting and Clinical Psychology, 45,* 891–895.

Ziegler, E., and Levine, J. (1981) Age on first hospitalization of schizophrenics: A developmental approach. *Journal of Abnormal Psychology, 90,* 458–467.

Zigler, E., and Hodappm R.M. (1986) *Understanding mental retardation.* New York: Cambridge University Press.

Zigler, E., and Butterfield, E.C. (1968) Motivational aspects of changes in IQ test performance of culturally deprived nursery school children. *Child Development, 39,* 1–14.

Zigler, E.F., and Phillips, C. (1961) Psychiatric diagnosis and symptomatology. *Journal of Abnormal and Social Psychology, 63,* 69–75.

Zilborg, G., and Henry, G. (1941) *A history of medical psychology.* New York: W.W. Norton.

Zitrin, C., Klein, D., and Woerner, M. (1978) Behavior therapy, supportive psychotherapy, imipramine, and phobias. *Archives of General Psychiatry, 35,* 307–316.

Zubrin, J., and Spring, B. (1977) Vulnerability: A new view of schizophrenia. *Journal of Abnormal Psychology, 86,* 103–126.

Zucker, R. (1986) The development of abusive and addictive behaviors over time: An interactional framework. Nebraska Symposium on Motivation: Alcohol and Addictive Behavior. Lincoln, Neb.

Zuckerman, M., Buchsbaum, M., and Murphy, D. (1980) Sensation seeking and its biological correlates. *Psychological Bulletin, 88,* 187–214.

Zuercher, E. (1980) Cortical evoked potentials in schizophrenia. Unpublished paper, University of Louisville.

Zung, W. (1965) A self-rating depression scale. *Archives of General Psychiatry, 12,* 63.

Name Index

Subject Index